PEOPLE, POLITICS, AND GOVERNMENT

Political Science: A Canadian Perspective

Second Edition

JAMES JOHN GUY

Collier Macmillan

To my wife Patti,
my daughter Katha, and my son Trevor

Collier Macmillan Canada, Inc.
1200 Eglinton Ave. East, Suite 200
Don Mills, Ontario
M3C 3N1

Canadian Cataloguing in Publication Data

Guy, James John, 1943 –
People, politics, and government

2nd ed.
Includes bibliographical references.
ISBN 0-02-953927-7

1. Political science. 2. Canada — Politics and government. I. Title.

JA66.G89 1990 320 C90-093703-4

1 2 3 4 5 94 93 92 91 90

PHOTO CREDITS

Cover: Canapress

1. Canapress
2. Bettman Archive
3. Reuters/Bettman Archive
4. AP/Wide World
5. AP/Wide World
6. Canapress
7. Government of Israel
8. Office of the Ombudsman of Ontario
9. Reuter Photo
10. John McNeill, *The Globe and Mail*
11. Canapress
12. Canapress
13. Amnesty International
14. Canapress
15. UN Photo
16. TASS

Illustration on page 446, Bernard Bennell, *The Globe and Mail* (Georges' Bank)

Every effort has been made to trace the source of each photograph and illustration that appears in the book. The publisher will appreciate any additional information regarding sources and will include it in future editions.

Contents

Tables

Figures

Tables

Figures

Foreword

This revision of Professor Guy's popular introduction to Political Science stands as a noteworthy achievement. Every instructor hoping to motivate uninitiated students with a thoughtful text which engages the reader need look no further. Given the growing number of noteworthy options, such a statement cannot be made lightly. It can be justified, however, because of several years of successful usage as assessed by many instructors and thousands of students.

At the outset, as the first five chapter headings indicate, this book answers the obvious but important questions asked by inquisitive beginners. What is Politics? What is Political Science? What is an Ideology? What is a Nation-State? What is Government? The chapter on ideology, an important addition to this revision, deals not only with the usual perspectives but also with related issues including "The End of Ideology" and feminism.

Chapters six through twelve, forming a cohesive structure-function overview, describe the branches and processes of government. An excellent chapter analyses "Constitutions and Constitutionalism." While the reader encounters illustrations from numerous political jurisdictions, examples dealing with the Canadian, American, authoritarian and totalitarian regimes appear with regularity. This timely shift from Western Europe to Second and Third World examples, while still exposing students to comparative politics, provides welcome realism and diversity.

Instructors wishing to introduce students to global politics will find the last four chapters very useful. The treatment is logical and lucid. Chapter 13 surveys "The International System" giving extended attention to the UN. NATO, COMECON, OAS and multinational corporations receive appropriate attention. Many readers will especially welcome the discussion of the Canadian-American Free Trade Agreement.

Chapter 14 describes "International Law," particularly its sources and significance. Chapter 15 explores the nature and role of "Diplomacy" while Chapter 16, "Challenges and Change in the Nuclear Age" analyses "The Challenge of Peace" as well as "Arms Control," "Nuclear Proliferation," "Population," and "Hunger."

This text brings some major strengths to a first course in Political Science. Definitions are presented clearly and simply, although some readers might question the broad usages of "nation-state." Fortunately, the author frequently cites alternative views and definitions that compel readers to grapple with issues. Throughout the volume one encounters numerous elaborations dealing with practical concerns.

Tightly yet lucidly written, the book incorporates masterful use of examples and well-conceived charts and graphs. Each chapter concludes with a brief bibliography and a very useful glossary with the defined terms clearly identified in the text.

Without employing any one methodological framework, Professor Guy has provided us with a highly readable and logically organized text. It places Political Science in academic, historical and geographic context, enables students to understand their own political setting, and subtly moves the students from the familiar to the unfamiliar. In doing so it appropriately combines description, structure-functionalist analysis, comparison and behavioural illustration.

In sum, this up-to-date treatment may well be the best introduction, with an appropriate Canadian emphasis, currently available.

John H. Redekop
Professor of Political Science
Wilfrid Laurier University

Acknowledgements

Once again, there is much thanking to be done. So many people both in Canada and the United States contributed to the first edition. It is gratifying, therefore, that *People, Politics, and Government* is now widely used in Canada, and that as a result, a second edition is justified.

Revising, I have discovered, is not an easy task. Those familiar with the first edition will notice many changes, yet much of the organization remains the same. Comments by reviewers led to the inclusion of a new chapter on ideologies and to various additions and deletions to all other chapters. Feedback from students in our undergraduate courses was also a significant part of the preparation of this new edition.

Many people have assisted in these revisions. As always, Bill Gallivan, our Vice-President Academic of the University College of Cape Breton, gave full support during the rewriting stages of this text by funding research trips to Ottawa and Washington, D.C., and by personally encouraging this project.

One of the most thorough reviews I have seen of any book was conducted by Dr. John H. Redekop of Wilfrid Laurier University, most of whose perceptive recommendations were included in this edition. The book is better for them, and owes much to Professor Redekop's insights. Dr. Lance Leloup of the University of Missouri drew upon his special expertise in the writing of a current major American-government textbook and provided welcome advice regarding the United States' electoral system, as well as on other matters. A large debt is also owed to Dr. David Milne of the University of Prince Edward Island for his valuable review of the chapter on constitutions. My dear friend and colleague, Dr. Mohini Gupta, generously contributed her comprehensive knowledge of the transitions taking place in the Soviet Union and East European states. She was always there to answer questions, to encourage me, and to provide valuable advice. Another colleague in our department, Dr. Marcel Leroy, read carefully through the first edition and made helpful suggestions relating to his fields of demography and international relations. I especially acknowledge the theoretical instructions of Teresa O'Brien, professor of sociology, whose expert guidance helped in the preparation of the section on feminist thought in the new chapter 3. As well, historian Dr. Brian Tennyson, Director of our Centre for International Studies and himself widely published, deserves acknowledgement for his help in identifying difficulties in the early drafts of the book and for his compassion during the writing of the second edition. As always, I owe Dr. Denis Stairs of Dalhousie University my appreciation for his original contribution and for his scholarly example.

To Derek Burney, Canada's ambassador to the United States, a special thank you for permitting me to include his profile in the chapter on diplomacy. He and his staff were most co-operative, providing documentation on his daily schedule and speeches. To Yves Fortier, Canada's ambassador to the United Nations, and his staff, my sincere appreciation for giving valuable time and expertise on multilateral diplomacy. To Supreme Court Justice Claire L'Heureux-Dubé, thank you for generously sharing your experiences on the high bench. You have provided a unique opportunity for political science students to gain some insight into the life of a Canadian woman doing a very special job in our governmental system.

I would also like to acknowledge the professional help so faithfully provided by the staff of Collier Macmillan throughout the preparation of this edition. Every author needs an empathetic managing editor like Patrick Gallagher, who skilfully escorted this project through the complexities of the editorial process for both the first and second editions. I appreciate his patience, encouragement, good humour, and effective direction. Once again, good fortune provided me with the masterful editorial services of Lydia Burton, who meticulously repolished the entire manuscript, and provided suggestions for dealing with ancillary materials. The production process was again ably co-ordinated by Gaynor Fitzpatrick with the assistance of Paula Fedeski-Koundakjian.

Public thanks are also due to loyal typist Sherry Spracklin, who typed the instructor's manual with such precision. And last, but not least, my wife Patti excelled in the application of her psychiatric counselling skills to an incurable client — me!

PEOPLE, POLITICS, AND GOVERNMENT

1

What Is Politics?

Pro-democracy students erect their "Goddess of Democracy" in Tiananmen Square, May, 1989

ALL OF YOU HAVE SOME IDEA of what politics is. Headlines abound with political information from different societies around the world: "Mulroney's government gives priority to reducing Canada's deficit"; "Massive exodus and protests in East Germany lend speculation to German re-unification"; "International policy response needed to address the threat of global depopulation caused by AIDS virus." Today's headlines make very clear the intricacies of political relationships that take place in various societies. Every society is an organized community of individuals and groups that aspires to achieve a distinctive social order and survival. Politics is the means by which it creates this order. People see society and its politics from particular vantage points and interpret what is observed by their own experiences and values.

Many political scientists and political activists* have defined politics in an attempt to provide an understanding of the political world. David Easton sees politics as a "process by which values are authoritatively* allocated in society."[1] Harold Lasswell referred to politics

*Asterisked words are in the glossary at the end of each chapter in which they appear.

simply as "who gets what, when and how."[2] Lenin, the great Bolshevik revolutionary, saw politics as "who does what to whom"[3] and Mao Tse Tung defined it as "bloodless war."[4] Chancellor Bismarck of Prussia asserted that politics was the art of getting things done. He defined politics as "the doctrine of the possible, the attainable."[5]

In all of this there is much room for disagreement. The world does not consist of a political reality that everyone sees in exactly the same way. Politics is highly complex social behaviour driven by distinctive cultural and institutional variables. Political science starts with the Aristotelian premise that we are basically political animals – not just from force of habit but because we could not survive otherwise.

In Canada, politics is seen as both an institutional* and a behavioural* phenomenon. For example, Professor John H. Redekop defines it this way:

> Politics, then, refers to all activity whose main purpose is one or more of the following: to reshape or influence governmental structures or processes; to influence or replace governmental office holders; to influence the formation of public policies*; to influence the implementation of public policies; to generate public awareness of, and response to, governmental institutions, processes, personnel and policies; or to gain a place of influence or power within government.[6]

Institutions are excellent places to start looking for politics but we should be prepared to discover political elements at other levels of human interaction. Politics is a recognizable characteristic of people acting towards, responding to, and influencing one another in the public milieu. It may manifest itself as group demands for more order, justice, and harmony in a society. One person may feel that voting for a particular party or candidate in an election will bring job security and a higher standard of living. Another will complain that there is too much government intervention in society and will support a party that advocates reducing bureaucratic regulation. A women's organization might pressure a provincial government to censor pornographic materials in sex stores and organized labour may lobby cabinet ministers to create more jobs. These actions are examples of traditional political behaviour. But less traditional activities are just as political in their social effect as are voting, supporting a party, or lobbying: for example, refusing to place money in banks that invest in South Africa; crossing or not crossing picket lines; or joining a group of citizens that takes legal action against a company using dangerous chemicals to spray forests near populated areas. All these activities involve people in the political structures of their society. Political activities of these kinds are inextricably linked to the pursuit and balance of private and social interests. Indeed, at every level, politics is the harmonization of the conflicting needs and demands of people in a changing world.

Politics as Behaviour

Some social scientists have pointed out that politics is a natural result of people interacting with their environment. This has been stated as a behavioural equation, PB = F(HE),[7] where political behaviour is a function (or product) of the relations humans have with their environments. A number of important theoretical studies have identified the two primary dimensions of political behaviour as the psychological and the social.[8]

From the psychological perspective, political behaviour appears as thought, perception, judgement, attitudes, and beliefs. The psychological basis of politics is also seen in the constructs of personality, expectations, and motivations that explain individual and group responses to environmental stimuli. For example, some studies point out that leaders are more likely to possess certain personality characteristics to a higher degree than do followers.[9] Leaders are found to demonstrate a higher rate of energy output, alertness, originality, personal motivation, self-confidence, decisiveness, knowledge, and fluency of speech than do followers. The psychological dimension of politics is also a working aspect of selling issues and candidates. Modern election-campaign strategies apply advanced propaganda and entertainment techniques to gather crowds for rallies and to influence voter behaviour in most countries. Images and issues can be carefully crafted to appeal to the widest possible range of voters. The psychological manipulation of voter preferences today is built into the campaign strategies of most candidates for public office.[10]

The social basis of politics is found in actions such as voting, protesting, campaigning, lobbying, and caucusing. In the broadest social sense, political behaviour may be observed in any institutional or behavioural setting. It is often revealed as aggression, co-operation, compromise, negotiation, posturing, decisiveness, assertiveness, dominance, and virtually any human strategy that leads to decisions that have social impact. In short, political behaviour is both the essence and form of politics.

What better place to witness these two dimensions of political behaviour than at the leadership conventions of the Conservative and Liberal parties in June 1983 and June 1984 respectively.[11] Not only were the candidates for the leadership of these parties presenting their ideas in formal speeches to the delegates who attended, but many other examples of political behaviour were evident. At both conventions, enthusiasm was high and the opening ceremonies became contests to see which camp had the strongest lungs. There were not only vocal battles for attention: posters, banners, and placards bounced up and down in eager hands, balloons floated through the arena, and hats and T-shirts sporting different alliances weaved through the hall.

Much of the wheeling and dealing for the votes of the delegates went on during the convention festivities. Some of the best side-shows Ottawa has seen took place around the activities of these conventions: at each convention, when the delegates arrived in Ottawa, the candidates were waiting with all the paraphernalia that have become so much a part of selecting political leaders in Canada. Hotel lobbies were filled with booths that were plastered with pictures of the candidates. Campaign buttons appeared everywhere and there seemed to be an endless flow of beer and liquor. Bars opened early and closed late. The methods may vary in each political party but the goals remain the same: to get and keep the delegate's vote. At both conventions candidates wooed delegates with food, fireworks, music, and giant movie screens flashing well-known faces. In some instances teary-eyed orators, lavishing praise, introduced their candidates with appeals to the emotions of the delegates. Campaign strategists made sure that support for their candidates appeared on placards at every corner of the convention floor. Who candidates talk to, look at, and walk toward all become psychologically dynamic gestures in the process of selecting a political leader.

For the candidates themselves, image, win-ability, and what one conservative delegate called "the sizzle factor" supersede the issues raised and the policies debated by the party intelligentsia. The ultimate test that demonstrates the leadership qualities of a candidate is his or her individual character. Character shows itself as the respect candidates display towards the delegates, and the coolness and grace they display under fire, when events take a difficult turn.

For candidates, the pressures of politics are enormous. They have just completed exhausting tours around the country. They have invested themselves, their time, and their money. As tension builds on the floor of the convention hall, their emotions become quite raw. Television viewers have memories etched in their minds of the moment in the Conservative convention when John Crosbie watched Michael Wilson and Peter Pocklington walk in front of him and march toward Brian Mulroney: we saw him sag; we saw his people sag. No one exaggerated the stress and intensities of the emotions involved. Issues were of secondary importance at both conventions. Most of the undecided delegates seemed drawn to the gleam and sparkle of the candidate they thought looked like a Canadian prime minister.

Party conventions are ideal places to witness the psychological and social determinants of political behaviour because we can see how the environment sets the stage for political action and that politics as a form of behaviour cuts across many levels of social conduct. Imitation, frivolity, faddism, mimicry, and emotion are as fundamental to political behaviour as are decision making, elections, authority, and consensus.

Politics as Culture

Just as agriculture describes the ways of farming and horticulture describes the ways of growing plants, so political culture refers to ways of conducting politics. We could think of a political culture* as the accumulation of beliefs, customs, expectations, attitudes, traditions, skills, symbols, and values in a given political system (see figure 1.1). All these components are a product of a society's political experience from its remote and recent past. They are inputs into the political environment of a society in its quest to survive and maintain social order. Because every society has a unique past, every political culture is unique and many nation-states (such as Canada and the Soviet Union) even experience different political subcultures flourishing within them. Although many political cultures exist throughout the international system, each reflecting distinctive qualities, certain components are found in all the ways of conducting politics:

- *Political customs* are conventional and accepted practices that may be recognized as a functional part of the political system and may be reinforced through the legal actions of

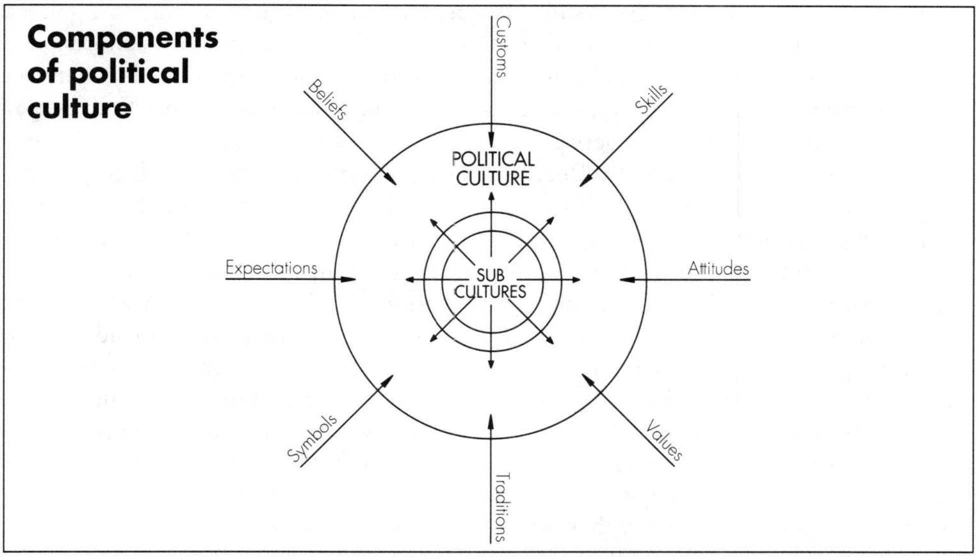

Figure 1.1

the state, e.g., when a cabinet minister resigns because of inappropriate behaviour or when he or she cannot subscribe to the policies of the government.

- *Political beliefs* are integrated coherent convictions of unprovable assertions that are based on one or more fundamental assumptions about political behaviour, e.g., that humans are basically selfish and governments should legislate and enforce the sharing of resources.
- *Political expectations* are normative assertions about what people believe ought to happen in the political world, e.g., that governments should not engage in patronage.
- *Political symbols* are things that represent something else, e.g., the maple leaf is a symbol of Canada.
- *Political attitudes* are learned predispositions that relate to political issues, events, personalities, and institutions in either a favourable or unfavourable manner and in a more or less consistent or characteristic way.
- *Political values* are attitudes and standards of judgement about what things are important, desirable, and right, e.g., Canadians consider it desirable and proper for people to pursue their own goals and interests as individuals under the law.
- *Political traditions* are customs legitimated by long and continued practice, e.g., during a royal visit, the Queen participates in ceremonies normally carried out in her name by the Governor General, such as the opening of Parliament or the granting of general amnesty.
- *Political skills* consist of the knowledge, procedures, strategies, and tactics for achieving desired social goals, e.g., lobbying, negotiating.

There are many different political cultures. In each one, people share similar ideals, similar procedures of government, and similar patterns of political behaviour that are learned and passed on from generation to generation. We are all very much part of our own political culture and we identify with it to distinguish ourselves from other political cultures.

Gabriel Almond was the first political scientist to bring to our attention the link between political behaviour and the wider phenomenon of carrying political knowledge from the past into the present. For Almond, "every political system is embedded in a particular pattern of orientations to political action."[12] Once established, a political system tends to generate informally its own support mechanisms within a society. These usually take the form of certain norms and values that are regarded as virtues and recognized by succeeding generations of political actors. For example, candidates to Canada's Parliament have learned that legislators must be loyal to their party positions – because the survival of the parliamentary system requires it. But south of the border, different values are adopted by novice congressmen and women. In the United States, the expectation is that representatives will usually act independently and will advance the interests of their constituency first.

Samuel Beer and Adam Ulam theorized that a political culture transmits to people "how government ought to be conducted and what it should try to do."[13] This ubiquitous nature of culture is what prompts people to expect certain qualities and values in political behaviour and to behave politically the way they do. For example, in Canada and in the United States people believe that their constitution, as the basic law of the land, will last indefinitely and be amended only from time to time. But in the twenty Latin American republics, where there have been more then 200 written constitutions since 1810, people have come to expect that constitutions can be whimsically abandoned by any government that gains power. This attitude is in line with what Sidney Verba contends about political culture: that it is a "system of beliefs about patterns of political interaction and political institutions."[14]

We can identify three general qualities of political culture.[15] First, there is widespread awareness of the rules and structures of the political system. Canadians are generally conscious of the presence of Parliament and how it operates as a political and lawmaking institution. The formal and informal political relationships of politicians are understood and centre around this institution in most cases, most of the time. Second, politics and the political system are widely accepted. Not only are people committed to the roles* and functions* of political institutions, but they usually comply with the written and unwritten rules of the system. Compliance is the invisible glue of any political system; without it, the political and social fabric of nation-states would fall apart. In Canada, there is widespread acceptance of the legitimacy of Parliament. People respect its procedures and comply with the laws it generates. Sometimes people violate the cultural expectations of a political system: In 1989 former Conservative MP Michel Gravel was sentenced to one year in jail and a fine of $50 000 after pleading guilty to charges of political corruption for accepting bribes totalling $97 500 and for influence peddling. Finally, the third element of a political culture is the expectation of behaviour within the political system. People are sensitive to the growth and size of government as an encroachment in their lives. They hold government accountable for its actions and deem certain behaviour appropriate or inappropriate for political actors.

Because of size and ethnic composition*, some nation-states contain more than one political culture. Usually in multi-ethnic and multinational states (which contain a number of linguistic and ethnic minorities), there are distinctive regional political cultures or political subcultures that constitute the political system. A regional political culture has been defined as "a set of values, beliefs, and attitudes which residents of a region share and which, to a great or lesser extent, differentiate them from the residents of other regions."[16]

Steven Ullman observes that while a homogeneous political culture is detectable across a wide range of Canadian political behaviour, regional political cultures can also be identified. In some instances it appears along provincial boundaries, as well as in regions that may consist of one or more provinces. One soon discovers that a Cape Breton coal miner, a Montreal taxi driver, a Saskatchewan wheat farmer, an Alberta oil executive, and a student at the University of Victoria do not share the same political values and beliefs about Canada's political destiny. In the Canadian political culture, a majority of people hold in common certain fundamental attitudes and beliefs regarding the role of Parliament, the ethical behaviour of politicians and bureaucrats, and the legitimacy of national legislation and certain governmental programs, such as unemployment insurance and medicare. But one would also find basic differences in attitudes and values of Albertans and Maritimers over the extent to which provincial and federal governments should be actively engaged in the economy. Simeon and Elkins have explained the presence of regional subcultures in Canada by pointing to the many differences in the historical development of different parts of Canada.[17] Unique patterns of settlement and ethnic composition are detectable across Canada's wide expanses. As a result political subcultures have flourished on the basis of provincial self-determination and regional isolation. Indeed, Canada is a country divided by its economics and politics and united perhaps only by its media and a national communications system.[18]

All political cultures, whether national or regional, nurture symbols with which people identify. A political symbol* is a meaningful object that represents some shared value or goal of a community of people. Thus the Canadian flag, which is a rectangular, multicoloured piece of cloth, represents "the true North strong and free," democracy, justice, and other values. Canadians have come to make a psychological association between the flag as an object and the values it represents. The significance of the flag is much greater than its physical appearance. Similarly, the House of Commons, which is little more than an ornate building on a large lawn, has come to stand for the majesty, prestige, and authority of Canadian government and politics. All Canadians understand that the House of Commons is a shorthand reference for the institutional machinery and the decision-making process of the federal government in Canada. Everyone makes the association between the terms and their meaning; everyone shares the symbol as part of the political culture.

Each political culture or subculture has many political symbols. Every political system has its symbol of power and legitimacy: the Crown, the White House, or the Kremlin. Every political system has its symbol of representation: Parliament, Congress, the Knesset, a Diet, or an election. Every political system has its symbol of authority: a coat of arms, the Stars and Stripes, the hammer and sickle, or a constitution. Symbols direct our political actions and serve to impose cultural expectations on our behaviour and preferences; they bind us as a group and unite our loyalties.

Another aspect of political culture is the political style* of a society.[19] Every political system develops its own characteristic style of politics that reflects its people's historical experiences, traditions, and values. We have in Canada a highly competitive, open political system that invites voluntary participation of people who want pragmatic solutions to social problems. Domestically, Canada has achieved a high degree of bargaining, compromise, and negotiation in the area of interprovincial and federal politics. The intensities of political competition are high at all levels of the Canadian political system and with no major regional differences.[20] This has made politics in Canada a healthy exercise for both the citizen and the professional politician.

Internationally, Canada has often engaged in the politics of mediation and developed the style of a peace broker in international relations. No other state shares Canada's distinction of having served in every peace-keeping force assembled by the United Nations.

South of the Rio Grande exists an exciting world of unique political cultures. Here we discover the politics of *continualismo, imposición,* and *personalismo.* Continualismo* has been widely practised throughout Latin America. It is a strategy to keep an executive or junta in office beyond the terms and limits set by the constitution. The methods usually involve changing the constitution so as to legitimize the continuation of an individual or group of individuals in power. By changing the constitution of Nicaragua, Anastasio Somoza Sr., who took office in 1937, extended his term of office in 1939, and served to 1948; he then returned to office in 1950 until his assassination in 1956. In Argentina, Juan Perón changed a 100-year-old constitutional provision against re-election and won the election in 1951.

Imposición* is similar in style to continualismo but involves tampering with the election process rather than the constitution. A government may rig the election, restrict party competition, ban certain parties, or control the media during the campaign. From 1964 until it withdrew from politics in 1985, the military government in Brazil had imposed an artificial two-party system on voters and guaranteed the success of a military president by controlling the electoral college.

Another Latin American political style is found in the phenomenon of personalismo*. Politicians project strong features of their personalities to attract popular support. People are encouraged to show allegiance and loyalty to a political leader because of his or her personal charisma and mystique rather than to the institutions of government or the rules of the political system. The attractiveness of a leader's personality is the primary means for mobilizing mass support and centralizing political authority in the hands of one person. José María Velasco Ibarra, the five-time president of Ecuador over a thirty-eight year period beginning in 1933, was so sure of his ability to gain public support from the force of his personality that he was quoted as saying, "Give me a balcony anywhere in the world and I will get elected."

It is necessary to know that politics as culture is an important way of understanding the uniqueness of every political system*. Our political culture is a looking glass through which we observe and judge other political cultures. We must constantly be aware of how our own values fix our political evaluations of the other people who make up the international system. We must learn that our views of national unity, honesty in government, regular and peaceful succession of political leadership, and economic growth are not shared by all people. We must also learn that elements of Canada's political culture may be inconsistent with one another and not equally shared among all social groups.

Politics as Values

Sociologists tell us that all societies are made up of groups* that share certain values. Within groups, values are widely believed to be desirable for their own sake and are used as standards to judge the behaviour of others. Values reveal themselves as human preferences and priorities, as beliefs about duty, about right and wrong, and about what ought to be done in certain situations. Seymour Lipset found that Canadians tend to value authority more than do Americans.[21] For him, Canadians are more law abiding and more inclined to recognize the authority of the police than are Americans. By comparison, Americans value personal freedom so highly, they tend to resist regulations and are more likely to feel hostile to authority figures.

Political values* are shared beliefs that provide standards for judging human thought and action. They may be viewed as pressures that motivate social behaviour within a political culture. Politics results from the interplay of values among individuals and groups pursuing different goals for their own benefit. Within every society or among societies, politics is the process of competition and co-operation by which values gain priority.

These priority values are authoritatively allocated by the political system in order to legitimize their binding effect on the lives of the majority of people. One value that has become an integral part of the fabric of Canadian society is *equality*. Because of this value, various groups have fought for the authoritative allocation of equal treatment in Canada. For example, in 1990 Canadian women celebrated their seventieth anniversary as "persons" under the British North America Act. In 1920, Judge Emily Murphy, Nellie McClung, and three other women from Alberta successfully took legal action that affirmed that Canadian women should not be classed with lunatics and children as people who were not responsible for their actions. Similarly, the federal government granted Canadian Indians full citizenship only in 1960. It was 1967 before a Supreme Court order halted the prohibition that Canadian Indians were not legally entitled to drink alcohol. And, as recently as 1989, the Canadian Human Rights Commission ordered the Armed Forces to open all combat roles to women. The point is that a belief in equality held by a majority of Canadians does not mean that this standard has applied in practice to all groups in Canada.

Values in a society provide people with a way of judging whether they are satisfied or dissatisfied with the distribution of social rewards that flow from community expectations. Politics is the process* that settles claims people make on their political system so that they feel part of the same set of shared social values.

Harold Lasswell[22] lists eight values that generate politics and are pursued by people in all societies. In varying degrees people make demands on the institutions of society and thus engage in political behaviour for at least these values.

Power

Power is a primary currency of political behaviour and it weaves its way into most arenas of human interaction. People want to experience power and are fascinated by those who appear to be in positions of influence. They have a natural curiosity about the political impact of people like K.C. Irving and Ken Thomson, two of Canada's seven known billionaires, or about the methods and tactics used by cabinet ministers in managing the Canadian government.

In Canada, power and political institutions are intimately related. As a value, however, Canadians prefer to think of power not in coercive terms but rather as authority that is granted by consent. In other words, rulers must be recognized as having the right to control the behaviour of other people. Canadians accept traditional authority because they believe the monarchy and its Canadian representative constitute the formal executive of government. Power and authority do not come from personal characteristics or from the office held, but are often vested in persons who Canadians have traditionally consider rightful leaders. However, the real basis of institutional power in Canada is derived from legal and procedural authority. This authority is granted by the position; it is not in the person. The rights, privileges, obligations, and power come with the office. When an individual leaves that office, the next person to occupy it is granted the same rights and obligations.

When in an office of power, a person is expected to behave in accordance with certain rules and values. Robert Coates, who was appointed minister of Defence in the first Mulroney government was forced to resign because of media reports questioning his moral conduct while on an official visit to West Germany. He was reported to have violated the rules of behaviour that were required of a person in his position and he lost all powers and privileges. Sinclair Stevens was found to have violated federal conflict of interest guidelines on fourteen separate occasions from 1984 to 1986 while he was minister for Regional and Industrial Expansion. Steven's alleged breach of executive trust led to his resignation as minister and ultimately convinced the prime minister that signing his nomination papers to run in the 1988 federal election was a political liability.

At first glance, power appears to be only an institutional or governmental phenomenon. However, in reality, power is more properly understood as a relationship among individuals, groups, and societies. In this regard Robert Dahl sees power as "the capacity to change the probability of outcomes,"[23] and Karl Deutsch sees it as the "ability to make things happen that would not have happened otherwise."[24] For both men, power involves access to a position of regulation and control where decisions can be made concerning the thoughts, feelings, and behaviour of others and oneself. All people desire to expand their capacity to gain and share power and they demand these opportunities from their political system.

Wealth

Wealth has been a political issue since the dawn of time. It enables people to satisfy their material needs, individually and collectively, in society. But invariably wealth leads to the exercise of political power. The political nature of wealth has always revolved around its possession, use, and distribution in a society. All political systems are sharply affected by the internal divisions of income and wealth. Wealthy economies like Canada's and those of Western Europe have more equitable income distributions than poorer countries such as Tanzania and Mexico.[25] The association of industrialization* and wealth has been significant historically and tends to be significant today. The global inequalities of wealth seen in most preindustrial societies are the primary causes of the political instability of so many developing states. It is an important reason to explain the susceptibility of poorer societies to radical ideologies and egalitarian political movements.

By 1989, Canada's net worth was just over 2 trillion dollars – nearly a million dollars for each Canadian if the country was liquidated and the wealth divided equally among its 26 million people. This national balance sheet, calculated by Statistics Canada, shows tangible assets – houses, durable consumer goods, business and government buildings and equipment, land, and money owed to individuals, businesses, and governments – totalling $4.6 trillion. When financial liabilities amounting to $2.5 trillion are subtracted from tangible assets our net worth is $2.1 trillion. Collectively, Canadians are very wealthy; however, many individuals never share in the affluence of the economy. In Canada, wealth is a widely valued commodity but is usually accompanied by its attendant poverty. One out of every twelve Canadians lives on welfare and one in six children grows up in a poor family. The Anti-Poverty Association estimated that over 5 million Canadians were living below the federal government's poverty line in 1990. Statistics Canada reported that 4 million Canadians were below that line at $11 118 income for a single person and $19 623 for a family of three.

At first glance it appears that the problem lies at the economic extremes in Canada. People tend to blame both the achievers and the victims. Few studies in Canada have explored the role that the middle class itself has played in the perpetuation of economic disparities across the country. Ian Adams and others note the political clout of the middle sectors in preserving the present tax system, corporate autonomy, and a collective-bargaining system that is grossly inequitable.[26] With a per capita gross domestic product in excess of $14 000, Canada's middle class ranks as one of the most affluent in the world.

As Canada has moved into the advanced stages of industrialization and technological innovation, its total wealth has dramatically increased. Leo Johnson has observed that while Canada's wealth and living standards have generally improved, the middle and upper strata of income earners do proportionately better than lower-income groups.[27] The rich are getting richer and the poor are getting poorer. Yet, in spite of greater inequality, most Canadians still believe that economic mobility is possible and they do not see themselves eternally tied to their present situations by fate or political design. Wealth remains an important political and social value in Canada.

Health

Canada's great wealth is used to purchase health and well-being. Even though most of the health and welfare services are within the constitutional jurisdiction of the provinces, the largest department of the federal government is Health and Welfare Canada, which spends approximately 40 percent of the annual government budget. Canadians, through their federal government, have made considerable efforts to improve public health. By the mid

1990s a newborn Canadian female will have about an 81-year life expectancy and a male about a 75-year life expectancy. This statistic contrasts with countries such as Nepal and Afghanistan where life expectancy is well below the age of 50 for both males and females.

Canadians take their health very seriously as witnessed by the role the federal government has played in health services since the passage of the federal Medical Care Act in 1966. By the 1990s, nearly 9 percent of Canada's GNP had been annually spent on health-care services. This is primarily attributed to political decisions. There is a widely held value that access to good health care is in the national interest and that individuals should not be left vulnerable to the high costs of medical services. Canada ranks with Sweden, Switzerland, the Netherlands, Germany, and Britain for its exceptionally well-developed arrangements for health care in the community, including care of the elderly and those with handicaps. But in the early years of the next century, Canada's aging baby boomers will drive up future health-care costs, forcing politicians to consider new policy directions to care for the aged. According to Statistics Canada, the number of Canadians 65 and older is likely to double in the next fifty years and the very old – those over 85 – will increase twice as fast.

Enlightenment

In industrial societies, enlightenment (or education) is one of the main sources of upward mobility. While there are still great differences between rich economies and poor economies, education stands out as a primary value in all societies. Levels of literacy among people 15 years of age and older range from 1 percent in Gabon to 99 percent in Canada and the United States.[28] Similar contrasts are found with respect to university and college students. The number of university students per 1000 population ranges from 0.2 in Ethiopia and Malawi to 43 and 46 for Canada and the United States respectively.

Despite the popular expectation that there is equality of educational opportunity in Canada, wealth and social class are still significant factors in determining access to university. Martin and Macdonnel showed that educational opportunities vary provincially.[29] A person from Alberta, British Columbia, or Ontario is more likely to acquire a university education than someone from the Atlantic provinces or Quebec. This ensures continued social differences across the country. Native Canadians in particular are excluded from the benefits of university education. Fewer than 1 percent of natives attend university, compared with 14.5 percent of the population aged 18 to 24.[30] Education is a global political value because it is closely related to skill and productivity. It is an important political resource because those who possess it improve their own welfare and make demands on the political system. Yet, despite its importance, poor nations have great difficulty making strides in education. It is difficult for a poor country to spend the required amount of its GNP on education because that means sacrifices elsewhere.

Skill

Work and employment are the basis of all cultures. It is no wonder that they should be so highly prized as political values in society. Employment links a person to a network of socially rewarding interactions. Without work, people feel disfranchised from their social and political systems. In short, they become alienated.

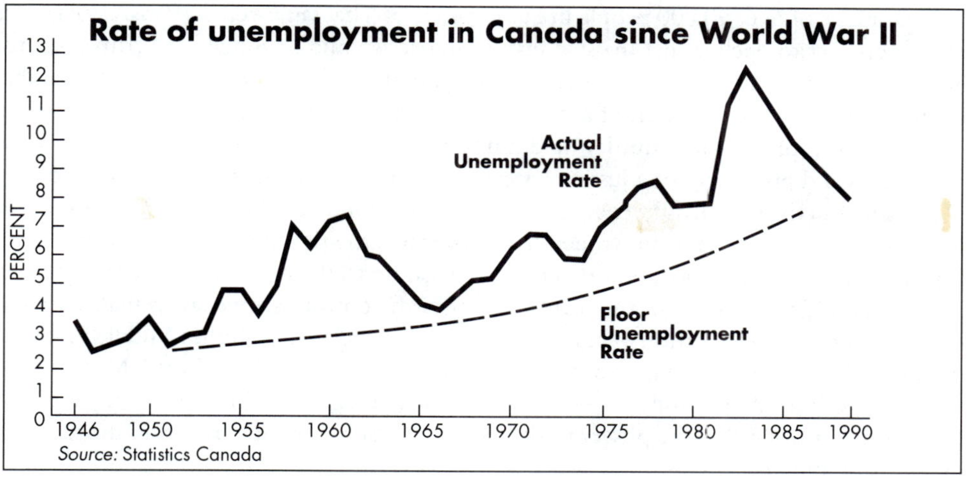

Figure 1.2

At the peak of unemployment levels in 1983, 1 346 000 Canadians or about 12.5 percent of the labour force could not find jobs – the highest rate since World War II (figure 1.2). Because of general public concern, unemployment was recognized by the federal government as the major socio-economic problem in Canada, ranking higher than inflation and interest rates as a national priority. By 1989, the national rate of unemployment had fallen to 7.8 percent.

Work and skill have been seriously affected by national policy in Canada since 1966. At that time the Canadian government consolidated its work-power policy to co-ordinate labour-market developments and immigration. Canada Manpower Centres were established to provide services to individuals seeking a job. Employment counsellors were hired to make placement referrals and allowances were taken out of general taxation to administer training. As a consequence, the Canadian government has assumed many responsibilities in relation to matters of job placement, income support, and mobility grants. Today, Canada Employment Centres try to match workers to jobs by funnelling information from employers to prospective employees. Occupational mobility and the maintenance of skills in the marketplace have necessarily been elevated to the highest level of political concern in a country as large and as complex as Canada. Because politics is now blamed and credited for the job market, it will continue to be regarded as an important political value.

Justice

Never before in human history have justice and righteousness been so passionately and universally pursued. The groundswell of humanity's concern for peace was demonstrated in June 1982 when United Nations Secretary General Pérez de Cuéllar was presented with a disarmament petition with 90 million signatures on it. In 1981 the first Latin American congress of families of "missing" was held in San José, Costa Rica, to denounce the disappearance of over 90 000 people in Latin America. That same year in Paris, associations of lawyers met to declare that massive disappearances should be judged as "crimes against humanity." And in Canada the Marshall Inquiry painfully deliberated the circumstances that led to the wrongful conviction of a young Micmac Indian, Donald Marshall, who served eleven years in prison for a murder he did not commit. Its recommendations focussed on the failures and prejudices of a justice system reputed to be one of the best in Canada.

Throughout the world, different perceptions of justice and morality are held. For example, in Spain, Portugal, and Ireland women have never had the right to either contraception or abortion. In Denmark, abortion on demand is legal up to the twelfth week of pregnancy. In Japan and Cuba abortion is the main form of birth control. Islamic law remains unclear on contraception and abortion but generally both are illegal in the Muslim Middle East with the exception of Tunisia, where abortion was legalized in the 1970s. In the Middle East, women risk death if the family learns of an illegitimate pregnancy. In Canada, the Supreme Court ruled in 1988 that the power to decide on abortion justifiably rested in the hands of individual women.

We have difficulty in establishing this value because there is not just one justice but many. Justice and morality cluster, compete, and conflict. Most debates about justice are not debates between right and wrong but between rights and rights – which makes their resolution endlessly complicated.

Respect

The rights and freedoms people demand from their communities are based on the need for human respect. The right to privacy, freedom of speech, freedom of religion, and freedom of assembly are some of the many ways in which people derive respect and dignity.

The need for respect surfaces in areas of international relations as well. Debtor militancy among the economies of the Third World is a message to the banking systems of the wealthy countries that they should respect the impoverished economies of the developing world. At the Olympics, where respect is literally put to the test, politics transcends the spirit of the games when states count their medals as tallies of national strength. And what remains of the separatist movement in Quebec is still, in large part, a demand for respect of the sovereign aspirations of an independent French-speaking republic.

Respect for the territorial integrity of states and the principle of non-intervention have become most important in the international law of the twentieth century. The charters of the United Nations, Organization of American States, and the Organization of African Unity make frequent references to these norms of international behaviour.

The need for respect may often appear hidden behind rhetoric and human aggression. Terrorist groups, unions, interest groups, and governments are all social and political manifestations of this powerful value in politics.

Affection

At the first glance, love and affection seem distant from politics. But upon closer examination we can see how the need for human affection touches every level of society, including the political system. For Plato and Aristotle, people and politics are part of a cosmic order built for the perfection of human beings as they relate with one another in society.[31] Politics must establish the framework within which love is possible, even though it cannot specify exactly how it shall be sought.

Although it can always be shown that politics does much to destroy good will among humans, there is also evidence that political behaviour fosters friendship and co-operation. Each day governments extend courtesies to one another through cultural, diplomatic, and scientific exchanges. For example, from 1983–88 Canada annually gave from four to eight immature bald eagles from Cape Breton to the United States Fish and Wildlife Service to re-establish its eagle population. And as an act of gratitude toward the City of Boston, which was the first community to come to the rescue of the citizens of Halifax after the Halifax explosion in December 1917, the province of Nova Scotia gives Bostonians a large spruce Christmas tree, ceremoniously lit by the premier each year. Similarly, the CANADARM was a gift of the Canadian government to the U.S. space shuttle program. The Soviet Union sponsors youth festivals, sends its performing artists abroad, and provides its Friendship of Nations University in Moscow to the youth of less developed countries. As well, the United Nations sponsors national and international programs aimed at improving cultural co-operation and international friendship among states.

Hundreds of treaties of friendship and mutual aid are signed by governments each year. In fact, the greatest proportion of interactions and transactions among the states of our international system each day are amicable. Never before in history have so many international organizations been established for peaceful and friendly purposes.

At the national level, many governments are genuinely concerned about generating friendly relations among citizens. In Canada, a number of federal government departments, like the Department of Communications, work to foster such an environment. They represent the political values of Canadians to co-operate and collaborate with one another. They reflect the idea that friendship, love, and affection can be encouraged within formal institutional settings in addition to the personal and social contexts in which we assume these values will surface. If we look closely we can see that politics often does succeed in fostering the growth of affection among people.

Politics as Conflicting Interests

Democratic politics invariably generates competing interests on all issues. In Canada issues such as the political equality of women, the size of the national debt, and the privatization of certain crown corporations stimulate the competition of divergent interests to seek solutions to these perceived social and economic problems.

Some issues, more than others, can dramatize the role of politics in the process of harmonizing individual and group interests. When the Supreme Court of Canada made its historic decision in January 1988 to strike down the 1969 abortion law as unconstitutional it triggered a flurry of competing interests across the country. The 200-page judgement placed the issue right back into the political arena, reopening emotionally heated debates on abortion at all levels of Canadian society. Almost immediately, pro-choice and pro-life groups organized demonstrations (even to the point of arrest and conviction for criminal contempt and public mischief), initiated face-to-face lobbying with parliamentarians, and conducted cross-national education campaigns to draw support to their respective positions. The Campaign Life Coalition, which opposes therapeutic abortion and claims a membership of 200 000, urged members to support anti-abortion MPs. They also campaigned against prominent pro-choice supporters such as Joe Clark, and invited the internationally acclaimed Mother Teresa to address groups in Ottawa. The Canadian Abortion Rights Action League, which claims a much smaller membership, encouraged its members to support pro-choice candidates.

Each individual contemplating an abortion was also challenged by the decision. For Dr. Henry Morgentaler the Supreme Court decision was the culmination of almost two decades of legal defiance, during which time he had performed an estimated 20 000 abortions. For politicians, the decision created agonizing deliberation. Abortion is an issue most politicians want to avoid: it cuts across party lines, divides party members, and can cost traditional party support. Party strategies of compromise and equivocation on the abortion issue break down under the pressures of translating religious and philosophical beliefs into public policy. To balance the rights of the unborn and the rights of a mother creates an issue with no middle ground.

Under the 1969 abortion law, which created the now defunct Section 251 of the Criminal Code, an abortion was lawful only when a properly constituted hospital committee certified that the continuation of the pregnancy would be likely to endanger the life or health of the mother. All five of the judges who composed the majority position in the Supreme Court's decision in the Morgentaler case found that the committee procedure was contrary to Section 7 of the Charter of Rights and Freedoms, which guarantees the right to life, liberty, and security of the person. To the government this meant that no new legislation with similar administrative practices would be acceptable. Government strategists knew that any new law to restrict abortion would be in open contradiction of the Charter. One province – Nova Scotia – outlawed free-standing abortion clinics by making it illegal to perform abortions anywhere other than in government-approved hospitals.

In the summer of 1988 the Mulroney government proposed a compromise motion, subject to a free vote, to establish a general policy that would guide the Cabinet in drafting legislation to replace the abortion law. The motion, which called for relatively easy access early in pregnancy with tougher restrictions coming later, was defeated 147–76 by a coalition of anti-abortion Tories, pro-choice New Democrats, and Liberals who favoured compromise but rejected the particular plan offered by the government. The tortuous Commons debate went into the early hours of the morning throughout a week of bitter deliberation, leaving the government with no clear guidance on which policy to pursue. One of the five defeated amendments to the motion brought together all twenty-three women present in the House at the time in strong opposition. This non-partisan female force of unity prevented the anti-abortion motion, which would have banned abortions except when two doctors decide that the life of the mother is threatened. After all was said and done during the free vote, the government did not venture to stake out a formal position that might alienate half the voters in the country or its deeply divided Tory caucus. As the likelihood of an election increased dramatically in the late summer of 1988, Canadians were left without any law on abortion. The issue remained a matter decided between a woman and her doctor, without any guidance from government. Growing national sentiment demanded that any proposed law would be a compromise to allow early abortion as a condition to prohibit late abortion. Based on a 1988 Decima poll, one in ten Canadians opposes abortion under any circumstances while about one-third favour abortion on demand. Of the rest, 60 percent approve of abortion under special circumstances. Pro-choice supporters feel that women do not need a law to help them make decisions on abortion.

But the abortion controversy remained unresolved as the Mulroney government prepared for a fall election. In the interim, former Manitoba cabinet minister Joseph Borowski, a vocal anti–abortionist, appealed to the Supreme Court of Canada to overturn a 1987 Saskatchewan Court of Appeal decision that had rejected Borowski's claim to grant the fetus the right to life, liberty and security of the person. But the Supreme Court reserved decision on the appeal because Canada no longer had an abortion law. And, in March 1989, the Supreme Court refused to decide the issue of whether the fetus has constitutional rights, positing that it would not deal with the question in the absence of an abortion law.

Provincial courts in Ontario and Quebec added fuel to the political flames across the country by handing down rulings that prevented women from obtaining abortions. One Ontario court decision granted an injunction to prohibit a woman from undergoing an abortion. It took a decision on appeal in the Ontario Supreme Court to set aside the injunction. But the Quebec Supreme Court upheld an injunction preventing a woman, Chantal Daigle, from having an abortion by interpreting the Quebec Charter of Rights and Freedoms as giving the fetus the right to life. In the case of Chantal Daigle, the Supreme Court of Canada unanimously overturned the Quebec court's injunction (the appellant had already travelled to the U.S. to abort her 22-week-old fetus).

In 1989, the Law Reform Commission of Canada recommended amendments to the Criminal Code that would balance the interests of the mother and the fetus. Mothers' rights would weigh more heavily up to twenty-two weeks, a period of time after which the fetus can usually survive outside the womb. Abortions would be permitted before then if a woman and her doctor feel her physical or mental health are threatened. After twenty-two weeks, a second medical opinion would be required and abortion would be allowed only if there was a threat to the woman's life or a serious threat to her physical health. An abortion would be permitted at any time if the fetus is found to have a lethal defect. Mental or physical handicap is in itself not a reason to permit abortion under the recommendations.

Canada's foremost governmental institutions, Parliament and the Supreme Court, provincial legislatures and provincial courts, could not or would not provide a decisive solution to this issue. In this regard, politics is a process between and within communities whereby divergent groups co-operate or struggle in order to satisfy their basic needs. The political process forced the federal government to attempt the difficult task of framing new abortion legislation. The new legislation amended the Criminal Code to allow a woman to have an abortion at any stage of pregnancy if one doctor agrees that the woman's physical, mental or psychological health is threatened. The politics of conflicting interests was thus reborn.

Politics as Nation-Building

Nation-states are not born; they are built. And politics plays a major role in their construction. The economic and social base of any society requires political direction. At various levels, politics constructs the building blocks of national development – the infrastructure* of a community. In the broadest sense the infrastructure of a society consists of systems of transportation, communication, education, power grids, the industrial and technological base, and the political system. These all form the structural components of a nation-state.

In the same way that a house is constructed from various building materials, in different patterns and designs, rapidly or slowly according to the will and power of its builders, so a

1970 – 2000: Urban population as a percentage of total population

	1970	1980	1990	2000
World total	37.4	41.2	45.2	50.1
Developed regions	66.2	71.9	77.0	81.4
Underdeveloped regions	25.0	29.8	35.0	40.8
Canada and U.S.	74.2	78.8	82.9	86.4
Europe	64.7	69.6	74.3	78.7
Oceania	70.2	73.1	75.8	78.2
USSR	56.6	64.2	70.8	76.3
Latin America	56.9	63.8	69.7	74.8
East Asia	28.5	32.9	37.7	43.2
Africa	21.9	27.1	32.5	37.7
South Asia	21.1	25.0	29.6	35.0

Source: Demographic Yearbook 1982 (New York: United Nations 1984)

Table 1.1

nation-state develops from its resources, according to different plans, quickly or gradually from the will and skills of its citizens.

The political system organizes, plans, and directs policies towards its developmental goals. Public policies are intimately related to nation-building at all levels of government. Public policies make us richer or poorer, happy or angry, live or dead. Public policy is what a government *does* as well as what public officials sometimes choose *not* to do. In the final analysis, therefore, societies survive and change on the basis of "whatever governments choose to do or not to do."[32] Government policies on municipal services, education, health, welfare, agriculture, business, defence, and relations with other states are all part of the nation-building process. Given the wide range of public concerns, governments must constantly assess their goals by rendering judgement on the feasibility of means, the range of possible choices, and the possible consequences of the choices they make when measured against the alternatives.

Municipal or Local Government

Political-science research has only recently begun to discover the important role that cities and towns play in national development. The political decisions and actions of local governments transform the landscape of a country. They plan and regulate local construction and land use and provide important services like utilities and transportation.

By the year 2000, most people of the world will live in cities (table 1.1). At that time the gradual shift of political and economic power to urban centres will be irreversible, making cities the primary centres of human development and important decision-making units of most political systems. In 1950 there were 76 cities in the world with a population over one million; the United Nations projects that by the end of the century there will be 440 such cities, 284 of them in the developing world. Already the physical expansion of the corporate limits of cities has created overwhelming human problems and added many jurisdictional questions to the national and subnational legislatures of most countries. As cities and towns have grown, so have public demands for increased responsibilities and services. In some cities, such as Mexico City and São Paulo, these demands are a response to unmanageable and ungovernable social conditions.

The result is that the division of powers and responsibilities between national governments and local governments carries momentous significance for the politics of development. Usually the cost of administrating public services goes beyond the financial capacities of cities, so other levels of government share costs or completely finance the administration of services (table 1.2). National governments are increasingly dependent on cities as economic and social centres of development. Thus, municipal problems have become national problems and municipal successes have become national successes.

In Canada, over 4000 municipalities and countless boards, commissions, and other local bodies contribute to the growth and development of Canadian society. But their contributions have not been without recurrent financial problems and a general public attitude that local government should be primarily concerned with administration and efficient service delivery, but not with politics.[33] Canadians have not linked urban growth with

General municipal services			
Locally financed		**Cost-shared**	
Fire protection	Planning and maintenance	Public education	Transportation
Refuse collection and disposal	Municipal libraries	Health	Public housing
Police	Water supply	Hospitals and medical care	Public welfare
Parks and recreation			Pollution control

Table 1.2

national development and have been reluctant to give greater autonomy to local governments. Under Section 92 of the Constitution Act, 1867, the provinces were granted full responsibility for municipal institutions and, thus, local governments have remained what a report by the Federation of Canadian Municipalities called "puppets on a shoestring."[34] Despite the fact that in the 1990s over 80 percent of all Canadians live and work in cities and receive the most personal essential services from their municipal governments, local administrations remain the most neglected and least regarded of all three levels of government. Unlike municipal governments in Europe and most parts of the United States, Canadian municipalities are not much involved even in the direct delivery of social services. In the years ahead public opinion may reverse its sentiments about the role of local governments in Canada's national development and draw closer to Sir Ernest Simon's view that "the City Council's services mean the difference between savagery and civilization."[35]

Subnational Government

In geographically large states, nation-building requires the co-operation of two or more levels of government, each with its own special jurisdictions, political institutions, and popular support. In Canada, provinces have special powers reserved for them in the Constitution Act, 1867, listed under Section 92. In addition to ten provincial political systems, Canada has two large territories that together make up 40 percent of the entire area of the country and yet hold only 0.2 percent of Canada's population. The Yukon Territory is governed by a commissioner as head of government and an elected legislative body called the Yukon Legislative Assembly. The Northwest Territories – the largest region within Canada – is governed by an appointed commissioner and a council made up of twenty-four elected members.

The Constitution Act, 1867, enumerated fifteen classes of subjects that have given provinces exclusive and substantive lawmaking powers and elevated them to economic instruments of nation-building. The provinces have responsibility for local governments, jurisdiction over education, control of provincial crown lands, natural resources, and the provincial administration of justice. They also have concurrent powers with the federal government in agriculture and immigration. Historically, the politics of federal and

Provincial gross domestic product 1987

	$BILLIONS
British Columbia	61.636
Alberta	58.982
Saskatchewan	17.291
Manitoba	20.049
Ontario	224.674
Quebec	131.872
New Brunswick	10.588
Nova Scotia	13.374
Prince Edward Island	1.608
Newfoundland	7.138
Yukon and Northwest Territories	2.235
Total (gross domestic product)	549.397

Source: Statistics Canada, *Provincial Economic Accounts* (13-213), *Annual Estimates 1986–87* (1989)

Table 1.3

provincial relations have transferred additional spending powers to the provinces, particularly under successive Liberal governments since 1968. The federal government spends billions annually in the areas of health, welfare, and post-secondary education but allows provinces to administer and influence the policy direction of these programs.

Any account of the contribution of the provinces and territories to nation-building should include some remarks about their economic importance in the Canadian economy (table 1.3). Each province of Canada generates a gross provincial product that is a constituent part of the gross domestic product (GDP), which is the total value of all goods and services produced within national boundaries.

British Columbia offers a primary product and resource economy to Canada. The United States, the United Kingdom, and the Pacific Rim countries are the main importers of fish, pulp and paper, primary metals, and manufactured goods produced in British Columbia. Table 1.3 shows that British Columbia contributed $61.636 billion to Canada's gross domestic product of $549.397 billion in 1987. Its sister province, Alberta, has also assumed a special role in the process of nation-building in Canada because approximately half the national value of petroleum, natural gas, sulphur, and coal comes form there. While it is also true that Alberta has a strong agricultural sector, the province's economy is struggling to avoid the dangerous pitfalls of non-diversification. Next to it, Saskatchewan has become a major participant in Canada's international trade. It generates important international sales for Canada in wheat, barley, canola, flax-seed, and other feed crops, especially to the Soviet Union and the People's Republic of China. The principal industries of Manitoba include the manufacture of agricultural implements, machinery, clothing, and transportation equipment. Along with Saskatchewan, Manitoba sustains Canada as the sixth leading agricultural producer of wheat and cereals in the world. As the wealthiest and most diversified provincial economy, Ontario's gross provincial product of $224.674 billion represents over 40 percent of Canada's gross domestic product. Ontario is the manufacturing and industrial heart of the country, as well as the host of the largest employer in the country – the federal government of Canada. Quebec adds $131.872 billion to Canada's GDP, accounting for one-quarter of Canadian manufacturing output in the areas of textiles, food processing, pulp and paper, and high-tech equipment. Quebec is also a major producer of gold, iron ore, copper, asbestos, and hydro-electric power. Nova Scotia ranks sixth in the size of its gross provincial product. Its principal industries in manufacturing, fishing, mining,

Federal transfers as a percentage of provincial revenues

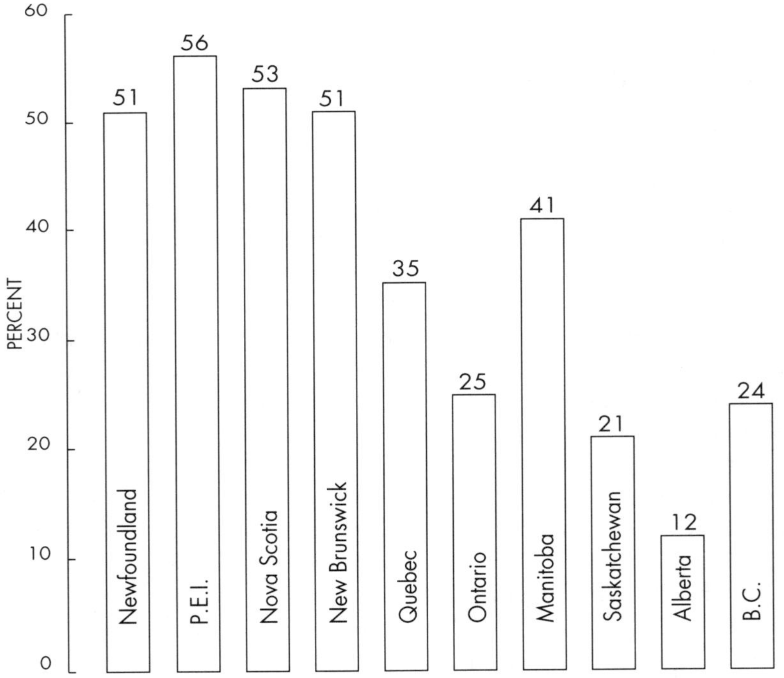

Source: Statistics Canada, Provincial Economic Accounts, 1988

Figure 1.3

tourism, agriculture, and petroleum refining promise to expand its role in international trade, as well as in offshore resource development. New Brunswick ranks after Nova Scotia in gross provincial product and derives its economic opportunities from forest products, food processing, mineral production, and agriculture. High rates of unemployment, negative provincial migration, and the burden of high welfare costs have severely hampered any growth arising out of its services and industries. Similarly, Prince Edward Island – Canada's smallest province in area, population, and gross provincial product – has relied heavily on the federal government to subsidize infrastructure development and to enhance services to its growing tourist industry, which now is second only to agriculture for value added to Canada's GDP. Newfoundland, the youngest province, has added much nation-building resource potential to Canada: fishing, mining, offshore oil and gas, pulp and paper, hydro-electric power, and iron-ore development are important contributions to Canada's national wealth.

All these provinces constitute just 60 percent of the area of Canada. Sprawling across the top of the Western hemisphere are the Northwest Territories and the Yukon. They encompass an area nearly one-and-a-quarter times the size of India with a population of only 70 000 people. These territories are just beginning to attract Canada's business pioneers in the areas of mining, hydrocarbon exploration, and oil exploration and refining. Together they generated $2.23 billion to Canada's gross national product in 1987.

National Government

The ultimate instruments of nation-building are held by national governments. They are the final arbiters of politics and legitimate decision making in most countries. National governments control the overall capacity of a political system to affect every level of society by their sheer magnitude, scope, and economic presence.

From the perspective of public policy, nation-building in Canada has had an important regional* dimension that is far reaching for all three levels of government but, in particular, the federal government. Since the 1950s new federal policies and programs have been introduced in rapid succession. Mid-1950's "rural adjustment" programs were followed in the 1960s by a policy focus on "growth centres," which in turn led to more comprehensive regional federal/provincial development strategies under the General Development Agreement approach of the 1970s and the Economic and Regional Development Agreement in the 1980s.[36] Billions of dollars have shifted from the national treasury through federal transfer payments to adjust and diminish regional economic differences in Canada. Because the pace of development has been very uneven in Canada, as a result of its unique size, distribution of population, and regional resource endowments, the federal government transfers payments to provincial governments in an effort to equalize the benefits of development across the country (figure 1.3). The heavy reliance of the four provinces of Atlantic Canada on transfer payments, as shown by the contributive percentages these payments constitute of their provincial revenues, is indicative of the severity of regional disparities in eastern Canada.

Ever since it was elevated to the level of public policy in Canada, regional development has been politically driven. Indeed, the federal structure of Canada's political system tends to reinforce the focus of public policy on regionalism and regional solutions to economic development. Yet the concept has never been adequately defined either in economic or political terms. Some economists even reject the idea that "region" is a valid concept for economic policy analysis. They hold that economic development can only be directed at people, as opposed to places or regions.[37] In short, regional development means different things to different people but appears to have been politically instituted in intergovernmental affairs in Canada.

Lucian Pye noted the centrality and competence of politics in the process of nation-building.[38] His position is that political development is a prerequisite of national development. For him, the quality of politics determines the capacity of a political system to execute effectively and efficiently public policy in the best interests of the nation-state. National governments integrate a set of complex political and economic structures in order to achieve desired national goals – such as energy self-sufficiency, economic independence, universal medical services, or economic prosperity. For example, Canadian governments have created crown corporations to facilitate the process of nation-building and province-building in areas of the economy where the private sector cannot or will not assume the cost and risks of development.[39] Such economic institutions now number over 400, comprising major contributors in such fields as coal, steel, oil, gas, forestry, railways, potash, ferry services, and manufacturing ventures.

In Canada, the job of nation-building has always been initiated, controlled, and directed by the federal government. The Constitution Act, 1867, granted the federal government the nation-building powers it needed to expand the role of the state directly and indirectly into the lives of individuals and groups, and into the jurisdictions of other levels of government. It is important to note that the division of powers outlined in our constitution clearly gives most powers to the federal Parliament, establishing it as the dominant decision-making authority in Canada. For example, the power of the federal government to *disallow* provincial legislation flows from a separate applicable grant of authority in the Constitution Act, 1867. The "peace, order and good government" clause of the constitution grants residual power* to the federal Parliament, giving it the necessary legal basis to involve itself in areas of jurisdiction that appear to be exclusive to the provinces, such as culture, education, and local government. This constitutional legitimacy, when combined with federal spending and taxing power, has provided the government with the means for expanding the national state apparatus to build Canada.

The size of the government sector has grown steadily since Confederation and rapidly since World War II. Total government spending as a percentage of gross national expenditures (the total output of the economy) grew from 23.7 percent in 1947 to over 42 percent in 1989. The number of federal government portfolios grew from 19 in 1947 to 40 in 1984 and 39 in 1988, indicating the expanding role of government in allocating the resources of the people and the never-ending politics of nation-building in Canada.

What Is Political Socialization?

The master concept used by political scientists to account for the ways in which the content of a political culture is transmitted to new generations is political socialization. In various ways every society teaches its members the political values, traditions, norms, and duties that it deems desirable and acceptable. All individuals experience the subtle pressures that entice them to internalize* their society's norms. Even though individuals in democracies may be dissatisfied with political leadership, they have learned to accept elections – rather than riots or insurgencies – as the best route to political change. In totalitarian societies, individuals learn that only one political party has the undisputed right to interpret and implement political goals, without dissent or competition from individuals or groups.

Political science sees socialization of political behaviour as both a *process* and a *goal*. As a process, political socialization has been defined by Easton and Dennis as "those developmental processes through which persons acquire political orientations."[40] For Roberta Sigel, "political socialization refers to the learning process by which the political norms and behaviours acceptable to an ongoing political system are transmitted from generation to generation."[41]

The goal of political socialization in some political cultures is to mould a child or adult to a prescribed set of conventions in which people are usually not treated as active innovators and modifiers of their own political learning. Following the successful Cuban revolution, children were housed, socialized, and educated by state organizations. Adult political values were shaped by organizations like the Committees for the Defense of the Revolution (CDR), which still induct people into Cuba's revolutionary political culture.

Political socialization may also be incidental to other life experiences or it may be as deliberate as a state-monitored program of indoctrination. As a general rule, democratic political systems provide a subtle environment in which political information is transmitted in a casual manner. In most totalitarian and authoritarian states, however, political stimuli may be organized and engineered so that the political consequences of socialization are those approved by the regime.

Profile of the Political Self

Much more research is anticipated on the psychological processes involved in early political socialization because little is known about them. It is very difficult to get into the heads of children as they acquire the initial political stimuli in their lives. Many political scientists who have specialized in this area have based their theories of observation on their own children or on relatively small numbers of randomly selected children. However, their work has been extremely important in helping us to understand how children first learn about politics.

At the outset we should avoid making the dangerous assumption that early socialization engenders indelible lifestyles, especially with regard to political behaviour. Adult character is highly malleable and continues as such well into old age.[42] Nevertheless, it is useful for us to focus on early or primary political socialization as an attribute of the child's development of "self."[43] Each person's self-development is unique and may not follow the stages of expected chronological human growth from that of a child to an adult. Some children may be more politically aware than their parents, even though the opposite is normally true. While research observations can be made about political learning in children, adolescents, and adults, understanding the political "person" in all of us requires a knowledge of our "self" and its general learning experiences.

The American sociologist Charles Horton Cooley saw the self as a looking glass in the process of socialization, political or otherwise.[44] Our political behaviour is a reflection of how we see ourselves in a complex world. Self-image determines our general interest in politics and affects our political identities. We learn political behaviour that satisfies the needs of our self as we pass through various levels of human development.

Political socialization is a life-long process intimately tied to self-definition. The foundations of political behaviour are laid in childhood and begin as children interact first with parents and later with peers, teachers, and other adults. Political socialization also occurs as we are exposed to messages from radio, television, and other mass media. Beyond these, it is linked to the preservation of political culture because the process of absorbing political values and inculcating them in new members is done by teaching and learning. Each political system tries to teach new members, especially children, what the accepted behaviours, norms, and values are. The goal is to condition the self-defining individual to accept the means society uses to achieve social order. If political socialization is effective, new members adopt supportive attitudes toward officeholders, political procedures, institutions, and the ways policy decisions distribute rewards and punishments.

Political Socialization and the Child

David Easton and Robert Hess found that even though children do not develop a political vocabulary until the ages of 11 or 12, many basic political attitudes and values have been firmly established by the time the child begins elementary school. James Chowning Davies discovered that before schooling starts, a child's familiarity with power is well at work within the framework of the family.[45] Later, in school, children learn that there are public dimensions in their lives. Government policy dictates that they be in school, that they get immunized against disease, and that public property does not belong to them and should be respected.

Despite the apparent regulatory nature of the political world, Easton and Dennis point out that the North American child "learns to like the government before he really knows what it is."[46] Early in their lives, children naturally develop favourable feelings toward the symbolic and ceremonial character of the state and government. The flag, the national anthem, emblems, the military, and the head of state are all presented as special representations of the majesty of the state and country.

This is particularly true for most Canadian youth. In a sample of 6000 Canadian children, Carroll, Higgins, and Whittington found that students from grades 4 to 8 held high levels of affection for the Queen, the governor general, and the prime minister.[47] Party identification also tended to increase from grades 4 to 8, with some changes in affection noted toward the prime minister. Ronald Landes discovered that Canadian children possess more knowledge about leaders than about institutions and processes.[48] The low-to-moderate level of political awareness in children suggests the variable importance of politics in their growth. Formal politics, its institutions, and its actors are not central factors in a child's development. However, the underlying currents of political behaviour, such as competition, co-operation, compromise, power, and manipulation, are learned during childhood and, with experience, are linked to later adolescent and adult political behaviour.

Political Socialization and the Adolescent

During adolescence people become increasingly aware of the existence of authority outside the family and school. Adolescents become familiar with institutions of authority such as the courts, Parliament, and municipal government. At this stage, the individual begins to express independent political views and to distinguish parental influence from general social ones. Adolescence is a period of biological maturation and change, and the formation of social and political attitudes are also part of this development.

Politicization may become highly personalized during adolescence. It may reveal itself as political cynicism*, political efficacy*, apathy*, or participation*. Susan and Ted Harvey showed that individual variations in adolescent intelligence affect knowledge of political facts and political tolerance.[49] During adolescence, individuals demonstrate different capacities for learning political information and reflect different levels of maturity with respect to opinion formation and expression. Again, this observation supports the importance of individual development as a process that is idiosyncratic to the person.

Political Socialization and the Adult

Because of the widespread belief that politics is the domain of adults, much more is known about adult political socialization than about that of children and adolescents. Adult socialization refers to changes in learning and attitudes that take place after the adolescent years. Because adult political socialization is a continuous experience, we should avoid the assumption that young people are usually more liberal and that aging leads to political conservatism. Robert Sigel and Marilyn Hoskin noted that adults change political attitudes regularly throughout their lives in response to issues that affect self-interest.[50] A person who at 35 held politically conservative views on social and economic assistance may at age 65 show strong support for government-sponsored programs.

Changes in adult values and behaviour from those of childhood and adolescence may result more from changes in personal roles than from age. Between the idealized state of adulthood and the reality of life as a parent, a spouse, and a breadwinner, there is sometimes quite a difference. Adults quickly learn that their political and economic freedoms are only relative. Politically they must make trade-offs between the independence they long for and the social and economic responsibilities life places upon them. Most important of all, they learn that there is still much to learn politically at all stages of adulthood. Taking on a new job or profession, becoming a parent, moving to a different community, and experiencing upward or downward social mobility are more directly related to changing political attitudes and behaviour than is age.[51] Each change in adult role affects political behaviour and alters the socio-political belief system of a person. The value and beliefs learned in childhood may no longer be adequate or relevant to the adult who experiences role change.

In many countries today adults experience a political *re-socialization* that is forced upon them by a government agency such as the secret service or the military or because a government with different ideological positions has come to power. The term *brainwashing* is used to describe an attempt to change attitudes or ideologies against a person's will. Brainwashing is a translation of an expression used by the People's Republic of China for purifying the mind of any political beliefs in the old order that existed before the Chinese revolution. With this extreme form of political socialization, the old mistaken ideas are washed away and the "right" political values are put in place. Both re-socialization and brainwashing are incisive methods of adult political learning. In democratic countries like Canada, adult political socialization is a gradual life experience, emerging as a person changes roles.

Because we are describing political socialization as a process of attitudinal behavioural change and not as a product of specific age categories in adult life, it is important to study the social context of political socialization. What are the environmental agents of socialization? How do they influence the way we learn about politics?

Agents of Political Socialization

The agents of political socialization most frequently identified by political scientists have been the family, school, peers, and the media. By agents we mean those social institutions and experiences that condition, indirectly influence, or directly determine the development of a person's political views and actions. The politicization* of an individual is affected not only by exposure to the most common agents of socialization but also by the degree to which the agents themselves are politicized. Thus, a person whose parents have little interest in politics is less likely to acquire political knowledge than one whose parents are highly active and motivated politically. The greater the exposure a person has to politically charged agents of socialization, the greater the likelihood that the values will be assimilated and internalized.

Figure 1.4 shows the approximate exposure to three of the most familiar agents of socialization. In Canada, as in most other Western countries, people learn the norms and expectations of their community from their parents, from teachers at school, and from their friends and associates. These are the primary sources of political information for most people. They help to shape our attitudes, values, and political behaviour throughout our lives. In figure 1.4, the age of a person is represented on the horizontal line from birth to age 50. The vertical line shows exposure as the percentage of interactions people experience with the agents that have a significant socializing effect on them.

Even though the family is neither instituted not designed as an agent for transmitting political values, it is considered by many scholars to be the most important source of political socialization. In our society the child's exposure to family influences remains high until late adolescence, when other agents of socialization begin to attract as much or more attention. But the family may intentionally or unintentionally influence a person's predispositions toward authority, party identification*, and general political norms and behaviour throughout a great part of life. Because most of our early personal development takes place at home, we can understand how the family contributes so much to the profile of our political self.

Canadian children spend a substantial portion of their working hours in a school setting. For many, attendance at a university prolongs this exposure into early adulthood. Because of their constant influence in the formative years of life, schools rival parents as agents of teaching important values and norms in a community. Because most schools in Canada are tax–supported public institutions that determine teaching standards and follow standardized curriculum guidelines, they inadvertently serve to transmit socially and politically approved values. Schools usually promote positive orientations toward the political and economic system and introduce students to the rituals and symbols of the political process. Teachers, whose credentials are normally set by provincial governments, also transmit political skills and values over and above those in the curriculum. The schools, the teachers, and the curricula constitute a learning culture through which we all must pass.

Finally, figure 1.4 shows that as the family influence wanes, there is increased contact with peers. Peer groups* are normally formed among individuals who share common backgrounds, outlooks, and values. In Canadian society peer groups occupy an important position for influencing adult socialization in all matters – including politics. For most of us, peers affect us before we enter school. With peers, we are first introduced to the value of equality: being equal among equals. We learn to share, compete, co-operate, compromise, and manipulate those in equal standing to ourselves. We also learn about leadership and the unwritten rules of being recruited and accepted by a group. In adult life, peer groups become the most significant agents of political socialization, particularly when politics is important to the group itself. Because of the personal nature of most peer-group relationships, they function as subtle pressure groups on individuals by communicating political values and encouraging certain standards of political conduct.

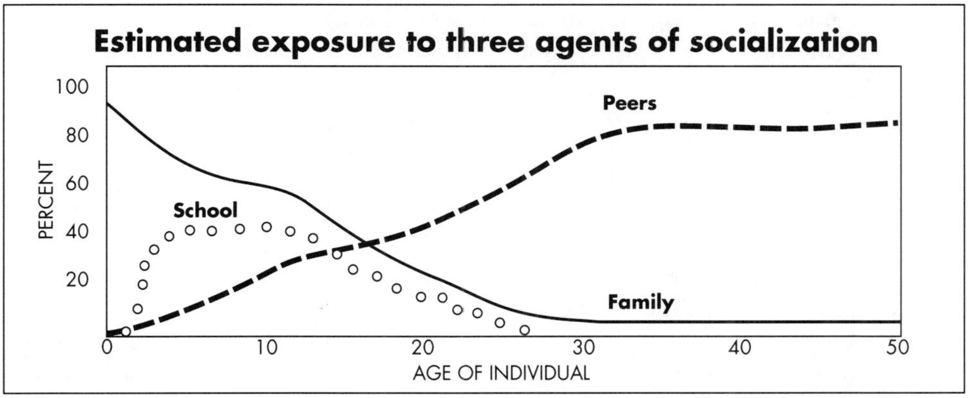

FIGURE 1.4

Another source of political socialization cannot be ignored: the mass media. The impact of the media on children and adults has been the focus of increased government and scholarly attention in recent years. In Canada, the mass media have played a major role in politicizing the population, as well as in nation-building and in fostering cultural identity.[52] Most newspapers and magazines are highly political in content and coverage. Radio and television are universal media that link Canada's 10 million square kilometres of area with coverage of politics, economics, and cultural happenings across the country. The media act as independent agents of political socialization, bypassing parents, the education system, and peers. Canadians spend 50 percent more time (about 25 hours per week) watching television than on any other leisure activity. The Royal Commission on Newspapers in 1981 discovered that the electronic media (television, followed by newspapers, radio, and magazines) are considered the most influential and believable of all media sources. Television especially plays a central role in the formation and change of political orientations among Canadians by structuring their attitudes about politics and the information on which these attitudes are based.

Expressing Public Opinions

Every political opinion is learned and is an indication of how much we have learned about politics. Usually, political opinions express our political values in day-to-day terms: they indicate how people feel about their representatives, their institutions, their national goals. Political opinions reflect upon our ideology, our values, our behaviour, and our expectations. To be sure, many opinions lead to no action, but most political opinions imply that political behaviour will follow. It is because of this expected linkage between opinion and action that democratic theorists lay such great emphasis on the role played by public opinion in political affairs.

We can trace the appreciation of the importance of public opinion from the earliest writings of political philosophers to the present day. Although Greek and Roman philosophers described it as "mass opinion," they quickly identified its importance to the world of politics. Among modern political theorists, Jean-Jacques Rousseau was the first to make use of its present meaning by employing the phrase "L'opinion publique" in regard to his notion of "general will."[53] Since the eighteenth century, public opinion has been courted by politicians, condemned by philosophers, catered to by business and governments, feared by military leaders, and analysed by statisticians. Public opinion is perceived to have such power that British Columbia prohibits the publication of public-opinion polls during election campaigns and federal members of Parliament (MPs) have introduced bills in the House of Commons to do the same in national elections.

The passion for expressing opinions is universal. Scholars, newspapers and television journalists, politicians, interest groups, government agencies, and most citizens are all willing to generate or try to fathom Canadian public opinion. Political scientists are interested in the formation and expression of opinions to the extent that they influence and change public policy.[54] By observing the role of public opinion in the formation of public decisions we heighten our understanding of extra-institutional factors that affect government actions. We learn if there is congruity between public policy and public preferences.

What Is Public Opinion?

All opinions amount to an expression of attitudes. In our society opinions constitute an expression of personal and group power. We build and destroy governments with opinions. In our legal system, opinions judge the behaviour of individuals and corporations. They represent the anticipations of people and reinforce or change the most fundamental beliefs of society. They operate as forceful and dynamic social messages representing any collection of articulated individual opinions.

In everyday discourse, public opinion refers to general public attitudes toward everything from athletics to the zodiac. But political opinions are specific and relate to all matters of government and political affairs. So, as students of politics, we should consider V.O. Key's definition of public opinion as "those opinions held by private persons which governments find it prudent to heed."[55] For purposes of political analysis, public opinions become significant when they link the opinions of people to political action and government attention. They reflect how people interpret their political culture and the extent to which political socialization is succeeding or failing.

Often, people make the incorrect assumption that there is only one "public" when referring to political opinion. This interpretation of public opinion is sometimes misleading because on very few issues in a country is an entire public concerned. We assume that "the people" really is one enormous individual with a single opinion, quite probably one that agrees with our own. For analytic purposes, however, it is important to be careful with aggregate references to "Canadians" or "Americans," keeping in mind the actual diversity of views that individual members of a given segment of the public may hold on most questions. It is true that for issues of widespread impact such as war, inflation, unemployment, capital punishment, and universal medicare, the general public will voice related opinions that are measurable as a national response. But only on a relatively small number of issues does a public respond organically. It is much more accurate to hold that there are many publics with special interests in issues of a local nature. For example, most Manitobans may not be concerned about the state of fishery in British Columbia. In fact, all across Canada there are many special publics as distinct from the general public.

Properties of Political Opinions

Political opinions have several distinctive characteristics. First, they have *content*. They are about something political – candidates, events, issues, or parties. Second, they have *direction*; that is, an opinion is not a simple statement about an alleged fact: it indicates or implies a value preference. A Canadian's opinion about the Organization of American States (OAS), for example, will express approval or disapproval of the organization, as well as his or her understanding of what the OAS is and does. The direction of an opinion informs us whether the public response is positive, negative, or indifferent. Third, opinions have *intensity*, which is an emotional characteristic of public opinion that tells us how committed people are to the position they have taken. In May 1980, intense clusters of Quebec opinion polarized in about a 60/40 percent distribution of divided expressions of self-determination. Intensity not only involves the "extremeness" of an opinion, but also the extent to which the issue is *salient* to a person; that is, how much he or she really cares about it. On the question of Canada's membership in the OAS, very few Canadians hold intense opinions. More significant is that the intensity of opinions held by a small group of people who constitute a "special" public opposed to, or in favour of, membership can influence a foreign-policy decision affecting most people, who are generally unconcerned. In the case of Quebec, the results of the referendum indicated the intensity of the conflict in that province. While appearing to be a victory for federalists, the referendum also served to dramatize how severely public opinion had polarized in Quebec.

The intensity of opinions is of great importance to government decision makers. If people hold opinions of low intensity on an issue, government may decide to proceed with a particular policy direction that is not very popular. Or intensity may reflect a strong consensus compelling a government to act or not to act with its policy ambitions. In Canada, governments spend millions of dollars each year on public-opinion surveys to test just how people will react to their policy initiatives. Between June 1987 and October 1988, just prior to the federal election, various departments of the federal government commissioned over 260 public-opinion surveys. All provincial governments are frequent users of opinion polls to measure the intensity of public reactions to their policies.

The *stability* of public opinion is another characteristic of particular interest to governments. Stability is the degree to which the direction and intensity of an opinion remain the same over time. Some people may adhere to a particular viewpoint for decades, while others shift position frequently. People also vary greatly in the consistency of their opinions. A Canadian may believe that government spending should be increased, but if he or she also wants taxes reduced, we would regard the opinion as inconsistent. Changes in opinion may require a modification of policies and programs by governments. The stability and volatility of public opinion are important measures for government decision makers and a constant challenge to political leadership.

Measuring Public Opinion

Nearly two centuries ago, the great French social theorist Alexis de Tocqueville argued that a society is a democratic one when elected officials pay attention to their electorates. When governors do not know what the people really want it is impossible for them to be responsible. A great deal of effort had to go into finding out what the public thought about particular issues. Before the 1930s governments, historians, and political observers had to guess at public opinion by analysing newspaper stories, political speeches, voting returns, and travellers' diaries. The founding fathers in both Canada and the United States felt that they could tap into public opinion by implementing representation by population in the legislative structures of each country. The framers thought that attitudes and actions in the legislatures would reflect public opinion on a wide variety of issues. However, after much experience with these legislative structures of government, it became evident that bills passed by a majority of elected representatives do not necessarily reflect the opinions of a majority of citizens.

In the nineteenth century, newspapers and magazines often enlivened their coverage of politics by conducting straw polls or mail surveys of their readers. The difficulty in relying on the results of these polls was that the method of *sampling* was not random. Not until the 1930s were efficient new scientific surveys and sampling techniques pioneered by Georges Gallup, Elmo Roper, and Archibold Crossley, all of whom had developed modern polling methods in American advertising and marketing research. The "little" Gallup poll was based on the theory that a sample of individuals selected by chance from a population would be "representative" of the entire population, so that a few thousand interviews representative of the total population would be far more effective in tapping public opinion than millions of ballots collected in a biassed or haphazard fashion. This means that the traits of individuals in a sample – their attitudes, beliefs, political characteristics, and so on – will reflect the traits of the entire population. Sampling theory does not posit that the sample will exactly match the population, only that it will reflect the population within some predictable degree of accuracy.

Three factors condition the degree of accuracy on the sample. One is that the sample must be taken randomly, so that each individual in the population has the same chance of being selected. In Canada, direct random sampling is complicated, given the size and dispersion of the population. Instead, pollsters first divide the country into geographical areas, then randomly choose areas, and eventually sample individuals who live in those areas. The second factor that affects the accuracy of sampling is the amount of variation in the population. It is important to stratify the sample so that the same variations in the population, i.e., linguistic, racial, gender, etc., are reflected in the sample. Finally, the size of the sample also affects the accuracy. The larger the sample, the more accurately it will reflect the population. For example, a sample of 400 individuals will predict accurately to a population within 6 percentage points (plus or minus), 95 percent of the time. Most national samples, such as the Gallup or Reid polls, are accurate within 2.5 to 4 percentage points, 19 times out of 20.

The results of public-opinion polls are often displayed in charts like those in figure 1.5, which depicts three idealized patterns of distribution – normal, skewed, and bimodal. Two basic elements that contribute to the shape of the opinion distribution are the percentage of the population that holds the opinion (vertical axis) and the direction and intensity of the opinion (– to ++, horizontal axis). Different patterns of public opinion affect the options open to policy makers. Opinions that are normally distributed permit government policies to range on either side of the centrist position (note the portion of the population with no opinion or weak opinion that clusters around the centre). Thus the pattern (a) is permissive because leaders may act freely without fear of much public reaction. The patterns in (b) are skewed to the pro side or con side of an issue and represent the consensus pattern of opinion. In these patterns the options open to leaders are more limited because most people have made

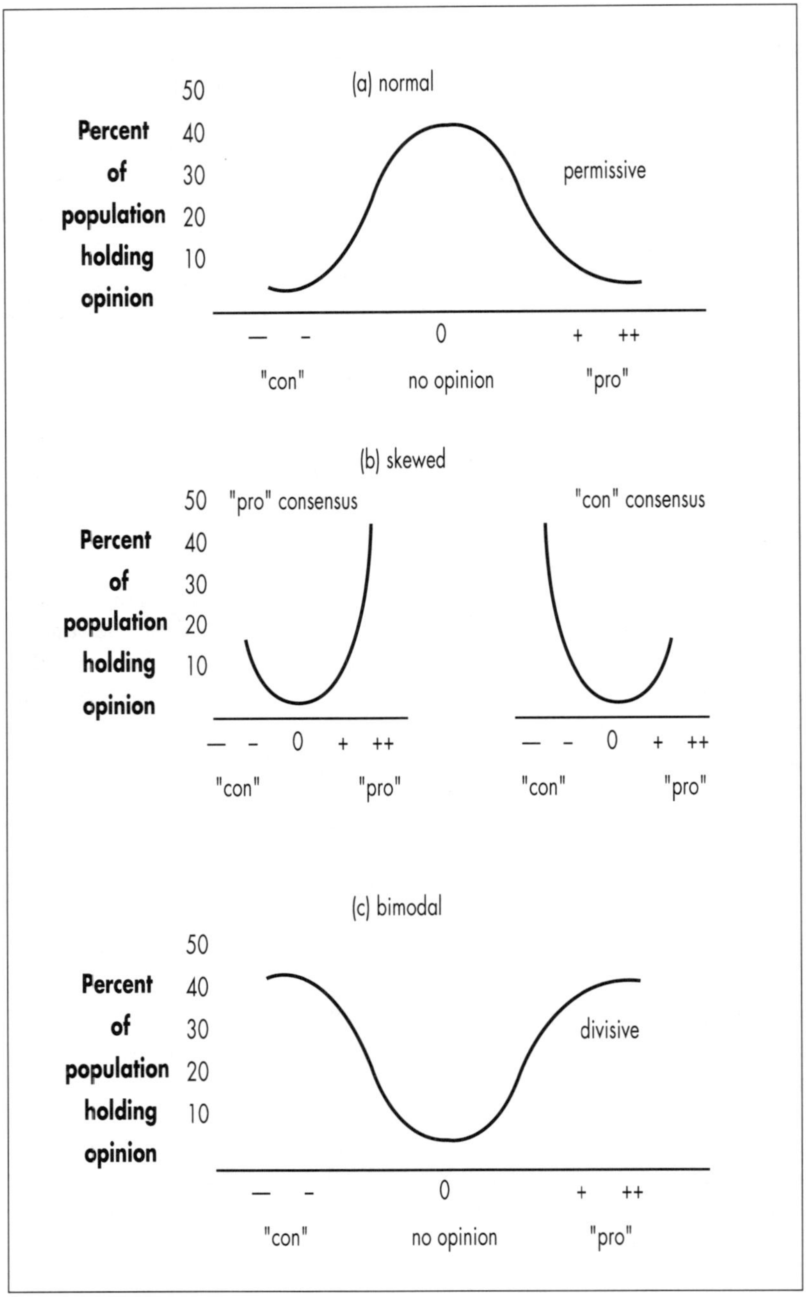
(a) normal
Percent of population holding opinion
50
40
30
20
10
permissive
— - 0 + ++
"con" no opinion "pro"
(b) skewed
"pro" consensus
"con" consensus
Percent of population holding opinion
50
40
30
20
10
— - 0 + ++
"con" "pro"
— - 0 + ++
"con" "pro"
(c) bimodal
Percent of population holding opinion
50
40
30
20
10
divisive
— - 0 + ++
"con" no opinion "pro"

Figure 1.5

up their minds and hold an opinion on one side of the issue. It would be politically perilous for government to ignore such a consensus of opinion, pro or con. The pattern of public opinion in (c) is conflictive and divisive. In such a bimodal distribution, opinions divide almost evenly over an issue. Bimodal distributions of opinion have the greatest potential to generate political conflict, especially if people on both sides feel intensely about the issue.

Accurately measuring something as complex as public opinion has stimulated public doubts about the roll of polling in a democracy. Do polls simply measure public sentiments from time to time or do they influence political behaviour when they are widely published or released during election campaigns? There is growing academic suspicion that the predictive value of polls influences undecided voters, politicians, and governments; encourages or discourages volunteer campaign workers; and positively or negatively affects the fund-raising efforts of political parties.[56] Increasingly, observers are noting that elections are *poll-inspired* and election campaigns are *poll-driven.* But if polls do have extensive persuasive effects, people are not willing to admit that they do. Pollsters in a Globe-Environics survey tested respondents after the Canadian federal election in 1988 and found that only 13 percent admitted public-opinion polls influenced their voting decision. Of the rest, 85 percent stated that they were not influenced and 2 percent refused to answer. Another "poll on polls," conducted by Gallup, found almost the same results, with most voters saying they were not influenced by published polls.

There are three kinds of polling organizations: (1) professional organizations that conduct public-opinion surveys and marketing research for both political and non-political clients, such as Gallup and Harris; (2) political pollsters who usually work for a candidate or a political party, such as Decima for the Conservatives and Goldfarb for the Liberals; (3) media pollsters, survey research conducted by the electronic or print media, e.g., CBC or CTV. In the 1979 and 1980 federal election campaigns, only a handful of national polls were conducted by professional polling companies and TV networks. By 1984 the federal election inspired eleven independent national polls. During the 1988 election campaign twenty-six independent national polls were completed, an average of four polls a week – the most polling ever conducted during any Canadian election.

Governments and politicians are interested in polls and increasingly conduct their own polling not only to find out whether they are winning or losing but also to learn if they are popular or unpopular with certain groups. Learning which groups are not supportive enables governments and politicians to make special appeals in that direction.

Because public attitudes are often unstable or uninformed, critics of Canadian political opinion argue that we are too easily manipulated into thinking one way or another by polls. During election campaigns people learn that political parties and their candidates are "sold," not unlike automobiles or toothpaste. If the government or the media can deliberately manipulate our political attitudes does this mean that we are ignorant or that our democracy is a sham?

In the final analysis, politics is an inescapable process: it cannot be separated from the rest of society. Politics omits very little about human existence. It must be observed and studied by all of us if we want to understand the world we live in. As students of political science we have already begun to consider what broad cultural traditions give shape to the phenomenon of politics. We ask what it is, how we come to learn about it, and how we express it: in everyday language, who gets what, when, and how? This question requires us to look at ourselves and to look at how people "do" politics. Politics, then, is about us as we live in the midst of a community of others.

REFERENCES

1. David Easton, *A Framework for Political Analysis* (Englewood Cliffs, NJ: Prentice-Hall 1965), 50; Alan Ball, *Modern Politics and Government* (London: Macmillan Education Ltd. 1988) 3–15.
2. As Harold D. Lasswell so aptly put it in the title of his book, *Politics: Who Gets What, When, How* (New York: McGraw-Hill 1936; republished, Cleveland: World Publishing Co. 1958).
3. V.I. Lenin, "Left Wing Communism: An Infantile Disorder," in *Selected Works* (New York: International Publishers 1943).
4. Quoted in Stuart Schram, *The Political Thought of Mao Tse Tung* (New York: Frederick A. Praeger 1969), 287.
5. Hugh Percy Jones, *Dictionary of Foreign Phrases and Classical Quotations* (Edinburgh: John Grant 1923).
6. John H. Redekop, "Canadian Political Institutions" in his *Approaches to Canadian Politics* (Scarborough, ON: Prentice-Hall Canada Inc. 1983), 149 .
7. Harold D. Lasswell and A. Kaplan, *Power and Society: A Framework for Political Inquiry* (New Haven: Yale University Press 1950), 4-6; J.C. Davies, *Human Nature in Politics* (New York: Wiley 1963), ch. I.
8. See Leroy Rieselbach and George Balch, *Psychology and Politics: An Introductory Reader* (New York: Holt, Rinehart and Winston Inc. 1969), 4.
9. See Alan Elms, *Personality in Politics* (New York: Harcourt, Brace Jovanovich Inc. 1976), 83; Ralph Stogdill, *Handbook of Leadership* (Glencoe, IL: Free Press 1974).
10. See Dan Nimmo and Robert Savage, *Candidates and Their Images* (Pacific Palisades, CA: Goodyear Publishing Co. 1976), 25–39.
11. Canadian Broadcasting Corporation, "The House," aired June 11, 1983 and June 16, 1984.
12. Gabriel Almond, "Comparative Political Systems," *Journal of Politics* XVIII no. 3 (1956): 396.
13. Samuel Beer and Adam Ulam, *Patterns of Government* (New York: Random House 1958), 12.
14. Sidney Verba, "Conclusion: Comparative Political Culture," in Lucian W. Pye and Sidney Verba, eds., *Political Culture and Political Development* (Princeton: Princeton University Press 1965), 515.
15. Lewis Bowman and G.R. Boynton, *Political Behavior and Public Opinion* (Englewood Cliffs, NJ: Prentice-Hall Inc. 1974), 5–8.
16. Stephen Ullman, "Regional Political Cultures in Canada: A Theoretical and Conceptual Introduction," in Richard Schultz, Orest Kruhlak, and John Terry, eds., *The Canadian Political Process* (Toronto: Holt, Rinehart and Winston of Canada Ltd. 1979), 7.
17. Richard Simeon and David Elkins, "Regional Political Cultures in Canada," *Canadian Journal of Political Science* VII (September 1974): 397; and Roger Gibbins, *Regionalism: Territorial Politics in Canada and the United States* (Toronto: Butterworths 1982).
18. See Robert Fortner, "Communication and Canadian National Destiny," *Canadian Journal of Communication* 6 (Fall 1979): 43; Jean-Louis Gagnon, "Community, Identity, Unity," York University, Gerstein Conference on Mass Communication and Canadian Nationhood, April 10, 1981; Warner Troyer, *The Sound and the Fury* (Rexdale, ON: John Wiley & Sons 1980).
19. Jarol Manheim, *The Politics Within: A Primer in Political Attitudes and Behavior* (New York: Longman Inc. 1982), 56; Lucian W. Pye and

Sidney Verba, eds., *Political Culture and Political Development* (Princeton: Princeton University Press 1965), 544–60.

20. See J.A.A. Lovink, "Is Canadian Politics Too Competitive?" *Canadian Journal of Political Science* 6 (September 1973).
21. Seymour Lipset, *The First New Nation: The United States in Historical and Comparative Perspective* (Garden City, NY: Doubleday 1967), 240–2, 284–5.
22. See Lasswell, *Politics: Who Gets What, When, How?*. It is interesting to compare Lasswell with William Glasser, "Our Basic Needs – The Powerful Forces that Drive Us" in Glasser, *Control Theory: A New Explanation of How We Control Our Lives* (New York: Harper & Row 1984), 5–13.
23. Robert Dahl, *Modern Political Analysis* (Englewood Cliffs, NJ: Prentice-Hall Inc. 1965), 50.
24. Karl Deutsch, *Politics and Government: How People Decide Their Fate* (Boston: Houghton Mifflin Co. 1980), 26.
25. See World Bank, *World Development Report, 1988* (New York: Oxford University Press 1988).
26. See Ian Adams, W. Cameron, B. Hill, and P. Penz, *The Real Poverty Report* (Edmonton: M.G. Hurtig Publishers 1971).
27. Leo A. Johnson, "Precapitalist Economic Formations and the Capitalist Labour Market in Canada, 1911–71," in James E. Curtis and William G. Scott, eds., *Social Stratification: Canada*, 2nd ed. (Scarborough, ON: Prentice-Hall 1979), 143.
28. UNESCO, *Statistical Yearbook, 1988* (Paris: UNESCO 1988).
29. Wilford Martin and A.J. Macdonnel, *Canadian Education: A Sociological Analysis* (Scarborough, ON: Prentice-Hall 1978).
30. *Canada Year Book 1988* (Ottawa: Statistics Canada 1987), 4-1–4-28.
31. See Plato, *The Symposium*, trans. by Walter Hamilton (New York: Penquin Books 1980), and Christopher Morris, *Western Political Thought*, Vol.1: *Plato to Augustine* (London: Longmans, Green and Co. Ltd. 1967), 35–79.
32. Thomas R. Dye, *Understanding Public Policy*, 4th ed. (Englewood Cliffs, NJ: Prentice-Hall 1981), 1.
33. See Donald Higgins, *Local and Urban Politics in Canada* (Toronto: Gage Educational Publishing Co. 1986), 31–63, 85–116.
34. Canadian Federation of Mayors and Municipalities, "Puppets on a Shoestring" (Ottawa, April 28, 1976); see also Federation of Canadian Municipalities, Resource Task Force on Constitutional Reform, *Municipal Government in a New Canadian Federal System* (Ottawa 1980, and second report, 1982).
35. Quoted in K.G. Crawford, *Canadian Municipal Government* (Toronto: University of Toronto Press 1954), 4; see also Robert Dahl, "The City in the Future of Democracy" *American Political Science Review* LXI (December 1967).
36. See Clyde Weaver and Thomas Gunton, "From Drought Assistance to Megaprojects: Fifty years of Regional Theory and Policy in Canada," *The Canadian Journal of Regional Science/La Revue Canadienne des Science Regionales* V (Spring 1982).
37. See David Alexander, "New Notions of Happiness: Nationalism, Regionalism and Atlantic Canada," *Journal of Canadian Studies* 15, no. 2 (1980) 29; and Donald Savoie, *The Canadian Economy: A Regional Perspective* (Toronto: Methuen 1986), 20.
38. Lucian Pye, *Politics, Personality and Nation-Building* (New Haven, CT: Yale University Press 1963), 1–14.
39. See Robert Adie and Paul Thomas, *Canadian Public Administration* (Scarborough, ON: Prentice-Hall Canada Inc. 1987) 388–95.
40. David Easton and Jack Dennis, *Children in the Political System* (New York: McGraw-Hill 1969), 7; see also Robert Coles, *The Political Life of Children* (Boston: Atlantic Monthly Press 1986).
41. Roberta Sigel, "Assumptions about the Learning of Political Values," *Annals of the American Academy of Social and Political*

Science 361 (1985): 1; M. Jennings and R. Niemi, *Generations and Politics* (Princeton: Princeton University Press 1981).

42. R.G. Niemi, "Political Socialization," in J.N. Knutson, ed., *Handbook of Political Psychology* (San Francisco: Jossey-Bass 1973), and J.N. Knutson, "Pre-political Ideologies: The Basis for Political Learning," in R. Niemi, ed., *The Politics of Future Citizens* (San Francisco: Jossey-Bass 1974), 80.

43. Harold Lasswell, "The Political Personality," in Leroy Rieselbach and George Balch, eds., *Psychology and Politics* (New York: Holt, Rinehart and Winston Inc. 1969), 47.

44. See Charles Horton Cooley, *Human Nature and Social Order* (New York: Schocken 1964). As applicable to Canadians, see David V.J. Bell, "Political Culture in Canada," in Michael S. Whittington and Glen Williams, eds., *Canadian Politics in the 1980s* (Toronto: Methuen 1981),108–25.

45. James Chowning Davies, "Political Socialization: From Womb to Children," in Stanley Renshon, ed., *Handbook of Political Socialization* (New York: Free Press 1977), 142–7.

46. David Easton and Jack Dennis, "The Child's Image of Government," *The Annals of the American Academy of Political and Social Science* 361 (1965): 56.

47. The principals in the survey were T.G. Carroll of Brock University, Donald Higgins of St. Mary's University, and Michael Whittington of Carleton University. The findings of this study are summarized in Richard Van Loon and Michael Whittington, *The Canadian Political System: Environment, Structure, and Process* (Toronto: McGraw-Hill Ryerson Ltd. 1981), 120.

48. Ronald Landes, "The Use of Role Theory in Political Socialization Research: A Review, Critique and Modest Proposal," *International Journal of Comparative Sociology* 17, nos. 1-2 (March–June 1976): 59–72.

49. Susan Harvey and Ted Harvey, "Adolescent Political Outlooks: The Effects of Intelligence as an Independent Variable," *Midwest Journal of Political Science* 14 (November 1970): 592; see also Alexander Astin et al., *The American Freshman: National Norms for Fall 1984* (Los Angeles: UCLA Graduate School of Education 1986), 64.

50. Roberta Sigel and Marilyn Hoskin, "Perspectives on Adult Political Socialization - Areas of Research," in Allen Renshon, ed., *Handbook of Political Socialization: Theory and Research* (New York: Free Press 1977), 267.

51. See Richard Merelman, "The Family and Political Socialization: Towards a Theory of Exchange," *Journal of Politics* 42 (May 1980): 461–86; M.K. Jennings and R. Niemi, *Generations and Politics* (Princeton: Princeton University Press 1981), 90–1.

52. See Arthur Siegel, *Politics and the Media in Canada* (Toronto: McGraw-Hill Ryerson Ltd. 1983).

53. Paul Palmer, "The Concept of Public Opinion in Political Theory," in his *Essays in History and Political Theory in Honor of Charles H. McIlwain* (Cambridge, MA: Harvard University Press 1936).

54 See Benjamin Page and Robert Shapiro. "Effects of Public Opinion on Policy," *American Political Science Review* 77 (1983): 175–90; see also "The Linkage of Policy to Participation," in Alexander Heard and Michael Nelson, eds., *Presidential Selection* (Durham, NC: Duke University Press 1987).

55. V.O. Key, *Public Opinion and American Democracy* (New York: Alfred A. Knopf 1961), 14.

56. See C. Anthony Broh, "Polls, Pols and Parties," *Journal of Politics* 45 (August 1983); also Edwin Diamond and Stephen Bates, *The Spot: The Rise of Political Advertising on Television* (Cambridge, MA: MIT Press 1984).

SUGGESTED READINGS

Steven Brooks, *Public Policy in Canada: An Introduction* (Toronto: McClelland & Stewart 1989).

Robert Campbell and Leslie Pal, *The Real Worlds of Canadian Politics* (Peterborough, ON: Broadview Press 1989).

Irving Crespi, *Public Opinion, Polls, and Democracy* (Boulder, CO: Westview Press 1989).

Robert Brym, *Regionalism in Canada* (Toronto: Irwin Publishing 1986).

R. Kenneth Carty and Peter Ward, *National Politics and Community in Canada* (Vancouver: University of British Columbia Press 1986).

Donald Higgins, *Local and Urban Politics in Canada* (Toronto: Gage Educational Publishing Co. 1986).

Michael Gibbons, *Interpreting Politics* (Oxford: Basil Blackwell 1988).

Gilbert Stelter, *Canada's Cities: Historical Readings on Urbanization* (Toronto: Copp Clark Pitman 1989).

Richard Lau and David Sears, eds., *Political Cognition* (Hillsdale, NJ: Erlbaum 1986).

John Porter, *The Measure of Canadian Society* (Ottawa: Carleton University Press 1987).

GLOSSARY

political activists: People who are distinguished by the extent of their involvement in politics, and by the methods they use to initiate change in the political system.

authoritative: The characteristic of a person, group, institution, or government that makes legitimate either in reality or in appearance the acts and commands exercised in its name.

institutional: Established patterns of human behaviour consisting of structured economic, political, or social interaction within a framework of common goals and values.

behavioural: Any human activity, ranging from internal psychological responses (as in thought, perception, judgement, and opinion), to overt, observable, and physical actions.

public policy: The formal process of choosing, formulating, and implementing the goals, values, and practices of a society.

political culture: All the learned behaviour, beliefs, customs, and institutions a people use to do politics.

institutional role: consists of those actions, behaviours, and outputs typically performed by a political or legal body, in accordance with the prescriptions of a constitution, set of by–laws, or rules and regulations endorsed by state authority.

institutional function: The actions and performance of political organizations, their leaders, and administrators that contribute to the adaptation and survival of a political system.

ethnic composition: The presence of diverse social groups in society, distinguished by language, national origin, customs, religion, and race.

political symbol: Any thing or person that generates political significance beyond what it is itself, e.g., a flag, a governor general, a legislature.

political style: The characteristic behaviour patterns of an individual, group, or a state.

continualismo: The practice of many Latin American chief executives to extend their terms in office beyond the limits set by constitutions or political promises.

imposición: The practice in many Latin American states of pre-selecting a candidate and manipulating the political process to ensure that candidate's election.

personalismo: The individualization of the political process. Political power flows from the force of personality rather than from institutions.

political system: All interrelated institutions, practices, and traditions that enable a society to make authoritative, binding and coercive decisions extending to all its members.

group: Two or more people who interact in patterned ways, share beliefs, values, and goals, and have a sense of membership or belonging.

political values: Those beliefs, goals, and standards that a society professes and tries to achieve.

process: Any rational sequence of related actions or operations leading to a desired goal or result.

industrialization: The process by which a society comes to be characterized by an economic system and a mode of social life based on machinery and the factory system of production.

infrastructure: The social and political substructure of a community that includes the institutions, laws, economy, communication, transportation, and education systems.

regionalism: The identification of subnational cultural, economic, and political interests that are articulated and defined in relation to a particular area of a country.

residual power: Jurisdictions or powers that are not specifically enumerated in a constitution, delegated to a specific government, or implied from powers that are delegated to a recognized government.

internalize: The process of adopting a society's norms as part of the individual's personality and notion of self.

political cynicism: Expressed feelings of doubt, distrust, and sarcasm aimed at the competence, credibility, and honesty of people in government and politics.

political efficacy: The belief that one's participation in politics has some impact on political outcomes and government decisions.

political apathy: Feelings of inattentiveness and/or non-involvement in political affairs, based on the attitude that perceived benefits in political participation are less than the anticipated costs of lost time or income.

political participation: Actions of private citizens by which they seek to influence or support government and politics.

politicization: To transform an activity that apparently has no political connotations into one that fulfills political ends.

party identification: The sense of psychological attachment or positive state of mind a voter has for a party, which is not the same thing as voting for a party in any given election.

peer groups: People who are similar to an individual in age, gender, economic, social, and political background.

2

What Is Political Science?

Italian political philosopher Niccoló Machiavelli, 1469-1527

EACH DAY CANADIANS ARE BOMBARDED with information from the media about political events occurring at home and around the world that evoke curiosity and spark our interest. On the radio we hear that after 27 years of imprisonment under apartheid, Nelson Mandela is released in South Africa. In the newspaper we read that many federal government departments still continue to waste and mismanage public monies despite the auditor general's long-standing struggle to make Ottawa more accountable for its spending decisions. On television we watch a documentary on the economic unification of Europe by 1992. We analyse these data, draw our own conclusions from them, and decide to act or not to act as a result of our evaluations. This constant barrage of information leaves us feeling overloaded and somehow threatened by the apparent complexities of the political world. But, like untutored music-lovers who discover after some instruction that they can understand music, we, too, can acquire appreciation of politics and government.

An understanding of politics is not a gift; it is an achievement. Learning to cope with the vast amounts of political information that come to us every day is a matter of training. We need to place the data in proper perspective by imposing some organization and structure on the flow of world events. First we must be motivated to learn about the political personalities and decisions that affect our lives. Then we must apply a methodology* to our process of learning that will provide a system for receiving new information. The information received becomes a contribution to a growing body of knowledge, rather than a hodgepodge of seemingly unrelated events.

This book is designed to rouse your interest in politics and to provide you with a number of different perspectives for understanding world affairs. It is probably impossible for any introductory text to teach students to think like political scientists, whose field, the study of political behaviour*, is expansive and requires a great deal of instruction, experience, and reading to master. But this book will give students a good start in that direction. The course is a general introduction to political science for Canadians rather than one restricted to Canadian government and politics. Wherever possible, a Canadian example has been used in order to relate to the country in which you are now studying and to the events about which you hear in the news. But the scope of the book deliberately ventures far beyond Canada and draws examples from political systems in every corner of the world.

Like you, political scientists want to learn about politics in a meaningful way. Over the years they have built a recognized academic discipline designed to discover the purpose and significance of all political behaviour. Nothing in politics just happens: events can be explained if a systematic approach to information is used. An introductory text in political science has the dual function of showing the student what information is politically relevant and how to organize that information in a coherent way.

One of the important tasks of political science is to study in a systematic and orderly way how politics affects the lives of people. People are both the causes and victims of politics. The needs of people, their values, their beliefs, and their share of worldly possessions are the stuff of politics. For this reason, a knowledge of politics brings us closer to a knowledge of ourselves. Whether we are aware of it or not, each of us has a political dimension. Nothing occurs in politics that in some way does not relate to our attitudes and behaviour.

All political analysis reduces itself to a study of people engaged in the form of behaviour that we call political.[1] None of our institutions (such as parliaments, congresses, and political parties) or processes (such as legislation, administration, and revolution) exist apart from the political behaviour of people. When we look at political phenomena from this perspective we see the world of politics not only as an institutional mosaic but also as groups of people interacting with each other because of different personal preferences and expectations. It is in this context that we can define political science as the study of people as individuals or groups, engaged in political behaviour of all kinds – in institutions, states, and international organizations.

Allied Fields of Study

Political behaviour does not occur in a vacuum. It is a highly complex aspect of general social behaviour.[2] It often appears as aggression, co-operation, institutionalization, negotiation, organization, and revolution. Because of the all-inclusive nature of politics, political scientists cannot approach the study of politics in a narrow fashion. They must draw from many other fields of knowledge that, in various ways, explain human behaviour. For this reason, political science is truly an eclectic* discipline. Even though political science collaborates with many other bodies of knowledge, it still retains its own character. It is not philosophy, although philosophy is inherent in its nature; it is not history, sociology, or economics, although it embodies something of all of these. In fact, there are at least eight specialized fields of study from which political scientists now frequently gather relevant information to construct theories about political behaviour. A thumb-nail sketch of each of these fields will help you understand the eclectic nature of political science.

Anthropology

Anthropology has elements of both a social and a natural science. Briefly put, it is the study of humankind in its primitive and preindustrial forms using the insights of archaeology, biology, cultural history, and physiology.

Political science has drawn on the findings of political anthropology to learn about the political behaviour of ancient peoples. For example, accumulated data from anthropological and archaeological sources have contradicted the assumptions of political theorists such as Hobbes, Locke, and Rousseau. These thinkers held the view that human beings entered into a social contract* for protection and survival, and that this prepared the way for the creation of democratic and non-democratic forms of government. Anthropologists have informed us that a social contract like the one assumed by early political theorists was never a consideration of preliterate peoples. Anthropology gives the student of politics insight into a great variety of political systems starting from the earliest examples of human political cultures to the present.

Economics

Economics – widely recognized as the most highly developed social science – studies human behaviour as it is manifested in the production, distribution, and use of goods and services. In Canada approximately 42 percent of our gross national product* (GNP) is spent by governments at all levels: federal, provincial, and municipal. As governments have taken a greater role in making decisions that affect our lives, also has politics increasingly encroached upon the distribution of goods and services. In today's world, the problems of inflation, recession, unemployment, and economic growth are as much related to political behaviour as they are to economic behaviour. Governments now run businesses, promote industries, intervene in the operation of the marketplace, and redistribute wealth. For these reasons the disciplines of economics and political science have drawn closer in recent years. Once only the preserve of economic analysts, the goals of economic policy in Canada have been the target of political-science research since the 1960s.

One of strongest areas of interest to political scientists is international economics. An understanding of this important field is essential for analysing international relations. Newspapers abound with stories about international monetary crises, the need for a new international economic order (NIEO), economic integration, and global trade. International economics provides the political scientist with the necessary analytical tools for evaluating the role of government policies on exchange rates, interest rates, commodity prices, the balance of payments, and many other factors in a world composed of interdependent national economies.

Geography

Geography is the study of the relationships that humans have with their natural environment – the social as well as the spatial and physical aspects of the environment. Geographers are interested in ecological problems created by industrialization and urbanization as well as in the whole range of economic behaviour resulting from our proximity to land, water, and natural resources.

In Canada, politics is intrinsically bound to geographic factors: regionalism is as much a political as a geographical fact of life. The Maritimes, Prairies, and British Columbia are geographically remote from each other, yet they share a common alienation from the centre of political power in Ottawa. Canada's geographical divisions have not always been conducive to political unity, making Canada an entity constantly at war with its own geography.

The term *geopolitics** is often used to describe the character and structure of the international political system. No state is made up of institutions alone. States are territorial units that often develop relations with other states based on geographical proximity, collective security, and regional economic integration.

History

History, as most of us are aware, is the study of the past. Historians have provided political scientists with a chronological framework for understanding past political ideas and events. While it is true that political scientists are usually more interested in current problems, many contemporary political institutions and events can only be understood by the chronological organization of information generated by historians. For example, the development of multiculturalism in Canada has been well documented by Canadian historians. From this documentation political scientists have been able to place the multi-ethnic character of Canada in political perspective. In the late eighteenth century, Canada's population was not as diversified as it is today. In 1790, the overwhelming majority of Canadians were French. One hundred years later, people of British origin accounted for 59 percent of the population, 30 percent were French, and only 11 percent were other nationalities. Since the 1940s, Canada has become a country of wide population diversity, with over 26 percent of the population belonging to neither of the two founding European peoples. Political scientists have noted the effects of multiculturalism* on Canadian elections, campaigning, political parties, pressure groups, and intergovernmental relations. Some political scientists have adopted the historical approach to politics as their primary research methodology. Others have used it to enrich their scientific methods of political inquiry.

Philosophy

Philosophy is the branch of inquiry concerned with the world of ideas, knowledge, and being. Philosophy has provided modern political science with a rich tradition of writers whose works constitute the subfield of political inquiry known as political philosophy. Politically philosophy, which is part of political science as a discipline, considers questions of social and economic values, political reality, and intellectual approaches to political analysis.

Historically, philosophy has been associated with normative theory. The philosopher is concerned with political values, moral judgements, and ethical and metaphysical questions – with what "ought" to be our social and political goals. These issues are difficult to test scientifically because concepts such as justice, happiness, and freedom resist measurement, and the philosopher will not hesitate to use logic, intuition, speculation, and personal conviction to describe or explain political reality.

In contrast, the scientific method usually dictates that scholars focus their attentions on falsifiable hypotheses*, avoid value judgements, and shun intuition as a reliable source of truth. Thus, political philosophy retains an important role in modern political science by daring to tread where science fears to go. Political philosophers can speculate and dream without the constraints of a rigorous scientific methodology. This encourages the development of creativity, which is so necessary in a social science that is often asked to measure the immeasurable.

Psychology

Psychology studies the relationship between mental process and human behaviour. Because of its advanced experimental and scientific methodologies, psychology has earned the reputation of an advanced social science.

It is in the field of social psychology, however, that psychology comes closest to political science. Social psychologists have answered many questions on how a person's attitudes, beliefs, and general personality traits are keys to understanding his or her social behaviour. The political psychologist is interested in how we develop our political selves from childhood to adulthood. Psychological research has contributed to our understanding of the personality characteristics of leaders, personality dynamics in voting behaviour, and the psychological factors behind political conflict.

Because political behaviour is so much influenced by personality, we are inclined to ask how expectations, motivations, and perceptions affect our political system. Are there distinct personality types drawn to the House of Commons? Are politicians driven by the genuine wish to help people or is their altruism a disguise for selfish career goals? Although personality is not always a prime factor in explaining political behaviour, it cannot be ignored. Indeed, the more that politics is studied as a behavioural phenomenon, the greater the tendency to call on psychology for insights.

Finally, political scientists have learned much from psychology's use of interviews, questionnaires, and survey techniques. Increasingly, political researchers are generating their own data to test hypotheses by using these methods of social research. Because of its utility, the application of psychological-testing approaches to the world of politics has gained recognition from political scientists all over the world.

Sociology

No other social science has as much affinity to political science as does sociology. Sociologists study social relationships as they manifest themselves in human group experiences. Because sociology is concerned with the comprehensive study of group behaviour, it is of special interest to political science. In almost all instances, groups are the basis of political behaviour. That politics is a group process can be seen in the behaviour of political parties, interest groups, legislative bodies, and public bureaucracies. To the political sociologist, the state is but one of many groups interacting in a society. This pluralistic approach to politics posits that power is shared among a multiplicity of groups that are competitive with the state.

The label *political sociology* refers to the sociology of politics. Political sociologists identify politics as cultural phenomena: the way we "do" politics is a reflection of the way we do other things in a particular social setting. Political sociology is concerned with the social foundations of political power, the effects of group conflict on political institutions, and the many social variables affecting political action. In Canada, political sociologists might consider whether Canadian society is pluralistic by questioning if various groups compete for political and economic power. If competition is found not to exist or to be weak, then they would want to know whether there is actually a coalition of groups unified as an élite who shape government policies to meet their demands.

As political scientists penetrate every level of society in search of answers to political problems, the distinction between sociologists who study politics and political scientists who adopt a sociological approach to politics has virtually disappeared.

Social Work

There is a continuing disagreement among social scientists about whether social work is actually a social science. As a practice, social work is a service profession that intervenes to help clients obtain their entitlement in a changing social and political system. But, in Canada, professors of social work and field workers also conduct research into social and political problems to build a theoretical knowledge base for social-work practice.

It is odd that political scientists have only recently discovered the contributions of social-work research to their field, because obviously the social-work profession is a front-line observer of the failures and weaknesses in our political system. Social workers address the problems of child neglect, domestic violence, drug abuse, violations of human rights, women's rights, native rights, and the effects of unemployment on the lives of people. From the research of the social-work profession, political scientists have become increasingly aware that stress can be politically generated, and can have widespread social ramifications, such as suicide, depression, and social disintegration. Often, in contrast to political scientists, social workers have been leaders in prescribing legislative and structural reforms at the political level. As political scientists seek to build a more relevant social science that can improve society, there is renewed concern for a value-centred discipline capable of political action. In this regard, social work may be to political science what engineering is to physics.

Statistics

When states first began to collect information about their citizens these numbers were appropriately called "statistics." Today, the discipline of statistics, with its methods for collecting, presenting, analysing, and interpreting data, has gained momentum in its applications to many fields of knowledge. Social science practitioners in such fields as anthropology, economics, political science, psychology, and sociology are all expected at least to have what is called statistical literacy. In fact, it is virtually impossible to become professional in any of these fields without having learned to gather and interpret statistics for analytical purposes.

A knowledge of statistical methods enables political scientists to form hypotheses for testing, to gather population samples from which to infer the probability of outcomes, to interpret the many charts, graphs, and tables that describe the political world, and confidently to plot patterns and trends of political behaviour. The political-science profession has become increasingly competent in the use of statistical techniques in research. Today, practitioners collect their information for analysis with statistical tools.

Computers have greatly simplified calculations used in statistical analysis. Software packages contain computer programs that perform particular types of statistical analysis, and a large number have been written for users at many levels of expertise. These packages now permit the user to apply a wide variety of statistical techniques to the same data with only minor changes in commands.

The Evolution of Political Science

In one sense the study of politics is as ancient as recorded history. In another sense, "political science" is a product of the twentieth century. The growth of political science as a modern academic discipline took a lot of time before the characteristics fundamental to a bona fide social science were present.

Philosophers have been writing about politics for thousands of years. Some of them, notably Plato and Aristotle, made contributions to the study of politics that are still relevant today. However, political science as such did not exist until this century and was not generally included among the social sciences until sixty years ago. As this section will reveal, most of the evolution of political science has occurred gradually over the centuries. In fact you are about to trace the emergence of a very old discipline.

The Greeks

We can trace the beginnings of the study of government and politics to the Greeks over 2400 years ago. The Greeks used the word *idiot* to refer to anyone who had no interest in politics. They took politics so seriously that they studied it as the "queen of the sciences." To them the study of government was architectonic*, i.e., a highly organized and structured approach to building a society and its political institutions.

The enduring contribution of the Greeks to political science lies in the way they thought about politics. They saw it as a natural form of human behaviour and tried to detect recurrent regularities in political behaviour from which to generalize about society. We know the Greeks did not apply the same scientific methods currently used by modern social scientists. But they did possess a "social science attitude" through which they applied independent objective reasoning to the Hellenic world of politics.[3] In fact, the word politics itself is derived from the Greek word for city-state, πολισ (polis). To the Greeks, the polis was the centre of the political universe.

Plato (427–347 B.C.) is credited with writing the first major utopian study, widely regarded as a classic in political science. In *The Republic* he displays the critical attitude that is necessary for the proper study of government and prescribes reforms and models for politics as actually practised. He elevated the study of politics to an independent academic enterprise when he founded an academy near Athens. Some have called it the first school of political science and law.[4]

Plato's student, Aristotle (384–322 B.C.), succeeded in overcoming the tendency of earlier writers of political thought to mix allegory, legend, and myth with political analysis. His use of systematic reasoning and critical inquiry in the *Politics* led him to conclude that "man is by nature a political animal." Aristotle held that all people are politicians, even though those in public office appear to be more political than others.

Aristotle is usually thought of as the father of modern political science. When he established the Lyceum in about 335 B.C., he employed special research assistants to compile information for political analysis. In fact, the Lyceum was dedicated to the scientific study of politics, using principles of knowledge from every known field of study. As far as we know from his work at the Lyceum, Aristotle was the first to recognize the eclectic nature of political inquiry and to encourage it in an institutional setting. We must credit Aristotle with nurturing the genesis of a modern political science, even though many other conditions had to evolve before it became the modern scholarly enterprise of today.

Another Greek student of politics, Polybius (204–122 B.C.), initiated the historical approach to the study of politics. In his intensive studies of the polis he linked the formation of foreign policy to complex institutional factors found in aristocracy, democracy, and monarchy. In his great political analysis of Rome, he attempted to trace the chronology of Roman political power. Polybius became a specialist in political history and was the first in a long line of specialists to develop the study of politics into subfields.

We can see that the Greeks viewed politics as an activity that is observable, classifiable, and understandable. Even in ancient times, it was clear that the serious study of politics was the only way to reform the weaknesses of a political system and to preserve the strengths of a civilization.

The Romans

Roman political thought made two special contributions to the study of government. The Romans focussed their political inquiry on the study of law and on public administration*. Knowledge of the law was an important stepping-stone to many appointive positions of government in the Roman Empire. The successes of the empire were mainly the result of the Roman genius for the universal application of law and the imperial administration.

Cicero (106–43 B.C.) took the lead in studying and writing about Roman government and politics. His two major works, *The Republic* and *The Laws*, provide us with a clear analysis of how the Roman political system fused *ius civile* (civil law), *ius gentium* (law of man), and *ius naturale* (natural law). Indeed, he was the only outstanding Roman of his time who took an objective interest in law and administration as aspects of a unique governmental system that aspired to rule the world. Without Cicero, the study of politics for the advancement of knowledge under the Roman Empire would not have taken place.

The Mediaeval Period

The mediaeval period lasted roughly from the fall of Rome in the fifth century to the Renaissance in the fourteenth. The astonishing growth of Christianity during this period turned the minds of the great writers from the general study of political affairs to theological and ecclesiastical concerns. In the words of Dunning, "the Middle Age was unpolitical."[5] The most notable writers were Augustine (354–430), John of Salisbury (1120–1180), Thomas Aquinas (1226–1274), and Marsiglio of Padua (1275–1343). Although they wrote to influence governments and rulers, they did so as dutiful sons of the Church and with the main goal of positing theological doctrine. Thus, the attitude of the Church toward society and the state became the subject of extensive controversy.

Augustine's great book, *The City of God*, was inspired by shock at the sacking of the "Eternal City" of Rome in 410; it was his attempt to explain such a devastating occurrence. In this book, Augustine posited two cities – the city of God and the city of man. Peace, harmony, and justice are found in the city of God, whose citizens are motivated by the love of God. The citizens of the city of man are motivated by love of self and this city is, therefore, imperfect and doomed to end. Although Augustine was speaking primarily of two spiritual states, the city of God could also be identified with the Church, and the city of man with the Roman Empire.

John of Salisbury posited the supremacy of ecclesiastical over temporal power. He held that a monarch must rule in conformity with Church principles or risk being overthrown.

Thomas Aquinas, the "Angelic Doctor," saw himself primarily as a theologian rather than as a political philosopher. Although agreeing with Aristotle that the purpose of the state is to direct a person to virtuous living, Aquinas held that human virtue was only attainable through the knowledge of God. For him the state was theologically oriented. Marsiglio of Padua is widely considered as the bridge between the mediaeval period and the Renaissance. As a practising physician, his scientific outlook made him sceptical about the dogmatic character of much of mediaeval thought. Marsiglio broke with the Middle Ages by rejecting the supremacy of theology over politics. His use of common sense, objective observation, and critical analysis made him a modern thinker with whom contemporary social scientists can identify.

With the exception of Marsiglio, these Christian writers reflected the non-political ethos of the Middle Ages. They did not take a secular* approach to political affairs, nor did they consider political problems as important as religious concerns. Because the Christian Church so dominated intellectual and social life in the Middle Ages, existing political thought centred on moral questions of "ought" (dogma) rather than scientific questions of "is" (facts). But during the central Middle Ages, a new institution emerged that would profoundly affect intellectual life in Europe and the world to the present day. This was the university, which ranks as the most enduring mediaeval contribution to modernity. The rise of universities spawned the growth of an intellectual class of people committed to original and independent thought.

The Renaissance

The Renaissance was a period of transition from the mediaeval to the modern world. Mediaeval Europe had been a fragmented feudal society with an agricultural economy, and its thought and culture were largely dominated by the Church. During the Renaissance, Europe witnessed a growing national consciousness and political centralization, developed an urban economy based on organized commerce and capitalism, and saw ever-greater secular control of thought and culture. People appreciated and even glorified the secular world, secular learning, and purely human pursuits as ends in themselves. Between the fourteenth and sixteenth centuries, intellectuals shook off the religious and institutional restrictions of mediaeval life to rediscover worldly things and a new place for the individual in a changing society.

The dawn of the Renaissance is identified with the writings of Dante Alighieri (1265–1321). Dante's work ushered in a revolutionary period of changing social values and a revival of interest in learning about Greece and Rome. Dante's most important political work, *De Monarchia*, contributed to political thought by stressing the need for monarchical world government, and by arguing that the pope and the emperor derive their authority directly and independently from God. Modern political science is indebted to Dante for his practical analysis of the instruments for the peaceful settlement of disputes between states. In *De Monarchia*, Dante envisioned a world order supported by global institutions that would legislate, arbitrate, and adjudicate peace.

Perhaps the best-known Renaissance thinker, whose works revived the national, secular, and scientific spirit that had lain dormant since the Greeks, is Niccolò Machiavelli (1469–1527). If the most important discovery of the Renaissance was man, the most important discovery of Machiavelli was political man. Of Machiavelli, the seventeenth-century philosopher Francis Bacon wrote: "We are much beholden to Machiavelli and others that wrote what men do and not what they ought to do."[6] Machiavelli asserted that the true guide to the science of politics was realism*, and that all human behaviour must be observed for what it is, not for what it should be. In the study of political behaviour, Machiavelli cautioned observers to distinguish between ethics and politics.

In *The Prince* and later in *The Discourses on the First Ten Books of Titius Livius*, Machiavelli pointed out that when humans occupy positions of power, ethics and morality tend to become lower priorities. For this reason Machiavelli is labelled as if he invented assassination, corruption, and political expediency. But he never advocated immorality for its own sake; rather, his amorality reflected a scientific objectivity in the study of human political behaviour. As a modern student of politics, Machiavelli replaced the "ideal" with the "actual." By doing so, he offered the first rigorous analysis of power politics* in understandable language.

The Reformation

During the Reformation, politics once again became a subject in the writings of theologians. Appalled by the corruption of the Church and by its abuse of political power, reformers like Martin Luther (1483–1546) claimed that salvation was achieved through the faith of the individual Christian and not through the practices of the Church. Luther also weakened the Church's political authority by claiming that political leaders had power over the Church. Luther received much support from German princes who were resentful of the political power of the pope, who to them was an Italian ruler. John Calvin (1509–1564) was converted to the ideas of the Reformation, but he went much further than Luther. Calvin was determined to establish God's "Holy Commonwealth" on earth, and he established a theocracy* in Geneva, which he himself ruled with great strictness. Both Luther and Calvin saw themselves as free critics of the political and social order. But the study of politics became a popular intellectual concern with the rapid spread of the printing presses in over 250 European cities. This dramatically increased the output of political information, so necessary for the development of modern political science.

Jean Bodin (1530–1596), a political theorist who wrote prolifically for a conservative group known as the "Politiques," coined the term "sciences politiques" (political science). For him, political science was concerned with the study of sovereignty, the functions of government, and all institutions that make law. Even though this was a much more restricted definition of what is today regarded as political science, it was an important step in the evolution of the discipline. The emergence of politically independent states provided students of politics with materials for comparative political studies. This stimulated a scholarly curiosity about the various forms and functions of government and about the political behaviour of executives and legislators. The study of politics had become a self-conscious activity. Already the core of political inquiry was recognizable and distinguishable from other fields of study.

The Age of Reason

The late seventeenth century, known as the Age of Reason, nourished a belief in the positive consequences of the free and unprejudiced use of the human intellect. This liberation of thought extended especially to political questions. People everywhere asserted their own ideas on the rights of individuals and the responsibilities of governments. The most outstanding political writers of the time considered such things as the dispersion of powers in government and in whom the supreme authority of the state should gather. Access to political information was almost limitless. Controversial political ideas were circulated in books, periodicals, and newspapers. Never before in European history had so many people shown so much interest in politics.

Thomas Hobbes (1588–1679) advocated absolute government to control human behaviour, based on a special social contract binding on all citizens to protect them from the ruthlessness of their own selfish human natures. Hobbes is an important part of the philosophical tradition of political science. He employed the deductive* method of reasoning whereby his assumptions about human nature were used as premises for building an appropriate political system.

His contemporary, John Locke (1632–1704), used the same method of reasoning as Hobbes, but Locke held a much more optimistic view of human nature. He felt that government should be limited, accountable, and changeable to give people the freedom to be themselves rather than to protect them from themselves. The text of the United States Declaration of Independence is a purely Lockean document. But the spirit of Locke's *Two Treaties of Government* (1690) can also be found in part I of Canada's Charter of Rights and Freedoms, where the inalienable rights of individuals are listed (sections 1–31). Political science is indebted to Locke for his advocacy of freedom of speech and inquiry. Without such freedom, an independent social science dedicated to the open discussion and critical analysis of government and all forms of political behavior could never have flourished.[7]

Charles de Secondat, Baron de Montesquieu (1689–1755), argued for a separation of powers among the executive, legislative, and judicial branches of government so that no one branch could ever dominate the political system. His revolutionary framework of government was later incorporated into the Constitution of the United States as well as the constitutions of most Latin American states.

The Enlightenment

The Enlightenment was an intellectual groundswell in support of reform and change in eighteenth-century European society. The writers and critics who forged this new social attitude came to be known as the "philosophes." The names Voltaire, Diderot, Rousseau, Hume, and Kant are but a few associated with those intellectuals who wanted to reform thought, society, and government for the sake of human liberty. Their demands for freedom shaped the constitutions and institutions of every modern democratic state.[8]

With the Industrial Revolution (beginning in the mid eighteenth century) came a new era of revolutionary thought and events, e.g., the American Revolution (1776) and the French Revolution (1789). This new age of revolution unleashed two complementary developments that advanced the growth of the social sciences: first, a widespread trust and belief that science and its exacting methods of inquiry would lead to the most reliable understanding of human behaviour; second, that the specialization of human skills and knowledge associated with the rapid growth of towns and cities was an incentive for people to choose a professional career in the study of social and political affairs.

Many of the intellectual responses to the Industrial Revolution were attempts to build an alliance of scientific methods and human knowledge. Thomas Malthus (1776–1834) used geometric and arithmetic projections to show that human population would out-strip food supply. David Ricardo (1772–1823) developed his Iron Law of Wages, linking the rise and fall of wages to the rise and fall of the birth rate. The British Utilitarians* attempted to quantify political reform by advancing the scientific principle of utility – the greatest good of the greatest number. Jeremy Bentham (1748–1832), James Mill (1773–1836), John Stuart Mill (1805–1873), and Sir Edwin Chadwick (1800–1890) all proclaimed a rational, scientific approach to political and economic affairs so that no single group would receive privileged consideration. This new attitude toward the study of political matters led to a greater use of the empirical method*, i.e., learning that came from actual experience, through the senses, and that was subject to testing for verification.

By the middle of the nineteenth century, even Darwin's theory of evolution and natural selection exerted influence on the study of political affairs. Concepts such as political "system," open system, closed system, feedback, and adaptation, widely used by present-day political scientists, were all inspired by biology.[9]

Karl Marx and his collaborator Friedrich Engels attempted to apply science to international politics and world history. They presented their scientific philosophy of history to explain the development of mankind as a dialectic of class struggles leading to new social orders – from feudalism to capitalism and from socialism to communism (*The Communist Manifesto* 1848). Marx's scientific method for discovering socio-political truth has its pitfalls when measured by twentieth-century standards. But his determination to derive an exacting method of studying political economy contributed to the birth of a real science of politics. Not long after his death in 1883, the most concentrated effort to apply scientific methods to political inquiry would take place in the United States.

Modern Frameworks

Political Science in the United States

The emergence of modern political science and its establishment as an independent self-conscious discipline is intimately tied to the growth of universities in the United States.[10]

By 1875 British, French, and German scholarly influences in political studies had reached the United States, revealing themselves in the formation of university programs especially designed to train people in political science.

In June 1880, Columbia University (then called Columbia College) established its School of Political Science, headed by John W. Burgess. Within a few years the school launched the *Political Science Quarterly*, which quickly gained world recognition for the quality of its publications and continues to maintain its reputation today. At Johns Hopkins University, Herbert Baxter Adams developed a program of advanced training and research in history and political science in 1876, followed by the establishment of the Johns Hopkins Historical and Political Science Association in 1887. From the experience of these two universities the teaching of political science as a unique academic discipline spread rapidly to the leading academic centres of the United States.[11]

Impressed by the achievements of the natural sciences, the first generation of American political scientists began to encourage the research of new knowledge using scientific methods that had already proved their potency in such fields as biology, mathematics, and physics. This approach was a departure from the European tradition of philosophical speculation, logical deduction, and the use of formal, legal, and historical methods. The gradual "Americanization" of political science brought with it a commitment to use the most modern approaches in studying politics and to distinguish the analysis of political behaviour from the total social environment. But we should not neglect the role of a small group of "realists" who were critical of the formalistic character of political inquiry during this period and who urged students of politics to focus on the "facts" to find out how government really works. Their influence encouraged researchers to study what the political system *is* rather than what it *should be.*

The American Political Science Association (APSA) was born in 1903 in a period of intellectual ferment and political reform that came to be known as "progressivism*." In the opening years of the twentieth century, progressives were concerned about whether science and technology could help the United States remain an industrial giant with the same democratic ideals inherited from the past. Many of the original 214 members of APSA were progressives who wanted "to assemble on common ground those persons whose main interests (were) connected with the scientific study of the organization and function of the state."[12] As the first modern organization of its kind, APSA was the single most decisive factor that determined the professional status of political science. Almost immediately, political science gained international respect as a unique academic pursuit.

The *American Political Science Review* began to publish in 1906 and attracted manuscripts from around the globe. It became the model journal of political science and was followed in 1907 by the *American Journal of International Law* and the *Academy of Political Science Proceedings* in 1910. Decade by decade the number of journals increased to reflect the multiple interests and the newer methods of studying political science. By the 1990s there were nearly 200 political-science journals published in the United States alone.

While the drive to Americanize political science characterized the first decades after the creation of APSA, European influences continued to hold their ground as departments of political science spread across the United States. The continental influence was sustained by the migration of European-trained political scientists, some of whom would complete their studies and begin new careers in the United States. Many of the émigrés were gifted scholars whose names are known the world over: Hannah Arendt, Karl Deutsch, William Ebenstein, Heinz Eulau, Carl Friedrich, Ernest Haas, Stanley Hoffman, Hans Kelsen, Henry Kissinger, Hans Morgenthau, Franz Neumann, and Leo Strauss. They, along with U.S.-born and -trained practitioners, have been instrumental in developing the two master approaches to the generic study of politics in the twentieth century – the traditional and behavioural approaches.

The Traditional Approach

Despite the drive toward scientism* in the interwar years, European influences firmly embedded the traditional approach to political science in the United States. It should be noted that "traditionalism" was not identified as a conscious, coherent movement or persuasion in political science until after World War II. The term was invented by a small group of American researchers who advocated scientific approaches to the study of politics and who wanted to stigmatize their academic opponents. Despite this mixed purpose, what is now referred to as traditionalism remains important because without it the modern study of politics would not have achieved its present status as a credible social science. The works of Francis W. Coker (*Recent Political Thought* 1934), Charles McIlwain (*The Growth of Political Thought in the West* 1932), Robert Murray (*The History of Political Science from Plato to the Present* 1930), and George Sabine (*A History of Political Theory* 1937) all demonstrated a common devotion to the traditional approach in order to arrive at academic excellence in the analysis of political truth.

Traditionalism in American political science embraces a wide variety of European approaches to political inquiry. Practitioners of political and social philosophy believe that a knowledge of classical political literature is essential for prescribing moral choices in the modern world. Like their European colleagues, they are political counsellors who offer general advice to the rulers and the ruled.

Traditionalists see themselves as practical observers rather than scientists. This is not to intimate that they are anti-science, but to them politics is an art that resists study by scientific methods. All political systems have information that is scientifically and technologically inaccessible. Policy questions relating to ethics, fairness, and justice readily lend themselves to traditional approaches of investigating political phenomena. On many issues, traditionalists see no need to separate facts from values; they recognize an intrinsic relationship between human political behaviour and morality. Politics is best understood through informed judgement derived from careful study and observation, often by suggesting what ought to be done in order to perfect or ameliorate a situation.

Let us outline the main components of the traditional approach that became so prevalent during the interwar years and continues today as an accepted practice in the international political-science community:

- *Methodology:* The general characteristics of traditional political analysis are descriptive and explanatory. To the researcher, a situation or event is knowable to the extent that it can be described and explained. The orderly understanding of the world of politics proceeds from descriptive questions of "what" to explanatory questions of "why." A description of facts is explained through the personal talents and informed judgement of the observer who applies his or her creative imagination to the task at hand. Quantitative methods are rarely applied because traditionalists doubt whether human political behaviour can be scientifically measured.
- *Historical analysis:* Historical methods are used for political research. The researcher collects information and evaluations of a particular subject by using primary sources, such as public documents, to develop a chronology of events or ideas that leads to a conclusion.
- *Institutional analysis:* Analysis focusses on the structures and functions of political institutions through careful observation. The researcher presupposes that all significant politics takes place in institutional settings. The analyst accumulates facts from official government documents and records as source materials. The study of institutions provides answers to questions of authority, power, and legitimacy.
- *Legal analysis:* Formal legal terms, practices, and institutions in a political system are studied. This usually involves the analysis of charters, constitutions, the process of law making, and interpretation. The judicial focus is instrumental in prescribing legal and political reform at the national and international levels.
- *Philosophical analysis:* The deductive method of reasoning is used to analyse normative political theory*. The analyst deduces political rules, values, and institutional needs from general premises about human nature and human behaviour. On the basis of the philosophical approach, traditionalists prescribe normative solutions to political problems. In their view no political inquiry into social problems can remain completely free of normative judgements or prescriptions. This may appear as a set of ideological convictions that map out an interpretation of the political world so as to reform the fabric of society.
- *Careerism:* There is a belief that political science should be used to prepare people for government service in public administration and diplomacy, teaching, political leadership, and service to international organizations. Political science has special responsibilities in public affairs to instruct democratic principles of government, in addition to training political researchers and teachers.

The Behavioural Approach

Traditional political science did not remain unchallenged for long. The scientific intent of the founders of APSA began to appear frequently in the works of Charles E. Merriam (*New Aspects of Politics* 1925), G.E.G. Catlin (*Science and Method of Politics* 1927), Stuart Rice (*Quantitative Methods of Politics* 1928), and Harold Lasswell (*Psychopathology and Politics* 1930). They were the first in a long line of American political scientists who would aspire to a greater degree of precision in the analysis of political phenomena by using the skills of science and by integrating concepts that were applied in other social sciences, such as sociology and psychology.

The term behaviouralism was recognized as part of a larger scientific movement occurring simultaneously in all of the social sciences, now referred to as the behavioural sciences. For political scientists, behaviouralism emphasized the systematic understanding of all identifiable manifestations of political behaviour. But it also meant the application of rigorous scientific and statistical methods to standardize testing and to ensure value-free inquiry into the world of politics.

The rise of behaviouralism in political science was greatly aided by major advances in survey and polling techniques and the use of computers to store and process information in all areas of human activity. This stimulated an information revolution in the mass production of scientifically generated data, particularly in the social sciences. After World War II, a growing number of American political scientists regarded behaviouralism as the only acceptable approach to valid empirical generalizations about political life. Those who had worked as public employees during the war discovered that governments were more attentive to recommendations derived from scientific research and theory. Thus, behaviouralists advocated the use of scientific methods to enhance the credibility of potential analysis and to add more weight to their policy suggestions.

Since that time, American behaviouralists have claimed considerable success in assembling theoretical hypotheses in political science. They have postulated that a science is as applicable to human political behaviour as it is to all other forms of animal behaviour. To them, science can help explain, predict, and construct generalizations about the political world, though the moral ramifications of particular studies using scientific method have yet to be drawn. However, behaviouralists believe in remaining neutral with respect to prescribing morals and values for a society. These are questions of concern for politicians and electorates. For the behaviouralist, the role of political science is primarily to gather and analyse facts as rigorously and objectively as possible.

By letting the facts fall where they may, the analyst surrenders the moral implications of the data to other people. The following is an outline of the components of behaviouralism:

- *Approach:* The primary focus of political analysis is on actual observable behaviour of individuals and groups rather than just on institutions where peripheral political behaviour may be overlooked. The analyst seeks to discover patterns and regularities of behaviour that can be expressed as verifiable generalizations.
- *Methodology:* The scientific method of inquiry is used to generate data for analytical purposes. The method involves essentially four steps:
  1 organization and collection of information;
  2 classification of variables*;
  3 formation of hypotheses on the interrelationship of variables;
  4 testing hypotheses.
- *Eclecticism:* Political science developed as an eclectic discipline that integrates relevant findings from related natural and social sciences into a body of political knowledge. By

working closely with other social sciences, political science contributes to a bank of testable knowledge leading to models* of human political behaviour.

- *Goal:* A body of empirical generalizations stating relationships among variables for the purposes of explanation and prediction is assembled. This knowledge is codified into logically related sets of theoretical propositions that provide answers to political questions of cause and effect. Behaviouralism is capable of constructing theories out of research from pure science, e.g., knowledge of politics for its own sake; or from applied science, e.g., knowledge of politics for immediate application to problem solving.
- *Professionalism:* Behavioural political scientists strive to conduct value-free* inquiry. Practitioners avoid mixing their moral standards, ethics, and personal preferences with the design and conclusions of research projects.

Behaviouralism spread rapidly across the United States after World War II, reaching its peak in the 1960s. The behavioural movement aspired to establish political science as a social-science discipline, meeting all the criteria by which any behavioural science is judged. There is no question that behaviouralism has had a permanent effect on the basic values and objectives of political science.

But as behaviouralism matured, it soon became obvious that the emphasis on methodology had sacrificed relevance for exactitude. Widespread frustration with the obsessive scientism of orthodox behaviouralism led to the formation of the Caucus for a New Political Science in 1967.[13] This group of predominantly younger political scientists called upon the American Political Science Association to recognize the limitations of scientific detachment. They encouraged the APSA to redirect its energies toward a post-behavioural synthesis of methodology with relevant policy considerations and political reform.

Post-Behaviouralism

Post-behaviouralism called for a literal re-vision or viewing again of the aims of political science.[14] Still in ascendancy, post-behavioural political science has proved to be a healthy reassessment of basic goals and values within the discipline. The essence of the post-behavioural revolution is that political science has a public purpose. Not only must it strive for generalization, verifiable understanding of political processes, but it must deliberately address the most urgent political problems of the contemporary world in an intelligible and relevant way. The credo of post-behavioural political science asks its practitioners to commit themselves to making this a better world. Thus the object of contemporary political research should be to apply the precision of scientific inquiry to improve political systems. Post-behaviouralists are confronting pertinent issues at every level of society by advocating political action and reform for problems of the aged, domestic violence, education, health and welfare, sexual equality, and unemployment, to name but a few. The possession of expert political knowledge and the skills to gather it in exacting ways places special social responsibilities on the political scientist to act in the service of society. For some like Haas and Kariel, not to act on this knowledge is "immoral."[15] In making the connection between having the knowledge and using it as a social obligation, post-behaviouralists belong to a tradition inherited from the Greeks through to the establishment of American political science.

Other implications flow from this post-behavioural shift to relevance. First, political scientists must be able to communicate with the victims of society, not just the élites in government, business, academia, and the military. Practitioners must aim their expertise at all society, not just at a privileged segment. Second, the choice of research projects is crucial and must reflect an immediate concern for the struggles of the day. The call to respond to the most pressing political issues facing societies leads to the politicization of the profession. American post-behaviouralists acknowledge that no group in society is spared from the effects of political crisis and therefore can remain aloof. Universities as well as professional associations cannot stand on the sidelines of political turmoil.

The main arguments for a post-behavioural political science are found in works by David Easton ("The New Revolution in Political Science" *APSR* 1969), George Graham and George Carey (eds., *The Postbehavioral Era: Perspectives in Political Science* 1972), Henry Kariel (*Saving Appearances: The Re-establishment of Political Science* 1972), and Marvin Surkin and Alan Wolfe (eds., *An End to Political Science: The Caucus Papers* 1970). Their criticisms of the state of the profession pointed out three problems: first, excessive concern over the application of scientific technique was severely limiting the choice of research projects; second, pure science was replacing relevance; third, academic neutrality was blocking effective political action.

Post-behaviouralism has resulted in a healthy scepticism that rejects the idea of postponing burning issues in times of stress until a sufficient body of systematic theory grows out of the extensive analysis of lesser matters. The components of post-behaviouralism are:

- *Approach*: Political science is a composite of both traditional and scientific knowledge. One task of the political scientist is to apply an eclectic approach that combines the use of precise measurement and prescriptive analysis. The practitioner makes value judgements based on data derived from scientific inquiry.
- *Methodology:* A great variety of methods can be used to evaluate political problems effectively. Methodology can no longer be treated as a restricted preserve of either traditional or behavioural persuasions. To the post-behavioural political scientist, methodology is concerned not only with technique but also with broader questions of values like justice and morality.
- *Scope:* Political science has a public dimension that imposes professional responsibilities and moral obligations upon practitioners. The responsibilities flow from the fact that political scientists are privy to a large body of accumulated knowledge that may be used to train new professionals and to help people understand and change their political world. The moral obligations require political scientists to direct their special skills to the public good.
- *Policy engineering:* Political scientists should focus their insights on problems of political

organization and behaviour with the object of improving society. This is a professional orientation that combines values and goals, not always scientifically derived, to prescribe practical ways of reforming society.

It is in the contexts of traditionalism, behaviouralism, and post-behaviouralism that we can best appreciate the development of American political science. These three approaches have advanced the organization and respectability of political science as a modern social science everywhere in the world. They represent the broadest and most comprehensive efforts on the part of American practitioners to learn about the complexities of politics.

The American ascendancy in political science has had enormous impact on the moods, values, and methods of the international political-science community. No other national association of political science has escaped its influence, nor has remotely rivalled its wealth, power, and resources. W.J.M. Mackenzie estimated 75 percent of the world's political scientists are presently employed in the United States.[16] The overwhelming preponderance of American political science has given it a global perspective on politics. In fact, much of what is known about political systems anywhere is largely the result of political research conducted in the United States.

Political Science in Canada

Prior to the twentieth century, political science scarcely existed as a subject in Canadian colleges. Political studies first appear in 1877 at Queens University, then at the University of Toronto in 1888, where a professorship of Political Economy and Constitutional History was established. In its infancy in Canada, political science was assumed to be a natural part of economics, history, and philosophy. There was still some reluctance to lend the air of academic respectability to politics, let alone to recognize political science as an independent academic pursuit.

McGill University opened its Department of Economics and Political Science in 1901, and shortly thereafter the internationally acclaimed Stephen Leacock was chairman from 1908 to 1936. The spread of separate political-science departments occurred in a halting, hesitating way from the turn of the century to the 1950s. The University of Saskatchewan established its department in 1910, but many of Canada's universities, like McGill, only offered courses in political studies as adjuncts to other departments, such as economics, history, and philosophy. Thus the organization of political instruction and the development of political research grew very slowly. In fact, as late as 1958 Canada had only produced an academic core of political scientists totalling thirty-three.[17] But despite its meagre size, the determination of this small, highly competent group of political scientists enabled the discipline to reach a self-consciousness of a different character from that of the powerful branch across the border.

From the beginning, Canadian political scientists, even those who would have accepted the label "scientist," were much less concerned with the need to define the scope and methodology of their discipline than were their U.S. colleagues. Early Canadian practitioners were much more flexible in adopting traditional approaches from Europe and were more tolerant of disciplinary developments.[18] W.J. Ashley, the British academic who first headed the department at the University of Toronto, laid the foundations for an eclectic political science by calling for the study of all important values, ideas, and subjects related to politics. British imports into the Canadian academic milieu greatly influenced the character of political studies in Canada. This influence is explained in part by a common language but also by the closer congruity of governmental institutions, as well as great similarities in the intellectual approaches to problem solving.

When the Canadian Political Science Association (CPSA) was formed in 1913, its first president, Adam Shortt, presided over political science as well as economics, sociology, and anthropology. This small but diversified association of professionals attracted members from many fields: administrators, journalists, lawyers, and politicians. And, unlike its American counterpart, the CPSA was organized to develop the study of politics by simply "studying political problems," not with a mission to marry science to political inquiry. Upon its establishment, the CPSA gave recognition to political science as a pluralistic discipline: no methodological design was implied or intended.

On the eve of World War I, Canadian political science was not of a clear and single mind with respect to the orientation the discipline should embrace. Its differentiation from other disciplines was far from complete, the emergence of a Canadian contingent of political scientists was still to follow, and the struggle for separate departments of political science would begin over forty years later. The establishment of the CPSA was a tremendous step forward and was decisive in determining much of what would happen to political science in future decades. But the outbreak of the war would slow its progress until 1929–30, when the CPSA revived its annual meetings and began to encourage a healthy pluralism in adopting approaches to political affairs.

The formation of an autonomous, domestic, university-based political science began in Canada after World War I.[19] At this time, a small number of able and influential political scientists established their presence not only by writing but also by teaching at Canadian universities. For illustrative purposes a few names will suffice: Henry F. Angus, Alexander R. Brady, H. McD. Clokie, James A. Corry, Robert M. Dawson, Eugene Forsey, Robert A. MacKay, Crawford B. MacPherson, and N. McL. Rogers. Their contribution to Canadian political science had been to provide a substantive bloc of reputable works, such that it is impossible to imagine what the present contours of the discipline might have been were it not for their efforts.

In 1935, the *Canadian Journal of Economics and Political Science* (CJEPS) became solidly established as the central publishing organ of the CPSA. At this time political scientists shared the journal with economists, and it provided extensive coverage in both fields. For many years the combined journal was able to accommodate the critical writings of both disciplines. But eventually the CJEPS was unable to provide the necessary exposure for the many specializations emerging in the study of political affairs. However, during its tenure it furnished a national forum of communication for Canada's sparse population of political scientists and helped disseminate professional political analysis to a small but attentive public. By 1968 a sufficient number of scholarly manuscripts were reaching the editorial desks of the CJEPS to warrant a separate journal, the *Canadian Journal of Political Science.*

During the interwar period political science gradually became academically established. Usually it was first introduced at the university level simply as a subject of study. In piecemeal fashion, political science gradually spread across the country and appeared as an independent academic discipline under separate departments: University of British Columbia in 1920, Acadia University in 1927, University of Ottawa in 1936, and the Université Laval in 1939.

Following World War II, a number of important works were published focussing on Canadian government, especially its "political" aspects: H. McD. Clokie, *Canadian Government and Politics* (1944); J.A. Carry, *Democratic Government and Politics* (1946); and R.M. Dawson, *The Government of Canada* (1947). These distinguished works by Canadians were instrumental in encouraging colleges and universities to recognize political science as a desirable academic field of study in Canada.

The establishment of separate departments of political science proceeded swiftly in the late 1950s and the 1960s. From 1958 to 1969, over thirty institutions either separated political science from other departments or established new departments.[20] The rapid spread of political science across Canada's leading academic centres presented major complications for a fledgling discipline seeking to build a distinctively academic enterprise. The number of political scientists teaching at Canadian universities grew from 33 in 1958 to over 500 in 1970.[21] Yet between 1960 and 1970 when faculty positions grew by 475, only 27 doctorates were awarded in Canada to political scientists.[22] This led to the widespread recruitment of qualified non-Canadian political scientists, many of whom were drawn from the United States. They brought with them the various tenets and methodologies of American political science. By 1970, nearly half of the more than 500 political-science professors in Canada were foreign born. And although some had become naturalized Canadians, only 63 percent of the total number were Canadian citizens.[23]

In the minds of some, this staffing represented a threat to the national distinctiveness of the discipline. Many expressed fears that as the job market tightened Canadian political scientists would not be able to find jobs. But since the majority of important departmental decisions still rested in the hands of Canadian political scientists at the associate- and full–professor levels, these fears proved ungrounded, if indeed they were ever well founded. The situation eventually corrected itself so that by 1981 over 80 percent of the newly appointed political scientists were Canadian citizens and the outlook for the 1990s predicted a competitive but optimistic market for trained graduate students.

There is no denying that American political science has played a major part in the history of Canadian political science. But while the discipline in Canada has been strongly influenced by the moods and values of American political science, it has not been overwhelmed by them. Canadian political scientists have remained masters in their own house, combining and preserving the generalist influences from Europe with the trend-setting behavioural and post-behavioural influences from the United States.

During its short history, Canadian political science has nurtured its own identity and has earned the respect of the international political-science community. Its healthy self–image is reflected in the current focus on Canadian institutional and behavioural studies. Of the more than 800 professional political scientists in Canada, 43.6 percent of them regularly conduct research into the study of Canadian problems.[24] The Stein, Trent, and Donneur survey shows that 27 percent of practitioners have research interests in foreign and cross-national politics, while the general field of international relations attracts about 10 percent of Canada's political scientists, representing a vigorous dispersion of professional interest in both domestic and external affairs. Many practitioners have advised successive governments in Canada at all levels.

Canadian political science also owes a large debt to francophone influences. Because of its varied Canadian and European heritage, francophone political science has enriched the quality of political research in Canada by its eclectic approach to the discipline.

In 1978 the Société québecoise de science politique (SQSP), formerly founded in 1964 as the Société canadienne de science politique, was a successful attempt to function autonomously from the CPSA. With its own journal, *Politique*, established in 1982, and a membership of about 200, the SQSP offers an interdisciplinary character to political research. Beyond a doubt, political science in Quebec has successfully asserted its claim as a recognized academic pursuit.[25] In addition to the many universities in Quebec, the Colleges d'enseignment général et professionnel (CEGEPS) have departments of political science.

It is obvious that the academic presence of political science is nearly complete in Canada. The establishment of a firm organizational basis for political-science research has also been achieved. By the 1990s, Canada could rely upon an impressive entourage of its own experts to conduct independent political research into national and international affairs.

Political Science in the International Community

In 1949 the United Nations Educational, Scientific, and Cultural Organization (UNESCO) co-ordinated the establishment of the International Political Science Association (IPSA).[26] As of 1990, thirty-seven national political science associations were listed as collective members of IPSA, along with 500 individual memberships. The association has been active in promoting the development of political science in the international community. It publishes the *International Political Science Review, International Political Science Abstracts*, and the *International Bibliography of Political Science*. In 1973, Montreal hosted the first IPSA World Congress to be held outside Europe. Professor Jean LaPonce of the University of British Columbia became its first Canadian president.

Political scientists in democratic countries tend to engage in open criticism of national and international issues. Each national association of political scientists bears the stamp of its own unique political culture, traditions, and ideologies. British political scientists have tended to remain loyal to the traditional historical and philosophical approaches.[27] Only since the mid 1970s has behaviouralism had any impact. However, post-behavioural sentiments have steadily penetrated the methodologies of British political science. Since World War II, many Italian political scientists have focussed on the factors that led to fascism before and during that war. In Sweden, the traditional orientation of political science is used to trace the development of Swedish political institutions from the Middle Ages to the present. In West Germany, political science reflects a conservative concern with constitutional and administrative law, as well as a cautious surveillance of democratic and antidemocratic thought. Throughout the democratic countries of Europe, the reconstructive pressures of post-behaviouralism have influenced both research and teaching. But there is a very real sense that an understanding of the political world can still be achieved without the ubiquitous imposition of scientific methodology, and model or theory building.

Political science in "authoritarian" states tends not to be open or critical, at least as a visible legitimate discipline. In Argentina and Brazil (even under new governments), political scientists are cautious and sensitive to government censorship and political repression. In Guatemala and El Salvador, social scientists are closely watched and their politics are constantly scrutinized by government officials.

In the "totalitarian" socialist states, the development of political science as an autonomous discipline has been slow. During the Stalinist years in the Soviet Union, social sciences had to be congruent with the hardline Marxist-Leninist dogma of the regime. After Stalin, more objective social-science research began to surface in Soviet society but it was viewed with great suspicion and its conclusions were usually not considered in the preparation of official data and statistics. The discipline of political science (*politologiia*) tended to concentrate its critical energies on the West and avoided the perilous occupation of delving into the political pathologies of the Soviet system.[28] By 1960, the Political Science Association of the USSR was established, although it had questionable autonomy in matters of independent research. At the official level, social scientists, such as political scientists, social psychologists, and sociologists, were viewed suspiciously because of their "propensity to seek out problems." Today, the Soviet Academy of Sciences has its Association of Political Sciences, which produces a yearbook. In it, Western political science trends are examined and researchers seem to have acquired a considerable knowledge of foreign methodologies.[29] In general, Soviet political scientists still support the ideological positions of their government and tend to avoid critical research in sensitive areas of Soviet politics. But, *glasnost'*, and *demokratizatsiya* have encouraged social scientists to speak out more freely and critically of Soviet social and political institutions and to publish their findings. Indeed, Gorbachev at the 19th Communist Party Conference in July 1988 called for more democracy and extolled the merits of *glasnost'* even though serious criticisms of previous leaders, such as Stalin and Brezhnev, were inevitable in the Soviet press and academe.

Poland, Yugoslavia, and Hungary have been more receptive to Western influences in political science, particularly American and Western European political science. Poland has a national political-science association with sixteen regional chapters no longer completely under the influence of Marxist-Leninist approaches. Many of the 1000 members of the Polish Association of Political Science employ Western concepts and techniques. Many are now openly supportive of pluralism and a multi-party system. In Yugoslavia, the University of Zagreb opened its school of political science in 1962. Yugoslav political scientists reflected the independent thrust of Titoist* political philosophy and have been influenced by the traditional and behavioural styles of American political science. In Hungary political scientists observe a more pluralistic political and social system and, like other members of the intelligentsia, engage in wider expressions of critical thought.

Political science has had a long and honourable history. For centuries political philosophers have been analysing basic questions about the politics of people in society. What is justice? What forms of government are best? Are rulers accountable? When and why must people obey? These are ancient issues, yet they engage us at every turn in our modern world. The great writers of the past – Plato, Aristotle, Machiavelli, Augustine, Hobbes, Locke, and Rousseau – can still inform us about these matter, even today.

Pre-scientific thinking about political behaviour and governmental institutions was characteristically devoted to describing what should be, rather than studying what is. Early political theory was concerned with redesigning society according to the philosopher's own favoured system of conduct rather than with carefully observing how a polity actually operates.

Not until the first decades of the twentieth century did most political theorists seek to discipline their theorizing and subdue their concerns for political reform with rigorous methods for systematically observing the society around them. These new political scientists were far from being the first students of political behaviour, but they were the first to adopt an empirical perspective and the scientific method in such studies. Many of them learned that modern methodologies could be directed toward the questions of political and social reform that had been posed by earlier students of politics. Today, all political scientists share with their ancestors the basic premise that the serious study of politics is crucial to the survival of humankind.

REFERENCES

1. Heinz Eulau, *The Behavioral Persuasion in Politics* (New York: Random House 1963), 3.
2. S. Sidney Ulmer, *Introductory Readings in Political Behaviour* (Chicago: Rand McNally & Co. 1961), 74.
3. William Anderson, *Man's Quest for Political Knowledge: The Study and Teaching of Politics in Ancient Times* (Minneapolis: University of Minnesota Press 1964), 336.
4. See Henri Marrou, *A History of Education in Antiquity*, trans. by George Lamb (New York: Sheed & Ward 1956), 64.
5. William Dunning, *A History of Political Theories* (London: Macmillan and Co. Ltd. 1923), 131.
6. Francis Bacon, *The Advancement of Learning Book II*, compiled by F.G. Selby (London: Macmillan and Co. Ltd. 1895), 116.
7. Donald Kagan, Stephen Ozment, and Frank Turner, *The Western Heritage since 1300* (New York: Macmillan Publishing Co. Inc. 1983), 619–43.
8. Peter Gay, *The Enlightenment: An Interpretation 1* (New York: Alfred A. Knopf Inc. 1967), 4.
9. See Herbert Spiro, "An Evaluation of Systems Theory," in James Charlesworth, ed., *Contemporary Political Analysis* (New York: Free Press 1967), 164.
10. See Lawrence Vesey, *The Emergence of the American University* (Chicago: University of Chicago Press 1965).
11. See Anna Haddow, *Political Science in American Colleges and Universities,*

1636–1900 (New York: Appleton-Century 1939).

12. Albert Somit and Joseph Tanenhaus, *The Development of American Political Science: From Burgess to Behavioralism* (Boston: Allyn and Bacon 1967), 55; see also Raymond Seidelman, *Dischanted Realists: Political Science and the American Crisis, 1884–1984* (Albany, NY: State University of New York 1985); and Mark Kesselman, "The Conflictual Evolution of American Political Science: From Apologetic Pluralism to Trilateralism and Marxism," in David Greenstone, ed., *Public Values and Private Power in American Politics* (Chicago: University of Chicago Press 1982).

13. P.S.: Newsletter of American Political Science Association1 (Winter 1968): 38–40, and 2 (Winter 1969): 47–9; and David Ricci, The *Tragedy of Political Science* (New Haven, CT: Yale University Press 1984), 304–7.

14. James Farr, "The Revision of Political Science," paper delivered at the 1983 Annual Meeting of the American Political Association Chicago, September 1–4, 1983; Louis Cantori, "Post-Behavioral Political Science and the Study of Comparative Politics," in Louis Cantori, Andrew Ziegler, Jr., *Comparative Politics in the Post-Behavioral Era* (Boulder, CO: Lynne Rienner Publishers 1988), 417–26.

15. Michael Haas and Henry Kariel, eds., *Approaches to the Study of Political Science* (Scranton, PA: Chandler Publishing Co. 1970), 525.

16. William M.J. MacKenzie, *The Study of Political Science Today* (London: Macmillan 1971), 32.

17. G.H. Thorburn, *Political Science in Canada: Graduate Studies and Research* (Ottawa: A Study for the Healy Commission 1975), 79; see also Ian Drummond, *Political Economy at the University of Toronto: A History of the Department* (Toronto: University of Toronto Press 1983).

18. Michael Stein, John Trent, and André Donneur, "Political Science in Canada in the 1980s: Achievement and Challenge," paper delivered at the Congress of the International Political Science Association, Rio de Janeiro, August 9–14, 1982, 1; see also John Trent and Michael Stein, "The Interaction of the State and Political Science in Canada: A Preliminary Mapping," paper presented at the XIVth World Congress of the International Political Science Association, Washington, DC, 1988, 1–34.

19. Alan Cairns, "Political Science in Canada and the Americanization Issue," *Canadian Journal of Political Science* 8 (June 1975): 193–5.

20. See Stein, Trent, and Donneur, "Political Science in Canada," 3–4.

21. See Cairns, "Political Science in Canada and the Americanization Issue," 205.

22. Interim Report of the Select Committee on Economic and Cultural Nationalism, "Colleges and Universities in Ontario" (Toronto 1973), 13–14.

23. N.H.W. Hull, "The 1971 Survey of the Profession," *Canadian Journal of Political Science* VI (March 1973): 89–120.

24. Stein, Trent, and Donneur, "Political Science in Canada," 37; see also Trent and Stein, "The Interaction of the State and Political Science in Canada: A Preliminary Mapping." op. cit., 1–34.

25. See Raymond Aron, "Reflexions sur la politique et la science politique française," in *Revue francaise de Science Politique* 5 (1) (1985): 55:22; Léon Dion, "Politique et Science Politique," *Canadian Journal of Political Science* 8, no. 3 (1975): 367–80; Michel Leclerc, "Pour un sociologie critique de la science politique québécoise: une impossible hagiographie," *Les Cahiers de L'ACFAS* 1, no. 1 (1985): 32.

26. See UNESCO publication 426, *Contemporary Political Science* (Paris:UNESCO 1950).

27. See Jack Hayward, "United Kingdom," in William Andrews, ed., *International Handbook of Political Science* (Westport, CT: Greenwood Press 1982); and Jack

Hayward, "Cultural and Contextual Constraints upon the Development of Political Science in Britain" paper presented to the International Round Table on the Comparative Study of the Development of Political Science, Cortona, Italy, September 21–27, 1987.

28. See " The Social Sciences: A New Ideology," in Moshe Lewin, *The Gorbachev Phenomenon: A Historical Interpretation* (Berkeley, CA: University of California Press 1988), 85–100; see also Archibald Brown, *Soviet Politics and Political Science* (London: Macmillan 1974).

29. *Pravda*, February 6, 1987.

SUGGESTED READINGS

Terence Ball, ed., *Idioms of Inquiry: Critique and Renewal in Political Science* (Albany, NY: State University of New York Press 1987).

Stephen Brooks and Alain Gagnon, *Social Scientists and Politics in Canada* (Montreal: McGill-Queen's University Press 1988).

Mary H. Curzon, ed., *Careers and the Study of Political Science: A Guide for Undergraduates*, 4th ed. (Washington, DC: American Political Science Association 1985).

Ada Finifter, ed., *Political Science: The State of the Discipline* (Washington, DC: American Political Science Association 1983).

M. Lal Goel, *Political Science Research: A Methods Handbook* (Ames, IA: Iowa State University Press 1988).

Andrew Jones, *Politics and Paradigms: Changing Theories of Change in Social Science* (Stanford, CA: Stanford University Press 1986).

Michel Leclerc, *La Science politique au Québec* (Montreal: L'Hexagone 1982).

Jarol Manheim and Richard Rich, *Empirical Political Analysis in Political Science* (Mississauga, ON: Copp Clark Pitman 1986).

Richard Nathan, *Social Science in Government* (New York: Basic Books 1988).

Jon Pammett and Jean Luc Pepin, eds., *Political Education in Canada* (Halifax, NS: The Institute on Research and Public Policy 1988).

Alexander Rosenberg, *Philosophy of Social Science* (Boulder, CO: Westview Press 1988).

Herbert Weisberg, *Political Science: The Science of Politics* (New York: Agathon Press 1986).

GLOSSARY

methodology: The process of gathering, measuring, analysing, and evaluating knowledge within a particular discipline.

political behaviour: Human responses to the world of politics in the forms of perceptions, attitudes, beliefs, thoughts, and values as well as overt actions such as campaigning, protesting, and voting, and even corrupt political practices.

eclectic: In political science, an approach to knowledge that draws information from other disciplines by selecting and combining the appropriate methods and conclusions for political research.

social contract: A theory of popular sovereignty based on the notion that humans had originally consented to a binding social agreement.

gross national product (GNP): The sum of all goods and services that a country produces in a designated fiscal year.

geopolitics: An approach to politics that explains political behaviour in terms of geographic factors, such as size, location, climate, topography, proximity to other nation-states.

multiculturalism: The belief in a social pluralism that postulates the sharing and preservation of ethnic customs and cultures within the framework of a nation-state.

hypothesis: Any tentative statement that describes or explains the relationship between or among variables.

architectonic: In the language of Aristotle, this term refers to the master art that prescribes the content of all other arts, occupations, and skills of life.

public administration: The subfield of political science that studies the bureaucratic skills and technologies used for the administration of public policy.

secular: A term referring to those political and social philosophies that advocate the separation of worldly things from religious and sacred interests.

realism: The disposition to see things as they are, rather than as they ought to be, and to recognize that political actors are motivated by power and self-interest.

power politics: The description derived from the German *Machpolitik*, and *Realpolitik*, which sees the world of politics as essentially conducted among groups with power.

theocracy: A term coined by the Jewish historian Josephus, who described government as embodied in the Torah, where divine laws are treated as civil obligations. As commonly used, the term came to mean government by priests.

deductive reasoning: The process of reaching conclusions by reasoning from the general to the particular.

Utilitarians: Those who in the nineteenth century advocated the concept of utility as the foundation of morals or the Greatest Happiness Principle, which posited that actions are right in proportion as they tend to promote happiness, wrong as they produce its opposite.

empirical method: An approach to knowledge that uses sense, observation, and experimentation as the most reliable source of information.

progressivism: A set of beliefs and attitudes favourable to political, economic, social, and cultural reform or change.

scientism: The belief that scientific method is applicable to all human problems and that it will generate the only possible solution to them.

normative political theory: Philosophical positions promoting a subjective preference for certain standards of human conduct in the realm of politics.

variable: Any characteristic or property of something that contains two or more values that change in degree and help explain a particular event or phenomenon.

hypothesis: Any tentative statement that describes or explains the relationship between or among variables.

model: A set of assumptions a researcher accepts as true that influences the perception of that which is being observed.

value free: The predisposition of a social scientist to pursue research objectives without the intrusion of personal opinions and values, which might otherwise distort conclusions.

Titoism: The socialism of Marshal Tito who, as leader of Yugoslavia, refused to be absorbed into the Soviet bloc, advanced a neutralist foreign policy, encouraged the development of market forces in the socialist economy, and tolerated small scale private property in the means of production.

3

Contemporary Political Ideologies

At the Brandenburg Gate, Berlin, November 1989

What Is an Ideology?

DURING THE ENLIGHTENMENT, the French philosopher Antoine Destutt de Tracy coined the word "ideologie" to mean the "science of ideas" – the study of the origins, evolution, and nature of ideas. Many philosophers of the time (the philosophes) believed that the application of human reason to society could reveal laws in human relationships that would unfold into dogmatic* patterns of belief systems, setting ideals, ends, and purposes for communities to pursue.[1] Until the Enlightenment, ideologies were primarily religious: the world was perceived and explained in terms that linked political and economic beliefs with religious ones, for example those of Buddhism, Calvinism, Catholicism, Islam, and Shintoism. The writers and critics who forged the "enlightened" ideas of the eighteenth century felt that the future of humankind lay not so much in the blind adherence to divine commandments but rather in the application of human reason* to economic, social, and political challenges.

The term "ideology" enjoyed good standing until the nineteenth century, when Napoleon began to call his political enemies "ideologues" because they advocated liberal ideals, and held utopian* and antireligious views. A negative connotation attached to the word and continues to this day in some countries of the world, depending on how the term is used. To many Americans and Canadians, ideology is to politics what superstition is to religion. In societies founded on philosophical pragmatism* and freedom, where individual choices determine leadership*, programs of action, and reforms, people distrust the intellectual and emotional commitment required to sustain what in their minds is an ideology. They see ideologies as abstract, utopian systems of ideas that demand a blind and uncritical allegiance of believers to fixed prisms of thought.

To so view ideology serves no useful purpose to scholarship or understanding because, in varying degrees, all societies are ideological. An ideology is a value system through which we perceive, explain, and accept the world. Ideologies give us a total view of things and claim to supply answers to all questions. Karl Deutsch holds that ideologies are like maps in that they outline "a simplified image of the real world."[2] To some degree, consciously or unconsciously, all people are ideologues in that they map out their interpretation of the real world and its significance to their world. Robert Dahl emphasized this fact when he said "Prior to politics, beneath it, enveloping it, restricting it, conditioning it . . . is ideology."[3]

Contemporary ideologies, such as anarchism, capitalism, conservatism, communism, and socialism, contain mainly socio-economic elements that dominate the beliefs people adopt and the biases* they reflect. Ultimately these systems condition people's political behaviour. Political ideology may be defined as a "belief system that explains and justifies a preferred political order for society, either existing or proposed, and offers a strategy (processes, institutional arrangements, programs) for its attainment."[4] Robert E. Lane classified a number of important functions of political ideologies.[5] They are summarized as follows:

- Ideologies present a simplified "cause and effect" interpretation of a complex world.
- Ideologies integrate a theory of human nature* with life's basic economic, social, and political values.
- Ideologies appear normative and moral in tone and content.
- Ideologies draw their philosophical premises from constitutions, declarations, manifestoes, and writings.
- Ideologies constitute a broad belief system and advocate reforms in the basic fabric and structures of society.
- Ideologies address fundamental questions about leadership, recruitment, political succession, and electoral behaviour.
- Ideologies have the effect of persuading and propagandizing people who learn not to be influenced by opposing views.

Because ideologies are value-laden belief systems they often come into conflict and competition: thus, conservatism vs. liberalism, capitalism vs. socialism, and nationalism vs. internationalism. Some political cultures appear more ideologically based than others. But whether an ideology is prominent, as in the Soviet Union or Cuba, or subtle, as in Canada or Australia, there is an ideological base to all political cultures.

Political ideology should be distinguished from other forms of political thought, such as political philosophy and political theory. Political philosophy is a detached and often solitary "search for the principles of the good state and the good society."[6] The political philosopher asks fundamental questions about the nature of political society and often prescribes moral and ethical* solutions for what "ought" to be a better polity. Political theory attempts to formulate testable and verifiable generalizations drawn from relatable variables that explain a particular political phenomenon. Where the political philosopher is rational* and deductive, the theorist is empirical and descriptive* of "what is" rather than "what ought" to be. The words of Carl Friedrich help us to further clarify the distinctions we have just made:

> Ideologies are action-related systems of ideas. They typically contain a strategy for its realization, and their essential function is to unite organizations which are built around them. It is confusing and fails to provide the opportunity for political analysis, to call any system of ideas an ideology, such as the philosophy of Aristotle or the Theology of the Old Testament. Such systems of ideas *may* provide the *basis* for an ideology, but only after being related to action in a specific sense and for a specific situation. Ideologies are sets of ideas related to the existing political and social order and intended either to change it or defend it . . . what makes them (ideas) "ideology" is the function in the body politic.[7]

The action-related character of ideologies to which Friedrich refers is significant. History confirms that ideologies energize people, capture their imaginations, and motivate them to dismantle old orders or construct new ones.[8] Ideologies tend to inspire organizational behaviour that always reflects itself at the political level. The ideological message is mobilized and carried by political elites*, political parties, insurgent groups, pressure groups, education systems, and the media. Once in place an ideology is culturally transmitted through families, peer groups, and other agents of political socialization. In the final analysis, societies exercise political power on the basis of their ideological perspective.

The Components of Ideologies

Ideologies address fundamental questions about the nature of society and its political character. We can identify some of the most common themes found in modern political ideologies: (1) the disposition of human nature; (2) the role of the individual in society; (3) the role of the state; (4) the sources and limits of political authority; (5) a preferred economic and social order. These are some of the important elements analysts look for when examining the contents of ideologies.

Human Nature

One theme found in many ideologies addresses the question of human nature. Are human beings born basically good or bad, or does social conditioning determine their character? Is it possible to perfect human nature or is it fundamentally unalterable? Modern attempts to answer this question scientifically have been inconclusive. Convincing facts fall on all sides of the question and ultimately are answered by our own value preferences.

Whatever view is expounded has immediate implications for the economic, political, and social preferences that flow from an ideological belief system. The conservative view, as propounded by Russell Kirk, asserts that human nature is unchangeable and that the purpose of social and political institutions is to control the pejorative tendencies in human behaviour.[9] Belief in the inherent goodness of human nature leads to the corollary that people should not be too closely controlled and directed by government. At the same time the belief that people are perfectible can lead to ideological prescriptions of radical, social, and institutional change as exemplified in Marxism*.

In choosing from the many ideological options open to societies a choice automatically implies a view of human nature. The democrat regards people as basically rational and trustworthy, neither mired in sin nor dependent on a superior social order for self-fulfilment. In contrast, the authoritarian sees people as capricious individuals, who, without the guidance of the party or the state, would have no predictability and direction in their lives. Emotion is thought to be much more determining in human behaviour than rational judgement.

The Role of the Individual

Through the centuries, political thinkers have wrestled with fundamental questions. Where does the individual fit into the total scheme of things? Does the state and its government serve the interests of individuals or are individuals subservient to the goals of the state? Where do we draw the line on the role of the individual in the political and social system? Many ideologies take into account the social obligations of individuals. They hold that those who live in society are not isolated individuals. Invariably, the way in which people act as individuals affects the opportunities for the self-development of others. And so other questions arise as to whether the state and its analogous institutions of government should try to regulate the inevitable conflicts that result from the free thoughts and actions of individuals.

To the doctrinaire socialists who adhere closely to the ideology of Marxism, the individual's welfare is subordinate to the welfare of the whole society. To them, the many will benefit most if the interests of individuals are not taken to represent the well-being of everyone. Even modern liberals concede that "the greater liberty of one is the lesser liberty of another."[10] But government is understood by contemporary liberals to be the necessary instrument for equalizing and thus maximizing individual freedom. A fundamental tenet of liberalism is the obligation to respect and protect each person's rights and to safeguard them from deprivation by other individuals or groups. One of the prominent ideological conflicts in the contemporary world pits the role of individuals in democratic societies against the collectivist positions expounded in socialist and communist doctrine.

The Role of the State

Throughout the intellectual history of political ideas the state has been the focus of much ideological controversy. In times past, the state was posited to have derived from the will of God, the fall of man, the social contract*, the process of natural evolution, the family, and the institution of private property. The controversy continues well beyond the notion of how the state originated because ideologies also differ sharply on its role in the political and social system. In some ideologies the state appears as a necessary evil or as a target for destruction. Some anarchists, libertarians, and ultra conservatives see the state as a set of institutions that attracts uncontrollable corruption, impedes economic and social progress, and threatens human liberty. In other ideologies the state represents the highest of human endeavours: Its purpose is viewed as raising civilized standards; its hallmark as justice; and its essence as law, founded on right, reason, and popular consent.

Most modern ideologies, with the exception of some strains of anarchism, believe that humans need a state apparatus of some kind to cope with the myriad problems associated with surviving in a competitive international community. The great ideological debates are not presented simplistically in terms of state or no state. Rather they are focussed on the degree of state intervention, the scope and character of political authority, and the methods of administration necessary to achieve the goals of public policy. Included in the ideological treatment of the role of the state are competing views on the functions of permanent and bureaucratic governments, the nature of sovereignty* by which the state can exercise legitimate force to regulate the affairs of its citizens as well as its relations with other states.[11] In some ideologies the concept "sovereignty" often denotes the supreme and final power of the state, above and beyond which no other power exists. Others concede that actually there is no such thing as absolute, utterly unqualified state power, and hence no absolute sovereignty. With respect to domestic or internal sovereignty there are wide variations among ideologies about the location and scope of sovereign power: Where does sovereignty reside – in the people or in the state? Is sovereignty divisible or indivisible? Who may express sovereignty?

Political Authority

One inevitable component of most modern ideologies is the consideration of the source and scope of political authority. Political authority is usually portrayed as a form of power based upon the recognition it receives from those over whom it is exercised. For some this authority is derived from the consent of the governed, while others point to the source of political authority as the coercive will of the state or dictators. Democracy and liberalism hold authority to be subjective, psychological, and moral in essence: authority is an influence that is intimately related to legitimacy, the belief of a citizenry that a government has the right to rule and that a citizen ought to obey the rules of that government. Whereas, in the ideologies of Fascism and Marxism-Leninism, authority is portrayed as something that flows objectively from the coercive arm of the state, government, and party institutions. The hallmark of totalitarian authority is the rigid hierarchy and the rank subordination of followers to the authority of a single or collective leadership. Authority, when attached to the state, is distinguishable more by command than by voluntary acceptance or compromise, more by dogmatic assertion than by consensus*.

Political authority has relevant meanings common to all ideologies. One is the *credibility* of the political communication – be it a law, regulation, decree or succession of power – that it is believed (almost regardless of its content) because it is derived from a source that is legitimized by force or procedure. A second is that political authority is to be obeyed, not always blindly or uncritically, but because compliance ensures the legitimate performance of the political system. In essence, political authority is a communication between leaders and the led, enabling them to relate to each other in such a way that the political system survives, be it a democracy or dictatorship.[12]

The Economic and Social Order

Ideologies usually reflect upon those desirable economic and social conditions that mobilize human beings for productive purposes. How will society organize, protect, and distribute the products of human labour and ingenuity? What social and political institutions should be in place to facilitate the required economic and social order? Who should reap the benefits of economic productivity and its attendant wealth?

Aristotle perceptively noted the economic and social basis of politics. Since his disclosures, the interdependence of socio-economic factors and politics has been omnipresent in the literature of Western political ideologies, even long before Marx and Marxism.[13] Mediaeval political thinkers, who in most cases were members of the clergy, recognized the obligations of monarchs to protect the economic and social well-being of their subjects. And the revolutions of the seventeenth and eighteenth centuries brought about extensive reviews of the ideological assumptions about the nature of production, distribution, ownership, and wealth in society. Changes in the ways these activities are performed will inevitably produce sweeping changes elsewhere in society. Ideologies reconcile a society's values with its structures.

The Marxists have searched for a more equitable way of organizing society and of ensuring that the satisfaction of individual economic needs does not contradict the fulfilment of social needs. Anarchists, insofar as they are willing to entertain the concept of order at all, insist on the free and spontaneous association of citizens in the economic and social life of society. For most anarchists the highest social order, and the only moral one, derives from each person's enlightened understanding of the social and economic interdependence of society. For capitalists, the economic and social system works best and the competitive ideal is most likely to be achieved when people are free to decide for themselves what they want and what they are willing to pay for it.

The End of Ideology

Although there is extraordinary diversity in the scope and content of ideologies, they perform similar functions. Most of the time people are not even aware that ideologies influence and condition their social behaviour. But they do consciously or unconsciously justify many of our thoughts and actions. Ideologies make us feel comfortable or uncomfortable about the institutions, leaders, and expectations of the political society we have created. They can divide or unite us. They can move us to act or to acquiesce.

Legitimation

The process whereby ideology gains acceptance for itself in the eyes of those who are influenced by it is legitimation. For some Marxists, legitimacy is the major function of ideology because it represents the prescribed political institutions and processes in such a way that political obligation seems natural and right.[14] From an ideological perspective legitimacy is a relative term. What is deemed legitimate by one ideology may not be regarded as legitimate in another. But generally an ideology will advance the belief that a political system is valid and justified and will be recognized as such by those over whom its authority is exercised.

In capitalist societies stratification* tends to be widely accepted and even defended – not just by people identified as privileged but often by those in the lower stratum as well. Sociologists sometimes refer to this form of ideological legitimation as *false consciousness* because members of the lower stratum of society often accept the ideology that justifies the system oppressing them. Instead of blaming the system, they attribute their low status to "luck," "fate," "nature," or the "will of God" – factors usually beyond their control. However, when an ideology facilitates *class consciousness* – an objective awareness of the lower stratum's common plight as an oppressed group – this group begins to question the legitimacy of the system or the ideology that sustains the system. The lower stratum may then be attracted to a different ideology, one that justifies its own class interests and consequently may seem revolutionary to the dominant stratum.

Leadership

One goal almost always articulated in ideologies is leadership.[15] With the exception of anarchism, which is an ideology founded upon the absence of leadership, all ideologies address this phenomenon on the social and political level. Who may lead us? How should we choose our leaders? When and how should leadership change? Ideologies often contain specific references to the nature of leadership and how it should shape the collective patterns of society. But, although ideologies may prescribe certain desirable leadership characteristics, the personal qualities of a single highly placed decision maker may themselves become a factor of power or revolutionary change: Castro in Cuba, de Gaulle in France, Tito in Yugoslavia, Nehru in India.

From the ideological perspective, leadership is closely related to authority, power, influence, and political succession. Leadership was a central feature of Fascist and Nazi ideologies as expressed in the concepts of *Il Duce* and the *Fuhrerprinzip*, whereby the leader embodied the state and for this reason had to be obeyed. With Marxism, leadership was intrinsic to the "dictatorship of the proletariat," which would bring under state control all the means of production, communications, transportation, and commerce. Lenin instituted the leadership of an elite revolutionary party in order to develop revolutionary consciousness among the masses. The party would become the vanguard of the people without necessarily having the support of the people. These patterns of leadership are not compatible with democratic thought. Democracy requires that the system of leadership recruitment be open, that the right and opportunity to seek the leader not be arbitrarily denied to any individual or category of persons. For democrats, a leader is someone who has legitimately won popular support, be it of a majority or of a minority. The procedures of democracy are organized to facilitate a consensual relationship between a leader and followers.

Purpose

One common attribute in the major ideologies is an end, goal, or purpose. Most of these ideologies hold a paramount concern with material abundance as the leading goal or purpose of the political system. Liberalism was the first ideology to articulate this end clearly and to develop the institutions designed to produce its systematic realization. Conservatism also keeps a watchful eye on national growth and the preservation of wealth. Communism, born much later, focusses on the possibility of overcoming scarcity, showing a passion for accelerating the pace of economic superabundance. This need to speed up economic growth and development is also a constituent in the indigenous revolutionary ideologies of the less-developed countries. The Fascists also had material abundance as a priority, although their methods differed considerably from those advocating liberal democratic values, as did their ideas about who would share in the national wealth.

Ideological conceptions of purpose also focus on what governments are expected to do.[16] The idea of "constitutional government" as expressed in the great democratic ideologies posits that the polity is not omnicompetent but should be restricted to specific social functions. The classical form of liberalism limited these to the preservation of order and property. Modern liberalism has added the concept of "welfare" to the proper province of government, and diminishes the previously legitimate area of unrestricted individual action. Quite to the contrary, Nazism subjugated the role of government to the state by postulating the idea of the *volkstadt* in which there was no distinction between governmental institutions and national relations. All political and governmental activity would bear immediately on society but all social activity needed the endorsement of the state. Nazis openly admitted to the role of government and party as "totalitarian."

Critique

One important psychodynamic of many ideologies is criticism. Karl Mannheim, best known for his development of the sociology of knowledge, saw the significance of differing and opposed positions in ideologies.[17] Mannheim distinguished two kinds of ideological thinking. One is utopian, which is the thinking of reformers who are unhappy with the status quo and want to tear it apart in order to build new institutions and values. The other is in defence of the status quo that is under attack.

Democrats, who believe that criticism is necessary for political systems to function, are themselves the target of severe attacks from opposing ideologies. The very nobility of democracy's goals invites an especially caustic flow of criticism regarding the gap between theory and practice. The heaviest attacks are concentrated on the practice, rather than the ideals of democracy. Virtually every democratic government in history has generated elements of aristocracy* and oligarchy*. Maurice Duverger defined democracy as government *of* the people by an elite sprung *from* the people.[18] Many democratic legislatures (particularly upper houses) give added weight to age, wealth, conservatism, and social status, resulting in an unacknowledged fusion of democracy with oligarchy.

For Marx, the fundamental contradiction of capitalism was the private ownership of the means of production, founded on the economic principle that the distribution of wealth is based on private and personal advantage: such a development would inevitably generate a society of immense inequality, causing many men, women, and children to suffer from poverty and want. According to Marx, capitalist ideology justified the use of the institutions of the state and their most characteristic expression – law – as a means of consolidating and perpetuating the socio-economic domination of the bourgeoisie*.

Prescription

Many ideologies are concerned with the normative implications of political organization and behaviour: the way the state and society should be organized and the way citizens should relate to these prescribed structures and social values. Almost invariably, empirical assertions are brought forward supporting assumptions that certain conditions exist, followed by normative assertions that a certain political order is preferred. As transmitted throughout a society, ideologies are a variable blend of facts, values, and propositions about what is and what ought to be. Each ideology, by means of its own logic and evidence, claims to possess the path to progress and directs its followers to implement its goals.

Anarchists prefer no government and reject the state, contending that individuals must have maximum choice to achieve the highest levels of morality, fulfilment, and perfectability. They therefore prescribe a society of individuals under no coercion. Nationalists, in contrast, prescribe a strong government and a competent state so as to unify the national character of a preferred group. The moral corporate personality of the nation is institutionally protected against the whims of individualism or the cultural incursions of other nations. In its extreme, as national socialism, the nation is seen as superior to the individual as well as to all other nations. Liberal democracy commits the state and government to the protection of the individual, while at the same time acknowledging the presence of the community and the nation as the collective expression of individualism.

The prescriptive dimensions of an ideology are what stir people to act and collectively arouse their intensive commitments toward achieving the goals put forward. Hardly any period in history or any part of the world has been without groups espousing ideological prescriptions on the way society should be organized. These ideological predilections often include an interpretation of the past, an evaluation of the present, and a vision of the future. They serve as both the foundation and justification of the desired political system and ultimately will depend on the passion, the drive, and the methods employed by those who have accepted the ideology.

Democratic Ideologies

Democratic thought is traceable to the Greeks. During the fifth century B.C. the Athenians, in particular, used the term *democracy* to refer to government by the many, as contrasted to government by the few (oligarchy), or by one person (monarchy). In his famous "Funeral Oration" Pericles (495–429 B.C.) declared that "our [Athens'] constitution is named a democracy, because it is in the hands, not of the few, but of the many."[19] The idea that the ultimate political authority lies with, and should flow from, the general public remains central to all conceptions of democracy to the present day.

The first great political theorist to consider democracy as a coherent system of thought was Aristotle, the Athenian philosopher who lived between 384 and 322 B.C. Aristotle saw democracy as direct popular government, which he thought would degenerate into mob rule because it lacked institutions capable of ensuring individual liberty and of controlling self-seeking interests. Direct democracy was too unrestrained and unstable, so Aristotle enlarged the concept by combining it with other elements: popular sovereignty, majority rule, and minority rights, which formed what he called constitutional government or polity. Aristotle's assessment of democracy in the *Politics* had remarkable range and prescience: he saw as necessary for constitutional democracy the presence of a large middle class and a fairly even distribution of property: "It is clear therefore that the political community administered by the middle class is the best ... in which the middle class is numerous ... it sways the balance and prevents the opposite extremes from coming into existence."[20]

The earliest Greek democracies were city states. They emphasized the equality of all citizens in their right to participate in the life of the community. Participation was widespread, with decisions based on oratory and face-to-face discussion. Citizens took part in such processes as jury trials and lawmaking, but more important than any other political rights was a broad notion of civic spirit. We are indebted to antiquity for the earliest examples of democracy in theory and practice. But many of the fundamental principles we now accept as generic to the ideology took many more centuries to develop. Indeed, democracy in its first manifestations was quite limited because slaves, women, and outsiders were excluded from citizenship.

Since Aristotle's time, many philosophers have contributed to the development of democracy. But the foundations of modern democratic ideology were fashioned in the seventeenth, eighteenth, and nineteenth centuries. The great thinkers of the time, John Locke, Jean Jacques Rousseau, Thomas Jefferson, Thomas Paine, Jeremy Bentham, James Mill, John Stuart Mill, and Alexis de Tocqueville all contributed to the present composition of modern democratic ideologies. But, in the theoretical construction of democratic theory from Aristotle to Locke to Rousseau, one critical element was missing: close attention to the practical governmental institutions through which constitutional democracy could protect minority rights and achieve social balance. The debates over the creation of the best institutional framework for democracy resulted in three distinctive ideological orientations: liberalism, conservatism, and socialism.

Liberalism

Liberalism as a discernible ideology in the eighteenth and nineteenth centuries was an outgrowth of an earlier revolt against oligarchic government, one that culminated in the "glorious revolution" of 1688 in England.[21] The Industrial Revolution stimulated a demand to free the taxpayer from arbitrary government action. This demand for freedom of action came primarily from the rising industrial and trading class and was directed against restrictions imposed by the government (in legislation, common law, and judicial action) upon the freedoms of economic enterprise.

Liberals derived their political ideas from the writers of the Enlightenment, the model of liberties available to the English middle class, and the so-called principles of 1789 as embodied in the French Declaration of the Rights of Man and Citizen. Liberal politicians in Europe wanted to establish a framework of legal equality, religious toleration, and freedom of the press. Their general goal was to construct a political structure that would limit the arbitrary powers of monarchical government against the persons and property of individual citizens. They generally believed that the legitimacy of government was not inherited but rather emanated from the freely given consent of the governed. The popular basis of this kind of government should be expressed through elected, representative, and parliamentary bodies. For liberals, free government required that the political executive must be responsible to the legislature rather than to the monarch.

The British philosopher Leonard Hobhouse prepared a list of liberal principles drawn from a penetrating analysis of the evolution of liberalism:

- *Rule of Law:* Liberals fought to limit government power by proclaiming the supremacy of law so as to secure the legal equality of all individuals and to protect the rights of people from arbitrary interference by officials.

- *Responsible government:* The democratic principle that all public officials are accountable to the people and can rule only by their consent.
- *Civil liberties:* At the basis of these lie the freedoms of thought, expression, association, religion, and the press.
- *Constitutionalism:* By means of a fundamental charter, social contract, or convention, to outline, define, limit the exercise of governmental power by law.
- *Individualism:* The principle that the chief function of government is to foster the well-being of each person and to permit them to reach their fulfilment.
- *Majority rule:* The principle that public decisions are weighted in favour of the greater number of citizens.
- *Popular sovereignty:* The source of all government and public authority flows from the people.
- *International co-operation:* Liberals called for the reduction or elimination of all trade barriers, tariffs, quotas, and other instruments of economic protection in order to foster international interaction.[22]

These ideological prescriptions may seem quite ordinary for us today. However, such democratic guarantees existed in none of the major European countries in the late seventeenth and eighteenth centuries. The people who espoused these changes in governments tended to be those who were excluded from the existing political processes but whose new wealth and education made them feel that such exclusion was unjustified. Liberals were usually intellectuals or people involved in the rapidly expanding commercial and manufacturing segments of the economy. The existing monarchical and aristocratic regimes often failed to recognize them as newly empowered groups or to provide for their economic and professional interests. In the chaotic years of eighteenth-century Europe, these groups organized for the purpose of winning control of government. They stressed the values of liberty, human dignity, and individualism, and they advocated political democracy. They sought to establish a constitutional order that would protect civil liberties, limit government, permit political competition, and separate church and state. The twentieth century has witnessed a further transformation of democratic liberal thought from its earlier legal forms to an ideology that postulates the "best" society rooted in individual freedom, social concern, and human dignity. Liberalism abandoned its eighteenth-century advocacy of the economic freedoms of laissez-faire capitalism. By the twentieth century it had postulated new roles for democratic government: to address the economic and social maladjustments of industrialization, to redistribute wealth, and to develop a policy framework for the health, education, and welfare of all citizens. One outstanding intellectual who helped to develop the rationale to support a greater government role in modern society was John Dewey (1859–1952).[23] This popular American philosopher noted the intimate connection between political democracy and economic well-being in society. For him, the political system had to guarantee a dignified life to all citizens.

Contemporary liberalism is a loosely knit mosaic of beliefs, practices, theories, and differing pragmatic approaches to solving economic, political, and social problems. Liberals believe that a strong central government is necessary to protect individuals from the inequities of technological society and that the growth of government has enhanced, not diminished, individual freedom. They see the role of the state as correcting the injustices of the marketplace, not supplanting it.

Conservatism

The term "conservatism" was coined from the French word *conservateur*, the label given to French writers and statesmen who demanded a return to pre-revolutionary conditions after the fall of Napoleon I. The birth of conservatism is usually associated with the publication of Edmund Burke's *Reflections on the Revolution in France* (1790), which excoriated the French revolutionaries for the arrogance with which they assumed they could alter the natural continuity of history.[24] The defeat of Napoleon and the diplomatic settlement of the Congress of Vienna re-established the conservative social and political order in Europe. Legitimate monarchies, aristocracies, and the established churches made up the main pillars of conservatism. These institutions were ancient but the conscious allegiance of the throne, wealth, and altar was new and made them reluctant allies. Conservatives knew they could be toppled by liberal political groups who hated them. They regarded themselves as surrounded by well-organized enemies; they felt permanently on the defensive against the forces of liberalism, nationalism, and popular sovereignty. A sense of alarm felt by European aristocrats, families of long-established wealth, and the clergy encouraged them to organize their own political groups.

Classical conservatism combined the ideological perspectives of Burke with thinkers such as Thomas Hobbes and David Hume. Hobbes had asserted that human nature was essentially selfish, requiring the restraint of coercive governmental power in order to tame the tendencies of people who satisfy their needs at the expense of others in society. Conservatives saw this selfishness expressed as social whim, demands for rapid or radical change, and licence for unfettered individual freedoms. David Hume, in his *Treatise of Human Nature* (1740), argued that given the tendency of human reason to reach selfish conclusions it was necessary for people to be bound by laws, conventions, and institutions that had proved their social wisdom over time.

Burke presented his conservative views of the world with power and conviction.[25] He held that humankind was wise, but that the individual was not. Burke confirmed the fundamental conservative distrust of human nature: as individuals, people were basically weak, given to passion and instinct, and generally untrustworthy. Such characteristics required institutional restrictions on human behaviour, through law, government authority, and other social constraints on individual freedoms. The role of the state was seen essentially as an agency to control people for their own good. Burke also stressed the organic nature of society – the idea that society is an organism to which all people in a community belong. The institutions that have evolved within this organic social system cannot be cut away without endangering the life of that organism, just as removing the internal organs of any living being would destroy that human organism. Thus, society is not merely a social contract as the liberals advocated, but an indissoluble and perpetual convention that assigns duties and responsibilities to be carried out from one generation to the next. Individuals are temporary and perishable. But society as an organic expression is a partnership between those who are dead, those who are living, and those yet to be born. As a product of evolution rather than revolution it is much larger and more enduring than any individual. Therefore, the interests of society must transcend individual interests.

In the early part of this century, the British political writer F.J.C. Hearnshaw set forth a classical statement of the principles of conservatism:

- *Reverence for the past:* Societies accumulate wisdom from their customs and traditions, and respect the accomplishments of their ancestors.
- *Organic conception of society:* Societies are greater than the sum of their parts and take on a corporate or communal identity and unity.
- *Constitutional continuity:* Constitutions are indissoluble conventions that carry the proven political norms and practices of the past into the present.
- *Opposition to revolution:* Conservatives reject radical change because it destroys proven customs and institutions.
- *Cautious reform:* Change should be evolutionary and carefully deliberated.
- *The religious basis of the state:* The state has a moral, religious, and sacred character beyond its political and legal personality.
- *The divine source of legitimate authority:* Political and legal authority is divine in its origin.
- *The priority of duties to rights:* Conservatives recognize that individuals have civic duties as well as personal rights and are obligated to fulfil them in the interests of the body politic.
- *Loyalty:* Conservatives demonstrate loyalty to church, family, school, party, institutions, and country.
- *Common sense and pragmatism:* Conservatives are people of practical action rather than theory; devoted to sound administration rather than prolific legislation.[26]

Modern conservatism is much less the body of coherent beliefs (as outlined by Hearnshaw) than a modern attitude or a state of mind. Conservatives usually want to preserve the status quo or return to a preferred previous state of affairs. In the 1990s, conservatism aspires to reduce social spending, reform the taxation laws to encourage investments, deregulate business to promote economic growth, and rebuild national defence. In other economic matters, conservatives draw upon many of the ideas of nineteenth-century liberalism. Conservatism has become essentially a defence of economic individualism against the growth of the welfare state. In its earlier manifestations conservatives were the supporters of strong government. They believed that only a government of a talented and propertied elite could preserve the sacred rights of humans. As the voting franchise extended to more and more people during the twentieth century, conservatives lost their faith in central government and focussed on the rights of property independent of the state, and on the rights of individuals to be free of government interference. Thus, contemporary conservatives oppose any increase in the role of the state in the economy and contend that a vibrant and unfettered private sector can best create jobs for the poor, immigrants, and minorities. Welfare programs, conservatives argue, only create a permanent class of the poor who are dependent on the state and who have little incentive to enter the work force.

On social and cultural issues conservatives come close to Burkean ideals. They prescribe that the state should promote virtue and social responsibility, improving the moral climate of society. As such, they are against abortion, pornography, and oppose affirmative rights for groups such as homosexuals. Conservatives challenge the idea of quotas and other affirmative policies: they argue that human rights guarantee equality of treatment, not equality of social results.

Democratic Socialism

Socialism is articulated by democratic as well as non-democratic ideologies. Unlike other systems of thought, it has enjoyed political prominence throughout recorded history, emerging in both primitive and modern societies as a rationale for societal planning and social equality. The prominence of socialist thought and practice over time in most parts of the world may have resulted from the very nature of society: men, women, and children surviving together as families, tribes, villages, cities, and nation-states. All societies have had to make choices regarding the reconciliation of the individual's welfare to the welfare of the whole society. The early socialists lacked any meaningful following: their doctrines were blurred and were viewed as bizarre by their contemporaries.

Among the first to articulate this social bias was a group of writers called *utopian socialists* by their later critics.[27] Thomas More (1478–1535), Francis Bacon (1561–1621) and Tommaso Campanella (1568–1639) were considered utopians because they were idealists whose ideas were visionary. These utopians looked nostalgically at earlier societies as though they were without selfishness and social antagonisms. They were called socialists because they criticized existing economic systems. One such early socialist pioneer was the French aristocrat, Claude Henri, Count of Saint Simon (1760–1825), who believed that private wealth, property, and enterprise should be socially administered by experts at arm's length from these assets to alleviate poverty and social dislocation. He came to be regarded as the father of modern technocracy.

The major British contributor to early socialist thought was Robert Owen (1771–1858), a successful cotton manufacturer. Owen held a partnership in a large British cotton factory at New Lanark, Scotland, where he put socialist ideas to practice, organizing the industry so that workers and managers lived together and produced their goods in co-operation. Although his experiment failed in New Harmony, Indiana, Owen contributed to socialist thought by his belief that the practicality of co-operative production under humane working conditions was possible. Charles Fourier (1772–1837), a contemporary of Owen, advocated the construction of morally liberated agrarian communities called *phalanxes* that would permit individuals to perform different tasks to avoid boredom and dullness. Fourier believed that societies would be more productive if social stratification and labour specialization were eliminated.

In the later part of the nineteenth century the democratic socialists who exerted the most influence were associated with the Fabian Society. Founded in 1884, the society took its name from Q. Fabius Maximus, the Roman general who defeated Hannibal by waiting a very long time before attacking. By acting out this strategy the society advocated a gradual approach to major social reform. Some of its notable members were Sidney (1859–1947) and Beatrice (1858–1943) Webb, H.G. Wells (1866–1946), Graham Wallas (1858–1932), and George Bernard Shaw (1856–1950). They believed that through democracy the great social questions of the day could be addressed. They wanted to replace individualism with state action. In their view the goals of socialism could be achieved without revolution.[28] This belief was echoed in the work of the German socialist revisionist Eduard Bernstein (1850–1932), who questioned whether Marx had been correct in his pessimistic appraisal of capitalism and the necessity of revolution. In his *Evolutionary Socialism* (1899), Bernstein pointed to the rising standard of living in Europe and the failure of Marx's predictions to materialize. Revisionists wanted socialist parties to gain control of governments in their respective countries, but the socialism to be thus established would be more moderate and limited than the sweeping transformation of society urged by doctrinaire socialists.

In the twentieth century, democratic socialism is a political and economic ideology that aims at preserving individual freedom in the context of social equality achieved through a centrally planned economy. While a private sector of the economy will continue to exist under socialism, major industries and corporations would be owned by the state in the national interest and, thus, the government would be responsible for planning and directing the economy. Under socialism the state takes ownership of only strategic industries and services, such as railways, airlines, mines, banks, radio, TV, telecommunications, medical services, universities, and important manufacturing enterprises such as chemicals and steel. Decisions concerning foreign investments, wages, and prices are placed in the hands of public institutions. The tax system is designed to prevent excessive profits or an undue concentration of wealth. No democratic socialist state aspires to communism. What separates democratic socialists from non-democratic socialists is the latter's acceptance of violent revolution: democratic socialists advance peaceful and constitutional change. But although socialist societies may redistribute wealth more evenly than capitalist ones, they are less efficient at creating wealth in the first place. The twentieth century has gathered persuasive evidence that socialist societies are more bureaucratic and less productive than capitalist ones.[29]

The contemporary descendants of evolutionary socialism are the social democratic and labour parties of North America, Western Europe, and Latin America. They have often abandoned the more radical elements of their ideology (for example, nationalization of industry and opposition to capitalism). Where they have gained power, they have pursued policies aimed at creating a welfare state and winning votes – all within the capitalist framework.

Communist Ideology

The idea that there should be no private property and that all things should be held in common is an ancient one. In the book of Genesis everything comes from God and no one has inherent rights of possession. In Deuteronomy, all debts are automatically cancelled every seven years in the "year of release," according to the ancient Hebrew beliefs of egalitarianism, welfare and communist norms. In Leviticus, the "year of Jubilee" is described as the time every fifty years when all the accumulated inequalities of land distribution are eliminated and the land is redistributed equally among Hebrew tribes. In the sixth century, Christian monasticism repudiated private ownership and called for a return to the ancient principle of equality believed to have been prominent in a "golden age" of communal life. In sixteenth-century Austria – 300 years before Marxism – the Hutterites practised social and economic communism and proclaimed that all humans should live in communal societies. The utopian socialists wrote of societies organized according to communist principles founded among the earliest human communities.

The person who had the most profound impact on modern notions of communism was Karl Marx (1818–1883). His socialist philosophy eventually triumphed over most alternative versions of socialism in Europe – even though varying interpretations, criticisms, and revisions of his monumental work continue to the present.[30] As a student at the University of Berlin, Marx immersed himself in Hegelian philosophy, which introduced him to the idea that all phases of human history are the inevitable product of class and ideological conflict. French utopian socialists gave Marx his focus on the ideals of communal life. And British economists, notably, Adam Smith, David Ricardo, and Thomas Malthus, who shared the view that the condition of the working class could not be improved, gave him a pessimistic focus. In 1844 Marx met Friedrich Engels, another young middle-class German, whose friendship with Marx led to an intellectual collaboration of enormous ideological consequences. In 1847, they wrote *The Communist Manifesto* for a newly organized secret Communist League. They had adopted the name *communist* because the word was much more emphatically radical than *socialist*. Communism implied the outright abolition of private property and required the extensive reorganization of society. A work of less than fifty pages, the *Manifesto* would become the most influential document in modern European history. By the time *Das Kapital* (vol. 1, 1867) was published, predicting the disintegration of capitalism, Marxism had emerged as the single most-important strand of socialism in Europe.[31]

Under the influence of Hegelian thought, Marx and Engels contended that human history must be understood rationally and as a whole. The basic means of production in an economy facilitates the structures, values, and ideas of society. The lesson from history is that the organization of the means of production generates conflict between the classes who own the means of production and those who work for them. History is driven and unfolds by this necessary conflict. Marxian analysis was, therefore, conditioned by the assumption that the path to socialism lay with revolution rather than reform. The era of the utopian community had ended.

The fundamental concepts of Communism flow from the theoretical contributions of Marx, Engels, V.I. Lenin, Leon Trotsky, Josef Stalin, Josip Tito, Nikita Khrushchev, Mao Tse Tung, and Mikhail Gorbachev. They include materialism, historical inevitability, alienation, labour theory of value, class struggle, dictatorship of the proletariat, the revolutionary role of the vanguard party, and imperialism.

Materialist Conception of History

Marxism begins with the "materialist conception of history," which asserts the human necessity to produce and acquire a means of subsistence. In order to understand the historical significance of materialism Marx asks us to look at the role of labour, the abundance or lack of raw materials, and the instruments of production available in society. This material basis for the "mode of production" determines the political, moral, legal and religious superstructure* of society and is the driving force of societal development from lower to higher stages. That is, the material lives of people determine their ideology and their supporting institutions. Changes in material conditions necessarily bring about changes in the social and political structures of society. Thus, history is the product not of deliberative decisions or ideas, but of material processes and conditions that are identifiable, observable, and predictable.[32]

Historical Inevitability

Marx borrowed the philosophical premise from Hegel and others that history moves in anticipatory and calculable directions.[33] Marx and Engels developed a theory about the movement of history that purports to explain why one economic system (mode of production) would give way to another and why prediction is possible to the final historical stage of human development, which is communism. They devoted much of their work to plotting the development of human history from primitive communism through slavery and feudalism to capitalism and socialism. Much of their work, however, sharply focussed on capitalism and its inevitable collapse rather than on the future of societies. Capitalism marked a transient stage of historical development destined to disintegrate because its antagonistic classes – capitalist and proletariat* – will clash, resulting in a victorious worker's revolution.

The identification of the inevitability of historical forces was regarded by Marx and Engels as the "scientific" quality of their analyses. Thus, the scientific study of history was the analysis of the way in which humans respond to material change in their societies and the capacity to predict the consequences of these changes.

Alienation

The Marxian theory of alienation seeks to explain how individuals living in a capitalist society lose their understanding and control of the world around them and in the process become something less than full human beings. Under capitalism, the source of alienation is the organization of work. Workers feel dissociated from the process of production because they compete with other workers, receive only a small portion of the value of what they produce, are divided and specialized in what they produce, and do not own the means of production or have much say in how the means are used.

Marx believed that the capacity to work is a distinctive human characteristic. All other species, he argued, are simply objects in their worldly environment; human beings are the sole subjects in the hierarchy of existence because they consciously act on and change the environment, shaping their lives, cultures, and personalities in the process. Because workers in a capitalist system have diminished responsibilities and are reduced to a minute part of the work process, they perceive themselves as mere cogs in the productions of society. Work becomes an enforced activity, not a creative or satisfying one, essentially because the profit produced by the labour of the worker goes to someone else. Marx did not see capitalism as the original source of alienation but he believed that under capitalism alienation is maximized.

Labour Theory of Value

Marx witnessed some of the worst manifestations of capitalism while he lived in England. From his experience he concluded that the majority of men, women, and children suffered from poverty and need. They were the victims of a mode of production that permitted the few who did not do manual labour to enjoy most of the wealth produced by labourers. Thus, the capitalist mode of production extracts surplus value from wage-labour to the benefit of a capitalist class. As Marx saw it, the true value of any commodity is derived by computing the labour that is necessary to produce it (labour theory of value). Because capitalists are not labourers they do not produce value. At the same time, workers are not compensated for the total value of the goods they produce and what the capitalist withholds from the worker is surplus value. The surplus value is used to expand capital, a process conditioned by competition. The accumulation of capital generates increasing demands for labour. But simultaneously, accumulation leads to the concentration of capital, which places greater amounts of capital in fewer and fewer hands.

Ultimately, the fundamental contradictions of capitalism are linked to the labour theory of value. The natural tendency for capitalists to expand surplus value, or profits, feeds the impoverishment of workers, creates under-consumption, and results in surplus production.

Class Struggle

Marx recognized that many different social classes had emerged at different times under different modes of production. For example, in preindustrial Europe, the aristocracy who owned the land were the ruling class, and the peasants who tilled it were the workers. During the industrial period two classes alone – the bourgeoisie and the proletariat – were the forces that shaped the economic destiny of the period. But, for Marx, social classes were more than ranks in a hierarchy: they were the building blocks of society. Social classes arise from the "relations of production." Accordingly, the major classes of the modern era are the landowners and capitalists, and the class of wage-earners. In the course of time classes become self-aware. This class consciousness leads to organization, politicization and ultimately confrontation. Because the state is a prominent component of the superstructure that reflects the ideology of the ruling class, its coercive power is applied against the challenges of the proletarian class.

Out of this situation revolutions are born. Marx saw history as a dialectic* of revolutionary change. For him, the dialectic is a process of class conflict and struggle involving social and political contradictions as *thesis* and *antithesis*, producing a conflict out of which a new and higher social order, *synthesis,* emerges. Marx and Engels asserted that class conflict would be resolved in the final proletarian revolution resulting in the final historical synthesis – communism.

Dictatorship of the Proletariat

According to Marx, after the inevitable revolution, a short period of socialist transition would take place following the collapse of capitalism. The dictatorship of the proletariat is the state under the control of the proletarians, defending the gains made during the revolution and guiding society through the inequalities and deprivations resulting from the transformation to communism. By means of its political dominance the proletariat is able to bring under its control all the means of production: industry, land, business, communications, transportation, and commerce.

The term dictatorship was never fully explained by Marx, although it may have been used rhetorically to add legitimacy to state representation of workers' interests in the period of transition. The state is a committee of proletarians making decisions, drafting laws, and taking action on behalf of the proletarian class. Marx argued that the advent of a socialist revolution would mean the disappearance of a class-based state apparatus. For this brief period the proletariat is the ruling class that prepares the way for a classless society.

The Vanguard Party

V.I. Lenin (1870–1924) was a determined, restless Bolshevik* revolutionary who studied the strengths and weakness of Marxist theory as it could apply to a revolution occurring in a backward country such as Russia. In his work, *What Is to be Done?* (1922) Lenin explained why the autocratic conditions of Russia demanded a unique kind of organization to guide the revolution to fruition. Lenin rejected Marx's concept of a mass party composed of workers because revolutionary consciousness had not developed sufficiently in the small

Russian working class during and after the revolution. For him, the Russian proletariat was diminutive, disorganized, easily subverted, and without a clear understanding of its revolutionary mission. Only a small élite, made up "of people who make revolutionary activity their profession" could lead the people with any disciplined determination.

Lenin was arguing that the socialist revolution was inevitable for Russia only if a specially constituted vanguard party made it so. In fact, one of his theoretical contributions to Marxism was that socialist revolution can take place in a pre-capitalist society if it is properly planned and engineered. In 1905 Lenin complemented his organizational theory for the party with a program for revolution in Russia. His *Two Tactics of Social Democracy in the Bourgeois-Democratic Revolution* (1905) urged that the socialist revolution unite the Russian proletariat and the peasants under one party organization. Lenin grasped better than any other revolutionary the profound discontent in the Russian countryside, even after the revolution. He knew that an alliance of workers and peasants in one party would be a formidable revolutionary combination.

Imperialism

In 1916 Lenin published *Imperialism: The Highest Stage of Capitalism*. In it he elaborated on Marx's assertion that monopolies are a natural tendency in developed capitalist economies. Monopolies will ensure their further expansion by penetrating and exploiting new markets in foreign economies. Otherwise, continued exploitation of a domestic market would result in Marx's prediction of severe social crisis and ultimately economic collapse.

Lenin observed that advanced capitalist economies had temporarily postponed social and economic chaos by entering new markets in the developing economies of the world. New markets absorbed excess production that could not be sold in the domestic economy because of the impoverishment of the masses. Thus, imperialism and colonialism were seen as a consequence of monopoly capitalism. Lenin's observations altered Marxism by linking colonialism with the spread of capitalism in the developing world and by advancing the possibility that revolutions need not occur necessarily in the most advanced industrialized economies.

Leninism

Lenin escorted Marxism into the twentieth century by applying its will, action, and initiative to a real revolution. Marx aspired to a Lenin when he said "the philosophers have *interpreted* the world in various ways; the point however is to *change* it."[34] Until Lenin's revolutionary activism, Marxists believed that the dialectic movement of history was determined by class forces that were beyond the control of any single individual. Lenin's main contribution to Marxism was that voluntarism and organization can generate socialist revolution independent of any movement of history. For Lenin, revolution was not necessarily spontaneous; rather it could be calculated and orchestrated by a disciplined, militant party organization: "The organization of the Party takes the place of the Party itself; the Central Committee takes the place of the organization; and finally the dictator takes the place of the Central Committee."[35]

Another important principle developed by Lenin in his theory of party organization was *democratic centralism*. Under this principle, democratic participation by means of free discussion is permitted for all party members until a decision is taken, at which time no further debate or dissent is tolerated and party members are expected to support fully the decision. Democratic centralism became a fundamental decision-making component in Soviet totalitarianism because it reinforced the control of the party and the government over ideological opposition. The Leninist variant of Marxism was essentially party-centric: (a) a party of professional revolutionaries, (b) the democratic dictatorship of the proletariat under the leadership and structure of the party, (c) *partinost*, the notion of partisan party-mindedness, which advances the party as the repository of ideological truth.

As discussed, Lenin's theory of imperialism altered Marx's position that revolutions will occur only in the advanced capitalist economies. A corollary to Lenin's rationalization of engineered revolutions was his "theory of the weakest link." In it, Lenin held that the greatest possibilities of revolution are not found in capitalist economies but in the weakest links of the capitalist chain, where the proletariat and/or the peasantry was more susceptible to revolutionary mobilization. Russia was portrayed as the weakest link in the chain of European capitalism prior to 1917. Lenin expressed confidence in the ability of Russia to attain socialism.[36]

Trotskyism

Lenin's intellectual comrade during the Bolshevik revolution was Leon Trotsky (1879–1940). He and Lenin believed that socialism could not be built in a single country that was surrounded by class enemies. After Lenin's death in 1924 Trotsky argued that Russia should be the base for world revolution. As an ideology Trotskyism was an appeal to unite the proletariat in all countries so as to establish a world Communist commonwealth. Trotsky believed that the Russian Revolution had declined because it created a bureaucratic ruling élite that was exploiting its own proletariat. He called for "permanent revolution" on an international scale, eventually to overwhelm the forces of capitalism everywhere in the world.

Leon Trotsky's brilliant organization of the Red Army under Lenin secured the Bolshevik victory in the Russian civil war. But he wanted to use the Red Army along with indigenous cadres of other countries, such as those in Poland, Germany, Austria, Hungary, and France, to instigate revolution in them. Trotsky further argued that the revolution in Russia could succeed only if new revolutions took place elsewhere in the world. He later lost his revolutionary power and influence when, following Lenin's death, Stalin outmanoeuvred him in the party strife of the late 1920s. By 1927 Trotsky had been removed from all his offices, expelled from the party, and exiled to Siberia. In 1929 Trotsky was exiled from Russia and eventually took up residence in Mexico, where he was assassinated in 1940, presumably by one of Stalin's agents.

Stalinism

After the removal of Trotsky from all positions of influence, Josef Stalin (1879–1953) was firmly in control of the Soviet state. Stalin transformed Marxism by urging that socialism should be achieved in one country, namely Russia. This doctrine of "socialism in one country" was intended to modernize and industrialize the newly formed Soviet Union, not only that it might become a powerful socialist state in its own right but also that it might serve as a model and a base for expanding communist revolutions.

Stalin held that socialism would develop only by iron-willed methods of state, beginning with the implementation of a series of five-year plans to construct heavy industry, collectivize agriculture, and educate a pool of skilled workers, scientists, and bureaucrats.[37] Stalin far exceeded his czarist predecessors in the intensity of state coercion and terror he brought to the task of modernization. During the Great Purges, one of the most mysterious and horrendous dictatorial events in this century, Stalin institutionalized state terrorism to achieve socialist economic and political goals. Stalinism came to mean ruthless style, bureaucratic centralization, and the domination of the state and party by a single individual.

Stalin believed that the interests of world communism and Soviet communism were identical. The enemies of the Soviet Union were therefore the enemies of global socialist revolutions. "Capitalist Encirclement" threatened the security of the Soviet Union and intensified as the socialist state advanced toward communism.

Titoism

Marshal Josip Broz Tito (1892–1980) pursued an independent course toward socialism and consequently was bitterly denounced by Stalin. Tito's socialism was characterized by a refusal to be absorbed into the Soviet bloc, a neutralist foreign policy, and a domestic economy that resembled market socialism in a free-enterprise economy. Tito did not accept the direction and control of the Communist Party of the Soviet Union and advocated instead that individual communist parties owed their loyalty to their own country. Tito's theory and practice of national communism was therefore a rejection of the monolithic approach to world communism envisioned by Stalin. This division in the ranks of communism generated by a renegade leader had major implications within the Soviet bloc as well as in the Cold War politics of the period.

Titoism became a model of peaceful transition from capitalism to socialism through the procedural use of parliamentary institutions and working-class parties. Tito practised a non-coercive style of communist government and conducted normal international relations with many states in the West. Titoism reflected the spirit of Marxism through its more humanistic approach to socialist goals. Yugoslavian socialism under Tito became known for its free exchange of ideas, its economic incentives, workers' right to strike, its democratic process in worker/managerial relations, and its independent judiciary.

Khrushchevism

Stalin's successors, all attempted to rectify, at least in part, the systemic neglect of consumers, peasants, urban dwellers, and the aged. Nikita Khrushchev replaced Stalin as First Secretary of the Communist Party in 1953, and by 1958 had consolidated his power after removing Nikolai Bulganin as the Chairman of the Council of Ministers.

The Khrushchev era, which lasted until the autumn of 1964, witnessed a marked departure from Stalinism, though not from all methods of totalitarian repression.[38] In 1956 Khrushchev attacked the policies of Stalin and denounced him as a criminal against socialist justice in a long secret speech before the Communist Party Congress in Moscow. The speech sent shock waves throughout the Soviet Union as well as through its sphere of influence in Eastern Europe. Khrushchev repudiated Stalin's "cult of personality" and, in his view, attempted to restore the "true" approach to Marxism-Leninism. Some intellectual liberalization followed along with a thaw in the cultural life of the country. But this change appeared tolerable only in comparison to what had preceded it. Gradually, the strongest supporters of Stalin's policies were removed, but none were executed. A less-tyrannical approach to government and party control seemed to solidify under Khrushchev's stewardship.

In 1956 the Soviet Union adopted the phrase "peaceful coexistence" in regard to its relations with capitalist states, especially the United States. The policy implied no less competition with the capitalist world but suggested that war might not be the best way to pursue communist expansion. For Khrushchev, communism would replace capitalism by peaceful competition and the historical transition from socialism to communism would take place in about twenty years, by 1984: "The party solemnly proclaims the present generation of Soviet people shall live in Communism."[39] Khrushchev also revised the Marxist-Leninist assertion that the state and classes would eventually wither away by predicting that the Communist party should remain as the directing force of communist society after the final historical transition.

Maoism

Mao Tse Tung (1893–1976) inspired, led, and built the largest socialist revolution in world history. He believed his ideological positions to be genuine Marxism. Highly critical of the Soviet Union, which he accused of having abandoned Marx's vision, Mao guided China towards socio-economic equality and authentic Marxist communism. Mao tried to eliminate all social distinctions of rank and status. During the Great Proletarian Cultural Revolution*, which ran its course during 1966–69, professional work was downgraded; professors were stripped of their titles, no university degrees were granted, and military rank was abolished. The Chinese all wore the same loose-fitting garments, the "Mao tunic." Private ownership of land was abolished and peasants were grouped into communes under the slogan "Let everyone eat from the same pot." The communes had production quotas and food was prepared and consumed communally, not by individual families. In the Leninist tradition, all authority was concentrated in the party under Mao.

Mao saw the "dictatorship of the proletariat" as a "people's democratic dictatorship" led by an alliance between workers and peasants. Under its leadership Mao envisioned a planned, classless, highly egalitarian, and self-reliant Chinese society in which the means of production are owned and regulated by workers. People would share a high level of communist consciousness and morality, which, Mao held, would generate a new Chinese consciousness in a society freed from all contradictions.

Mao's theory of revolution coincided with Trotsky's idea of permanent revolution against the bastions of capitalism throughout the world. To facilitate a permanent world revolution, Mao advocated fighting guerrilla wars in agrarian societies to spread communism globally. The transition to communism would not occur merely as a class revolution but as a social and cultural revolution – a transformation that could require violence and permanent political struggle. Revolutionary warfare involved the establishment of hidden base areas, the codification of guerrilla tactics, and the organization of the peasantry into a hierarchy of overlapping military, paramilitary, and political units. Mao also stressed the need to engineer the revolution in three carefully defined stages: (1) organization, (2) guerrilla warfare and (3) conventional war.

The monumental split between Mao's China and the Soviet Union confirmed the polycentric* character of the Soviet bloc, commencing with the expulsion of Yugoslavia from the Cominform* in 1948. By the early 1950s, China had embarked on an independent socialist course, and advanced the cause of world communism by supporting wars of national liberation in the underdeveloped world. Not until the Sino-Soviet Summit of 1989 did an official rapprochement appear to heal the ideological rift between the two states.

Gorbachev's "New Thinking"

Gorbachev's call for "new thinking" as expressed in *Perestroika: New Thinking for Our Country and the World* (1987) constituted an open attempt at ideological reform in the Soviet Union. In 1986, the Twenty-seventh Congress of the CPSU gave Gorbachev the opportunity to revise the stale ideological legacy of Brezhnev, Andropov, and Chernenko under whose leadership the forces of economic stagnation and political corruption had worsened in the Soviet Union after Khrushchev. Although it is true that in 1983 Iuri Andropov launched a campaign of systemic "reforms" against corruption and lax labour practices, Gorbachev was the first Soviet leader in the post-war era to go beyond mere reform to "restructuring" of the Soviet economic system.

Gorbachev admitted that the Soviet economy was flawed – that the central planning process operated as a "braking system" on economic growth, that production was shoddy and inefficient, that the economy was not innovative, and that labour was wasteful and subsidized. At the January 1987 Central Committee plenary session, Gorbachev defined restructuring as the "energetic deliverance of society from the distortions of socialist morality," "the profound renewal of all aspects of life," and the "transformation of the economic, social, and spiritual spheres."[40]

The "Law of the USSR on Individual Work Activity," which took effect, on May 1, 1987, legitimized most of the productivity of the "second economy," where private enterprise has flourished since the revolution. The individual labour of citizens and their families covers a wide range of handicraft and service activities that are registered and supervised by the executive committees of local soviets. Another law on state enterprises, proclaimed in June 1987, was drafted to co-opt the role of the central bureaucracy in the economy and thus to diminish the need for a "shadow" economy. In effect, the law on state enterprises is an attempt to displace the administrative forces of conformity and central planning in the economy with more natural economic forces affecting supply and demand, wages and prices, and interest and finance.

Another important instrument of restructuring is *glasnost'*, a component of the notion of "socialist democracy" undertaken by Gorbachev. *Glasnost'* was an ideological means of directing public attention to the failings of previous leaders as well as a method for mobilizing public support for Gorbachev's restructuring. The concept resembles the old Bolshevik principle of "criticism and self-criticism," almost totally abandoned during the Stalinist period because of the harsh penalties attached to dissent. Gorbachev stated that *glasnost'* was needed to assure fulfilment of the objectives outlined at the Twenty-seventh Congress. Subsequently Gorbachev advocated "vocality" and "publicity" to enhance public participation in the governmental soviets, and to encourage public initiative and involvement as a means of "overcoming . . . passivity, civic colourlessness, apathy, [and] unself-reliant thinking."[41]

Gorbachev announced the "acceleration of social and economic development" to prepare the Soviet Union for its inexorable movement toward modernization. In conformity with Marx, Gorbachev defines communism as a "classless social system with a single form of public ownership of the means of production."[42] But unlike Marx, Gorbachev's communism will not produce a stateless system that would whither from obsolescence and conscientious maturity: "The activity of state agencies will require a non-political nature, and the need for the state as a special political institution will gradually disappear."[43] As for the time frame required to achieve communism, which Khrushchev was so willing to forecast a quarter century before him, Gorbachev would only decline such speculation: "The only thing that can be definitely said today is that the fulfilment of the present program extends beyond the confines of the current century."[44]

Nationalism

The roots of nationalism can be traced deep into the past, appearing as it did when England, France, and Spain were transformed from feudal principalities to national monarchies and when their people regarded themselves as English, French, and Spanish nationalities rather than as Yorkshiremen, Gascons, and Andalusians.[45] Somewhat later, during the Hundred Years' War (1337–1453) England and France drew upon strong feelings of national sentiment to centralize their governments and economies, and to wage war. Much later, in the seventeenth century, the Treaty of Westphalia (1648) nurtured distinctive nation-states, each with its own political, cultural, and religious identity; it unleashed the forces of competitive nationalism in the modern world. In the following century, writers of the Enlightenment had generally championed a cosmopolitan outlook on the world but the political leaders of the time fashioned a national perspective characterized by autocracy, censorship, and repression. Napoleon demonstrated the power of nationhood. His toppling of ancient political structures, such as the Holy Roman Empire, demonstrated the need for a new type of political organization in Europe. Nationalism proved to be one of the strongest motivating forces of the nineteenth and twentieth centuries, demonstrating its powerful tendencies to unite people on the one hand and to destroy millions on the other.

German Romantic* writers portrayed nationalism as the glorification of individual cultures.[46] Johann Fichte (1762–1814) challenged the younger generation of Germans to recognize the national duty that historical circumstances had placed on their shoulders. He called for the revival of the German nation so as to receive the gratitude of later generations. Johann Herder (1744–1803) saw human beings and societies as developing organically, like plants, over time. He urged the collection and preservation of distinctive German songs and sayings and seized upon the conception of the *volksgeist* or national spirit. Perhaps the most important person to develop the ideology of nationalism during the Romantic period was G.W.F. Hegel (1770–1831), who recognized that the individuality and worth of each separate people and culture constituted one of the spiritual forces at work in changing world history.

These Romantic writers defined *nation* in terms of common language, common history, common customs, and a homeland. This cultural nationalism would later become transformed into a political creed that ideologically asserted the unique spirit of belonging together and the corporate nature of the polity. The belief spread rapidly that every people, ethnic group, or nation should constitute a separate political entity and that only when it so existed could the nation be secure in its own unique character.

French nationalism also reflected a romantic and culturally homogeneous character. Writers such as Voltaire, Montesquieu, and Rousseau advanced a cultural nationalism, observing that each people had a language, history, and world view of its own, which must be preserved and perfected. They then passed on to a political nationalism, holding that in order to preserve the national culture, each nation should create a sovereign state. All persons of the same nationality should embody the same state.

The nineteenth century saw the nascent emergence of the *nation-state*, the political consolidation of one or more nations under the jurisdiction and administration of a single state. Prior to this time, the characteristic political organizations were small states comprising fragments of a nation, such as were present in Europe – Hanover, Baden, Sardinia, Tuscany, and the two Sicilies – and the large sprawling empires made up of all sorts of peoples, distantly ruled from above by dynasties, such as the Romanov, Habsburg, and Ottoman. For many people in the nineteenth century, nationalism, the winning of national unity and independence, and the creation of the nation-state became a kind of secular faith.

At about this time governments recognized that they could not effectively rule, or construct the full powers of a state, without enlisting the membership and support of their subjects. The consolidation of the nation-state had some noteworthy phases: In its territorial phase, it meant the union of pre-existing smaller states; and psychologically, it meant the construction of new relations between the government and the governed, the inclusion of new strata of the population into political life, and the creation and extension of representative institutions. As an ideology, nationalism came to mean the will of a particular nationality or group of nationalities to accept the power of a state to administer its interests, such as with the creation of a new Italy, a new Germany, and a new Canada. But it also meant in some cases the power of a state to maintain national unity as in the United States when President Lincoln used national force to repress Southern independence by force of arms.

During the nineteenth century, nationalism was not doctrine so much as it was a state of mind, arousing the emotional responses of people when national interests were questioned. In many societies nationalism was blended with conservatism, liberalism, socialism, or republicanism. Within the confines of these ideological prisms patriots began to call for the preservation of their historic cultures. Intellectuals collected folk tales and ballads, studied languages, and composed lexicographies of their mother tongues. They encouraged their compatriots to give up "foreign ways" and began the writing of heroic histories. The nineteenth century had generated the ideological prescription that the only legitimate basis for political organization was nationality. The result of this belief was the spread of national independence movements and the consequent development of an international system of sovereign nation-states.

Nationalism in the contemporary state system is in many ways similar to and an extension of its nineteenth century predecessor. However, nationalist sentiment has taken on a more doctrinaire form in the present century. The contemporary ideology of nationalism accepts the idea that the human species will naturally form into nations that reflect a particular character. Each nation enjoys the right of self-determination and possesses many legal rights and duties when represented by a state apparatus that is recognized by other states as independent in the international community. Loyalty to the nation is seen to supersede other loyalties. Human freedom and harmony are said to be enhanced by an international system formed on the basis of independent nation-states.[47]

Totalitarian Nationalism

In its extreme during the twentieth century, nationalism manifested itself as the irrational ideologies of fascism and national socialism (nazism). Latent in German thought in the nineteenth century, nationalism became an obsession. One eminent German historian, Leopold von Ranke (1795–1886), in his work *Latin and Teutonic Peoples*, taught that the Germans had a mission from God to develop a pure culture "corresponding to the genius of the nation." Such cultural nationalism was further considered by many philosophers and other intellectual authors who contributed to the development of anti-democratic thought. Friedrich Nietzsche (1844–1900) wrote about the "heroic man," the "superman," the "spineless multitude," and the "slave morality" and influenced the superiority theories of Adolf Hitler. Another German philosopher, Arthur Schopenhauer, who wrote *The World* *as Will and Idea*, advocated the idea of subjective truth, which inspired Hitler's use of propaganda to distort reality and engage in psychological warfare*.

Even though there are important theoretical differences between Italian Fascism and German National Socialism, both emphasized the historical importance of building state institutions that united the common cultural identities of the people. These ideologies invariably focussed on the nation rather than the individual and on the superiority of the state over the citizen. There was never the emphasis on individual rights, natural rights, or social contract that had formed the basis of liberal democracy.

In ancient Rome, the *fasces* (a bundle of rods tied to an axe) symbolized the unity of the nation facilitated by an administrative state. In the twentieth century, governments regarded as fascist were intensely nationalistic, imperialistic*, anti-democratic, anti-Marxist, and anti-Semitic. They expressed a deep pride in their past cultural achievements and a bitterness that – despite a self-proclaimed cultural superiority – the less-cultured nations exercised real political and military power in the world. The Fascist and Nazi attitudes towards wars and quest for empires was related to cultural glorification and expressions of racial superiority. Mussolini often referred to Italy's *sacro egoismo* as the rationale for territorial aggrandizement and irredentism*. The Nazis likewise called for the union of all Germans to form the "Great Germany" and demanded more living space "for the nourishment of our people and for settling our excess population."[48] Those who did not share in the superpatriotism of the period and the resurrected glory of the past were treated as "un-German" or "aliens."

The underlying nationalist ideology of nazism was racist. Hitler embraced the image of the "Aryan race" as a blond, blue-eyed, and uniquely gifted "master race," which had diluted its genetic heritage by intermarriage with "lesser breeds." The fear of intermarriage with whomever was deemed the bad race became linked with all kinds of sexual fears and phobias. In the Nuremberg Laws (1935) proclaimed by the Nazis, and analogous to South African *apartheid* legislation and U.S. miscegenation statutes, German Jews were denied their citizenship, and intermarriage between Germans and Jews was outlawed.[49] Anti-Semitism thus became a fundamental policy of the Nazi government.

Fascist ideology had rejected the political inheritance of the French Revolution and the democratic traditions of liberalism. Sovereignty was vested in the national state: all individuals existed to enhance the power of the state and the nation it represented. The mystical entity of the nation was viewed as an organic body headed by the *Fuhrer* and sustained by unity, force, and discipline. This new philosophy of statecraft drew heavily upon the historic nationalism which it greatly exaggerated. The organic theory postulated the nation as a living organism within which the individual person was but a single cog. Individuals possessed no independent existence, receiving all worth from the nation that nurtured them. Law itself was defined as the will of the nation operating through the institutions of the Nazi state. The new national order was designed to be monolithic: Germany ceased to be a federal state, and old states such as Prussia and Bavaria were abolished so that the historic process of national unification could be finalized.

Anarchism

The Greek word *anarchos* means without a leader or chief. Like the Greek cynics, who first developed the doctrines of anarchism, modern anarchists believe that government and the state apparatus are unnecessary for the meaningful arrangement and operation of society.[50] They are essentially optimistic about human nature, believing that the inherent goodness in people alleviates the need for political and organizational constraints on their behaviour. Today, anarchists are not universally agreed on what kind of economic order is desirable. The debate over the economic system currently splits anarchism into two schools. One school believes that only capitalism can be combined appropriately with anarchism, while the other school advocates returning to an agrarian economy based on socialist economic principles. As for social justice, all anarchists advocate that we should live in a society where there is no compulsion of any kind. For them, social justice is the chance to lead the life that best suits each individual.

Because anarchists are philosophically opposed to all forms of political organization, very few anarchist political parties have ever been established. They are anti-political in that they do not believe that the electoral system can bring about real change in society. They are against the excesses of organized political power, and they have tried to establish a countervailing force at the base of society, e.g., through tenants' associations, daycare associations, housing, and municipalities. In Montreal, anarchists work through the Civic party or the Montreal Citizens Movement to bring about change at the municipal level. Instead of forming political parties, anarchists prefer to project themselves as a movement, advocating and co-ordinating their goals within the organizational framework of established labour, communist, and socialist parties. In Latin American countries, such as Argentina, Chile, and Mexico, and the European countries of France, Germany, and Spain, *anarcho-syndicalism* has appeared in various labour parties. The central element of anarcho-syndicalism is workers' control. This group argues that society should be organized on the basis of the control of each industry by the workers in that industry. Then representatives from each industry come together to administer the economic life of the whole country.

In the context of communist and socialist parties, anarchists frequently identify with the theories of Peter Kropotkin, Alexander Berkman, and Herbert Reid.[51] Kropotkin argued that co-operation rather than conflict was a natural law of human nature. He and Herbert Reid believed that the ultimate level of co-operation will only be possible when people are able to do away with coercive institutions. Berkman's contribution to anarchist thought emphasized the need to develop a society without any social coercion. He contended that capitalism created economic inequality and governments perpetuated that inequality with laws that protect those who own the means of production. To many anarchists of the left, capitalism, government, and the law are the roots of all evil. For them, the emphasis of anarchism is on the voluntary association of individuals in a variety of forms, one of which is the society or commune that makes political decisions by consensus.

The vitality of anarchism as an ideology has varied throughout this century. In the United States and Canada, anarchists helped establish co-operatives and libertarian communities.

Because of the popular fears and misunderstandings of anarchists at the turn of the century, they were the only group restricted from immigration into the United States because of their political beliefs. Anarchism as a movement appealed to the peasants and labourers in certain parts of Europe, especially Spain.[52] The Confederation National de Trabajo formed in 1911 had 700 000 members by 1918; by the 1930s, the Federacion Anarchista Iberica held over 200 000 members, some of whom wanted to form a syndicalist party.

In the period from the mid 1930s to the 1960s, not much was heard of anarchism in any part of the world. However, by the late 1960s, a growing number of academics began to publish manuscripts on anarchism. Students who rioted in Paris carried the anarchist banner in June 1968. By the mid 1970s, the black flag of anarchism was frequently seen in anti-war and disarmament demonstrations in Europe and North America. In spring 1982, the Montreal-based Anarchos was established as a North American centre for anarchist research. Anarchos is a clearing house of information and serves as a vehicle of public education in the Western hemisphere. Today, in many countries, people actively engaged in the peace movement share anarchist beliefs about the dangers of nuclear war. Anarchists point to the absurdity of nuclear-weapons' competition among organized political systems. They explain the tensions of global politics in terms of the competitive interaction of states, with organized governments as both the actors and targets of human aggression. Thus, anarchists want to dismantle the sovereign state system and replace it with a global society of autonomous groups that interact for political purposes on bases other than those now subsumed under the concepts "state" and "government." They argue that there is a need to go beyond disarmament. Humans still have the knowledge to rearm after disarmament would take place. Therefore, there is the need to change institutions to mitigate against the possibility of a new arms' race. Weapons must be dismantled, say the anarchists, and the global arms' industry must be abolished.

Ideologies of Development

The political ideologies that are most popular among the developing nation-states have eclectic roots in the great systems of nationalist, democratic, non-democratic, and socialist thought.[53] Most modern ideologies of development date to the end of World War II, when a number of European colonies in Asia and Africa began their struggle toward political independence. The republics of Latin America have had a much longer period of independence after their revolutionary insurrections of the early nineteenth century. But the widespread adoption of development ideologies south of the Rio Grande is also a post-war phenomenon. To be sure, the origins of modern development thought go back to Marx, but never before did his critical observations succeed in crystallizing into so many divergent ideological perspectives than in the latter part of the twentieth century. Many leaders in the developing world often interpret and apply traditional ideologies in different ways, usually by adding indigenous qualities and characteristics to the phenomenon of political and economic development.[54]

Pragmatism is essentially what distinguishes developing ideologies from their generic forms. Practical solutions within the framework of nationalism, socialism, and other ideological prisms are attempted as the vehicle for economic and political modernization. Pragmatism is the underlying principle of operation: what is good for a developing society is what works well for it in the light of its own conditions. Hence, leaders in the developing world have taken from the ideological reservoirs of the First and Second Worlds what works best for them in their own political and economic circumstances. They have also felt equally free to reject the ideals of liberalism, capitalism, socialism, and communism, if, in their view, the application of such ideas would not work. Thus, an individualist, politically competitive, capitalist and market-oriented system might not fit easily into the political environment of some African states. A socialist economic philosophy, articulated by a single dominant party, may be more adaptive. State leaders search for a unique blend of ideological solutions to their national development goals.

The most common ideological goals of developing states can be reduced to four: (1) national self-determination; (2) economic development; (3) political and social modernization; (4) self-styled democracy. The ideological component of self-determination postulates the right of a people who considers itself separate and distinct from others to determine for itself its own economic, political, and social destiny. In Asia, Africa, and the Caribbean, the drive toward political independence included demands for a new national society based on economic, social, and cultural equality. Characteristically, these states adopt an ideology that prescribes a strong charismatic leader, a single party, a loyal but conspicuous military, and authoritarian methods to achieve national priorities. Economic development demands rapid agricultural, commercial, and industrial improvements led by a strong central government. The ideology calls for a "quick fix" to underdevelopment through land reform, the redistribution of wealth, nationalization of certain industries, and economic planning. Political modernization is portrayed as an ongoing, continuous process that leads to greater citizen participation, better representative institutions, and a more efficient and egalitarian decision-making system. Social modernization is an aspiration to advance the quality of life by improving the educational infrastructure, the system of transportation, communications, life expectancy, health-care facilities, and employment opportunities. Political democracy is self-styled with the means of a powerful executive supported by an acquiescent legislative branch of government. The evolution towards democracy is said to be "guided" or "directed" by an elite party organization through executive government directives.

Revolutionary Thought: Ideologies or Movements?

The meaning of *revolution* has changed considerably since it was first used as a political term in 1648 during the "Glorious Revolution" in England.[55] Initially a revolution was reactionary: it referred to a revolving return to some pre-established point or some pre-ordained order, e.g., the restoration of the English monarchy in 1660 was a "revolution." In the eighteenth century, as enlightened philosophies flourished, the term revolution came to mean progress, moving forward: ideas or actions that could alter history. By the nineteenth century, revolution was equated with liberation and freedom. Marx, for example, argued that the final revolution will end in communism with the elimination of class conflict and the ultimate abolition of the state. In the twentieth century the term revolution came to reflect three distinct processes: (1) destruction of an old regime; (2) a period of chaotic disorder; and (3) the creation of a new social order. Revolution became identified with the most radical and far-reaching kinds of societal change – a sharp break with the past and a change in the basic patterns of life, institutions, traditions, and social expectations.

As the twentieth century progressed, revolutionary thought revealed itself through many ideologies and movements, such as anarchism, communism, national liberation, and feminism.[56] More than in any previous century contemporary ideologies express the interests and goals of major social groups. The word *movement* suggests collective behaviour that is ideologically inspired, accompanied by a strong sense of solidarity and idealism, and has an emphasis on action. Movements are often a prelude to revolutionary change because they create or resist attitudes, behaviours, and institutions. Political and social movements depend on ideologies to establish their identities as well as to gain public visibility. A movement's ideology serves several functions: it provides direction and self-justification; it offers arguments for use in both attack and defence; and it is a source of inspiration for members.[57] Some movements are shapeless, without leadership or clear goals. Others are more directed and fundamentally more ideological.

There are broad distinctions among contemporary movements.[58] *Value-oriented movements* concentrate on matters of general social and political concern, such as democracy, peace, and nationalism. *Norm-oriented movements* have a narrower focus: for example, to establish or change a particular social or political practice, such as the use of alcohol, birth control, and gun control. A *power-centred movement* uses political muscle to achieve certain ends, such as the prohibition movement, movements organized around the abortion issue, and the civil-rights movement in the United States. Power-centred movements will sometimes use illegitimate means to meet their goals. A *persuasion-centred* movement uses education, including propaganda and legitimate political action to advance its cause, such as in some feminist, pacifist, and environmental movements. These movements tend to favour gradual change and compromise. *Participation-centred movements* focus on creating a unified group of committed members, such as utopian communities and many religious sects. *Revolutionary movements* seek fundamental changes in the entire social structure, usually combined with violent social conflict to establish a new political and social order.

The ideological perspective of the Algerian psychiatrist and theorist Frantz Fanon (1925–1961) is an interesting case in point.[59] While in Algeria, Fanon became a supporter of the revolutionary movement that eventually led to the French withdrawal from the country. He became one of the most widely read anti-colonialists. Fanon's revolutionary ideology rejected the Marxist assertion that the proletariat is necessarily the revolutionary class, and opted instead to identify the African peasantry as such. He emphasized the idea of revolutionary praxis*: acts of violence by black peasant "subjects" against white (and black middle-class) colonial "masters." Revolutionary action generates revolutionary consciousness. Fanon believed that the peasant masses would achieve national liberation once the first acts of violence materialized within the newly independent African republics. His advocacy of revolutionary praxis stimulated movements in Algeria, Kenya, Zaire, and the Portuguese colonies of Angola and Mozambique.

Another revolutionary theorist, Herbert Marcuse, rejected the working class as a group that has revolutionary potential. For Marcuse the possibility for revolutionary change is likely to be found in the substratum of a society's outcasts and outsiders, the exploited and the persecuted, the unemployed and the unemployable. Marcuse was essentially a Marxist influenced by Freudian psychology.[60] He developed a position of political and sexual liberation that he viewed as contrary to the prevailing trend towards repression and exploitation in advanced societies. Marcuse believed that there was a "logic to domination": people become conditioned to oppression usually by the infusion of carefully planned but limited affluence.

Regis Debray, the French philosopher who spent considerable time in Cuba after Castro came to power, saw revolution not only as containing elements of violence or military action but also as being a process by which the military within the revolution becomes the guerrilla foco* itself, generating theory and inspiration to the masses.[61] The guerrilla force is the party in embryo but war is necessary to make the revolution. In fact, the conditions for a successful revolution can be engineered.

These iconoclasts held that a political revolution (as opposed to any other basic transformation of society) aims to overthrow a government and destroy the power of the social groups that support it. The revolutionaries mobilize popular support through direct action, usually involving violence, and demand basic changes in the social order. Ideologically, this has translated into a number of fundamental precepts about revolutionary behaviour:

1. Organized armed forces are vulnerable to popular or trained guerrilla insurrections.
2. Violent action (praxis) can generate ideal conditions for revolution before these conditions may evolve naturally.
3. The rural setting is better than an urban one for the organization and initiation of violent revolutionary guerrilla warfare.
4. Guerrilla warfare is not decisive in itself. Revolutionary change requires the fundamental alteration of economic, social, and political institutions.

A political revolution should be distinguished from a political revolt or coup d'état, which merely replaces one set of leaders with another or only changes the form of government without affecting the social order.

Feminism: Ideology or Movement?

The political struggle for sexual equality is not new in North America: in 1848 some 300 women and men met at Seneca Falls, New York, to protest the oppression of women. This first manifestation of the "women's movement" had grown out of the social reforms of the 1830s and 1840s, when women were denied the right to speak out publicly against slavery.[62]

By the mid nineteenth century, the women's movement faded from view, subsumed within the Victorian cultural ideal of feminine purity and helplessness. The movement was revived during the reform-minded Progressive period in the early twentieth century. The Canadian women's movement was influenced by developments in Britain and the United States.[63] The political needs of working women and children were advocated by the National Council of Women, founded in 1893 by Lady Aberdeen, the British wife of Canada's then-governor general, the Earl of Aberdeen. The Toronto Women's Literary Club, the Women's Christian Temperance Union, and other organizations demanded the right to vote, gained in every province between 1916 and 1922 (except in Quebec, where women got the vote in 1940).

In Europe and North America, *suffragettes* devoted their energies to gaining the right to vote and to establishing greater access for women into the political system.[64] Women first won voting rights in New Zealand in 1893; Australia, Sweden, Norway, and Finland soon followed. In Russia, women participated in socialist/terrorist movements before and after the revolution: a woman led the assassination of the czar and many women fought as soldiers for the Bolsheviks. Under totalitarianism/socialism women seemed to gain greater opportunities (particularly in occupations) than in other countries.

In democratic states suffragettes made the erroneous assumption that the power of the franchise would bring about changes in the workplace, university, religion, and the family. In fact, the vote made very little difference in the lives of women. The high unemployment levels of the Great Depression sustained the widely held belief that men should get the few jobs generated in the economy. Not until World War II was this trend reversed. World War II served as a benchmark for opening paid employment opportunities to women. During the war, government propaganda declared that it was women's duty to work in factories and offices to support the war effort. However, after the war, women were encouraged to leave the labour force to assume their traditional role of homemakers so that returning veterans would find employment. Many women liked working and wanted to continue after the war ended. But peace terminated employment opportunities for most women, closing child-care centres and discontinuing training programs. Throughout the 1950s the women's movement entered a dormant period, lacking communication and organizational networks to facilitate the spread of its nascent ideology.

The 1960s saw most of the elements of a successful political movement come together: organization, leadership, an enlarging membership, and an ideology focussing a widespread sense of protest.[65] In Canada, established women's organizations, such as the Canadian Federation of University Women and the Fédération des Femmes de Québec, established a communications system among knowledgeable, politically active women. In the United

States, the 1961 President's Commission on the Status of Women led to the establishment of the National Organization for Women (NOW), the chief organization in the older, reform-oriented wing of the American women's movement. Betty Friedan's *The Feminine Mystique* linked the oppression of women to cultural variables and began to articulate the ideological basis of the contemporary women's movement in North America. Friedan's book encouraged millions of women to re-examine their social roles in economic and political terms.

By the 1970s the women's movement had evolved through the norm-oriented "women's rights" form to a value-oriented "women's liberation" form. In Canada, the National Action Committee on the Status of Women, the umbrella organization for most other contemporary feminist groups, was established in 1972. Feminists began to identify women's inferior position in society with male supremacy in the family and other social and political structures.[66] During this decade feminism began to win widespread public acceptance and gained new economic and legal advantages for women. Membership in the movement grew dramatically both in Canada and the United States, attracting predominantly white, middle-class, and college-educated people who supported programs that would benefit working-class and minority-group women.

At the end of the decade the women's movement took on the characteristics of a power-centred movement with detectable conservative, moderate, and radical wings. It also developed an international character in that leaders and organizers in different countries became known to each other and communicated on a regular basis. Most of the countries of the world contain a visible women's movement, albeit with diverse ideological, political, and strategic goals.

Just as no single women's organization can represent the whole movement, so no unified political ideology is detectable either.[67] *Liberal feminism* (sometimes called reform or bourgeois feminism because it accepts the structure of the present system) calls upon the political and legal system to re-examine the degree to which individuals enjoy equal opportunities from the perspective of the inherited qualities of gender and race. This current of feminism wants society to remove all the barriers that actively and subtly discriminate against women. *Radical feminism* (sometimes called cultural or separatist feminism) points to the biological and psycho-social differences between men and women. It advocates the development of a women-centred culture with alternative lifestyles and antimilitaristic, non-hierarchical political and social structures based on co-operation. *Socialist feminism* (sometimes called Marxist feminism) identifies capitalism and its social and political superstructures as the systemic reasons for the oppression of women. This perspective posits that women are the proletarians in the gender division of labour and men are the bourgeoisie because they control the means of production. The initial advantage fell to men because of their greater physical strength and women's frequent pregnancies, but the advantage has been maintained by institutionalized norms and values that keep women in an inferior position. The Marxist framework has generally formed the ideological basis of the contemporary feminist movement.

Feminism has focussed on certain ideological factors present in most contemporary societies, regardless of their economic and political organizations. One is *patriarchy*. In feminist writings patriarchy refers to the dominance of social, economic, and political institutions by men.[68] A close correspondence is held between patriarchy and capitalism (state or private) in which both the generation and distribution of wealth reflects a male lineage. Historically, the idea that political authority is a male preserve has been the justification for the exclusion of women from access to social power. Both in and out of the family, human societies have been characterized by patriarchal authority whereby males have come to control economic resources, make consequential decisions, and have the final say in all matters related to the social good. Patriarchal authority is culturally transmitted and ideologically approved male supremacy.

Culture is the focus of socially mediated information about the role of women in society and male views of femininity.[69] In many cultures women are expected to be neat, pretty, sexually passive, emotional, understanding, cultured, child-oriented, slightly helpless, dependent, and in need of male protection. Culture conditions gender identity by creating stereotypes about men and women as reflected in children's books, the adult print media, television, and the movies. These stereotypes are reinforced by toys, games, and sports, and they influence the learning of gender identity in school, place of work, and at home. Culture subtly transmits the ideologies of oppression or liberation on matters of sex and gender.

Another focus of feminism is *epistemology*, the theories and methods of perceiving and thus acquiring knowledge. Feminists recognize that all knowledge is socially constructed and our perceptions and interpretations of the world are coloured by the society in which we live, as well as by our position within that society. Many feminists believe that the dominant ideology (including law, religion, political philosophy, and so on) is essentially sexist and serves the legitimized interests of the male ruling class.[70] All knowledge is therefore culturally conditioned. Feminists are concerned with the process by which knowledge arises in a particular culture, why it takes the form it does, and how it sustains the various stratifications within society. From the perspective of society, socialization is an important by-product of epistemology because through it, cultural perpetuation and continuity are achieved. In most contemporary societies, gender-role socialization assigns accesssory roles to women, as wives, mothers, and employees. Socialization ensures that individuals will develop a social character and will comply with a consensus among the majority of its members about the "correct" ways of behaving, thinking, interacting, and responding.

Feminist analysis also takes critical note of *history*, by exposing the actual and interpretative discriminations against women that have prevailed in previous generations. It notes, as well, the male influence on historical interpretation (particularly social and economic histories) that has tended to reinforce the ideology of subservience characteristic of the role of women in the past. Women have been granted invisible status within the profusion of historical analysis. Having only recently been given the rights of citizens, women have suffered society's refusal, throughout history, to include them in the public sphere. Feminists call for a reconstruction of historical interpretation to trace the moral and political beliefs about women to deeper metaphysical or even biological ones.

The movement and ideologies of feminism have matured rapidly, producing a body of knowledge of significant size. The impact of feminist political thought has enriched the intellectual history of the twentieth century. What remains to be seen is the extent to which the analytical frameworks of feminism can translate into the exercise of political power.

REFERENCES

1. See F.L. Baumer, *Main Currents of Western Thought,* 4th ed. (New Haven, CT: Yale University Press 1978), 373–6.
2. Karl Deutsch, *Politics and Government: How People Decide Their Fate* (Boston: Houghton Mifflin Co. 1980), 9.
3. Robert Dahl, *A Preface to Democratic Theory* (Chicago: University of Chicago Press 1956), 132.
4. R. M. Christenson et al., *Ideologies and Modern Politics* (New York: Dodd, Mead & Co. 1971), 5.
5. Robert E. Lane, *Political Ideologies* (New York: Free Press of Glencoe 1962), 14–15.
6. Andrew Hacker, *Political Theory: Philosophy, Ideology, Science* (New York: Macmillan 1961), 5.
7. Carl Friedrich, *Man and His Government: An Ethical Theory of Politics* (New York: McGraw-Hill 1963), 90.
8. See Barbara Ward, *5 Ideas that Changed the World* (New York: W.W. Norton & Co. Inc. 1959).
9. See Russell Kirk, "Prescription, Authority and Ordered Freedom," in F.S. Meyer, ed., *What Is Conservatism?* (New York: Holt Rinehart and Winston 1964), 33.
10. See R.M. MacIver, *The Web of Government* (New York: Macmillan 1965), 201.
11. Karl Loewenstein, "Political Ideology and Political Institutions," in Richard Cox, *Ideology, Politics, and Political Theory* (Belmont, Ca: Wadsworth Publishing Co. Inc. 1969).
12. Read Amos Perlmutter, *Modern Authoritarianism: A Comparative Institutional Analysis* (New Haven, CT: Yale University Press 1981).
13. See Kenneth W. Thompson, *The History and Philosophy of Rhetoric and Political Discourse,* vols. I, II, III (Lanham, MD: University Press of America 1987).
14. John Plamenatz, *Ideology* (New York: Praeger 1970), 13–15.
15. See Robert Tucker, *Politics as Leadership* (Columbia, MO: University of Missouri Press 1981), chs. 2 and 3.
16. See Roy Macridis, *Contemporary Political Ideologies,* 4th ed. (Boston: Little, Brown & Co. 1988), ch. 1.
17. See Karl Mannheim, *Ideology and Utopia,* trans. by L. Wirth and E. Shils (New York: Harcourt, Brace Jovanovich 1936), 36.
18. Maurice Duverger, *Political Parties* (New York: John Wiley & Sons, Inc. 1954), 425.
19. See Thucydides, *The History of the Peloponnesian War,* ed. by Sir Richard Livingston (New York: Oxford University Press 1951), 111–13.
20. *Aristotle in Twenty-Three Volumes,* XXI: Politics, trans. by H. Rackham (London: Heinemann 1977), Book III: 331.
21. Joseph Strayer and Hans Gatzke, *The Mainstream of Civilization* (New York: Harcourt, Brace Jovanovich Publishers 1984), 571–84.
22. Leonard T. Hobhouse, *Liberalism* (New York: Oxford University Press 1911).
23. John Dewey, "The Future of Liberalism," *Journal of Philosophy* (April 25, 1935): 225–30.
24. Donald Kagan et al., *The Western Heritage* (New York: Macmillan Publishing Co. Inc. 1983) 663–65.
25. See Rod Preece, "The Political Economy of

Edmund Burke," *Modern Age* 24, no. 3 (1980): 266–73.

26. F.J.C. Hearnshaw, *Conservatism in England* (London: Macmillan and Co. Ltd. 1933), 22–3; for contrast, see David Green, *The New Conservativism* (New York: St. Martin's Press 1987).
27. Macridis, *Contemporary Political Ideologies*, 53–6.
28. See Sidney Webb, *Fabian Essays in Socialism* (Gloucester, MA: Peter Smith 1967).
29. See Peter Berger, *The Capitalist Revolution*, (New York: Basic Books 1986).
30. See Alan Gilbert, *Marx's Politics: Communists and Citizens* (Boulder, CO: Lynne Rienner Publishers 1988).
31. See Albert Fried and Ronald Sanders, eds., *Socialist Thought: A Documentary History* (Garden City, NY: Anchor Doubleday 1964).
32. Karl Marx and Friedrich Engels, *The German Ideology* (Moscow: Foreign Languages Publishing House 1947); see esp. "The Material Basis of Ideology," 247–55.
33. Robert C. Tucker, ed., *The Marx-Engels Reader* (New York: W.W. Norton & Co. 1978), 3–12.
34. Karl Marx, *Selected Works* (New York: International Publishers, n.d.) 1: 473.
35. Quoted in Bertram D. Wolfe, *Three Who Made a Revolution* (New York: Dial Press 1948), 253; also published by Stein and Day 1984.
36. See Rolf Theen, *Lenin: Genesis and Development of a Revolutionary* (Princeton, : Princeton University Press 1980), and A.J. Polan, *Lenin and the End of Politics* (London: Methuen & Co. 1984).
37. See Robert Tucker, ed., *Stalinism: Essays in Historical Interpretation* (New York: W.W. Norton & Co. 1977).
38. See Roy Medvedev, *Khrushchev* (Garden City, NY: Anchor Doubleday 1983).
39. *Programme of the Communist Party of the Soviet Union* (Moscow: Foreign Languages Publishing House 1961), 128.
40. *Izvestia*, January 28, 1987, 2.
41. Ibid., February 19, 1988, 2.
42. *Kommunist*, no.4 (March 1986), 112.
43. Ibid., 113–14.
44. Ibid., 78.
45. See Hans Kohn, *Nationalism: Its Meaning and History*, rev. ed. (New York: Van Nostrand 1965).
46. See M. Lebris, *Romantics and Romanticism*, trans. by B. Bray and B. Swift (New York: Skira, Rizzoli 1981); and Franklin Baumer, ed., *Intellectual Movements in Modern European History* (New York: Macmillan 1965).
47. See Anthony Smith, *Theories of Nationalism* (New York: Harper & Row 1971), 21; Ernest Gellner, *Nations and Nationalism* (London: Cornell University Press 1983), 1–14.
48. See Raymond Murphy, ed., *National Socialism* (Washington: U.S. Department of State 1943), 222–4.
49. See Louis Snyder, ed. and trans., *Documents of German History* (New Brunswick, NJ: Rutgers University Press 1958), 427–8.
50. See Frank Harrison, *The Modern State: An Anarchist Analysis* (Montreal: Black Rose Books 1983); David Osterfeld, *Freedom, Society, and the State: An Investigation into the Possibility of Society without Government* (Lanham, MD: University Press of America 1983).
51. Lyman Tower Sargent, *Contemporary Political Ideologies: A Comparative Analysis* (Homewood, IL: Dorsey Press 1969), 159–78.
52. Hugh Thomas, *The Spanish Civil War* (Harmondsworth, Eng.: Penguin Books Ltd. 1965), 67–8.
53. Stewart MacPherson, *Social Policy in the Third World – The Social Dilemmas of Underdevelopment* (Brighton, Eng.: John Spiers 1985), 15–33.
54. Stephen Chilton, *Defining Political Development* (Boulder, Co: Lynne Rienner

Publishers 1987), 1–135; see Magnus Blomstrom and Bjorn Hettne, *Development Theory in Transition* (London: Zed Books Ltd. 1984), 8–26.

55. See Jack Gladstone, "The Comparative and Historical Study of Revolutions," *Annual Review of Sociology, 1982:* 200; Crane Brinton, *The Anatomy of Revolution* (Englewood Cliffs, NJ: Prentice-Hall 1952).
56. A.S. Cohan, *Theories of Revolution* (London: Thomas Nelson & Sons 1975), 162–75.
57. Ralph Turner and Lewis Killian, *Collective Behavior* (Englewood Cliffs, NJ: Prentice-Hall 1972), chs 16–19.
58. See Neil J. Smelser, *Theory of Collective Behavior* (New York: Free Press 1962); Mark Traugott, "Reconceiving Social Movements," Social Problems 26, (October 1978): 43; and Ted Gurr, *Why Men Rebel* (Princeton: Princeton University Press 1970), 22–58.
59. Frantz Fanon, *The Wretched of the Earth*, trans. by Constance Farrington (Harmondsworth, Eng: 1967), 101.
60. See Herbert Marcuse, *One-Dimensional Man: Studies in the Ideology of Advanced Industrial Society* (Boston: Beacon Press 1966), 19.
61. See Regis Debray, *Revolution in the Revolution?* trans. by Bolkye Ortiz (Harmondsworth, Eng: 1968), 105.
62. Jo Freeman, "The Origins of the Women's Liberation Movement," *American Journal of Sociology* 78, no. 4 (1973), 792–811; William Chafe, *Women and Equality* (New York: Oxford University Press 1977), 117–22.
63. See Catherine Cleverdon, *Woman Suffrage in Canada* (Toronto: University of Toronto Press 1950); Nellie McClung, *In Times Like These* (Toronto: University of Toronto Press 1972); and Gwen Matheson, ed., *Women in the Canadian Mosiac* (Toronto: Peter Martin 1976).
64. Lorna Marsdan and Edward Harvey, *Fragile Federation: Social Change in Canada* (Toronto: McGraw-Hill Ryerson 1979), 195.
65. Juliet Mitchell, "Replay to a Discussion on 'Women The Longest Revolution,'" *New Left Review* 41 (1967); Meridith Tax, "Woman and Her Mind," in Leslie Tanner, ed., *Voices from Women's Liberation* (New York: Mentor 1971), 10–15.
66. See Dorothy Smith, "An Analysis of Ideological Structures and How Women Are Excluded," *Canadian Review of Sociology and Anthropology* 12 (1975); Susan Griffin, *Woman and Nature: The Roaring Inside Her* (New York: Harper & Row 1978).
67. See Nancy Adamson, Linda Briskin, and Margaret McPhail, *Feminist Organizing for Change* (Toronto: Oxford University Press 1988), 3–25 Angela Miles, *Feminist Radicalism in the 1980s* (Montreal: Culture Texts 1985), 1–39.
68. See M. Grumet, "Pedagogy for Patriarchy," *Interchange* 12: -3 (1981): 165-84; H. Hartmann "Capitalism, Patriarchy, and Job Segretation by Sex," Signs 1: 3 (1976): 137–70; Roberta Hamilton, *The Liberation of Women: A Study of Patriarchy and Capitalism* (London: Allen & Unwin 1978).
69. Eileen Saunders, "Theoretical Approaches to the Study of Women," in James Curtis, et al., *Social Inequality in Canada: Patterns, Problems, Policies* (Scarborough, ON: Prentice-Hall Canada 1988), 248–63.
70. D. Smith, "A Peculiar Eclipsing: Women's Exclusion from Man's Culture," *Women's Studies International Quarterly* 1:4 (1978): 281–96.

SUGGESTED READINGS

Larry Arnhart, *Political Questions: Political Philosophy from Plato to Rawls* (Don Mills, ON: Collier Macmillan Canada Inc. 1987).

Norman Barry, *On Classical Liberalism and Libertarianism* (New York: St. Martin's Press 1987).

Diana Coole, *Women in Political theory: From*

Ancient Misogyny to Contemporary Feminism (Boulder, CO: Lynne Rienner Publishers 1988).

Fred Dallmayr, *Critical Encounters: Between Philosophy and Politics* (Notre Dame, IN: Notre Dame Press 1987).

Iain Hampsher-Monk, *The Political Philosophy of Edmund Burke* (Toronto: Copp Clark Pitman Ltd. 1987).

H. D. Forbes, *Canadian Political Thought* (Toronto: Oxford University Press 1985).

Asher Horowitz and Gad Horowitz, *Everywhere They Are In Chains: Political Theory From Rousseau to Marx* (Scarborough, ON: Nelson Canada 1988).

David McLellan, *Ideology* (Markham, ON: Fitzhenry & Whiteside 1986).

Michael Riff, ed., *A Dictionary of Modern Ideologies* (New York: St. Martin's Press 1987).

Max Skidmore, *Ideclogies: Politics in Action* (Chicago: IL: Harcourt, Brace Jovanovich 1989).

Robert Wesson, ed., *Democracy World Survey 1987* (Boulder, CO: Lynne Rienner Publishers 1988).

GLOSSARY

dogmatic: A fixed or firmly held belief on any subject.

reason: The distinctive human faculty that permits a process of thinking which leads to logical conclusions.

utopian: A term coined by Sir Thomas More, derived from the Greek *outopos*, "no place." More emphasized the word *eu*, meaning best, thus suggesting that Utopia was a non-existent best place in reference to an ideal and harmoniuos society.

pragmatism: A philosophical perspective traceable to the American writers William James and John Dewey, who stressed that concepts and actions should be evaluated in terms of their practical consequences and not necessarily according to theoretical rationales.

leadership: Those personal attributes and qualifications that enable an individual to influence or shape collective behaviour patterns of a group in the direction determined by the leader's values, without the presence of sanctions.

bias: The tendency, often unconscious, to interpret facts according to one's values and beliefs.

human nature: Those psychological and biological qualities universally characteric of the human species.

ethics: A set of rules and codes of morality that describes human goodness and rightness and embodies absolute rules upon which humans should pattern their conduct.

rationalism: The philosophical approach to reasoning that proceeds logically from a premise to a conclusion so as to make rightful choices or decisions based on the most efficient and appropriate goals and values.

descriptive: An analytical skill that involves applying appropriate conceptual labels to people, things, events, and ideas that are observed.

élite: Any select group of individuals enjoying privileged status in a society and often united by certain common ties, interests, or objectives.

Marxism: The revolutionary ideology founded by Karl Marx and Frederick Engels which focussed on concepts such as alienation, class struggle, the dictatorship of the proletariat, the revolutionary role of the national party, and national liberation movements.

social contract: An original agreement among individuals to create an organized political society.

sovereignty: The power possessed by the state to make decisions of last resort – decisions that cannot be overridden or reversed by any other human decision maker or agency.

consensus: A widespread agreement on a particular issue, policy, or course of action by those participating in the making of the decision without a formal verification of the statistical proportion of support.

stratification: A system of social inequality based on hierarchical orderings of groups according to their members' share in socially valued rewards.

aristocracy: A word from the Greek, meaning rule by the best, by which virtue is the title to power, but is more commonly described as rule by the privileged who may enjoy a hereditary status or whose power flows to them by virtue of their class position in society.

oligarchy: This word from Greek means rule by the few, where power is concentrated and not shared.

bourgeoisie: Taken from the French for town dweller, the term was used by Marx to identify the class of property and production ownership that flourished under capitalism.

superstructure: The legal, political, and social institutions that reflect, express, and consolidate the relations of economic power and the flow from the mode of production practised by a society.

proletariat: As used by Marx, the term referred to a class of labourers characterized as propertyless, rootless, poor, and mobile, which has nothing to sell but its labour power.

dialectic: A concept borrowed from Hegel by Marx; it asserts that all societies contain within them the seeds of their own destruction: the struggle of opposites generates social transformation.

Bolshevik: The Russian word for "member of the majority" that Lenin used to name the predecessor of the Communist Party of the Soviet Union (CPSU) in the years preceding the Russian Revolution.

cultural revolution: A mass proletarian movement against capitalist restoration and materialism, seen in China as occurring between old generation bureaucrats and technocrats, and Maoists.

polycentrism: The splitting of a political organization into three or more independent centres of power.

Romanticism: The cultural movement that began in eighteenth–century Europe, marking the transformation of intellectual thought from the rational to the intuitive as a means of perceiving and understanding the world. Romantics were fascinated by dreams and hallucinations that suggested a world beyond the empirical.

psychological warfare: A form of ideological or propagandistic terrorism based on political, economic, social, and military activities designed to weaken a perceived enemy's will to fight or compete.

imperialistic: An economic, political, or military strategy by which a state and its people are subordinated to the will of a foreign state.

irredentism: A word taken from the Italian expression "Italia irredenta," meaning Italy unredeemed, and referring to the desire of the people of a state to annex those contiguous territories of another country that is inhabited by the same linguistic or cultural minorities.

praxis: A term derived from the Greek for "action," which later came to refer to what people do as against what they think, an active means of shaping historical conditions to one's advantage.

foco: The revolutionary concept that asserts guerrilla war ideally begins by the creation of a focus or nucleus, a small band of guerrillas who operate in rural areas.

4

Nations, States, Rank, and Power

Azerbaijanis gather before a statue of Lenin

What Is a Nation-State?

SOME OF THE WIDESPREAD CONFUSIONS in our political vocabularies concern the meaning of the terms *nation*, *state*, and *country*. People may sometimes use these terms interchangeably in casual conversation but, for professional purposes, they should be distinguished. They have different meanings and require precise definition for use in political science and international law.

The term *state* refers to a legal/political and administrative entity composed of a governing central authority that makes and enforces laws and is recognized as the primary subject of the international legal system. The Montevideo Convention on the Rights and Duties of States (1933) laid down four criteria that states must possess to qualify as persons* under international law. The convention declared that a state must have (1) a permanent population, (2) a defined territory, (3) a government, and (4) a capacity to enter into relations with other states. In the contemporary international system there are over 170 such legal/political entities functioning as states and claiming international legal status. This status entitles them to sign treaties, form alliances, join international organizations, and exchange ambassadors.

States may be the hosts of many nations. In contrast to a state, a *nation* is a socio-cultural entity, made up of a group of people who identify with each other ethnically, culturally, and linguistically. A nation may not have a government or a geographically delimited territory of its own. But many nations may exist within the political and administrative jurisdiction of a state. For example, the Soviet Union is a multinational state comprising twenty-one major non-Russian nationalities (numbering in excess of 1 million; see table 4.1) and more than 100 distinctive ethnic groups. These together make up 44 percent of a population of 287 000 960. From table 4.1 we can see that the Soviet Union is not "Russia" - a term routinely used on Canadian television, radio, and in popular publications. To refer to the Soviets as the "Russians" is to misrepresent the multinational character of that state. A conglomerate of many nationalities exists within the Soviet state, of which ethnic Russians account for slightly over 50 percent. Indeed, the Soviet Union is an independent political apparatus that brings together existing nations under one totalitarian* administrative system.

Many scholars refer to the relationship between the state and the nationalities it serves as a *nation-state*.[1] The modern nation-state weaves together nationalities according to a deliberate political design: it determines official languages, creates a uniform system of law, controls the education system, builds a national bureaucracy to defend and socialize different people and classes, and fosters loyalty to an abstract entity, such as "Canada," the "United States," or the "Soviet Union." Today the nation-state is the most effective instrument of social and political integration, as well as the primary vehicle for national modernization. Only 175 such nation-states make up the present international system, yet together they host over 1400 nationalities existing in the world.[2]

The term *country* refers to the all-inclusive characteristics of a geographical entity – its physical, material, and socio-economic components. Use of the term country is widespread in political-science literature but can sometimes result in confusion if it is not properly clarified. To refer to the country of Ireland requires specific reference either to the six counties of Northern Ireland under Great Britain or to the twenty-six counties in the south that form the Republic of Ireland. The same problem exists with divided countries such as Germany and Korea.

The Growth in the Number of Sovereign Nation-States

By 2000 the modern nation-state system will have only existed for 352 years – less than 10 percent of the 5500 years of recorded human history. In 1648, the Peace of Westphalia terminated the Thirty Years' War of religion in Europe, bringing an end to the view of the world as an organized system based on a Christian commonwealth governed by the Pope and Holy Roman Emperor.[3] We know that countries such as England and France predate the Peace of Westphalia as sovereign political units. But at the time of the Peace of Westphalia the international system was transformed into a society of legally equal states, each exercising complete territorial jurisdiction* over well-defined boundaries.

Soviet nationalities: 1988

	POPULATION	PERCENTAGE OF TOTAL
Slavs		
Great Russians	150 388 500	52.4
Ukrainians	46 207 155	16.1
Byelorussians	10 332 035	3.6
Central Asians		
Kazakhs	7 175 024	2.5
Uzbeks	13 489 045	4.7
Turkmen	2 296 007	0.8
Kirgiz	2 009 006	0.7
Tadzhiks	3 157 010	1.1
Transcaucasians		
Georgians	4 018 013	1.4
Armenians	4 592 015	1.6
Azerbaydzhanis	6 027 020	2.1
Balts		
Estonians	1 148 003	0.4
Latvians	1 435 004	0.5
Lithuanians	3 444 011	1.2
Others		
Moldavians	2 870 009	1.0
Tartars	6 888 023	2.4
Germans	1 435 677	0.6
Jews	2 583 008	0.9
Chuvash	2 009 006	0.7
Bashkirs	1 435 244	0.5
Moravins	1 435 722	0.5
Poles	1 148 243	0.4
Total Population	287 000 960	

Sources: Yearbook USSR *'88'*; percentage of total population from USSR; Tsentralnoye Statisticheskoye Upravleniye, *Narodnoye Khozyaystvo v 1988 g.* (Moscow 1988)

Table 4.1

With the disintegration of the Holy Roman Empire into autonomous* political organizations, the modern nation-state came to dominate the international system as a legal/political entity subject to no higher secular authority. The doctrine of sovereignty thus became the first general principal of international law. It asserts that the nation-state is the supreme decision-making power within a geographically delineated frontier and is subject to external authority only by its consent.

A question of sovereignty arose in 1985 when Canada's historic claim to most of the Northwest Passage as territorial waters was challenged by the United States. The U.S. Coast Guard icebreaker *Polar Sea* passed through the arctic waterway without Canada's consent and proceeded as if the passage was an international strait open to all states. Canada's External Affairs Minister Joe Clark issued a strongly worded statement on the controversial voyage, stating that future use of the Arctic "shall only be on the basis of full respect for Canada's sovereignty." In January 1988, Canada and the United States signed an agreement on Arctic co-operation, under which U.S. icebreakers are required to receive Canadian permission before entering waters claimed by Canada. The agreement, however, avoided the issue of U.S. military vessels entering the waters of the Arctic and the Northwest passage as if they were international ocean highways open to entry by any nation-state without Canadian consent.

Out of the doctrine of sovereignty emerged the principle of the legal equality of states. This equality establishes that sovereign states enjoy the same rights and duties under international law, regardless of size, population, wealth, or military power. The principle is affirmed in the legal equation of one state, one vote, practised and enjoyed by all states in the international councils of the world.

The proliferation of states was a gradual occurrence from the Peace of Westphalia until the second half of the twentieth century when the decolonization* of the Western European empires escalated following World War II (see figure 4.1.) Since 1945, the number of nation-states has more than doubled from roughly 65 to about 175, with most of these newcomers appearing in Africa. The process of decolonization in the post-war period resulted in the independence of some 95 nation-states and over 1 billion people – all in the span of a single generation. Today, less than 1 percent of the world's population and territory remains without self-government. The emergence of new nation-states is likely to continue for some time, but at a much slower pace. One very recent addition to the international community is Vanuatu, formerly known as the New Hebrides. From 1906 to 1984 this collection of eighty scattered islands, inhabited by 121 000 people, was jointly ruled by Britain and France in what is called a condominium*. In the last century, the people of Vanuatu were regarded as the most bloodthirsty and savage cannibals in the Pacific. Today, Vanuatu is one of the newest of the world's independent nation-states, trying to find its own identity as a now-independent territory after a confusing but colourful history.

The Nation-State and the Components of Power

The preceding chapter considered the inter-personal nature of power as a phenomenon that permeates all human relationships and that is widely upheld as a value in our personal lives. The nation-state provides us with the most visible manifestations of this phenomenon because it is an organization specifically designed to accumulate, institutionalize, and

Independent nation-states, 1648-1990

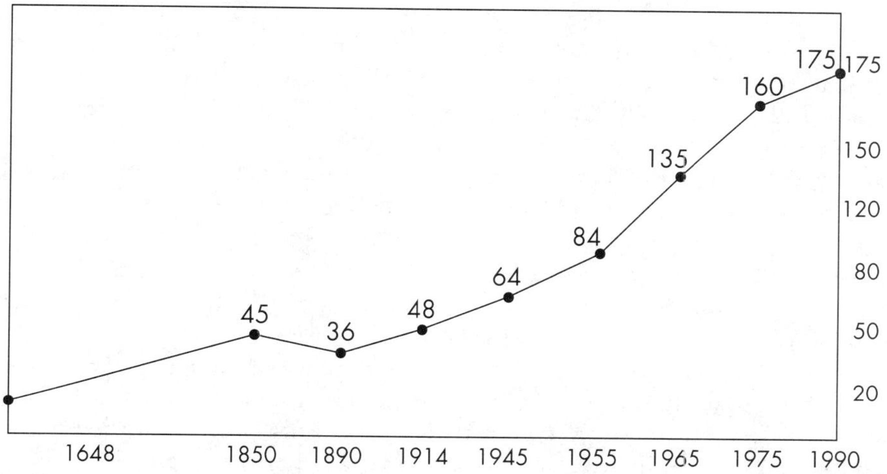

Sources: C.J.H. Hayes, *The Historical Evolution of Modern Nationalism* (New York: Macmillan 1948); Michael Wallace and David Singer, "Inter-governmental Organization in the Gobal System, 1815-1964: A Quantitative Description," *International Organization* 24 (Spring 1970): 272; for the period 1965-85, see John Paxton, ed., *The Statesman's Year Book* (London: Macmillan Press 1989), various years.

Figure 4.1

articulate power in a competitive international system. Indeed, the interactions of nation-states represent the most salient expressions of political power in the world community.

Most analysts of international relations see the power of a nation-state in terms of its capacity to influence other entities in its environment. Karl Holsti defines power as "the general capacity of a state to control the behavior of other states."[4] Karl Deutsch sees it as "the ability to prevail in conflict and overcome obstacles."[5] For Robert Dahl, power "is the ability to shift the probability of outcomes."[6] Dahl also sees it as a psychological relationship between those who exercise it and those over whom it is exercised. Each of these definitions is an attempt to explain a highly complex set of power components that cluster together, building the overall capacity and potential of nation-state. Ray Cline constructed a conceptual formula to illustrate the parameters of power at the disposal of a nation-state.[7] He states it as

$$Pp = (C + E + M) \times (S \times W), \text{ where}$$

Pp = perceived power
C = critical mass: size, location, population, and natural resources.
E = economic capability
M = military capability
S = strategic purpose
W = will to pursue national strategy

Perceived power expresses the psychological relationship between those who use power and those over whom power is exercised. It has both a domestic as well as an international dimension: the power of a nation-state is a product not only of its externally perceived power but also of its own self-perception. One of Prime Minister Trudeau's first foreign-policy statements in 1968 was to disclaim Canada's post-war international status as the smallest of the large powers by repositioning Canada's contemporary role to be "the largest of the small powers."[8] Trudeau's perception of Canada's power was a reflection of Canada's internal aspiration to relate its international role to domestic capabilities: "We shall do more good by doing well what we know to be within our resources to do than to pretend either to ourselves or to others that we can do things clearly beyond our national capacity."[9]

The perception of the power of a nation-state can flow from the characteristics of its critical mass, its economic capability, and its military capacity. But these elements alone will not determine the power potential of a nation-state. They must be brought together by the deliberate and planned strategy of decision makers who formulate foreign policies to use power in their national interest. Thus, strategic purpose coupled with the will to pursue a strategy of power are important considerations in realistically appraising the strength of a nation-state. Let us examine each of these various components of power.

Critical Mass

The tangible elements of national power are frequently identified as size, location, population, and natural resources. These elements affect the political conduct of people and are used in association with the study of national strength. Together they constitute the power inventory of a nation-state. They are measurable features that condition rank and status in the international system. We know that physical and demographic* resources may serve to enhance the power status of a nation-state, but they may also function to create major obstacles to development. For example, Japan has earned its reputation as an economic superpower* in the 1990s, but it is severely circumscribed by population pressure and the lack of raw materials. And Canada, the second-largest country in the world, with a population approaching 27 million, a modern economy, and vast natural resources, can only attain middle ranking in the international community. Both countries, for opposite reasons, must overcome obstacles created by their size and the distribution of their populations. In the final analysis, individual elements of national power must be seen in conjunction with other variables, usually of a political, social, and strategic nature.

Size

Political geographers inform us that the size of a nation-state – the amount of territorial space it incorporates – presents advantages and disadvantages to a government's ability to enhance its power profile.[10] After all, the total world land mass is limited and larger states do have greater access than do smaller states to the bulk of resources from which power can be derived. The Soviet Union (the largest nation-state) and the United States (the fourth-largest) are two superpowers blessed with the possession of a wide range of raw materials. The abundance of natural resources is the prime requisite for power, perhaps even more important than the capacity to exploit the resources. Countries like Australia, Brazil, Canada, China, and Mexico are nation-states with great potential for increasing their influence in world affairs based on their size and share of natural resources. Although it is true that size alone does not determine national power, it is also true that the world's two most powerful nation-states are very large.

With vastness in size come problems of social cohesion, economic disparities, political organization, and national control. Canada is a good example. The physical characteristics of Canada create enormous challenges for achieving political and economic integration. Canada's area is nearly 10 million square kilometres. The country spans seven time zones and possesses large natural internal barriers: the Appalachians, the Canadian Shield, the Rocky Mountains, the Great Lakes, and the Arctic desert. These features tend to divide rather than unify its population. In addition, Canada is a composite of six geographic regions: the Atlantic provinces, Quebec, Ontario, the Prairies, British Columbia, and the North, each with distinctive physical characteristics that tend to foster economic regionalism. Politically, Canada is at war with its geography. Of the world's sixteen federal states, Canada has the most decentralized federal system, with each Canadian province possessing significantly wider political powers and jurisdictions in economic, social, and cultural matters than do those in other federations. At the extreme, some provinces have even developed a special role in international affairs, as in the case of Quebec. For Canada, sheer size has made its functioning as an independent nation-state a political miracle.

The world's ten biggest countries by area

COUNTRY	AREA SQ. KM	PERCENTAGE OF WORLD TOTAL
USSR	22 402 200	16.5
Canada	9 976 139	7.3
China	9 596 961	7.1
United States	9 363 123	6.9
Brazil	8 511 965	6.3
Australia	7 686 848	5.7
India	3 287 590	2.4
Argentina	2 766 889	2.0
Sudan	2 505 813	1.8
Algeria	2 381 741	1.8
Subtotal	**78 482 162**	**57.8**
World	**135 830 000**	**100.0**

Source: The International World Atlas
(Maplewood, NJ: Hammond Inc. 1989)

Table 4.2

Table 4.2 lists the relative size of the ten biggest nation-states in the world. These ten countries control more than half the land surface of the globe. We can see from the table that size is not the most significant criterion upon which to judge the power profile of a nation-state: six of the ten biggest countries of the world are Third and Fourth World nation-states. And, in the cases of the USSR and Canada, size creates staggering political and economic problems in terms of national unity and development. Very large states often experience internal divisions because of natural barriers caused by vastness: Australia's central desert, the Soviet Union's eastern domain, and Canada's Rocky Mountain belt all exemplify this factor. Both Canada and Brazil have the problem of diminishing the "empty" aspect of their sparsely populated regions by encouraging population resettlement in these areas. Brazil relocated its capital, Brasilia, in the heart of the jungle just for the purpose of encouraging the westward migration of people. The African state of Sudan is so vast that it extends from Arab Africa into black Africa. The Arab population in the north, which concentrates in the capital of Khartoum, is racially and culturally distinct from the black Africans in the south. Very few nation-states have utilized and exploited the vast spatial characteristics of their terrains in an efficient way. The United States and China have succeeded in populating a large land area westward across rivers and mountains and then, with powerful central governments, inculcated a strong sense of national unity among their people.

Location

The location of a nation-state influences its power potentiality in strategic* as well as geographic ways. Location determines a country's neighbours, its access to the oceans, its proximity to the world's major trade routes, and its strategic importance in matters of collective security. Therefore, location is politically important to a nation-state for purposes of trade, transportation, defence, and attack. Although it is true that the location of a country is permanently fixed, the political ramifications of the space a state occupies constantly change as other nation-states evaluate its significance in terms of their national interest. For example, the strategic importance of El Salvador, Guatemala, Honduras, and Panama to the United States has recently and abruptly changed because of the presence of the Sandinista regime in Nicaragua, which nurtures relations with Cuba and the USSR. Since the Eisenhower administration the United States has assumed a domino theory* of foreign policy in the Central American region. Such a theory holds that if El Salvador becomes a Marxist state, the other states of Central America will quickly succumb to Marxism. These governments will become allies and, therefore, a threat to the United States. The policy of the United States government toward Central America reflects the geopolitical significance the United States attaches to states in the Western hemisphere such as El Salvador.

Access to oceans and important waterways is another critical factor in determining a state's power. Most of the nation-states of the world are adjacent to seas and oceans. From an economic viewpoint, oceans are highways of commerce linking the world's markets. They are extensions of the land-based commercial power of a nation-state. Strategically, access to oceans provides states with the military advantages of sea power. Today sea power is a crucial factor in both conventional and nuclear-war deterrence. The world's foremost sea powers possess the naval capability of massive retaliation from any point on the globe in response to a first strike from an enemy state. When, in April 1982, Argentina invaded the Falkland Islands, British warships were promptly dispatched as the decisive military response to the occupation. Every day states stalk each other on the high seas in an endless show of naval force.

Not having access to oceans and waterways also affects the power of a state. Because they do not have easy access to the international marketplace, the twenty-eight independent nation-states of the world that are landlocked have special economic problems (table 4.3). The export/import relations of such economies are dependent on the national policies of coastal states and are always subject to higher transportation and handling costs. At best, landlocked states must negotiate with coastal states to gain permission to carry on overseas trade without interference or harassment. In 1921 in Barcelona, the Freedom of Transit Conference was held that produced a convention to encourage signatories to assist landlocked states in the movement of goods to the nearest seaport without levying discriminatory taxes or freight charges on them. In 1965, the United Nations drafted a convention outlining concessions to landlocked states to provide them with customs exemptions, free storage, and free ports of entry.[11] Landlocked states must nevertheless enter into bilateral treaties with coastal states and bargain at a disadvantage.

Landlocked states

AFRICA	AMERICA	ASIA	EUROPE
Botswana	Bolivia	Afghanistan	Andorra
Burundi	Paraguay	Bhutan	Austria
Central African Republic		Mongolia	Czechoslovakia
Chad		Nepal	Hungary
Lesotho			Liechtenstein
Malawi			Luxembourg
Mali			Switzerland
Niger			San Marino
Rwanda			Vatican City
Swaziland			
Uganda			
Upper Volta			
Zambia			
Zimbabwe			

Source: The Statesman's Year Book, 1988-89
(New York: Macmillan Co. 1989)

Table 4.3

Location has had important political implications for Canada's international role. Canada's geographical position is unusual in that it shares a vast border with only one country and that country happens to be a superpower. The presence of only one powerful land neighbour has been the single most-significant factor in the history of Canada's external relations. A constant resistance against the tug of U.S. influence in domestic and external affairs has encouraged Canada to turn to oceans for contact with other countries. Geographically, Canada's location is unique because it is the only mainland country directly connected to three oceans. The total length of Canada's coastline, bordering on the Atlantic, Pacific, and Arctic oceans is over 36 000 kilometres, more than twice the circumference of the earth. These three ocean avenues have allowed Canada to diversify its international ties, as well as to enrich its natural-resource base. The Atlantic Ocean has maintained Canada's links with Europe, especially with Great Britain and France. The Pacific Ocean has opened ties with Asia and the economies of the Pacific Rim*. By the early 1970s, Japan had surpassed Great Britain as Canada's second most-important trading partner after the United States. The Arctic Ocean is vital to Canada for its vast untapped natural resources as well as for its strategic value in protecting the Western hemisphere.

Population

The nation-states of the world vary as much in population as they do in territorial size. Population ranges from the Vatican with a population of about 1000 to China with a population of over 1 billion people, or one-fifth of all humanity. When population is discussed as a global concern, the tendency for analysts is to focus on those nation-states with the largest populations (table 4.4). But it is interesting to note that over 120 of the states of the world contain populations of less than 20 million people. From the perspective of a majority of these states, not enough population is a more central concern in terms of economic growth and development than is overpopulation.

Difficult problems are often faced by large countries with small populations. For example, Canada's total population of 26 million inhabitants makes up only one-half of 1 percent of the global population, yet this population has the task of developing nearly 10 percent of the world's living room. Canadians must construct highways, railways, communication networks, and also participate in a military system that serves the Western hemisphere and Europe. They must economically exploit Canada's vast resources with a population slightly larger than that of the state of California. In the development of their capital projects, Canadians must depend heavily on foreign investment, over 80 percent of which flows from the United States. Other nation-states such as Australia, South Africa, Argentina, and Peru have similar problems. Even the Soviet Union, which has the third-largest population in the world, has most of its population clustered west of the Ural Mountains, leaving large expanses of territory unoccupied and undeveloped.

Like the factors of territorial size and location, the size of a nation-state's population is not necessarily an indication of its power. The effectiveness of the population, whatever its size, in contributing to the agricultural, industrial, and military capacities of the state in a highly competitive world is important, however. In addition, the size of a population must be analysed not only with respect to the space it occupies but also with respect to the resources at its disposal and the political and economic organization of the state.

The population of a nation-state is truly a national resource and includes all people capable of contributing usefully to the development of the country. It is made up of the male and female work force, the young and the elderly, the military, and the bureaucratic machinery of the state. The growth, distribution, density, and mobility of a population are factors that must be constantly evaluated to get a clear picture of the potential in a nation-state. For Canada, a population increase can contribute to the productive strength of the country only because the problems of food supply, welfare, education, and other factors are adequately met by the economic system. But for Bangladesh, Ethiopia, and India, population increases are too burdensome for the capabilities of the economy: this problem nullifies the benefits of human resources. Bangladesh, for example, ranks first in density of population and is twenty times as crowded as the world in general. For some nation-states a growing population may be a source of power and productivity, but for many it is an unwanted consumer of limited resources of food, clothing, housing, and education.

Natural Resources

The natural resources of a nation-state generally refer to the resources found on, above, and under the surface of the earth. A country's soil, animal life, forests, vegetation, water, sunshine, climate, and minerals are natural resources. For example, Canada is the second most powerful country in the world after the Soviet Union in terms of hydro-electricity. By 1990, Canada's waterways produced over 75 percent of its electrical power. The lack

Leading nation-states in population 1988

COUNTRY	POPULATION	PERCENTAGE OF WORLD TOTAL
China	1 279 010 000	23.3
India	846 000 000	15.4
USSR	287 000 960	5.3
United States	246 600 800	4.6
Indonesia	166 400 060	3.1
Brazil	138 400 000	2.7
Japan	121 500 030	2.3
Nigeria	118 000 000	2.2
Bangladesh	114 000 000	2.1

Source: World Development Report 1988
(New York: Oxford University Press 1988).

Table 4.4

or abundance of resources like these can be crucial in developing the power potential of a nation-state. For some countries, such as Australia, Canada, the United States, and the Soviet Union, nature has provided an extravagant resource endowment. But for others, such as Chad, Ethiopia, and Mali, nature's provisions have not been so generous. For these states, the hope of achieving any measure of self-sufficiency and industrial diversification from an accessible resource base is scant. Sometimes, however, the sheer will and capacity of a population to industrialize from imported raw materials can propel it to economic superiority: Japan has little locally accessible natural resources. But Japan is an exception. For most of the economies of the world, national power is directly related to the possession of and accessibility to raw materials and the capacity to use them to produce goods. Without a solid agricultural base and access to raw materials, nation-states cannot develop into prosperous industrial economies.

Tables 4.5 and 4.6 show the leading agricultural and mineral producers of the world. It is immediately apparent that no national economy is completely self-sufficient in respect to foodstuffs or natural resources. Economic interdependence* is a basic law in the modern

Leading agricultural producers of the 1980s

PRODUCT	LEADING PRODUCERS (PERCENTAGE OF WORLD TOTAL)
Cereals	China (18.0), United States (17.2), USSR (11.6), India (9.2), France (3.0), Canada (2.6)
Cocoa	Ivory Coast (20.9), Brazil (18.9), Ghana (16.4), Nigeria (11.2), Cameroon (7.1), Ecuador (6.1)
Coffee	Brazil (22.1), Colombia (15.8), Ivory Coast (5.1), Indonesia (5.0), Mexico (4.6), Ethiopia (4)
Cotton	USSR (23.6), China (19.3), United States (15.1), India (10.0), Pakistan (5.0), Brazil (4.3)
Maize	United States (43.1), China (15.2), Brazil (5.2), Romania (2.9), Mexico (2.8), Canada (1.4)
Rice	China (35.6), India (20.8), Burma (3.3), Japan (3.1), Vietnam (2.5), Brazil (2.4)
Soya	United States (59.3), Brazil (18.1), China (12.1), Argentina (4.2)
Sugar	Brazil (9.7), USSR (8.9), Cuba (7.9), United States (6.1), France (5.0), China (4.3)
Tea	India (31.1), China (17.5), Sri Lanka (10.1), USSR (6.6), Turkey (6.4), Japan (5.2)
Tobacco	China (17.1), United States (14.9), Brazil (7.6), India (7.4), USSR (5.7), Japan (3.1)
Wheat	USSR (22.0), United States (14.5), China (12.2), India (7.1), France (5.3), Canada (4.3)

Source: 1988 CRB *Commodity Year Book*
(New York: Commodity Research Bureau 1988).

Table 4.5

Leading mineral producers of the 1980s

MINERALS	LEADING PRODUCERS (PERCENTAGE OF WORLD TOTAL)
Asbestos	Canada (42.7), USSR (32.3), S. Africa (6.3), Zimbabwe (6.3), United States (4.2)
Bauxite	Australia (28.3), Guinea (16.0), Jamaica (13.9), USSR (5.3), Brazil (4.8), Surinam (4.7)
Chromium	S. Africa (34.0), Philippines (6.0), Zimbabwe (5.9), Turkey (4.0), Finland (1.8)
Cobalt	Zaire (51.0), Zambia (9.2), Australia (5.8), Canada (5.1), Philippines (5.1), Finland (4.4)
Copper	United States (19.5), Chile (13.3), USSR (11.9), Canada (8.8), Zambia (7.3), Zaire (5.8)
Industrial diamonds	Zaire (31.5), USSR (27.7), S. Africa (16.7), Botswana (14.1), Ghana (3.2)
Iron ore	USSR (28.3), Brazil (11.5), Australia (10.6), United States (8.7), China (8.2), Canada (5.5)
Lead	United States (13.2), Australia (11.3), Canada (10.3) Peru (6.0), Mexico (4.4), Yugoslavia (3.5)
Molybdenum	United States (62.0), Chile (11.1), Canada (10.3), Peru (0.9)
Nickel	Canada (26.5), New Caledonia (7.0), Cuba (5.5), United States (2.2)
Phosphates	United States (31.7), USSR (17.5), Morocco (13.7), Tunisia (3.2), Jordan (2.9)
Platinum	USSR (48.0), S. Africa (45.7), Canada (5.0), United States (0.9)
Silver	Mexico (14.0), Peru (13.4), Canada (10.6), United States (10.4)
Tin	Malaysia (25.0), USSR (15.0), Thailand (14.0), Indonesia (13.0), Bolivia (10.0), China (5.9)
Titanium	Brazil (26.3), India (17.5), Canada (15.2), S. Africa (8.6), Australia (6.6), United States (6.0)
Tungsten	China (26.0), USSR (16.9), Australia (6.3), United States (6.1), Bolivia (6.1), Canada (5.2)
Zinc	Canada (17.1), Australia (8.7), United States (5.3), Mexico (4.3)
Natural gas	United States (36.5), USSR (29.0), Canada (5.0), United Kingdom (2.5), Romania (2.2)

Source: 1988 CRB Commodity Year Book
(New York: Commodity Research Bureau 1988)

Table 4.6

international system. The uneven distribution of arable land and raw materials is the primary motivation for national economies to engage in international trade. Never before in human history have nation-states relied so much on each other to obtain the essentials of life. Since World War II, the growth of international trade in goods and services has greatly expanded: it is estimated that it now totals US$2.45 trillion ($2456 billion) per year.[12] The material resources of a nation-state, derived from its agricultural and industrial output, help determine its power potential. States use this power to influence the behaviour of other states either by imposing their will on them or by resisting the influence they attempt to exert. Natural resources and the extent to which they are exploited determine the economic power of the state.

Economic Capability: The Political Dimension

All independent states exercise effective organization and control over their territorial boundaries. The politico-territorial organization of a state is not just the organization of geographical space, but also the foundation of its economic capacity. The way a state divides or centralizes political power and the decision-making functions of government translates into economic advantage or disadvantage. Economic capacity is almost always a product of political organization. Thus a reunited Germany under a confederal state system of two governments or a unified federal system would greatly enhance the economic power of that country.

The political system establishes the communications and transportation networks, the arrangements of the land-tenure system, and the application of an overriding structure to enhance human opportunity and exploit natural resources. For example, an efficient communications network is of vital importance for political and economic cohesiveness in a nation-state. In Canada, the federal government has invested heavily in developing a comprehensive network of communications for purposes of national integration. Canada's communication system is technically the most advanced in the world. With the launching of the *Anik* satellite series in 1972, Canada became the first state to establish a national telecommunications system based on signals from space. The *Anik* satellites at present in orbit can transmit information of the highest broadcast quality to the remotest parts of Canada. The application of this advanced technology in the field of communications is crucial for Canada's national defence, as well as for the maintenance of cultural identity.

The manner in which a nation-state has organized its government, its economy, and its defence is an important indication of the internal institutional power of the state and its perceived external power in the political world. The political organization of a nation-state, as distinct from its form of government, is either unitary or federal.

Unitary States

The unitary state is the most common type of political organization, accounting for 90 percent of all independent nation-states. A unitary state is one in which all sovereign power resides in the national government: all other units of government are merely its subdivisions. Any delegation of power to regions, districts, or municipalities is largely at the discretion of the national government and may be legally reduced, increased, or removed even if only for reasons of administrative efficiency. In this type of political organization, the national government can impose its decisions on local governments, regardless of the unpopularity of these decisions. This high degree of political centralization is not always intended to foster economic efficiency: rather it is frequently implemented to facilitate political and social control.

As a general rule, unitary states, such as Japan and France, enjoy a high level of internal homogeneity and cohesiveness. But some unitary states, such as Spain and South Africa, lack social homogeneity and are geographically large enough to warrant federal systems. In Spain, the existence of four spoken languages – Spanish, Portuguese (in Galicia), Basque, and Catalan - serve to divide rather than unify the affairs of state. In 1910 the Union of South Africa joined four provinces – Cape Colony, Transvaal, Natal, and the Orange Free State, each with its own special social characteristics and distinctive physical geography – under a unitary system that continues to exist today. Unitarism has provided both Spain and South Africa with a political structure that maximizes the authoritative power of the central government.

The average unitary state is small and densely populated with one core area*. There is a direct one-level relationship between the people and their national government (figure 4.2). People are not burdened with the complications and duplications of government services. One central agency designs school curricula, issues licences and permits, raises taxes, and plans the economy. All governmental units are administrative subdivisions of the same government so that, under normal conditions, unitarism has cost-efficient benefits.

Many former colonial territories have embraced the unitary form of political organization. All the former French territories adopted the unitary system of political organization. Most British-influenced states in Africa - Kenya, Sierra Leone, and Ghana - are unitary. All

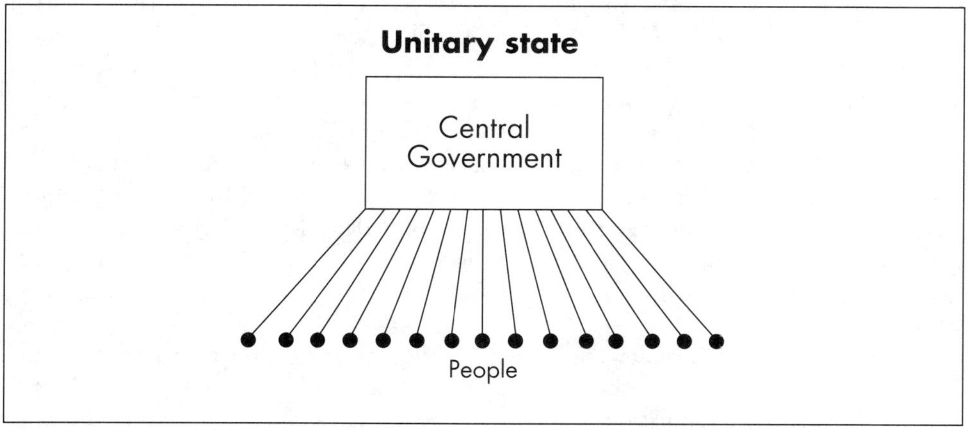

Figure 4.2

Arab states in the Middle East are unitary; the majority of emergent black African states also chose this form of political organization. All Central American republics are unitary states; in South America, Colombia, Ecuador, Peru, Chile, Bolivia, and Paraguay function as unitary states.

China holds the distinction of being the largest unitary state in the world. Among Southeast Asian states, all are unitary except Malaysia. Again, the European influence has made a strong contribution to the establishment of unitary systems in this part of the world. The unitary system is also popular because of the facility that this system gives to the consolidation of power. A unitary state can exercise full control over all areas of a country without the complications of contested jurisdictions from subnational components.

Federal States

Only sixteen of the world's nation-states are politically organized as federal systems (see table 4.7). Yet over 50 percent of the world's people live in a federal system. No simple generalization can be made about the size of federal states. A mutually interdependent political relationship links a system of national and subnational governments according to legal and constitutional prescriptions. Although it is true that a federal structure is especially suitable for large states, it is also true that many unitary states are larger than the federations of Switzerland, Yugoslavia, or Malaysia. Geography is but one of the many divisive complications. All federal states have human as well as geographic factors that divide them. The federal structure is amenable to countries occupied by people of widely different ethnic origins, languages, religions, and political cultures. India, which has the world's second-largest population and a federal system of government, has 14 main languages and over 200 secondary ones. Both the USSR and Canada have complicated federal systems where these social differences have regional expression in that some peoples see different parts of their country as a homeland.

The word *federal* finds its origins in the Latin *foederis*, meaning "league." It implies an alliance of a state's diverse internal regions and people. K.W. Robinson says that "federation does not create unity out of diversity; rather, it enables the two to coexist."[13] The federal arrangement is a political balance of constantly shifting centrifugal and centripetal forces in a country. *Centrifugal* forces move power away from the political centre of a state to the component areas. These are many and varied: regional loyalties, different historical experiences, distinct forms of economic specialization, differences of language, culture, and population densities, as well as remoteness from the federal capital. In contrast, *centripetal* forces centralize political power and control at the federal level of government. They eliminate separatist* pressures by diminishing the perception of internal differences, encouraging a loyalty to the nation-state, unifying the economy, and centralizing political decisions.

Table 4.7 is a list of all the federal states in the world. It identifies the formal name of each state, gives its founding dates, the number of subnational units federated, as well as its territorial area, current population, and type of federation. In every example of a federated political organization there exists a constitutional division and sharing of powers among the

Federal states

NAME	DATE FORMED	NUMBER OF UNITS	AREA (MILLION) SQ. KM	POP. (1989)	CAPITAL CITY	TYPE OF FED.
Republic of Argentina	1816	24	2.8	31 060 000	Buenos Aires	Centralized
Commonwealth of Australia	1901	6	7.7	16 091 000	Canberra	Matured
Brazil	1889	22	8.5	138 400 000	Brasilia	Centralized
Canada	1867	10	9.9	26 146 000	Ottawa	Conciliatory
Federal Republic of Germany	1955	11	0.25	62 715 000	Bonn	Matured
Union of India	1950	21	3.2	781 400 090	New Delhi	Conciliatory
Malaysia	1963-65	3	0.13	15 557 000	Kuala Lumpur	Conciliatory
Mexico	1824	29	2.0	80 024 000	Mexico City	Matured
Republic of Nigeria	1960	12	0.92	103 100 000	Lagos	Centralized
Confederation of Switzerland	1848	25	0.04	7 541 400	Berne	Conciliatory
United Republic of Tanzania	1964	2	0.94	21 733 000	Dar es Salaam	Centralized
United Arab Emirates	1971	7	0.84	1 327 000	Dubai	Conciliatory
Union of Soviet Socialist Republics	1922	15	22.4	287 000 960	Moscow	Centralized (transitional)
United States of America	1782-87	50	9.3	246 600 800	Washington	Matured
Republic of Venezuela	1830	20	0.91	18 900 600	Caracas	Matured
Socialist Federal Republic of Yugoslavia	1946	6	0.26	23 123 000	Belgrade	Centralized (transitional)

Source: *The Statesman's Year Book, 1989-90* (New York: Macmillan Press Co. 1989); United Nations, ***Population and Vital Statistics Reports*** [quarterly] (New York: Statistical Office 1989).

Table 4.7

various levels of government. Simply put, federalism means that more than one unit of government has responsibility for a citizen living in any part of the country (figure 4.3). The subnational units are well defined geographically. They are called states in the United States and Mexico, provinces in Canada, Lander in West Germany, cantons in Switzerland, and republics in the USSR.

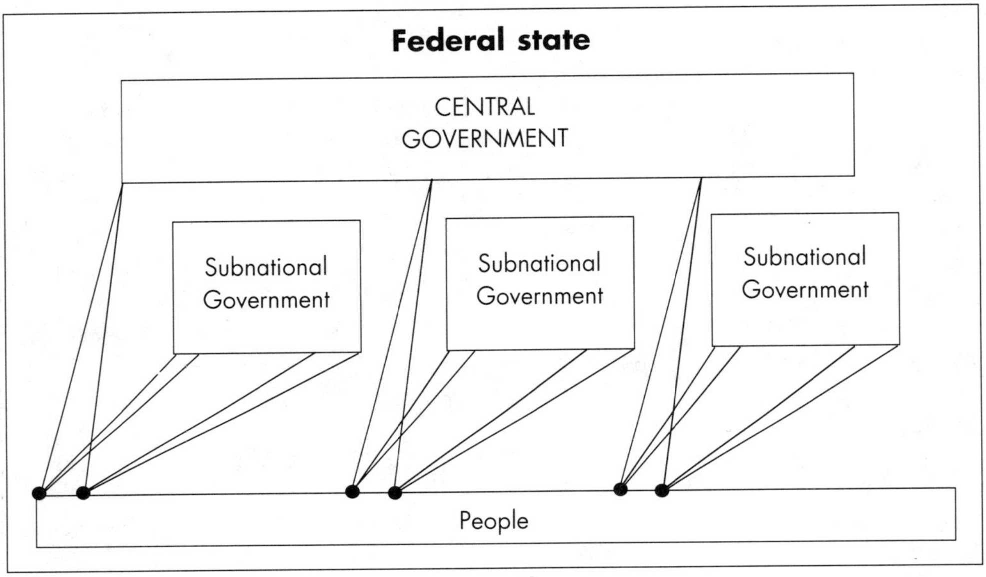

Figure 4.3

There are three types of federations among the sixteen nation-states that practise federalism: mature federations, conciliatory federations, and centralized federations. A *mature federation* is one that over time has achieved national, economic, and political integration among people of diverse ethnic origins. In this type of federation the constituent parts share a mutual interest in the goals of the national government and have a stake in supporting the original divisions of power and jurisdiction. The component parts accept their constitutionally designated autonomy and are willing to yield powers to the federation in order to make viable the larger economic and political unit. Six nation-states fall into this category, with the United States and Australia as prime examples.

Conciliatory federations are characterized by a high degree of constitutionally designated centralization, but an ongoing process of compromise and negotiation between the national government and the subnational units produces a rough equality of autonomy in matters affecting jurisdictions and the divisions of power. Unlike those in mature federations, the various entities that make up conciliatory federations have retained their own identities, with their own laws, policies, customs, and languages. These federations appear inherently contentious, and perhaps even contradictory as a form of political organization. Jurisdictional* disputes frequently arise. Constant bickering punctuated by charges of usurpation of power characterize the relationship between the central government and the governments of the lower units. In this type of federalism, no level of government can effectively govern without the co-operation of the other levels. Nevertheless, conciliatory federalism is much more responsive to local and regional needs than would be a unitary state. Five states can be labelled conciliatory: Canada, India, Malaysia, Switzerland, and the United Arab Emirates. All these federations have required a great deal of compromise and adjustment since they were formed.

Canada's experience illustrates the nature of conciliatory federalism.[14] The Constitution Act, 1867, placed in the domain of the federal government four important powers that strongly favoured centralized government. These powers – the residual power, the declaratory power, and the powers of disallowance and reservation – gave the federal government the sovereign capacity of a unitary state cloaked in the guise of federalism. The *residual power* is enshrined in the "Peace, Order and Good Government of Canada" clause that – in circumstances such as those that encouraged the government to invoke the War Measures Act in 1970 and wage-and-price controls in 1975 – permits the federal government to penetrate provincial jurisdictions. The *declaratory power* allows the federal government to displace provincial powers if, in the view of Parliament, such an action is "for the general Advantage of Canada or for the Advantage of Two or more of the Provinces." *Disallowance* is a pre-emptory power of the federal government to void a provincial law within a year of its passage. *Reservation* allows all federally appointed lieutenant-governors to reserve royal assent on a provincial bill, placing the final decision before the federal Cabinet.

Much has changed in Canada's federal character since 1867.[15] At the outset of Canadian federalism the character of the system was "quasi-federal" because the national government assumed major administrative responsibilities for the bulk of public services. In the period between 1896 and1914 provinces demanded more power and consultation from the federal government.[16] "Emergency federalism" characterized the war period, when Parliament delegated sweeping authority to Ottawa to levy personal and corporate income taxes, to apply wage-and-price controls, and to prohibit strikes in wartime. This quality of federalism would return just prior to and after the Great Depression until the end of World War II. But during the 1920s provincial autonomy grew as a result of revenues drawn from licensing automobiles, and taxing gasoline and liquor. The late 1940s and 1950s saw the forces of centralism return to Canadian federalism. What has been called "Father knows best" federalism resulted from the enormous postwar taxing powers of the federal government and its ability to penetrate the administrative purview of the provinces by funding certain shared-cost programs. "Cooperative federalism" began in the 1960s as provincial governments experienced unprecedented demands for expanded services in health, education, welfare, and resource development. Today, all provinces spend over half their budgets in these areas. As well, the rise of nationalism in Quebec spawned the concurrent spread of provincial autonomy in the other provinces.

By the 1990s Canada, with all the requisites of a highly centralized state, had become the most decentralized federation in the international system.[17] Over the decades this dramatic change of character was brought about largely from provincial challenges to federal autonomy. Many of these challenges were supported by a number of judicial decisions that ruled on the side of the provinces in jurisdictional disputes with the federal government. In addition, since the 1940s, the federal government has been reluctant to use its four autonomous powers against the provinces. As the provinces have gained more ground against the federal government they have developed a confrontational attitude, tantamount to the role of the opposition parties in the House of Commons. Another major cause of decentralization lies in the changing priorities of Canadian society since the nineteenth century. When the Constitution Act, 1867, was adopted, provincial powers in the areas of education, health, municipalities, and welfare were of minor importance. Today, Canadians no longer consider the role that provincial governments play in their lives as secondary to that of the federal government.

Centralized federations include nation-states that have federal constitutions on paper but in practice are run like highly centralized unitary states. Argentina, Brazil, Venezuela, Nigeria, the USSR, and Yugoslavia are centralized federations.

The Soviet Union is the world's largest federal state and the best example of a centralized one, although it is undergoing transitional pressures. The USSR is divided into fifteen Soviet Socialist Republics, roughly corresponding to each of the major nationalities living in the country. The Russian Soviet Federated Socialist Republic (RSFSR) is by far the largest, extending from west of Moscow to the Pacific Ocean in the east. The fifteen republics have equal constitutional standing in the union, but the RSFSR exercises political leadership and dominates political affairs in the Soviet Union. With over half the country's population, most of the major cities (including the capital), and over three-quarters of the land area, the RSFSR is the nucleus of the Soviet Union. The Russian language is compulsory in all other republics, but the languages of these other areas are not compulsory in Russia. The constitution permits each republic to carry its own foreign policy, to issue its own currency, and even to secede* from the union. None of this is permitted in practice.

The Soviet political framework primarily protects the interests of the RSFSR; it is a federal state in name only. The federal pattern is not an actual division of powers between the Soviet state and its fifteen union republics. Instead it serves the ideological designs of the Communist Party, *perestroika* notwithstanding. The federal design of the Soviet Union gives formal recognition to the heterogeneity of the Soviet people – their cultures, languages, religion, and ethnic origins. Democratization has unleashed latent forces of nationalism and separatism in the Soviet Union. The federal structure of the state is inevitably altered under such pressures. Since the Gorbachev revolution the Soviet federal system has been rocked by demands from the Crimean Tartars about grievances festering for fifty years, nationalist demonstrations in Moldavia and the Ukraine against Russification*, secessionism along the Baltic coast, and sectarian violence between Armenians and Azerbaijanis.

Yugoslavia is another centralized federal state experiencing major structural change. Because of immense internal cultural diversity, the unitary framework of political organizations adopted in 1919 eventually failed. A federal constitution was drawn up in

1939 in which the Croats, Serbs, Slovenes, and other minority groups gained regional autonomy. In 1953, Yugoslavia created six autonomous republics under the watchful scrutiny of the national government. They are best seen as administrative vehicles of the national government and its policies. Each autonomous republic has limited legal authority, subject always to political checks from national officials at higher levels. In 1989, the southern province of Kosovo erupted in violence when Serbs demanded administrative control over the republic. All of Yugoslavia's republics have recently begun to challenge openly the power and authority of the central government, perhaps ultimately moving in the direction of a less-centralized federation.

Economic Organization

Political organization is as essential for the economic structure and strength of a nation-state as it is for the administration of political power. The national economy is the organized process of developing markets for its natural resources, industrial production, agricultural output, and technological innovations. All nation-states must choose not only how their natural resources should be exploited to meet social needs but also how to distribute the goods and services produced from them. Essentially, these political decisions determine the economic organization of a nation-state. The economic institutions established within states to solve the problems of what commodities to produce, how to produce them, and how to distribute output and income constitute the economic system.

In the world today three main types of economic systems are distinguishable among nation-states: the capitalist system, the socialist system, and the mixed economic system. The *capitalist system* is characterized by the widespread practice of private enterprise, by the private ownership of resources, and by a limited amount of government intervention in the economy. Theoretically, in this type of economic organization, the productions, pricing, and distribution of goods and services are determined by millions of individuals, each attempting to maximize personal gain. Of course, in the real world these factors are also determined by large domestic corporations, multinational corporations, and the political actions of other states. A pure capitalist economy does not exist in the international community. Capitalist economies are more or less organized as free-enterprise* economies. In a *socialist system*, all resources are theoretically owned and controlled by the state for social purposes. In a politically directed economic system the supply, demand, and prices of goods and services are determined by government policies. In many economies the two systems have merged into a hybrid organization called a *mixed economy*. In this system, control of the economy is shared by public and private institutions.

The differential performance of these three economic systems has produced what some analysts have referred to as five worlds of development in the international community.[18] The *First World* includes the advanced industrialized nation-states of Europe, North America, and Asia that have adopted a more or less capitalist, market-oriented economy. Canada, Japan, the United States, the economies of Western Europe, New Zealand, and

Australia clearly qualify as the First World. The economic power of these nation-states translates into foreign-policy objectives that influence global development, economic growth, or recession. From an economic point of view, First World states are the most powerful in the world. They control the world's financial and banking communities and extend credit to all levels of the international economy. The *Second World* includes almost all people of the world's centrally planned, so-called communist states. The only exceptions are Yugoslavia, which has retained a somewhat mixed economy, and Cuba, which is generally regarded as a Third World country. China also deserves special and separate status because it is the largest communist state in terms of population but contains an agrarian* Third World economy on the threshold of modernization. The *Third World* is made up of large numbers of less-developed countries (LDCs) that need time and technology to build modern developed economies. The nation-states in this category include the revenue-rich members of OPEC (Organization of Petroleum Exporting Countries), as well as countries that possess other key natural resources: Chile, Zaire, and Zambia (copper), Morocco (phosphates), Malaysia (tin, rubber, and timber). Into this group also fall the nation-states of Brazil, Ivory Coast, Mexico, Nigeria, and Venezuela, which are widely viewed as potentially wealthy economies if the process of modernization is not interrupted by political instability or severe international recession. They are highly dependent on other economies for trade and investment capital. The Third World must also overcome severe domestic problems related to rapid urbanization, high concentrations of wealth and land ownership in the hands of the few, low levels of literacy, and galloping inflation*. However, economists are much more optimistic about the developmental fate of these economies because they possess valuable resources, which, if properly organized and managed, can propel them into the First World class of nation-states. The *Fourth World* consists of less-developed nation-states that possess enough raw materials to build a modern economic infrastructure*. Unlike Third World economies, this development not only hinges on foreign investment and time but also on substantial financial assistance and special policy treatment by the rich industrial powers. Otherwise, the Fourth World has little hope of achieving self-sustaining economic growth. This category includes Benin, China, India, Kenya, and Sri Lanka. They show low per capita savings and generally poor economic performance. The *Fifth World* comprises those national economies that are doomed to remain on permanent dole. They have very few easily exploited resources and are unable to grow enough food to feed their starving populations. The most notable in this disparate group of poverty-ridden economies are Chad, Ethiopia, Guinea-Bissau, Mali, Mozambique, and Nepal.

In the 1990s, nation-states are reassessing their power potential with a new awareness of the importance of the economic parameters* of power. Economic might breeds political power. First World states have the capacity to save money, to lend it, and to reinvest it in their economies. In such economies, economic growth enhances the standard of living, permitting better employment, education, and health benefits. Economic strength also enables First World nation-states to control their destinies in a competitive international system. They are in the strongest position to influence international trade and monetary

Gross national product (GNP) per capita of selected First, Second, Third, Fourth, and Fifth World states

CATEGORY	GNP PER CAPITA IN U.S. DOLLARS (1986)
First World states	
Canada	14 120
Great Britain	9 280
Sweden	14 821
Switzerland	17 680
United States	17 480
Second World states	
Czechoslovakia (transitional)	9 748
German Democratic Republic (transitional)	10 496
Poland (transitional)	6 467
Soviet Union	7 403
Yugoslavia (transitional)	5 596
Third World states	
Brazil	2 950
Chile	1 903
Cuba	2 948
Ecuador	1 354
Syria	1 974
Fourth World states	
Benin	461
China	396
India	262
Kenya	390
Sri Lanka	398
Fifth World states	
Chad	117
Guinea-Bissau	181
Mali	276
Mozambique	169
Nepal	170

Sources: Victor Showers, *World Facts & Figures,* 3rd ed. (New York: John Wiley & Sons 1989); United Nations, *World Economic Survey 1989* (New York: Statistical Office 1989);

Table 4.8

policy* so that it works in their favour. Finally, the nation–states of the First World are best able to carve out a sizable role for themselves in international affairs in terms of aid and investment. Industrialized* economies can also convert their economic assets into military and political ones.

Military Power

Force and the threat of force play a prominent role in international relations. Many of the states of the world use their military as an expression of national power. The ability to project military prowess beyond national boundaries is viewed by some analysts as the qualifying constituent of power among states.[19] It is tempting to assume that the possession of nuclear or conventional weapons is the most significant factor in the power equation of a nation-state. But a paradox emerges in a world of militarily credible states. Those states that have vast military strength cannot always exercise it as an effective instrument of national policy. Modern international law rejects violence as a means of settling disputes, except in cases of self-defence*. Although force continues to be used by some states, such acts are legally indefensible in the eyes of the international community, as exemplified by the U.S. invasion of Panama, 1989/90. As well, modern weapons of mass destruction are themselves a deterrence against their use. Most states believe that nuclear technology will not be used against them, so the capacity of nuclear states to coerce and intimidate other states may not often be greater than it would be in the absence of the nuclear threat.

Despite its vast military power, the United States has not been able to claim political victories in Cuba, Nicaragua, Vietnam, Cambodia, and Iran. Nor has Soviet military superiority prevented recent deviationist or independent tendencies in Poland, Romania, Yugoslavia, and Hungary. Defying superpowers is common sport among lesser states.

The Soviet Union and its allies are frequently cited as having been more successful than Western states in imposing their will on other states by using military force. In Hungary, Czechoslovakia, Angola, and Ethiopia, the Soviets approached their goals by means of military power. But even within its own sphere of influence, the Soviet Union has actually lost considerable power, and Eastern Europe remains fundamentally unstable from the Soviet point of view. In 1989, after nine years of humiliation, frustration, and defeat, the Soviet Union retreated from the military persistence of the *mujahedin* rebels in Afghanistan. In other parts of the world, where wars have raged between Iraq and Iran, Argentina and Britain, and in hostilities between Israel and the Palestine Liberation Organization in Lebanon, great-power influence could not prevent or terminate conflict. The fact that the large military powers have immense "superiority" over all other states does not give them control over events in the international system. Among members of the global community who are not important actors in the nuclear balance there is now a consensus among governments that limited local violence is tolerable.

Some analysts have noted that military power is more a result than a cause of international tensions. The underlying causes of competition for power among states are widely regarded as economic and social. For the United States, the military preparedness of Cuba and Nicaragua is not the real threat to American security. No one doubts the superiority of U.S. forces in an all-out military confrontation with these states. What is of central concern is the spread of economic and social systems opposed to the capitalist model and the consequences of this on American interests in Central and South America. It is an oversimplification to argue that military capabilities and the power of a state are synonymous. Political reality today tells us that power is also expressed in terms of trade, aid, economic productivity, and scientific and technological advancement.

The extent to which military capability enhances the power of a state is open to debate. The fact that more states are acquiring advanced weapons gives the impression of a global grab for power. In the 1990s, Argentina, Iraq, Iran, Pakistan, South Korea, and Taiwan, among other states, are expected to join the eleven-member nuclear club*. Would Argentina have been a more successful combatant against Great Britain over the Falkland Islands by possessing nuclear weapons? Does Pakistan graduate from the Fourth World to the Third World with a nuclear arsenal? Would nuclear weapons promote Canada from the rank of middle power to superpower? The proliferation of sophisticated military technology may make states more dangerous, but not necessarily more powerful.

In 1989, the governments of the world spent US$1 trillion on defence. Many spent their money on military personnel, equipment, and weapons to maintain internal security, not to build reputations of power among the other nation-states in the international arena. It is also noteworthy that a large number of the world's states in Africa and Latin America do not even view their militaries as having an external defence function. They are not threatened by their neighbours nor are they prepared to extend their sovereignty over other peoples. In these states, the military is used primarily to repress the domestic population. Even in states that have trained their militaries primarily for external defence, the armed forces can be ordered against the people. Such was the case in China in 1989 when an unleashed military began to massacre its own people in Tiananmen Square. Thus, before we can generalize about the relationship between power and military capacity, we must consider the strategic purpose of each state's defence.

National Will and Strategic Purpose

The tangible elements of power, i.e., population, geography, and natural resources, remain stagnant without national will and strategic purpose, the intangible elements of power. Together they enable a state to influence and control the behaviour of others. Although **will** is difficult to measure, some analysts rank it as the most important determinant of power.[20] Hans Morgenthau sees it as "the degree of determination with which a nation supports the foreign policies of its government in peace and war".[21] Support may be enthusiastic toward a particular strategy or it may be sluggish and apathetic.

The will of a population and its leadership can often compensate for the lack of economic and military resources within a nation-state. Recent history abounds with examples of powerful states deferring to or losing influence in seemingly less-powerful states. National will is the force that enabled North Vietnam and the Vietcong to repel the United States, even though the United States held superior economic and military strength. In 1980, the determination of Iran paralysed the efforts of the United States to rescue its diplomatic personnel. Eight U.S. presidents have roared at Fidel Castro's Cuba only to confront an impenetrable wall of national determination. Afghan guerrillas confirmed the worst fears among Soviet military strategists that a protracted exchange of force would demonstrate the vulnerability of the USSR to an insurgency.

However, national will can also temper leadership to refrain from exercising the full economic and military powers at its disposal. During the Vietnam War, the political establishment in the United States favoured using more military might against Vietnam. But by 1975 the groundswell of American popular disgust with the war discouraged the U.S. government from continuing its combat commitment to South Vietnam and Cambodia.

In Canada, a conservative public has kept a watchful eye on the development and direction of Canadian foreign policy*. Canadians have been a major source of restraint on their political leaders in carving out a distinctive role for Canada in international affairs. In recent years they have encouraged their foreign-policy makers to pursue goals more in tune with Canada's national capabilities.

Canada emerged from World War II with the enhanced status of "a minor great power."[22] Post-war politicians seized the opportunity to project Canada as a second principal Western power. As a chief participant in the creation of the United Nations, the North Atlantic Treaty Organization (NATO), the North American Defence Agreement (NORAD), and as an intermediary in Commonwealth disputes, Canada stood as a rising power with a global perspective in international politics.

This pattern of internationalism* in Canadian foreign policy did not change until Pierre Elliott Trudeau shifted public opinion in favour of a more hemispheric and continental focus for Canada. Under Trudeau, Canada developed a foreign policy that saw itself primarily as an independent North American nation–state, capable of exercising a responsible role in managing global order. As Peyton Lyon noted, Canada had taken "a giant step in the direction of continental isolationism ... One that will be much cheaper, and more sharply focused on national interests."[23]

In the 1970s, Canadians insisted on a counterbalance to the extremes of superpower diplomacy by encouraging a set of policies that would build Canada's reputation as a mentor state in East-West relations.[24] At the summit level, Canada has projected this image very well: Canada is widely regarded as a peacemaker, a powerful negotiator, and an advocate of parliamentary diplomacy*. Viewed as an equal among participants, Canada's acclaimed negotiating skills have sustained the momentum of the annual "Summit Seven"* meetings around the world. At Cancun in 1981, Canada led the cause of the LDCs by fostering the

North-South dialogue*.

In the 1990s, the decline of U.S. global hegemony may elevate Canada to a position of much greater influence in international affairs. A calculation of the critical elements of power as it is perceived and used by analysts such as Cline in international politics now places Canada as high as fourth and seldom below tenth as the most powerful country in the world.[25] Yet Canadians have consistently rejected the military road to power, favouring economic strength and diplomatic skills as the most desirable indicators of rank and status. The meteoric rise in the importance of national resources in the 1980s – especially food and fuel – has provided Canada with the opportunity of becoming a principal power in continental politics.

What conclusions can we draw about state actors from the various parameters of power discussed in this chapter? All states are structurally designed to accumulate and articulate power in various ways. As the main currency of international politics, power is the capacity of an actor to change the behaviour of other actors. Some states express their influence in economic ways, through trade, aid, and investment. Others use their political skills in bilateral and multilateral negotiations to gain important concessions from the international system. A number resort to military strategy and force to exercise power. However, most states combine their economic, political, and military capacities for the purpose of persuading or coercing the other states with which they interact.

Sometimes expected conclusions about power are confounded. The Vatican, an independent state of 104 acres, with less than 1000 people, and no military or natural resources, exercises powerful influence in every corner of the world. This example shows that size, location, population, resources, and military preparedness are significant in some situations and meaningless in others.

For the analyst such paradoxes lead to frequent failures of power predictions in international affairs. In many cases, intuitive notions of power are as relevant as the systematic empirical study of power relations. Even in Cline's equation for measuring national power, the elements of strategic purpose and the will to pursue national strategy are immeasurable. But his analytical* design is flexible enough to incorporate the intangible elements of power as variables that can change the power formula. It enables the researcher to challenge the classical assumptions that size and military capability are decisive determinants of national power.[26]

But in focussing only on the domain of power within a state, the Cline framework cannot consider the complete array of factors in the international environment. States are no longer the only significant organizations: multinational corporations, terrorist groups, and non-governmental organizations (NGOs) must also be taken into account as important components in the international power structure.

In subsequent chapters, we will analyse how these other actors affect the behaviour of states. We will observe that power is dispersed among non-state actors that also share in the international power equation. We will learn that the state-centric model of the global political system has become obsolete and that the presence of non-state actors cannot be ignored.

REFERENCES

1. Leonard Tivey, *The Nation-State* (New York: St. Martin's Press Inc. 1981), 13–39.
2. See George Peter Murdock, *Atlas of World Cultures* (Pittsburgh, PA: University of Pittsburgh Press 1981), 3.
3. Leo Gross, "The Peace of Westphalia, 1648–1948," in Robert S. Wood, ed., *The Process of International Organization* (New York: Random House 1971), 42.
4. K.J. Holsti, *International Politics, A Framework for Analysis* (Englewood Cliffs, NJ: Prentice-Hall Inc. 1988), 141.
5. Karl Deutsch, "On the Concepts of Politics and Power," *Journal of International Affairs* 21, no. 2 (1967): 334.
6. Robert Dahl, "The Concept of Power," *Behavioural Science* 2 (July 1957): 201–15.
7. Ray S. Cline, *World Power Trends and U.S. Foreign Policy for the 1980s* (Boulder, CO: Westview Press 1980), 113; and John Rourke, *International Politics on the World Stage* (Guilford, CT.: Dushkin Publishing Group 1989), 211–38; for a critique of Cline, see David Baldwin, "Power Analysis and World Politics," *World Politics* 31, no. 2 (1979): 164.
8. Quoted in Kim Richard Nossal, *The Politics of Canadian Foreign Policy* (Scarborough, ON: Prentice-Hall Canada Inc. 1985), 12.
9. Office of the PM, press release, May 29, 1968.
10. See Harm J. de Blij, *Systematic Political Geography* (New York: John Wiley & Sons, Inc. 1973); Albert A. Rose, *A Geography of International Relations* (Dayton, OH: University of Dayton Press 1965).
11. United Nations, Report of the Committee on the Preparation of a Draft Convention Relating to the Transit Trade of Land-Locked Countries, March 1965.
12. United Nations. *Monthly Bulletin of Statistics* (New York: May1988).
13. K.W. Robinson, "Sixty Years of Federation in Australia," *Georgia Review* 50 (January 1961): 2.
14. D.V. Smiley, *Canada in Question: Federalism in the Eighties*, 3rd ed. (Toronto: McGraw-Hill Ryerson 1980), 22–7; see also Peter Aucoin, ed., *Regional Responsiveness and the National Administrative State* (Toronto: University of Toronto Press 1985)
15. See A.W. Johnson, "The Dynamics of Federalism in Canada," *Canadian Journal of Political Science* 1, no. 1 (1968): 18; Arend Lijphart, "Consociation and Federation: Conceptional and Empirical Links," *Canadian Journal of Political Science XII*, (September 1979): 499–515.
16. See Robert Adie and Paul Thomas, *Canadian Public Administration* (Scarborough, ON: Prentice-Hall Canada Inc. 1987), 425–74.
17. See Alan Cairns, "The Other Crisis of Canadian Federalism," *Canadian Public Administration* XXII (Summer 1980): 175 –95; see also Bruce Pollard, *Managing the Interface: Intergovernmental Affairs Agencies in Canada* (Kingston, ON: Institute of Intergovernmental Relations 1986).
18. See Hollis B. Chenery, "Restructuring the World Economy," *Foreign Affairs* 53 (January 1975): 258–63.
19. See Ruth Leger Sivard, *World Military and Social Expenditures 1982* (Leesburg, VA: World Priorities 1982); Andrew-Pierre, *The Global Politics of Arms Sales* (Princeton: Princeton University Press 1982); and Seymour Melman, "Limits to Military Power", *International Security* 11, no. 3 (1986) 72–88.
20. See Cline, *World Power Trends*, 143 and William P. Bundy, "Elements of National Power," *Foreign Affairs* 56 (October 1977): 1–26; Luigi Sensi, "Superpower Interventions in Civil War,1945–87," paper presented to the International Studies Association, St. Louis, MO, 1988.
21. Hans Morgenthau, *Politics among Nations: The Struggle for Power and Peace* (New

York: Alfred A. Knopf Inc. 1973), 135.

22. See Peter C. Dobell, *Canada's Search for New Roles: Foreign Policy in the Trudeau Era* (London: Oxford University Press 1972), 1.
23. Quoted by Peter C. Dobell, "A Review of a Review," *Journal of Canadian Studies* 5 (May 1970): 34.
24. See Michael Tucker, *Canadian Foreign Policy: Contemporary Issues and Themes* (Toronto: McGraw-Hill Ryerson Ltd. 1980), 10-12; see also J.L. Granatstein, *Canadian Foreign Policy: Historical Readings* (Mississauga, ON: Copp Clark Pitman 1986).
25. Cline, *World Power Trends.* See also Peyton Lyon and Brian Tomlin, *Canada as an International Actor* (Toronto: Collier Macmillan Canada Inc. 1979), 58–75; David Dewitt and John Kirton, *Canada as a Principal Power: A Study in Foreign Policy and International Relations* (Toronto: John Wiley & Sons 1983), 38.
26. Klaus Knorr, ed., *Power, Strategy and Security* (Princeton: Princeton University Press 1983), 14–15. See also Paul Kennedy, *The Rise and Fall of the Great Powers* (New York: Random House 1988).

SUGGESTED READINGS

Herman Bakvis, *Federalism and the Role of the State* (Toronto: University of Toronto Press 1987).

Seweryn Bialer, *Politics, Society, and Nationality inside Gorbachev's Russia* (Boulder, CO: Westview Press 1989).

Szymon Chodak, *The New State: Etatization of Western Societies* (Boulder, CO: Lynne Rienner Publishers 1988).

Douglas Dowd, *The Waste of Nations* (Boulder, CO: Westview Press 1989).

Daniel Elazar, *Federation as Grand Design: Political Philosophers and the Federal Principle* (Lanham, MD: University Press of America 1987).

Robert Keohane and Joseph Nye, *Power and Interdependence* (Glenview, IL: Scott, Foresman and Company 1988).

Peter Leslie, *Federal State, National Economy* (Toronto: University of Toronto Press 1987).

Peter Morriss, *Power* (New York: St. Martin's Press 1987).

Harold Seidman and Robert Gilmour, *Politics, Position, and Power* (New York: Oxford University Press 1988).

Andrew Vincent, *Theories of the State* (Oxford: Basil Blackwell 1988).

GLOSSARY

persons: Legal entities that are subject to international law and have the capacity to enter into binding relations, with all concomitant rights and duties of such relations.

totalitarian: The systematic use of political and social control by a government or party organization potentially over every facet of private and public life by means of technology.

jurisdiction: The recognized right of a state to exercise control over people, property, territory, and events within a given geographical area.

autonomy: The freedom that permits political systems and subsystems to manage their own affairs without external interference.

decolonization: The forces of national self-determination that led to the rapid dwindling of empire and the birth of new, independent nation-states.

condominium: A dependent territory governed jointly by two or more states, neither or any of which have exclusive jurisdiction.

demographic: Referring to the components of national and global population change that take place from time to time and place to place.

superpower: The perceived status assigned to nation-states by virtue of their size, population, industrial-technological capacities, and military prowess that enables them to exercise influence throughout the entire international system.

strategic: Concerns the capacity of a state to utilize location, natural and human resources, military strength, economic advantages, and other political or social variables for the purpose of enhancing its perceived power among other states.

domino theory: The foreign-policy theory elevated to high policy levels under U.S. President Dwight Eisenhower and his secretary of state, John Foster Dulles, that asserted that communism would spread from one country to another and states would fall under the influence of communism like dominos.

Pacific Rim: A group of countries identified for purposes of trade and other international relations by their proximity to the Pacific Ocean. They include Australia, China, Hong Kong, Indonesia, Japan, Malaysia, New Zealand, Philippines, Singapore, South Korea, Taiwan, and Thailand.

economic interdependence: The degree to which the economic performance of a nation-state is dependent on the international economy.

core area: A relatively small portion of a country in which the political power of the entire state is concentrated, usually where a nation-state originated.

separatist: The aim of a group within a society to renounce its allegiance to the state and to form a sovereign state of its own.

jurisdiction: The constitutional sphere of authority exercised by a state and its constituent structures over economic, political, and social matters.

secede: The voluntary withdrawal of a state, nation, or subnational government from some federation of which it forms a part.

Russification: The imposition of the use of the Russian language on national minorities through the education system, the media, party membership, and other institutional representations within the Soviet state.

free enterprise: An economy in which people are permitted by law to start enterprises of production, distribution, or exchange under private rights of ownership.

agrarian society: A society in which a significantly large number of members (peasant class) are involved in agricultural pursuits on plantation systems of forced or transeient labour.

galloping inflation: An increase in the general price level that proceeds at an exceptionally high rate from month to month.

infrastructure: The network of roads, dams, power plants, and communication, irrigation, and transportation systems that constitute the structural framework of a society.

parameters: Political scientists sometimes use the term to mean limiting conditions that serve as boundaries or constraints on the operation of economic or political variables.

monetary policy: embraces all measures intended to affect the growth, utilization, efficiency, and diversification of the financial system, especially measures intended to encourage the growth of savings in the form of financial assets, to develop money and capital markets, and to allocate credit between different economic sectors.

industrialized economy: An economy that relies primarily on mechanized production for its subsistence.

self-defence: The anticipatory right of all states to retaliate against armed attack in kind in the interests of national security.

nuclear club: States with one or more

nuclear weapons and extensive delivery systems.

foreign policy: Governmental actions with respect to foreign governments, their nationals, and international agencies.

internationalism: The idea that political activity should define its objectives not in terms of the constitution, history, or geographical boundaries of any particular state but in terms of the global community of states.

parliamentary diplomacy: The use of debate, negotiation, and voting in international organizations to settle international issues.

Summit Seven: Annual summit meetings of leading Western industrial states to develop and synchronize economic policies in the capitalist international economic system. Participating countries are Canada, France, Japan, Italy, United Kingdom, United States, and West Germany.

North-South dialogue: On May 1, 1974, a majority of Third World nation-states at the United Nations drafted a "Declaration on the Establishment of a New International Economic Order" and a "Programme of Action" followed in December by a "Charter on the Economic Rights and Duties of States." These efforts led to the ongoing dialogue pledged at Cancun, Mexico, in 1981 to close the gap between the rich nations of the North and the poorer nations of the South.

analytical: To separate an object of inquiry into constituent parts in order to study its nature and to determine the relationship of the parts to each other and to the whole.

5

Government

Nelson Mandela with South African President F.W. de Klerk soon after Mandela's release

What Is Government?

ANTHROPOLOGISTS TELL US that about 30 000 years ago the human species began to organize into societies. Primitive communities attempted to regulate human behaviour with respect to food gathering, family life, and protection from predatory animals. The social system may have been informal, folk-sustained, uncentralized, and non-institutional – but it did contain a *social government*. *Political government*, the centralized system that maintains an institutionalized system of order within a society large or small, first appeared only about 10 000 years ago when the first civilizations developed in Asia Minor and northern Mesopotamia. As people gradually concentrated in cities, social controls were needed to maintain order in a more complex organizational system. Government by political elites and by detailed law codes was developed to maintain control over these populations.

The word "govern" is derived from Middle English *governen* and the Old French *governor*. The Latin *gubernare* (to direct, steer) is taken from the Greek *kyberman* (to steer, govern). The Greeks combined the notions of steering and government in the concept of *kybernétés*, the word for "steersman" or "helmsman" of a ship (a person who governs a ship by operating the rudder). The image of "the ship of state" appears in the writings of many political writers, especially in those of Plato and Aristotle.

The American political scientist, Karl Deutsch, has adapted the modern concept of cybernetics (the science of communication and control) to the study of government. For Deutsch, "steering depends on a country's *intake* of information through its 'receptors' (such as embassies abroad or statistical offices at home) from the outside world, the recall of other information from *memory* (including memories about where one wants to go), the transmission of commands for action to 'effectors,' and the *feedback* of information from the outside world about the results of the action just taken."[1]

Modern governments are elaborate networks for transmitting and receiving information. Governments gather and store information on attitudes and events occurring in their domestic and external environments. In Canada, all three levels of government process information on every aspect of Canadian life. Municipal governments monitor where we build and renovate our homes for tax purposes. Health and Welfare Canada informs us that "most Canadians don't smoke" from research it conducts on drug addiction across the country. Revenue Canada tells us that in terms of income, West Vancouver, B.C., is the wealthiest city and Longueil, Quebec, is the poorest city in Canada. The Department of External Affairs knows that all the states in the Western hemisphere favour Canada joining the Organization of American States (OAS). Such knowledge was part of the basis for changing public policy towards that organization.

The idea of government as steerer affords us the opportunity to distinguish it from the concepts of state and politics. Many people erroneously consider the state synonymous with government and politics. The *state*, the most formal of political organizations, is one of the hallmarks of civilization. Inherent in the concept of the state is the idea of permanent bureaucracy, public and sovereign, which the state can use to administer the affairs of its citizens as well as its relations with other states. As we have already noted, states are primary legal units in the international community, recognized as such because they have a population, occupy a defined territory, and have an effective government capable of entering into binding agreements with other states. The international rights and obligations of a state are not affected by a change of government. The states of Germany and Italy paid compensation for wrongful acts committed against other states by their Nazi and Fascist governments. However, a *government* is an organized group of people who – for a time – control the executive, legislative, and administrative machinery of a state by allocating authoritative decisions and steering the political system in the direction of specific policy goals. Governments are political; they rise and fall, while states are bureaucratic and more enduring. *Politics* is influential behaviour that leads to the making of public decisions, either within or outside the institutional frameworks of government. All political behaviour has an impact on the community. Thus, the activities of a group of women to start a community crisis centre for rape victims are as political as the decisions of politicians to fund the project at various levels of government. Although it is often convenient for us to identify politics with government, we should be aware that many political decisions are made outside government. *Politics is the articulation and when possible the harmonization of conflicting values and preferences, while government is the institutionalized process of allocating and distributing these values as binding decisions on people.*

In a country of over 26 million diverse people, living and interacting in different regions, from different ethnic backgrounds, conflict in Canada's social system is unavoidable. Politics is an inescapable process that serves to harmonize conflict in human affairs. Government is the set of organizations within which much of that process takes place. But why government? What is its purpose? For political philosophers, such as John Locke and Jean Jacques Rousseau, government is essential to civilization. To government falls the task of ensuring human decency and restraint. "Taxes," wrote the American Justice Oliver Wendell Holmes (1902–1932), "are what we pay for civilized society." The English philospher Thomas Hobbes wrote that in the absence of government, life among individuals would be "solitary, poor, nasty, brutish, and short."

Throughout history philosophers have posited that government in varying degrees is essential to protect people from one another, by force if necessary. If people kill or assault one another or steal from each other, government must intervene to protect society. If it does not, civilization is simply not possible. People could not enjoy the fundamental pleasures of life – a walk in the park, a hockey game, a concert – if their physical well-being is constantly threatened by others whose violent acts go unhindered or unpunished. Although anarchists would disagree, government is essential to non-violent human liberty.

Every political-science student quickly learns that governments differ in many ways: in size, ideology, degree of centralization, openness, legitimacy, effectiveness, and the degree and kind of political participation by individuals and groups outside the centre of authority. Correspondingly, there are various ways in which governments may be classified by structure and character from democratic to authoritarian and totalitarian, open to closed, leftist to rightist.

Traditional Classifications of Government

The earliest and most famous classifications of government were developed by the Greeks. Although they are rudimentary by today's research standards, the Greek typologies* were the first serious attempts to build a systematic body of knowledge about existing governmental structures and institutions.[2] The Greek historian Herodotus grouped all governments into monarchies (government by one), aristocracies (government by elites), and democracies (government by all). Nearly a century later, Aristotle revised the typology to include six types of government (table 5.1). He made the distinction between natural forms of government (where the ruling authority governs according to constitutional guidelines in the best interests of society) and the degenerate forms (where the ruling authority uses the powers of government for selfish gain). Thus, as rulers depart from constitutional guidelines, kings become tyrants, aristocrats become cliquish oligarchs, and democrats become selfish demogogues*.

Throughout history, many political theorists have constructed typologies for classifying various systems of government. Classical comparisons were essentially normative in that

Aristotle's typology of government

IDEAL FORM	NUMBER OF RULERS	DEGENERATE FORM
Kingship	Rule of one	Tyranny
Aristocracy	Rule of the few	Oligarchy
Polity	Rule of the majority	Democracy

Table 5.1

they pertained to value judgements and perfective standards, and prescriptive in that they asserted the means of achieving desired social goals. Plato and Aristotle compared and described governments in order to discover their ideal form. Plato was primarily interested in studying the "ideal forms" of government. His typology was designed to prescribe the best form of government without necessarily referring to a real situation. Aristotle, in contrast, rejected Plato's forms and described forms of government that actually existed, while passing normative and prescriptive judgements on them. In the fifteenth century, Machiavelli saw advantages in the republican form of government and urged political expediency for princes to unify states. Later, Thomas Hobbes, in his *Leviathan*, recommended an absolute monarchy as the preferred form of government to contain the destructive tendencies of people in society. In contrast to Hobbes, John Locke concluded that the sovereign trust can safely reside in the people and is revocable from government if its leaders and institutions should become absolutist and arbitrary. Thus, his comparative choice strongly favoured a constitutional democracy, holding governments constantly responsible to popular scrutiny.

By the eighteenth century, theorists focussed on reforming political institutions rather than advancing hypothetical forms of government. Montesquieu compared monarchical and parliamentary institutions, advocating a separation of powers among the executive, legislative, and judicial branches of government. James Madison and others in the *Federalist Papers* incorporated this experimental model of government in the United States Constitution of 1787.

The comparative study of political institutions grew steadily during the nineteenth century. Theorists assumed that the British and American models of government were the best. Other countries were measured by comparison with these two models. In Europe, the political order seemed to stand still. For nineteenth-century students of comparative government, the empires were in their heaven: all was right with the world. But not for long.

One of the most renowned critics of traditional governmental systems in Europe was Karl Marx. For Marx, various types of government were the products of class struggle, where the dominant class came to control the political institutions by virtue of its economic strength. But Marx's influence as a political analyst was posthumous. With the exception of Latin America, the break-up of Europe's large empires* and the consequent explosion of new states and their governments was a twentieth-century phenomenon. Other critics of the traditional typologies identified with Marx's elitist assumptions about class and group power. Two Italians – Gaetano Mosca (1858–1941), the political theorist and politician, and Vilfredo Pareto (1848–1923) – seriously challenged the principle of majority rule in democratic governments and posited the hypothesis that small minorities control the reins of government.[3] From their viewpoint, the important analytical focus was not the formal processes of government institutions but the sociology of government, i.e., how is an elite recruited and over whom does it exercise its power?

Comparative Government in the Twentieth Century

The field of comparative government is based on the assumption that students of government can better understand how societies are ruled if they compare political cultures and institutions across national boundaries. Analysts learn by making comparisons, by distinguishing similarities and differences, by measuring performances, and by contrasting the succession and durability of political systems. Thus, we examine the broader contexts of modern governments as they appear in democratic, authoritarian, and totalitarian forms. The special qualities and features of each governmental system can be measured against the background of problems that are common to all governments. In the present world, all governments attempt to tackle many of the same problems but do so according to the narrower confines of each society's peculiar way of doing politics. Even though all governments are different they try to control the many by the few, giving them more in common with each other than with their own citizens. In taking a comparative perspective, we learn that governmental institutions are the products of those behavioural patterns by which people seek order and stability. No government can be understood without giving principal consideration to that fact.

Since the turn of the century, the comparative study of government has undergone many changes. The emergence of political science as an academic discipline influenced the nature and scope of political inquiry into the dynamics of government. Comparative studies were broadened to include the whole world, not just Western governments, and focussed on the gap between the rich and poor countries. The imprint of behaviouralism on political science shifted the concentration of study toward politically relevant social behaviour and the environmental process of government. Analysts began to construct a political sociology of government. David Truman advanced the proposition that governments were an outgrowth of group competition and interaction.[4] Truman's group theory encouraged political researchers to look behind the institutional facade of government to discover the social variables of political power. In emphasizing the sociological basis of government, group theorists had penetrated a vital area of political knowledge, laying the foundations for the more sophisticated concepts of political culture and political modernization.

The concept of political culture (a term invented by political scientists Gabriel Almond and Sidney Verba) opened new vistas for learning about the evolution of modern governments.[5] Political culture can be simply defined as the way citizens orient themselves to politics and government. Drawing heavily on the insights of psychology and sociology, political scientists were able to isolate the particular actions, attitudes, values, and skills that culturally determine the persistence and maintenance of certain types of governmental systems (table 5.2). They called attention to the fact that the cultural environments of governments differ in countries of different historical experience, even though their political systems are typed as democratic, authoritarian, or totalitarian. Almond and Verba found that if there is general popular acceptance and expectation of democracy, the government will probably administer democratic institutions. Similarly, if people have come to accept and expect authoritarian institutions, there will probably be repression and tyranny.

Citizen expectations of government performance

Qualities of	Democratic	Authoritarian	Totalitarian
durability	+	/	+
accountability	+	–	/
pol. competition	+	/	–
adaptability	+	–	–
civil order	+	X	X
legitimacy	+	/	+
human rights	+	–	–
rule of law	+	/	X
pol. violence	–	X	/

Legend
High + Relatively high X Relatively low / Low –

Source: Adapted from Roy Macridis, *Modern Political Systems* (Boston: Little, Brown & Co. 1986)

Table 5.2

A range of similarity may exist among political cultures that generate similar types of government even though the political institutions appear to be quite different. Canada and the United States are two similar political cultures that have produced markedly different democratic institutions. In many ways, Canadians are more like Americans than any other people one might select for comparison. Both countries span a continent with all of the diversity of territory, settlement, and development that this implies. Both are sociologically similar nation-states, settled by immigrants from abroad, with histories deeply rooted in Anglo-Saxon and European traditions. Many other national attributes that underscore their likeness would lead one to expect very similar systems of government. Yet Canadians borrowed heavily from the British system of parliamentary and cabinet government, whereas Americans chose a different path in 1787 and adopted a republican form of government with a novel presidential/congressional scheme.

Political scientist Allan Kornberg addressed himself to the comparison of political practices in Canada and the United States.[6] His analysis led him to the conclusion that while there are striking similarities in the political cultures and folkways of each country, divergent political practices can be explained as a result of differing responses to the form of democratic institutions. The institutions in both states, through the process of political socialization, instil certain expectations and behaviour patterns in their citizenry. Canada and the United States both achieve democracy, but through uniquely different institutional forms.

Classifying Today's Governments

For political scientists, the tasks of classifying governments is a challenging one. Clearly, the notion of political culture has been a valuable tool for understanding the similarities and differences among systems of government. Political culture sensitizes us to the distinctive character of each government as a particular type of political system. Its overall value has been to look beyond traditional labels to the patterns of belief and behaviour that shape and support each government. The basic message derived from the analysis of political culture has been that every government is different. This conclusion has made it difficult for political scientists to assemble typologies that can neatly classify governments into "either/or" categories. For example to say that Canada and Mexico are democracies is as much of an oversimplification as to say that the Soviet Union and Yugoslavia are totalitarian. The political cultures of these countries have constructed political systems of varying degrees of democracy and totalitarianism. Canadians enjoy more elections, more party competition, and a greater amount of government accountability than do Mexicans. Similarly, the relative openness of Titoist* political philosophy endures in Yugoslavia and predates the appearance of *glasnost'** and *perestroika** in the Soviet Union. Some governments are more democratic than others, just as some are more coercive than others.

Instead of thinking of governments in a compartmentalized fashion, we should consider a continuum of governments running from democracy to totalitarianism, as represented in

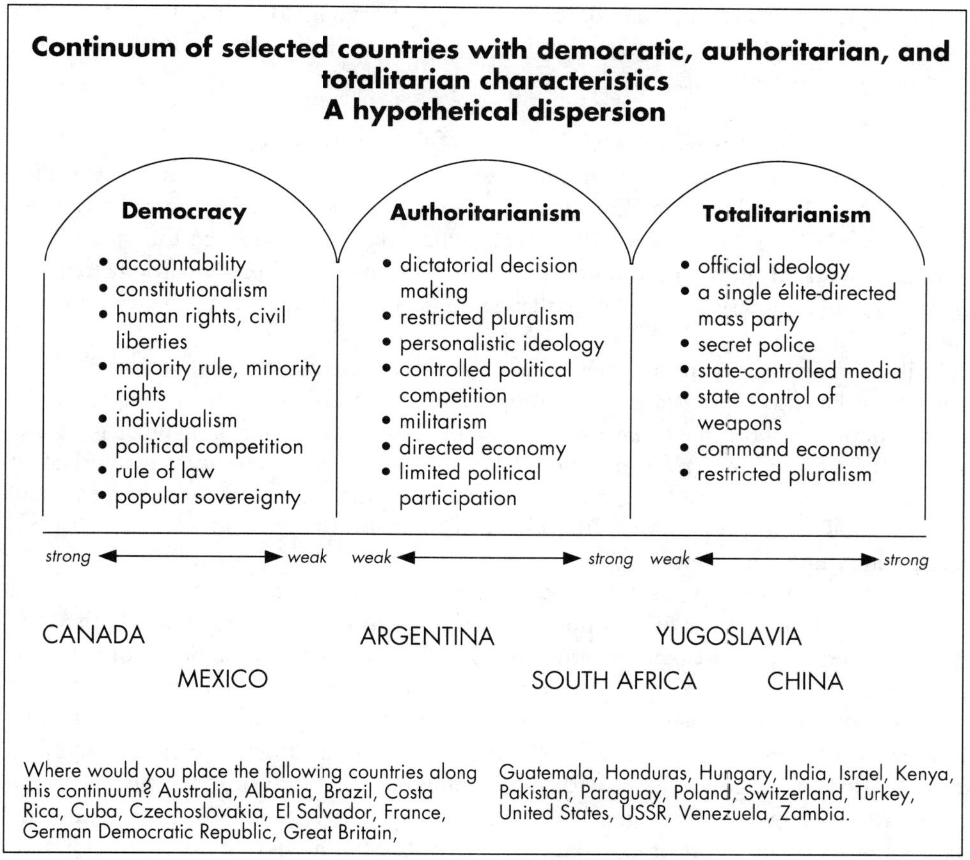

Figure 5.1

figure 5.1. All governmental and state systems are potentially transitional. The most spectacular transitions have unfolded in Eastern Europe, especially in Hungary, Poland, the German Democratic Republic and Czechoslovakia, where democratization has altered the institutional structures of these political systems beyond recognition. The continuum is analytically more sophisticated than a typology because it permits the analyst to distribute governments according to a range of perceived criteria detected in the political culture. Thus, if due process of law or party competitiveness are found to be stronger in one democratic state than in another, the former would appear closer to the generic type. Each observer may choose to scatter states along the continuum somewhat differently. But the figure presented here will serve to magnify the variations within and between forms of government.

The improper identification of governments is a common occurrence in the media, as well as among those who conduct national or international affairs. In a world of 175 states, it is not surprising that significantly different ways of governing do exist. It is important for us to realize that although it is possible to classify governments under general categories, every political system is unique.

Democratic Forms of Government

The word *democracy* comes to us from the Greek *democratia*: *demos* for people and *kratia* for government. Throughout the history of governments, democracies were not always viewed in such high regard. Even the Greeks who invented it believed that democracy could only work in small communities where all citizens could directly participate in the making of public decisions. They feared that democracies would eventually degenerate into unrestrained mob rule.

Until the nineteenth century, there was continuing mistrust in the ability of ordinary people to make rational decisions about complex social matters. In fact, the Athenian model of direct democracy has been a rare occurrence in history (the Athenian general assembly, the North American town meeting, and the Israeli kibbutz). In recent times an ambivalent Winston Churchill said that "democracy is the worst form of government ... except for all the others." This remark captures the mixed feelings prevalent about democracy even among renowned democrats.

Despite widespread scepticism, democracy is what Bernard Crick describes as "the most promiscuous word in the world of public affairs."[7] Even Libya's Khadafy has applied the term in a rather unique adaptation to his country: "Democracy – it has been construed to be a Greek word, but originally it is an Arabic word from two parts – *demo*, which in Arabic means the continuation, and *cracy*, the chair. And, therefore, the continuation of the people on the chairs of power is democracy."[8] Almost every state in the international system claims a democratic form of government with all the trappings: a constitution, elections, and the appearance of popular sovereignty. Yet we actually live in a sea of non-democratic governments. Canada is one of approximately thirty-five countries that closely corresponds to the modern qualities of a liberal democratic system in the 1990s; three-fifths of humankind live under some form of dictatorship, in either authoritarian or totalitarian regimes.[9] Because only a minority of the world's states host credible liberal democratic systems, it is necessary to examine the basic characteristics of this form of government. All democratic systems exhibit the following attributes, although the institutions and procedures for their implementation tend to vary in each state:

- *accountability* of all public officials directly and indirectly by constitutional limitations, fair elections, and public opinion;
- *constitutionalism*, whereby the scope of government authority is limited in a written or unwritten constitution that can be tested in an independent judiciary;
- *human rights* and *civil liberties* protected by a constitution or government legislation to guarantee freedoms and safeguards against the arbitrary abuse of legitimate power;
- *a doctrine of individualism* that relegates government to the service and protection of each person, so that individuals can realize their full capabilities;

Basic institutions of Canadian government

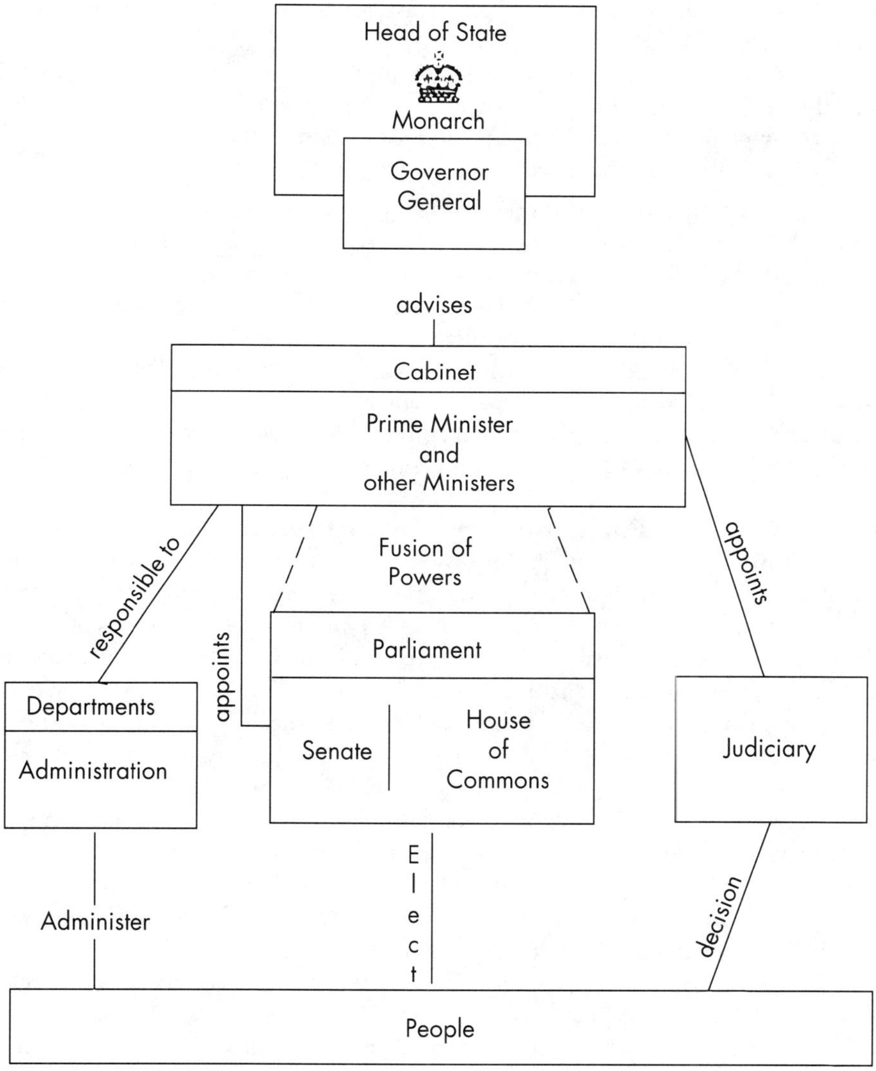

Figure 5.2

- *majority rule* and *minority rights* that govern the decision-making apparatus in the political system, permitting consensus to override dissent but giving the minority the right to challenge the majority;
- *political competition* flowing from the principle of pluralism* that allows individuals and groups to compete for political power;
- *popular sovereignty*, demonstrating the basic democratic principle that people directly or indirectly are the ultimate source of political authority; and
- *rule of law*, which proclaims the legal equality of all individuals and the supremacy of law over unlimited personal and bureaucratic power.

Two types of democratic government have evolved in the Western world and are prevalent today. One is the parliamentary form of government (also referred to as cabinet government), modelled after the British system. The other is the presidential form of government, modelled after the American system. Both are general political frameworks into which power, authority, and democratic values are allocated by different institutions. Some countries, such as France, Finland, and Portugal, combine some of the characteristics of a presidential system with those of a parliamentary system. In practice, the institutions that characterize democracies include an executive and legislative branch of government, an independent judiciary, a bureaucracy, and competitive political parties.

Parliamentary Government

Among the democratic countries, the most widely practised form of government is the parliamentary system, which places sovereignty (the legitimate right to govern) in parliament. A parliament is a legislative body usually comprised of two houses of assembly. The Canadian Parliament consists of the Queen and her Canadian representative, the House of Commons, and the Senate (as shown in figure 5.2). As well as in Canada, the parliamentary form of government appears in countries where monarchies have become constitutional democracies, e.g., some members of the Commonwealth and Scandinavia; but it also appears in other countries, such as France, Germany, and Italy.

The parliamentary executive comprises a *head of state* (monarch or president) and a *head of government*, usually called a prime minister (chancellor in the German Federal Republic), who is nominally selected and sworn into office by the head of state. The prime minister or head of government in turn chooses the cabinet, which is collectively responsible to parliament. The cabinet is the most visible and central executive committee of government in the whole parliamentary system. It guides, directs, and virtually drives the process of parliamentary government. In terms of policy and lawmaking, the cabinet is the government. The supremacy of parliament is premised on the assumption that a government should be formed from among members of parliament (MPs). The political executive is thus fused to the legislative branch of government that collectively embodies the sovereignty of the people. Unlike other forms of government, the executive in the parliamentary system is dependent for both its authority and tenure in office on maintaining the confidence of the parliament.

In Canada, the essential fusion of the executive and legislative branches of government is accompanied by the belief that Parliament is supreme. Canadian political culture dictates that sovereignty resides in Parliament; laws cannot be made or amended, taxes cannot be raised or monies borrowed unless formal parliamentary approval is granted.[10] But, in Canada as well as in some other parliamentary systems, the government has differentiated itself more and more from Parliament, placing itself in a strong position to control policy and legislation. Both the prime minister and the Cabinet, known collectively as the government, usually enjoy majority support in the House of Commons, the only popularly elected house in the Canadian Parliament. The continuous support of the majority party assures the legislative confidence of Parliament and is regularly demonstrated when the government submits its programs and policies for approval.

However, *majority governments* are not always elected. Occasionally *minority governments* are formed in the House of Commons and provincial legislatures. Such was the case in June 1979 when Prime Minister Joe Clark's new government captured 136 seats (6 short of a majority), becoming Canada's eighth minority government in 60 years. The defeat of the Clark government came after only six months in office on a non-confidence motion* that fatally attacked the Tory budget. Minority governments are vulnerable to the whims of partisan politics in the House of Commons. In these circumstances the Cabinet tends to be much more responsible to Parliament in order to maintain the necessary support to sustain the government. In the period from 1972 to 1974, a minority Trudeau government successfully wooed the New Democratic Party's support by making adjustments to its legislation and by being more consultative with the opposition.* At the provincial level, in 1988, Manitobans elected a minority Conservative government led by Gary Filmon. When he called his legislature into session, Filmon had some difficulty producing legislation that won both the support of his twenty rurally based right-wing members in the Conservative caucus and the powerful Liberal opposition led by Sharon Carstairs.

Because majority governments have so much control over the direction and passage of legislation, the continuing supremacy of parliament falls squarely on the shoulders of the opposition.[11] Given the desired tendency of the Canadian parliamentary system to develop strong executive authority based on a cohesive party majority, it follows that the opposition has a crucial role to play in the democratic process. The role of the opposition is to criticize government proposals, its behaviour, and the administration of its policies.

On rare occasions Canadian legislatures have produced no opposition. In the election of 1987, a rejuvenated Liberal party in New Brunswick, led by Frank McKenna, won all the fifty-eight seats in the provincial legislature – an electoral accomplishment seen only once before in Canadian history, when in 1935, the Liberals of Prince Edward Island took all thirty seats under Premier Wallace Lea. Single-party legislatures challenge the assumptions of parliamentary democracy, which rest upon the presence of an elected opposition to provide legitimate checks on the actions of government. When this occurs the role of the opposition can fall upon backbenchers who may use legislative rules and procedures to critically question ministers. In addition, many expect the media to play a key role in scrutinizing government initiatives as an extra-legislative opposition. Some rely on the vigorous opposition of defeated parties and interest groups outside the legislature to raise the dust generally and to keep a close watch on government business. In the final analysis, however, only an opposition present in the legislature can effectively represent the interests of those who did not vote for the government.

Inside legislatures, opposition parties tailgate governments by forming a shadow cabinet*. In 1988 John Turner assigned one critic for each of the thirty-nine ministers in the Mulroney Cabinet. The shadow cabinet is expected to recommend new policies or changes to existing policies, as well as to work vigorously to criticize the government.

Many of the strengths and weaknesses of the parliamentary system are determined by the quality of the opposition. An obstructionist opposition prevents the government from getting on with the business of running the country in an efficient way, thus interfering with the spirit of parliamentarianism. Sometimes, in the collective mind of the opposition, delaying the passage of a bill* is a patriotic act. Such were the sentiments of the opposition Conservative members of Parliament in March 1982 who walked out of the House of Commons, allowing the division* bells to ring for two weeks and forcing a government compromise on the energy security bill. On rare occasions, opposition parties find themselves in complete agreement with the government, allowing a piece of legislation to pass without a whimper. In October 1987, a bill to increase legislative salaries and pay raises to MPs for extra duties whizzed through the House with the blessings of all three parties.

In Canada, the rules and procedures of the House of Commons[12] permit the opposition to "oppose" the government by the technique of filibuster* or endless debate, where every member of the opposition speaks as long as the rules allow during each stage of the debate. Such a strategy can effectively delay, if not bury, the passage of government legislation. The opposition frequently uses the threat of filibuster to gain concessions from the government on the content of legislation before the House. The rules give the government an ace in the hand by providing for closure*, whereby the government, by means of the Speaker's ruling, limits the tenure of debate to not more than ten sitting days of Parliament. The Conservative government invoked closure three times after it introduced its free-trade legislation in December 1988. Since 1969, a change in the standing orders* of the House of Commons has substantially strengthened the ability of a government to control the length of debate. For example, Standing Order (SO) 75(c) allows the government to unilaterally limit debate at each stage in the passage of a bill. The severe competition for time in Parliament usually leads to deals between the government and the opposition parties. Hence, resorting to the extreme tactics of filibuster and closure by parliamentarians is rare because it tends to turn public opinion against the protagonist.

The basic tenet governing parliamentary practice is *accountability*: the ultimate responsibility of all public officials is to the people.[13] In the parliamentary mould, two competing principles are in a constant state of reconciliation. One is that the government does represent the majority of seats in the House of Commons and should design and implement policies in their interests. The other is that the opposition represents the concerns of those who do not identify with the elected majority and whose rights and interests should also be protected.

In the Canadian parliamentary system, accountability is facilitated by what Van Loon and Whittington call the "general audit function."[14] These are rules and procedures that allow members of Parliament to publicly scrutinize and criticize the government record. Party cohesion and discipline guarantee that most of the surveillance function of Parliament is conducted by opposition parties. But government backbenchers* may also avail themselves of the same procedures to question and criticize their government's performance. Sometimes backbenchers in a government with a large majority will publicly question and criticize the government's policies.

The process of general auditing is witnessed in a number of parliamentary debates and procedures. Standing Order 38(1) of the House of Commons requires a debate on the "Address in Reply to the Speech from the Throne"*. The Throne Speech Debate endures for eight days and usually elicits expressions of undaunted support from the government of the House to pessimistic appraisals of government intentions from the members of the opposition. The Throne Speech Debate gives backbenchers the opportunity to bring to public attention the most salient issues in their constituencies, as well as to criticize or applaud the government.

Another important general audit function of the Canadian Parliament is seen in the 25 supply days allocated to the opposition (5 days in the fall, 7 days before March 31, and 13 days before the end of June). These "opposition days" are intended to give members of Parliament time to criticize the spending policy of the government. The opposition chooses the topics for debate and their motions enjoy precedence over government business. Each speaker is recognized for twenty minutes during which time government business (ways and means) is discussed. The opposition always uses its allocated days to expose cases of wasteful government spending, mismanagement, and wrong-doing.

The most widely observed parliamentary debate is the Budget Debate. Parliamentary accountability is at its height, preceded, however, by another sacred tradition of British cabinet government – pre-budget secrecy. The budget is traditionally kept top secret until the finance minister reads the speech in the House of Commons in order to prevent anyone from profiting from inside knowledge. The premature release of information contained in a budget would pre-empt the privilege of Parliament as the only legitimate forum to hear firsthand the financial and monetary direction the country will take over a designated period of time. In 1989, the release of Finance Minister Michael Wilson's fifth budget was precipitated by an unprecedented leak, when details were broadcast on the Global television network one night before the budget was scheduled to be tabled in the House of Commons. According to the customs of parliamentary accountability a minister of finance should resign when there is a serious breach of budget secrecy. Wilson defied the tradition by clinging to his portfolio despite fierce opposition to his tenure. Normally, the country watches attentively as the minister of finance brings down the budget by tabling the government's ways and means motions. The Budget Debate begins with the minister's speech and lasts for six days, during which time members of Parliament speak to the ways and means proposals contained in the budget. The debate is an occasion for the opposition parties to raise issues of national significance, such as economic policy, unemployment, and tax policy.

Another important dimension of parliamentary accountability in Canada is the Question Period. Standing Order 39(5) sets aside forty minutes a day while the House is sitting for MPs to ask the government "questions on matters of urgency." Opposition members seize the opportunity to embarrass ministers by confronting them with intrusive questions about their actions, words, and policies. If not satisified with the minister's reply, a member will call for a supplementary question in order to clarify an evasive point in an answer. These televised exchanges are often quite humorous as members banter and heckle each other across the floor of the House.

Sometimes MPs simply require information from the government. Such questions are written and placed on the Order Paper*. The answers to both the written and oral questions are printed verbatim in *Hansard**.

As a final recourse for a member who feels a question was not fully answered, a member can serve notice that the matter will again be raised "on the adjournment" of the House. Questions raised on the adjournment are debated at the end of the daily sitting period when a member with a question can speak for seven minutes and other members have three minutes in which to make comments. These adjournment debates are yet another example of parliamentary accountability.

The parliamentary form of government has long been the object of careful study by history and political-science scholars such as Walter Bagehot and Sir Ivor Jennings.[15] Since World War II, a great amount of research has concentrated on the less formal elements of parliamentary government. It has investigated the legislative and executive behaviour within parliamentary institutions such as roll-call analysis, intraparty decision making, correlation of the background of legislators, and the role of interest groups on the parliamentary process. Much more can be learned by detailed analysis of the components of parliamentary systems. Especially important is an understanding of the factors of stability and the efficiency of parliamentary government. The main laboratories of modern-day research are the governments of Western Europe and the Commonwealth countries. But there is a need to develop hypotheses on the general applicability of parliamentary government to developing states.

Thus far, the evidence concerning the adaptability of parliamentary government in states outside the Western mould is not yet conclusive. Most of the new African and Asian states, once under British control, have tended to adopt the parliamentary form of government without the monarchy. The most successful application of this form of government by a non-Western state has been Japan, formerly an imperial power.

The rules of parliamentary government are difficult to apply even within nation-states that have traditions of democracy. For the newer states, the difficulty is maintaining a strong executive that remains responsible to a legislative body.

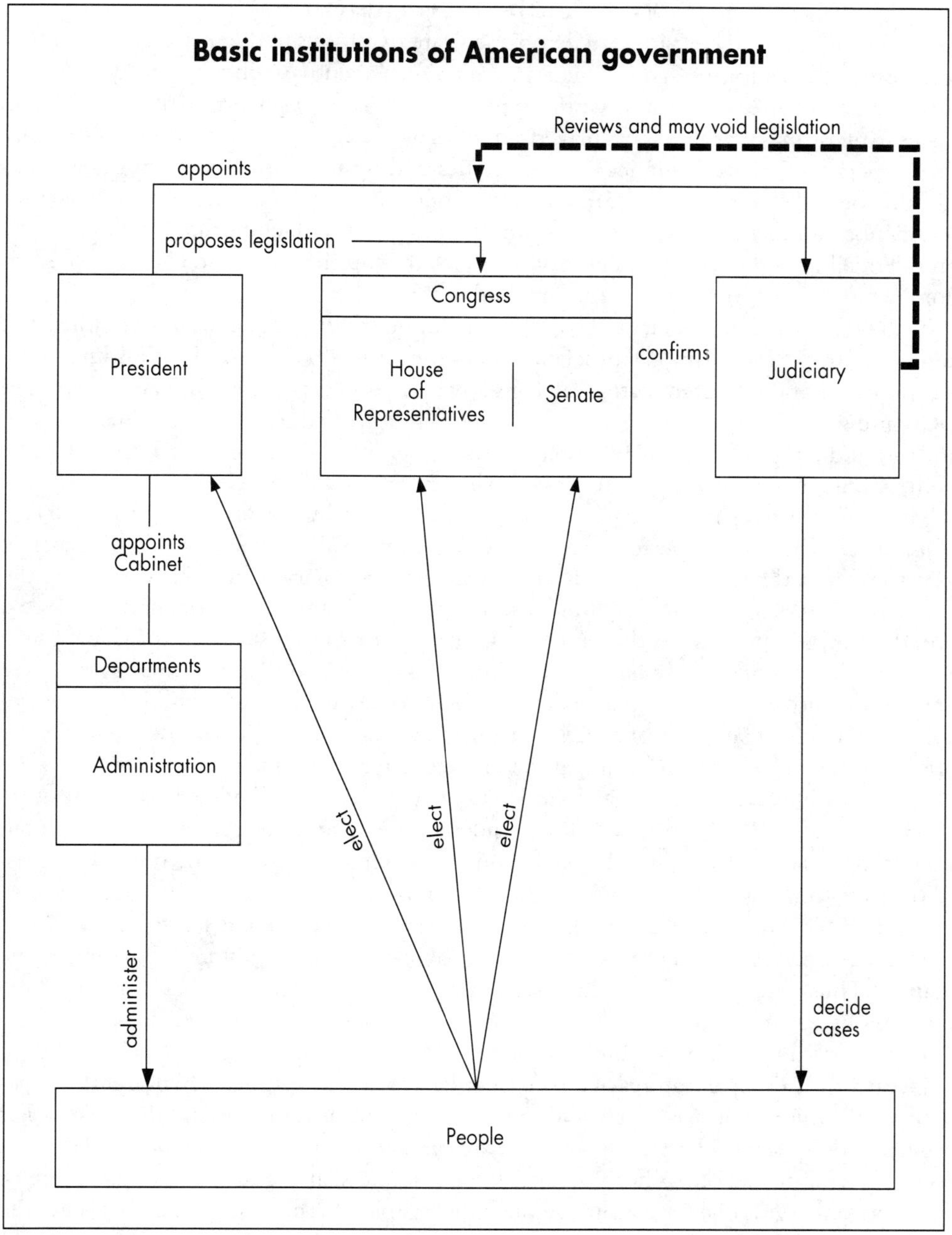
Basic institutions of American government
Reviews and may void legislation
appoints
proposes legislation
President
Congress
House of Representatives
Senate
confirms
Judiciary
appoints Cabinet
Departments
Administration
elect
elect
elect
administer
decide cases
People

Figure 5.3

Presidential Government

"Presidentialism" and "presidential democracy" are two terms frequently used by political scientists to label a form of government in which the executive is institutionally separated from the legislature. The oldest working presidential form of government is the United States. American government has played a model role for many political systems, especially those operating in Latin America where varieties of this model are more common than in Europe or Asia (see figure 5.3). However, fidelity to the constitutional dictates of presidential democracy is another question. In many states of Central and South America, presidentialism is the facade of authoritarian dictatorship. In these systems, the president dominates all institutions of government and is above the law.

In all presidential democracies, however, the unique feature of government is the strict adherence to the constitutional proclamation of the *separation of powers*.[16] According to the Constitution of the United States, "all legislative powers herein granted shall be vested in a Congress" (article 1), "the executive Power shall be vested in a President" (article 11), and the "judicial power ... shall be vested in one Supreme Court, and in such inferior Courts as the Congress may from time to time ordain and establish" (article 111).

The principle of separation of powers has two functional dimensions. First is the *separation of personnel*, whereby no person may hold office in more than one of three branches of government at the same time. Thus, unlike the parliamentary form of government, the executive cannot simultaneously hold a seat in the legislature. If a U.S. senator is elected president or is appointed to the Supreme Court, he or she must resign the Senate seat. Second is the system of *checks and balances*. Under this system, powers are shared by the three branches of government so that no one branch comes to dominate the governmental apparatus. In effect, all three branches share executive power. The executive power of the president to veto* a bill by returning it to Congress can be overridden by a two-thirds vote in the House of Representatives and the Senate. Article 1, section 7 of the U.S. Constitution also provides for a "pocket veto"*. If a president neither signs nor vetoes a bill within ten days of its passage by Congress, the bill becomes law without his signature unless Congress adjourns within ten days. President Franklin D. Roosevelt holds the record for the most vetoes (625) of which 263 were pocket vetoes and 9 were overridden. The Supreme Court can declare an Act of Congress unconstitutional and block the actions of the executive branch. Thus, executing, lawmaking, and judging are divided and shared by all three branches of government.

To understand the distinguishing characteristics of presidential democracy it is necessary to identify the principal features of the presidential type of government. In political systems such as the United States, Mexico, and Venezuela, the president represents the majesty and pageantry of the state. The president is both the *ceremonial* as well as the *political* head of state. As the ceremonial or titular head of state, the president is analogous to a monarch. He or she is the only symbolic representative of all the people. As the political head of state, the president heads the government and is responsible for supervising the national bureaucracy, executing legislative decisions, and enforcing court orders.

In presidential systems, the constitution specifies a fixed term for the president, who is usually directly elected. In the United States, as a matter of form, the president is indirectly elected by an electoral college. But, in fact, the election of the president is the result of a popular vote, and most voters so perceive it. In France, the president is directly elected for a seven-year term and is eligible for a second term. In the U.S., the fixed term of an independently elected executive means that the president cannot dissolve the legislature and call a general election as in the parliamentary system of government. But in France, where the constitution is both presidential and parliamentary, the president can dissolve the legislature at any time and call for an election. The U.S. president cannot be removed from office during the fixed four-year term except through the legal process of impeachment*. In France, no impeachment procedures exist but the president can be tried by a special tribunal for acts of treason or for acts contrary to the Criminal Code.

The presidential form of government seems to focus primarily on the executive branch. But, in actual fact, it is a multi–dimensional form of government based on balancing the competitive forces among executive, legislative, and judicial institutions. Under this arrangement, the executive institutions carry out the decisions of the two other branches of government; the legislative institutions deliberate and decide on making general laws; and the judicial institutions apply these laws to particular cases.

In the presidential system, the general audit function is a product of political competition among institutions. The elaborate machinery of lawmaking is meant to ensure that laws are formulated carefully and that the bulk of the population – as well as major interest groups – perceive the laws passed as legitimate.

Authoritarian Government

Authoritarian regimes are familiar phenomena to political scientists. The genesis of authoritarianism and its many similarities to totalitarianism are well known, but as we shall see, the two systems of government are quite different from each other.[17] Today, most of the states of the world are governed by authoritarian regimes. Depending on which conceptual boundaries are applied the numbers vary, but approximately 125 states may be typed as authoritarian, 10 as totalitarian, and 40 as democratic. Democratization in East Europe and elsewhere will alter the dispersion of these classifications.

Authoritarianism, sometimes referred to as corporatism*, is a system of government principally characterized by autocratic* decision making, restricted pluralism, and limited public participation.[18] Just as democracy is an outgrowth of a cluster of cultural determinants that leads to a pluralistic, politically competitive and open polity, so is authoritarianism a product of unique historical variants within a political culture. The non–democratic cultural tradition in authoritarian states allows new autocratic regimes to exploit a pattern already well established. That pattern reveals itself historically as a tendency to concentrate all political power in the hands of a few, to distrust democratic institutions, and to regard political succession* as a violent and unstable event.

Four types of authoritarian governments manifest themselves in the international system. *Tyrannies* are governments dominated by an absolute civilian or military rulership that arbitrarily exercises political power in a highly repressive and often personalistic* fashion.

Governments in contemporary South Africa, El Salvador, and Uganda are some examples. *Dynastic regimes* are monarchies wherein members of the royal family exercise absolute political powers ascribed by religious law, custom, and inheritance. Examples of these are Saudi Arabia, the Gulf Emirates, and the Sultanate of Brunei. *Military regimes* are governments in which the executive, legislative, judicial, and administrative institutions are controlled by members of the armed forces. A multitude of African examples exist in states such as Chad, Guinea, and Burkina Faso. *Single-party regimes* are governments instituted with the support of only one political party that dominates the electoral system exclusively. States such as Egypt, Kenya, Iraq, Syria, and Tanzania provide examples of this type of regime. The chief characteristics of the authoritarian type of government are:

- Political leadership tends to be elitist, personalistic, and sometimes charismatic. Political power is personalized rather than institutionalized, resulting in subjective decision making, rather than a government of procedural institutions and laws. Personalism is an effective means for attracting mass support and centralizing government power. People are encouraged to identify with the leader rather than institutions or the ideals of a formal governmental system.
- There is usually an absence of an official, undisputed ideology that prescribes a national or international mission for the government. If an ideology exists, it is superficial and is frequently sacrificed for pragmatic considerations.
- A plurality of interest groups may exist by permission or tolerance but they are licensed or closely monitored by the government. If they support the regime their activities go unhindered, but if they oppose the government they are usually harassed or repressed.
- The political-party system may appear to be competitive but is always dominated by one political party: the government party. Opposition-party competition is usually legal, provided it remains weak and devided.
- A constitutional façade based on liberal democratic norms masks authoritarian operating structures. Authoritarian regimes practise a type of legalism that embraces law and regulation but its purpose is to control people, not to limit government.
- The economy is "directed" to the problem of securing economic development and modernization. But authoritarian governments generally do not attempt to control every aspect of human economic activity. Free enterprise, free markets, and other components of laissez-faire principles are permitted in the economy.
- Authoritarian regimes usually have a strong military component that from time to time intervenes in the political process. The presence of the military in an authoritarian state ranges from holding a veto over the actions of a civilian government to direct intervention in the political process to instituting a military regime.
- The government limits and controls popular participation in the system. Political mobilization is encouraged by the government only for support of its economic and political policies. Contemporary authoritarian systems, particularly one-party dominant states, permit the symbolic involvement of citizens through elections, referendums, and plebiscites.

Civilian Authoritarian Regimes

To a greater or lesser degree, all authoritarian governments are dictatorial. Dictatorship may manifest itself in a number of different civilian and military forms. *Caesarism* is the kind of dictatorship in which the leader enjoys absolute power by virtue of control over the military. The military is the coercive arm of the civilian dictator.[19] It can be summoned to neutralize political enemies, as well as to repress dissidents in the population. Thus, most civilian dictators court the loyalty of the military by catering to its materialistic needs, such as regular pay raises, fringe benefits, overseas travel, and access to state-of-the-art equipment and hardware.

The Caesaristic dictator often has the support of the masses, a modern political machine, and a program combining personal charisma with a socio-economic plan of action for modernization. Many people regard the dictator as the only salvation for the country.

Caudillismo – from the Spanish word *caudillo,* meaning man on horseback – is a type of dictatorship that has been a principal feature of Latin American politics since the nineteenth century. The strongarm style of rule is based on the force of personality (*personalismo*) of the *caudillo*, not on an ideology as a program of action. The *caudillo* comes to power on the back of a personal mystique, using charm and effective oratory to capture the support of the people. By appealing to the forces of nationalism and high ideals, the *caudillo* gains mass appeal.

However, behind this popular façade is almost always a repressive dictatorship that uses the loyalty and physical power of the military to maximize personal gain and effectively control opposition. Political rights and liberties are often suspended: restrictions are placed on the activities of political parties and interest groups; and newspapers are monitored or bridled. Elections become an event of the past or the future and the authority of the judiciary is curtailed. Whatever opposition exists is kept weak so as not to seriously challenge the political strengths of the *caudillo*. Some of the most infamous Latin American dictators who have led authoritarian regimes in the twentieth century have been Anastasio Somoza and his son Anastasio Somoza Debrayle in Nicaragua, François Duvalier and his son Jean-Claude Duvalier in Haiti, and Raphael Trujillo in the Dominican Republic.

Military Government

Militarism – the intrusion of the armed forces into the political life of a country – is a salient feature of authoritarian governments all over the world. Since 1945, over two-thirds of the states of Africa, Asia, the Middle East, and Latin America have experienced varying degrees of military government.[20] Cycles of military intervention alternating with civilian rule are a typical pattern within authoritarian states. After Jean-Claude Duvalier fled to France in 1987, Haiti was ruled by General Henri Namphy until the elections in November of that year saw Leslie Manigat, a lawyer, assume the presidency. Not long after, Namphy returned to power in a coup that generated violence throughout the country. On September 18, 1988, only four months after a military coup had toppled a civilian president, Brigadier General Prosper Avril came to power by yet another coup, soon after to be threatened by attempted coups against his regime.

Usually, during periods of political and economic crisis, the armed forces are likely to step in. In many cases, any circumstance that threatens the status quo is enough to bring the military running from the barracks. In the post-war period, the armed forces in Latin American countries are inclined to attribute their political intrusions to the threat of communism. But often the rationale for military intervention is civilian corruption or government mismanagement. One reason that is openly admitted to by military officers is adventurism. Soldiers have guns, tanks, and planes – the most persuasive tools for acquiring the ultimate power of the state. Such was the case in 1989 when Paraguayan General Alfredo Stroessner gave up power the same way he got it – in a *cuartelazo**. Stroessner's hostile successor, General Andres Rodríguez, promised to expunge rampant government corruption, and to place Paraguay on a course toward democracy. Stroessner, who had ruled Paraguay for thirty-four years, used a blend of military force, political patronage, self-discipline, and terror to stabilize a state that before him had endured twenty-two presidents in thirty-one years.

By definition, military regimes are those in which the armed forces have seized power by a *cuartelazo* or a coup d'état* and have taken command of the highest positions of government. A military council or *junta* is usually formed to control all executive and legislative functions. Many military governments create mixed military/civilian executives to enhance the legitimacy of the regime. Civilians are almost always included in the cabinet and high bureaucratic positions as advisers in the formation of government policies. But their presence and influence is largely at the sufferance of the military governors.

From the beginning of their tenure in power, the military portrays itself as a group of responsible and patriotic officers who are temporarily forced to take the reins of government away from incompetent civilians or a previously inept military regime.[21] Ostensibly, their goals include altering the system of government to rid it of excessive, corrupt, and inefficient partisan politics. Often, intrusive actions are taken to protect a corrupt military leader, such as Panama's president General Manuel Antonio Noriega, who was indicted in Florida on drug-smuggling and money-laundering charges. The 15 000-member Panamanian Defence Forces annulled the elections held in May 1989 when results showed that the opposition had won.

Initially, the military is concerned with economic problems it claims resulted from civilian rule: high inflation and unemployment, wasteful government spending, and balance-of-payments deficits. Viewing itself as an "iron surgeon," it often employs drastic economic measures to correct the malaise in the economy. It restricts the supply of money to address inflation and invites foreign investment to reduce unemployment. Cutbacks in social security, medical, and education programs are implemented to reduce public spending. But progressive measures to redistribute wealth and institute land reforms are usually avoided in the military's strategy to reconstruct the economy. The basic contours of the social system are preserved or only mildly altered. Military governments will usually eliminate or extensively limit the political rights of the civilian population. Some political parties, newspapers, and trade unions are permitted to operate under the close scrutiny of government authorities. Almost always, the existing leadership of political organizations and labour unions are purged and replaced by people acceptable to the regime.

The immediate reasons for limiting political competition and muzzling the media are quite apparent. The military takes power to prevent certain changes. It will not provide former rulers and their supporters with the means to challenge them. Because the justification for taking power was to prevent civilian performance failures, the military is determined to neutralize the power potential of those responsible for these failures.

If the significance of a particular form of government depends upon the frequency with which it occurs, then the study of military government is paramount. Given the frequency of military interventions in Western as well as non-Western systems, military governments must be viewed as a global political phenomenon.[22] Since 1945, only Costa Rica and Mexico among the twenty Latin American republics have institutionally neutralized the threat of military intervention. Between 1945 and 1990, close to 60 percent of all Latin American presidents have been military men. During the same period in nine of the eighteen Asian states, military officers carried out successful coups against established governments. By 1990, nearly two-thirds of the Middle Eastern and North African states had experienced at least one attempt by the military to seize political power. Algeria, Egypt, Iraq, Libya, the Sudan, and Syria were particularly affected. In the brief independence period of tropical Africa since the 1960s, over half the civilian governments have been overthrown – in Congo, the Central African Republic, Dahomey (now Benin), Ghana, Nigeria, Togo, Uganda, and Upper Volta (now Burkina Faso).

Research confirms that the most likely aftermath of military government is military government. As states spend more of their GNPs each year on militarization, the greater will be the frequency of military intervention in politics.

Totalitarian Dictatorship

Totalitarianism is a uniquely novel product of the twentieth century, quite distinct from modern authoritarianism and far removed from the autocracies of the past. Under authoritarian dictatorship, average citizens retain a great degree of control over their private lives and usually are not cognizant of the all-pervasive influence of government in society. In contrast, the essential trait of totalitarianism is its claim upon every aspect of a citizen's life to the service of national goals as determined and interpreted by the rulers. In the totalitarian state, the regime's presence is "totalistic" in that no realm of private and social life is completely immune from its control.[23]

The recent emergence of totalitarianism (since World War I) is attributable to breakthroughs in mass-communication technologies as well as in techniques of social control and manipulation discovered from experimental research in social psychology. By means of these devices, totalitarian states are characterized by a system of government in which one party enjoys a monopoly of political, economic, judicial, and military power. The party has the capacity to penetrate all levels of society, to determine its values, and to direct the lives of individuals towards the achievement of its prescribed ideology.

George Orwell alarmed the democratic world with his nightmarish novel *1984,* an icy satire of life under totalitarian government. Orwell's vision of totalitarian government portrayed a society with the political and technological capacity to remould and transform people according to an official plan. With modern electronic devices the government spies on its citizens: television cameras scan the streets; listening devices monitor private conversations; even private thoughts and actions are known to the state. Watched by an ever-present "Big Brother," people are completely controlled by the government. They are subjected to constant censorship and surveillance and indoctrinated in daily "two-minute hate" sessions, directed against a phantom enemy with whom they are endlessly at war. In the end, the hero becomes a mindless robot, believing everything the government tells him to believe, fearing what he is told to fear, and hating what he is told to hate.

In hindsight, Orwell's novel was a projected exaggeration of the most menacing and horrific features of totalitarianism. But all totalitarian governments have the institutional and technological capacity to achieve the most repressive forms of social control. In the Soviet Union, the KGB (Committee of State Security) with its half-million members has ensured the compliance of Soviet citizens by means of torture, harassment, and fear. Often, recalcitrant citizens have been subjected to threats, molestations, questioning, searches, eviction, firing, and imprisonment.[24] And, in Cuba, the 6000 Committees for the Defence of the Revolution (CDRs) keep close watch on the social and political behaviour of Cubans.

One of the most comprehensive analyses of totalitarianism was conducted by Carl Friedrich and Zbigniew Brzezinski.[25] They identify six essential characteristics of this twentieth-century phenomenon:

- An official undisputed ideology that encompasses all aspects of human life: history, the economy, and all social and political institutions, as well as one that prescribes an international mission of global conversion or domination.
- A single, elite-directed mass party, led by a dictator and a core of militants dedicated to realizing the goals of the ideology. Recruitment of party membership is controlled, usually about 15 percent of the population. The organization of the party is linked to the formal institutions of government and touches every level of society.
- A secret-police apparatus that uses modern communications technology and psychological methods to ensure mass allegiance to party ideology.
- The monopolized control of the mass media in order to indoctrinate the masses in the official ideology. The media function as organs of mass propaganda to educate citizens about the goals of the state.
- The monopoly of weapons' control to prevent the possible armed resistance of dissidents.
- A centrally controlled "command economy" in which most means of production and consumption are owned and planned by the state according to ideological prescriptions.

The Soviet Union may be departing from the traditional expressions of totalitarianism explicit in the analysis of Friedrich and Brzezinski. In Poland, the election of Solidarity's

Tadeusz Mazowiecki as prime minister in 1989 marked the first time an East Bloc nation-state formed a non-communist government in over forty years. Likewise in Hungary, forces of political reform succeeded in generating a multiparty system to challenge the one-party dominance of the Communist party.

The reversal of the totalitarian rule that has prevailed in Eastern Europe for nearly half a century could actually facilitate the rebirth of socialism in a new democratic form: more enlightened, efficient, and accountable. But such tumultuous change inevitably brings uncertainty. As totalitarianism continues to fade toward the end of the century, whatever fills the vacuum remains to be seen. Much depends on the responses of the democratic states of the West.

Mikhail Gorbachev's call for *glasnost'* (openness, as in public airing and public disclosure), *demokratizatsiya** (democratization), and *perestroika* (restructuring) reflect the "new political thinking" pervading Soviet officialdom.[26] The inclusion of these concepts within the ideological framework of the Communist party and governmental system is not meant to replace socialism with a Western-style democracy; but, rather, to modernize and revitalize socialism so as to reverse the forces of economic stagnation that stultify the achievements of communism.

Perestroika, as a new stage in Marxist socialism, means structural changes to the governmental apparatus of the Soviet Union. It involves streamlining the government and military bureaucracies, distancing the judiciary from politics, recruiting reform-minded citizens into the party leadership, and even permitting multi-party competition. It means removing restrictions on small-scale free enterprise and infusing the profit principal in the 48 000 state-owned enterprises operating in the country. Many Soviet industries have moved toward Gorbachev's goal of *khozraschot* – self-financing and self-management.

Glasnost' has encouraged the Soviet media and intelligentia to communicate more freely on historical and contemporary issues, allowing open criticism of past leaders and loosening the censorship of fault-finding journalism.

Demokratizatsiya introduced more open political competition within the CPSU (as well as in other East European communist parties) and gives citizens the right of judicial appeal against certain decisions by Communist party officials. Popular referendums on regional and social issues facilitate greater public participation in government decisions. Parliamentary democracy, which permits political competition with the Communist party, is present in the Soviet Union where Gorbachev instituted a more powerful head of state, elected by secret ballot among a 2250 Congress of People's Deputies created to review annually constitutional, economic, and social questions. His later demands for political party competition supported these innovations.

The long-range effects of these new policies are difficult to predict. The Communist party is not easily transformed or reformed. An amorphous mass of party and governmental officials, civil servants and managers was firmly entrenched in the old hard-line ethos of the Soviet system. Stalin's legacy of centralized planning, collectivized agriculture, heavy industralization, and repressive governmental style produced a formidable and rigid social and political system. Under Soviet totalitarianism the state has ordered the people to be free. Only time will tell whether this is a revolution without change. In order to move along a continuum from totalitarianism to authoritarianism or democracy, the Soviet polity would have to de-emphasize ideology, permit a greater degree of social and political pluralism, provide greater religious freedoms, less press censorship, a wider spread of private enterprise, freer access to more foreign literature, greater artistic freedom, and permit much more emigration.

Two models of totalitarianism have appeared in the twentieth century: right-wing totalitarianism and left-wing totalitarianism. Italian Fascism and German National Socialism are the two generic examples of right-wing totalitarianism. But Fascism and Nazism were not uniquely Italian and German experiences.[27] Both were parts of an ideological movement that swept Europe in the period between the two world wars. Right-wing totalitarianism first appeared in Italy, where by 1922 Mussolini had gained complete control of the Chamber of Deputies. By 1933, in Germany, the National Socialists were the only legal party under the iron grip of Adolf Hitler. Germany and Italy aided Francisco Franco and his Falangist party in Spain and inspired Juan Perón in his successful quest for power in Argentina.

These totalitarian governments of the right reflected remarkable similarities with totalitarian communism. They had a high degree of centralized governmental decision making. A single party monitored, controlled, and infiltrated government at all levels with a prescribed ideological mission. The party was elitist and claimed to be the vanguard of the people. Leadership tended to be absolute, charismatic, and personalistic. The scope of secret-police actions was comprehensive, arbitrary, and unaccountable except only to the highest party leaders. Fascism proclaimed a romantic ideology of mythic consensus, homogeneity, and personal comfort in conforming to social roles. Human dignity was to be achieved by the integration of individuals into an all-encompassing corporate moral order, represented by the fascist state. But none of the fascist regimes revolutionized their societies; rather they built a powerful governmental apparatus for social control and expected individuals to glorify the goals of the state.

Totalitarianism of the left is the more revolutionary of the two models. In the Soviet Union, China, and Cuba, this form of government has fundamentally changed all levels of society so that previous social and political structures are no longer recognizable. Upon assuming power these governments take immediate action to collectivize almost every facet of private property and to bring it under state control. In agriculture, the land-tenure system is restructured into collective and state farms, permitting only a minimum amount of private ownership of land. In the Soviet Union, farmers are allowed to grow fruit and vegetables, on small private plots of land. Under Gorbachev's reforms collective farms are beginning to sell produce through their own outlets in competition with state stores. The current Soviet leader has applied the profit principle to agriculture, calling for a sharp increase in small-scale farming to supplement the inadequate output of the collective farms. Farmers may now lease land from large collective and state farms to increase production and prevent chronic food shortages. In Cuba, about 25 percent of the land is privately farmed because state management is impractical, but private growers are usually told what to grow and most of their produce is sold by state-managed food stores.

Non-democratic socialist states nationalize the means of production in their industrial and commercial sectors. This action has usually extended to individual entrepreneurs, artisans, street vendors, taxi drivers, and other small commercial services. But some governments are encouraging economic innovation by permitting the spread of private enterprise in these sectors. In the Soviet Union, the "individual labour law," passed in 1987, legalizes small-scale service businesses owned and operated by individuals or families. Owners of private automobiles are now allowed to use their cars as taxis during their time off from regular state jobs. Skilled workers, such as carpenters and plumbers, can legally take on private work. Today, in China, it is possible to purchase a computer or a modern sound system from private businesses all over the country.

In all societies that try to regulate almost everything, black economies* and black markets* (second economies) have come to play a large part in the economic structure of the country. Economies that are centrally planned by the government are not able to accommodate the natural everyday forces of supply and demand that inevitably accrue in all societies. Gorbachev articulated the problem at the 19th Communist Party Conference in 1988 when he called for the overhaul of Soviet market philosophy because of "the vicious circle of production for the sake of production and the plan for the sake of the plan." In the past many people have resorted to illegal sources to procure goods and services needed from day to day. Black-market capitalism grew naturally in all totalitarian socialist states at least in part because of the absence of privately motivated market mechanisms based on profit.

The absence of an official acceptance of the profit principle created far-reaching consequences for labour as well as for managers. Productivity has consequently remained low in comparison to the leading Western economies. Historically, unions remained under the control of the party, which placed pressures on workers to meet or exceed the targets of government planners.[28] The unions exercised the will of the party and the government and thus were unable to initiate reforms in a stagnant economic system. In carrying out the directives of the government and party, unions contributed to the litany of economic problems that includes shortages of food and consumer goods, and the overproduction of unwanted consumer products. Gorbachev's call for "new thinking" is an attempt to democratize productivity and to shift the role of government from control to responsiveness. Unlike his predecessors, he has assiduously courted the dictum that adaptability and change will stimulate the capability of the regime to generate reforms and to accommodate institutional and socio-economic changes.

This chapter has provided a survey of governmental regimes within the threefold typology of democratic, authoritarian, and totalitarian governments. The overall evaluation of the performance of any of these types of government requires us to ask whether they promote human dignity. To what extent is human well-being enhanced by the presence of the regime? Do people feel they can participate in the decisions of the system? Are the rights of individuals respected by the government and its officials? Does the government respond to the most necessary demands of its citizens? What about the functional performance of a government? How well does it manage the natural and human resources under its jurisdiction? Does it use its capacity to generate good for all of its citizens most of the time?

In the following chapters we will learn that governments are multi-dimensional, usually comprising four branches: the executive, legislative, bureaucratic, and judicial. Each can be compared as a separate part of a political system, and each must be understood as a constituent element of the whole polity.

REFERENCES

1. Karl W. Deutsch, Jorge Dominguez, and Hugh Heclo, *Comparative Government: Politics of Industrialized and Developing Nations* (Boston: Houghton Mifflin Co. 1981), 13.
2. Leslie Lipson, *The Democratic Civilization* (New York: Oxford University Press 1964), 19–45.
3. See James H. Meisel, *Pareto & Mosca* (Englewood Cliffs, NJ: Prentice Hall 1965), 57–62, and 141–60.
4. David Truman, *The Governmental Process* (New York: Knopf 1951); see also Jeffrey Berry, *The Interest Group Society* (Boston: Little, Brown & Co. 1984).
5. Gabriel Almond and Sydney Verba, *The Civic Culture Revisited* (Boston: Little, Brown & Co.1980).
6. Allan Kornberg "Caucus and Cohesion in Canadian Parliamentary Parties," *American Political Science Review* LX (March 1966): 83–92
7. Bernard Crick, *In Defence of Politics* (London: Weidenfeld & Nicolson 1964), 56.
8. See Patrick Watson and Benjamin Barber, *The Struggle for Democracy* (Toronto: Lester & Orpen Dennys Ltd. 1988), 79.
9. See Kenneth Janda, Jeffrey Berry, and Jerry Goldman, *The Challenge of Democracy* (Boston: Houghton Mifflin Co.1987), 55; Robert Wesson, ed., *Democracy World Survey 1987* (Boulder CO: Lynne Reinner Publishers 1988), 1– 9; Amos Perlmutter, *Modern Authoritarianism: A Comparative Institutional Analysis* (New Haven: Yale University Press 1981); Irving Howe, ed., *1984 Revisited: Totalitarianism in Our Century* (New York: Harper & Row 1983).
10. John H. Redekop, *Approaches to Canadian Politics* (Scarborough, ON: Prentice Hall Canada Inc. 1983), 151–2.
11. See Michael Atkinson, "Parliamentary Government in Canada," in Michael Whittington and Glen Williams, eds., *Canadian Politics in the 1980's* (Toronto: Metheun 1981), 260–73; see also A. Paul Pross, "Parliamentary Influence and the Diffusion of Power," *Canadian Journal of Political Science* 18 (June 1985): 235–66.
12. See Mark MacGuigan, "Parliamentary Reform: Impediments to an Enlarged Role for the Backbencher," *Legislative Studies Quarterly* (November 1978); House of Commons: Special Committee on Standing Orders and Procedures, *Third Report* (Ottawa: 1982); and John Stewart, *The House of Commons: Procedure and Reform* (Montreal: McGill-Queen's University Press 1977).
13. See Canadian Study of Parliament Group, "Seminar on Accountability to Parliament" (Ottawa: Queen's Printer, April 7, 1978).
14. Richard Van Loon and Michael Whittington, *The Canadian Political*

System: Environment, Structure, and Process (Toronto: McGraw-Hill Ryerson Ltd. 1981), 630–6.

15. See Norman St. John-Stevas, *Bagehot's Historical Essays* (New York: Doubleday & Company Inc. 1965); and Sir William Ivor Jennings, *The British Constitution* (Cambridge: Cambridge University Press 1950).
16. Gabriel Almond and Bingham Powell Jr., *Comparative Politics Today: A World View* (Glenview, II: Scott, Foresman & Co.1988), 50–65.
17. See Roy Macridis, *Contemporary Political Ideologies* (Glenview, II: Scott, Foresman & Co. 1988), 229–31.
18. See Roy Macridis, *Modern Political Regimes* (Boston: Little, Brown & Co. 1986), 125–259.
19. See Herbert Tillema and John Van Wigen, "Law and Power in Military Intervention" *International Studies Quarterly* 26 (June 1982): 220–50; and Berth Duner, *Military Intervention in Civil Wars: The 1970s* (Aldershot, Eng.: Gower 1985).
20. Eric Nordlinger, *Soldiers in Politics, Military Coups and Governments* (Englewood Cliffs, NJ: Prentice-Hall Inc. 1977), xi.
21. See Henry Bienen, ed., *The Military Intervenes: Case Studies in Political Development* (New York: Russell Sage Foundation 1968); see Milten Leitenburg, *Aspects of Military Intervention and the Projection of Military Power* (Frankfurt: Hessische Stiflung Für Friedens und Konfliktsforschung 1985).
22. Morris Javanovitz and Jacques van Doorn, eds., *On Military Intervention* (Rotterdam: Rotterdam University Press 1971), 306; and Sheldon Simon, ed., *The Military and Security in the Third World: Domestic and International Impacts* (Boulder, CO: Westview Press 1978), ch.1; and David Singer and Melvin Small, *Resort to Arms: International Civil Wars 1816–1980* (Beverly Hills, CA: Sage 1982).
23. See Hans Buckheim, *Totalitarian Rule* (Middletown, CT: Wesleyan University Press 1972); and Darrell Hammer, *The USSR: The Politics of Oligarchy*, 2nd ed. (Boulder, CO: Westview Press 1986).
24. Ladislav Bittman, *The KGB and Soviet Disinformation: An Insider's View* (New York: Pergamon-Brassey's 1985); Jeffrey T. Richelson, *Sword and Shield: The Soviet Intelligence and Security Apparatus* (Cambridge, MA: Ballinger 1986), ch. 7.
25. Carl J. Friedrich and Zbigniew Brzezinski, *Totalitarian Dictatorship and Autocracy* (New York: Praeger Publishers 1956), 9–10.
26. Mikhail Gorbachev, *Perestroika: New Thinking for Our Country and the World* (New York: Harper & Row Publishers 1987), 17–59.
27. Ernst Nolte, *Three Faces of Fascism* (New York: Holt, Rinehart and Winston Inc. 1966), 3–10.
28. See Jay B. Sorenson, *The Life and Death of Soviet Trade Unionism 1917–1928* (New York: Atherton Press 1969); Leonard Schapiro and Joseph Godson, eds., *The Soviet Worker: Illusions and Realities* (New York: St. Martin's Press 1981); Mervyn Matthews, *Poverty in the Soviet Union: The Lifestyles of the Underprivileged in Recent Years* (New York: Cambridge University Press 1986).

SUGGESTED READINGS

Karen Dawisha, *Eastern Europe, Gorbachev and Reform* (Cambridge: Cambridge University Press 1988).

Larry Diamond, Juan Linz, and Seymour Martin Lipset *Democracy in Developing Countries: Persistence, Failure, and Renewal* (Boulder, CO: Lynne Rienner Publishers 1989).

Anthony Jones, *Perestroika: Gorbachev's Social Revolution* (Boulder, CO: Westview Press 1989).

Everett Carl Ladd, *The American Polity*, 3rd ed. (New York: W.W. Norton & Co.1989).

A.F. Mullins Jr., *Born Arming: Development and Military Power in New States* (Stanford, CA.: Stanford University Press 1987).

G. A. O'Donnell, P.C. Schmitter, and L. Whitehead, *Transitions from Authoritarian Rule/ Prospects for Democracy* (Baltimore: Johns Hopkins University Press 1987), 4 vols.

David Roth, Paul Warwick, and David Paul, *Comparative Politics: Diverse States in an Interdependent World* (New York: Harper & Row, Publishers 1989).

Giovanni Sartori, *The Theory of Democracy Revisited* (Chatham, NJ: Chatham House Publishers 1987).

Joseph Vining, *The Authoritative and the Authoritarian* (Chicago: University of Chicago Press 1989).

Patrick Watson and Benjamin Barber, *The Struggle for Democracy* (Toronto: Lester & Orpen Dennys Ltd. 1988).

GLOSSARY

typology: The systematic classification and grouping of phenomena by class or type.

demagogue: A political leader who takes advantage of social and political unrest by making emotional and prejudiced appeals to the general population for political gain.

empire: Originally referred to territory governed by emperors but has fallen almost entirely into disuse, it now refers to large areas of land and peoples conquered and coerced by a foreign power.

Titoism: The socialism of Marshal Tito, who governed Yugoslavia from 1944-1981, and followed an independent domestic and foreign policy from other states in the Soviet bloc.

glasnost': Gorbachev's policy of open public airing and disclosure about public affairs in every aspect of Soviet life.

perestroika: The term covers the full range of institutional reforms advanced by the supporters of Mikhail Gorbachev that have and will effect the social, cultural, economic, and political life in the Soviet Union.

pluralism: The existence of diverse social forces, such as political parties, political-action groups, labour unions, social and religious groups, and service clubs.

non-confidence motion: When a legislative assembly passes a vote of non-confidence in government (ie., the cabinet), the prime minister and the cabinet must resign and request the dissolution of parliament.

opposition: Members of a Parliament who do not belong to the government party.

shadow cabinet: A group of opposition legislators specifically assigned to observe and criticize cabinet ministers.

bill: A proposal placed before an assembly that must pass through various stages of scrutiny before becoming law.

division: The process of voting in a legislative assembly, committee, or political convention.

filibuster: A time-consuming tactic used by legislators to prevent the passage of a proposed bill or amendment by taking as long as possible to delay a piece of legislation.

closure: A device used by the governing party to end debate in the House of Commons and to force a vote.

standing orders: Established rules and procedures of Parliament, each house having its own, which from time to time may be altered or suspended.

backbenchers: All of the members of the legislature in the British model of parliament who are not members of the cabinet or leaders of the opposition parties.

Speech from the Throne: The traditional opening ceremony for each session of Parliament that outlines the proposals of the prime minister and the Cabinet, and is read by the governor-general or the Queen.

Order Paper: The daily agenda for the House of Commons.

Hansard: A official record of the proceedings of the House of Commons and the Senate.

veto: The U.S. president may reject any bill or joint resolution passed by Congress, with the exception of proposed amendments to the U.S. Constitution.

pocket veto: The U.S. president may refuse to sign a bill passed by Congress within a ten-day period before adjournment.

impeachment: The power of the U.S. Congress to indict a president, or members of the cabinet and judiciary, by a single majority vote in the House of Representatives, followed by a trial in the Senate, where a two-thirds vote of members present can convict and remove the president from office.

corporatism: A principal form of contemporary right-wing government that attempts to organize society along non–conflicting functional lines, so that workers, peasants, the Church, business, and other institutions are directed to contribute to the goals of the state.

autocratic: The quality of absolute power invested in a single ruler who exercises authority without being accountable to any person or institution.

political succession: The designated constitutional or extra-constitutional methods used to fill vacated offices of government.

personalistic: A characteristic of governing whereby the personality of the ruler dominates the institutions, structures, and constitutional prescriptions in a political system.

cuartelazo: A barracks revolt, used to refer to a military coup d'état.

coup d'état: A sudden political or military action, frequently initiated by people possessing some authority, to overthrow an existing government by force.

demokratizatsiya: The process initiated by Mikhail Gorbachev that shifts decision making from the party to the people and groups of people.

black economy: Economic activity that is not recorded in the national income accounts, although it does involve the actual production of goods and services. It is carried out either by barter or for cash that is not declared as income for taxation purposes.

black market: An illegal market created when the demand for a commodity, which is controlled and rationed by the state, exceeds the legal supply such that people are willing to pay a much higher price than the controlled price to obtain greater amounts of the commodity.

6

Executives

Benazir Bhutto takes the oath of office following her election as Pakistan's prime minister

Resources Used by Executives

Of all the branches of government, the executive is the oldest and the most universal institution. Archaeological evidence in the Middle East indicates that the institution of kingship* was already well established over 5000 years ago.[1] From the very beginning of human experience with organized structures of government, the executive has been the focal point of political power and effective decision making. Even today, in the mind of the public, the executive is synonymous with government. Every political system has an executive in which leadership is concentrated in the hands of a single individual or a small elite group. Whether in democratic or non-democratic political systems, executive power is inevitable. In this modern world of few democracies and many autocracies*, executives have come to be the major and sometimes the sole actors in every organized system of government. This importance occurs because all political executives have access to a wide range of available political resources, usually inaccessible to other branches of government.[2]

Information

One important political resource available to executives is information. Because executives are primary decision makers, they are privy to classified information flowing from within the country, as well as internationally from other governments. For this reason, executives tend to know much more than either assemblies or judiciaries about what is going on in government. Executives can control, to a great extent, what other participants in government get to know because they generate considerable information themselves and can act in secrecy. In Canada, the Cabinet exercises extensive control of government information with the assistance of the Prime Minister's Office* (PMO), the Privy Council Office* (PCO), and the Treasury Board*. Sometimes called the "gatekeepers," these three bodies advise the prime minister and the Cabinet on the advisability and financial feasibility of pursuing a given policy.[3] All administrative and security information is filtered through these offices to the prime minister and the Cabinet. At this level information is carefully guarded; even backbenchers on the government side of the House must wait for access to information in secret caucus and remain silent according to the written and unwritten rules of party discipline.

In the United States, the president and his appointed cabinet draw and control vital information from four sources: the Executive Office of the President* (EOP), the National Security Council* (NSC), the Office of Management and Budget* (OMB), and the Council of Economic Advisors* (CEA).[4] The doctrine of executive privilege* allows a president to guard secrets in matters of national security, internal bureaucratic discipline, and individual privacy. Even executive decisions can be made within the bounds of secrecy and are accountable only through the works of congressional investigation, journalism, and judicial testimony.

In non-democratic states, executives enjoy a vast amount of information control. In communist states, the first secretary of the Central Committee of the Communist Party commands the flow and dissemination of political information thereby wielding extensive control over what the government knows and ultimately what the people know. In 1989 the Chinese government embarked upon a national propaganda campaign denying that anyone had been massacred in the uprising in Tiananmen Square. Until *glasnost'*, all Soviet newspapers were regulated by the party and its ubiquitous organs. *Pravda* (The Truth), the most important Soviet newspaper, is published by the Central Committee; *Izvestia* (The News) is an organ of the Soviet government. Lower-level newspapers depend on the Soviet central news agency TASS, which censors and edits information throughout the country in accordance with executive directives.[5]

In all states, executives are privy to the most vital secrets of state. They participate in the formation of policy, where information may be deliberately kept scarce. In many non-democratic states, executives acquire direct or indirect control of the communication facilities in the country and have the coercive powers to destroy all rival centres of information and communication. Usually, military intelligence* is the major clearing house for political information in a non-democratic state, although it may also be so in democratic states.

Organization

A second political resource readily available to the executive branch of government is organization. All executives are surrounded by some form of civil or military bureaucracy, as well as a political-party organization. In Canada, the prime minister and the Cabinet enjoy a virtual monopoly of power over the organization of government.[6] Canada's political executive has instant access to an army of bureaucratic expertise from which to draft and legislate policy. Not only do the PMO and PCO provide essential expertise for executive decision making, but the entire civil service is also at the disposal of the prime minister and the Cabinet. The political executive can draw from ministerial staffs, the party structure, and the government caucus to provide information and advice on policy initiatives.

In the United States, the White House staff is only a small part of the presidential establishment, but it links the president with the vast organizational machinery of American government.[7] Under the numerous agencies of the EOP, NSC, OMB, and CEA, over 3 million executive-branch employees serve the president. Every year those executive agencies bring forward their new proposals for legislation, both to improve the handling of existing programs and to innovate with new ones. Unlike the Canadian executive, which is fused to the legislative process and thus to the entire bureaucracy of government, the U.S. Congress is a genuinely independent body, with a separate bureaucracy of its own to serve it. Because the executive leadership and the legislative bureaucracy do not necessarily work in concert, there is always a tension between the president and the other organizations of government.

In autocratic states, executives have much more direct control over the various organizations of government. In the absence of a competitive and accountable political system, non-democratic executives have distinct organizational advantages over their democratic counterparts. In some East European political systems, the organizational structure of government is dominated by the highest echelons of the Communist party. The ministries and bureaucracies are implementing agencies, or simply function as legitimators* of policy after the decisions have already been reached by the executive.

Legitimacy

Another important political resource available to executives is legitimacy: the exercise of political authority in a way that is perceived as rightful and is accepted by the members of the political community. One test of legitimacy is the degree of coercion the executive must employ to achieve acceptance and obedience. The more coercion, the less legitimacy.

No executive can claim to rule on the basis of force alone, because that procedure will allow equal legitimacy to any dissenting groups or opposing movements. In democratic political systems, executives have legitimacy because they adhere to constitutional principles and follow standard procedures when establishing policy. Judgements about the wisdom or morality of a particular executive decision may vary, but legitimacy goes unquestioned. For example, in Canada the Cabinet's strategy for reducing the deficit may leave much to be desired, but most Canadians would still consider as legitimate the budgetary laws passed for dealing with these problems under the current rules. In the United States, President Ford's decision to pardon former president Nixon for any crimes committed while in office was generally accepted as the legitimate exercise of presidential power, even though most Americans disputed the wisdom, merit, and morality of Ford's action.

Even in dictatorial regimes, executive institutions are protected from the adverse consequences of unpopularity by the appearance of legitimacy. In these types of political systems, legitimacy attaches to executive institutions because people sense that they are firmly established and here to stay. The legitimacy of the executive is not based merely on coercion but also instilled quite early in the civilian population through the processes of political indoctrination* and socialization. Especially in totalitarian regimes, children from early years are taught to trust and respect political authority, often symbolized by executives. In these political cultures, authoritarian patterns of the family and schools serve to reinforce the legitimacy of the political executive as an institution.

In authoritarian regimes, dictatorial executives have decisive control over government but choose not to control a wide range of social and private behaviour. Thus, executive legitimacy is frequently based on personalism and popularity in the absence of an official ideology to legitimize executive power. Popular support is the predominant source of legitimacy in the modern authoritarian executive; without it even a monopoly of political violence will not prevent a change of power at the top. Legitimacy enables the authoritarian executive to play the largest and most important role in the exercise of political authority.[8] Not only does it permit the executive branch to dominate the process of executing rules, but it also allows the executive to exercise an ever-enlarging share in the process of rule making and rule adjudication, usually exercised by the legislature and judiciary.

Economic Power

Economic power is another major resource often favouring the executive branch of government. Because of their dominance in the structure of government, executives appropriate to themselves a vast share of the economic resources of their country. These resources are available to them through taxation and confiscation, but may also be derived from the profits of state enterprises. Other instruments of control, i.e., regulation and nationalization, are available to executives to obtain the financing of their policies or to eliminate the rival centres of economic power in the country.

In Canada, the political executive (the Cabinet) wields enormous economic power.[9] It is through the Cabinet that revenues are raised, finances managed, and policies planned and legislated within the confines of the budgetary process of government. The Financial Administration Act is the legislation that gives the Cabinet full control of the budgetary process. The Treasury Board, a statutory committee of Cabinet, oversees the economic power of the Canadian government. It advises the Priorities and Planning Committee of the Cabinet about the financial feasibility of government goals. The Department of Finance is the revenue-raising organ of the Canadian executive. Its authority extends over all aspects of the taxation system, and it co-ordinates its efforts with the Cabinet committees directly responsible for the making of public policy.

In the United States, the economic policy of the national government receives its most overt expression in the executive budget. Every year the president makes thousands of decisions to spend money on particular projects. Those include dams, environmental programs, urban-renewal projects, highways, airports, university facilities, and numerous other public works. Increasingly, presidential discretion has played a greater role in deciding where and when a particular project will be implemented. Different presidents have different attitudes about the extent to which political considerations should dictate decisions concerning federal expenditures. Nevertheless, even the most conservative administration will recognize that funding for some categories of projects can be allocated in accordance with political considerations favourable to the executive. Because members of the House of Representatives and the Senate are always eager to obtain federal projects for their constituents, the White House can use this executive economic power — which in some cases is at the sole discretion of the executive branch — to lure favourable votes in Congress.

In authoritarian states, the economic powers of the executive are often corrupted. It is not uncommon to find the highest public officials with their hands deep in the national till, taking public property including land, money, and lucrative concessions through criminal as well as legal activities. In Latin America, many dictators have taken advantage of their economic powers to amass great personal wealth.[10] The former president of Panama, General Manuel Antonio Noriega, received millions in kickbacks for the role he played in the illegal cocaine trade throughout the Western hemisphere. After his overthrow in 1955, Juan Perón of Argentina is believed to have taken an estimated US$700 million with which to live luxuriously in Spain. Both Fulgencio Batista of Cuba and Perez Jiménez of Venezuela personally accumulated US$250 million while in office. In Nicaragua, the Somozas came to control over one-fifth of the economy, amassing a family fortune approaching US$1 billion. No source of easy money was overlooked. Besides helping himself to a large proportion of funds in the national treasury, Anastasio Somoza Debayle extracted large-scale profits from the funds and supplies sent from abroad after the devastating earthquake of 1972.

Totalitarian executives exercise economic powers largely through party channels and the state apparatus. In most totalitarian socialist states, the single most-powerful individual is not a government official but rather the general secretary of the Communist party. Thus, the ideological priorities of the highest party officials determine the direction of economic planning and investment in the economy. In political systems such as these, the executive can mobilize the entire resources of the country to achieve its economic goals. These executives wield the decision-making capacity to improve the standard of living and the material well-being of their citizens. In almost every totalitarian state heavy industry and defence-related industries have had priority over light industry and consumer goods. But with the Gorbachev revolution in the Soviet Union a reduction of military expenditures and investments in heavy industry stimulated the production of goods and services in light industries and consumer goods.

Modern Executive Functions

Even though political styles and organizational structures differ remarkably across the international system, executive functions do lend themselves to generalization. In all cases executive behaviour is a product of the political culture; the roles and functions of modern executives are determined by the ways people think about and do politics.

Symbol and Ceremony

All the symbolism and ceremony in the executive branch of government is centred on the *head of state**. In Canada, the pomp and circumstance surrounding the formal delivery of the Speech from the Throne rivals the regal splendour of British imperial majesty. The appearance of the president of the United States before a joint session of Congress to deliver the State of the Union address has the magnificence of a Hollywood spectacular. The impressive array of Soviet officials standing elevated on Lenin's mausoleum, reviewing crowds of flag-waving citizens, projects the power and vibrance of the Soviet polity. In most countries there is a separation of personnel within the executive (see table 6.1).

There are a number of advantages to having the separation of the head of state and the chief executive.[11] For many states it is important to have some office (and the person who occupies it) independent of the deeply enmeshed political battles of government. The head of state transcends the brush-fires of partisan politics and can foster both unity and

Types of executives

Country	Head of State	Head of Government
Canada	Governor General	Prime Minister
France	President	President
Great Britain	Monarch	Prime Minister
United States	President	President
Soviet Union	President	President
Federal Republic of Germany	President	Chancellor

Table 6.1

continuity within the nation-state. In Canada and Great Britain, the reigning monarch or the official representative of the reigning monarch is the living symbol of the state and acts independently in the interests of the community as a whole. The head of state opens Parliament and attends public functions at which the majesty of the state is to be given symbolic or ceremonial representation. When there is an election, or when a government falls, the head of state formally appoints the political executive. In this way the head of state is the transmitter of legitimacy and the personification of the state.

Heads of state, like those in Britain, Canada, the Netherlands, and Norway, who are seemingly only figureheads subject to overriding powers of the political executive, often exercise considerable de facto executive power and influence. For example, when there is doubt about who leads a majority party or when no party commands a majority, the head of state can decide who should be prime minister designate.

In political systems where the ceremonial and political executive are the same person, there is always the risk that the president will use symbolic authority to enhance political power or that involvement in politics will hamper the unifying and ceremonial functions of the executive. In the United States the dual role of the president in the affairs of *state* and *government* has given the presidency almost continuous media exposure and, thus, preeminent power among competing political institutions.[12]

Leadership

The executive has evolved to become the locus of leadership in all modern political systems. It is where political power gravitates, concentrates, and disseminates through the various levels of government. The leadership qualities of those entrusted with the destiny of a state can activate every factor of power and extract inordinate advantages from limited resources. There is no question that a society's success or failure, indeed its very survival, depends in large part on the quality and competence of the executive leadership it is able to attract.

In fact, the ability of a single highly placed decision maker to mobilize other human resources is itself a factor of power. No political leader can do the job alone. Thousands of other people must be included in the process of leadership if the resources of a state are to be used to maximum capacity. The role of the political executive in recruiting other human talent is therefore paramount. Presidents, prime ministers, and first secretaries have extensive appointive powers, not just to fill a cabinet, politburo, or judiciary, but to place key personnel in the bureaucratic machinery of the state.

In times of peace or war, the political executive must effectively lead the people and the institutions that constitute a state. In the nuclear age, the role of leadership is particularly crucial because world leaders carry the heavy burden of maintaining international peace or, at least, of avoiding nuclear war. Executives in states that possess nuclear weapons hold the fate of all of humankind in their hands: they have the final responsibility for using weapons of global destruction. Ultimately their decisions reach far beyond their national constituencies.

Even in the realm of domestic economic problems, political leadership has global implications. Executives who do not manage their economies well threaten the security of the international economy. Leaders in countries like Brazil and Mexico can destabilize the economies of the developed world by failing to manage their huge public debts. Similarly, leaders in Canada and the United States can make matters worse for the debt-strapped developing countries by sustaining heavy deficits, thus contributing to huge interest rates that compound the indebtedness of the underdeveloped world.

Policy Initiation, Formulation, and Implementation

Despite widespread public sentiment for the legislative branch of government today, the fact remains that executives are the nerve centres of modern government decision making. Ever since the beginning of organized government, making and enforcing binding rules has been the preserve of the executive branch of government. For centuries executive political structures functioned without separate legislative agencies for making laws. Today, after only a brief ascendancy in the history of government, legislatures are on the decline.[13]

Not surprisingly, the modern executive is the most important structure of policy making in all governments around the world. Public policy* may be defined in a variety of ways, but it is generally the result of whatever executives choose to do or not to do with the resources available to them. Financing AIDS research, cutting or raising taxes, increasing defense spending, or launching a bill to establish a centre on substance abuse, are all examples of public policies. Nowadays the executive initiates new policies and programs and, depending on the division of powers between the executive and the legislature, has a substantial role in their adoption. Under any system — democratic or non-democratic — the executive oversees the implementation of its policies with the assistance of an army of professional administrators.

Often it is only the political executive that can adequately communicate with the general public on questions of public policy. By means of press conferences, statements, and speeches in parliament, and frequent exposure on radio and television, the political executive has many opportunities to communicate important information to the public about domestic and foreign-policy issues. These high-level communications are an advantage to executives seeking public support for their policies and programs.

Supervision of Administration

Every executive is responsible for implementing legislative decisions and enforcing court orders. To fulfil this role, political leaders must supervise the bureaucratic machinery at the national level. In many states the national bureaucracy is an immense, complicated organization. In the U.S. political system the national bureaucracy is a multi-layered system of organizations, crisscrossed between the executive and legislative branches of government. The president of the United States has his own administration, separate from Congress, which itself controls a vast bureaucratic machine. In Canada, the national bureaucracy comes under the purview of the Cabinet which supervises the various departments of government, boards, commissions, and crown corporations. The administration of government is a fusion of executive and legislative functions, unlike the separate administrations operating in the United States.

In the final analysis, the role of the executive and its administrative bureaucracy is to apply laws, to make sure that the programs of government are put into action, and to enforce new statutes. Of course, the executive also initiates programs, as when the minister of Finance announces a new tax reform or when the prime minister and the minister of External Affairs embark on new foreign-policy directions for Canada.

Diplomatic and Military Functions

Diplomacy and defence have remained primary responsibilities of the executive branch of government throughout history. Both diplomatic and military matters have always been intrinsically tied to the security of the state, thus requiring the decisiveness and secrecy of executive decision making. Diplomats are appointed representatives of the head of state and are, by custom and convention, personifications of the sovereign authority of the executive wherever they are accredited. All diplomats take their directives from, and are responsible to, the political executive. The principal executive powers in the area of diplomacy are those of (a) sending and receiving diplomats, (b) recognizing new governments and establishing or withdrawing diplomatic relations, (c) determining and implementing foreign policy, and (d) negotiating treaties and agreements through normal diplomatic channels and at the summit level. In fact, in most states, tradition, constitutional interpretation, and decree have established the head of government as the sovereign power in foreign affairs, making this person the chief diplomat. In Canada, depending on the importance of a particular foreign-policy matter, either the prime minister or the minister of state for External Affairs fulfils such a role.

In all states where there is a military, the control of the armed forces is an exclusive function of the executive. In some states, the military accepts a distinctly subordinate position to the civilian chief executive, whether president, prime minister, party chairman, or monarch. In other states, there is virtually no distinction between the highest ranking members of the military and the executive branch of government. On matters of internal security or foreign involvements, the executive can summon the legitimate physical force of the military to protect the interests of the state.

Canada's Department of National Defence is one example of military subordination to civilian control. At the top of the organizational scheme of Canada's Armed Forces is the minister of Defence, who is chairman of the Defence Council, which meets once a week with its mixed staff of civilian and military advisers. In the United States, the president acts in his duties as Commander-in-Chief of the armed forces. The Constitution vests in the president extensive military powers for preserving internal order and defending the country against external aggression. To these ends, the president may decree partial or total mobilization of the armed forces to cope with a serious internal or external threat.

Judicial Functions

In the judicial realm, many political executives have assumed or have been conferred extensive authority. Usually in accordance with the constitution, the executive is required to oversee the general administration of justice and to guarantee its impartiality and fairness to all citizens. That is why one of the most important judicial functions of the executive is the power to appoint judges. The chief executive is charged with enforcing the law by ensuring that judicial decisions are carried out. Executives are responsible for the operation of the courts and must make sure that the official conduct of judges comports with national dignity and with their official responsibilities.

Among the important judicial powers, an executive is usually authorized to grant pardons* and reprieves*, both as a means of mitigating possible judicial malpractice and in the spirit of justice and mercy. Another executive judicial power is amnesty* – a blanket pardon extended to large groups, usually political offenders and conscientious objectors. Less than 24 hours after taking the oath of office, President Jimmy Carter granted an amnesty to the U.S. military deserters of the Vietnam War.

In some states, a blanket executive amnesty for illegal immigrants has been a useful tool. It allows governments to grant a large number of people a swift change of status, thus avoiding costly and lengthy proceedings and addresses the problem of illegals filtering into the economy. Since World War II, Canada has offered seven partial immigration amnesties, allowing more than 140 000 people, who would not have qualified as refugees, to jump, in effect, to the head of the immigration lines. But in 1989, Canada's Immigration Minister, Barbara MacDougall, refused to grant an amnesty to a backlog of 85 000 applicants because it would mean ignoring the 1 million applicants who each year seek entry through conventional channels.

Classifying Executives

There are four classifications of the executive branch that are the most salient aspect of modern government. Executives in the principal modern states may be classified under these four types, corresponding to the governmental systems discussed in the last chapter: parliamentary, presidential, authoritarian, and totalitarian. Within these classifications, the methods of selection, tenure in office, and public accountability of executives vary enormously. But these broad generalizations enable us to recognize the important differences among the various types of executives in the world.

The Parliamentary Executive

The parliamentary executive is the most widely adopted form of democratic leadership. It is used by most of the world's political democracies: Australia, Austria, Belgium, Canada, Denmark, Finland, West Germany, Iceland, India, Ireland, Israel, Italy, Japan, Luxembourg, Netherlands, New Zealand, Norway, Sweden, and the United Kingdom.

In these states the executive is divided into two parts: a head of state and a head of government. The main political function of the head of state is to appoint the head of government. For the most part the powers of the head of state are essentially formal, although many governments entrust this person with the authority to protect and defend the political system. The head of government is the more important politically. Whether called prime minister, premier, or chancellor, he or she is the leader of the majority party in the parliament or a person able to form a coalition that will sustain the confidence of the House*. The political executive chooses the cabinet, which is a collective body politically responsible to the parliament. Theoretically, parliament is supreme over the executive. But no matter what constitutional documents may say about fusion of powers or legislative supremacy, the executive is de facto the essence of government and the embodiment of authority. The legislature may have critical functions, but its position is always defined by its relationship to the executive.

THE EXECUTIVE IN CANADA

The Constitution Act, 1867 (Section 9), affirms that executive authority is vested in the Queen and exercised by her appointed representatives, the governor general, and the lieutenant governors. In 1947, the legitimizing authority of the Queen was delegated to the governor general but it was not effective until 1977.[14] However, in practice the governor general plays only a passive executive role by following the advice of the prime minister and the Cabinet. In actual fact the governor general is acquiescing to the will of the Canadian electorate when it gives one party a majority of seats in the House of Commons. The govenor general can use some discretion for ensuring that there is always a government in office, for example, in a situation where partisan politics prevents the formation of a government or when no party receives a majority of seats after an election.

Under the Canadian constitution, the governor general has the right to be consulted, to advise, and even to warn the political executive if it abuses its powers. Considerable differences of opinion may be found concerning the advantages of the Crown as a formal appendage to executive government in Canada. But a brief summary of the duties of the governor general indicates the significance of the office as both a formal and effective part of Parliament: (a) The governor general summons, prorogues,* and dissolves* Parliament; (b) the governor general appoints the prime minister and the Cabinet and swears them into office; (c) the governor general signs all bills, conferring royal assent* before they become law; (d) the governor general must be advised of and signs all orders in council* issued by the Cabinet; (e) the governor general signs Letters of Credence of Canadian ambassadors and accepts similar credentials of ambassadors and high commissioners appointed to Canada. As the personification of the Crown, the governor general is above all political affiliations and is in a position to represent and speak for Canada at home and abroad.

Notwithstanding the legal supremacy of the formal executive over the political executive in Canada's Constitution, the office of governor general has essentially become symbolic and ceremonial by custom and convention. As the representative of the head of state, the governor general accepts the credentials of diplomats, entertains other heads of state and political executives, bestows honour on Canadians, and generally embodies the majesty of the Canadian State. Hence, this person is a symbol of the unity and continuity of Canadians.

The Letters Patent of 1947 provide for the replacement of the governor general should this person die, become incapacitated, or be absent from the country for a period of more than one month. The replacement is the Chief Justice of the Supreme Court of Canada and if that post is vacant, the senior *puisne* justice who is appointed as the Administrator of Canada, and who assumes all of the formal executive powers and serves until the governor general can return to the office.

Canadians have been appointed to the office only since 1952. Thus, by 1990, of the twenty-four governors general, only seven will have been Canadians. History has shown that the importance of the office depends a lot on the personal dynamism and esteem of the incumbent. The appointment of Jeanne Sauvé for a five-year term as governor general in 1984 produced a "first" for the Canadian political system, but only one of a long list of "firsts" for the new governor general. In 1989, her term of office was extended by seven months to mid January 1990. She became the first woman in Canada, and the third woman in the Commonwealth, to become a governor general. In 1972, Jeanne Sauvé became the first woman from Quebec to be appointed to the federal Cabinet and, in 1980, the country's first woman Speaker of the House of Commons. Her successor at Rideau Hall is Ray Hnatyshyn, former PC justice minister.

The office of governor general has never had the full support of Canadians.[15] One reason for this attitude is a lack of public awareness of the significance and role of the Crown* as a functional institution in the Canadian political system. A poll conducted by Data Laboratories Research Consultants for *Weekend Magazine*[16] found that 42.5 percent of Canadians identified the prime minister as head of state. Some 14.3 percent named the governor general as head of state, and 36.7 percent recognized the Queen as head of state. Another reason is the reluctance of many French-speaking people in Quebec and other parts of Canada to identify with the symbolism of the British Crown.

Another feature of Canada's formal executive is the Queen's Privy Council (section 11, Constitution Act, 1867). Originally a private advisory body to royalty, the Privy Council evolved to become the legal precursor of the modern-day Cabinet. Neither the prime minister nor the Cabinet are mentioned in the Constitution and thus have no legal existence whatsoever apart from the fact that they form a committee of the Privy Council. In order to transfer constitutional legality from the formal executive to the political executive in Canada, members of the Cabinet are sworn into office as members of the Privy Council. Thus, Cabinet decisions are issued as "orders in council." The Privy Council is made up of all present and former Cabinet members, regardless of party affiliation, and other persons appointed by the governor general on the recommendation of the prime minister.[17] Hence, we find that in the 1990s there are over 100 members of the privy Council, yet the Cabinet ranges in size from 30 to 40 people. Even though former Cabinet ministers remain Privy councillors for life, they may not advise the government of the day. The full Privy Council meets rarely, usually to honour a visit by the Queen or other members of the Royal Family.

Two other bodies formally attached to the Privy Council are the Privy Council Office (PCO) and the Treasury Board.[18] The role of the PCO has evolved from that of a body responsible for dealing with the occasional formalities of the Privy Council to a major prestigious policy-advising agency of the federal government. The PCO, with a staff of over 300, briefs the prime minister, the plenary cabinet and its subcommittees on the activities of the government and matters of national policy. The whole structure of the PCO, with its three principal divisions (Plans, Operations, and Senior Personnel), is headed by Canada's highest-ranking civil servant, the Clerk of the Privy Council, who is also the Secretary to the Cabinet and sets Cabinet agendas, takes minutes at Cabinet meetings, and transmits Cabinet decisions to the bureaucracy.

The Treasury Board, like the Cabinet, is formally a committee of the Privy Council, headed by a cabinet minister who is called the President of the Treasury Board. Its original function under the jurisdiction of the Department of Finance until 1966 was as an overseer of the budgetary process of government, to ensure that public funds were being spent only on authorized government projects. Today, as a separate government department, the Treasury Board not only keeps track of current and projected expenditures, but also, with its large secretariat, operates as a board of management for the government, providing highly influential advice in both financial management and the overall personnel management of the public service. The financial management of contemporary government priorities and objectives would be chaotic were it not for a central monitoring agency like the Treasury Board. By means of a management system, such as the Policy and Expenditure Management System (PEMS), the Treasury Board can apply controls on the spending demands of federal departments as each ministry trys to gain a greater share of the government budget.

CANADA'S POLITICAL EXECUTIVE

The focus of leadership and political power in Canada culminates in the prime minister and the Cabinet, which derives its legality and legitimacy through the House of Commons and by constitutional convention and custom.[19] The prime minister is uniquely powerful because of his prerogatives* to call an election, to gain public visibility, to instruct the formal executive, to lead a political party, and to form a government.

The authority to advise the dissolution of the House of Commons at any time is an important strategic power enjoyed by the prime minister. The political careers of all members of Parliament are challenged by an election. Consequently, the timing of an election is crucial. Usually, the prime minister will go to the polls when the government party enjoys a safe margin of popularity over the opposition parties. Such appeared to be the case when Brian Mulroney called an election in the fall of 1988, after a Gallup poll showed the Progressive Conservatives attracting 43 percent of decided voters, the Liberals with 34 percent, and the New Democratic Party with 23 percent. Sometimes what appears to be a propitious decision to call an election turns against the prime minister and members of the prime minister's party bear the brunt of bad judgement. Such was the fate of the Liberals in Canada, for example, when John Turner decided to call a snap election in the summer of 1984. The Liberals were enjoying an 11 percent-point lead in popularity over the Conservatives, but won only 40 seats in that election, down from 147 in 1980. And

John Turner earned the dubious distinction of serving the second-shortest term in office as prime minister after Sir Charles Tupper, who governed for only 69 days in 1896.

Another dimension of executive power flows from the fact that the prime minister tends to dominate public perceptions of national politics. In Canada, everything about a prime minister seems to be a source of fascination to the mass media: what the PM has for breakfast and dinner, how the PM spends leisure time, what the spouse does, how they decorate 24 Sussex Drive, what pet animals the family keeps. This extremely high level of visibility can be an important political resource. But, by the same token, the singular visibility of the prime minister so dominates public perceptions of the political world that every action - casual or official - occupies a crucial place in the emotions of the public. This high visibility and role of political leader means that the pm is held accountable when things go wrong, regardless of any actual responsibility for them. Usually, however, the prestige of the office can be used by the prime minister in a highly personalized way to gain political advantage. Standing at the centre of Canadian politics, the prime minister can steal the show from most political opponents by capturing the lion's share of news coverage. No matter how narrow the electoral margin that brought the government to power, the prime minister will find that many Canadians approve of what is done simply because the prime minister does it.[20]

One of the most distinguishing features of prime ministerial power is the unique relationship this person has with the formal executive. The prime minister is the sole link between the formal and political executives. Only the prime minister can advise and instruct the governor general to prorogue and dissolve Parliament. It is the prime minister who formally recommends those who are appointed to the Privy Council and the Senate. It is also the prime minster who connects the Cabinet and, indeed, Parliament with the governor general. Thus, on the initiative of the prime minister, constitutional legitimacy is transferred from the formal executive to the political executive.

Prime ministerial power is also enhanced by leading a political party, usually one with a majority of seats in the House of Commons. Because the prime minister is seen by the governing party as the architect of electoral victory, i.e., the person who attached the party to the reins of political power in Canada, the PM is virtually in an impregnable position. As a rule, the rank and file are highly supportive of a successful leader. The party caucus* can be a much more critical body because it consists of the prime minister's rivals for office. But the prime minister, by virtue of having powers to appoint party faithfuls to rewarding government positions in the public and diplomatic service, as well as on the bench, is able to command the loyalty of the caucus. In addition to the Cabinet, the heads of crown corporations, deputy ministers, and other key mandarins in the public service are among more than 3500 Canadians appointed under the authority of the prime minister. The people surrounding the prime minister are among the most influential on Parliament Hill, and their ranks always include friends and advisers who helped during the election campaign. For example, in 1984, Bernard Roy, the campaign director for the Progressive Conservative party in Quebec and best man at Brian Mulroney's wedding, was appointed the prime minister's principal secretary, the most important political adviser to the head of government. When Roy resigned in 1988 he was replaced by Peter White, a prominent businessman, who had worked as a special assistant to the prime minister from 1984 to 1986.

In the House of Commons party discipline places the prime minister at the apex of the apparatus of government. As government leader, the prime minister has control over the political futures of the party's elected members. When Progressive Conservative MP Dan McKenzie voted against amendments to the Official Languages Act in 1988 he was fired from his job as parliamentary secretary to the Minister for Veterans Affairs. Others who opposed the amendments faced the possibility that the prime minister would refuse to sign their nomination papers in the next federal election. Similarly, Mulroney expelled Montreal MP Suzanne Blais-Grenier, a former Cabinet minister, from his caucus, after her allegations that people pay kickbacks to the Progressive Conservative party to get government business could not be substantiated. The possibility of transforming backbenchers into ministers and vice versa is a continuing asset to the prime minister in the process of encouraging undisputed party loyalty and support. In addition, the Senate has long been treated by the prime minister as a place to put political workhorses out to pasture. The great majority of Canadian senators have their posts because — and only because — of prior loyalty to the prime minister. One of the provisions of the Meech Lake Accord (Constitution Amendment, 1987) would require that Senate vacancies be filled by persons whose names have been submitted by the government of the provinces to which the vacancies relate.

We have yet to account in full measure for the conventional prerogatives of the prime minister. Nothing demonstrates the strength in the office of the chief political executive so forcefully as the power to form a government by appointing a Cabinet.[21] As an organization in its own right, the Cabinet is the executive council of the Canadian government, the key decision-making forum for initiating laws and policies, raising and spending public monies, and a source of advice to the prime minister pondering major decisions.

The prime minister chooses who will enter the Cabinet, how large a body it will be, and the extent to which individual Cabinet ministers exert influence on the direction of public policy in Canada. It has been said that the prime minister is the first among equals (*primus inter pares*) in relations with his Cabinet colleagues. But no Canadian Cabinet has ever operated as a body of individuals equal in power.

Even among the various ministries, a pecking order exists beneath the prime minister. The departments of Finance, Justice, and External Affairs wield much more influence in the inner circles of Cabinet power than do Communications or Indian and Nothern Affairs. The prime minister chairs the plenary Cabinet and its most important Priorities and Planning Committee. As such, he is the co-ordinator and arbitrator of the executive decision-making process. In 1989 prime minister Mulroney announced the most radical shake-up of the Cabinet system in twenty years. First, Mulroney removed the power of most ministers to spend their department's budget. Under this system, only two Cabinet committees, Priorities and Planning and Treasury, will have the power to authorize any government spending. The aim – tighter centralized control of the purse-strings – is to ensure that when new programs are brought forward the money is there to pay for them. Borrowing an idea from Australia and the United Kingdom, the PM now chairs a new Expenditure Review Committee with the power to cut programs, a sign of concern for the spiralling government deficit. Another small cabinet group, the Operations Committee, is now the political nerve-centre of the new Cabinet, underlining how much power Mulroney is concentrating in the hands of just a few (eight) trusted colleagues. Another new Cabinet committee is the Environment Committee, with the power to veto programs from other departments that could damage the environment. The upgrading of the environment ministry promises to be a popular move, which is not likely to be the case for the new government's other priority – cutting the deficit.

Having appointed the ministers to the Cabinet, as well as to its standing committees, the PM retains a large amount of authority and power over their political destinies. By means of the *cabinet shuffle* the PM can promote the most loyal and promising ministers or demote those whose performance is less than satisfactory. Sometimes a prime minister will appoint an *interim* Cabinet to finish old parliamentary business before making more permanent appointments. Such was the case in 1988, when Brian Mulroney appointed an interim Cabinet to guide the Free Trade Agreement (FTA) through the final stages of ratification before implementing its provisions on January 1, 1989. Because six Cabinet ministers had gone down to defeat in the 1988 federal election, Mulroney gave other ministers additional responsibilities until he named a new Cabinet in January 1989. The principle of Cabinet solidarity* ensures that collectively the Cabinet is one with the prime minister and that recalcitrant ministers will either acquiesce in the corporate will of the government or resign.

Traditionally, ministers appointed to the Cabinet were assigned portfolios* to head a major government department. In fact only the prime minister and the government leader in the Senate were appointed without portfolios and did not and still do not carry any departmental responsibilities. Today, the only administrative responsibility of the prime minister is the Privy Council Office. The Ministries and Ministers of State Act 1970 (Revised 1985) places the present designation of Cabinet ministers into five categories.[22] The first are the ministers of regular government departments, such as minister of Finance. The second designation is for ministers who are assigned parliamentary responsibilities without heading a department or ministry, such as House Leader. The third category includes ministers of state who are assigned a junior portfolio, such as junior Finance minister. The fourth category is for ministers of state appointed to assist a regular minister, such as the minister of state for Science and Technology under the Department of Industry, Science and Technology. The last category consists of ministers without a portfolio appointed as undesignated ministers of state, who are assigned to assist a minister with a portfolio.

Although Cabinet ministers are appointed by the prime minister and owe their primary allegiance to this person, they must develop good relations with the departments they run. These departments are headed by career civil servants called *deputy ministers,* who usually remain at their posts regardless of which political party gains control of the government.[23]

Deputy ministers advise their political bosses on policy matters, plan and control expenditures in the department, scrutinize the organization and structure of the department, and assume the wider responsibilities of co-ordinating departmental activities with those of other government departments.

Quite understandably, deputy ministers who are the permanent heads of the department will have administrative interests that may be different from those of the minister and the prime minister they serve. Usually, deputy ministers are fiercely dedicated to the programs they administer. They expect that the minister who heads their department will take their advice and avoid the many transient political pressures that cause Cabinet ministers to alter the administration of government programs. They want the minister to represent the interests of the department to the prime minister. As a result, the minister is somewhat at cross–purposes between the bureaucratic and political forces of government. This is augmented by the fact that ministers are responsible only for their part of government and thus lack the prime minister's need to balance a wider range of interests.

Ministers are not totally without ways of dealing with centrifugal tendencies of the bureaucracy. Cabinet ministers are accompanied by an entourage of aides, executive assistants, and *parliamentary secretaries,* who are directly responsible to them. Parliamentary secretaries are members of Parliament who are designated by the minister to assist in the political operation of the department. In the last ten years, ministerial aides, executive assistants, and parliamentary secretaries have occupied an increasingly important place in the functioning of the Cabinet. As the complexity and size of the bureaucracy increase the challenges to ministerial control, the staff acts as a buffer to the growing colonization of the political adminstration by the civil service. One major function of the minister's staff is to protect and advance the political interests of the department and the Cabinet, including liaison with Parliament, press relations, control of the minister's schedule, travel, and relations with major interest groups and party figures. Ministers also have assistants to perform such inevitable but disagreeable tasks as refusing access, discharging employees and officials, and denying requests for special consideration. The parliamentary secretaries have some input into the development of new programs and legislation. They also serve to take the heat off the minister from time to time in the House of Commons by standing in to answer sensitive questions directed at the department from members of the opposition. Sometimes, as well, when the minister has accepted an engagement to speak in a politically hostile area of the country, the parliamentary secretary is sent instead to vicariously deflect the political flak away from the minister. Despite such stratagems, all Cabinet ministers are aware of the many difficulties involved in gaining control of the very bureaucracy that is one of the bases of their power. The prime minister is also aware that ministers will sometimes have an adversary relationship with career civil servants. The prime minister and the Cabinet are preoccupied with speed and the political perspective of the executive process, which inevitably grates on bureaucrats accustomed to a specialized and long-term perspective.

One executive support agency that facilitates both speed and efficiency for the political executive is the Prime Minister's Office (PMO). The prime minister has appointed his most loyal and trusted advisers to this executive body. They assist in almost everything, from drafting the Speech from the Throne to guiding the prime minister through the maze of political and bureaucratic hurdles confronting executive leadership in Canada. The PMO co-ordinates with the Privy Council Office to develop a national policy framework, including a public relations strategy for the government. The PMO is therefore a practical policy think-tank charged with an advisory capacity about the political fortunes of the prime minister and his cabinet. On a daily basis the PMO answers the prime minister's mail, schedules his appointments and invitations, and keeps a close watch over the patterns of popularity and unpopularity that affect the political executive.

At the outset, a prime minister must decide how large the Cabinet will be and who will be in it.[24] Many factors affect the prime minister in determining the size and composition of the Cabinet. One is the mood of the country and in the PM's party about whether the government, as at present constituted, is too big or too small. Since John A. Macdonald's first thirteen–member Cabinet in 1867, Canada had, by the 1990s, one of the largest cabinets among the democratic countries of the world. In the last twenty years the wholesale growth of governmental responsibilities has prompted the enlargement of cabinets. Trudeau's largest Cabinet had 37 ministers, 9 above the largest convened under Pearson. Under John Turner the size of the Cabinet was reduced to 29, the same number of ministers as in the short-lived Clark government. But the largest Cabinet in Canadian history was assembled by Brian Mulroney in 1984; it totalled 40, including the prime minister, selected from among 210 Tory MPs. After the 1988 federal election Mulroney's Cabinet consisted of 39, including the prime minister, drawn from 169 Progressive Conservative MPs.

Another factor of major importance for the prime minister when forming the Cabinet is the principle of representation. Today, the general political parameters a prime minister must follow in striking a Cabinet roster cut across economic, geographic, gender, linguistic, political, and social criteria. In some cases the choices for representation with major portfolios are well signalled. There is always the exigency of forming a national government. This means that, to the extent it is possible, every province should be allocated at least one Cabinet minister. When this is not possible because representatives have not been elected to the governing party's caucus from every province, the prime minister sometimes appoints senators to the Cabinet to represent these provinces, or gives a minister from a neighbouring province special ministerial assignments in a province with no government representation. For example, in 1989, Elmer MacKay, Nova Scotia's only voice in the Cabinet as minister of Public Works, was also given special duties with respect to Prince Edward Island, where voters failed to send a single Conservative member to Ottawa.

In 1984, with 210 MPs from whom to choose, Brian Mulroney assembled a Cabinet that was more representative of the entire country than any since former prime minister Pierre Trudeau's first term in office. By carrying all ten provinces Mulroney was able to form a truly national government and to shift a significant amount of power to the West from its traditional concentrations in central Canada. The 1988 election reduced Mulroney's numerical choices significantly but still gave him the capacity to construct a national cabinet. With the exception of Prince Edward Island, which returned four Liberals, all provinces provided Mulroney with candidates for possible Cabinet posts. Once a national Cabinet is formed, the success of the prime minister will depend in large measure on reconciling the various competing elements within the government and within the party caucus. A representative geographic selection of ministers, while appearing to unite the country, can divide a cabinet because so many conflicting interests have a powerful voice in the decision–making process of the country.

To complicate the job of making a representative government along provincial and regional perimeters, the prime minister must also try to balance the composition of the Cabinet according to economic, gender, linguistic, and social variables. Every effort must be made to include people to represent the business community, native people, women, Catholics, Protestants, Jews, and those of French and other non-English origins.

John A. Macdonald once said: "Like any cabinet maker, I do the best I can with the lumber you furnish me." In 1984, Canadians gave Brian Mulroney a mill-worker's dream. With the exception of native representation, Canada's eighteenth prime minister amassed a government that included almost all important geographic and social criteria.

The Cabinet must also be representative of gender. In 1984, Mulroney named a record six women to his first Cabinet from the twenty-eight elected nationwide, doubling the previous record of three. However, these six women comprised only 15 percent of the Cabinet but represent over 50 per cent of the national population. Prior to the appointment of the six women ministers by Mulroney, only eight women had ever sat around a Canadian Cabinet table. Women were given some tough portfolios with External Relations, Energy, Mines and Resources, and the Environment, a signal that when women are elected with the right credentials, they do not have to sit as backbenchers. In 1989, Mulroney's first cabinet shuffle again included only six women, selected from thirty-nine elected to a larger House of Commons.

There is also an obvious political or partisan dimension to cabinet making. The prime minister may place heavy emphasis on loyalty in the selection, drawing on personal memory of early campaign and convention supporters. Shortly after Mulroney, then a Montreal lawyer and corporate executive, announced he was running for the Conservative party leadership in 1983, he spread the word around Parliament Hill that aspiring Tory MPs had one week to sign up in support of his campaign if they had any hope of getting into the Mulroney Cabinet. The first members of the Progressive Conservative caucus who met with Mulroney at the Chateau Laurier Hotel all received Cabinet posts in his first government. But, while loyalty may determine a prime minister's selection of some Cabinet ministers, it cannot be the main reason for the selection of all ministers: experience, talent, and popularity are among the other important factors affecting a prime minister's choice.

As the only person capable of making a government once Canadians have decided who goes to Ottawa, the prime minister must aim above all else to provide the political glue for national unity and is the one pan-Canadian figure in our political system.

The Presidential Executive

The modern presidential type of chief executive began with the U.S. Constitution of 1787. Despite its great success in that country, it has not been as widely embraced as has the parliamentary type of executive. The presidential executive is most commonly found in Latin American states because of their historical links with the American experience. It has also been installed by Liberia and the Philippines, as well as in some of the newer African countries like Burundi, Mali, and Nigeria. Sri Lanka adopted the presidential executive in 1978, as did Guyana in 1980. While a growing number of states from around the world are adopting this type of executive, many of its advantages have not been widely recognized. The presidential executive establishes a solid and stable centre of power in the executive branch, an advantage particularly appropriate to newer states requiring a strong democratic central government. The presidential system provides that the head of state, who is also the head of government, is elected for a definite term of office. The president has the entire country as a constituency and is independent of the legislative branch of government. The president acts as the official ceremonial head and as leader of the government that proposes, directs, and enforces the country's public policies.

THE EXECUTIVE OF THE UNITED STATES

In the United States, the president is indirectly elected by an *electoral college* for a fixed term of four years. In the electoral college, each state has a number of electoral votes equal to the size of its congressional delegation: e.g., California 47, New York 36 (figure 6.1). If a presidential candidate wins a plurality of votes in a particular state, he or she also wins all of the electoral votes for that state. Of a total of 538 electoral votes, 270 are required to elect a president. The largest states are hotly contested during a presidential election because they yield the greatest number of electoral votes. Thus, a minimum winning coalition of states needed to secure 270 electoral votes and win the presidency would be California, New York, Pennsylvania, Illinois, Texas, Ohio, Michigan, Florida, New Jersey, Massachusetts, and Wisconsin. In 1984, Ronald Reagan won 525 electoral votes and his opponent, Walter Mondale, won only the District of Columbia and the state of Minnesota, giving him 13 electoral college votes. In the 1988 presidential election George Bush did not match the enormous landslide of his predecessor but took 40 states for 426 electoral votes against Michael Dukakis who won only 10 states and the District of Columbia for 112 electoral college votes.

According to the twenty-second amendment (1951) of the U.S. Constitution, "no person shall be elected to the office of President more than twice." The only legal way a president can be removed from office is through the process of impeachment. By a simple majority vote, the House of Representatives can vote to *impeach* the president as well as other members of the executive. Once this happens, the Senate convenes as a court, chaired by the Chief Justice of the Supreme Court, to weigh the evidence for and against the president. It takes a two-thirds majority of the Senate to convict the accused. The only president in U.S. history to stand trial before the Senate was Andrew Jackson in 1868. However, the

Senate failed to convict him by one vote; thus many American historians argue that no U.S. president has ever been impeached.

To qualify for holding the office a president must be a "natural born" citizen, at least thirty-five years of age, and have held residency in the United States for fourteen years. If a president is impeached, dies, resigns, or is incapable of performing duties of the office, the presidency goes to the vice-president, then, in order of succession, to the Speaker of the House of Representatives, the president pro tempore of the Senate, and then to Cabinet officials.

The U.S. Constitution briefly enumerates the executive authority of the president in general terms: that he "shall take care that the laws be faithfully executed" and that he shall "take an oath to preserve, protect and defend the Constitution." Provision is also made in the Constitution for the president's relations with the other branches of government.[25] From time to time the president must give Congress a report called the "State of the Union Message" and may recommend policies and programs for its consideration. The president is authorized to call special sessions of Congress and most bills and joint resolutions passed by Congress must be signed by the president. Some exceptions are joint resolutions, which are rarely signed; a president may decide not to sign a bill and it might well die unless the veto can be overridden by a two-thirds vote in each house.

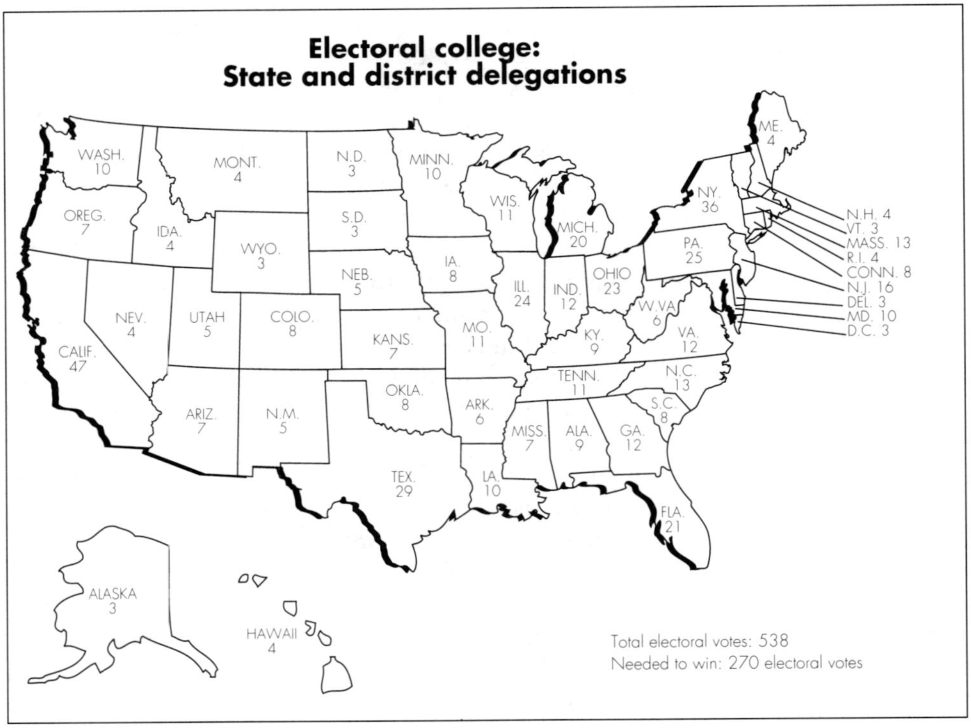

Figure 6.1

In the United States, the work of the federal executive is conducted by thirteen departments and a host of non-cabinet agencies like the Central Intelligence Agency (CIA), and the Federal Trade Commission (FTC). Each department is headed by a *secretary* appointed by the president and confirmed by the Senate. Thus there is a secretary of State, of Commerce, of Treasury, and so forth. The vice-president, the secretaries, and several other executive officials make up the *cabinet* in American government. From election day in November to Inauguration Day on January 20, a president or president elect has about eleven weeks to select a cabinet and form the next administration. As in Canada, the term cabinet does not appear in the Constitution but any comparisons with the Canadian Cabinet, which plays a major leadership role in Canada's political life, would be totally misleading. The American cabinet is *not* the executive council of government. Its meetings are infrequent, brief, and often superficial. Most presidents use cabinet meetings to inform their secretaries of new directions in the strategies of the executive and to inform one department what other departments are doing. For actual consultation on policy matters, presidents use hand-chosen advisers. Traditionally, only one or two members of the president's cabinet have a significant advisory function. For the most part, the cabinet is chosen to satisfy different functions in the president's party, i.e., the secretary of Labour is usually someone associated with organized labour and the secretary of Commerce is a prominent business person.

One expert on the American presidency, Richard Neustadt, has written that "a President is many men or one man wearing many hats."[26] There are several major roles that any president must carry out: head of state, head of government, party leader, chief legislator, commander-in-chief, and chief diplomat.

As the *head of state*, the president is the central figure in the elaborate ceremonial life of the country. The president speaks and acts on behalf of all of the people and is the foremost symbol of the political community. It is the president who greets foreign dignitaries in the name of the United States, makes the annual state of the union address, opens a National Arts Centre, and proclaims National Codfish Day. In so doing, the president shows that he is the personal embodiment of the United States of America.

In sharp tension with his ceremonial role as head of state, the president is also *head of government*. As chief of the executive branch of government, the president controls a vast portion of the federal bureaucracy. Because of the separation of powers, he does not have full control of the permanent civil service but he does have considerable influence over it. In the United States the federal civil service consists of over 5 million people (3 million civilians and about 2 million military service personnel). In addition to appointing the cabinet, the president appoints approximately 7000 people and through them supervises and directs federal policies in the complicated network of the federal government. These "president's people" link the executive with the other branches of the federal bureaucracy and are crucial appointments for the success of any administration. So important are these appointments to the executive control of government that modern-day presidents establish special personnel-selection teams to search for loyal and qualified individuals. The president guides the operation of government through the cabinet, the White House advisers (also known as the domestic council), the executive office of the president, and the Office of Management and Budget. The National Security Council plays a similar role with respect to foreign policy. As head of the government, the president steers the other branches of government in the direction of the administration's policies.

The tensions between the ceremonial and political functions of the president are especially evident in the role as *party leader.* As partisan leader, the president leads one political faction of the country against all others, yet as the head of state, the president must represent and unify all factions. Because the president has such vast powers of appointment and is the leader of a successful political party, it is not surprising that top-level policy-making positions will be offered to members of the president's own party. Party patronage is used to reward those who have been loyal to the president, a loyalty expressed as campaign contributions or other influential support that enabled an individual to win the party's presidential nomination, and then the presidency itself.

In addition to job patronage, the party expects its leader to take the lead in raising campaign funds and to endorse and campaign on behalf of party candidates at the national, state, and local levels. Hence, it is always difficult for the American chief executive to appear above politics as the embodiment of the lofty aspirations of the state, yet at the same time to be politically responsible to the party.

Closely associated with the president's role as party leader is that of *chief legislator,* proposing a legislative program and urging Congress to pass it. What is distinctive about the U.S. political system, unlike most other parliamentary democratic governments, is that executive leadership and the legislature do not necessarily work in concert. Often, the policy views and political interests of these two independent institutions are not identical. Each year numerous executive agencies come forward with the president's proposals for legislation, both to improve the administration of existing programs and to innovate with new ones. Not all members of the president's party will automatically vote for what is proposed, but the executive program will definitely be a partisan focus for the party's congressional membership. The president will make use of every available leverage to influence and gain the support of Congress.[27] All congresspersons are interested in directing the highly desirable patronage appointments of the president to their own political supporters. They know that the pork barrel* in Washington will contain lucrative federal projects for their constituents. In addition, Congress does take note of the popularity of the president when considering executive requests, although it often ignores such requests. But by appearing on television, a president can gain the support of millions of Americans in a single speech. And when all else fails, the president can exercise the *executive veto.* Sometimes, this alone is enough to persuade Congress to frame its legislation to the president's liking.

U.S. MILITARY AND DIPLOMATIC EXECUTIVE POWER

One constitutional power of the president that has great significance far beyond the national boundaries of the United States is that of *Commander-in-Chief.* Since 1776, presidents of the

United States have involved their country in six "undeclared wars" and in 128 instances (including Lebanon and Grenada in 1983, and in the Persian Gulf in 1988), U.S. presidents have ordered the armed forces to take military actions abroad without obtaining prior congressional authorization. However, the president can only act alone for a limited time when – as Commander-in-Chief – military action is initiated. In order to continue military actions abroad, the president requires congressional co-operation to engage the armed forces and use public funds. The Vietnam experience demonstrated that once a president commits U.S. troops into combat, Congress is expected to support the executive decision by providing staffing and funds for the continuation of the military operation. The War Powers Act of 1973 requires that if a president commits armed forces anywhere without a declaration of war, a written report must be submitted to Congress within 48 hours of any such commitment. Under these circumstances, the armed forces must terminate their mission within sixty days after the president reports to Congress unless Congress (1) declares war, (2) authorizes a continuation of the use of armed forces, or (3) cannot convene because of an armed attack against the United States.

Both tradition and constitutional prescription have established the president as the *chief diplomat*. The Constitution outlines the foreign policy responsibilities of the president to "make treaties," to "receive ambassadors and other public ministers," and to exercise "the Executive power." But the Constitution requires that treaties need the support of two-thirds of the Senate and that the appointment of diplomats needs the advice and consent of the Senate. More important, the power to declare war is a joint legislative and executive responsibility. The executive power allows a president to enter into an agreement with a foreign executive and bypass treaty procedures that require Senate approval. Executive agreements have been routinely formulated by presidents since World War II in Europe, Asia, and Latin America. By tradition the president has acquired many foreign-policy powers. Because, unlike the Congress, the president is in "continuous session" and international events happen quickly, requiring an immediate executive response. The president is always poised to act, aided by huge intelligence operations and instant contact with a network of embassies and consulates spread throughout the world. The options open to the chief executive with respect to world affairs range from the use of summit diplomacy (when international urgencies demand the president's participation) to the deployment of military forces anywhere on the globe.

Much of the history of the United States – its highest and lowest points – has been written largely as a result of the political behaviour of its presidents. More than other executives, the president of the United States can alter world history. In the words of William Young, "The President of the United States of America is, without question, the most powerful elected executive in the world."[28]

The Authoritarian Executive

The formal constitutional framework for most authoritarian executives today fictitiously appears as either democratic, parliamentary, or presidential systems.[29] But what the constitutions may prescribe is one thing, while the practice of executive power is sometimes quite another. In all authoritarian states, instead of being constitutionally limited and responsible, the executive so far overshadows the other branches of government that for all practical purposes the president or prime minister *is* the government. "L'état c'est moi," boasted Louis XIV of France; in all authoritarian states the executive comes close to being a twentieth-century version of the French monarch.

One of the key characteristics of the authoritarian executive is the dominance of the individual person, often a charismatic leader, in the political life of the country. Political power is highly personalized rather than institutionalized, usually despite constitutional guarantees to the contrary. Other centres of power exist besides the ruler, sometimes acting as a check on the extensive powers of the political executive. Such institutions as the church, the military, economic organizations, the bureaucracy, and political parties are often the only sources of restraint on arbitrary government.[30] However, the power relations among these groups are manipulated or controlled by the ruler, so that none of them is able to establish an independent position of power or threaten the dominant position of the executive.

The most common form of authoritarian executive today is *military rule*, already well entrenched in the Latin American region and now appearing increasingly in the newer states of Asia, Africa, and the Middle East. In this type of executive, a military junta* (or council) collectively exercises executive powers. Juntas are usually made up of three ranking officers of the army, navy, or air force who preside over the executive branch of government following a successful coup d'état.

Regardless of whether the executive appears in the civilian or military mode, the powers of the authoritarian president or prime minister are great – far greater than in most democratic states. In many cases, the executive exercises a broad collection of legislative, administrative, and judicial powers. Included among these many powers is the authority to issue decrees, form a cabinet, make administrative and judicial appointments, declare a state of siege, suspend the constitution, command the military, control finance and public revenues, grant pardons, and intervene in local government.

One very important power of the authoritarian executive is the authority to issue *decrees*. Decrees are laws issued by the executive rather than passed by the legislature. The decree power gives the executive supraconstitutional legislative authority because decree laws have the same legal standing as congressional laws, and are recognized with the option to bypass the legislature or to neutralize the electoral process.

Authoritarian executives cannot run a national administration single-handedly.[31] Next in importance to the president or prime minister are ministers, who act as chief advisers and head and supervise the various administrative departments of government. Collectively they constitute the cabinet. In selecting a cabinet, the executive takes into account such human virtues as loyalty, dependability, and competence. But in all authoritarian regimes the main criterion for executive appointment is trustworthiness. The cabinet must be made up of trusted confidants and advisers because the very life of the dictator will depend on their loyalty and faithful performance of duty. The chief executive may frequently make changes in the cabinet for reasons of political expediency. Frequent personnel changes have a definite psychological impact on the citizenry, showing it who is unquestionably the boss, thus reinforcing and maintaining the strong centralized power of the chief executive. In August 1984, Costa Rica's president, Louis Alberto Monge, asked fifteen members of his cabinet to resign, as well as thirty of the state's thirty-three ambassadors because of rumours among them that a coup was imminent. The housecleaning was aimed at restoring public confidence and asserting Monge's control of the government.

Within the framework of authoritarian government, the chief executive has virtually unlimited power to appoint administrative and judicial officials. In the appointment of high officials, such as ambassadors, ministers, judges, and ranking officers of the armed forces, many constitutions usually require that the choice of the chief executive be approved by a senate, or some other body. This approval is more fictitious than real, becuase legislatures tend to be weak and ineffective as a check on the authoritarian leader and function as bodies that give unquestioned support to executive initiatives.

One of the most important powers of the authoritarian executive is the authority to proclaim a *state of siege*, also known as the suspension of constitutional guarantees. This emergency power is used when the state is threatened by a foreign invasion or by serious internal disorder. Amid hyperinflation, widespread food riots, and looting, the President of Argentina declared a 30-day state of siege in June 1989 to control civilian uprisings throughout the country. Military governments declare a state of *martial law*, which is similar to the state of siege, the main difference being that under the latter the civilian police and regular organs of civilian government continue to function; while under the former, civilian control is replaced by the military. This special emergency power grants extraordinary powers to the president or prime minister and authorizes the executive to take drastic steps that affect all aspects of national life. The president or prime minister can divert a larger portion of the national budget for military purposes and indefinitely suspend the private rights of citizens that may by guaranteed by the constitution. In 1988 martial law was declared in Algeria, Burma, South Korea, and Haiti in order to crush democratic uprisings in each country. In South Africa, the Internal Security Act of 1982 prohibits all gatherings of people intent on protest or open criticism of the government. The South African executive declared a "state of emergency" in 1985, giving authorities unlimited powers to arrest without warrant, to search and seize, to disregard court orders, and to bar the media from reporting critically on any government action. In similar fashion, the Venezuelan government evoked a state of emergency to quell public outrage at an austerity program recommended by the International Monetary Fund (IMF).

Yet another area in which authoritarian executives enjoy unique powers is *internal intervention*. Intervention is the coercive action undertaken by the national government in the affairs of subnational units, particularly in federal states, as well as in the financial institutions, the judicial system, and the media of the country. The practice among federal states varies, but intervention can be extensive, such as the replacement of state and provincial governors, legislators, and other officials whom the president deems a challenge to executive authority and national autonomy. In 1984, the military government of

Nigeria ordered the replacement of eight of the nineteen state governors in an attempt to rid the country of corruption. Authoritarian executives also have very broad powers over the financial institutions of the country. Under this unusual grant of power, a president or prime minister can authorize a new monetary system, reorganize the structure of financial institutions, and modify the banking system. Executive intervention in the judicial system usually takes place when courts are denied the power to interpret the laws passed by the political system. It is not uncommon in authoritarian states to see the executive interrupt the process of justice, to pack the courts with supportive judges, or to simply ignore the judicial branch of government. Dictatorship almost invariably plays havoc with judicial independence. Finally, the main threat to the media in authoritarian states comes from the president or prime minister. In almost all cases, authoritarian executives strongly resist the critical scrutiny of a free press. Restrictions on the freedom of the press are usually imposed by decree, ostensibly under the authority of the constitution. Under Nigeria's sweeping press law, the military has virtual control over all new media operating in the country. According to its provisions, the government is protected from a critical media; even if the truth of allegations is proved, an editor, publisher, or writer will be censured or jailed.

The Totalitarian Executive

The models of the totalitarian executive have been produced historically in fascist and so-called communist states.[32] In today's international system the fascist model is no longer present and there is a much closer correspondence between dictatorial, socialist, or "communist" states and totalitarianism. However, since Gorbachev's revolutionary initiatives toward the structures and functions of Soviet government and its relationship with the CPSU, the character and style of traditional "communist" leadership is changing throughout the communist world. Still, executive power in these states is exercised mainly through party channels. The executive authority of the party, which is the distinguishing trait of communist states, initiates and co-ordinates the major decision-making and policy directions of the country. The state apparatus is subordinate to the party executive. It is the instrument the political executive uses to enforce and administer party policy through the government ministries.

Many communist states are headed by a collective executive, called a *politburo* or *presidium* as in Kampuchea, and the USSR. Some are headed by a *council of state*, as in China, Ethiopia, and Mongolia. These collective bodies are made up of high-ranking state officials headed by a chairman who sometimes also serves as head of state. Other communist states have single-person executives, as in Cuba, Laos, North Korea, Vietnam, and Zimbabwe.

In communist political systems, the party and the state apparatus are constitutionally and organizationally distinct but they overlap in personnel, thus interlocking the power of the Communist party with the bureaucracy of the state. This fusion of party and state authority is represented at the highest levels in a politburo, presidium, or council of state. There is no question that this is the most important executive decision-making organ in totalitarian socialist states. Members of this body are elected by a majority vote of the party's central committee, an unwieldy plenary committee of the party membership. Whatever the degree of executive power, the Communist party in all "communist societies" controls and co-ordinates government activities; it exercises "sovereign" authority. Thus, the executive organ of the party dominates the executive structure of government and the policy process. And the formulation of policy, normally the preserve of the cabinet in Western parliamentary systems, is really the province of the party elite in communist states.

All the executive powers so far discussed are initiated by the party and implemented by the government. In many communist states, it is only the party and not the government that issues directives and administrative orders that have the weight of law. Thus, the basic executive function of the top party leadership is to control a complex and interlocking network of bureaucratic and governmental structures, enabling a small group of people to control society. At present, the Politburo of the Soviet Union numbers eleven full and eight candidate members but can vary in size. If the process of democratization continues on its present course it is almost certain that executive powers will be affected by popular pressures for a more pluralistic political system.

Although in theory the Politburo of the Soviet Union and the executive organs of communist parties in other totalitarian states operate collectively and by consensus, in traditional practice one person usually has come to dominate the executive. This reality illustrates a characteristic tendency of communist political systems to concentrate executive power in the hands of an elite. The leader often becomes the embodiment of the state apparatus and the continuing revolution, as has been demonstrated in such executives as Castro in Cuba, Mao Tse Tung in China, Kim Il-Sung in North Korea, Enver Hoxha of Albania, Ho Chi Minh in Vietnam, Tito in Yugoslavia, and Robert Mugabe in Zimbabwe. All these people initiated the revolutions that brought communist or socialist totalitarian rule to their countries. Even leaders who succeeded the original revolutionaries as modern communist executives, like Gustav Husak in Czechoslovakia, Erich Honecker of the German Democratic Republic, Nicolae Ceausescu of Romania, Wojciech Jaruzelski of Poland, and Mikhail Gorbachev of the Soviet Union, sustained the same absolute power as their original counterparts.

One of the important differences between totalitarian and authoritarian dictators is that the former are less inclined to subvert the aims of the party for personal reasons and ambitions. While the "cult of personality" does surface in many communist states, political power still tends to be institutionalized more than it is personalized. People may adulate the leader, but their allegiance and loyalty remain with the ideological ideals of state institutions and organizations.

REFERENCES

1. David Rodnick, *An Introduction to Man and His Development* (New York: Appleton-Century-Crofts 1966), 53–64.
2. Robert Fried, *Comparative Political Institutions* (New York: Macmillan Company 1966), 7; see also Gabriel Almond and G.Bingham Powell Jr., *Comparative Politics Today: A World View* (Glenview, IL: Scott, Foresman & Company 1988), 113–115.
3. See Marc Lalonde, "The Changing Role of the Prime Minister's Office," *Canadian Public Administration* 14 (Winter 1971): 487-537; Robert Adie and Paul Thomas,

Canadian Public Administration (Scarborough, ON: Prentice-Hall 1987), 224–27.

4. Edward Greenberg, *The American Political System*, 5th ed. (Glenview, IL: Scott, Foresman & Company 1989), 273–89.
5. Almond and Powell Jr., *Comparative Politics Today: A World View*, 341–2; see also John Reshetar, *The Soviet Polity: Government and Politics in the USSR* (New York: Harper & Row 1989), 278–81.
6. See Richard Van Loon, "Cabinet Organization: The PMO, PCO, Policy Control and Expenditure Management," in Paul Fox, ed., *Politics Canada* (Toronto: McGraw-Hill Ryerson Ltd. 1982), 443–60.
7. Everett Ladd, *The American Polity* (New York: W.W. Norton & Co.1989), 223–6.
8. See Marian Irish and Elke Frank, *Introduction to Comparative Politics: Thirteen Nation-States* (Englewood Cliffs, NJ: Prentice–Hall, Inc. 1978), 99–102.
9. See Michael S. Whittington and Glen Williams, eds., *Canadian Politics in the 1980's* (Toronto: Methuen 1981), 292–309.
10. See Thomas Skidmore and Peter Smith, *Modern Latin America* (New York: Oxford University Press 1984), 379; Alexander Edelmann, *Latin American Government and Politics* (Homewood, IL: Dorsey Press 1969), 329.
11. See Joseph LaPalombara, *Politics within Nations* (Englewood Cliffs, NJ: Prentice-Hall, Inc. 1974), 190–6.
12. Greenberg, *The American Political System: A Radical Approach*, 234.
13. Dell Gillette Hetchner and Carol Levine, *Comparative Government and Politics* (New York: Harper & Row Publishers 1981), 190–1.
14. Rais Khan and James McNiven, *An Introduction to Political Science* (Homewood, IL: Dorsey Press 1984), 188.
15. See W.L. White, R.H. Wagenberg, and R.C. Nelson, *Introduction to Canadian Politics and Government* (Toronto: Holt, Rinehart and Winston Ltd. 1981), 128–9.
16. "Canadians Think the Queen Is just Fine," *Weekend Magazine*, October 2, 1977, 4; and Richard Van Loon and Michael Whittington, *The Canadian Political System: Environment, Structure and Process* (Toronto: McGraw-Hill Ryerson Ltd. 1981) 121–2.
17. See Ronald Landes, *The Canadian Polity: A Comparative Introduction* (Scarborough, ON: Prentice-Hall Canada Inc. 1983), 115.
18. See Van Loon, "Cabinet Organization," in Fox, ed., *Politics Canada*, 449–51; Canada, Treasury Board of Canada, *Role of the Treasury Board Secretariat and the Office of the Comptroller General* (Ottawa: 1984).
19. Canada, House of Commons, *Debates*, January 29, 1934, 42; and October 31, 1945, 1681.
20. Leon Dion, "The Concept of Political Leadership," *Canadian Journal of Political Science* 1 (March 1968): 9; and David Roth et al., *Comparative Politics: Diverse States in an Interdependent World* (New York: Harper & Row Publishers 1989), 256–300.
21. W.A. Matheson, *The Prime Minister and the Cabinet* (Toronto: Methuen 1976), 47–78; see also E. Forsey and G. Eglington, *The Question of Confidence in Responsible Government* (Ottawa: Special Committee on Reform of the House of Commons 1985).
22. See Robert Adie and Paul Thomas, *Canadian Public Administration* (Scarborough, ON.: Prentice-Hall Canada Inc. 1987), 213–33.
23. See A.W. Johnson, "The Role of the Deputy Minister," in Kenneth Kernaghan, ed., *Public Administration in Canada* (Toronto: Methuen 1985), 289–98; Timothy Plumptre, "New Perspectives on the Role of the Deputy Minister," *Canadian Public Administration* 30 (Fall 1987): 376-98; Gordon Robertson, "The Deputies Anonymous Duty," *Policy Options* 4 (July/August 1983): 11–13; and Gordon Osbaldeston,

Keeping Deputy Ministers Accountable (Scarborough, ON: McGraw-Hill Ryerson Ltd. 1989).

24. See Matheson, *The Prime Minister and the Cabinet*, 22–46.
25. See Erwin Levine and Elmer Cornwall Jr., *An Introduction to American Government* (New York: Macmillan Publishing Co. Inc. 1983), 169–210.
26. Richard Neustadt, *Presidential Power* (New York: New American Library 1964), viii.
27. See Hedrick Smith, "Taking Charge of Congress," *New York Times Sunday Magazine,* August 9, 1981.
28. William Young, *Essentials of American Government* (New York: Appleton-Century-Crofts 1964), 251.
29. Perry Anderson, *Lineages of the Absolutist State* (London: Veros Editions 1979).
30. David Collier, ed., *The New Authoritarianism in Latin America* (Princeton: Princeton University Press 1979), 285–318.
31. See James Malloy, ed., *Authoritarianism and Corporatism in Latin America* (Pittsburgh: University of Pittsburgh Press 1977).
32. David Roth and Frank Wilson, *The Comparative Study of Politics* (Englewood Cliffs, NJ: Prentice-Hall Inc. 1980), xxiv.

SUGGESTED READINGS

Peter Calvert, *The Process of Political Succession* (New York: St. Martin's Press 1987).

James Davies, *The American Presidency – A New Perspective* (New York: Harper & Row 1987).

Irving Janis, *Crucial Decisions: Leadership in Policy Making and Crisis Management* (New York: The Free Press 1988).

Barbara Kellerman, *Leadership: Multidisciplinary Perspectives* (Englewood Cliffs, NJ: Prentice-Hall 1986).

Gary King and Lyn Ragsdale, *The Elusive Executive* (Washington, DC: CQ Press 1988).

Olga Narkiewicz, *Soviet Leaders: From Cult of Personality to Collective Rule* (New York: St. Martin's Press 1986).

Leslie Pal and David Taras, *Prime Ministers and Priemiers* (Scarborough, ON: Prentice-Hall Canada Inc. 1988).

W. Rosenbach and Robert Taylor, *Contemporary Issues in Leadership* (Boulder, CO: Westview Press 1989).

Kenneth Thompson, *The Virginia Papers on the Presidency* (Lanham, MD: University Press of America 1988).

Richard Watson, *The Presidential Contest*, 3rd ed. (Washington, DC: Congressional Quarterly Press 1988).

GLOSSARY

kingship: A society with its political power concentrated in a hereditary king or monarch who rules in the name or guise of the gods.

autocracy: A form of government in which power is held by a single person unencumbered by legal or other restraints.

Prime Minister's Office (PMO): An executive agency of government that functions as a source of advice to the prime minister on policy matters and matters related to public opinion concerning the government.

Privy Council Office (PCO): An executive government agency to advise on government matters and to communicate and coordinate Cabinet decisions with relevant officials.

Treasury Board: A statutory committee of Cabinet charged with overseeing the budgetary process of government.

Executive Office of the President (EOP): The office containing the major staff organizations of the president, such as the White House Office and the Office of Emergency.

National Security Council (NSC): An executive office agency charged with advising the president on matters related to national security.

Office of Management and Budget (OMB): A federal agency, created in 1970, within the executive office that replaced the Bureau of the Budget, which was formed in 1921 to handle the preparation of the annual budget.

Council of Economic Advisors (CEA): An executive office agency established in 1946 to analyse the U.S. economy, advise the president on economic programs, and recommend policies for economic growth.

executive privilege: The right of executive officials to refuse to appear before or to withhold information from a legislative committee.

intelligence: Information gathered by a government about the capabilities, strengths, weaknesses, and intentions of other states.

legitimators: Agents and or institutions that process political activities or decisions so that they are widely held to be rightful or justified in the political and social system.

indoctrination: The deliberate transmission of specific ideas, attitudes, or patterns of behaviour in congruence with an official ideology or set of policy goals.

head of state: The ceremonial executive who formally represents a nation-state.

public policy: The culmination of the whole political system from which governmental actions or inactions are directed at a society's goals, priorities, and problems, based on the human and physical resources available to decision makers.

pardon: An executive annulment of a penalty already prescribed.

reprieve: The executive postponement of the carrying out of a sentence.

amnesty: An executive determination that an entire class of people shall not be prosecuted, or will be, because of special circumstances, exempted from the application of the law.

confidence of the House: The support of a majority of the elected members of the House of Commons.

prorogue: To end a parliamentary session that is not followed by a general election.

dissolution: To terminate a parliamentary term that is followed by a general election.

royal assent: The final step in the passage of a bill, whereby the Crown accepts and signs it into law.

orders in council: Laws and decrees passed by the Cabinet without reference to the House of Commons.

Crown: Reference to the composite character of sovereign power in a monarchy and a symbol of the institutions of state as in crown law, crown lands, crown courts, crown office, crown debts, etc.

prerogative: An exclusive right inherent within an office or position that may be constitutional or may have developed out of custom and tradition.

caucus: A private meeting of political party members.

Cabinet solidarity: Once a Cabinet decision has been made, all Cabinet members are obliged to support it in public even if they had opposed it earlier. Any member unwilling to do this is expected to resign.

portfolio: The office and duties of a Cabinet minister who is in charge of a government department. Some portfolios are "senior" (e.g., the minister of Finance) and co-ordinate their vast responsibilities along with a "junior" portfolio (e.g., the minister of state for Finance).

pork barrel: The public treasury that is drawn from by public officials legislating out of special interests for their own constituents or for their own political image.

junta: A Spanish word for a board or council, but in politics the term usually applies to a group of military officers who collectively exercise the powers of government.

7
Legislatures

The Knesset, Israel.

Assemblies

COMPARED WITH THE EXECUTIVE BRANCH of government, the legislature is a relatively new creation among political institutions. The only legislature to survive to the present without changing its earliest forms is the British Parliament. Dating back to the eleventh century, the English legislative structure has become the prototype of the modern legislature, inspiring many variations on the parliamentary model, even among authoritarian and totalitarian regimes. When William of Normandy conquered England in 1066, he imposed Norman feudal* institutions on his new subjects. These included the Curia Regis, an assembly of nobles to advise the king, and the Curia Regis Magnae, a large assembly of lesser nobility that met three times annually to counsel and present petitions to the king.

Over time, English kings summoned this Great Council with increased frequency. Made up of knights, burgesses, and members of the clergy, the council met separately from the barons to advise the king and approve taxes for projects that affected their constituencies. Eventually, this body of advisers came to be the House of Commons and the assembly of nobles became the House of Lords. Originally, neither institution was intended to be democratic. But by the nineteenth century the British Parliament came to symbolize modern democracy.

Most modern states have developed a legislative branch of government consisting of bodies of elected or appointed individuals called parliaments, congresses, assemblies, diets, or chambers. Only Oman and Saudi Arabia, both absolute monarchies, do not have some kind of legislative assembly. In all other states, the role and function of the legislature are determined by the type of political system, i.e., democratic, authoritarian, or totalitarian. It is significant that despite the character of a regime, nearly all modern nation-states find it necessary to maintain some form of representative assembly either as an effective lawmaking body or as a symbol of government legitimacy. Even in the most repressive regimes, the legislature contributes to the formal proclamation of the law by lending popular endorsement to the lawmaking initiatives of the executive.

Number of Legislative Chambers

Parliamentary bodies can be *unicameral* (one chamber), *bicameral* (two chambers), or *tricameral* (three chambers). Today, unicameral national assemblies outnumber bicameral assemblies by a ratio of three to two.[1] On the eve of World War I, most of the world's political systems had bicameral national assemblies. But as new nation-states emerged, more and more political systems adopted the unicameral form of legislature. The largest number of unicameral legislatures is found in Africa, Asia, Central America, and the Middle East. One-house assemblies can also be found in homogeneous nation-states with democratic traditions, such as Denmark, Finland, and New Zealand. Even in those states with bicameral national assemblies, many of the subnational legislative bodies are unicameral: for example, the Diets (Landtage) of the Lander in the German Federal Republic (except Bavaria), Canada's provincial legislatures, those of the states of India, and that of the state of Nebraska in the United States.

Approximately two-thirds of all democratic governments have bicameral legislatures.[2] The centre of political power is always located in the "lower house," which tends to have a larger elected membership and shorter terms of office. Examples of such houses are the Canadian *House of Commons,* the French *National Assembly*, the Swiss *Nationalrat,* and the U.S. *House of Representatives*. The second chamber, usually called the "upper house," has the smaller membership, longer tenure, and is selected in different ways. For example, the members of the Canadian Senate are *appointed* by the governor general on the advice of the prime minister and must retire at age 75. In the United States, senators are *elected* in state-wide constituencies for six-year terms. In contrast, members of the Austrian Bundesrat are elected by the legislatures of the various Lander (lands).

One justification for bicameralism in democratic federal states is that it permits a system of dual representation for the constituent parts of the union. This certainly applies in democracies such as Australia, West Germany, Switzerland, and the United States. But, in Canada, the traditionally inferior legislative role of the Senate to the House of Commons has diminished its ability to represent effectively regional and provincial interests.

Another asserted advantage of bicameral legislatures is that they prevent concentrations of legislative power in one assembly and provide a second forum for deliberating legislation. In democracies, a second chamber is considered to be a necessary conservative influence that reduces hasty or impulsive decision making in a lower house. In the United States, the Senate performs this conservative function with respect to the House of Representatives. But as a deliberative body it also has important checks on the initiatives of the executive branch of government, with its power to confirm presidential appointments and ratify treaties.

In some states the second chamber is particularly well suited for advising the lower house, as does the Federal Republic of Germany's Bundesrat (upper house), whose members are state government officials advising the Bundestag (lower house) of ramifications of national legislation on the Lander. In Canada, the largely symbolic upper house has considerable legislative powers on paper but is limited by its non-elective character from conducting any legitimate deliberation in the lawmaking process. The Senate, as presently mandated, functions as a house of formal reward for party stalwarts who have paid their political dues. Thus, as the Canadian Senate demonstrates, the mere presence of a second chamber is no guarantee that bicameralism is functional or even appropriate to fulfil the representative needs of a state.

But two chambers can be particularly adaptive to multi-ethnic and multinational states because the legislatures provide political representation of these special groups. Sometimes an upper chamber is a power concession made to special groups in order to reduce political tensions. The bicameralism of the Soviet Union and Czechoslovakia and the multi-chambered arrangement of Yugoslavia are formal attempts to give symbolic concessions to special groups. The basic rifts between the Russians and the Ukrainians, the Czechs and the Slovaks, and the Serbs and the Croats are recognized by the political system and, to some extent, mitigated by bicameral legislatures.

There are no hard or fast rules to explain why a particular state adopts a unicameral or bicameral legislature. Legislative structure depends on the traditions, needs, and goals of a political system or regime. Some East European and Asian socialist states (Bulgaria, the German Democratic Republic, Hungary, Romania, Mongolia, North Korea, Vietnam, and China) have adopted unicameral legislatures for ideological reasons, one being that "the will of the people must be one." In these states, a second chamber is associated with the privilege of the bourgeois state. One East European exception is Poland, which in 1989 established a new second chamber – a 100-seat Senat (Senate). In authoritarian regimes, the unicameral legislature facilitates centralized political control and functions as a rubber stamp for the actions and policies of the dictator.

But there can be any number of reasons why it is expedient for a political system to use single or multiple chambers in the legislative process. For reasons of efficiency and the centralization of decision making, Sweden reduced its bicameral parliament to a single chamber in 1971. Pakistan reverted to bicameralism in 1973, as did Spain in 1977, when its new bicameral parliament, the Cortes, was constituted. And, more recently, the Philippines reverted to a bicameral Congress after the elections of 1987. In 1984, South Africa adopted a tricameral parliamentary system, with one house legislating for whites, one for mixed races, and a third chamber for Indians.

Size and Tenure of Assemblies

The size of most legislatures is determined by constituency* representation as it relates to total population. Some legislatures use a system of functional representation* whereby people are represented according to occupations rather than according to where they live. For example, in Ecuador's upper house, Senators represent occupational groups in agriculture, commerce, industry, journalism, and labour. Similarly the 60-member Irish Senate (Seanad Éireann) employs functional representation: 11 are nominated by the prime minister, 6 are elected by universities, and 43 are elected from special panels of candidates representing the public services and other interests, such as the arts, languages, literature, agriculture, banking, labour and industry. In Indonesia, the 460-member House of Representatives has 360 elected representatives and a functional group composed of 100 representatives who gain their seats from the support of professions and occupations. But most legislatures follow the principle of representation by population.*

As a general rule, as population varies so does the representative size of legislatures. In Canada, under federal law, independent three-member commissions in each province redraw constituency boundaries once every 10 years. Using data from the 1981 census, the size of the House of Commons was increased by 13 seats from 282 to 295 effective July 13, 1988. The new boundaries gave Ontario an increase of four seats to 99, Alberta increased by five seats to 26, and British Colombia increased by four seats to 32. The total number of MPs from each of the remaining provinces, Yukon, and the Northwest Territories remained unchanged. But within each province, the boundaries of many constituencies were redrawn to adapt to population swings while producing ridings with roughly the same number of electors.

Many less-populated states in Africa, Asia, and Latin America have lower houses with fewer than 100 members. For example, the National Assembly of Botswana has 36 members, the House of Representatives in Gambia has 42 members, Gibraltar has only a 19-member House of Assembly, and El Salvador's National Assembly elects just 52 members. Another large group of states, such as Austria, Colombia, Mexico, and Venezuela, have legislatures with between 100 and 200 members. Canada, with its 295-member House of Commons, falls into a group of states with relatively larger lower houses. The more populous countries tend to have lower houses ranging in size from 400 to 3000 members: West Germany's Bundestag has 497 members; and China's National People's Congress has 3000 members; Taiwan's National Assembly has 1285 members; Great Britain's House of Commons has 635 members; Japan's House of Representatives has 511 members; and the United States House of Representatives has 435 members.

Most upper chambers have fewer members than do lower houses, ranging from 25 to 1200 members. Paraguay's Senate has 30 members; Canada's Senate has 104 members; the French Senate has 318 members; and the British House of Lords has approximately 1200 members.

It is difficult for large legislatures, like those in China, Great Britain, Japan, and the United States, to deliberate the intricacies of complicated issues and to reach a collective decision easily. In most democratic states, even if all other commitments (servicing constituents, ceremonial functions, studying community problems, electioneering, and political party work) allowed time enough for legislators to meet and deliberate, no one of them could be reasonably informed about the variety of matters that require legislative action. How, for instance, can a Canadian MP become sufficiently knowledgeable so that he or she can deal in quick succession with legislation on freight rates, tariff policy on textiles, immigration quotas for Chilean nationals, and a mutual defence treaty with the United States? Most legislative leaders are aware that the larger the legislature and the more complicated the issues, the less likely the legislature as a body will deal effectively with them. Larger legislatures delegate the drafting of legislation to small groups of legislative experts. Out of the necessity to cope with the modern lawmaking process, many legislatures have established committee systems*. In Canada, the use of legislative committees began in the mid 1960s; in the United States, a much longer history of standing committees* and subcommittees* has been the response to complex congressional matters.

Like size, the length of legislative terms in lower houses varies considerably. The United States House of Representatives has a two-year term; Australia, Mexico, New Zealand, and Western Samoa have legislatures with three-year terms; Canada, Great Britain, France, Ireland, Italy, and South Africa all have five-year legislative terms; a term of six years is found in the Philippines and Sri Lanka.

Many upper chambers differ in tenure from their legislative counterparts because of the divergent systems of representation and the sometimes different ways of selecting representatives for upper houses and lower houses. Members of upper chambers are selected by *appointment, indirect election,* or *popular election.* In the United Kingdom and Luxembourg they are appointed for life. In other states they are appointed by the head of state on the advice of the head of government for limited terms, as in the Bahamas, Canada (to age 75), and Jamaica. Indirect election is conducted in Austria, France, and the Netherlands, for fixed terms. Directly elected upper chambers are found in Australia, Colombia, Italy, the United States, and Mexico.

Functions of Democratic Legislatures

Because legislatures are a product of a unique political culture found in every country, they differ in organization, power, and structure.[3] Some legislatures are organized and structured along oligarchic and racial lines, as in the Union of South Africa where a powerful white elite controls the legislative balance of power in a nation-state of predominantly coloured and mixed races. Independent legislatures, exemplified by the Congress of the United States, reflect a tradition of institutional competition in the lawmaking process. Some legislatures are weak, as in Great Britain and Canada, where Parliament is dominated by majority parties that control all executive posts. Many legislatures are captive, as in totalitarian and authoritarian countries, where real power is solely an executive exercise and the legislature serves primarily to legitimize executive decisions. But whether they are – as democratic or non-democratic institutions – oligarchic, independent, weak, or captive, legislatures perform similar functions in a political system. They represent people, formulate, initiate, and enact laws, control public finances, check the executive, adjudicate on executive behaviour, and amend constitutions.

Representation

Hanna Pitkin defines representation as "re-presentation, that is, making present of something absent – but not making it literally present. It must be made present indirectly, through an intermediary; it must be made present in some sense, while nevertheless remaining literally absent."[4] That is precisely what a legislature does. It makes present an authorized sample of the population representing all the rest who must remain absent from the decision-making process of society. In Canada, the average number of constituents each member of Parliament represents is 85 800. Legislatures are a social compromise between the principles of "perfect" democracy (direct popular participation in the lawmaking process) and the realities of indirect representation in modern complex nation-states. Because there is no way for entire societies to assemble, deliberate, debate, and decide, we compromise our commitment to these principles by instituting representation by which a select group of people meet and decide on the issues of the day, but are ever conscious of the interests and preferences of those who sent them to the meeting.

Representative assemblies have proved to be enormously popular in Canada. In addition to Parliament, we have provincial legislatures, town and city councils, school boards, and various regional boards and commissions. Today about a quarter-million Canadians hold office as elected representatives. In Canada, representative institutions have diffused well beyond formal government. No political ideal, with the possible exception of majority voting, is so deeply a part of Canada's political culture as is the institution of representative assemblies.

In modern democratic legislatures, representation is based on three principles: *authorization, accountability,* and *responsibility.*[5] Authorization means that a representative is one who is given the right by a constituency to act on its behalf. Accountability means that representatives are responsible to the people by means of *elections,* initiatives*, referenda*, petitions*, recall*, *public opinion polls,* and roll-call voting* in legislatures. Responsibility is the way the representative acts. Some argue that true responsibility is acting in the best interests of the constituency, regardless of whether constituents* agree with the actions of the representative. Others argue that true responsibility means that representatives should act as their constituents want them to act.

Making Laws

In most democratic legislatures, the formulation and initiation of policy has become an executive function. Canada, Great Britain, and other parliamentary systems operate legislatures that fuse executive and legislative powers according to the majority principle: the political party that enjoys the support of a majority of seats in the legislature forms an executive that drafts and initiates legislation. These "government" bills are introduced by a minister. Then, as a body, the legislature debates and enacts government bills into law. As a general rule in parliamentary democracies, any member, whether on the government or opposition side, may introduce a bill. But the success rate of private-member bills is extremely low because of the urgency of government bills and the power of the executive to mobilize disciplined party support. In fact, for this reason, some states do not permit individual legislators to introduce bills of their own. For example, in the West German Bundestag (lower house), individual members who want to initiate a bill must form a "fraktion" (a group of at least fifteen members) before the bill can be introduced.

Increasingly, in the United States, rule initiation originates in the executive branch, where one of many agencies drafts a proposal and finds a sympathetic legislator to introduce the bill in Congress. But even in the U.S. political system, unless there is widespread support for a proposed bill, the legislation will die. In the 99th Congress (1986), 3835 bills were introduced and only 341 became law.[6]

In the world's two major democratic political systems, the parliamentary and presidential, the support and leadership of the executive must accompany the role of the legislature in the enactment of law. The parliamentary system is particularly well suited to executive leadership in the legislature through the prime minister and the cabinet, as the Canadian experience has shown. The presidential system is much more complicated because the president and the cabinet are not present in the congress. But, in both systems, the increasing complexities of government have made the legislature dependent on the executive for the initiative and proclamation of the laws. Essentially the function of the modern legislature is to criticize, examine, amend, adopt, and (from time to time) reject legislation.

Control of Public Finances

The power to scrutinize and control public finances varies widely among legislatures. In Canada and the United States, executive budgets are drawn up and submitted to the legislature for approval. In states with an elected cabinet, like Canada and Switzerland, the budget is approved or rejected in its entirety by the legislature. If it is rejected, the government is defeated, the Cabinet must resign, and Parliament is dissolved. If approved in Canada, the House of Commons has an important audit function that guarantees a measure of financial control. The Canadian auditor general reports directly to the House of Commons and conducts audits of government spending to assure the legislature that the provisions approved in the budget are implemented honestly. Unlike other executive officers, the auditor general is an employee of Parliament, not of the Cabinet. In France and West Germany, the executive has greater power of the purse than does the legislature.

The French president can overrule* legislative disapproval of the budget by executive order. The German chancellor may also bypass the legislature and authorize* expenditures by executive prerogative*. In the United States, the president can only veto the entire budget or accept the entire budget. But the president may refuse to spend the money.

Perhaps the oldest and most enduring function of the legislature is the power to levy* taxes. But as with so many other legislative functions, the raising and spending of revenues have shifted primarily from legislative to executive control. Most democratic legislatures now only retain the power to scrutinize and revise budgets proposed by the executive branch. The pressure for higher tax revenues comes largely from the increased cost of executive programs – costs of defence and domestic policies. As these programs become more and more costly, the executive is forced to demand new revenues. The legislature is always in a tricky political position – caught between the desire for increased government spending and public resistance to paying the cost through higher taxes.

Checks on the Executive

The universal expansion of executive authority has steadily increased the importance of the legislature to check and supervise the executive branch of government. These tasks are accomplished in a variety of ways. In democratic parliamentary governments, the function of supervision is built into the system by the fusion of the executive with the legislature. Ministers must be members of the legislative body and are responsible to it, as in Australia, Canada, Great Britain, and Ireland. In other states, cabinet ministers are not members of either house but the legislature has the power of approving executive appointments, as in France, the Netherlands, and Norway. In the United States, the Senate must approve executive appointments for ambassadors, the cabinet, and federal judges and other officers.

Executive acts may be subject to legislative approval, like the ratification of treaties, issuance of decrees, and declarations of national emergency. In Canada, there is no constitutional requirement for the parliamentary ratification of treaties.[7] The decision to accede and ratify a treaty is an executive act legitimized by the royal prerogative. Most treaties are simply tabled in the House of Commons. But major multilateral treaties are by tradition submitted to Parliament before ratification.

One of the most effective means of controlling the executive is legislative scrutiny. In democratic states, legislators can supervise the policies and activities of executive members by asking questions in oral and written forms. In Canada, Great Britain, and the Commonwealth countries, the parliamentary question period is an effective device for gaining information about government actions. In other parliamentary systems the process of interpellation* is a more pointed method of legislative scrutiny of the executive. In Japan, opposition parties can question or interpellate government ministers and their assistants in the various committees drafting legislation before it goes to a full or plenary session of the Japanese Diet. The objectives of opposition legislators are to embarrass, delay, and even shape government-sponsored legislation. In Belgium, Italy, Netherlands, and Switzerland, interpellation forces specific questions that are unsatisfactorily answered to debate and formal vote, sometimes resulting in a motion of censure against government. The functions of discussing, criticizing, and reviewing executive initiatives constitute an important check on powerful executives.

Judicial Role

Some democratic legislatures have the power to adjudicate the behaviour of executive officials. The Constitution of the United States gives Congress the power to impeach* any civil officer of the national government: the House hears the evidence and decides to impeach; the Senate sits as the court, with the power to convict on a two-thirds vote of its members. In France, the National Assembly and the Senate can decide to impeach the president and the ministers of state, but the accused must be tried by the High Court of Justice. In Canada and Great Britain, Parliament does not impeach members of the executive because the House of Commons has the power to defeat a goverment whose members have acted illegally or unethically. Most parliamentary systems permit a prime minister to remove a minister from the cabinet who has been found guilty of a crime. But usually such persons retain a seat in the legislature unless, by a unanimous vote, they are stripped of their parliamentary privileges.

In Canada, the House of Commons has investigated the activities of MPs to determine if they could hold their seats. For example, in 1890 the House reviewed a previous conviction for forgery and the allegation that an MP's conduct was corrupt on a matter involving the granting of timber permits. And on two occasions Louis Riel was expelled, once because he failed to obey a House order to appear in his seat, and then for having been judged an outlaw for a felony. The House demonstrated its right to expel an MP when, in 1946, Fred Rose was convicted and sentenced to six years' imprisonment for conspiring to commit offences under the Official Secrets Act. Since then a number of MPs who have been convicted in the courts (for example Michel Gravel, 1988, and Richard Grise, 1989) have resigned before the House could exercise its right to expel a member.

Amending Constitutions

The legislatures in most democratic countries have certain powers over the amendment* of the national constitution. Since many consititutions were originally drafted by national legislatures, it is appropriate that they are authorized to exercise some role in the process of constitutional reform. In some states, such as Great Britain and New Zealand, constitutional change is primarily a function of the national legislature. In other states, such as Australia, France, and Switzerland, constitutional amendments are proposed by the national legislature, then ratified by voters in a nationwide referendum. In the United States, Congress has the power to propose a constitutional amendment by a two-thirds vote, then the proposed amendment must be ratified by three-quarters of the states in order to be adopted. In Canada, constitutional reform is a lengthy and complicated process involving five different methods, depending on the nature of the amendment. In three of the methods, the legislative assembly of each province, or of those provinces to which the amendment applies, must approve of the proposed constitutional amendment.

In general, legislatures are involved in basically three methods of amending constitutions. One is by the action of the legislature alone, with certain variations in the usual requirements for passing a law. For example, Ecuador requires that a constitutional amendment must be approved by unanimous vote of the total membership. Another method of amendment involves a proposal by the legislature followed by a constitutional convention to ratify the amendment, as employed in Argentina. A third method, practised in federal states, gives a distinctive role in the amending process to the subnational units.

Canada's Legislative Assemblies

Canada's bicameral Parliament consists of two houses: the *House of Commons* and the *Senate*. Elected members of the House of Commons are called *members of Parliament* (MPS); members of the Senate are called *senators*. In Canada, the House of Commons is modelled after the British lower house. The country is divided into political constituencies that are roughly equal in population, each sending a representative to Ottawa. Originally the Senate was modelled after the British House of Lords. But in Britain there is no limit on the membership of the House of Lords: new appointments may be made from any constituency. However, the Constitution Act, 1867, states what the number of senators should be from each province and thus limits the size of the Senate. The Constitution stipulates that there must be a session of the Parliament of Canada at least once each year and that the maximum life of a Parliament between elections is five years. Under certain emergency conditions, such as war, this normal tenure can be extended.

The House of Commons

If Parliament is the symbol of political authority in Canada, the House of Commons is where the actualities of this legislative authority are exercised.[8] The principal divisions of legislative power do not run between Parliament and Cabinet, but within the House of Commons between the majority party (which controls the Commons and Cabinet) and the opposition.

These divisions are reflected in the structural composition of the House of Commons, between the government and the members of the opposition, with the *Speaker* as the presiding officer of the House. On the Speaker's right sits the government, and on the left sits the opposition, an adversarial positioning of political opponents in the legislative framework. The political executive sit in the first two rows on the government side of the House. In the rows surrounding the prime minister and the Cabinet sit majority-party backbenchers. The leader of the opposition and the shadow cabinet sit directly across the centre aisle, facing the government. Behind them sit opposition backbenchers and the furthest seats from the Speaker are filled by the minor parties and independents.

By presiding over the debates and acting as the administrative head of the House of Commons, the Speaker plays a central role in the legislative process.[9] The Speaker is a bilingual member of the House who is elected by that body for the duration of Parliament on the nomination of the prime minister. As the presiding officer of the House of Commons, the Speaker is expected to be non-partisan* and impartial in applying the rules and procedures and in recognizing members who want to debate. During each sitting of the House, the Speaker rules on time limits for debate, on parliamentary privileges when they are violated, and on motions of adjournment and closure. In case of a tie, the Speaker casts the deciding vote. As the administrative head of the House of Commons, the Speaker is responsible for preparing and defending the internal estimates, which are the costs of staffing and operating the lower house.

Concurrent with the election of the speaker is the election of a *deputy speaker*.[10] The deputy speaker replaces the Speaker when he or she is absent and acts as the chairperson of the committeees of the whole. Like the Speaker, the deputy speaker can be selected from either the government or opposition sides of the House, although the conventional practice is for the government to select both people. In the unlikely but possible case that both the Speaker and deputy speaker are absent, the House of Commons will temporarily appoint the *deputy chairperson of committees* from the government side of the House to the Speaker's chair*.

The House of Commons is headed by a permanent civil servant, the *Clerk of the House*, whose job is to supervise all the permanent staff of the House of Commons and to prepare and deliver the daily order paper to the Speaker. The Clerk provides the minister of Justice with two copies of every bill tabled in the House. The Clerk may be thought of as a deputy minister whose department is made up of the officers and staff of the House of Commons.

Party whips are important in the organization and structure of the House of Commons. Named after the "whippers" in the organization of the traditional English fox hunt who kept the hounds from straying, they are chosen in party caucus as special officers of their political parties. A whip seeks to assure that all party members are present for important votes. The authority of the whip is accepted because MPs recognize that only by voting as a bloc can their party continue to be effective in the House of Commons, as government or opposition. To defy the whip by abstaining or even voting for the other side is to seriously challenge party discipline. Such actions may result in MPs losing the support and respect of their party colleagues. So, in addition to ensuring party discipline, the party whip must educate party members about the ramifications of party policies so that these are as palatable to as many members as possible. Whips are the party negotiators who decide among each other what items on the agenda are subject to political compromise and how much debate will be expended on them.

Working alongside the whips are the *House leaders* of the various parties. The House leaders guide the flow of business through the House of Commons. On the government side, the House leader is a Cabinet member responsible for the organization of government business and its quick passage through the House of Commons. Like the party whips, House leaders negotiate the apportionment of time to be spent on legislation and other matters of procedural business.

The structure and functions of the House of Commons are also determined by its committee system.[11] The basic challenge to the House of Commons is how to organize its 295 diverse members in order to get things done. One major response to the challenge since the mid 1960s is the specialization of parliamentary business in numerous legislative committees. Currently, there are twenty-six *standing committees* and four joint committees made up from members of the House and the Senate. The Striking Committee* decides on the membership of the standing committees. Each party caucus provides the Striking Committee with the names of qualified committee candidates, thus preventing the government from assigning the least experienced and least able opposition members to important standing committees (table 7.1) Under the Standing Orders of the House of Commons, adopted in June 1978, these committees are permanent and are struck at the commencement of each session of Parliament to consider all subjects arising from the process of lawmaking in Canada. Committee assignments are party-based and reflect the percentage of seats a party commands in the Commons. For example, the Conservative party has over 70 percent of the seats in the House and enjoys approximately the same proportion of positions on each committee. Committee power is more closely concentrated in the House when there is strong majority government. But opposition parties can be more influential in committees in a minority-government situation.

A number of factors influence MP requests for committee assignments. One of these is the desire to be where the action is. MPs also want to serve on committees that handle the broadest central concerns of government – like the Public Accounts Committee. Another major motive of House members in requesting committee assignments is being in a position to influence public policy. Some committees are attractive to members because they play important roles in the key areas of government decision making, like taxing and spending, the economy, and social welfare.

However, the main function of the House of Commons is the passage of legislation.[12] Legislation is the formal process of converting a proposed bill into law. Bills may be proposed and introduced to the House of Commons as a *private-member's bill* or as a *government bill.* A private-member's bill can be introduced by any member of Parliament on either the government or opposition side of the House. Usually, at the time they are introduced, these kinds of bills do not have the support of the government and almost never become law. Opposition members who introduce private-members' bills recognize these facts, using the opportunity to generate public opinion that will influence the direction of a particular government policy. A government bill is a policy proposal or a money bill* requiring legislation that is introduced in the House by a Cabinet minister. The responsible minister calls for the drafting of legislation by the Department of Justice. The draft is then approved by the responsible minister before it is presented to the Cabinet Committee on Legislation and House Planning. Once this committee has approved the draft bill, it is then signed by the prime minister and introduced in the House of Commons in its *first reading* by the responsible minister. During this stage the title of the bill is read, followed by a short explanation of its contents. At the *second reading,* the bill is debated and a vote is taken on

Standing Committees of Parliament

House of Commons	Senate
Aboriginal Affairs and Northern Development	Selection
Agriculture	Agriculture and Forestry
Communications and Culture	Banking, Trade and Commerce
Consumer and Corporate Affairs	Energy and Natural Resources
Elections, Privileges and Procedure	Fisheries
Energy, Mines and Resources	Foreign Affairs
Environment and Forestry	Internal Economy, Budgets and Administration
External Affairs and International Trade	Legal and Constitutional Affairs
Finance and Economic Affairs	National Finance
Fisheries and Oceans	Official Languages
Government Operations	Scrutiny of Regulations
Human Rights	Social Affairs, Science and Technology
Justice and Solicitor General	Standing Rules and Orders
Labour, Employment and Immigration	Transport and Communications
Management and Members' Services	
Multiculturalism	
National Defence	
National Health and Welfare	
Official Languages	
Public Accounts	
Regional Industrial Expansion	
Research, Science and Technology	
Scrutiny of Regulations	
Secretary of State	
Transport	
Veterans' Affairs	

Table 7.1

principle to approve or reject it in total. If it is "approved in principle," and it usually is, the bill is then considered by the appropriate standing committee, where it is given a clause-by-clause examination. At the *committee stage* the bill is debated and witnesses may be called to testify about their positions, pro or con. All standing committees are empowered to make amendments to the original draft, if necessary. It should be noted that money bills, unlike other bills, are not considered by standing committees; rather, they go before the Committee of the Whole*. When the committee has completely examined the bill to its satisfaction, it reports the bill with any recommended amendments back to the House of

Commons. In this *report stage,* the opposition will vigorously debate the bill and try to reintroduce the amendments it made at the committee stage. Any final changes the government wishes to make must also be made at this time, before the bill goes to its *third reading.* In almost all instances, a bill passes quickly through its third reading. However, if revisions made during the committee stage are unacceptable to the full House, the bill can be rejected. After a bill is finally passed through the House of Commons at this third reading, it is then introduced in the Senate, where it receives a *pro forma** repetition of the legislative process of the House. Once a bill is passed by Parliament, it is presented to the governor general who confers *royal assent* by signing it into law. *Proclamation* follows royal assent and a new Canadian law has finally been enacted.

The Senate

Anyone reading the Constitution Act, 1867, would have to conclude that the Senate and the House of Commons are about equal in power.[13] But, because the Senate is an appointed body, it has usually avoided the exercise of its constitutional powers in a manner that would challenge the popular legitimacy of the House of Commons. However, controversy flared in May 1989 when the Senate's Liberal majority proposed an amendment to a supply bill authorizing the Mulroney government to borrow about $33 billion, even though the bill had been approved in the House of Commons. They also called upon the president of the Treasury Board and the minister of Justice to justify the way the government had spent $7.5 billion by using the governor general's special warrants*. The issue was whether Parliament has control over Canada's finances. By stalling the bill, the Senate created a new round of demands for reform, even outright abolition. On paper, the Senate can amend or reject a bill passed by the House of Commons; this activity is as important a part of the lawmaking process as are royal assent and proclamation. The Senate last defeated a House of Commons bill in 1939 and from 1960 to 1989, fourteen bills sent from the Commons to the Senate failed to receive royal assent. In 1988 former Liberal leader John Turner directed the Liberal majority in the Senate to delay enabling legislation for the Canada-United States free-trade agreement. Notwithstanding the fact that a federal election intervened, the Senate was exercising its right to delay a bill. Although the Senate powers of *delay, rejection,* and *amendment* have been but rarely exercised, the formal role of the Senate in the passage of legislation remains mandatory. It is closer to the truth to say that with Canada's Senate there is little at issue but much at stake.

Nevertheless, the Senate remains an integral part of Canada's Parliament.[14] All senators are formally summoned by the governor general who appoints them on the advice of the prime minister. Under the terms of the *1987 Constitutional Accord* (not yet ratified by all provinces) the federal government must appoint senators from lists supplied by the provinces when making appointments to the upper house. In 1987, Senator Gerald Ottenheimer was selected from a list of five names submitted to the prime minister by the Newfoundland government, making him the first appointment to the Senate within the provisions of the *Meech Lake Accord*. Presently, the Senate has 104 seats, allocated on the basis of four representative divisions: Ontario and Quebec each have 24 seats; the three Maritime provinces share 24 seats (10 each for New Brunswick and Nova Scotia, and 4 for Prince Edward Island); the four Western province share 24 seats; Newfoundland has 6 seats; and the Yukon and Northwest Territories have 1 each.

Originally, the Fathers of Confederation expected the Senate to do two things: first, to play a legislative-review role by acting as a check against the majority in the elected House of Commons, and second, to represent the various regions of the country. The Senate has usually not been able to do either effectively. As a legislative-review body, the Senate lacks the authority to exercise its substantial powers because the public does not think it has the legitmacy to use them. In fact, the Cabinet has assumed the Senate's legitimate role as a forum for regional representation. As well, first ministers' conferences have given provincial governments a special voice to provide their own views on national issues and policies. What has been referred to as "executive federalism" is the direct result of frequent federal/provincial negotiations for settling questions of regional concerns. Finally, political parties, especially their elected representatives, have assumed the responsibility for the expression of regional viewpoints. Thus, regional representation at the national level is carried out by a variety of means, although it has been argued that these different ways of speaking for the regions are not sufficiently visible to the Canadian public.

Much recent action and discussion about Senate reform has revolved around creating a permanent solution to this problem of inadequate institutional regional representation. Interest in changing the Senate is demonstrated by a wide range of publications and proposals. Senate reform was an important provision in the constitutional proposals made by Quebec in its submission to the Constitutional Conference of 1968. The Government of Canada drafted white papers on Senate reform in 1969 and 1978. A Special Joint Committee of the Senate and the House of Commons on the Constitution published its report in 1972. But in 1978, the Supreme Court of Canada struck down an attempt by the Trudeau government to replace the Senate with a House of the Federation because the provinces had not given their consent. And in 1985, the Mulroney government moved to draft a Constitutional amendment that would prevent the Senate as presently constituted from ever repeating its stalling action on important government business. This amendment could prove to be daunting. Constitutionally, the Senate's powers could be curtailed only with the consent of at least seven provinces representing 50 percent of the Canadian population – and even after that, the Senate could itself delay changes in its powers for 180 days.

Reports were also prepared on reforming the Senate by the governments of British Columbia (1978) and Alberta (1982 and 1985), the Ontario Advisory Committee on Confederation (1978), the Progressive Conservative Party of Canada (1978), the Canada West Foundation (1978, 1981), the Canadian Bar Association (1978), the Pepin-Robarts Task Force on Canadian Unity (1979), La Fédération des francophones hors Québec (1979), the Goldenberg-Lamontagne report of 1980, and the Royal Commission on the Economic Union and Development Prospects for Canada (1985) [the Macdonald Commission]. The future role of the Senate was also a major part of the deliberations of the Federal-Provincial Continuing Committee of Ministers on the Constitution from 1978 through summer 1980. In its "beige paper," entitled "A New Canadian Federation," the Quebec Liberal party recommended an intergovernmental council that would operate independently of Parliament, but would perform some of the functions proposed for a reformed Senate.

In 1985 a Special Select Committee on Senate Reform established by the Government of Alberta recommended a "Triple E" Senate, in which members are directly *elected* based on *equal representation* from each province to a Senate with *effective* powers. Since 1985, important progress has been made toward Senate reform. In 1986, all premiers agreed at the Annual Premiers' Conference in Edmonton that Senate reform is a priority for constitutional change. In the same year the federal government pledged to address Senate reform in a new constitutional amendment. The 1987 Constitutional Accord (not yet ratified) was signed by the First Ministers on June 3, 1987, bringing Quebec into the Canadian constitutional family. The accord contained a provision for annual conferences of first ministers to address Senate reform. This was the first time that both the federal and provincial governments had agreed to concrete measures to reform the Senate. The accord promised that Senate reform would be the next priority in building national reconciliation.

Some of the recommendations for a Triple E Senate include:

a A Senate of sixty-four senators, seated as delegations of six, representing each province and two for each territory, elected from single-member districts with plurality.

b The Senate will have the powers to initiate any legislation (except money or taxation bills); to amend any bill after which the House of Commons would consider the amendment; to veto any bill except a supply bill; to hold a 180-day suspensive veto over constitutional issues; to vote on money or taxation bills within 90 days, and on other bills within 180 days once received from the House of Commons; to ratify all treaties except military treaties; to vote on French- and English-language issues requiring a "double majority" of either French- or English-speaking senators with a majority of all Senators, depending on the issue.

c Each provincial delegation will select a chairman, who with an elected speaker, will compose an eleven-member Senate Executive Council, which will determine the order of business in the Senate and appoint the membership to its committees.

The architects of a new Canadian Senate have many options from which to choose. They can reconstruct the second chamber in such a way that its present legislative-review and legislative-support functions are effectively enhanced by means of new methods of appointing or electing senators. For example, in 1989, Alberta's Conservative government introduced legislature enabling that province to hold Canada's first election for a federal senator during the municipal election held in October. To give senators more representative legitimacy in the eyes of Canadians, the federal government and the provincial governments could share a method of appointment, giving people of all regions in the country a feeling of being effectively represented. Another recommended method of appointment would remove the federal government entirely from the process and give the power of appointment solely to the provinces, thus institutionalizing provincial and regional input into the national legislative process. This process would also give the provinces additional powers beyond those already delegated to them in the Constitution. Provincial delegates appointed to a reformed Senate would have review and veto powers over the federal lawmaking process. The British Columbia paper (1978), the Pepin-Robarts Task Force (1979), and the Alberta government paper (1982) all echoed this view.

Another possible way of choosing senators is by indirect election – a Senate elected by the provincial legislatures. Such is the practice for electing members to India's Rajya Sabha by the state legislative assemblies. In 1978 the federal government proposed a Senate selected by means of proportional indirect election. Under the terms of the proposal, the Senate would reflect the proportional popular performance of political parties in the most recent federal election. The proposal was criticized because it would not guarantee the representation of important regions in the country if political parties were unsuccessful in gaining seats nationally.

In the reports by the Fédération des francophones hors Québec (1979), the Canada West Foundation (1981), and the Macdonald commission (1985), direct election of the Senate was proposed. In these and other reports it has been argued that direct election would give Canadians a feeling that the regions of the country have national as well as provincial representation. The Macdonald commission advocated an elected Senate, based on proportional representation, with the power to hold up legislation for six months. An elected Senate would be a direct voice of the people from various regions, rather than of political parties or governments. In this regard, the Senate might also be designated to reflect the existence of certain minorities, especially Canada's aboriginal peoples.

There is no doubt that there are many ways to reform the Canadian Senate. What is certain is that the present means of legislative review and regional representation are inadequate and perceived as such. Because of this, many Canadians continue to ask whether they should follow the example of other federations that assign a more functional use to the second chamber.[15]

The United States Legislature

The United States has a bicameral national legislature called the Congress. Congress is divided into the *House of Representatives* and the *Senate*. Members of the House of Representatives are called *representatives,* also congressmen and congresswomen. Members of the Senate are call *senators*. This structure was the result of a compromise that resolved a most important conflict of the Constitutional Convention (1787). The smallest populated states feared that representation by population would favour the largest populated states of the union. Therefore, they insisted that one House – the Senate – should represent each state equally and that the approval of both Houses should be required to pass a law. The Senate has 100 members: 2 from each of the fifty states, elected for six-year terms. One-third of the senators are elected every two years. There are 435 members of the House of Representatives. This number, fixed by legislation, is divided among the fifty states in proportion to population. No matter how small the population of a state is, it is entitled to at least one representative. When states gain or lose population (taken by census every ten years) they also may gain or lose representatives.

Despite the outward appearance of the separation of powers, the Congress of the United States shares its powers with the president and the Supreme Court.[16] Although the Constitution designates the Congress as the legislative branch, the president is very much a part of the lawmaking process. If the president opposes legislation passed by Congress, he can refuse to sign it and can return it to Congress, giving reasons for so doing. This is called a veto. The fate of such a bill would then be up to Congress. If Congress passes the bill by a two-thirds vote of each House, it overrides the veto and the bill becomes law without the signature of the president.

Legislative Leaders and Committees

As with all legislatures, Congress has its legislative leaders who organize the lawmaking process. Each House of Congress has two sets of leaders: those who achieve strong positions (mostly committee chairpersons) by virtue of their seniority, and those who are elected to the positions of congressional leadership.

The Speaker of the House of Representatives is elected by the majority party and acts as the head of that party in the House. The Speaker is more than a party figure; this person presides over the House and is next in line of presidential succession after the vice president. The minority party in the House has no officer similar to the Speaker. Otherwise, the leadership organizations of the two parties are similar. Each party has a floor leader*, a whip, and a number of assistant whips in charge of floor business. On the majority side of the House, the Speaker joins these officers, acting as party spokesmen, and representing House Democrats or Republicans to the president and the general public.

Party organization in the Senate also takes a similar form. The U.S. vice president is the presiding officer of the senate. He has relatively little influence there except to cast the deciding vote in case of a tie or to issue a decision on a congressional ruling.

What role do party leaders play in the legislative process of Congress? The majority leadership in both Houses manages legislation after it comes out of committee. Majority leaders schedule and delegate the workload on a bill as it passes through each stage of legislation. They are at the centre of a network of information about legislation and must be consulted on every bill and kept informed on its progress. Although U.S. congressional leaders have a great deal of influence, they do not enjoy the same degree of influence over their fellow lawmakers as do their Canadian counterparts.[17] They cannot tell their party members how to vote or expect them to follow orders. Party discipline is weak in Congress. Party leaders cannot even control how much campaign assistance will go to individual candidates for the House and Senate. Because they only have marginal influence in keeping their party members in office, they exercise only marginal power over them in Congress.

The congressional committee system is by far the most important element in the legislative organization of Congress.[18] Members of the House and the Senate establish their reputation from the committee work they do. The Congress is much too large for all its members to collectively make important public decisions. No congressperson can possibly learn about every issue before the legislatures. Only through the committee system can the work of Congress get done. Each bill must go through the hands of at least one, and often more than one, committee in each House. The vast majority of bills flow through standing

Standing Committees of Congress

House of Representatives	Senate
Agriculture	Agriculture, Nutrition, and Forestry
Appropriations	Appropriations
Armed Services	Armed Services
Banking, Finance, and Urban Affairs	Banking, Housing, and Urban Affairs
Budget	Budget
District of Columbia	Commerce, Science, and Transportation
Education and Labor	Energy and Natural Resources
Energy and Commerce	Environment and Public Works
Foreign Affairs	Finance
Government Operations	Foreign Relations
House Administration	Government Affairs
Interior and Insular Affairs	Judiciary
Judiciary	Labor and Human Resources
Merchant Marine and Fisheries	Rules and Administration
Post Office and Civil Service	Small Business
Public Works and Transportation	Veterans' Affairs
Rules	
Science and Technology	
Small Business	
Standards of Official Conduct	
Veterans' Affairs	
Ways and Means	

Table 7.2

committees for their scrutiny and approval or disapproval. There are sixteen standing committees in the Senate and twenty-two in the House (table 7.2).

These standing committees are subdivided into subcommittees that do specialized work within the overall jurisdiction of the full committees. The party composition of standing committees is roughly equivalent to the relative party strength in each House, and the chair of the committee and subcommittee is usually held by a ranking member of the majority party.

The U.S. Congress also conducts select committees*. Ordinarily, select committees do not play a significant role in the process of passing a bill. But there are times when select committees capture a prominent role in the legislative process, as did the Senate select committee that investigated Watergate.

Finally, two other kinds of congressional committees deserve attention. Joint committees* are those made up of an equal number of senators and representatives. The chairs of these committees are alternated between both Houses from Congress to Congress. Joint committees rarely have anything to do with initiating legislation but do long-term studies on important questions like taxation. Joint conference committees* are also composed of equal membership from both Houses and function to iron out any technical difficulties a bill encounters because of the procedural differences between the Houses.

Because of its size and political complexities, Congress can be viewed as a collection of committees that meet together only to approve what each has accomplished separately. The committee system has earned a great deal of respect among U.S. legislators. Congresspersons will rely on expert opinion and intelligence gathering before deciding the direction of their votes.[19] For them the "committee" has done all the credible groundwork, held hearings, studied the issues, and consulted with experts and interested parties. Consequently, committee opinion is usually respected.

How Bills Are Passed

The U.S. legislative process follows an often slow and formidable path, although political will in the Congress can speed a bill through a labyrinth of hurdles. A bill may be formally introduced by any member of a particular House. Sometimes companion bills are introduced in the other House simultaneously in order to speed up the process of legislation. In addition, any number of members of Congress may sponsor a bill. Presidential bills are introduced by a member of the president's party who has seniority on the standing committee that will hold hearings on the bill.

When the bill is introduced on the floor, it is read and immediately assigned to the appropriate standing committee handling such matters. The subcommittees of the parent committees are then assigned the job of investigating the purposes of the bill, determining its value, and amending it in accordance with the wishes of the subcommittee, and then re-submitting it to the parent committee. Sometimes the full standing committee will specifically investigate certain provisions of the bill. This action is followed by hearings of the parent committees and subcommittees. These hearings perform several broad functions. One is to assist congresspersons in collecting information and opinion from the interested parties. Within this process, special-interest groups will have their say. As the bill passes through the hands of these committees, it may come to bear only a slight resemblance to the original draft or even the intent of it.

Many riders or amendments may be added along the way. Once the committee reports a bill out by returning it to the legislature, it is scheduled for the second reading, debate, and voting on the floor of the House by the Rules Committee. If a bill survives the second reading, it is engrossed* by printing the amendments in final form and given a third reading. This reading is by title only, unless a member requests that the bill be read again in full. The speaker asks for a vote after the title is read and the bill is either defeated or passed. As in

Canada, the third reading is merely pro forma, because the sentiments of the House have had opportunity for expression in the Committee of the Whole, where the entire legislative body sits as one large committee.

All revenue bills are required by the Constitution to originate in the House of Representatives. Once passed in the House, they are taken up by the Senate. But all other bills may originate in either the House or the Senate. If one House passes the bill first, it then goes to the other House where it goes through the same process. Bills must eventually pass both Houses in exactly the same form before being sent to the president for signing. Even after a bill authorizing a new government program becomes law, the new program must still get an appropriation of money if it is actually to get under way. Appropriations bills* go the to House and Senate appropriations committees. These committees regard themselves as having a special role to play in protecting taxpayers from unnecessary federal expenditures.

The primary concern of Congress is the thousands of bills and resolutions that are introduced each year. The number of bills and resolutions introduced in one Congress has been as high as 44 000, but between 15 000 and 20 000 is more usual. The odds are that over 90 percent of these legislative proposals will be killed or permitted to die in committee.

Although the U.S. Congress was born in an age of great legisltive activity, much has changed in the last 200 years. Today most observers agree that the branch of government first mentioned in the Constitution has been greatly surpassed in power by the executive branch. A frequently advanced reason for the decline in the power of Congress has been its inability to organize and legislate rapidly on the ever-changing social exigencies of American society.

Functions of Non-Democratic Legislatures

Authoritarian Assemblies

At first glance, legislatures in authoritarian and totalitarian states resemble democratic lawmaking institutions. In most cases their members are elected, they elect or appoint presiding officers, they meet regularly, make speeches, vote on proposed legislation, and formally enact laws and constitutional amendments. But on closer examinations, we see that the roles they play in their respective political systems are quite different from those of democratic legislatures.

In authoritarian states, the character of the policy-making process is strongly influenced by the concentration of power in the hands of the political executive. The very personal way in which power is exercised means that the legislature has little actual autonomy and cannot play a strong independent role in the policy-making process. In all authoritarian states, the vital centre of governmental power is the executive itself; political parties, legislatures, and courts are not important challenges. Any institutional constraint on these powerful executives remains extremely weak. It was President Mobutu of Zaire who completely side-stepped the legislature when he declared that even his speeches have the force of law. By means of presidential decrees and without any legislative consultation, Mobutu introduced sweeping institutional changes, subject to no legal or political challenges.

In many African states, legislatures are colonized by a single party or a dominant party under the influence of the military that tolerates only marginal opposition.[20] In these authoritarian political systems, the legislature functions to uphold the government rule of the incumbent regime. As a result, the vitality of democratic accountability is severely weakened. The legislatures provide merely ceremonial and decorative functions. In some states, such as Kenya, the National Assembly provides an arena in which members can successfully represent the claims of their constituents to gain minor amenities like a paved road or a new school. But legislators cannot effectively challenge the executive leadership in areas of general policy.

Constitutionally, legislatures are theoretically equal partners with the other political branches of government – the executive and the judiciary. However, in all authoritarian states, this equality is more fiction than fact. In states such as Guatemala and Honduras, the legislative body is always overshadowed by the president and does not even hold as much independence or influence as the judiciary.

There are many reasons for the predominance of authoritarian executives and the minor supportive role of the legislatures. One is that in many states the legislature is a hand-picked body of the executive. The 1974 Constitution of Zaire, for example, gives the president the power to name members to the leading organs of the state, such as the legislature and the supreme court. Often it is impossible for legislators to be elected or re-elected without the personal approval of the president. In Mexico's single-party dominant system, the president, who is always the nominee of the Partido Revolucionario Institucional (PRI), has such control over the electoral process that he not only influences who the next presidential nominee will be, but has final approval over the party's slate of candidates to both Houses of Congress. And in Zambia under President Kuanda, all candidates for the National Assembly had to be members of the United National Independence Party (UNIP) and had to be confirmed by the president. Even in states where the president does not personally endorse party candidates for the legislature, legislators often owe their election almost entirely to the influence of political executives and are, therefore, beholden to them.

Legislators in authoritarian systems are well aware that in a contest of power among the branches of government the executive holds most of the trumps, especially the high ones, such as the support of the armed forces and the national police. In a showdown of political power, executives will even use these trumps against members of the legislature.

Many other factors contribute to the inconsequential role of legislatures in authoritarian states. The widespread presence of illiteracy, poverty, and lack of political experience have contributed substantially to the weakness of legislatures. This is particularly true in Niger, with an adult literacy rate of 5 percent and a per capita GNP of US$410.[21] The legislature is virtually dysfunctional. Low levels of literacy, education, and information curtail the formation of a participant political culture. Many people are denied the privilege of voting because of illiteracy in states such as Brazil and Ecuador. Even when suffrage is extended to a wider population, the great majority of citizens in authoritarian states hardly know what is going on in government and are uninterested in the legislature's work, its problems, or its degree of independence.[22] Conversely, the continuing tradition of strong executive leadership that can capture the emotions of the masses serves to relegate the functions of any representative bodies to a position of minor importance.

The net result is that legislatures tend to function as rubber stamps. In authoritarian states, open debate is mainly window dressing for the international community. Usually, the legislative order of business, even the outcome of the proceedings, is a foregone conclusion. Most of the important bills considered by the legislature have already been formulated or decreed by the executive. In the final analysis, legislation is the process by which dictators whip legislators into line behind the policies they feel are in the national interest. Often the bureaucratic machinery of the state is well under way, implementing the policies as they are being considered by the legislature. By 1988, fifteen years after the coup d'état that imposed a bureaucratic authoritarian regime on Chile under Augusto Pinochet, over 1000 decrees issued by the executive had been stamped with congressional approval.

Totalitarian Assemblies

Legislatures in totalitarian socialist states, modelled after democratic parliamentary assemblies, function quite differently. They have functioned to legitimize the policies and rules of the executive levels of government, which in this case is the party leadership. For this reason, assemblies in these states have tended to remain subordinate to the Communist party. The impact of democratization, however, has altered the relationship between the party and the legislative branch of government in some governments.[23] We must, therefore, view the totalitarian model of government as transitional under the reforms initiated as *perestroika, glastnost',* and *demokratizatsiya.* As a result the predominant role of the party will change over time.

All so-called totalitarian states have unicameral legislatures, except three: Czechoslovakia, the USSR, and Yugoslavia, which have bicameral bodies. In 1989 the Soviets began an experiment with democracy as members of a new-styled parliament, the Congress of People's Deputies, began their deliberations amid ambiguity about their legislative role in the era of *perestroika.* Until that time there was no precedent for this type of legislative reform in the Soviet Union since the Bolshevik revolution in 1917. Having succeeded in the first contested elections in Soviet history, deputies were given the mandate from their constituents to deliberate on questions such as deteriorating economic conditions, taxation, violence in several republics, nascent independence movements within the three Baltic states, the conduct of foreign policy, and proposals to protect press freedom and human rights. Under constitutional reforms initiated by Mikhail Gorbachev, the Congress is the highest legislative body in the Soviet Union. It is expected to hold one session a year to elect a president, a vice-president, and the chairman of the Supreme Court.

The Congress also elects a smaller legislative body, which retains the name of the old legislature: the Supreme Soviet. The revitalized Supreme Soviet consists of 542 deputies,

271 in a Council of the Union and 271 in a Council of Nationalities (figure 7.1). The membership of the Supreme Soviet rotates each year over a five-year term. About 20 percent of its membership will be replaced annually so that each of the 2250 deputies has a chance to serve on the smaller body. The Supreme Soviet can call general elections, endorse or reject cabinet appointments, establish or abolish ministries, and bring officials to account for their actions.

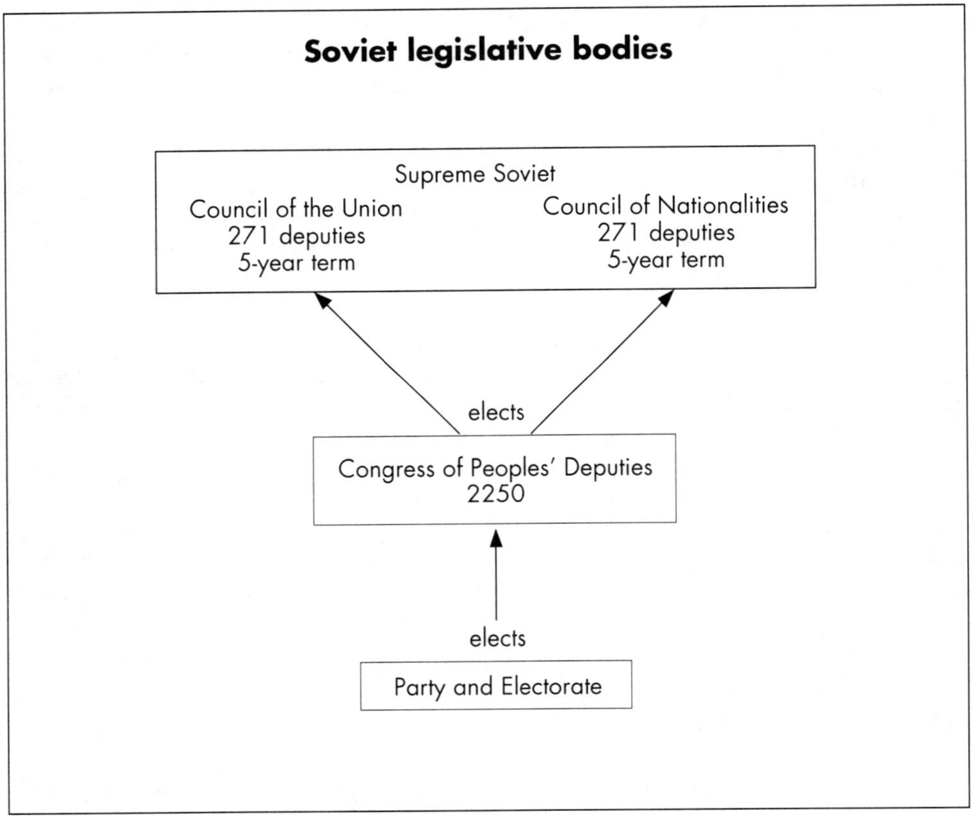

Figure 7.1

The Supreme Soviet is now authorized to ratify or reject treaties, veto government decrees, and settle constitutional disputes between the 15 constituent Soviet republics and the national government.

In the voting by the Congress for the first revitalized Supreme Soviet, the Communist party and other organizations under its control were guaranteed 750 of the 2250 Congress seats before the balloting even started – a provision created to protect the Communist party. Nevertheless, 90 percent of the new deputies elected to the new Congress were members of the Communist party. Notwithstanding the rhetorical appeal of *perestroika* in the formation of new legislative institutions, one person still retains a preponderence of political power.[24] As Soviet President and Secretary-General of the Communist party, Mr. Gorbachev can personally determine the distribution of institutional power. The Soviet Union has retained its one-party character and its dictatorial disposition by a single individual.

Unlike the dual chamber system of the USSR, China is a unicameral state. According to the Chinese Constitution of 1982, "the highest organ of state power" resides in the National People's Congress (NPC). The NPC has over 3000 members and is the largest legislative assembly in the world. Its delegates are elected every five years but its awesome size prevents it from being an effective decision-making body. The meetings of the NPC are short and mostly ceremonial because its deputies ratify the major reports presented to them by the Chinese Communist party. In 1989 the regular session of the NPC was cancelled by the party because of the political instabilities generated by the student uprisings across the republic.

The four levels of Chinese government include national, provincial, county, district, and township (figure 7.2). Each level has a legislature called a people's congress defined constitutionally as the "local organ of state power."[25] Like the NPC, these local congresses meet irregularly and briefly. The standing committees of the people's congresses have the role of supervising the government organizations and of keeping the goals of the party well entrenched in the administrative structure of government. Congresses at the national and provincial levels are indirectly elected for five-year terms by lower-level congresses. But congresses at the county, district, and municipal levels have three-year terms and are elected directly by the voters. The district and township congresses are directly elected and administer government programs at the grass-roots level.

The 1982 Constitution gave formal and legal approval to several new tendencies in Chinese politics. It increased the legislative powers of the congresses and clearly specified the roles of the party, state, and government in the political system. The effort to give the legislative structures of government a greater role in the political process indicates the willingness of the Chinese Communist party to institutionalize the decision-making process.

Almost all contemporary political systems have legislatures in which individuals assemble to either make laws or formally enact laws proposed by the executive branch of government. A legislature's relationship to the political executive varies significantly from polity to polity. It is always affected by the degree of democratic, authoritarian, and totalitarian ideology practised by political leaders and accepted by the people in a state. Other factors include the number and nature of the individual houses of the legislature, the power of committees, and the political customs and mores practised in a state.

Legislative power is seldom separate from executive power. However, how closely connected they are or what the balance between them may be depends on the state's constitution and whether it prescribes a parliamentary system, a presidential system, or some blend of the two – as in authoritarian and totalitarian polities. Where legislatures merely function to formalize decisions made elsewhere about the laws that govern people, it is

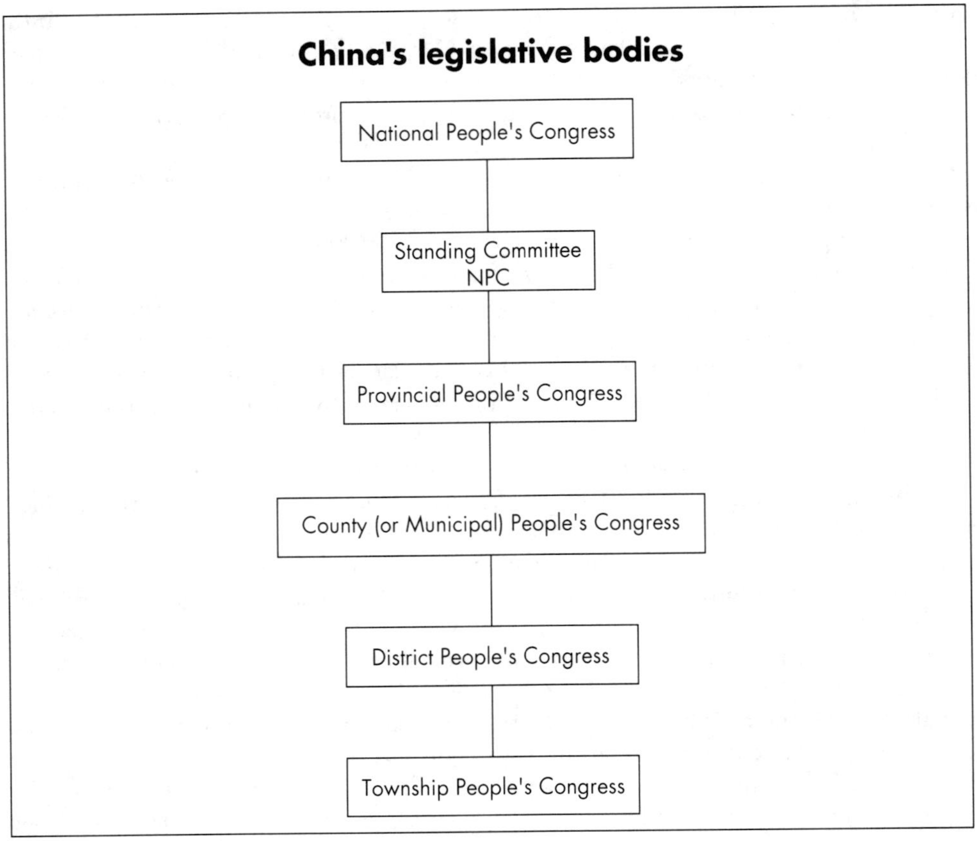

Figure 7.2

important to find out where laws are really being made and exactly what procedures are being followed. In some states, a great amount of effort is made to show that lawmaking is the job of the legislature, but in practice that body has progressively surrendered a larger and larger role in the exercise of lawmaking to the executive branch.

We have seen that the lawmaking function is usually assigned to representative legislatures if not as an effective body than as a formal, symbolic one. In all probability, however, the power to make laws is not held exclusively by the legislature but is shared to a greater or lesser extent with others outside that body.

REFERENCES

1. Dell Gillette Hitchner and Carol Levine, *Comparative Government and Politics* (New York: Harper & Row, Publishers 1981), 202.
2. Based on comparisons of legislatures described in John Paxton, ed., *Stateman's Year Book, 1988–9* (London: Macmillan Press 1989).

3. See M.L. Mezey, *Comparative Legislatures* (Durham, SC: Duke University Press 1979), ch. 4; and Robert Fried, *Comparative Political Institutions* (New York: Macmillan 1966), ch. 2.
4. Hanna Fenichel Pitkin, "The Concept of Representation," in Pitkin, ed., *Representation* (New York: Atherton Press 1969), 16.
5. Arend Lijphart, *Democracies* (New Haven, CT: Yale University Press 1984), 90–105.
6. See D. Stephenson Jr. et al., *American Government* (New York: Harper & Row Publishers 1988), 376.
7. Hugh Kindred et.al., *An Introduction to International Law: Chiefly as Interpreted and Applied in Canada* (Toronto: Emond Montgomery Publications Ltd. 1987), 137–8.
8. Michael Atkinson, "Parliamentary Government in Canada," in Michael Whittington and Glen Williams, eds., *Canadian Politics in the 1980's* (Toronto: Methuen 1981); see also Peter Hogg, "Responsible Government," in R.S. Blair and J.T. McLeod, eds., *The Canadian Political Tradition* (Toronto: Methuen 1987), 17–41.
9. Ronald Landes, *The Canadian Polity* (Scarborough, ON: Prentice-Hall Canada Inc. 1983), 156–8.
10. Standing Order 33(1); see also Gary Levy, "A Night to Remember: The First Election of a Speaker by Secret Ballot," in Paul Fox and Graham White, *Politics: Canada*, 6th ed. (Toronto: McGraw-Hill Ryerson 1987), 519–24.
11. Richard Van Loon and Michael Whittington, *The Political System: Environment, Structure and Process*, 4th ed.(Toronto: McGraw-Hill Ryerson 1987), 616-–24; Michael Rush, "Parliamentary Committees and Parliamentary Government: The British and Canadian Experiences," *Journal of Commonwealth and Comparative Politics* XX (July 1982): 138–54.
12. See K.C. Wheare, "The Decline of Legislatures," in Mark Dickerson, Thomas Flanagan, and Neil Nevitte, *Introductory Readings in Government and Politics* (Toronto: Methuen 1987), 290–6; and Eugene Forsey and Graham Eglington, "Twenty-Five Fairy Tales about Parliamentary Government," in Paul Fox and Graham White *Politics: Canada,* 507–13.
13. Robert Jackson and Michael Atkinson, *The Canadian Legislative System* (Toronto: Macmillan of Canada 1980), 88.
14. See Landes, *The Canadian Polity,* 170, esp. his reference to Allan Kornberg and William Mishler, *Influence in Parliament: Canada* (Durham, NC: Duke University Press 1980), 17–18.
15. Canada, "Reform of the Senate: A Discussion Paper" (Ottawa: Government of Canada 1983); Roger Gibbins, *Senate Reform: Moving toward the Slippery Slope* (Kingston, ON: Institute of Intergovernmental Relations, Queen's University 1983), 1–50; and Canada. *Report of the Special Joint Committee of the Senate and the House of Commons on Senate Reform* (Ottawa: January 1984).
16. See Robert Lineberry, *Government in America* (Glenview, IL: Scott, Foresman & Co. 1989), 378–421.
17. Steven Smith and Christopher Deering, *Committees in Congress* (Washington, DC: Congressional Quarterly Press 1984).
18. Everett Ladd, *The American Polity,* 3rd ed. (New York: W.W. Norton & Co. 1989), 166–73.
19. Joel Aberbach, "The Congressional Committee Intelligence System: Information, Oversight and Change," *Congress and the Presidency* 14 (Spring 1987): 51–76.
20. See Ruth Collier, *Regimes of Tropical Africa: Changing Forms of Supremacy* (Berkeley, CA: University of California Press 1982); see also John Harbeson, *The Military in African Politics* (New York: Praeger 1987).
21. World Bank, *World Development Report, 1989* (New York: Oxford University Press 1989).

22. Gabriel Almond and G. Bingham Powell Jr., eds., *Comparative Politics Today* (Glenview, IL: Scott, Foresman & Co. 1988), 126; Paul Best, Kul Rai, and David Walsh, *Politics in Three Worlds: An Introduction to Political Science* (New York: Macmillan Publishing Co. 1986), 154–95.
23. See Gail Lapidus, *State and Society in the Soviet Union* (Boulder, CO: Westview Press 1989).
24. See Leon Baradat, *Soviet Political Society* (Englewood Cliffs, NJ: Prentice-Hall 1988).
25. See James Wang, *Contemporary Chinese Politics: An Introduction* (Englewood Cliffs, NJ: Prentice-Hall 1985).

SUGGESTED READINGS

Vernon Bogdanor, ed., *The Blackwell Encyclopaedia of Political Institutions* (Oxford: Basil Blackwell 1988).

Roger Davidson and Walter Oleszek, *Congress & its Members*, 3rd ed. (Washington, DC: CQ Press 1989).

Robert J. Fleming, *Canadian Legislatures: The 1987-1988 Comparative Study* (Ottawa: Ampersand Communications 1988).

C.E.S. Franks, *The Parliament of Canada* (Toronto: University of Toronto Press 1987).

Inter-Parliamentary Union, *Parliaments of the World: A Comparative Reference Compendium*, 2nd ed. (London: Gower 1986).

Kenneth Lieberthal and Michael Oksenberg, *Policy Making in China* (Princeton: Princeton University Press 1988).

Michael Mezey, *Congress, the President and Public Policy* (Boulder, CO: Westview Press 1989).

D.G. Morrison et al., *Black Africa: A Comparative Handbook* (New York: Paragon House Publishers 1988).

Lisanne Radice, Elizabeth Vallance, and Virginia Willis, *Member of Parliament: The Job of the Backbencher* (New York: St. Martin's Press 1987).

Frederik van Zyl Slabbert, *The Last White Parliament* (New York: St. Martin's Press 1987).

GLOSSARY

feudalism: A social and economic system characterized by a strict hierarchical organization, e.g., from "lord" to "serf," whose relationships were based on rights and duties assigned by eccliastical law and a system of production based on the exchange of services.

constituency: A legislative district or riding from which an individual or group of individuals is chosen to represent in a public fashion the interests of people, known as constituents.

functional representative: The concept that legislators should represent economic, political, or social groups, rather than general units of the population.

representation by population: Representation within a legislative body based on the principle that each legislator represents approximately equal populations.

committee system: The complex and formal arrangement whereby a legislative body investigates matters deemed worthy of possible legislative action by the use of committees composed of legislators.

standing committee: A permanent or regular committee created by a legislative body to consider matters on which the legislature may act.

subcommittee: A supplementary group of individuals appointed by the chairperson of a legislative committee to investigate legislative matters and report to the larger committee.

initiative: An electoral process whereby designated percentages of the electorate may initiate legislative changes by filing formal petitions to be acted upon by the legislature or the total electorate in a general election or referendum.

referendum: An electoral process by which legislative or constitutional questions are referred to the total electorate.

petition: A method of placing a candidate's name on a primary- or a general-election ballot by submitting a specified number or percentage of voters' signatures to appropriate officials.

recall: A procedure enabling voters to remove an elected official from office before his or her term has expired.

roll-call voting: A "yea or nay" vote in a legislative body where each member's vote is required to be recorded.

constituent: A resident in a legislator's district or constituency.

overrule: To supersede a legislative initiative by a subsequent action or decision.

authorize: To empower by granting a right or mandate to act in a certain way.

executive prerogative: Usually refers to a special privilege, power, or immunity vested in an executive office or person who alone enjoys particular rights and capacities in contra-distinction to others.

levy: To assess or raise taxes with the authority of the state.

interpellation: A procedural action by a legislative member to interrupt the order of the day by asking a minister or committee official to explain some matter belonging to his or her jurisdiction.

impeachment: The procedure to formally bring charges against an officer of the government.

amendment: A change made to a bill.

non-partisan: Political conduct showing no preference for any political party or ideological position.

Speaker's chair: The Speaker's chair of the Canadian House of Commons is a replica of the Speaker's chair in the Palace of Westminster that was destroyed during an air raid in 1941.

Striking Committee: A selection committee that decides on the membership of all other committees.

money bill: Financial bills that authorize taxation and appropriations or expenditures that must be introduced first into the House of Commons by a minister of the crown.

Committee of the Whole: The entire parliamentary body.

pro forma: As a matter of form.

governor general's special warrants: Extra-parliamenatry executive borrowing privileges, authorized under Canada's Financial Administration Act and used only in emergencies for urgent and unforeseen government expenditures.

floor leader: A person who is in charge of getting a U.S. congressional bill passed, or in the case of opposition, of getting it defeated.

select committee: A legislative committee of the U.S. Congress established for a limited period of time for a special purpose.

joint committee: A congressional committee struck on special subject-matter areas, made up of members of both Houses of the U.S. Congress.

joint conference committee: A congressional committee composed of members of the U.S. House and Senate to resolve differences resulting from conflicting interpretations of the same bill.

emgrossed: To copy the rude draft of a legal instrument, such as a bill or agreement.

appropriation bills (U.S.*):* A congressional enactment to authorize government expenditures.

8

The Administration of Government

Roberta Jamieson, Ombudsman of Ontario

Development

MANY PRIMITIVE SOCIETIES compiled and stored information on tilling, hunting, fishing, animal husbandry, and human population for the purposes of social administration* and survival.[1] Egypt, China, and India produced highly developed bureaucratic mechanisms before Europe had emerged from barbarism. In much of the world, the history of the development of government has been the history of the development of bureaucratic administrative machinery to replace rule by local tribal chiefs, feudal lords, and royalty. Gradually, European countries forged an effective central administration that enabled them to overcome feudal pluralism to rule a united country.

The full-blown model of the modern administrative state was Prussia. Under Frederick William I (1713–1740), a pattern for a professional administrative corps was organized, embracing many of the characteristics now generally recognized as normal adjuncts to the public service.[2] Frederick William I was the first to establish universities to train government bureaucrats. Recruitment and selection were by competitive examination after the completion of specialized training, and career tenure was the normal expectation. It was this well-organized and efficient government administration, as much as any other single factor, that enabled Prussia to emerge as the leader among the competing German princedoms that existed until the late nineteenth century. The Prussian model was copied by many other continental states, most notably by eighteenth-century France. Under the centralizing leadership of Napoleon, France developed a professionalized civil service*, with a hierarchical* structure of offices and officials – uniform throughout the country – following elaborate patterns of law and administering rules established by the executive, legislative, and judicial branches of government. The term bureaucracy* is derived from the French "bureaus," which were the desks of government officials that came to symbolize the authority and administration of the public service.

In Britain, the painful struggle for parliamentary supremacy was as much pursued to control the centralizing governing apparatus that successive kings and queens had developed as it was to control the monarchs themselves.[3] Monarchs could rule only through their servants in the administrative structure: control of the one could not be asserted without control of the other.

The development of administrative government in both Canada and the United States owes much to Britain; thus, public administration in North America is more like that of our English cousins than like the continental model. Eighteen sixty-seven Canada, with its simple economy, relatively sparse population, wealth of resources, and remoteness from the broils of the old world, in fact needed but a minimum of government of any kind. The problem of administrative development in Canada and the United States was one of overcoming a tradition hostile to bureaucracy and deeply rooted in political cultures that stressed egalitarianism*, equal opportunity, and a militant antigovernment approach to staffing the political system.

In the late nineteenth century, Canadians were not prepared to assign more than a rudimentary role to government involvement in their lives.[4] There were no personal or corporate income taxes, no family allowance, no Canada Pension Plan, and no medicare. CBC radio and television did not exist, nor did the Canada Council, Investment Canada, the Canadian International Development Agency (CIDA), or Atomic Energy Canada Ltd. Government consisted of Parliament, postal service, customs and immigration, a system of courts, and public works. The public service of the day was largely unprofessional by current standards, made up of people whose only expertise amounted to reading, writing, and perhaps some bookkeeping.

Until the early twentieth century, administrators were selected and obtained tenure* as a consequence of partisan preference through an elaborate system of patronage*: the characteristics of a professionalized bureaucratic service on the European model were conspicuously absent. During the 1920s, under Mackenzie King, the Canadian civil service was upgraded from an essentially clerical force into a highly qualified group of professional policy advisers. When R.B. Bennett was elected in 1930, he kept on the senior civil servants who were appointed by Mackenzie King. The tradition of a non-partisan civil service was firmly established. Deputy ministers were and still are the most powerful civil servants in Ottawa. Today more than 600 000 people work directly for the federal government, in its departments, crown corporations, agency corporations, and other federal bodies, such as the armed forces. The Canadian system, because of its federal structure, is much less centralized than the British or French systems. Never before have so many Canadians been so involved with bureaucracy or so affected by it. If provincial and municipal administrations are added to the federal total, government administration presently employs over 12 percent of the total labour force in Canada.

Distinctive Characteristics of Bureaucracy

The first systematic study of bureaucracy was conducted by the German sociologist Max Weber* (1864–1920).[5] His classic studies formulated an ideal set of features for any public bureaucracy.[6] However, no modern government administration is bureaucratic in the strict interpretations of his definition. Weber himself always emphasized the exaggerations and simplifications of his model. The constituent elements of his formulations are present in varying degrees in such diverse organizations as the Secretariat of the United Nations, the Vatican's Curia (which has handled the business of the world-wide Catholic Church over the past 1800 years), and Revenue Canada Taxation. The six principal attributes of bureaucracy are:

- Organizational tasks are distributed among the various positions as official duties. Implied is a clear-cut division of labour among positions that make possible a high degree of specialization*.
- Positions or offices are organized into a hierarchical authority structure. This hierarchy takes the shape of a pyramid wherein each official is responsible for the decisions and actions of subordinates, as well as responsible to a superior.
- A formally established system of rules and regulations governs officials and their actions. The regulations ensure the uniformity of operations, regardless of changes of personnel, and together with the authority structure, make possible the co-ordination of various organizational activities.
- There is a specialized administrative staff whose task it is to maintain the organization and, in particular, the lines of communication within it.
- Officials are expected to assume an impersonal orientation in their contacts with clients and with other officials.
- Employment by the organization constitutes a career for officials. Typically an official is a full-time employee and looks forward to a lifelong career in the agency.

Administrators and political scientists today feel that Weber's bureaucratic ideal has drawbacks in its application to modern democratic administrations, as well as to the authoritarian administrations it originally described. In the Weberian model, the bureaucracy is politically neutral, carrying out public policies regardless of which party or government faction is in power. But in all modern political systems the process of decision making itself is inexorably affected by those agencies of the state created to administer government programs and policies. The bureaucracies of modern democratic and non-democratic governments do more than merely implement decisions authorized by law or by executive fiat.[7] Today, a bureaucracy's functions include the provision of policy information and advice to elected officials – and therein lies a source of potent influence over the shaping of policy decisions. There are some who can persuasively argue that bureaucracies govern when no other branch of government is setting policy at all! In other words, public planning* in many states reflects the power of the modern administrator over the elected or appointed representative. The permanent official, able to spend a career accumulating expertise in policy areas, has a massive advantage over the nominally powerful politician and is not the captive of a stratified hierarchical government as described by Weber. Late twentieth-century bureaucracies are human institutions and are not as impersonal or predictable (nor are they as efficient) as the Weberian ideal would have them.

As well, in all modern political institutions, the administrative apparatus can be viewed as people performing the special functions of government. If the structural form represents the framework within and around which administrative activity is oriented, the lifeblood of the system is the people who staff the various departments and agencies and carry out the functions of government.

Functions of Modern Government Bureaucracies

We noted that modern states, regardless of their philosophical persuasion, require vast amounts of governing. All such national communities must perform a variety of administrative functions, which include the implementation and formulation of policy and regulations, performing services, and gathering information. The point is not how these functions are set – whether by elections, legislatures, and referenda, or by dictators and monolithic parties – but that however set, these functions must be implemented. And implementation requires bureaucracy, no more or less in the Soviet Union than in Canada.

Implementation of Policy

The primary function of all government administrations is the execution and enforcement of the laws and regulations passed by the executive and legislative branches of government and ruled by the courts. In this regard, bureaucratic activity affects everybody, every day. In the process of implementing government policies, bureaucracies assess our property values, issue our drivers' licences, collect our taxes, pay our pensions, execute court orders, and send us our family allowance cheques. Many people earn their livings in bureaucratic jobs. Some of us may be arrested, prosecuted, and defended in court by officials who carry out the laws and policies of government. Public bureaucracy determines whether we can build a house, add on to the one we own, or pave our driveways. It follows us through life, recording our marriages, the birth of our children, and finally our deaths.

The administration of government also affects the quality of our lives. In the Soviet Union before *perestroika*, the State Planning Committee (Gosplan) set all the economic priorities of the country. The administration of these policies determined how much meat Soviet citizens ate, as well as the availability of the appliances and utensils on which to cook it and with which to eat it. Public administration can affect the quality of life of other people in the international community. In Ottawa, the Department of External Affairs administers Canada's foreign policies, not only through a world-wide network of embassies and consulates, but also through the international divisions of other domestic departments such as Agriculture, Communications, and Fisheries and Oceans.[8] Its policies towards other countries vis-à-vis trade, investment, and development assistance create jobs for Canadians, as well as provide benefits to the people of the countries where these policies apply.

The patterns of administration vary from state to state with respect to arrangements, structures, and techniques.[9] In the Western world, two general patterns of administration have evolved: the Anglo-American type and the continental European type.

The Anglo-American pattern grew out of basic distrust of centralized authority and encouraged the accountability of administrators through legislative and executive controls of their activities. Differences are also apparent among Anglo–American administrations. Unitary governments like Great Britain's exercise a great number of centralized administrative services, usually because their areas are relatively small. But the federal systems of larger countries such as Australia, Canada, the United States, and India have intermediate levels of administration under the separate jurisdictions of provinces and states. Because of their federal structures, the administrations of these states are much less centralized than the British and, to some extent, much more accountable.

The continental type of administration maintains a tradition established under previous monarchical rule of administrative control from the centre. Local levels of administration are organized as appendages of the central government. In France, the ministries of the national government dominate local administration through *tutelle administrative* (administrative tutelage). One deviation from the continental model is West Germany, where the Lander (states) conduct most administrative functions, enforce federal laws, and supply federal services. But the public funds allocated to these programs originate at the federal level.

Authoritative governments at various levels of economic development reflect an affinity for the continental European administrative model.[10] Their administrative structures – for reasons associated with political control – appear to allow only very limited autonomy to local bureaucratic initiatives. The national administrative organizations of authoritarian states tend to be elitist, hierarchical, and departmentalized in the application of national policies. This is particularly true in many African and Latin American states. Authoritarian states in these regions of the world are characterized by centralized bureaucracies that include the usual ministries, departments, and bureaus organized under the direct control of the executive. Because all these governments have embraced policies of development, decentralized agencies have been permitted to form, composed of independent and semi-independent organizations that are removed from executive control. These include credit banks, development corporations, national oil and mining companies, and regional development agencies.

Today, many authoritarian government administrations are a confusing jumble of "departments," "agencies," "sections," "offices," and "centres." Authoritarian executives have developed two control strategies over their administrations. The first is to staff as many key positions as possible with political followers, friends, and family. The second is to create a political and financial dependency relationship with the executive branch of government.[11]

Two major effects of these formal control systems characterized by executive decision-making procedures are red tape* and corruption. It is frequently observed that officials at all levels of public administration delay decisions for weeks and sometimes years, and accept bribes for special favours or even for the routine performance of their regularly constituted duties.

Totalitarian socialist states have created enormous administrative machines to achieve their ultimate goals of communism. Communist theorists regard the primary functions of the state apparatus to be the implementation of party directives as an expression of an official ideology. In China, the 1982 Constitution formalized the dominance of the party's central bureaucracy over all organs of government. In the Soviet Union, a massive bureaucracy (*apparatchiki*) administers party policies over the largest country of the world. Three types of ministries – *All Union* (federal), *Union Republics* (federal and republic), and *Republic* (local) – administer the complex socialist political and economic system. Because of the enormity of these administrations, the management of totalitarian government has been usually inefficient and characterized by apathy, corruption, delay, and confusion. Before *perestroika*, the "principles of central planning" created a kind of bureaucratic despotism from which the economy and Soviet society were administered by an enormous bureaucracy that generated economic stagnation. *Perestroika* calls for the replacement of centralized administrative management and planning methods with decentralized local and industrial self-management decision making.

Formulation of Policy

In modern democracies, the vast house of bureaucracy has come to have an immense impact on the creation of public policy.[12] Today, public administrators have assumed the important task of initiating policy proposals based on the changing needs of their departments and the people they serve. The fact that civil servants often formulate policy proposals that are then passed by a congress or parliament is a source of concern to the public and their elected officials because it means that politicians may be colonized by administrators.[13] In a democracy, it is one thing for administrators to exert influence* on the lawmaking process, but quite another for them to draft the laws. However, access to information, expertise, and the organizational wisdom of government departments makes many administrators much more than just advisers to their political bosses. In Canada's Department of External Affairs, for example, civil servants enjoy a virtual monopoly over information and the analysis of that information. Senior civil servants take the lead in recommending changes to the minister in the complicated matrix of Canadian foreign policy.[14] Because politicians rarely have alternative sources for analysing the intricacies of Canada's external relations, they tend to accept the authority of bureaucratic policy.

Much of the legislation passed by democratic legislatures is broadly framed, which allows bureaucratic agencies a great deal of discretion in the implementation of programs and policies. Government departments and agencies need loosely outlined rules so that they are able to meet new situations as they arise. But often the details of a program are left to the discretion of administrators out of political necessity. The end result is that administrators have broad powers to fill in the specific details of a policy.[15] In this process they have much to say about how a policy is applied. When a bureaucracy fills in the details of a policy or program, its direction is generally consistent with administrative policy. It is, in fact, in the business of making policy.

The steady growth of all governments, both federal and unitary forms, has been one of the most distinctive trends of the twentieth century.[16] As a result, the number of public servants has expanded dramatically in every country, constructing an elaborate administrative apparatus. The discretionary policy-making powers of public servants permit them to play a major part in the decision-making processes of modern governments. Over the years, students of public administration have written extensively about the implications of the growth of the administrative state and its effects on the relationship between bureaucracy and democracy. The exercise of decision-making powers that are largely anonymous and indirectly accountable blurs the line between political and administrative authority.

Regulation

Many of us meet bureaucracy head-on when it applies the plethora of regulations* that governments generate and update each year.[17] Things seem to be done to us or for us according to stringent regulations that demand our acquiescence and always the completion of forms. Encounters with bureaucracy are very often shaped by books of rules, manuals of procedure, and forms to fill out.

In Canada, numerous regulations flow from all the departments of the provincial and federal governments. Virtually every aspect of private, corporate, and governmental behaviour is regulated: airlines, atomic energy, customs and immigration, consumer and corporate affairs, labour, radios, sports, and televisions are some of the most visible areas of regulatory activity. In the decade of the seventies, the Economic Council of Canada reported that the federal government passed more statutes regulating the economy than had been passed over the previous thirty years.[18] Accompanying the dramatic increase in the number of regulatory statutes has been the proliferation of regulatory agencies by which governments seek to influence, direct, and control economic and social behaviour.[19] For example, in three areas of fundamental importance – telecommunications, transportation, and energy – regulatory agencies make decisions that have enormous impact on the allocation of Canadian resources, the organization of production and consumption, and on the distribution of income. The Canadian Radio and Television Commission (CRTC), the Canadian Transport Commission (CTC), and the National Energy Board actually make regulations in their respective fields that have the effect of law and directly affect citizens every day.

There is an extensive relationship between regulative bureaucratic agencies and the individual in contemporary Canada. In periods of high unemployment, the application of regulations of the Unemployment Insurance Commission and provincial welfare agencies affect the quality of life for millions of people.[20] In recent years, regulations in Canada have extended to include the prohibition of discrimination against minorities and women in employment, the control of pollution, and the commercial uses of metric and imperial weights and measures.

But Canada is not an exception. In the last century the regulative activities of modern bureaucracies have proliferated enormously all over the world. Industrialization and urbanization have produced problems in transportation, health, and the public order in all countries.[21] Growth in industry and technology has created problems with monopolies, industrial safety, the ethical applications of modern technologies, and labour exploitation. At the same time, the growth of science and the widespread attitude that people should control their environment have led to the recognition that social control can only be met through administrative action. Political modernization* is identified with the performance of regulatory activities.

Servicing

Many administrative agencies are created to provide government services of various kinds to individuals and groups in society. Environment Canada is one of the best examples of one important service agency administered by the federal government. Its inland and marine forecasts are vital to all modes of transportation, as well as to businesses, farming, and fishing. Canada's Department of Agriculture and its provincial counterparts conduct research on pest control, land management, livestock improvement, and the marketing and distribution of agricultural products. Employment and Immigration runs an extensive job-finding service in all important Canadian towns and cities. And the Department of National Health and Welfare funds and co-ordinates Canada's Medicare program with the departments of health in the provinces.

Because the efforts made by governments in different administrative service areas are a percentage of the gross domestic product (GDP) and a reflection of their political values, they vary from state to state. In 1987, Israel spent 25.7 percent of its GDP on defence and only 4.1 percent on health and other welfare services, whereas West Germany spent 3.2 percent of its GDP on defence and 22.9 percent on health and other welfare services.[22]

Education, social security, and health are administrative services provided by most governments but they are affected by levels of a domestic wealth. It is difficult for poor economies to allocate their financial resources to services like these when their budgets are limited. All the wealthier economies can afford to choose how and for what purposes to provide government services to their citizens.

Licensing

As an administrative function, licensing is both a means of control and a source of government revenue. It enables governments to set standards and qualifications on activities having public consequences. Driving a car, hunting, fishing, practising medicine or law, selling real estate, teaching in public schools, and owning and operating a radio or television station are just some of the areas in which governments impose licensing requirements.[23] In Canada and other federal states, most of these standards are set by the provinces; however, some licences are issued by the federal government. For example, the Canadian Radio and Television Commission (CRTC), under the Broadcasting Act, is delegated with the responsibility to license all radio, television, and cable television companies operating in Canada. However, in unitary states such as France, Great Britain, and Israel, the national government is the sole licensing authority.

In one sense, licensing involves the provision of a service, but in another sense it also involves a considerable amount of regulation. In the case of the CRTC, the agency was created in 1968 to protect the Canadian broadcasting system. Its objectives are to make sure that Canadians own and control the broadcasting system and to regulate programming so that it is of high quality for public consumption. Similarly, the regulatory functions of any agency are involved in the power to grant or withhold licences.

Gathering Information

All bureaucracies gather and store information from the outside world. In a government, the intake of information is a major function of public administration. Eventually information results in an output of policy or action by the political system. Governments gather information by means of administrative research, polls, public hearings, commissions, task forces, committees, and licensing.

In Canada, all government departments and administrative agencies generate and consume massive quantities of data about the private and corporate behaviour of Canadians, as well as about Canada's external relations with the international community. The Department of National Health and Welfare conducts research into the diseases that afflict Canadians. Consumer and Corporate Affairs co-ordinates information on businesses and corporations in Canada. And the Department of External Affairs receives vital information from its embassies around the world.

Many departments of government, in order to carry out their programs, gather information on the private lives of individuals. The Department of Justice is charged with responsibilities to fight crime and subversion. Its files hold information on even the most intimate aspects of the lives of individual citizens.

Most of the information collected by governments is not controversial. In Canada, the census gathers information about the population in order to help government make policy choices that fit the needs of the people. Canada's twelfth census, taken in 1986, contains nearly 50 million pages of data on almost everything Canadians have or do. Canadians willingly told the 32 400 enumerators whether they were athletes (1.8 million were) and how many flush toilets they had (more than 100 000 had none).

But there is always a potential danger in the collection of such data. Bureaucratic agencies know about our life histories, our financial affairs, our credit ratings, our reputations for loyalty, our politics, and our places of residence. Police investigations may detail and hold on file whatever stories a neighbour or even a stranger has told about us.

In these days of computerized data retrieval, this information can be pulled together and disseminated with frightening speed. Only such human factors as the good will and decent motives of most bureaucrats may save us from the worst invasions of our privacy. But people do lose jobs and suffer other hardships because of unsubstantiated rumours that are registered in their files. The private lives, opinions, and morals of individuals are becoming increasingly vulnerable to bureaucratic scrutiny. The sheer volume of personal information in data banks, both public and private, is a threat not only to our credit ratings but to our freedom to live as we choose.

In most countries, the public has no right of access to the vast store of information in reports, records, files, and statistics gathered by governments through their administrative agencies.[24] But a growing number of democratic governments have decided that this practice is wrong and should be reversed: all unclassified administrative documents ought to be accessible to the public, except for information classified as secret by law.[25] Usually called a freedom of information act, access act, or privacy act, this kind of constitutional and legislative provision is now operative in nine democratic countries. Sweden was the first state to grant the right of public access to government documents in its constitutional law over 200 years ago, in 1766. Other states have proclaimed access laws in more recent times: Australia (1982), Canada (Privacy Act, 1982, and Access to Information Act, 1983), Denmark (1970), Finland (1951), France (1978), the Netherlands (1978), Norway (1970), and the United States (1966, revised 1974). In Canada, two provinces, Nova Scotia (1977) and New Brunswick (1978) passed-access-to information legislation applicable to provincial administrative documents and government files. At the federal level, the Privacy Act gives citizens and residents access to information about them held by the government, protects their privacy by preventing others from gaining access to it, and gives them some control over its collection and use. The Access to Information Act gives the same people the right to examine or obtain copies of the records of a federal government institution, except in limited and specific circumstances. The Access Register and Access Request Forms are located in public libraries, government information offices, and in postal stations in rural areas.

Controlling Bureaucracy

All states have developed a variety of formal and informal controls* on bureaucratic behaviour (table 8.1). One of the obvious major government controls external to the administrative apparatus of a state is the political executive. Presidents, prime ministers, and ministers formally control the bureaucracy through their powers of appointment and removal.[26] They also have the power of the purse from which bureaucracies are funded and programs are planned. While it is true that political executives cannot get along without bureaucracies, it is also true that there is a mutual dependence and reciprocal control between executives and bureaucracies. The executive can tame an autonomous administration by threatening to reduce government spending and by cutting back the size of the civil service. Where the executive chooses to allocate financial resources among administrative agencies, and where it decides to change the lines of administrative authority will bring bureaucratic implementation into greater conformity with the goals of the elected government.

Assemblies and courts are the other branches of government that exercise significant external controls on a bureaucracy. Public inquiries, auditors reports, questions of parliamentarians, congressional hearings, and judicial decisions all have an effect on bureaucratic performance. These formal controls work to secure a responsive, effective, and honest civil service.

Controls on bureaucratic behaviour

	Formal	Informal
EXTERNAL	Political executives: (presidents, prime ministers, premiers, governors) Elected assemblies: (parliaments, congresses, city councils) Courts Ombudsman	Public opinion Media Pressure groups Electorate University public administration programs
INTERNAL	Public Hearings Inquiries Royal commissions Decentralization and deregulation	Professional standards Upgrading Accountability

Source: Adapted from Mark Nadel and Frances Rourke, "Bureaucracies," in Fred Greenstein and Nelson Polsby, eds., *Handbook of Political Science*, vol. 5 (Reading, MA: Addison-Wesley, 1975), 416

Table 8.1

Legislatures can compel a bureaucracy to change administrative policy by creating a new law or revoking a department's or agency's powers. In all parliamentary systems of government, bureaucracies must defend their budgetary requests before an appropriate legislative committee or cabinet minister.[27] In many countries, especially in the United States, the power of the purse is as much a legislative as an executive power. The mere threat of withholding funds can force a change in administrative policy. In Canada and Great Britain, individual members of Parliament indirectly exercise restraints by becoming experts on particular subjects. An MP can ask a question of any minister concerning the administrative policies and practices of his or her ministry. Asking questions is the principal method by which backbenchers can review and criticize the action of the civil service. In general, the committee system of parliament or congress supports the scrutinizing role of the legislature over the bureaucracy.

Then there are the courts. They have the final authority to interpret the law and to rule on the proper administration and enforcement of laws in society. When private citizens or corporations feel that an administrative practice is unfair or that an administrator has stepped outside of his or her jurisdiction, they can seek a legal remedy through the courts. In a landmark decision in 1988, two federal cabinet ministers—Joe Clark and Flora MacDonald—were found guilty of contempt of court because of the behaviour of their officials in an immigration case. The decision of the Federal Court of Appeal meant that cabinet ministers could now be held accountable for what their bureaucrats do or do not do in an official capacity. The two ministers were held responsible for $65,000 in court costs, a bill the government had to pay. For the first time in Canadian history, it has been made clear that ministers are responsible to the courts for the way they run or do not run their ministries. The case was seen as a major step to evening the odds for citizens who take on the government in court. In the past, governments could fail to produce evidence for one reason or another and citizens could not pinpoint the blame at a particular bureaucrat. Now with the legal capacity to blame the minister the courts have greatly enhanced the direct control and accountability of bureaucrats in their official functions. In Canada and the United States, a remedy may take the form of a *writ of mandamus* (a court order requiring a public official to do his or her duty as the law dictates), a *writ of injunction* (a court order prohibiting an official or a private citizen from performing a particular action), or a court decision resulting in the payment of damages or the determination of responsibility for the abuse of administrative powers. But legislatures and courts are not always successful in keeping a close check on bureaucratic activities because they are primarily concerned with making and adjudicating laws, not watching over the administration of them.

Recognizing the limitations of legislative and judicial controls that leave the initiatives to elected officials or to the aggrieved, an increasing number of nation-states have created a special office of *ombudsman* (parliamentary commissioner) to advocate, investigate, and publicly criticize on behalf of citizens who complain about unfair bureaucratic treatment. Sweden was the first country to create a Justitieombudsman (representative of justice) in 1809. The Swedish Riksdag (parliament) appoints the ombudsman, who is empowered to hear and investigate citizen complaints of official arbitrariness*, negligence*, or discrimination*. The ombudsman has comprehensive jurisdiction, which includes the supervision of courts and the military.

The office of ombudsman has been adopted in about twenty-five democratic states, including Canada, Denmark, Fiji, Finland, France, Great Britain, Israel, New Zealand, and West Germany. Not all states have offices at the national level. Canada and the United States have no general ombudsman at the federal level. However, both have ombudsmen at the provincial and state levels respectively. In Canada, all provinces except PEI have ombudsmen to remedy complaints against provincial administrations.[28] In the United States, only Alaska, Iowa, Hawaii, and Nebraska have ombudsmen, but the office has been established in a number of U.S. cities, such as Atlanta and Seattle.

As an investigator and mediator appointed to protect the rights of individuals and groups in dealing with government, the ombudsman hears many complaints. When regular government agencies do not satisfactorily resolve problems the ombudsman is asked to investigate grievances. In general these involve a) claims for social assistance benefits or Workers' Compensation; b) property affected by work on highways; c) employment, or consumer services regulated by the province; c) difficulties in obtaining licences or permits; and d) any other matter regulated by provincial or municipal laws. In Canada, provincial ombudsmen do not have the authority to investigate grievances arising from decisions of the Cabinet, the law courts or judges, the federal government, private companies or individuals.

In April 1978, the Trudeau government introduced a bill to create a federal ombudsman, but it died on the order paper and the government was defeated in May 1979. The Clark government left it off their legislative agenda and the new Trudeau government, elected in February 1980, did not revive the bill. Thus far, the Mulroney governments (1984 and 1988) have not moved on providing a bill for a general ombudsman office to cover all aspects of federal administration. However, it is important to note that Canada has created ombudsman-like offices for special matters under federal jurisdiction. For example, there is a Commissioner of Official Languages who reviews complaints from the public that they were unfairly treated in their own languages by federal agencies. There is a Correctional Investigator who receives complaints from inmates about injustices in the penal system. Under the Access to Information Act, the government has established the office of Information Commissioner to deal with complaints about the wrongful denial of access to information. And, under the Privacy Act, the government empowers a Privacy Commissioner to investigate complaints about personal information retained by government agencies and to make recommendations to the institution involved if there is a denial of access. But all of these offices are highly specialized and in no way perform the comprehensive functions of a general ombudsman.

Among the extra-governmental forces and agencies that attempt to control bureaucracies are pressure groups and the mass media. Pressure groups attempt to reform the bureaucracy by using their own investigative staffs to challenge the efficacy of many types of social programs and to bring pressure to bear upon the government to change the programs. In Canada, the Canadian Federation of Independent Business (CFIB) has prompted many other organizations to use public opinion as a way to reform the tax collection methods of Revenue Canada Taxation. In the United States, Ralph Nader has gained prominence in connection with administrative reform in both public- and private-sector bureaucracies. The mass media provide still another avenue for taming an unresponsive bureaucracy.

Bureaucratic accountability is also affected by internal controls, such as professional standards and upgrading, as well as by advisory committees made up of people representing political parties and interest groups.[29] The variety and kinds of controls vary from country to country.[30] The term "administocracy" was coined by Guy S. Claire in the 1930s to refer to tensions between the ideals of popular sovereignty and the growth of an aristocracy of administrators within a democratic state.[31] In a democracy, a multiplicity of formal and informal controls function to keep a bureaucracy accountable. But in totalitarian and authoritarian political systems, many of these controls are lacking or so constrained as to be virtually ineffective. Political executives and legislators are not often responsibly elected and courts do not function as an independent branch of government. The roles of the mass media and pressure groups are not those of an external conscience for the bureaucracy or a forum for public grievances. Instead, bureaucracies are affiliated with the goals of an élite-directed party and government apparatus. In the absence of an open and pluralistic political system, the effectiveness of all controls on bureaucracy is very limited.

Canada's Public Service

Broadly speaking, the Canadian bureaucracy consists of the personnel in federal government departments (e.g., the Department of Finance), federal government agencies (e.g., the Bank of Canada and the Canadian Wheat Board), central control agencies (e.g., the Treasury Board and the Privy Council Office), and crown corporations (e.g., Air Canada and Petro-Canada). The great bulk of federal government employees are recruited by the Public Service Commission*, itself a central control agency that performs its wide staffing functions by means of competitive examinations and interviews in which merit is the determining factor. Legally, Canada's public employees are not appointed or removed from their positions for political reasons. Civil servants are directly responsible, through a chain of command, to their administrative superiors. It cannot be denied that political favouritism sometimes plays a part in the choice of job assignments and speed or delay in promotions, even though the public service in theory rules out politics. In 1988 a ruling by the Federal Court of Appeal struck down the law (The Public Service Employment Act) that restricted the political rights of federal public servants, on the grounds that it infringed on their freedoms of expression and association. The decision noted that the Charter of Rights and Freedoms does not alter the public interest in a politically neutral public service. It has simply added countervailing individual rights.

The basic structural units of the federal government are the more than thirty departments that exercise jurisdiction over national and international policies and programs. Beginning with the federal administrative establishment, the key political actor is the *Cabinet minister*, who functions as the formal department head and who is responsible for the administration of the government's policies through its public employees. The administrative efficacy of the minister in leading the department is often solely dependent upon the qualities of his or her personal leadership and aggressiveness.[32] But generally the energies of a minister are focussed and directed on the politics of Cabinet decision making. The minister tends not to tamper with administrative functions of the department itself. Instead, the minister must learn to deal with what one minister called the "civil service policy" and adapt the political exigencies of Cabinet and constituency pressures to the routines of the department's administration.[33]

The person second in the line of authority within a department is the *deputy minister* (DM), who is appointed by the prime minister.[34] Unlike other civil servants, the deputy minister retains an administrative position "at the pleasure" of the government. He or she does not enjoy permanent tenure and may be shuffled, demoted, or fired at the will of the prime minister. In January 1985, Prime Minister Mulroney announced what he called the largest single change of senior personnel in the history of the Canadian public service. He announced twenty-four appointments, seventeen of which were reassignments, while five were new people from outside the federal public service. All the appointments involved senior officials – powerful people in the Ottawa bureaucracy. Although deputy ministers are held accountable for the policies they helped to devise and for the loyalities they may have demonstrated toward the government that appointed them, most of the time they seem to be able to overcome their associations with out-of-favour governments and are kept on by succeeding governments as a source of useful advice. The two most important skills of a deputy minister – that of advising and departmental management – are indispensable to political ministers who need to take command of an administrative machine that was in operation long before they rose to power and will function quite well after they have gone.

In terms of the policy process itself, the deputy minister is a senior policy adviser not only to the minister, but to the entire government. The segmented process of federal decision making requires deputy ministers to advise other ministers and deputy ministers in order to co-ordinate Cabinet policies and programs. In particular, all deputy ministers must represent and co-ordinate their department's affairs with three central agencies: The Prime Minister's Office, the Privy Council Office, and the Treasury Board Secretariat. Over many years of gaining administrative experience, the deputy minister builds an important network of personal and professional contacts that is invaluable to the operation of the government. As administrative head of a department, the deputy minister is like the managing executive of a large corporation. As an executor of political policies, the deputy minister is an interdepartmental diplomat, a policy co-ordinator, and a negotiator.[35]

The deputy minister is at the top of a hierarchical chain of command within the structure of the department. The people who work at subordinate levels are almost exclusively civil servants who stay on over the years, in contrast to the political executives above them, who come and go with each changing government or Cabinet shuffle. All departments have certain characteristics that seem to be universal bureaucratic traits: (1) *specialization or division of labour** – individual jobs have specific tasks assigned to them irrespective of the individual who holds the job. (2) *Hierarchy or fixed lines of command* – each civil servant knows who the boss is, and whom, if anyone, he or she may supervise. (3) *Incentives* to attract people to work for the department and be loyal to its purposes. By far the most important incentive is the assurance that once someone has a job, he or she will keep it unless a gross transgression is committed.

Crown corporations are another important aspect of public administration in Canada. These are public enterprises in which the government has the controlling interest, and which provide goods and services to the public on an administrative or commercial basis. Since World War II public enterprises have rapidly expanded in the Canadian economy. Crown corporations have been used to meet national or local needs in the interests of the public where private enterprise and investment have not been ready or willing to take the risk to promote economic growth. The development of a national or provincial infrastructure has been costly and risky, culminating in the incorporation of such public enterprises as the St. Lawrence Seaway Authority, Ports Canada, and Air Canada. Private-sector corporate behaviour is profit-motivated; government-owned corporations consider factors such as unemployment, welfare, market failures, and national standards when operating in a community.

There are a number of different ways of defining crown corporations: the characteristic of government ownership is considered to be the most important legal criterion for defining a crown corporation. However, there is some disagreement as to what amount of government ownership determines the status of crown corporation. *Mixed enterprises* are companies, such as the Canada Development Corporation and Telesat Canada, in which ownership is shared by the government (in the name of the Crown) with the private sector. *Joint enterprises* are public companies, such as the Newfoundland and Labrador Development Corporation, and the North Portage Development Corporation, in which ownership is shared between governments, usually a province and the federal government.

From a functional perspective crown corporations reflect common criteria, whether they are provincially, federally, or jointly owned: (a) majority ownership is held by a government; (b) there is an arms-length management strategy, independent from government; (c) corporate goods and services are directed at the private sector, not the government; (d) prices for goods and services provided by crown corporations must be fair and competitive.

Federal crown corporations are accountable to Parliament under the Financial Administration Act (1952), as amended in 1984. This legislation applies only to corporations which are wholly government-owned, such as the Canada Development Investment Corporation and Via Rail Canada Inc. The FAA places crown corporation into three schedules, classified as B, C1, and C11. Under schedule B are crown corporations, such as the Canadian Centre for Occupational Health and Safety, the National Museums of Canada, and the Economic

Council of Canada. Formerly categorized as departmental corporations, they perform a wide range of administrative, advisory, regulatory, and supervisory functions of a governmental nature. Schedule C1 lists crown corporations, such as Loto Canada Inc., the Export Development Corporation, and the Federal Business Development Bank. These companies perform a variety of commercial, developmental, managerial, and service functions. They make up the majority of corporations listed under the act and experience varying degrees of ministerial direction. Schedule C11 includes most companies formerly categorized as proprietary corporations, such as Teleglobe Canada, Petro-Canada, and Canada Ports Corporation. These corporations are often in direct competition with privately owned companies and are expected to operate as financially self-sustaining.

Under the 1984 amendments, some crown corporations were dropped from the listings of the FAA. The Canadian Broadcasting Corporation, the Canada Council, the Canadian Film Development Corporation, and the National Arts Centre perform special cultural functions and are distanced from the political controls applied to other corporations. Some crown corporations, such as the Bank of Canada, the Canada Wheat Board, and the International Development and Research Centre, have been established by special legislation. They perform many diverse functions that require independence from political and ministerial control. For example, the Bank of Canada sets the prime lending rate on Canadian currency in order to keep the interest rate differential between Canada and the United States from becoming too great. In order for the Bank of Canada to manage and regulate Canadian monetary policy*, it must remain free from direct political interference. The governor of the Bank of Canada is frequently at the centre of momentous struggles-– involving the federal government, the provinces, and lenders and borrowers – over the bank's monetary policy on such questions as "tight money" or the most desirable political and economic means of combating inflation* or recession*.

Crown corporations have a working arrangement with the Public Service Commission that allows them almost complete discretion in hiring and promotion at all levels, particularly at management levels. The labour standards of the Public Service Commission are a model aimed at preventing arbitrary and unfair decisions and at equalizing promotion and pay policies for employees among the various crown corporations.

By the 1990s, nearly half of all federal government employees, or about 250 000 Canadians, were working for both classified and unclassified crown corporations. An additional 300 000 people were employed by federal departments of government such as National Revenue, External Affairs, and Consumer and Corporate Affairs. When the nearly 85 000 members of the Armed Forces are taken into account, over 600 000 people are employed by the federal government. By any measure, the bureaucracy is overwhelmingly the largest part of the federal government. In effect, this makes Canada's public service its own constituency, with the federal bureaucracy acting like any other pressure group by prodding, probing, expanding, and consolidating its own position in Canada's political system. The federal bureaucracy has grown large enough to constitute a fourth branch of government. Neither the mass media nor elected politicians and interest groups have the aggregate power of the federal bureaucracy.

A growing consensus among political scientists points to the conclusion that Canadian society may be *ruled* by the politicians but it is *governed* by the bureaucrats.[36] The bureaucracy makes thousands and thousands of interpretive decisions each day, thus having an enormous amount of supplementary lawmaking power after bills become laws. At the departmental level in Canada, the bureaucracy is a major initiator of public policy. Many proposals for new legislation come from senior civil servants who set the agenda of alternatives for the government behind the view of the public. It is true that the crucial initiative for the most important new legislation comes from the Cabinet. But even here the departmental civil servants provide much of the background and analysis, and they frequently draft the actual bill as well. Furthermore, they provide a significant share of the continuity and flow of information necessary to pass legislation.

The routine decisions of the Canadian government are a preserve of the federal bureaucracy. For example, the federal government is a very large buyer of goods and services. In some cases, it is the largest buyer, or the only one. The millions of decisions about what the government will or will not buy, or provide its money for, are made by career civil servants subject to very general supervision and guidelines. The collective impact of these decisions is the government's policy. Because the bureaucracy is so vast and complex, the sum of so many apparently small decisions has an impact rivalling that of the few obviously big ones. Canadians may be unwarranted in their easy use of the term "bureaucrat" as a purely negative stereotype. However, they are warranted in their desire to watch and evaluate the public service.

Public Administration in the United States

In the United States, the term bureaucracy in reference to the national government is used loosely to designate a group of administrative organizations serving the president, the congress, and the judiciary. Beginning with the federal administrative establishment, the primary units of the bureaucracy are the thirteen departments – collectively the largest part – most of whose heads carry the title *Secretary* and who make up most of the *cabinet*. Also included are the *independent regulatory commissions*, the *government corporations*, the *unaffiliated agencies*, and a host of *boards* and *administrations*.

The oldest and largest administrative units are the departments, which employ over 1.5 million of the nearly 3 million civilian employees working for the federal government in 1990.[37] The secretaries are appointed by the president and approved by the Senate. Most of the departments have more than one *undersecretary* who functions as the personal assistant to the secretary. Below the undersecretaries are the *assistant secretaries*, each of whom is responsible for a major division within the department. Each division is made up of *bureaus*. Each bureau is headed by directors or administrators who function as *bureau chiefs* and manage the administrative programs of the departments.

Independent regulatory commissions* are the other major components of the federal bureaucracy.[38] They are intended to make and administer regulatory policies in the public interest. The commissions, such as the Federal Trade Commission (FTC), the Civil Aeronautics Board (CAB), and the Federal Aviation Agency (FAA), are independent in the sense that, unlike the conventional departments, they are not in the chain of command leading to the president: the commissioners cannot be dismissed by the president at will. The commissions are quasi-legislative: they are empowered by Congress to make many supplementary laws of their own. They are quasi-judicial: they hold court-like hearings to make decisions affecting industry, commercial services, and private citizens. Most regulatory commissions deal with industries that are natural monopolies (such as electric power companies) or with business activities in which unrestrained competition damages the industry or the public interest.

Congress also uses the government-owned corporation* to pursue specified government policies.[39] These specially chartered corporations, such as the Federal Deposit Insurance Corporation (FDIC), the Tennessee Valley Authority (TVA), and the United States Postal Service, are created by the government to do a particular job. The FDIC is generally responsible for insuring the deposits of the banking public and the TVA makes and sells electric power to the vast region in the Tennessee Valley; it operates in much the same way as any large business corporation.

A host of other unaffiliated agencies*, boards, and administrations stand on their own, but are directly responsible to the president or Congress. Some of these agencies are very large, complex, and important. The Veterans Administration (VA) operates a national system of hospitals and administers veterans' programs employing nearly 200 000 people. It is larger than any of the departments except Defence. Other important unaffiliated bodies are the National Aeronautics and Space Administration (NASA) and the Environmental Protection Agency (EPA). Such agencies are often established in order to pioneer a particular policy area, NASA being an obvious case in point.[40] President Kennedy's promise to put a man on the moon before the year 1970 required an immense governmental effort in an independent agency. By the same token, when public concern with ecological issues grew in the early 1970s, the newly created EPA was sheltered under the president's wing.

The origin of a professional civil service in the United States was a product of an act of political violence. In the latter part of the nineteenth century, the patronage system (in which federal jobs were given as rewards for service to one of the political parties) flourished in the United States. A new president could make appointments to most of the administrative jobs in the federal government. "To the victor belong the spoils" was the caption of the spoils system* in U.S. federal politics. Old officeholders were simply turned out after a new president was inaugurated. In 1881, a crazed, unsuccessful spoils seeker shot and killed President James Garfield. After a great deal of pressure from reform groups campaigning against the patronage system, Congress passed the Pendleton Act (1883), establishing the Civil Service Commission (now called the Office of Personnel Management*); a merit system based on competitive examinations was created for hiring and promoting federal employees. Today, over 75 percent of all civil servants in the United

States are under the central merit system administered by the Office of Personnel Management. Most of the remaining federal employees are recruited by the separate merit systems of individual agencies such as the Federal Bureau of Investigation (FBI). There are over 1000 jobs not covered by civil service regulation that go mainly to people within the president's party (a mini-spoils system). Many of these appointees are close friends and supporters of the president.[41]

The Office of Personnel Management is the central employment agency for the national government. It advertises positions, receives applications, and, most important, establishes, administers, and evaluates a system of competitive recruitment. When a government department or agency wants to hire someone, the Office of Personnel Management is notified. It then supplies the names of the three top achievers on the appropriate exam to the recruiting agency. The administrator must select one of the three successful candidates.

In Canada, the fusion of powers brings the federal bureaucracy under the direction of the political executive; in the United States, the executive and legislative branches of government each have the power to create their own separate bureaucracy under the Constitution. The bureaucracy serves both executive and lawmaking functions of the president and the Congress. However, as in Canada, the American federal bureaucracy is involved in every stage of the policy-making process. It drafts the bills that eventually become laws, administers the execution of them, and interprets the patterns of detailed applications that determine what those laws eventually mean in practice. The more routine a policy decision, the larger part the bureaucracy is likely to play in it. The president and Congress play greater roles in what appear to be the major decisions. The only preventive controls available to deal with the bureaucracy belong to the president and the Congress. The checks-and-balance system is constantly brought into play by these two branches of government. Presidents must give the bureaucracy executive direction because they represent the entire country and must see to it that administrators follow that direction. The Congress, which represents the many regional interests of Americans, must be ever watchful of the bureaucracy, too. Through its powers of appropriation and investigation, the Congress has to check possible abuses of bureaucratic authority from the perspecitive of constituents and constituencies.

However, the U.S. federal bureaucracy has evolved to become a power with an independent life of its own. It is at least partially independent of the president, the Congress, and the courts. The federal bureaucracy is primarily directed by more than 5000 experienced career executives with permanent civil-service status.[42] These people occupy the "super grade" positions of the administration, and they remain in their position despite changes in the White House or the Congress. Career executives are protected from the perils of partisan politics and are expected to serve the "national interest" even through changes in the political fortunes of the two major political parties. As in Canada, the bureaucracy must be viewed as the fourth branch of government.

REFERENCES

1. Stanley Udy Jr., *Organization of Work: A Comparative Analysis of Production among Non-industrial Peoples* (New Haven: HRAF Press 1959), 10–35.
2. Donald Kagan, Steven Ozment, et al., *The Western Heritage since 1300* (New York: Macmillan Publishing Co. Inc. 1983), 550–3.
3. Joseph Strayer and Hans Gatzke, *The Main-stream of Civilization* (New York: Harcourt, Brace Jovanovich Publishers 1984), 550–9.
4. W.L. White, R.H. Wagenberg, and R.C. Nelson, *Introduction to Canadian Politics and Government* (Toronto: Holt, Rinehart and Winston of Canada Ltd. 1985), 145–56.
5. Stephen Sanderson, *Macrosociology* (New York: Harper & Row Publishers 1988), 442–3.
6. Max Weber, *The Theory of Social and Economic Organization* (Glencoe, IL: Free Press 1974), 334; and Talcott Parsons, ed., *American Sociology* (New York: Basic Books 1968), 57–9.
7. See Fred Greenstein and Nelson Polsby, eds., *Handbook of Political Science,* vol. 5 (Reading, MA: Addison-Wesley 1975), 373–40.
8. Kim Richard Nossal, *The Politics of Canadian Foreign Policy* (Scarborough, ON: Prentice-Hall Canada Inc. 1985), 136–7.
9. See F.A. Nigro and L.G. Nigro, *Modern Public Administration* (New York: Harper & Row 1977); and B.G. Peters, *The Politics of Bureaucracy: A Comparative Perspective* (New York: Longman 1978).
10. Yaacov Vertzberger, "Bureaucratic-Organizational Politics and Information Processing in a Developing State," *International Studies Quarterly* 28 (March 1984): 69–96.
11. See Gabriel Almond and G. Bingham Powell Jr., *Comparative Politics Today: A World View* (Boston: Little, Brown & Co. 1984), 109–12.
12. See Joel Aberback and Robert Putman, et al., *Bureaucrats and Politicians in Western Democracies* (Cambridge, MA: Harvard University Press 1981).
13. In reference to Canada, see Robert Lewis, "Ottawa's Power Brokers," *Maclean's,* May 24, 1982.
14. Mitchell Sharp, "The Role of the Mandarins," *Policy Options* 2 (May/June 1981): 43.
15. An analysis of this phenomenon is found in Seymour Wilson, *Canadian Public Policy and Administration: Theory and Environment* (Toronto: McGraw-Hill 1981), ch. 4.
16. See Seymour Wilson and O.P. Dwivedi, "Introduction" in Dwivedi, ed., *The Administrative State in Canada* (Toronto: University of Toronto Press 1982), 3–13.
17. Michael Hill, *The State Administration and the Individual* (Glasgow: Collins 1976).
18. Economic Council of Canada, *Responsible Regulation* (Ottawa: November 1979), 16; Hugh Segal, "The Acountability of Public Servants," *Policy Options* 2 (November-December 1981): 11–13.
19. Hudson Janisch, "Policy-Making in Regulation," *Osgoode Hall Law Journal* 17, no. 3 (1979): 46–106.
20. Herbert Kaufman, "Fear of Bureaucracy: A Raging Pandemic," *Public Administration Review* 41 (January-February 1981): 1–9.
21. See Arnold Heidenhiemer, Hugo Heclo, et al., *Comparative Public Policy* (New York: St. Martin's Press 1983); and Arpad Abonyi and Michael Atkinson, "Technological Innovation and Industrial Policy: Canada in an International Context," in Michael Atkinson and Marsha Chaldler, eds., *The Politics of Canadian Public Policy* (Toronto: University of Toronto Press 1983), 93–126.
22. United Nations, *Yearbook of National Account Statistics, 1987* (New York: United Nations 1989).
23. See Richard Schultz, "Regulatory Agencies and the Dilemmas of Delega-

tion," in Dwivedi ed., *The Administrative State in Canada,* 90–106.

24. See Heather Mitchell, *Access to Information and Policy Making: A Comparative Study,* Research Publication 16 (Toronto: Ontario Commission on Freedom of Information and Individual Privacy 1980); Murray Rankin, "The New Access to Information and the Privacy Act: A Critical Annotation," *Ottawa Law Review* 15, no. 2 (1983): 35–6.
25. Donald C. Rowat, ed., *Administrative Secrecy in Developed Countries* (London: Macmillan 1979); see also Donald Rowat, "The Right of Public Access to Official Documents," in Dwivedi, ed., *The Administrative State in Canada,* 177–92.
26. See Colin Campbell, *Governments under Stress: Political Executives and Key Bureaucrats in Washington, London, and Ottawa* (Toronto: University of Toronto Press 1983).
27. In reference to Canada, see Treasury Board, *Accountable Management* (Ottawa: March 1981).
28. Donald C. Rowat, "We Need a Federal Ombudsman Commission," *Policy Options* 3 (March-April 1982); K.A. Friedmann and A. G. Milne, "The Federal Ombudsman Legislation," *Canadian Public Policy,* VI (Winter 1980): 63–77.
29. Robert Best, "The Meaning of 'Merit' in Canadian Public Administration," in Robert Adie and Paul Thomas, *Canadian Public Administration* (Scarborough, ON: Prentice-Hall Canada Ltd. 1987), 55–95.
30. Donald C. Rowat, *Global Comparisons in Public Administration* (Ottawa: Carleton University Press 1981).
31. Guy S. Claire, *Administocracy* (New York: Crowell-Collier and Macmillan Inc. 1934).
32. Douglas Hartle, "Techniques and Processes of Administration," *Canadian Public Administration* 19 (Spring 1976): 31–2; Ian Clark "Recent Changes in the Cabinet Decision-making System in Ottawa," *Canadian Public Administration* 28, no. 2 (1985): 185–201.
33. Flora MacDonald, "Cutting through the Chains," *Globe and Mail,* November 7, 1980, 7.
34. Colin Campbell and G.J. Szablowski, *The Superbureaucrats: Structure and Behaviour in Central Agencies* (Toronto: Collier MacMillan of Canada Ltd. 1979).
35. See Richard Van Loon and Michael Whittington, *The Canadian Political System: Environment, Structure and Process* (Toronto: McGraw-Hill Ryerson Ltd. 1981), 391–3.
36. See J. Robert Prichard and Michael Trebilcock, "Crown Corporations in Canada: The Choice of Instrument," in Atkinson and Chandler, eds., *The Politics of Canadian Public Policy,* 199–222.
37. See John Langford, "The Identification and Classification of Federal Public Corporations: A Preface to Regime Building," *Canadian Public Administration* 23, no. 1 (1980): 76–30.
38. See Richard Schultz, *Federalism Bureaucracy and Public Policy* (Toronto: University of Toronto Press 1980); Kenneth Kernaghan and T.H. McLeod, "Mandarins and Ministers in the Canadian Administrative State," in Dwivedi, ed., *The Administrative State in Canada,* 17–30.
39. There were 2 890 144 in 1989; see U.S. Office of Personnel Management, Annual Report of 1989.
40. See James Wilson, *The Politics of Regulation* (New York: Basic Books 1980); see also Lance LeLoup, *Politics in America* (St Paul, MN: West Publishing Co. 1986), 423–56.
41. See Randall B. Ripley, *Congress, Process and Policy* (New York: W.W. Norton & Co. 1983), ch. 10; and James Wilson, *American Government,* 4th ed. (Lexington, MA: D.C. Heath & Co. 1989) 378–87.
42. See James Bennett, "How Big Is the Federal Government?" *Economic Review* 40 (December 1981); see also *Federal Employees' Almanac 1986* (Falls Church, VA: Federal Employees' Digest 1986).

SUGGESTED READINGS

Robert Adie and Paul Thomas, *Canadian Public Administration: Problematical Perspectives* (Scarborough, ON: Prentice-Hall 1987).

Frank Fischer and John Forester, eds., *Confronting Values in Policy Analysis: The Politics of Criteria* (Beverly Hills, CA: Sage Publications 1987)

Gordon Osbaldeston, *Keeping Deputy Ministers Accountable* (Scarborough, ON: McGraw-Hill Ryerson Ltd. 1989).

Kenneth Kernaghan and David Siegal, *Political Administration in Canada: A Text* (Scarborough, ON: Nelson Canada 1987).

David Kozak and James Keagle, *Bureaucratic Politics and National Security: Theory and Practice* (Boulder, CO: Lynne Rienner Publishers 1988).

Jeanne Kirk Laux and Maureen Appel Molot, *State Capitalism: Public Enterprise in Canada* (Ithaca, NY: Cornell University Press 1988).

Leslie Pal, *Public Policy Analysis: An Introduction* (Scarborough, ON: Nelson Canada 1987).

Davis Robertson and Dennis Judd, *The Development of American Public Policy The Structure of Policy Restraint* (Glenview, IL Scott, Foresman & Co. 1989).

David Roessner, ed., *Government Innovation Policy* (New York: St. Martin's Press 1988).

David Schuman and Dick Olufs III, *Public Administration in the United States* (Lexington, MA: D.C. Heath and Co. 1988).

GLOSSARY

administration: The ways in which the activities of an organization are managed in order to implement certain policies.

civil service: A term applied to the body of employees working for a government.

hierarchical: The term used to describe the relative positions of individuals or groups of individuals within a body or society and their relationship to power and control.

bureaucracy: A formal organization characterized by the rational operation of a hierarchical authority structure and explicit procedural rules. Bureaucracies tend to arise whenever the activities of a group of people have to be co-ordinated in terms of explicit impersonal goals. The rationality of the bureaucratic form gives it a superior efficiency to other methods of administration.

egalitarianism: The ideology that refers to the degree of equality between two or more individuals, populations, or large groups with respect to some specified characteristic, such as a right, a duty, or treatment.

tenure: A guarantee of permanent job security after a certain period in which the individual has proved his or her worth.

patronage: The practice of appointing political supporters to public office or to desirable positions on public boards, commissions, and committees.

Max Weber: A German sociologist whose work profoundly influenced Western social thought and sociological method.

specialization: The apportionment of various tasks or procedures among individuals in an organization so as to maximize efficiency and decision-making facility.

public planning: The process of determining the future economic, social, political, and physical arrangements of a community.

red tape: The phrase (derived from the red ribbons tied around official documents in the royal courts of Europe) that refers to the system of rules and procedures applied by bureaucratic organizations in their rountine affairs.

influence: A form of power that involves freely affecting the conduct of others in an intended way as distinct from control, coercion, force, or interference.

regulations: Rules that are usually written down in such documents as by-laws and operating manuals that define such diverse matters as decision-making authority, criteria for promotion, and the everyday operating procedures of an organization.

political modernization: The process of change in a political system based on the idea that public institutions should incorporate more people as participants who are differentiated, effective, and efficient in their performance, and on the notion that the character of these institutions is universalistic and egalitarian.

controls: The techniques and strategies for regulating human behaviour in any society.

arbitrary: The exercise of power by officials who use their authority for personal rather than institutional goals.

negligence: Omitting doing something that a reasonable person, guided by ordinary considerations, would do or the doing of some act that would ordinarily not be done.

discrimination: The according of different treatment to persons, bodies, or groups without sufficient reason or legal authority for so doing.

Public Service Commission: In 1967, the Canadian Civil Service Commission became the Public Service Commission, a central agency that under the Public Service Employment Act is empowered to recruit potential employees for public service through competitive examinations and interviews.

division of labour: The separation of work into distinct parts, each of which is completed by an individual or group of individuals for the purposes of increasing production, efficiency, and specialization of expertise.

private sector: In a mixed economy, that part of the economy which is not under governmental control, i.e. all private enterprise, private profit- and non-profit-making organizations and exchanges between individuals.

monetary policy: Actions that the Bank of Canada takes to change the equilibrium of the money market, that is, to alter the money supply, move the exchange rate, or both.

inflation: A sustained increase in the general price level.

recession: A period in which the total output of the economy declines.

independent regulatory commissions (U.S.)*:* Agencies of the U.S. federal government that combine the power to legislate and enforce the rules they make, and to try cases under their regulation.

government-owned corporations (U.S.)*:* Agencies of the U.S. federal government established to resemble private corporations for reasons of efficiency, regulation, and policy.

unaffiliated agencies (U.S.)*:* Agencies not a part of a government department that report directly to the president or to the Congress.

spoils system (U.S.)*:* The political advantage of a victorious president who appoints his supporters and those of the party to most of the jobs in the federal bureaucracy.

Office of Personnel Management: Originally called the Civil Service Commission, this agency is now the central employment agency for the rest of the U.S. federal government.

9

Law and the Judiciary

Ben Johnson during the Dubin Inquiry

The Meaning of Law

YEARS AGO A LEGAL EXPERT WROTE: "Those of us who have learned humility have given up on defining law."[1] One of the difficulties in arriving at a definition of law is that it pervades culture without any clear-cut edges. Law is not sharply separable from all other forms of human action. Moral and ethical principles are often the basis of law in society. But custom* and usage* may also gain legal import if a people regard them as culturally significant. When it becomes necessary for a society to protect what it deems socially important, rules and regulations are established for that purpose. Laws codify certain norms*, mores*, and folkways* present in every society. They set down the prescribed and proscribed behaviour in precise terms and usually include specific guidelines for the kind and length of punishment to be given to violators.

A law differs from a custom in the quality of its obligation. A person who violates a custom may be regarded as eccentric but cannot be legally punished for an infraction. For example, a person may not approve of the dress and mannerisms of a rock star but that person is not doing anything against the law. However, if someone rides a motorcycle beyond the prescribed speed limit or decides to undress in front of a policeman, that person may be liable to arrest. These distinctions sometimes appear arbitrary because some societies permit what others do not, and laws within a society may even change over a period of time. But laws are customs that persons *must* abide by or be prepared to accept the consequences. This means that laws must somehow be enforced; they are enforced by a legitimate agency that is recognized as having political and legal authority within society.

According to E. Adamson Hoebel, "law is merely one aspect of our culture – the aspect which employs the force of organized society to regulate individual and group conduct and to prevent redress or punish deviations from prescribed social norms."[2] A number of leading legal experts have defined law in terms of the judicial process. American Justice Oliver Wendell Holmes put it this way: "The prophecies of what the courts will do in fact, and nothing more pretentious, are what I mean by law."[3] B.N. Cardozo emphasized that law is a basis for prediction rather than a mere guess: "A principle or rule of conduct so established as to justify a prediction with reasonable certainty that it will be enforced by the courts if its authority is challenged is ... a principle or rule of law."[4]

Taken together these definitions contain the four essential elements of law:

- The first is a *normative* element – a standard or model of conduct that may perfect human behaviour or achieve some collective good.
- The second is *regularity* – that laws are made by a recognized political authority and are predictably and universally applied. The practical advantage of this element is that it emphasizes law as a process, not a series of particular commands. Law is a body of principles that is regularly enforceable on all persons and groups within a legal jurisdiction.
- The third essential element is that the courts will objectively *apply* and *administer* the law. The task of a court in actual litigation is to determine the facts of a case, to declare the rule that is applicable, and then to make a specific order that is the result of the application of the law to those facts that are considered relevant.
- Finally, for the law to have teeth there must be legitimate *enforcement* by a recognized legal authority.

The lawmaking process and its enforcement by a system of courts is a primary means of peacefully resolving disputes in most societies. In the present day, modern industrialized states have formal institutions and offices, such as legislatures, the police, lawyers, courts, and penal systems, to deal with conflicts that arise in society. All these institutions generally operate according to codified laws – a set of written or explicit rules stipulating what is permissible and what is not. Transgression of the law by people gives the state the right to take actions against them. The state has a monopoly on the legitimate use of ultimate force in any society because it alone can coerce its subjects into compliance with its legislation, regulation, customs, and procedures.

Sources of Law

The laws that humans abide by are drawn from several sources.[5] Throughout history legalists have struggled to distinguish the formal sources of law as derived from a deity, morality, nature, or human political and legal institutions. Ethical, moral, and natural principles have always been important guides to human behaviour, and many of these principles have been given legal sanction. But the principal source of legal practice within nation-states and for the international community has been positive law. *Positive law* is human-made law, derived from the will of the state as manifested in custom, legislation, statutes, treaties, and the decisions of courts.

Custom is a source of positive law because certain practices and usages are enforced by governments. For example, in many countries the custom that the chief wage earners (usually men) continue to provide support to spouses and childern during marriage breakdown and after divorce was legislated as law by governments. Custom provides the raw material from which many laws are enacted or adjudicated. *Judicial rulings* are another source of positive law because the decisions of judges add to the total body of law. *Legislation* in the form of constitutions, decrees, statutes, and treaties, is a final source of law. The sovereign authority of the state and its institutions are the sources of the validity of law in most legal systems. Many states regard law as valid because it is the expression of divine, moral, or natural justice, but in the modern world it is clear that legal validity of a system of law depends on its enactment and enforcement.

Law and Legal Systems

History reveals that every civilization has developed a recognizable legal system – a body of laws, rules, and regulations, enacted by a lawmaking authority that delegates judicial powers to special groups of people.[6] Western civilization developed two complete and influential legal systems from English *common law* and from Roman *civil law*.

English Common Law

Although the Romans had evolved a formidable legal system well over 1000 years before the appearance of what we now call Anglo-American law, it collapsed in Great Britain when Rome was forced to relinquish her frontiers in the face of barbarian onslaughts. The complete withdrawal of Rome's military presence from England in A.D. 410 meant the disappearance of Roman culture on the island.[7] On the European continent, civil law systems are directly traceable to the Roman influence.

After Rome recalled her armies from Britain in the fifth century, tides of invaders crossed the English Channel for the next 500 years. Each of these groups of arriving Angles, Saxons, Jutes, and Danes brought its own rules for settling legal disputes. Over the centuries these peoples carved out petty kingdoms where legal customs became fixed. Even the final successful invasion of 1066, led by the Norman conqueror William, did not affect the differing customary legal practices of these little enclaves, although it transformed the political life of England.

It remained for Henry II (1154–1189) to implant the unique legal practices of common law. King Henry II trained representatives called "justices" to travel throughout England and administer his land law (the basis of taxation and property rights), breaches of the "King's Peace" (criminal law), and the supervision of local officials. In this way, judicial administration was made the same in all parts of the country, and differing customs were united into a body of law, "common" to the whole kingdom.

In time these justices began keeping records of their decisions in legal disputes. Thus a body of precedent* was built up. Justices developed the practice of following the precedent called *stare decisis et non quieta movere* (let the decision stand and do not move what has been settled), which added the element of predictability to regularity in the evolving legal system. By referring to past situations, justices could make the same decisions in identical cases and arrive at judgements in legal disputes that were similar, but not the same. The system of relying on precedent made the law very conservative but it fulfilled the minimum requirements of justice in that it was predictable, regular, and evenly applied.

Alongside laws administered by justices grew the rules of *equity*. Because the king was believed to be the fountain of justice, the keepers of his conscience were empowered to dispense justice and fairness, or equity, in ruling on legal disputes. In deciding a case *ex aequo et bono* (out of justice and fairness), the justices were authorized by the king to apply equity by overruling other rules that stood in the way of a remedy. Thus, if a person maliciously killed a productive animal belonging to another person, he or she would not only be required to replace the animal but would also have to pay compensation for any losses the owner incurred while the matter was being remedied.

The practice of summoning a jury to assist in arriving at a ruling in criminal cases was also an English invention. Henry II recognized the potentialities of swearing in twelve men from the local area and four from surrounding towns to inform justices of persons suspected of grave infractions against the King's Peace. The use of a jury in civil cases grew from Henry's idea of using a group of neighbours to determine ownership and possession of disputed land. Once made available to the people, trial by jury established its superiority over trials by combat, ordeal, and swearing oaths that had been practised in England for half a millennium.

Gradually, the consolidation of English law into a complete corpus by absorbing independent systems of law (merchant law, admiralty law, probate law, etc.) gave England a body of law common to all in the realm. A later strand in the development of English common law came from the statutes or legislation enacted by Parliament. By the nineteenth century this legislation had acquired real significance because the needs of Britain's urban industrial society required an extensive recasting of traditional common-law practices.

After its successful revolution, the United States first reacted against the common law as a legacy from Great Britain. Some states even passed laws making it a criminal offence to cite English cases and judges began to turn to French codified law as a substitute. But the years of British predominance and the lack of a codified system obliged reluctant states to accept the common-law system. Louisiana is the only one of the fifty states that does not have its legal system based on common law.

Other states governed by common law are Australia, Canada (except Quebec), Ireland, and New Zealand, to name only a few. Common law has been a major influence in the legal systems of India, Israel, and Pakistan, the Scandinavian states, and the newer states of Africa and Asia. In all these legal systems many acts of the national assembly have displaced much of the traditional character of common law. But still their judges and attorneys bring the heritage of a thousand years of British legal development to the bench and to the bar.

Roman Civil Law

The most impressive intellectual achievements of the Romans had been in law, and the sharpest minds of the empire developed a comprehensive legal system. Roman law had developed over many centuries, creating voluminous legal records of generations of lawyers and government officials. The emperor Justinian (527–565) attacked the problem of codifying the law in his *Digest, Corpus Juris,* and the *Code*. These extracts dealt with the basic problems of law and justice but they also included a restatement of Roman law and legal experience that provided Europe and other parts of the world with a rich legacy. Justinian's Code became an essential part of Western legal tradition and affected every Western European country, as well as many legal systems in the new world.[8]

After Rome collapsed, Justinian's Code was challenged by the more primitive Germanic legal system, canon law, and disparate commercial and maritime legal practices. But Roman law was rediscovered in the twelfth century, after which it gradually reasserted its influence on the teachings and practices of European jurists and professors of law.

Throughout the countries of Europe the tendency has been established to codify* law in the legal system. France's Napoleonic Code, beginning with the Civil Code of 1804, was the first great modern contribution to the civil-law system. It was widely copied, as in Belgium, Italy, the Netherlands, Portugal, Spain, and Latin American Republics. The legal systems of Germany, Japan, and Turkey have also relied heavily upon a codified civil law. In the French and Swiss codes, as well as others, law is developed not by the courts through definition and interpretation, but rather by legislatures, ministries of justice, and academic institutions. Reason, logic, and legal expertise are accorded high value in civil law. The letter of the law rather than its spirit as derived by judicial interpretation and precedent is the dynamic force behind legal systems based on civil law.

Other Legal Systems

Islamic Legal Systems

The Islamic system of law governs nearly 800 million Muslims who live in many of the countries of Africa, Asia, and the Middle East.[9] Islamic law originated in the seventh century, based on rules regulating all areas of human conduct in traditional pastoral societies that possessed very few social and governmental institutions. Islam was the last of the three great world religions to emerge, and for many centuries it was more vigorous than either of its rivals – Christianity in the West and Buddhism in the East. Today it is the second largest of the world's religions.

The founder of Islam, Mohammed, left a collection of his revelations, which became known as the Koran. These revelations are at once a religion, an ethic, and a legal system. The Koran forbids wine drinking, usury, gambling, and bans certain foods, especially pork. There was also a rudimentary sacred code of law, the Sharia, designed to check the selfishness and violence that had prevailed among the Arabs. Arbitration was advocated to take the place of the blood-feud, infanticide was condemned, and elaborate rules of inheritance safeguarded the rights of orphans and widows. Mohammed also made an effort to limit polygamy by ruling that no man might have more than four wives simultaneously. Divorce was still easy, but the divorced wife could not be sent away penniless. These and other provisions were enough to furnish a framework for a judicial system.

Because the Koran was immutable law, it proved incomplete as the Muslim countries began to modernize, to have more contact with the West, and to establish sovereign national governments. In the nineteenth century, European legal codes were adopted to supplement Islamic law in Egypt and Turkey. In the twentieth century, Turkey abolished Islamic law altogether, as did Egypt as recently as 1956. However, in 1980 Egypt amended its constitution to make Islamic revelations the main source of its legislation. At present, twenty Muslim states combine some elements of Islamic law with European civil-law codes in commercial, criminal, and public law. These include Afghanistan, Iraq, Morocco, and Indonesia.

Some states, such as Bahrain, Saudi Arabia, and the United Arab Emirates, have attempted to reinstitute neglected Islamic traditions in the presence of renewed Islamic fundamentalism. Pakistan's Constitution of 1973 forbids the enactment of laws that are contrary to the injunctions of Islam. In that state, the traditional punishments of flogging, amputation, and stoning have been reinstituted as they were practised according to the Sharia. In Libya, Colonel Mohammar Khadafy has followed a similar path. Finally, in Iran, under the late Ayatollah Khomeini and his successor, Ali Akbar Hashemi Rafsanjani, Islamic fundamentalism combined with fierce nationalism, generating a great deal of internal instability and spreading political tensions in the region. Strong reactions against secular law have also surfaced in Malaysia, Syria, and Turkey, where waves of religious and political violence can further destabilize international relations in the Middle East.

Communist Legal Systems

What distinguishes communist legal systems from those in the West is the effective control of a single agency, the Communist party, to determine for all others what is in the best interest of the country.[10] In all totalitarian socialist states, law enforcement and legal scholarship are controlled by the party. The party influences judicial practices through the doctrine of *social legal consciousness,* which requires that lawyers and judges be guided by party policy when deciding cases. The fate of a defendant is decided on the basis of the regime's ideology.

Under the principles of socialist legality, the range of activities defined as criminal is extensive. Crimes such as murder and theft are treated in similar fashion to the West. But the severest punishments and widest interpretations of the law are crimes against the state, such as failure to meet production plans, inefficiency, and poor-quality production. Even harsher penalties are applied for political crimes, such as anti-state agitation, of which dissidents are frequently accused.

In all cases, the legal profession is controlled by the party. There are three professional elements in totalitarian socialist legal systems: (1) judges, who preside at court proceedings; (2) advocates and attorneys, who defend the accused; and (3) procurators, who prepare cases for trial. Judges are civil servants, who are usually members of the Communist party. Rarely can they conduct their courts independent of party influence.[11] Lawyers are also tied to the national party. At times they can exercise some independence in their defensive strategies but they are legally bound to uphold the interests of the state. Procurators tend to outshine both judges and advocates in prestige and government support. When applying and interpreting the law, they have extensive powers in the legal system. In addition to its preindictment, quasi-legal function, and its supervisory role over all investigations, the procuracy has a broader, autonomous, scrutinizing role over the entire state administration. Crimes against the state are considered especially serious and the procuracy is the arm of the legal system that simultaneously investigates and brings to justice anyone it deems to have violated state security. Even the KGB (State Security Committee) needs the written permission of a procurator to start an investigation or to make an arrest.

Most cases, civil and criminal, are heard in *people's courts,* although appeals can be made to higher courts. In some countries *comrades' courts,* staffed by volunteer citizens, hear cases. These courts hear a variety of cases from petty theft and public drunkenness, to violations of labour discipline. In China, people's courts and comrades' courts educate citizens in loyalty and compliance with party principles. In the Soviet Union, these courts tend to be more punitive, imposing fines, reprimands, and sometimes incarceration, depending on the seriousness of the offence.[12]

Combined Legal Systems

Many of the authoritarian states of Africa, Asia, and Latin America blend the customs, procedures, and codes found in other systems of jurisprudence into their own. Most of Africa was colonized by European powers that transplanted their legal traditions to each state. African legal systems reflect the civil-law codes of France, Germany, and the Netherlands, as well as British common-law practices, Islamic legal prescriptions, and customary tribal law. Particularly in states influenced by British jurisprudence, judges often exhibit remarkable dedication to the integrity of the legal process. In states such as Zaire, Kenya, Tanzania, and even South Africa, judges have displayed great personal courage when their verdicts were counter to the political sentiments of the authoritarian ruler.[13]

The legal systems of Latin America are also good examples of a blend of many influences. By far the major influence on the legal systems of Latin America has been Roman civil law. Bolivia adopted verbatim the French civil code. And Argentina, Colombia, Ecuador, and Paraguay modelled their codes after the French, German, and Swiss codes. The civil law as practised by Spain and Portugal was transplanted to the new world by the conquistadors. By the time of the independence of most Latin American countries in the early nineteenth century, civil law had taken firm root.[14] But while civil law has been a major influence, the legal systems of Latin America also strongly reflect the impact of English common law, especially the doctrine of *stare decisis* and the recognition of custom and usage as important sources of law.[15] The constitutional law and practice of the United States has also had considerable influence in Latin America, especially in the federal republics of Argentina, Brazil, Mexico, and Venezuela.

Finally, in Southeast Asia, Western powers exerted considerable influence on the legal practices and institutions of the region. Many legal systems refer to case procedents established under colonial rule. In the Philippines, courts cite legal precedents in the English and American courts, as well as legal decisions made before their independence.

The Judiciary

The administration of justice has been one of the most important functions of government since the dawn of recorded history. Courts first appeared in Egypt in 2900 B.C. At that time Egyptian kings began to delegate a large part of their judicial powers to a chief judge who heard and ruled on cases at the royal residence. Somewhat later, courts in Mesopotamia applied the Code of Babylon and the Code of Hammurabi. The Hebrews, Hindus, Arabs, Chinese, Greeks, and Romans had elaborate court systems to administer justice as a function of government.[16] In the new world, the Aztecs held courts and adjudicated market disputes in daily sessions. There were local courts, a court of appeal, and a supreme court; decisions were recorded by means of knots made of cords of various sizes and colours. There was also had an elaborate judiciary.

Courts today do not have to draw pictures to portray concepts of justice or knot variegated cords to record judicial decisions, but the administration of justice still remains an important responsibility of the judiciary. The modern judiciary can be ranked into two broad categories: courts of original jurisdiction, and courts of appeal. A court of first instance hears prosecutions and actions in criminal and civil cases. A court of appeal hears a case and rules to confirm or reverse a decision made by a lower court. In some states, appellate courts review the decisions of lower courts to determine if judicial errors have been made and whether a uniform interpretation of law is occurring. Thus, courts of appellate jurisdiction serve as a check upon errors of law that arise in the course of trials in lower courts. They also serve to give a losing party another chance to win a case. In all states the scope of appellate jurisdiction (that is, the type of cases and legal questions that may be appealed) is determined by rules of procedure established by the courts themselves or by a legislative body.

The Functions of the Judiciary

In all democratic states, the primary purpose of the courts is to uphold independently the constitution as the first law of the land.[17] What distinguishes the courts in democratic states from courts in authoritarian and totalitarian states is the relative neutrality and impartiality of judges when their own government is one of the parties before them. The degree of independence of the courts from the political and governmental system is an important measure of the ability of courts to act in justice and fairness to the litigants. In every country, judges are government officials, the laws they apply are made by the government, and, from time to time, the government may be one of the litigants. But, although politics can never be excluded from the appointment process of judicial officials, it is important to know to what extent a judicial system remains detached from the political system that appoints and funds it. *Judicial independence* protects the courts from outside interference and provides judges legal immunity from the consequences of their decisions. This principle of judicial independence is not a component of every judicial system, although most states outwardly proclaim it to be.

Adjudication

The judiciary differs from the executive and legislative branch of government by the way it conducts itself with respect to the lawmaking process. Courts do not initiate action; rather they wait until a case is brought before them. A case becomes an occasion for the courts to adjudicate and proclaim a general rule. The process of adjudication involves elaborate procedures for gathering evidence and establishing the facts in a case. Adjudication permits those actually affected by a law to bring forward the particulars of their case and to act for a reasonable interpretation of the law in the light of the evidence revealed. In court, arguments focus on the neutral principles of justice. To win, it is necessary to show that a claim is just, or that an indictment or settlement is just.

A final commentary concerning adjudication relates to the effectiveness of the courts to generate social reform. It is sometimes argued that a single, decisive ruling by the courts may initiate reform far quicker than years of lobbying and legislation. Judicial rulings enjoy a decisive authority and legitimacy not often accorded to the prescriptions of political institutions. Courts that interpret the law in a sense also create it.

Constitutional Interpretation

Probably the single greatest influence a court can have on the destiny of a particular nation-state is judicial review*. The practice, borrowed from the United States, where it has worked so well, is used in some form by the courts in most states today. Judicial review means that some courts may declare unconstitutional an executive, legislative, or judicial act that is judged to be in violation of the spirit and letter of the constitution. In the United States any court may examine the constitutionality of an act when deciding a case before it. However, the United States Supreme Court enjoys full judicial review and can interpret what the clauses of the Constitution mean and set aside acts of the Congress or of state assemblies as unconstitutional.

In Canada, the practice of limited judicial review has changed significantly since the entrenchment of the Charter of Rights and Freedoms in 1982. The Supreme Court of Canada now is responsible for interpreting and enforcing the Canadian Constitution and the Charter of Rights and Freedoms. Prior to 1982, the role of the Supreme Court of Canada was limited to the application of law as defined by statute or legal precedent to cases brought before it. Since the proclamation of Canada's patriated constitution, all law, the legislatures, even the federal Parliament itself is subordinate to the Constitution. Consequently there has been a dramatic increase in the power of judicial review in Canada, giving the Supreme Court the ultimate responsibility for interpreting the Constitution and for striking down laws that are in conflict with it.

In other states, the power of judicial review exists, but usually in a more limited form. For example, in Great Britain the doctrine of parliamentary supremacy limits courts in their power to review laws or acts of government when their constitutionality is challenged. Parliament in the British tradition best represents the national will; any law it passes should therefore be nullified or rescinded only by another legislative act. The High Court of Australia may determine only which level of government is supreme with respect to the powers outlined in the constitution. Such states are examples of limited judicial review because the supreme courts deal with the kinds of powers and jurisdictions that national and subnational governments may exercise.[18]

In Latin America about three-quarters of the states confer a limited power of review on the courts. The rest of the states combine the review function between the congress and the courts or make it solely the responsibility of congress.

A unique form of judicial review is Mexico's writ of *amparo**. Any citizen may apply to one of the federal courts to redress a law or an act of government that impairs the rights guaranteed to a citizen in the constitution. The writ applies to each case and does not declare any act of congress or the president unconstitutional. Rather it provides a remedy for a violation of individual rights in the instance for which *amparo* is applied. But in the process, a judicial review of the articles in the constitution does take place because others could have their rights impaired by the same provision under similar circumstances.

Law Enforcement and Administration

Judicial institutions perform the important function of upholding the law in a society. The imposition of fines and other punishments is a credible component of law enforcement as administered by the courts. Courts enforce compulsory adjudication by the issuance of writs and orders. Court orders direct police officials to execute the law.

Courts authorize warrants* of arrest, summonses* to appear in court, subpoenas* to summon witnesses, writs of mandamus* to order a party to perform an act required by law, writs of habeas corpus* to remove the illegal restraint of personal liberty, writs of prohibition* to stop a court proceeding beyond its jurisdiction, and injunctions to order a stop on certain actions.

In civil-law states, such as France, Italy, and Portugal, administrative courts issue writs and orders on the executive branch of government. In Greece and Japan, courts can interfere with executive actions if they clearly violate the constitution.

In many states, courts are assigned administrative responsibilities. In Canada and the United States, courts probate wills, manage estates of deceased persons, grant and revoke licences, grant admission to the bar or disbarment, administer bankruptcy proceedings, grant divorces, and naturalize aliens. In many countries, when elections are disputed, courts conduct recounts to verify the results.

Nowhere have the functions of courts been perfected. In most states, however, courts produce practical results that generally meet with public expectations.

Canada's Judiciary

Federalism determines the structure of the Canadian judiciary. There are separate federal and provincial courts, with the *Supreme Court* of Canada being a general court of appeal — the country's highest appeal court in all areas of law. But the system of courts is essentially hierarchical and unified (figure 9.1).

On the provincial level, the bottom of the hierarchy of courts takes the form of magistrates' or provincial courts. These courts hear criminal offences, small claims, and family and juvenile litigation. Each province exercises sole jurisdiction over the creation and staffing of these courts at this level. Consequently, the administration and procedure of provincial courts will vary from province to province.[19] But in all cases, judges are appointed by the lieutenant-governor in council*.

At the next level in most provinces are the *circuit, county,* or *district* courts. There are no county or district courts in Quebec or Prince Edward Island because the pre-existing county courts in these two provinces were fused with the Supreme Court (Superior Court in Quebec). The administration and jurisdictions of these courts are also the responsibility of each province, but they are presided over by a judge, who is appointed and paid by the federal government. Some provinces, like Ontario, have *surrogate* courts. These courts have jurisdiction over matters relating to the administration and settlement of wills (testamentary instructions). They settle claims against an estate and the appointment of guardians for the children of the deceased. Finally, provincial *superior courts* or *supreme courts,* the Superior Court in Quebec or Courts of *Queen's Bench* (as in Alberta, Manitoba, New Brunswick, and Saskatchewan) are the high courts of justice established by provincial statute. Supreme courts hear appeals from lower courts within the province and exercise unlimited jurisdiction in civil and criminal matters. The appointment of all supreme court judges is by the federal government with remuneration set by federal statute. Supreme courts exercise *concurrent jurisdiction* with lower courts for most indictable crimes* and *exclusive jurisdiction* for the most serious indictable crimes* such as murder.[20]

Federal courts consist of the Supreme Court of Canada, the Federal Court, the Court Martial Appeal Court, and the territorial courts in the Northwest Territories and Yukon.

The Federal Court, which replaced the Exchequer Court, was established by the Federal Court Act of 1970 with a trial division and an appeal division. It consists of twelve judges, four of whom must come from Quebec, with tenure until age 70. The Federal Court exercises original jurisdiction in matters involving claims against the Crown, interprovincial and federal/provincial legal disputes, citizenship appeals, and matters formerly the original jurisdiction of the Exchequer Court, relating to the Excise Act, Customs Act,

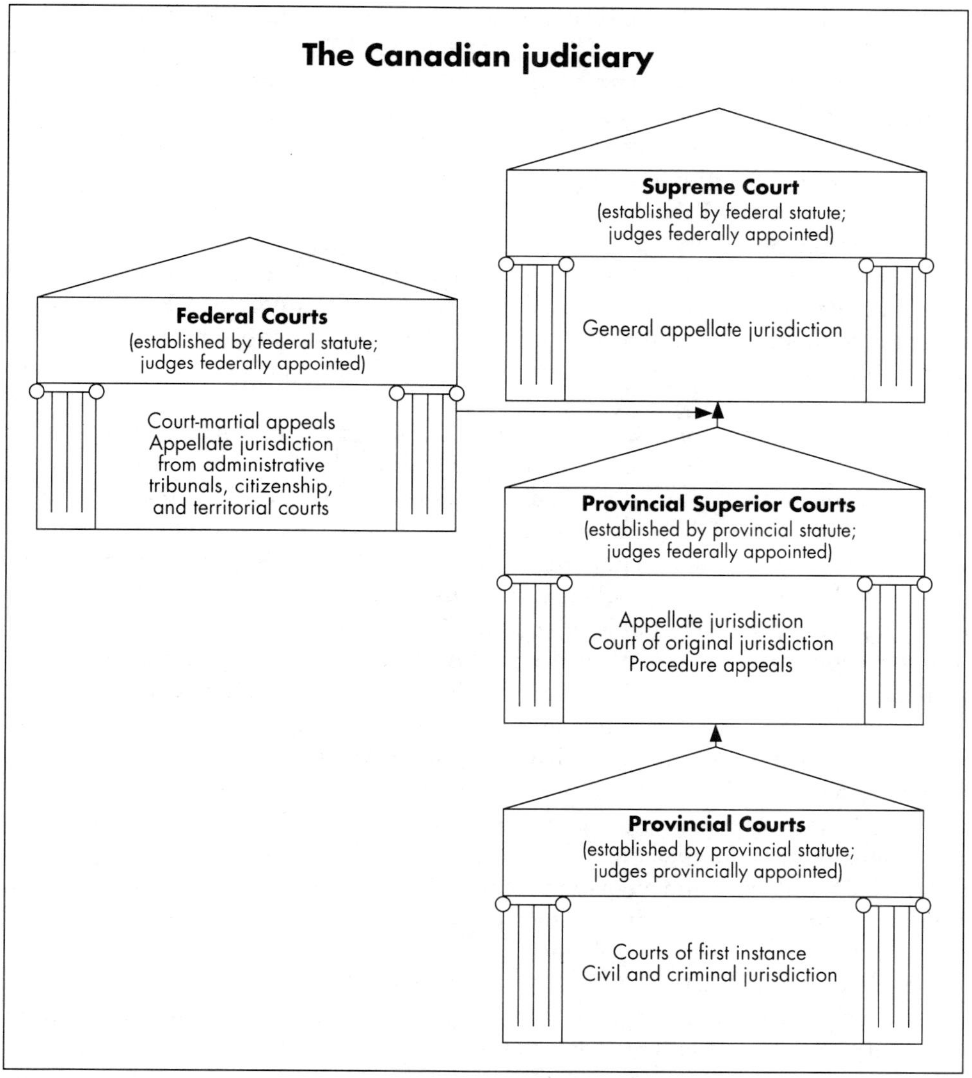

Figure 9.1

Income Tax Act, National Defence Act, Patent Act, and the Shipping Act.[21] The Federal Court serves to ease the load of appeals flowing to the Supreme Court, especially those of special national character, arising from federal boards, commissions, and tribunals.

The Supreme Court of Canada

The Constitution Act, 1867, gave no mention to the Supreme Court of Canada. The Fathers of Confederation granted statutory authority to Parliament, which, after having bills withdrawn to establish a final court in 1869 and 1870, succeeded in passing the Supreme Court Act, 1875. The fact that this federal statute gave existence, jurisdiction, and composition to the Supreme Court generated concern over the years among constitutional, legal, and political experts. Accordingly, in 1982 the Supreme Court of Canada was entrenched in the Constitution by sections 41(d) and 42(1)(d) of the Constitution Act, 1982. And, the Meech Lake Accord (Constitution Amendment, 1987), when ratified, recognizes the composition of the court as consisting of a *chief justice* and eight *puisne* (junior rank) *judges,* with at least three justices coming from Quebec to ensure that some justices have a background in the distinctive civil-law tradition of that province. In addition, the appointment process was entrenched, giving provinces for the first time a constitutional voice in the selection of Supreme Court justices by filling vacancies from provincial lists of nominees.

At first the court had only six justices and its first sittings were held in the Railway Committee Room of the House of Commons: thereafter the court sat in the old Supreme Court Building at the foot of Parliament Hill until 1946, when it took possession of its present building. But until 1949, the Judicial Committee of the Privy Council* in London was the highest court of final appeal for Canada. In that year the Supreme Court assumed that role and sits only in Ottawa. Since 1949, the composition of the court's bench has followed the pattern of appointing three justices from Ontario, three from Quebec, two from the western provinces, and one from the Atlantic region. This pattern had only one temporary deviation between 1979 to 1982, when there were two justices from Ontario, and three from the West.[22] All nine judges are appointed until age 75 by the governor general in council. Candidates must have at least ten years' experience in law practice. Normally, Supreme Court judges are selected from provincial courts of appeal; for example, Beverley McLachlin was appointed in March 1989 from the B.C. Supreme Court. But from time to time, practising lawyers are elevated directly to the high court, as exemplified by the appointment of John Sopinka in 1988; he replaced Justice Willard Estey as one of Ontario's representatives on the bench. Judges are removable from the Supreme Court by the governor general in council (on the advice of the Cabinet), accompanied by a joint address to the Senate and the House of Commons.

The chief justice (presently Brian Dickson) presides over and directs the work of the court as its principal administrator. For this he receives an annual salary of approximately \$163 800. His position is one of great judicial influence rather than one of power: the chief justice has only one vote, as do the other judges, in deciding cases. The other eight puisne justices, whose annual salaries are about $151 700, unavoidably bring their own personal values and political philosophies to the bench. These six men and three women, ranging in age from 56 to 73, have usually left more lucrative careers in law and teaching to accept prestigious judicial appointments — initially to the Supreme Courts of their home provinces.

The Supreme Court, notorious for its lengthy deliberations, has the capacity to hear only about 100 cases of the several hundred filed each year. As one justice told an interviewer: "We're like an oversold airline; we have an airplane with a hundred seats and a 1000 passengers trying to get in." There are two classes of people who have the automatic right to appeal: those whose acquittal of a crime was reversed by a provincial appellate court on an appeal from the Crown; and those whose conviction was upheld by an appellate court with one of the judges dissenting on a question of law. An appeal is accompanied by a lawyer's written arguments called factums*, which, together with the appeal books containing all of the trial transcripts and judgements from lower courts, frequently reach several thousand pages. One case involving Quebec's Bill 101, which legislated French as the only official language in that province, contained fifty-five volumes.

In response to a 1987 report on the Supreme Court by the Canadian Bar Association, the court instituted reforms to streamline its operations for faster more-efficient service. The court now limits most submissions to forty pages and permits lawyers to beam their arguments (video conferencing) to the Supreme Court's television screens via satellite.

In recent times the Supreme Court has not hesitated to pass judgement on basic political and moral questions: it unanimously ruled that Ottawa could not unilaterally change the structures and powers of the Senate without provincial consent; it ruled that evidence obtained illegally by the police was admissible in court; it upheld the requirement that the public must obtain a city permit for planned demonstrations; and it concluded that the results of a polygraph test used to determine who is telling the truth have no place in the legal system. Indeed, over the past two decades, the nine judges of the court have made important rulings on the guarantees of equality and individual freedom in Canadian society. Since the Charter of Rights and Freedoms became law in 1982 the Supreme Court has decided over sixty cases involving its provisions: in 1984, the court ruled that if police get authorization to bug private premises they also have the right to enter these premises secretly to plant the bug. In its ruling, the Supreme Court decided that even though Parliament does not say police can trespass, it undoubtedly means to do so. Dismissing an appeal from Alberta's attorney general in 1985, a unanimous Supreme Court struck down the federal Lord's Day Act because it compelled all residents to observe the Christian Sabbath thereby violating the right of individuals to determine their religious obligations. And, in a 5:0 decision in 1988, the court ruled that the provision banning the use of languages other than French on public signs (Bill 101) is invalid because it violates the Quebec Charter of Rights.

No branch of government is more removed from public scrutiny. The public's only real influence on the high court comes indirectly through the power to elect governments, which appoint justices to the Supreme Court. Appointments to the Supreme Court have never been an election issue in Canada. As a result, our judicial institutions are perceived to be beyond the scope of political influence, although, a recent judgement of the Federal Court removed the disqualification of judges from voting in federal and provincial elections. Change is rarely sudden in the Supreme Court. Governments may come and go, and with them their national policies, but the judges, whatever their political leanings, represent continuity and predictibility.

Profile of a Supreme Court Justice

Professionally, the justices of the Supreme Court of Canada have the collective reputation for intensity on the bench. They often work 80-hour weeks, including weekends, and at the average age of 64, make up one of the youngest benches in the history of the court. But as private citizens they do what most people do: raise their families, pursue recreation in sports such as swimming, tennis, and fishing, and go through the daily routines of managing their personal affairs. An unwritten rule of the court is that justices should lead restrained social lives and close their lifestyles to public scrutiny so that their judicial impartiality is preserved for cases pending their decisions. Other restrictions also affect judges' lives. They may not hold any other remunerative positions with federal or provincial governments, nor can they engage in business. They must live in the National Capital Region or within forty kilometres thereof. For reasons like these, a judge's life is a complex one.

Before they are appointed to the Supreme Court of Canada justices have earned solid reputations in the legal profession. Such is the case of Madame Justice Claire L'Heureux-Dubé, who is the second woman to be appointed to Canada's highest court. After graduating cum laude from the Faculty of Law at Laval University she was called to the Quebec Bar and practised law in her native Quebec City, where she quickly earned a distinguished record as counsel and justice from 1952 to 1973. In February 1973 she was appointed to the Superior Court of Quebec, and to the Quebec Court of Appeal in 1979 where she served as justice until her appointment to the Supreme Court of Canada in April 1987. Within a span of thirty-five years Justice L'Heureux-Dubé enhanced her professional experience as lecturer in Family Law in the Cours de formation professionelle du Barreau du Québec; was a counsellor of the Quebec Bar and served as delegate in its General Council; was a five-year member of the Conseil consultatif de l'administration de la justice de la Province de Québec; spent three years in a judicial inquiry into certain matters relating to the Department of Manpower and Immigration in Montreal; accepted a three-year term as vice-president of the Canadian Consumers Council; spent four years as president of the Family Law Committee and of the Family Court Committee of the Quebec Civil Code Revision Office; devoted a year as vice-president of the Vanier Institute of the Family and as chairman of the Editorial Board of the Canadian Bar Review.

Throughout her busy legal career in Quebec City, Madame Justice Claire L'Heureux-Dubé learned to work days and nights, including weekends, on matters of judicial importance. Likewise, on the High Court she begins most thought-filled weekdays in the same way. She gets up at six, often goes swimming at a downtown Ottawa hotel, eats breakfast, and reads the newspaper. By 8:00 A.M. she passes through the bronze doors at the entrance hall of the Supreme Court building, rides the elevator to the second floor, and enters the churchy atmosphere of her small book-lined chamber. There, she begins to read and answer correspondence, which might include memorandums to and from members of the court on current opinions circulated. She receives invitations of all kinds: requests to speak at lunches, dinners, and conferences. She is frequently asked to participate at seminars, conventions, and annual meetings. All these engagements must be organized around the schedule of the Supreme Court, which holds three sessions during the year and sits about twenty weeks from the end of September to the end of June.

Most of her office time is spent reading and writing. When she became a superior appellate court judge she earned a reputation as a good writer, an adventurous thinker, and a tireless reader. When Justice L'Heureux-Dubé arrives at her office the factums* for a case the court will hear are sitting on her desk. She must read these carefully because they contain the lawyers' presentations of the facts on which the legal contest is based as well as their refutations of the means of the adverse party. She must interpret these in conference with her colleagues. Thus, the job demands a cautious, professional approach, tactfulness, diplomacy, and most of all patience. Law clerks are assigned various tasks. Sometimes she will direct them in the research to be done, while in other circumstances she will request specific answers; when the research is completed, the law clerks and the justice will have discussions about it.

When in session, the court convenes after the morning recess from 11:45 AM to 1:00 PM, followed by a one-hour lunch at the Court House. The afternoon session begins at 2:00 PM and runs until 4:30 PM, followed by a half-hour conference of the court to discuss the cases of the day. The justices enter the court through the door directly behind the long elevated bench, wearing black silk gowns with white collar vests. But usually at the formal opening and closing of each session they will wear their bright scarlet robes trimmed with Canadian white mink, which they also wear at the opening of each new session of Parliament. The most junior justices sit on the far flanks and the others range closer to the chief justice, who occupies the centre position. A *quorum* consists of five members, but the full court of nine sits for most of the cases, unless illness prevents a full court.

Two or three days a month (motion days) are devoted to motion hearings. Motion days start at 9:30 AM and the court convenes at 10:00 or 10:30 AM and ends at about 4:30 with a one-and-a-half hour break for lunch. Court motions are requests by parties to have their cases heard by the Supreme Court. The court receives 20–30 motions a day. Justice L'Heureux-Dubé, like her colleagues, must consider the merits of a request before giving an opinion: each motion requires a judge to expend valuable reading and research time. Some are accepted, others are rejected. Those that are accepted have their day in court.

Unless by special leave* of the court, the only people who may argue before it, apart from the litigants themselves, are lawyers from any Canadian province or territory. When the arguments are being presented to the court, any justice may ask questions of the lawyers retained. Sometimes a decision will be rendered at the conclusion of the arguments, but usually decisions are reserved for further deliberation or to enable judges to write up their reasons. Decisions are that of the majority and need not be unanimous; dissenting reasons are given. On adjourning, the justices file out of the back door of the court to their conference rooms directly across the corridor. At this time, Justice L'Heureux-Dubé sits by a circular oak table and begins the ritual of discussing the case she has just heard. Each judge speaks to the points and issues raised in the case. The proceedings in this room are more confidential than federal Cabinet meetings. It takes a lot of time for a judgement to go through the process of writing, translating, and printing, but each judge must make his or her decision quickly.

The decisions of the Court are published in the *Supreme Court Reports* and lodged in the *Registry*, managed by the *Registrar* who holds the status of deputy minister responsible for the administration of the Supreme Court.

Justice Claire L'Heureux-Dubé, like most of her colleagues, performs an essential governmental task that is the peaceful settlement of legal disputes at the highest judicial level. Because of the enormous importance of the decisions to which she contributes, her professional conduct is necessarily solitary and isolated. When the court is not sitting, she deliberates, writes opinions, or attends conferences. Holidays are, most of the time, working holidays or short evasions from the heavy routine of judicial life.

The U.S. Judiciary

As in Canada, the laws that prevail in the United States facilitate the peaceful remedy of personal and group conflicts in a system of courts. At the state level the legal machinery is complicated because the court systems of the fifty states operate within a variety of organizational patterns of jurisdictional and appellate arrangements. This diversity reflects the decentralization of the U.S. legal system that has evolved in a large federal state[23] (figure 9.2).

At the lowest level are the local courts whose jurisdiction is limited to minor civil and criminal matters. They are called *municipal courts* in twenty-six states and *county courts* in the remaining states. In addition, many cities have *magistrate* or *police courts* that deal with traffic violations and misdemeanors punishable by small fines and imprisonment for periods of up to six months. It is at this level that one finds the *rural justice courts* staffed by justices of the peace, who are often untrained at law and largely uncontrolled. These courts had their origin in fuedal England, where justices of the peace enforced the King's Peace. Today, in the United States, they are gradually disappearing and being replaced by special courts that deal solely with one kind of legal problem. Thus, many states have domestic-relations courts, juvenile courts, and probate courts (to examine wills of deceased persons).

In all states, however, there is a distinction between the courts of general jurisdiction and those of special jurisdiction. The courts of general jurisdiction are responsible for major civil and criminal cases. These include trial courts, usually called superior courts, or circuit courts

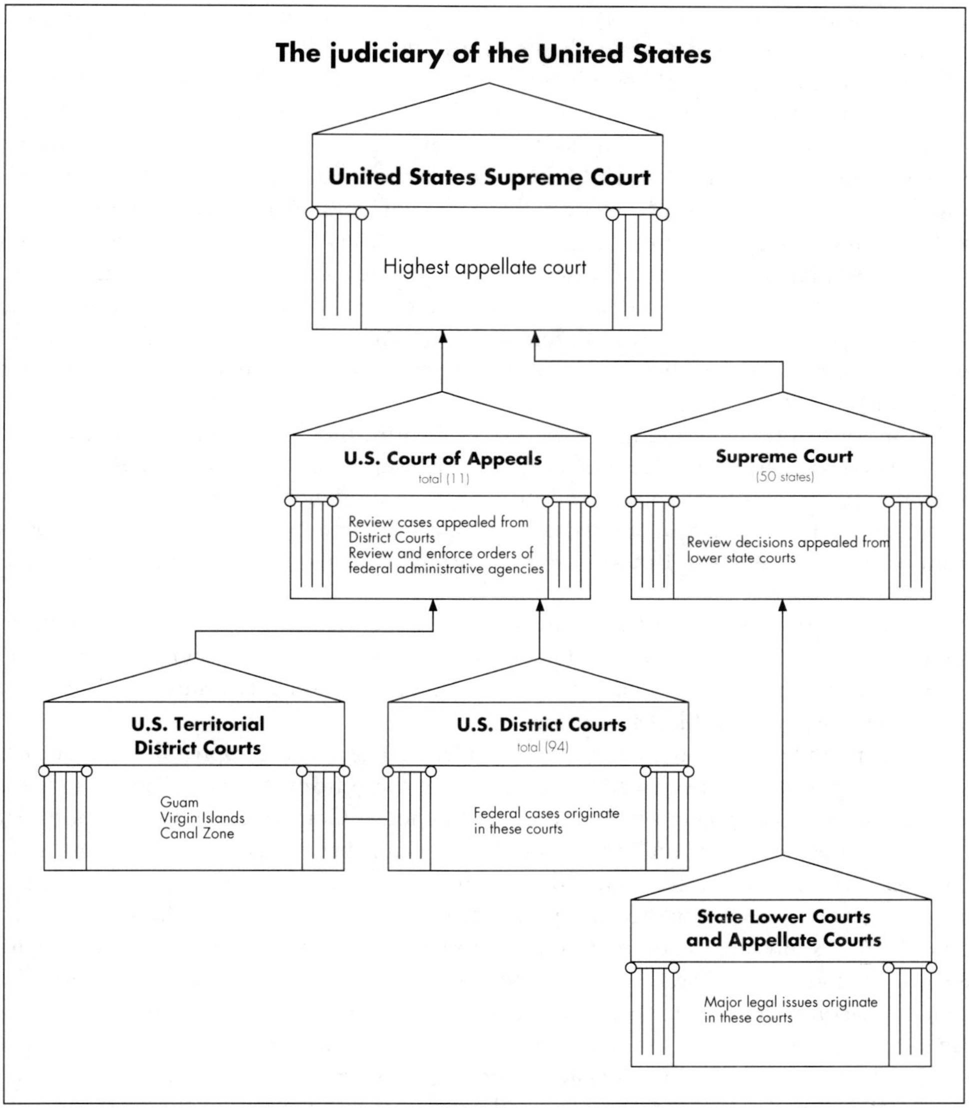

Figure 9.2

and appellate courts of various kinds. Every state has an appellate judicial structure that culminates in a supreme court.

State court judges are selected in a variety of ways. In general, most states elect their judges. Some states use executive appointment, subject to the approval of the state legislature. Four states use legislative election, an inheritance from the American Revolution. And, a few states use non-partisan selection by special nominating commissions made up of lawyers, judges, and distinguished citizens.

Compared to the judicial machinery of the states, the federal court system is less complicated. There are specialized courts to deal with matters relating to customs and patents. But, apart from these tribunals, U.S. federal courts are organized in a three-layered pyramid. Most cases that fall under United States law are settled in the ninety-four federal *district courts* with at least one in each state, the District of Columbia, and the commonwealth of Puerto Rico. Their basic authority flows from Article III of the U.S. Constitution, which extends the "judicial power [to] all cases, in law and equity, arising under this Constitution, the laws of the United States, and treaties made...under their authority and to the controversies between citizens of different states." At the second layer of the pyramid eleven (plus one in the District of Columbia) *courts of appeal* review the conclusions (decisions) of district courts.

At the apex of the pyramid the highest federal court, the *Supreme Court* of the United States, hears cases from two separate avenues. The Supreme Court hears cases on appeal from the circuit courts of appeal, and in special circumstances from the district courts. Because the court operates under a broad constitutional grant of power, it can take appeals from state judicial systems. But in matters of purely state law, the Supreme Court has no authority.

The Supreme Court is a single tribunal of nine judges that hands down full opinions in no more than 100–150 cases a year. The Supreme Court, however, disposes of over 3000 cases each year; in most instances this means that, after some examination, the court concludes that the appeal lacks merit.

All federal judges are appointed by the president, subject to the approval of the Senate. Senatorial approval means that senators, especially those from the state where a judge is selected, have a veto power over the president's choice. Consequently, the appointment of federal judges leads to complicated political bargaining between the Justice Department, the senators of the state concerned, and local party leaders. Unlike in Canada, where prime ministers show less concern for the political philosophies of potential Supreme Court candidates, U.S. presidents consider political philosophies very significant. When Ronald Reagan nominated Robert Bork in 1987 on his conservative judicial record, the Democrat-controlled Senate voted 58:42 to reject him. The next nominee, Justice Douglas Ginsburg, notwithstanding his conservative stripe, might well have won the approval of the Senate were it not for his admission to having smoked marijuana in his younger days. Finally, Reagan's third candidate, Judge Anthony Kennedy, met the approval of the Senate. Judges serve for life but can be removed for "cause" if impeached by the House and convicted by the Senate, following a special trial. Once a justice enters the Supreme Court's sanction, he or she can remain there for life. The Supreme Court is a gerontocracy*. At present many of the justices are 75 or older. The inevitability of death or retirement on the high court offers a historic opportunity for each president to fill several vacancies. Assuming that the appointees are relatively young, the president can set the course of the Supreme Court through to the end of the century.

Throughout much of its history, the U.S. Supreme Court has laid many cornerstones, some of which deserve special note. In the mastercase of *Marbury v. Madison* (1803), Chief Justice Marshall managed to divert the attention of the contesting parties from their petty quarrel to what was the most significant element in the decision — the bold assertion that the Supreme Court, on the basis of its interpretation of the Constitution, was empowered to set limits to what Congress could prescribe. This case laid the conerstone of judicial review by decisively establishing the Supreme Court's right to define the limits of government activity. In another case that dramatized the clash of federal and state powers, *McCulloch v. Maryland* (1819), the Supreme Court firmly established itself as the interpreter of the Constitution and justified the expansion of federal powers in the U.S. federal system. In the case of *Brown v. Board of Education of Topeka* (1954), the court ruled that in the field of public education the doctrine of "separate but equal" has no place, and thus racial discrimination could no longer be regarded as consistent with the constitutional principle of equality before the law. In the case of *Roe v. Wade* (1973) the Supreme Court extended the right of privacy to cover a woman's right to terminate a pregnancy free from government-imposed constraint at the beginning of pregnancy. But the court also recognized that, toward the end of pregnancy, government interest in protecting the fetus' right to life normally will outweigh a woman's right to an abortion. The U.S. Supreme Court is primarily a public tribunal. Almost all its cases are of two general types. First, the court tests state actions against federal law, including the Constitution, laws, and treaties of the United States. Second, it interprets the meaning and passes judgement on the constitutionality of the work of Congress, the president, and the administrative agencies. In its history of nearly 200 years, the United States Supreme Court has often aroused ambivalent emotions among the American people.[24] Viewed as the most politically neutral government body the Supreme Court elicits more deference from Americans than does the office of the presidency. In recent years, more than ever before, the Supreme Court has been regarded as the exemplar of democratic values, a role thrust upon it by the reluctance of other branches to act impartially on matters of political (or national) importance. But it has rarely stimulated a dispassionate response toward its judicial/political decisions, and the reason is plain: the Supreme Court is a unique judicial tribunal; it addresses the conflicting forces that contend in U.S. society, with decisions that mix law and politics. By so doing, it contributes to the formation of national policy and influences the direction of political change.

REFERENCES

1. B.N. Cardozo, *The Growth of the Law* (New Haven: Yale University Press 1924), 3.
2. E. Adamson Hoebel, *The Law of Primitive Man* (New York: Atheneum Press 1968), 4.
3. Quoted in H.A.L. Fisher, *The Collected Papers of Frederic William Maitland* (Buffalo, NY: W.S. Hein 1981), 173.
4. See Jerome Frank, *Law and the Modern Mind* (New York: Coward-McCann 1949), 46; Beryl Levy, *Cardozo and Frontiers of Legal Thinking* (Cleveland, OH: The Press of Case Western Reserve University 1969), 31.
5. George Paton, *A Text-Book of Jurisprudence* (London: Oxford University Press 1948), 52–5; see also Michael Zander, *The Law-*

Making Process (London: Weidenfeld & Nicolson 1989).

6. See Donald Black, *The Behaviour of Law* (New York: Academic Press 1976), ch. I.
7. Donald Kagan et al., *The Western Heritage since 1300* (New York: Macmillan Publishing Co. Inc. 1983), I–23 to I–41.
8. Joseph Strayer and Hans Gatzke, *The Mainstream of Civilization* (New York: Harcourt, Brace Jovanovich Publishers 1984), 160–7.
9. See John Esposito, ed., *Islam and Development: Religion and Sociopolitical Change* (New York: Syracuse University Press 1980), ix.
10. Peter Juviler, *Revolutionary Law and Order* (New York:Free Press 1976).
11. George Feifer, *Justice in Moscow* (New York: Simon & Schuster 1964), 239.
12. Gabriel Almond and G. Bingham Powell Jr., *Comparative Politics Today* (Glenview IL: Scott, Foresman & Co. 1988) 352–5.
13. See Joel D. Barkan and John Okumu, eds., *Politics and Public Policy in Kenya and Tanzania* (New York: Praeger 1979).
14. Alexander Edelmann, *Latin American Government and Politics* (Homewood IL: Irwin-Dorsey Limited 1969), 465–7.
15. Phanor James Eder, "The Impact of the Common Law on Latin America," *Miami Law Quarterly* IV, no. 4 (June 1950): 436–8.
16. Victor Barnouw, *An Introduction to Anthropology* (Georgetown, ON: Dorsey Press 1978), 202–3; see also W. Haviland, *Anthropology*, 4th ed. (New York: Holt, Rinehart and Winston 1985), 544–52.
17. Leonard Theberg, ed., *The Judiciary in a Democratic Society* (Lexington, MA: D.C. Heath 1979), ch. I; Mr. Chief Justice Brian Dickson, "The Judiciary–Law Interpreters or Law-Makers," *Manitoba Law Journal* 12, no.2 (1982).
18. E. McWhinney, *Judicial Review in the English-Speaking World* (Toronto: University of Toronto Press 1969); see also Jennifer Smith, "The Origins of Judicial Review in Canada," *Canadian Journal of Political Science* XVI (March 1983): 115–34.
19. David Bellamy et al., *The Provincial Political Systems* (Toronto: Methuen 1976), 374–7.
20. Perry Millar and Carl Baar, *Judicial Administration in Canada* (Kingston: McGill-Queen's University Press 1981), 75–106; see also Michael Detmold, *Courts and Administrators* (London: Weidenfeld & Nicolson 1989), ch. 1.
21. Revised Statutes of Canada, 1970, C.10.
22. Peter Russell, "Constitutional Reform of the Judicial Branch: Symbolic vs. Operational Considerations," *Canadian Journal of Political Science* XVII (June 1984): 227–52.
23. Robert Lineberry, *Government in America,* 4th ed. (Glenview, IL: Scott, Foresman and Co. 1989), 503–42.
24. See David O'Brien, *Storm Center: The Supreme Court in American Politics* (New York: W.W. Norton & Co. 1986).

SUGGESTED READINGS

Jack Batten, *Judges* (Markham, ON: Penguin Books Canada Ltd. 1986).

Lief Carter, *Law and the Judicial Process* (Glenview, IL: Scott, Foresman & Co. 1988).

Dieter Hoehne, *Legal Aid in Canada from Charity to Public Policy* (Queenston, ON: Edwin Mellen Press 1988).

Robert Katzmann, ed., *Judges and Legislators* (Washington, DC: Brookings Institute 1989).

Patrick Monahan, *Politics and the Constitution: The Charter, Federalism and the Supreme Court of Canada* (Scarborough, ON: Nelson Canada 1987).

Jeffrie Murphy and Jules Coleman, *Philosophy of Law* (Boulder, CO: Westview Press 1989).

Peter Russell, *The Judiciary in Canada: The Third Branch of Government* (Toronto: McGraw-Hill Ryerson 1987).

James Snell and Frederick Vaughan, *The*

Supreme Court of Canada (Toronto: University of Toronto Press 1986).

Neelan Tiruchelvam and Oki Ombaaka, *The Role of the Judiciary in Plural Societies* (New York: St. Martin's Press 1987).

Jerold Waltman and Kenneth Holland, *The Political Role of Law Courts in Modern Democracies* (New York: St. Martin's Press 1987).

GLOSSARY

custom: A conventional or accepted practice that may be recognized as legitimate behaviour and is reinforced by the actions of legal and political institutions.

usage: As it pertains to law, the manner of using, treating, or handling a legal matter in society.

norms: A cultural expectation that represents what most members of a society feel they ought to do in a particular circumstance.

mores: Those ethical rules that a society considers important, such as the prohibition of murder, theft, rape, and incest.

folkways: The trivial norms and conventions such as manners, dietary habits, and style of clothing that are shared by members of a society.

precedent: A common-law principle that recognizes the high persuasive authority of previous court decisions on cases of similar legal character.

codify: To arrange laws into a written systematic body, as opposed to unwritten mores, norms, and traditions.

judicial review: The power of a court, in the course of litigation, to declare the actions of other branches of government unconstitutional.

writ of amparo: A written legal order that grants a citizen judicial relief from the denial of personal rights that are guaranteed by the constitution.

warrant: A judicial writ issued to an authorized legal official requiring the official to arrest a designated party, or search certain persons or premises,or seize property.

summons: A written legal order issued by a judicial officer to a person who has had a formal legal complaint against him or her.

subpoena: A written court order that requires witnesses to appear before a court and produce testimony.

writ of mandamus: A written judicial order that compels a party to perform a certain act required by law.

writ of habeas corpus: A written judicial order demanding legal officials to immediately produce or release a prisoner and cite the reasons for his/her imprisonment.

writ of prohibition: A written judicial order demanding that a specified action cease.

lieutenant-governor in council: provincial cabinet directives.

indictable crimes: common law offences or statutory offences usually punishable by imprisonment.

Judicial Committee of the Privy Council: The British Privy Council committee that acted as the court of final appeal for Canadians until 1949, when the Supreme Court of Canada was established as the final arbiter in Canadian jurisprudence.

factums: A legal memoir that contains the facts upon which a contest is based.

leave of the court: Permission obtained from a court to take some action which, without such permission, would not be allowable.

gerontocracy: A government formed by the oldest people within the social and political system.

10

Constitutions and Constitutionalism

The signing of the Canadian Constitution

What is a Constitution?

THE WORD CONSTITUTION* carries an ancient, broad usage and a modern, narrow usage. The Greek word for constitution, *politeia*, means basically any form of government or regime as it functions in its entirety. Plato's six governmental forms were thus constitutions. The Greek *politeia* was the spirit (*ethos*) that animated the institutions of a government. The ancient Greeks saw the constitution as a cultural phenomenon – a formal expression of the way people do politics and the appropriate public attitudes that support a particular form of government.[1] Thus, to them a constitution is a product of culture, what modern political scientists call a "political culture." Hence, aristocracy, monarchy, or democracy are embodiments of the attitudes, customs, usages, and values of a people – an ideal summation of their collective behaviour. In the ancient view, constitutions *evolve* as the political needs of people change in society.

Today, in most countries of the world, the word constitution is understood in a much narrower sense. The modern format for a constitution as exemplified by many but not all democratic states, e.g., Great Britain, is that it be a written document adopted at a given point in time by a sovereign authority.[2] But many modern constitutions are merely showcases for the international community and provide some governments with a rhetorical opportunity to appear "democratic." The ancients stressed the *growth* of a constitution; modern governments stress the authoritative enactment* of a constitution as a single event. But most contemporary students of constitutional law recognize the unwritten* as well as the written* dimensions of modern constitutions. No constitution can be properly understood solely as a written document. Judicial interpretations as well as modern political customs, conventions, and usages modify and sometimes nullify the written assertions of all constitutions in operation today.[3]

Some scholars avoid the distinction between the written and unwritten features of a constitution and focus on the *formal* and *effective* elements of constitutions.[4] The formal constitution is the original documents, statutes, charters, and other authoritative sources that explicitly outline the structures and goals of a government. The effective constitution is the actual modus operandi of a political system that includes those customs and practices that in time evolve according to the spirit of the constitution, but are not specifically mentioned in the constitution. For example, Canada's formal constitution does not mention the federal Cabinet, the prime minister, political parties, or the federal civil service. Effectively, these important institutions of Canadian government have constitutional *legitimacy* by legislation, custom, and judicial interpretation. Similarly, according to its constitutional documents, Great Britain is a monarchy but effectively it is a parliamentary democracy. In the United States, members of the electoral college may elect any eligible person to the presidency. However, electors are effectively pledged to elect the same president selected by the American people in a national election.

For analytical purposes, political scientists define constitution in the widest possible context. As we shall use the term, a constitution is an entrenched* body of formal and effective rules and practices, written and unwritten, according to which the people and the political institutions of a society are governed.[5] This broad definition enables the political scientist to recognize the functional constitution operating in each political system. Because in most states many fundamental constitutional principles remain largely informal and unwritten, the political analyst must include the accumulated traditions, political mores, and practices of a people as constituent parts of all constitutions.

The Meaning of Constitutionalism

Constitutionalism* may be thought of as the superego of a democratic constitution. It is to a constitution what character is to an individual. The essence of constitutionalism is its belief system that asserts the need for formal limitations on political power: that is, that power is proscribed and procedures of government are prescribed in a constitution.[6]

Historically, modern constitutionalism grew out of the abuses of autocratic government in Europe during the fifteenth and sixteenth centuries. Constitutionalism was the major accomplishment of individualism in its attack on absolute government in Europe. In its purest form, constitutionalism treats government as a necessary evil: humans accept limited government to escape the chaos of anarchy. The term and its related concepts revolve around the idea that individual rights* should be protected by inclusion of those rights in a formal constitution.

At the turn of the century, constitutionalism almost disappeared from the standard vocabulary of students of politics, because of shifting academic fashions and a changing international system.[7] The rapid growth in the number of nation-states adopting authoritarian regimes, as well as the emergence of totalitarian dictatorships after World War I, challenged the ideal of limited government protected by a constitution. Even among the democratic states, social, economic, political, and military exigencies encouraged the rapid expansion of government into all the traditional private preserves of society. The legal ability of governments to ignore constitutional standards* became insurmountable and the practice of simply changing a constitution to meet the needs of autocratic executives became the rule rather than the exception..

Recent global concerns over the struggle for human rights and the almost universal phenomenon of violent political change have spurred a renewed academic interest in constitutionalism.[8] John Rawls, the internationally respected Harvard professor of philosophy, devoted one-third of his *Theory of Justice* to the analysis of constitutionalism in his just society. His position is that a virtuous republic is a product of a virtuous people. Hence, constitutionalism is only as meaningful as the people want it to be. Constitutionalism is the will of the people regarding the just forms of a society's political, economic, and judicial institutions.

Modern constitutionalism has much to do with public attitudes, standards, and expectations. A constitution and its rules grow out of a belief system that people support and tend to confirm. In order to be effective, the constitutional rules that govern the political behaviour and institutions of a people must be venerated. Otherwise, when constitutions become political liabilities to autocratic rulers, they will simply be replaced. For example, over 200 constitutions have been in force in the twenty Latin American republics since their independence in the period between 1810 and 1830. No constitution now in force in any Latin American country dates from independence. The average for all of Latin America is about ten for each country. Nearly half the constitutions currently in force were enacted since the 1960s. The reality of constitutionalism in Latin America is that many constitutional provisions are either ignored, suspended*, or rewritten at the whim of the government in power. For the rest of the world, only a dozen constitutions are in effect from the nineteenth century or earlier. Most of the constitutions in operation today were written following World War II.

Thus, in today's world, it would not be inaccurate for us to conclude that there are two concepts of constitutionalism. One concept, based on the Western democratic tradition, asserts that constitutions are created as the supreme law of the land. Their purpose is to guarantee that no public official should ever exercise unlimited authority or govern without accountability to the people. As an additional protection against autocratic rule, the individual is ensured certain inalienable rights and freedoms. The other concept, practised in non-democratic states, which are today the majority, no longer upholds these constitutional standards. Many of the constitutions of authoritarian and totalitarian states resemble political and ideological manifestoes, where platitudes are idealized or combined with organizational descriptions of democratic offices and agencies of government and parties.

It is important to note that just because a constitution exists is no guarantee that it really works. All independent nation-states, whether democratic or non-democratic, consider the promulgation* of a constitution a legitimizing step towards attaining full recognition as a legal entity in the international system. However, the practice of constitutionalism is the only measure we have of determining whether a nation-state has a working constitution.

The Features of Democratic Constitutions

All democratic constitutions actually *restrict* government power. Thus, while most constitutions appear to be democratic, in actual fact they do not work as a legal limitation on government authority. Those states that limit the powers of government by a written constitution or by statute and custom are called *constitutional regimes*; all other states are authoritarian or totalitarian regimes.[9] In order to evaluate the democratic character of a constitution, many political objectives, features, and procedures must be taken into account, including (a) the extent to which the constitution promotes the public good, (b) has procedures to make amendments, (c) places limitations on the various branches of government, and (d) enumerates individual rights and freedoms.

The Public Good

The Irish Constitution of 1937 provides that "the State shall endeavour to secure that private enterprise shall be so conducted as to ensure reasonable efficiency in the production and distribution of goods and as to protect the public* against unjust exploitation"; the Japanese Constitution of 1947 includes the right of "choice of spouse" and the right "to maintain the minimum standards of wholesome and cultural living"; the Italian Constitution of 1948 states that "the Republic favors through economic measures and other provisions the establishment of families and the fulfillment of their functions, with special regard to large families"; the Constitution Act, 1982 affirms that "Parliament and the Government of Canada are committed to the principle of making equalization payments to ensure that provincial governments have sufficient revenues to provide reasonably comparable levels of public services at reasonably comparable levels of taxation." All these are examples of constitutions in the Western democratic tradition that try to advance the welfare of all the people, rather than to increase the power of the state and government. Constitutions establish broad and *positive purposes* to enhance the public good and to achieve general public goals. They are not documents written primarily for governments; rather, they are *legal instruments* outlining the relationship of people to the governmental institutions of society. Constitutions establish the context within which people co-exist with government.

The concept of *majority rule* is the most widely applied principle to achieve the public good in all democratic constitutions. We see it at work in Canada's Constitution in deciding the most solemn constitutional questions by "resolutions passed by a majority of members of the Senate and the House of Commons." Even though it is difficult for the political system of any society to define the public good, the notion of majority rule set in the constitution serves as a guide and check on policy makers. Therefore, the public good can only be derived from the principles and rules of the game laid down in a constitution. Insofar as this is the case, the criterion for measuring the success of any democratic constitution flows from the question: Do all individuals and groups in society have an equal opportunity to benefit from the majority principle? Evaluating constitutions in terms of people is a relatively straightforward matter with regard to the public good: the constitution provides a framework within which the public good is attainable.

Amending Procedures

Most constitutions have certain procedures by which they can be formally amended. Constitutions vary with respect to flexibility and rigidity.[10] Only a few constitutions (e.g., those of Great Britain and New Zealand) are *flexible** to the extent that they can be amended by the same procedures used to pass ordinary laws. But many constitutions are *rigid** in the sense that they can be formally amended only by special procedures more complicated to enact than ordinary legislation.

Every special amending procedure is intended to ensure that constitutional reform is the result of sober deliberation. Amendments to the constitutions of many Western European states, such as Denmark, Ireland, and Switzerland, must be *approved by the electorate* in a referendum. In Belgium, the Netherlands, and Sweden, an amendment must be approved *by the national legislature*, that is subsequently dissolved, followed by a general election to return a new legislature, which must pass the amendment in its identical form.

Almost all amendment formulas are intended to prevent basic constitutional changes that are initiated by any level of government acting alone. In the United States, amendments are proposed by a two-thirds majority of Congress but ratification is empowered to the states, requiring the approval of thirty-eight out of fifty. In Canada, provincial legislatures must give their approval for amendments on the use of the English and French languages, the composition of the Supreme Court, and the alteration of provincial boundaries. And in Australia and Switzerland, a majority of national voters must also be accompanied by a majority of state and canton voters before the amendment is passed.

Finally, some amendment formulas are designed to protect the rights of linguistic, religious, and cultural minorities. The Swiss Constitution stipulates that Switzerland is a trilingual country, where French, German, and Italian have equal status under constitutional law. The Constitution Act, 1982, specifies that "English and French are the official languages of Canada and have equality of status and equal rights and privileges as to their use in all institutions of the Parliament and Government of Canada."

Limitations on Government

Constitutions operating in the Western democratic tradition adhere to the fundamental principle that proclaims the supremacy of law, establishing limits on public officials in the exercise of their powers.[11] Limitations on government are established through a number of constitutional devices, including a blueprint of the formal structures of government, sometimes a system of checks and balances, judicial controls – and in federal states – the distribution of powers among the various levels of government. By limiting the powers of government, its institutions, and personnel, a democratic constitution prevents the accumulation of personal power within the political system and is an instrument for protecting the rights of individuals from arbitrary interference by officials.

Federal constitutions can have a significant limitation on the accumulation and exercise of political power at one level of government. *Federalism* creates two spheres of government, a national system for the entire country and a subnational system of governments with specific powers over limited jurisdictions. In most federal systems, both levels of government can derive their legitimacy only from the delineated powers enumerated in the constitution and from the various judicial reviews and interpretations directed at resolving intergovernmental disputes. Federal constitutions vary considerably in their limitations of power among the different levels of government. In the United States, each state can legislate in any area not constitutionally reserved to the federal government or to the people. This strong national bias in the constitution has given the federal government the power to expand its activities into the areas of state jurisdiction. The Australian form is similar. In Canada, in contrast, powers are separately delegated to the federal government and the provinces, but Ottawa retains extensive residual powers. Areas of concurrent powers are specified in the Canadian Constitution. In the German Federal Republic, the Basic Law enumerates areas of exclusive federal jurisdiction and the concurrent powers exercised by the Federal and Land governments.

Enumeration and Protection of Civil Liberties

Most constitutions, whether upheld by democratic or non-democratic regimes, establish and outline fundamental rights and freedoms for citizens. The extent to which these civil liberties are guaranteed depends on how dedicated a government and its people are to the principles of democratic constitutionalism. The safeguard of the rights of the individual has been the testimony of democratic constitutionalism since the American and French revolutions. But the performance of contemporary governments in these matters varies from one extreme to another.[12] In states such as Australia, Austria, Belgium, Canada Iceland, Sweden, and the United States the protection of civil rights enjoys widespread constitutional and community support. However, in the most repressive regimes of

Albania, Bulgaria, Cuba, North Korea, Libya, and Vietnam individual rights are flagrantly violated by government policy, notwithstanding the community will or constitutional guarantees that formally promise to protect them.

Despite the entrenchment of individual rights in the majority of constitutions around the world, the power to violate enumerated freedoms exists in all states. In the late 1970s, Canada solemnly assured the United Nations that it is "unlikely" to use (nor has it ever used) its existing powers to execute children or pregnant women under military law. Among the many civil-rights issues confronting the United States, none is more troublesome than that of the black person's place in American society. The freedoms of speech, religion, assembly, the press, and others have much less significance to blacks in the face of both obvious and subtle white racial prejudice. In France, the constitutional right to free assembly seemed to disappear in light of the government's treatment of the Breton nuclear-power demonstrators in 1980. And, West Germany's penchant for psychologically debilitating isolation cells in its prison system tears deeply into the constitutional guarantees of "due process." Even Great Britain stands condemned for torturing suspected terrorists in the interrogation centres of Northern Ireland.

These infringements of individual rights, which do take place in the most democratic states, necessarily pale before the extreme violations in some countries. Between 1966 and 1970 thousands of Ibos lost their constitutional rights in the Biafran Civil War leading to the death and starvation of over 2 million people at the hands of the Nigerian government. The Ugandan constitution was rendered meaningless as the ruthless Idi Amin engaged in mass killings of over 300 000 people and imprisoned and tortured thousands of others from 1971 to 1979.

At the heart of democratic constitutionalism is the right to personal liberty. In Canada's Charter of Rights and Freedoms, this guarantee appears as the "right to life, liberty and security of person and the right not to be deprived thereof except in accordance with the principles of fundamental justice." But despite what a constitution says, infringements* upon elementary rights are common even in the most democratic as well as non-democratic states. In many Latin American states the infringement upon fundamental rights is so customary that most incidents go virtually unnoticed. In Asia, millions of people born into the lowest caste are kept in a state of servility and poverty by the upper classes. In the Middle East, many Islamic governments are intolerant of religious freedom as an individual right.

Closely associated with individual liberty is the *freedom of speech and the press.*[13] All states limit this freedom to some extent. In Great Britain and Canada, slander* and libel* can only be committed against individuals, who then can seek legal redress. However, in Italy, institutions such as the army, the police, and the church can regard statements made about them as slanderous and libelous, with due legal recourse. In Great Britain, an editor was convicted of blasphemous libel for publishing a poem depicting Christ as a homosexual.

Freedom of speech and the press exists in most states, at least according to their constitutions. In some this freedom is quite genuine and comparable to that of the most democratic states. In 1989 a U.S. Supreme Court decision seemed to go to the extreme on the issue of free speech when it ruled unaminously that a recent law banning dial-a-porn was unconstitutional. The court reaffirmed that people have the right to choose not only what they say but also to what they may listen. But in many states, including Canada, various restrictions are imposed on the press. In Uruguay, all authors as well as their publishers are liable to severe penalties if their words are interpreted as abusive by the government. Colombia's constitution restricts newspapers from accepting outside grants from a foreign government or corporations, except with the permission of the government. In Chile, restrictions on the freedom of the press have been heavily imposed by presidential decrees since 1973. Under Libya's sweeping press law, the government has virtual control over all news media in the country. The president is immune from criticism, and authors and publishers are censored. In Israel, the press enjoys a considerable latitude in its freedom to criticize but the government regulates news when it perceives that certain information threatens national security.

There are numerous constitutional provisions and laws aimed at guaranteeing the *freedom of association and assembly*. But these and many other rights, which look so impressive on paper, are frequently limited with impunity, even in those nation-states that have a democratic commitment to free associations. Many governments retain the power to determine when a peaceful assembly becomes a threat to the order of the state, as did Israel in trying to control Palestinian uprisings (*the intifadah*) in the occupied territories. In some states the formation of communist and fascist parties is illegal. Italy's constitution prohibits the Fascist party but the government has tolerated the formation of neo-fascist groups. In Latin America, five states – Brazil, Chile, Guatemala, Haiti, and Uruguay – not only have made the Communist party illegal, but actively persecute party militants. In others, such as Argentina, the Dominican Republic, Panama, Ecuador, and Honduras, the Communist party is illegal but functions at a low level. During the McCarthy era in the United States, a number of legislative proposals were made to outlaw the Communist party but federal courts ruled against them and the party regularly competes in elections today. Other democracies, such as Australia, Canada, India, Japan, and Scandinavian states, permit the Communist party to organize and run its candidates in any election.

A large number of authoritarian and totalitarian states permit only one party and make it illegal for opposition parties to participate in the electoral system. In totalitarian states, the party effectively controls the organization of groups such as labour unions, students, and women by extending auxiliary party organizations into all levels of society and mobilizing popular participation in them. Many people participate in such groups only because the organization has a monopoly on some activity they want to do, not because the organization can effectively manipulate party policies.

Compared with the highly combustible freedom of association, *freedom of religion*, which most constitutions profess, has been a sporadic issue that makes headlines from time to time. In the United States, laws restrict the Mormon practice of polygamy. And Canadian authorities have prosecuted the Sons of Freedom, a small but distinct subgroup of the

Doukhobors, for acts of violence and public nudity. In totalitarian states, restrictions on religious minorities have been instituted when religious beliefs are perceived as a threat by the government.[14] In the Soviet Union, Jews have been regarded by the regime as a dissident group spreading "Zionist propaganda." The restrictions placed on Jews to practise their religion and to emigrate became a thorny issue in Soviet/Western relations in the 1980s. By 1982, over 250 000 Jews had left the USSR because of religious persecution. By 1988 Gorbachev's policies of *perestroika* and *glasnost'* lessened Soviet restrictions against minorities. It remains to be seen whether these policies are permanent.

The majority of modern constitutions mention the rights to *privacy and private property*. The constitutions of France, Germany, Italy, Japan, and Turkey, for example, entrench the right to own private property, provided that such ownership does not conflict with the public interest. The U.S. *Bill of Rights*, adopted in 1791, is long on states' rights and property guarantees. But it took an extensive period of judicial interpretation to resolve the competing demands of property rights in this constitutionally egalitarian society. The U.S. Supreme Court has come a long way from its notorious Dred Scott decision in which it upheld the property rights of slave owners.

It is discouraging to many Canadians that the words "privacy" and "property rights" are not mentioned in either the Constitution Act, 1867, or the Constitution Act, 1982. It seems so basic – the inclusion of property rights in the Constitution – yet the proposed "enjoyment of property" has sparked controversy in the House of Commons and has been the subject of heated debate in provincial legislatures across the country. The proposal to protect property and privacy is opposed for various reasons by the governments of Alberta, Manitoba, Newfoundland, Prince Edward Island, Quebec, Saskatchewan, the federal New Democratic Party, and the Canadian Civil Liberties Association. The champions of a property-and-privacy amendment are the federal Progressive Conservative and Liberal parties, the governments of British Columbia and Ontario, the Canadian Bar Association, and the Canadian Real Estate Association. Nobody is opposed to the general principle that people should have the right to own their homes and farms. The concern is that, when interpreting a property-rights clause, the courts might place severe limitations on the legislative powers of governments to expropriate lands for public works, might award in favour of native land claims*, control land use and zoning, and place restrictions on the uses of public property. It will be interesting to see how the Supreme Court of Canada handles cases in which property rights and the right to privacy are invoked. Only time and jurisprudence will determine whether Canada's *Charter of Rights and Freedoms* is comparable or even superior to the U.S. Bill of Rights. The Canadian Court can benefit from the American experience.

Even with embracing constitutional guarantees, all governments place some restrictions on the rights to privacy and private property. By means of taxation, expropriation, and policies on land use and land reforms, governments in every corner of the globe have the powers to restrict the right to private property.

Canada's Constitution

The conventional traditions of British constitutionalism combined with the American penchant for a written document have been the two major influences on Canada's constitutional history. More than one document has had constitutional significance in Canada. In fact, much of what is described as the constitution of Canada is found in a number of documents and practices. Thus, Canada's Constitution includes the Constitution Act, 1867; the Constitution Act, 1982; the Constitution Amendment, 1987 (if ratified); the Supreme Court Act, 1875; the Statute of Westminster, 1931; the federal acts that admitted new provinces since 1867 (such as the Alberta and Saskatchewan acts of 1905); all statutes of the United Kingdom in reference to Canada, such as the British North America Act, 1871, now called the Constitution Act, 1871; and the various customs, conventions, judicial decisions, and statutes that are considered permanent components of Canada's political system.[15] Some of the unwritten practices of constitutional consequence are Cabinet solidarity, the dominance of the political executive over the formal executive, the role of the prime minister and Cabinet in Parliament, and the function of political parties in the parliamentary system.

The Constitution Act, 1867, is the heart of the overall Canadian constitutional framework.[16] Despite the political, social, and economic changes that have taken place in the country since the British North America Act was enacted in 1867, Canadians still legitimize their political decisions by rooting them in its constitutional authority. Canadians harken back to the Constitution Act, 1867, as the source of all political and legal authority. Even though the original document is in part ambiguous and omits much (as already noted, no reference to the prime minister or political parties, for example), it has acquired layered encrustations of precedent and tradition. The Constitution Act, 1867, is the symbol of Canada's legal and political diversities. For Canadians it is their first and highest secular law, containing the important principles of federalism and parliamentary democracy.

The Constitution Act, 1867, made Canada the third country in history, after the United States and Switzerland, to adopt a federal system of government. As part of the basic constitutional outline, the division of powers between levels of government persists as a major part of the institutional setting of Canadian politics. This system of federalism – in which the provinces retain an allocation of powers, autonomy, and sovereignty, even while they are subordinate to the sovereignty of the central government – is one of the most distinctive features of the Canadian political system. The essential legal characteristic of Canadian federalism is that both the federal and provincial governments enjoy exclusive* and concurrent* powers derived directly from the Constitution. The principle of federalism is a major component of Canada's political culture. It is an extremely important aspect of the workaday world of Canadian political life. Without understanding Canada's federal system, as outlined in the Constitution Act, 1867, it would be impossible to understand such factors as the distribution of popular support among the national political parties, voting behaviour in the House of Commons, the striking of a national budget, the pattern of policy outcomes, and the many other features of national politics. To a great extent, the provinces are the building blocks from which the national parties are built, and the operating agencies through which a large share of federal programs are carried out.

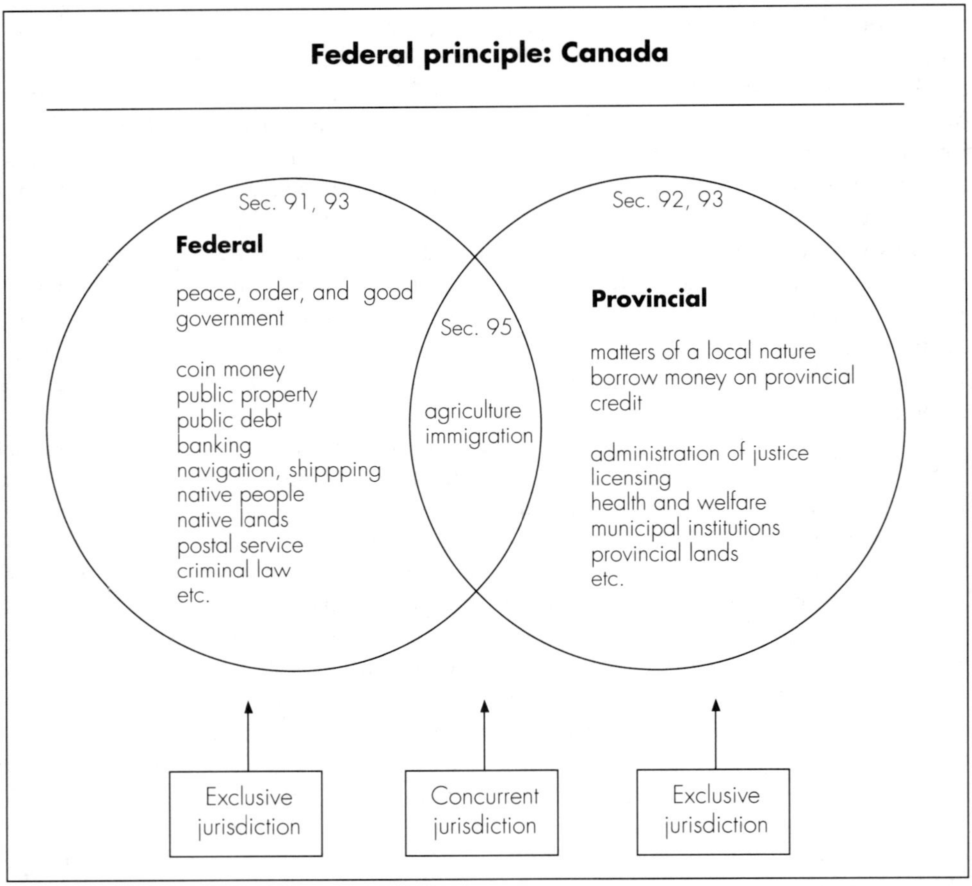

Figure 10.1

The Constitution Act, 1867, allocates and delineates the exclusive powers of the federal government under Section 91, and those of the provinces under Section 92 (see figure 10.1). Under Section 91, the federal government enjoys twenty-nine classes of political functions in addition to jurisdiction over public property and public debt, banking, credit, navigation and shipping, native people and their lands, postal services, and the criminal law. To the provinces, Section 92 allocated exclusive powers stated as "generally all matters of a merely local or private Nature in the Province." These powers included the borrowing of money based on the credit of the province, prisons in the province and the administration of justice, licensing to raise provincial revenues, health and welfare, municipal institutions, and the control of provincial lands. Section 93 gives the provinces control over the education rights of religious minorities. But it also gives the federal Cabinet and Parliament the right to scrutinize provincial laws and to pass remedial legislation should provincial action in the area of education run contrary to Section 93.

Federalism provided the provinces with an enormous number of chances for small victories in local affairs. But the intent of the Fathers of Confederation was that there indeed ought to be a central government with effective powers and institutions.[17] For them nothing else would guarantee political unity, provide a stable monetary system, and allow for the development of the economic resources of the country. But the most distinguishing powers that established the dominance of the central government over the provinces were in the area of taxation. The federal government has almost unlimited taxation powers under Section 91(3). It can offer to dispense huge sums of money to the provinces provided they spend the money according to policies established by the federal government. Section 92(2) gives the provinces the power of direct taxation to raise revenues for their purposes. The superiority of the federal taxation power has enabled Ottawa to expand its sphere of activity into many areas of provincial jurisdiction to the point where most of the provinces have become dependent on the national treasury. In addition, the Constitution Act, 1867, granted the Parliament of Canada the power to make laws for "Peace, Order and Good Government." The courts have interpreted these words as a residual power* to the federeal government, so that when a particular matter cannot be distinguished from the specific categories of powers enumerated in the Constitution Act, 1867, it moves under the authority of Parliament. On the surface, residual powers that favour the federal government would seem to permit Ottawa the potential, at least, to govern Canada as if it was a unitary state. But this has not happened.

Despite these powers, however, Canadian federalism ought not to be seen solely in terms of the constitutional capacity of the federal government to colonize provincial jurisdictions. The Constitution Act, 1867, does not tell us how Canadian federalism has actually evolved or how it presently works. Indeed, much of the transformation of Canada's federal system points in the direction of increased power and prestige for the provincial governments.[18] Since 1867, the expansion of governments at all levels in Canada has been enormous. But because of the present-day importance of property and civil rights, health and welfare, and provincial ownership of natural resources, the provinces have gained striking powers in most of the important areas of public policy affecting all Canadians, even in external affairs. Today, all areas of federal actions and policies must align themselves with the interests of the provinces. The vast size of Canada and the obvious geopolitical diversities that surface within the country enable the provinces to challenge and renegotiate federal powers. Socio-cultural diversities also exist to favour support for *provincial autonomy*, particularly in Quebec. The growth of Quebec nationalism and its example of constant resistance against federal incursions into provincial matters has affected the tone and solidarity of provincial politicians committed to local autonomy in many parts of the country.

Section 95 of the Constitution Act, 1867, refers to concurrent jurisdictions among the federal government and the provinces in the areas of *agriculture* and *immigration*. Here again, even though the Constitution gives supremacy to the Parliament of Canada, when conflicts arise on matters of concurrent jurisdiction, the federal government has been willing to negotiate its policies in these areas with the provinces.

In many other areas where exclusive federal jurisdiction is provided by the Constitution, the provinces have successfully challenged and penetrated the powers granted to Ottawa. In 1978 the Supreme Court ruled that the federal government had exclusive jurisdiction over cable television. But in the face of contravening provincial pressures, the government has been willing to bargain that jurisdiction with the provinces. In similar fashion, the provinces have gained special input into the formulation of *foreign policy*, particularly in the area of *trade*. In the past decade, the federal government has withdrawn its institutional involvement in municipal affairs by disbanding the Department of Urban Affairs in 1978, after seven years of persistent provincial resistance. And yielding to yet another provincial preserve, the federal government gave control of family allowances to the provinces and withdrew its direct involvement in post-secondary education.

Thus, with regard to federalism, the constitutional context of Canadian politics is complex. The Constitution Act, 1867, obviously leaves open the path of federal/provincial negotiation as a permissive political approach to the problem of constitutional jurisdictions. In this sense, the Constitution Act, 1867, does not close the question of divisional jurisdictions in Canada's federal system. It sets the context and establishes definite outer limits within which each level of government may choose to operate. A less formal way to say this is that the written Constitution does not tell us how Canadian governments and politics actually work. But the constitution is an important element in establishing the context – the political geography – within which politics and governments operate.

The Amendment Formulas

Before presenting a detailed description of the complicated process of amending Canada's Constitution, it is important to consider the conventional relationship that existed between Canada and Great Britain on constitutional change from 1867 to 1982. For much of Canada's history as an independent nation-state, the Constitution Act, 1867, lacked an amendment procedure in Canada.[19] Until 1949, the British Parliament amended the Constitution on all substantive matters by request from Canada through a joint address to the House of Commons and the Senate. From 1949 to 1982, amendment of the Constitution Act, 1867, could be passed by Canada to increase the number of senators by two, one each from the Yukon and Northwest Territories. But Parliament still could not amend the Constitution on a wide range of matters, including provincial jurisdictions, English and French languages, and provisions on the tenure of Parliament. In fact, Canada was the only democracy that could not reform its Constitution in its entirety without the parliamentary approval of another country.

Three months after his return to the office of prime minister in February of 1980, Pierre Elliott Trudeau pledged that his majority government would *patriate* the Constitution, give it a Charter of Rights and Freedoms, and an amendment formula. After a constitutional conference that ended in failure in September 1980, Trudeau moved unilaterally to patriate the Constitution. The Patriation Resolution* introduced in Parliament in October 1980 came up against considerable resistance from the Conservatives as well as from the provincial governments. Only two provinces, Ontario and New Brunswick, supported it. This state of affairs culminated in a number of court battles to determine the legality of unilateral patriation. In February 1981, the Manitoba Court of Appeals, in a close decision of 3:2, ruled that the Patriation Resolution was legal. Two months later, the Newfoundland Court of Appeals ruled unanimously against unilateral patriation. And in April 1981, the Quebec Court of Appeal ruled in favour of the federal proposal in a 4:1 decision. Finally, the Supreme Court heard arguments stemming from the Manitoba, Newfoundland, and Quebec decisions, and rendered its judgement on the Constitution Act on September 28, 1981. In a 7:2 decision, the court ruled that the federal government had the legal right to ask the Parliament of the United Kingdom to amend the British North America (BNA) Act, and to implement a Charter of Rights and Freedoms, without the unanimous consent of the provinces.

In the ensuing weeks, the Trudeau government bargained intensely with the provinces and reached agreement with all except Quebec on the final concessions of the Constitutional Accord. In December 1981, Parliament passed the Canada Act by a vote of 246:24 in the House and a vote of 59:23 in the Senate. In the same month the act was delivered to the British Parliament by the secretary to the governor general and Minister of Justice Jean Chretien. The British Parliament finally approved the Canada Act in March 1982 and on April 17 of that year the Queen proclaimed the Constitution Act, 1982, completing the process of patriation.

The Constitution Act, 1982, was Canada's last manifestation of independence from Great Britain. The formal amendment process had finally severed the need for Britain's legal imprimatur on Canada's first law of the land. It was the British Parliament's last bill that was binding on Canada.

However, without Quebec as a signatory of the accord, Canada would remain constitutionally impaired. But, with the defeat of the *Parti Québécois* government by Robert Bourassa and his Liberal candidates in December 1985, the way was cleared for a new set of negotiations to bring Quebec into the constitutional family as a full partner. In May 1986, at Mont-Gabriel, the new Quebec government laid out five conditions for its adhesion to the Constitution Act, 1982, in a manifesto entitled "Maitriser l'avenir." They were:

1. Recognition of Quebec as a distinct society
2. A larger provincial role in immigration
3. Provincial input into appointments to the Supreme Court of Canada
4. Limitations on federal spending power
5. A veto for Quebec on constitutional amendments

At the federal government's retreat at Meech Lake, Quebec, on April 30, 1987, Canada's first ministers agreed in principle on Quebec's five proposals. An all-night negotiating session at the Langevin Block in Ottawa that June resulted in the drafting of the *1987 Constitutional Accord*.

The Meech Lake Accord recognized that the legal, social, and political realities of Quebec are distinctive within the federal structure of Canada and deserve constitutional status. On immigration, the accord granted constitutional status to immigration agreements signed between the federal government and individual provinces, protecting them from capricious legislative change. The Senate got special consideration: the federal government would retain its right to appoint senators, but it would have to make its choice from among names supplied by the province where a vacancy occurs. Under the accord, Senate reform would be placed on the agenda of future constitutional conferences. Meech Lake gave the Supreme Court full constitutional status, entrenching the tradition of reserving three of the nine Supreme Court appointments for Quebeckers, and requiring Ottawa to select new Supreme Court appointments from lists of jurists provided by the provinces. On the matter of national programs Meech Lake confirmed Ottawa's constitutional right to initiate such programs while limiting its ability to force conditions on reluctant provinces: Any province that opts out of a federal program would be entitled to receive its share of federal funding – at the same time, it implements an acceptable program of its own. Finally, on conferences and amendments, the accord set an agenda for constitutional change: first ministers must meet at least once a year to consider new constitutional amendments, requiring *unanimous* consent of the House of Commons and the Senate and the legislative assembly of each province on a broadened slate of subjects, such as changes to the Supreme Court or the powers and composition of the Senate, and the establishment of new provinces.

Serious reservations about the agreement surfaced almost immediately after it was signed in June 1987. Francophones outside Quebec criticized the distinct-society reference and anglophones faulted the document for laying the foundation for future confrontations between the two founding peoples. Women's groups across the country lamented that the accord did not guarantee women's rights. Others argued that the accord did not reach out to natives and minorities. Representatives from Yukon and the Northwest Territories held that unanimity would make it difficult for the territories to become provinces. Two premiers, Manitoba's Gary Filmon and New Brunswicks's Frank McKenna, who were elected since the accord was signed, withheld the ratification of their provincial legislatures. The election of a Liberal government in Newfoundland in 1989 strengthened the resolve of those opposed to the Meech Lake Accord. The Liberal leader, Clyde Wells, opposed the accord because it eroded federal powers, gave Quebec special status within Confederation, failed to establish an elected senate, and required unanimity on important constitutional reforms. Soon after, Premier Joe Ghiz threatened to withdraw his support of the accord in protest against Ottawa's closure of the armed forces base at Summerside, P.E.I. Next, Saskatchewan's Grant Devine and British Columbia's William Vander Zalm expressed reservations about the accord. Then, another original signatory, John Buchanan, Premier of Nova Scotia, stated publicly that he would accept a companion agreement to Meech Lake, a "parallel accord." Such an appendage would permit the inclusion of new wording to the Meech Lake accord to address the concerns expressed by some premiers.

The procedures for amending the Constitution are listed in part v, sections 38–49 of the Constitution Act, 1982. There are five methods applicable to the broad areas of constitutional reform requiring the approval of the House of Commons and the Senate and the legislative assemblies of at least two-thirds (7) of the provinces with at least 50 percent of the population of all provinces. This is referred to as the 7-50 formula.

Method 1: The amendment is proclaimed by the governor-general for:

a. resolutions of the House of Commons and the Senate.
b. resolutions of the legislatures of at least two-thirds (7) of the provinces that have, in the aggregate, according to the latest Census, at least 50 percent of the national population.

The first method is used when constitutional reform is required that alters provincial legislative powers, proportional representation in the House of Commons and the Senate, Senate reform, changes in the Supreme Court of Canada, the creation of new provinces, or the expansion of existing provincial boundaries. The so-called *opting-out formula* is applicable here: a province can dissent from an amendment by passing a resolution supported by a majority of its legislative members, with the result that the amendment shall not apply. (Under Meech Lake the first method, the 7-50 formula, would apply to provincial legislative powers, the expansion of existing provincial boundaries, and a change in the distribution of powers between the provinces and the federal government. Opting-out is applicable: a province can dissent from an amendment by passing a resolution supported by a majority of its legislative members. The amended Section 40 would require reasonable compensation to a dissenting province for any amendment that transfers exclusive provincial legislative powers to the Parliament of Canada.)

Method 2: The amendment is proclaimed by the governor general for:

a. resolutions of the House of Commons and the Senate, and
b. resolutions of the legislative assembly of each province.

The second method is for the following matters: the Office of the Queen, the governor general and the lieutenant-governor of a province; the right of a province to a number of members in the House of Commons (not less than the number of senators by which the province is entitled to be represented), the use of the English or the French language, the composition of the Supreme Court, and an amendment to the formal amendment procedures outlined in part v. (Under Meech Lake the principle of unanimity applies for the following matters: the Office of the Queen, the governor general and the lieutenant-governor of a province; the right of a province to a number of members in the House of Commons not less than the number of senators by which the province is entitled to be represented in the Senate and the residence qualifications of senators, the principle of proportionate representation of the provinces in the House of Commons prescribed by the Constitution of Canada, the Supreme Court of Canada, the extension of existing provinces into territories, the establishment of new provinces notwithstanding any other law or practice, and an amendment to the formal amendment procedures.)

Method 3: The amendment is proclaimed by the governor general for any provision that applies to one or more, but not all provinces for:

a. resolutions of the House of Commons and the Senate.

b. resolutions of the legislature of each province to which the amendment applies.

The third method is applicable to amendments to alter boundaries *between* provinces and to the use of the English or French languages *within* a province or any other issue affecting only one province.

Method 4: Parliament may exclusively make laws amending the Constitution for matters pertaining to the executive and legislative branches of the federal government.

Method 5: The legislature of each province may exclusively amend the constitution of the province.

Rights and Freedoms

At the time of Confederation Canadians felt secure in adopting the British guarantees of individual rights and freedoms embedded in the traditions of common law. The Magna Carta (1215), the Habeas Corpus Act (1679), and the Bill of Rights (1689) seemed quite enough to protect Canadians for most of the century after 1867.[20] In 1960, however, the Diefenbaker government was determined to reiterate legislatively these assumed guarantees by passing its Canadian Bill of Rights. This measure suffers from an inherent weakness: because it is a legislative rather than a constitutional enactment, and can be rescinded by a simple act of Parliament. The Canadian Bill of Rights, in addition to the Charter, still protects citizens. But by entrenching these rights in a new constitution in 1982, Canadians could feel more secure in the knowledge that the rigid amendment formulas would work to prevent any rapid erosion of basic freedoms.

Thus, with the proclamation of the Constitution Act, 1982, which contains the 34-clause Canadian Charter of Rights and Freedoms, two important guarantees were branded on Canada's political culture. One was *substantive rights* that specify a condition of freedom and advantage that can be enjoyed for their own sake. Another was *procedural rights* that provided political and legal devices through which governments are controlled and the people protected from arbitrary action.

Clause 1 of the Canadian charter states that rights are subject "to such reasonable limits prescribed by law as can be demonstrably justified in a free and democratic society." On the surface, at least, rights are guaranteed in the Constitution, but they are subject to overriding by Parliament and provincial legislatures. Enactment of the charter has also placed the Supreme Court of Canada in the difficult position of arbitrating disputes to adjudicate on whether they are "reasonable" or have been "demonstrably justified."

Similarly, Clause 33 states that "Parliament or the Legislature of a province may expressly declare in an Act of Parliament or of the Legislature, as the case may be, that the act or provision thereof shall operate *notwithstanding* ... this charter." In effect, the Constitution allows the enactment of bills that say they operate notwithstanding the Charter of Rights and Freedoms. For example, Quebec premier Robert Bourassa used the notwithstanding clause to restrict English-language signs in the province. In other words, laws that infringe on the most fundamental rights of individuals may be passed, even though they contravene the spirit and letter of the charter. The danger in such clauses is that legislators can simply specify that their legislation is operative despite certain provisions in the charter. There is not much more assurance for Canadians between a legislated bill of rights or an enacted charter of rights if rights can be pre-empted by a "notwithstanding" clause. Only time and jurisprudence will tell whether Canada's Charter of Rights and Freedoms is a superior document.

But the Canadian charter does contain two major provisions that have received much praise from constitutional scholars. One is a clear statement of the *equality of men and women* (Clause 15 [1]). The second is Clause 15(2) that is an *affirmative-action provision.* It permits the adoption of laws, programs, and activities to advance the cause of groups that are disadvantaged because of race, national or eithnic origin, colour, religion, sex, age, and mental or physical disability.

All the other provisions in the charter resemble those of most democratic constitutions in the world today. Like many other Western documents, the charter affirms that "Canada is founded upon principles that recognize the supremacy of God and the rule of law." Under sections 2 to 5, it lists the basic *civil and political liberties* to which Canadians are entitled. Sections 7 through 14 outline the *legal rights* of Canadian citizens that also fall in line with other democracies, such as the United States, West Germany, Switzerland, and Sweden.

The Constitution of the United States

The first organic superlaw of the United States was the *Articles of Confederation**.[21] In 1777, these articles had been proposed to the states by the Continental Congress – the body of delegates representing the colonies that met to protest British treatment of the colonies and that eventually became the government of the United States. The proposed articles were finally ratified in 1781 and they provided for annual meetings of the states "in Congress assembled" to conduct the business of the United States, each state entitled to one vote. Soon after, the Articles of Confederation were widely viewed as unsatisfactory because the Government of the United States could not raise revenues on its own and the states were slow and often delinquent in submitting their appropriations so that the "confederate" government could operate. The perceived powerlessness of the U.S. Congress led it to call for a constitutional convention that would create "a more perfect Union."

This constitutional convention met in Philadelphia in 1787 to produce a relatively short but eloquent document, whose chief draftsman was James Madison. When this document was finally ratified by enough states in 1788, it became the Constitution of the United

States. This same basic document, amended only twenty-six times in over 200 years, governs one of the most dynamic societies in the world today.

The U.S. Constitution is clearly organized and provides a straightforward declaration of the supremacy of the rule of law, as well as an outline of the institutions of government.[22] Structurally the Constitution deals with the following: Article 1: the legislative powers of U.S. government; Article 2: the powers of the executive; Article 3: judicial powers; Article 4: general provisions relating to the states; Article 5: the amendment formula; Article 6: the supremacy of federal law; and Article 7: ratification* of constitutional amendments.

In all, four aspects of the American Constitution have contributed to its adaptability (1) the amendment process; (2) broad grants of institutional power and authority; (3) the growth of extra-constitutional practices permitted by the silence of the Constitution on key matters; and (4) the interpretation of constitutional generalities.

The Formal Amendment Process

The formal amendment of the U.S. Constitution has been infrequent and some of the amendments have been used for minor changes in the functions of government.[23] But most of the amendments have been significant in the adaptation of government to new social circumstances. The famous "Civil War Amendments" (thirteenth, fourteenth, and fifteenth) outlawed slavery, defined the privileges and immunities of citizenship, and provided the right to vote regardless of race, colour, or prior servitude. Other amendments have given new meaning to the Constitution and expanded some democratic rights, such as the direct election of senators, women's suffrage, repeal of the poll tax, and the lowering of the voting age to 18. One of the most consequential amendments, the sixteenth, ratified in 1913, authorized the income tax. Amending the U.S. Constitution is not an easy process. Amendments can be proposed by a two-thirds majority of both houses (357 of 435 members). Amendments are ratified when three-fourths of the states (38 to 50) approve them.

Broad Grants of Power and Authority

In some places the U.S. Constitution seems to have been written with deliberate ambiguity. Unadmittedly, the founding fathers used ambiguity as a strategy for winning the approval of the diverse factions that disputed the document. The vague phraseology contributed to the flexibility and accommodation the document provided for later generations to interpret some sections as giving broad grants of power and authority to *key institutions*. For example, the power of the Supreme Court to declare acts of Congress unconstitutional is neither explicitly stated nor denied in the Constitution. However, the Supreme Court ruled that it did have the power of judicial review, an interpretation of the words in the Constitution that greatly enhances its political significance. The executive powers of the president are not distinctly spelled out in the Constitution, either. But the words "the President shall take care that the laws be faithfully executed" have justified the creation of a huge bureaucracy to administer and execute the laws of the land.

The Silence of the Constitution

Flexibility and adaptability also flow from what is not written in the U.S. Constitution. As with the Canadian Constitution, political parties are not mentioned in the original document and the party system is extra-constitutional. Every major elected official, and most appointed ones, take office under the banner of a political party. All of this takes place outside of the framework of the Constitution. Because of the absence of precise terminology, political institutions have been able to adapt to the requirements of twentieth-century politics. To say that a constitution is flexible is another way of saying that it does not provide ready-made answers for new political questions and social issues. The capacity of American politics to redefine its institutions has been facilitated by this silence in the Constitution.

Constitutional Generalities

The U.S. Constitution is a document of general formulations that have been amenable to modern interpretation. In the modern world of American politics, this means that old words have been given new meanings and old institutions have acquired new functions. The original words of the Constitution have acquired *modern-day application.* The framers of the U.S. Constitution opposed the manner in which colonial officials arbitrarily searched private residences. The Fourth Amendment, ratified in 1791, declared that "the right of the people to be secure in their persons, houses, papers, and effects, against unreasonable searches and seizures, shall not be violated." Today, despite a technology that permits electronic surveillance, wiretaps, hidden microphones, and telescopic cameras, the principle inherent in the Fourth Amendment is sustained. The old argument that places individual rights above the government's right to know has been given relevance in the American legal system.

Similarly the electoral college is an example of new functions being assigned to old institutions. The electoral college, as laid down in the Constitution, was a method of choosing a president and vice-president by a small group of respected citizens. This small group of people composing the electoral college was to be chosen by the state legislatures. The electoral college continues to play a major role in selecting the president, but it does so by performing a function not at all envisioned by the framers of the Constitution. It has become an institution of popular democratic control.

The Federal Principle

One of the primary objectives of the framers of the U.S. Constitution was to allocate powers between the national and state governments within a federal structure, which at the time was a radically new idea in its application on a continental scale.[24] The basic constitutional outline permits the federal government and the government in each state to be separate in *scope* – in *whatever* areas of jurisdiction each may govern. But, the federal structure unites the national and state governments in *domain* – the people for whom they govern. In other words, the federal government and the government in each state operate directly on the individual, within their respective spheres of power. The so-called *residual powers*, not explicitly granted by the Constitution, either to the federal government or to the states, are now held to belong to the federal government.

Under the Constitution, some powers are forbidden to the national government, while others are granted exclusively to it. Many powers were forbidden to the states but several are shared by both the national and state governments (figure 10.2). The Constitution is rather hazy on state powers in that states can do what has not been specifically granted to the federal government or forbidden to the states. Since 1787, conflicts over what is exclusive and concurrent jurisdiction between the states and the federal government have often been adjudicated by the Supreme Court, sometimes ruling in favour of national institutions and sometimes ruling for the states. By means of Supreme Court decisions and federal and state legislation, the whole concept of federalism, as originally conceived by

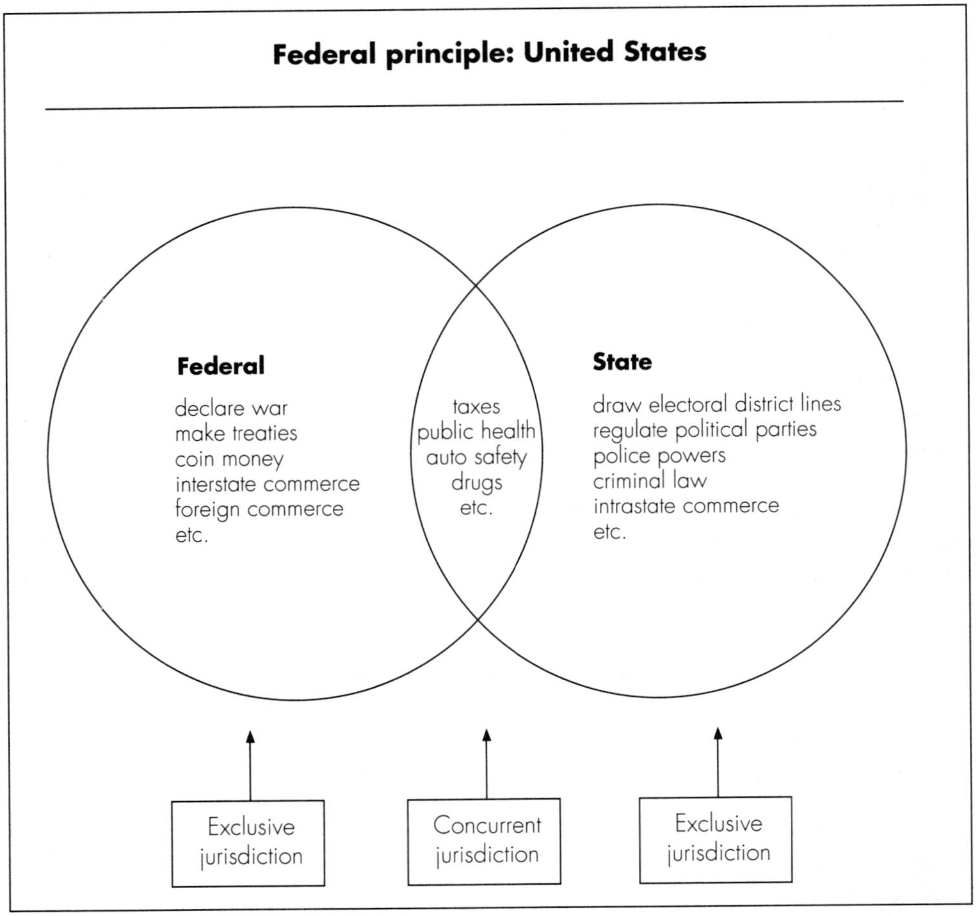

Figure 10.2

the framers of the Constitution, has been reinterpreted under the pressures of a changing society making new and different demands on government.

In recent years, the federal government has placed itself in the position of providing funds for the development of state-oriented programs over highways, schools, and public housing. Federal-guaranteed loans, grants-in-aid* to states, and outright grants of money to federally designated areas have all brought the federal government more into the private lives of Americans than ever before. The powers of the national government have also increased significantly through congressional legislative enactments, but so have those of the states. State governments are doing more than ever before in the fields of health, education, welfare, housing, and highway construction. So, while the government in Washington has grown, so have state governments. However, the ultimate vehicle of control is money. Without federal aid, many states simply cannot carry out programs they urgently need. And with federal money comes federal control. The unlimited taxation powers of the federal government have made it predominant: it can offer to dispense huge sums of money to the states with the proviso that they will spend the money according to policies established by the federal government. The states either do what the central government wants or they do not get the money.

As in Canada, federalism continues to be a dynamic political process. Like Canadian provinces, the states are political entities to be reckoned with. Their governments have powerful governors, legislatures, and bureaucracies. They demand that federal programs serve state interests. In this regard, the U.S. Constitution has provided the legal and institutional framework for the resolution of conflicting political interests. The result is a continuing battle over legal authority, bureaucratic jurisdiction, and constitutional legitimacy.

The American Constitution is an extraordinary achievement. For over 200 hundred years it has remained the vital foundation of American government and society. The American Constitution has also continued to evolve and change: first, it has been amended twenty-six times, and second, the power of judicial review has imposed important changes on the meanings of the original document. Through the interpretations of the Supreme Court, the Constitution has been elaborated, enlarged, and updated to meet new conditions in a rapidly changing society.

REFERENCES

1. Mark Hagopian, *Regimes, Movements and Ideologies* (New York: Longman Inc. 1984), 38–9.
2. K.C. Wheare, *Modern Constitutions* (London: Oxford University Press 1952), 2–3.
3. See Paul Sigmund, "Carl Friedrich's Contribution to the Theory of Constitutionalism – Comparative Government," in J.R. Pennock and John Chapman, eds., *Constitutionalism* (New York: New York University Press 1979), 34–9.
4. J.R. Pennock and David Smith, *Political Science* (London: Collier Macmillan Ltd. 1965), 241.
5. This definition is a modified version of the one given in Francis Wormuth, *The Origins of Modern Constitutionalism* (New York: Harper & Row Publishers 1949), 3.

6. William G. Andrews, *Constitutions and Constitutionalism* (Toronto: D. Van Nostrand Co. Inc. 1961), 13.
7. See Gordon Schochet, "Introduction: Constitutionalism, Liberalism and the Study of Politics," in Pennock and Chapman, eds., *Constitutionalism*, 5.
8. See John Rawls, *A Theory of Justice* (Cambridge, MA: Harvard University Press 1971); Harvey Wheeler, "Constitutionalism," in Fred Greenstein and Nelson Polsby, eds., *Handbook of Political Science: Governmental Institutions and Processes,* vol. 5 (Reading, MA: Addison-Wesley Publishing Co.1975), 1–91; Carl J. Friedrich, *Limited Government: A Comparison* (Englewood Cliffs, NJ: Prentice-Hall 1974).
9. Gabriel Almond and Bingham Powell Jr., *Comparative Politics Today, A World View* (Glenview, IL: Scott, Foresman & Co. 1988), 102–18.
10. See K.C. Wheare, *Modern Constitutions* (New York: Oxford University Press 1951), ch. 6.
11. Carl Friedrich, *Limited Government: A Comparison* (Englewood Cliffs, NJ: Prentice-Hall 1974).
12. Raymond Gastil, *Freedom in the World: Political and Civil Liberties, 1981* (Westport, CT: Greenwood Press 1981), 14–17.
13. Gordon Fairweather, "Press Freedom: More than a Platitude," Lecture in Honour of the 20th Anniversary of York University, Gerstein Conference on Mass Communication and Canadian Nationhood, Toronto, York University, April 10, 1981.
14. Almond and Powell, *Comparative Politics Today: A World View,* 326–27; also Ellen Jones and Fred Grupp, "Measuring Nationality Trends in the Soviet Union: A Research Note," *Slavic Review* 41 (Spring 1982): 112–22.
15. Ronald Cheffins and Patricia Johnson, *The Revised Canadian Constitution: Politics as Law* (Toronto: McGraw-Hill Ryerson Ltd. 1986), 12–24.
16. See Ronald Landes, *The Canadian Polity* (Scarborough, ON: Prentice-Hall Canada Inc. 1983), 74; David Milne, *The New Canadian Constitution* (Toronto: James Lorimer & Co. 1982).
17. Alexander Brady, "Background to the Constitutional Controversy and Settlement," in Paul Fox, ed., *Politics: Canada* (Toronto: McGraw-Hill Ryerson Ltd. 1982), 49–57;
18. Donald Smiley, *Canada in Question: Federalism in the Eighties* (Toronto: McGraw-Hill Ryerson 1980), 16–27; Garth Stevenson, *Federalism in Canada* (Toronto: McClelland & Stewart 1989).
19. See Garth Stevenson, "Federalism and Intergovernmental Relations," in Michael S. Whittington and Glen Williams, *Canadian Politics in the 1980s* (Toronto: Methuen 1981), 275–91; and Richard Simeon, "Meech Lake and Shifting Conceptions of Canadian Federalism," *Canadian Public Policy* XIV (September 1988) S7–S24.
20. See Marc Kilgour, "A Formal Analysis of the Amending Formula of Canada's Constitution Act, 1982," *Canadian Journal of Political Science* XV1 (December 1983): 772–7; and Robert Campbell and Leslie Pal, *The Real Worlds of Canadian Politics* (Peterborough, ON: Broadview Press 1989), 227–98; and Neil Finkelstein and Brian Rogers, *Charter Issues in Civil Cases* (Toronto: Carswell 1988), 3–73.
21. See Edward Corwin, *The Constitution and What It Means Today*, 14th ed., rev. by Howard Chase and Craig Ducat (Princeton: Princeton University Press 1978).
22. Joseph F. Costanzo, *Political and Legal Studies: Studies in American Constitutional Law*, vol two (West Hanover, MA: Christopher Publishing House 1982), 12–15.
23. James Wilson, *American Government,* 4th ed. (Lexington, MA: D.C. Heath & Co. 1989), 490–506.
24. See Daniel Elazar, "Constitutionalism, Federalism and the Post-Industrial

American Polity," in Seymour Martin Lipset, ed., *The Third Century* (Chicago: University of Chicago Press 1979), 80–107; see also Klaus von Beyme, *America as a Model: The Impact of American Democracy in the World* (New York: St. Martin's Press 1987).

SUGGESTED READINGS

Philip Anisman and Allen Linden, *The Media, the Courts and the Charter* (Toronto: Carswell 1986).

Gerald Beaudoin and Ed Ratushny, *The Canadian Charter of Rights and Freedoms* (Toronto: Carswell 1989).

A.P. Blaustein and J.A. Sigler, *Constitutions that Made History* (New York: Paragon House Publishers 1988).

Alan Cairns and Douglas Williams, eds., *Constitution, Government and Society in Canada* (Toronto: McClelland & Stewart 1989).

David Currie, *The Constitution and the Supreme Court: The First Hundred Years* (Chicago: University of Chicago Press 1987).

Malcolm Feeley, *Constitutional Law*, 2nd ed. (Glenview, IL: Scott, Foresman & Co. 1989).

Kenneth Fogarty, *Equality Rights and Their Limitations in the Charter* (Toronto: Carswell 1987).

Peter Hogg, *Meech Lake Annotated* (Toronto: Carswell 1988).

Joseph Magnet, *Constitutional Law of Canada* (Toronto: Carswell 1987).

Patrick Monahan, *Politics and the Constitution: The Charter, Federalism, and the Supreme Court of Canada* (Toronto: Carswell 1987).

Christopher Wolfe, *The Rise of Modern Judicial Review* (New York: Basic Books 1986).

GLOSSARY

constitution: The fundamental law of a nation-state, written or unwritten, that organizes government, assigns and limits political power, and clarifies the relationship between the people and their political leaders.

enactment: The formal process of giving validity to a bill or constitutional amendment.

unwritten constitution: A constitution that consists primarily of custom, convention, or statute that is not written down in one comprehensive document.

written constitution: The fundamenal law as it appears in one or more written documents.

entrenched: The provisions embodied within the protection of a constitution, subject to amendment procedures not affected by ordinary legislation.

constitutionalism: The principle of government that holds that political power should be defined and limited by fundamental rules, either written or unwritten.

right: A capacity residing in one person of controlling, with the assent and assistance of the state, the actions of others.

standards: Established practices to which other actions, commodities, and qualities are required to correspond.

suspended provision: A constitutional right that is temporarily stayed with the expectation that it will be resumed when certain conditions are met.

promulgation: The order that is given to cause a law to be executed and to make it public.

public: Pertaining to the state, nation, or whole community in the sense that whatever affects the whole body of people falls into the general domain.

flexible constitution: A constitution that is easily amended.

rigid constitution: A constitution that makes no allowances for amendments or that requires a procedure so difficult that it is almost impossible to add amendments.

infringement: To enter into the rights or permissions of another without consent or permission.

slander: The speaking of base and defamatory words tending to prejudice another in reputation, office, trade, business, or means of livelihood.

libel: To defame or injure a person's reputation by a published writing.

claim: Action at law for recovery of specific rights or permissions wrongfully taken and detained, with damages that the taking or detention has caused.

exclusive powers: Those political entitlements that, under a constitution, may be exercised only by either the national government or the subnational governments.

concurrent powers: Powers that are shared by the various levels of government constitutionally designated to exercise certain jurisdiction.

residual powers: Sometimes also called reserved powers that are potentially wide in scope and may be constitutionally or judicially allocated to the national government or the subnational units.

resolutions: A formal statement by a convention or a legislature or some other body that declares or decides on a motion before it.

Articles of Confederation (U.S.): The instrument of government that served as the basic document for the American states that had broken away from Great Britain between 1775 and 1781.

ratification: The validation, acceptance, or approval of an action of an official, an agency of government, a treaty, or a constitution.

grants-in-aid (U.S.): Monetary grants made available by one government jurisdiction to another, usually on the basis of precribed conditions designed to meet specific program objectives.

11

Political Parties and Pressure Groups

Lubicon band members block access to disputed lands

Development

IN ANCIENT ROME, REPRESENTATIVES SOUGHT their re-election and the election of their friends by identifying with a prominent group.[1] Because Roman suffrage was very limited, there was little need for using a label to attract voters, nor were these groups organized as extra-parliamentary bodies with an ongoing bureaucracy that functioned between elections.

The genesis of modern political parties as institutions representing a multiplicity of socio-political factors is traceable to the growth of parliamentary governments during the eighteenth century in Europe and the United States.[2] The first formal parties in England and the United States evolved from legislative factions that consisted of friendly groups of notables and were more like political clubs. To some degree these groups did organize for elections, maintaining an ongoing structure that worked systematically between elections.

They formed electoral committees made up of prominent citizens who sponsored candidates by raising funds necessary for the election campaign. The historic roots of modern democratic parties are found in the struggle of fledgling legislative bodies that challenged the autocratic prerogatives of the monarch. Initially parties were divergent groups – almost totally without ideologies or programs – that formed within an expanding electorate, taking opposite sides in the battle to demand recognition of voting franchise* and to dismantle property and class* qualifications as impediments to political participation.

By the end of the nineteenth century, the growth of democracy and the rise of industrial societies spawned a new kind of political organization, the *mass political party*, which continues to serve as an institution designed to mobilize public participation on a grand scale in support of candidates and political programs. Today, in the majority of states where they are permitted to function, political parties appeal to the widest possible interests in their respective countries. Almost all contemporary parties are mass parties. There are now more than 500 such political parties functioning in over 130 nation-states. Wherever there are more candidates than offices, there is a process of *competition* and *selection*, and the candidates supported by these mass-appeal parties are usually the ones that survive.

However, a number of contemporary states do not permit political parties to function at all. Approximately thirty states have either declared parties illegal or have discouraged their formation through repression. In the 1990s, a group of states from the various regions of the world have outlawed political parties. These include Chad, Cyprus, Ghana, Liberia, Niger, North Yemen, Rwanda, and Uganda. In another group of states, political-party systems have simply not developed. These include such states as Andorra, Bahrain, Bhutan, Brunei, Jordan, Kuwait, Oman, Nepal, Qatar, Saudi Arabia, Swaziland, Tonga, and the United Arab Emirates. In many of these states a surviving traditional kingship has prevented the evolution of a pluralistic* and competitive political-party system. The concentration of political power clusters around the monarch by custom and tradition. Contemporary states without political parties are found chiefly in the Middle East, Southeast Asia, and Sub-Saharan Africa.

What Is a Political Party?

One of the most general and flexible definitions of a political party was made by a Bahamian party leader, Sir Randol Fawkes: "A political party consists of a group of persons united in opinion or action, more or less permanently organized, which attempts to bring about the election of its candidates to public offices and by this means to control or influence the actions and policy of government."[3] A political group can be defined in terms of the purpose for which it was organized, the size and character of its membership, its structure, and the functions it performs. Leon Epstein points to the distinguishing characteristic of the party "label," because in his opinion size and membership are less significant components. He defines a party as "any group, however loosely organized, seeking to elect governmental office-holders under a given label."[4] The French scholar Maurice Duverger, in contrast to Epstein, focusses on "ideologies, social foundations, structure, organization, participation, strategy – all these aspects must be taken into account in making a complete analysis of any political party."[5]

These definitions make sense particularly when a political party is viewed from a behavioural perspective. In competitive party systems, all political parties have as their primary goal the conquest of *power* or at least some influence in the distribution of it. Political parties try to win seats at elections in order to take *control* of the offices of government. When this is not possible, they assume the strategy of an *opposition* to scrutinize government action and to offer *alternatives* to the electorate. In most cases, political parties seek *support* from a broad social base so as to claim representation and *legitimacy* in articulating the interests of the people. They are particularly adept at aggregating* as many interests as possible under a common organizational structure and some ideological identification, such as liberalism, conservatism, nationalism, socialism, or communism.

In authoritarian systems, one party or a small number of parties try to mobilize the backing of interest groups and voters. Where political competition is controlled or non-existent, the aggregation of many interests still takes place within parties, but the groups that are aggregated (such as unions, business organizations, and consumers) are mobilized to accept the party platform whether they support it wholeheartedly or not. In many totalitarian party systems, a single party controls group demands and tries to foster a monolithic consensus among the various groups in society.

Political parties can differ in several respects. A structural-functional definition and approach to parties sensitizes us to the fact that different structures may perform similar functions, and the same structures may perform different functions. Some parties, including the Liberal and Progressive Conservative parties in Canada and the Republican and Democratic parties in the United States, are basically of a *pragmatic/brokerage* type.[6] They are generally found in the well-developed party systems of the Western democracies. The Australian Liberal party, the British Conservative party, and the Swedish Moderate Coalition party are other examples. These parties are mass-appeal parties with no strong ideological commitments and no well-defined or differentiated party programs. Some analysts refer to these characteristics facetiously as "tweedledum and tweedledee," suggesting that brokerage parties sacrifice identity for electoral "market" success. Their chief goal is to elect their candidates to public office and to attract special-interest groups, giving them preferential legislative treatment in exchange for electoral and financial support.

The fact that pragmatic parties can embrace the original ideas and platforms popularized by other parties, even though the same policies may have been previously attacked or ignored, indicates something important about them. On close examination, one observes that mass parties are coalitions* of many dissimilar groups that, at times, seem only to share a common party label. Pragmatic parties are much more concerned with political success than with political philosophy, opting usually to put together a winning coalition of candidates rather than attempting to reconcile the doctrinal persuasion of the party label with the voters.

In contrast to the brokerage-type parties are the *ideological* parties, many of which were formed in the last century and the early part of the twentieth century.[7] Operating within democratic as well as non-democratic party systems, these parties are *doctrinal* in that they pursue a set of prescribed principles in a political system. Ideological parties based on socialism and communism are almost universal among the states of the world that permit political parties. Under the socialist label, they appear in the Netherlands and Norway as labour parties. Those based on Marxist-Leninist ideologies operate in numerous states, including Britain, Canada, France, Mexico, and the United States. Some ideological parties are organized around religious doctrines, such as the Swiss Evangelical party, Pakistan's Islamic party, and Israel's United Torah Front.

Since World War II, many doctrinal parties have become less ideological and more pragmatic. The communist parties of Yugoslavia and Cuba are good examples of this newer trend. The present Chinese Communist party (CCP) moved sharply away from Maoism by stressing the importance of material economic considerations (as opposed to subjective human factors under Mao) in development and the basic unity of Chinese society.

The characteristic of doctrinal pragmatism seems to be rooted in the high rate of ideological and social change in these countries. Modern socialists and communists find themselves obligated to innovate and reform, both politically and economically. In Western Europe, ideological parties have abandoned or substantially modified their former objectives of nationalizing* all basic modes of production in their economies.

One type of ideological party that deserves special mention is the *indigenous* or *nation-building* party.[8] Indigenous parties gear their platforms to the countries in which they are found. They build their ideologies from a multiplicity of political doctrines that are relevant to the national problems in their particular social and economic environment. Increasingly they have come to represent the peasant or tribal masses, the new proletariat and the middle sectors. Many indigenous parties adopt a platform of land reform, nationalization of industry, a full range of economic and social reforms, and an opposition to communism. In Latin America, the Peruvian Aprista party, Venezuela's Acción Democrática, Costa Rica's Liberación Nacional, Puerto Rico's Popular Democratic party, and Guatemala's Partido Revolucionario are indigenous parties with nation-building ideologies. In Africa, Botswana's Democratic party is a nation-building political party.

Another meaningful classification of ideological parties is in terms of party objectives. *Revolutionary* parties are dedicated to the fundamental transformation of the political, economic, and social system in a society. The formation of revolutionary parties has been encouraged by population explosion, growing urbanization, the concentration of land ownership, rigid class structures, and the support of revolutionary movements by external powers in the developing countries of the world. More direct and immediate factors contributing to the growth of revolutionary parties include the proven success of similar groups in other countries. For example, following the ascendancy of Fidel Castro in his successful overthrow of the dictatorship of Fulgencio Batista in 1959, Fidelista movements sprang up in many countries of Latin America. First appearing in Peru, then in Guatemala, Venezuela, Uruguay, Argentina, and Bolivia, they gradually became an increasingly contentious force throughout the region. Such movements have spawned a number of insurgencies against the governing elites present in most dictatorial political systems – oligarchies supported by the armed forces or direct rule by the military. In Nicaragua, the Sandinista National Liberation Front (FSLN) overthrew the Somoza regime in 1979 and established the Sandinista party, which competed and claimed victory in the controversial elections of 1984. In El Salvador the Marxist Farabundo Marti National Liberation Front is the revolutionary arm of the insurgent guerrilla groups. But the National Revolutionary Movement (MNR), founded in 1965, that later helped to establish and became part of the Democratic Revolutionary Front (FDR) is an example of a revolutionary party. It advocates a moderate form of democratic socialism and is affiliated with the Socialist International. Revolutionary parties tend to be elitist and monopolistic, suppressing competition and mobilizing the population around the goals of the regime's leaders, rather than fostering the participation and representation of various groups in society.

In contrast to pragmatic and ideological parties are *special-interest* parties. These parties organize around a particular issue or interest and usually attract the support of an intensely dedicated and well-organized segment of the electorate. By so doing, special-interest parties focus on a dominant issue that the major parties are unwilling to endorse and sometimes can take enough votes away from the larger parties to change the outcome of elections. Such was the intention of the Equality Party, formed in Quebec as an English protest movement prior to the 1989 provincial election. When special-interest parties form a government, they are hard pressed to act out their political goals as soon as possible. If unsuccessful, political support may wane within the party as well as in the electorate. In 1984, the Parti Québécois was cast in the throes of bitter crisis because former premier René Lévesque announced his decision to jettison the goal of independence, the very raison d'être of his party's existence for over sixteen years. His statement triggered a series of backbench defections and ministerial resignations, including his own, that nearly tore the party apart. Under the leadership of Lévesque's successor, Pierre Marc Johnson, the P.Q. struggled with the policy of "national affirmation," which preached that Quebec would somehow assert a separate identity within the Canadian federal system. While in opposition to the Liberals, the party gradually drifted into a kind of ideological wilderness, eroding its electoral base of support and bringing enormous internal party pressures on Johnson to resign. As soon as the P.Q.'s new leader, Jacques Parizeau, took office in Montreal in April 1988, he reaffirmed the successionist aspirations of the party, returning to its special-interest character and restoring sovereignty as the number one goal of its followers.

In 1980 a new political party, the Greens, was created in West Germany because the established parties generally had been unresponsive to environmental issues. To gain rapid electoral strength, the anti-Nato Greens allied themselves with other political groupings to form the Green Alternative List (GAL). This strategy led to their electoral success in six Land legislatures by the end of 1982. In the West German federal election of 1983, the Greens gained sufficient popular support to capture twenty-seven seats in the Bundestag, and in the 1987 election the party received 8.3 percent of the vote, up from the 5.6 percent they won in 1983.

Parties representing special interests have emerged in many countries around the world. For example, the Green Party of Canada ran sixty-eight candidates and the Confederation of Regions Western party ran fifty-five candidates in the 1988 federal election. The Netherlands Farmers party, the Finnish Center party, and the Australian National Country party are other examples of special-interest parties. In some states, women's parties have joined in the political competition of the party system. Referring to themselves ideologically as the "third dimension," the Women's Alliance in Iceland rejected the pyramidal structure of other political parties. Without formally choosing a leader, the Women's Alliance captured 20 percent of the popular vote, awarding them ten of the sixty-three seats in the Lower House of the Albingi (parliament) in the Republic of Iceland in 1988. In Belgium, the Women's Unity party was organized in 1972 and similar parties have formed in Canada, France, and Norway. The Feminist Party of Canada has not been electorally competitive in the provinces or at the national level and is said to be dormant.

Functions of Political Parties

The institutional character of political parties in most states where they operate makes them primary political units; politics and government would be impossible without them. Political parties vary a great deal in their structure, goals, and actual functions performed in the political system. They differ in political ideology, in adherence to democratic and constitutional methods, in their legislative platforms, in the size of their membership, and in their socio-economic bases of support. They operate in political cultures with different traditions of partisanship, degrees of popular participation, and legal requirements regulating party competition. The Communist Party of the Soviet Union (CPSU), the Progressive Conservative Party of Canada, and the Likud (consolidation) party of Israel all illustrate the degrees by which parties differ in ideology, organization, and function.

Political Socialization

All political parties are agents of political learning. They interpret political events, initiate new political philosophies, or combine old ones to form new policies and platforms* and transmit political messages to the people through their candidates and the media. In the Soviet Union, the CPSU and its allied youth organizations, the Young Pioneers and the Komsomol are crucial agents of political socialization.[9]

In Canada all political parties have a political socialization function, but on a more limited scale and in competition with other parties, groups, and the media. Canadian political parties are just one among many competing institutions that openly and legitimately transmit political information. The family, schools, neighbourhood and peer groups, churches, professional and work groups, trade unions, business associations, and mass media also share in political socialization.[10] The socializing activities of Canada's political parties take place in the riding associations and local clubs and societies affiliated with them. Riding associations seek to recruit and initiate new members. They canvass voters, distribute literature, and invite candidates to make speeches. At the leadership level of the parties, clubs, caucus meetings, and parliamentary committees are constantly training and indoctrinating party members.

Leadership Recruitment

Parties vary in their recruitment of members, candidates, and leaders.[11] The techniques of recruitment include appointment, election, and party conventions*, where political leadership is formally slated. In most party systems, the government party has access to a large number of patronage appointments that enhance executive leadership. In one-party socialist states, the communist party directly selects and appoints many political officials or supervises their selection and tenure. In Canada, the recruitment function is directly affected by the nominating functions of competing political parties. Political parties are the main vehicles of presenting and selecting Canada's representatives and their leaders. But people can enter the political system as *independents* without formal ties to any of the competing political parties. The success rate of independent candidates who ran in many Canadian ridings is marginal. Even though political parties are extra-constitutional organizations in Canada's political system, there is no question that they give Canadians primary access to the parliamentary process.

Interest Articulation

Another important function of political parties in pluralistic political systems is to convert opinions, attitudes, beliefs, and preferences into coherent demands on the political system.[12] A plethora of interests requiring political expression exists in all societies. These groups can call for the legalization of abortion, legislation to institute capital punishment, the control of interest rates, the adjustment of tax laws to favour certain groups, or any interest that demands political representation and public visibility. Political parties vary in the intensity and extent to which they make and articulate the interests that are present in society. And the processes of interest articulation differ among the various political party systems. For example, in the Soviet Union – with *perestroika* – associations and interest groups can be independent of the CPSU. In some one-party states, interest-group bargaining takes place but the articulation of interests is still decided by the central agencies of the party establishment. Spokesmen for heavy, light, and distributive industries, as well as the navy, air force, and army, are permitted to press their points of view on the party hierarchy.

In Canada, a wide range of social and economic interests are organized. Within a highly competitive political system, political parties seek to attract the support of many of these interest groups by articulating their demands as either government policies or as opposition strategies. But most of Canada's interest groups prefer to remain non-partisan, avoiding the politically hazardous tactic of affiliating with one of the parties competing in the political system. To win the support of the various interests, political parties invite economic, regional, and local interest groups to make their claims and influence party policy through the activities of the riding associations, annual party conferences, and in the party committees in Parliament.

The basic difference between the Canadian and non-democratic patterns of interest articulation lies in the Canadian system of autonomous groups and in the necessity that parties compete for their support. In most non-democratic states people have learned that they cannot efficaciously make demands on the government without fear of severe reprisals. Interest-group activity and interest articulation exist, but only on a relatively small scale and under controlled circumstances – carried on at the local level and satisfied within those limits.

Interest Aggregation

Interest articulation is the expression of group demands by means of campaigns, the mass media, direct action, petition, lobbying, and the interpenetration of elites. Interest aggregation is the joining of interests together in such a way that they are related to the selection of government and party leaders and to the making and administering of policy.

In the Soviet Union the aggregative process traditionally took place solely within the confines of one legal party – the Communist party.[13] The party made efforts to recruit people who represented the KGB, the Komsomol, the military, physicians, lawyers, engineers, women, and certain nationalities. Workers, peasants, women, and non-slavic minorities tended to be under-represented at the highest party levels. But, with *glasnost'*, Soviet elites are now more sensitive to interest aggregation as a social exigency and cultivate clientelistic ties with a wider sample of interest groups than they did formerly.

The aggregative function of Canadian parties cuts across a wide variety of organized economic interests and professional and non-professional groups. But interest groups are aware that the structure of government and the political party in power are the two political realities that can bring about the materialization of their demands. Thus, the Cabinet, which itself usually is a microcosmic representation of many organized interests, is the target of concentrated group pressures. Organizations such as the Canadian Chamber of Commerce, the Canadian Manufacturers' Association, the Canadian Federation of Agriculture, and the Canadian Labour Congress make annual submissions to the Cabinet. When government is unresponsive, they will usually turn to opposition parties to carry their banner. In all cases where parties wish to aggregate the interests of groups, a process of bargaining takes place in which inducements are offered to business and labour, specific industries and professions, and the various regions of the country. Even satirical interests may be aggregated by a political party as exemplified in the Rhinoceros party.

Policy Making and Implementation

In democratic political systems, political parties may play a crucial role in formulating and implementing public policy.[14] However, because of the competitive nature of democratic political systems, organizations other than political parties also shape the policy process. Besides political parties, interest groups and the civil service participate in policy making. Sometimes the party system itself reduces the ability of political parties to formulate and implement policies in line with their ideology and their base of popular support. Especially in European democratic countries, where multiparty systems abound, few parties ever gain a majority in the legislature at either the national or local level. In these states, parties need to participate in coalitions in order to form governments; this procedure usually requires the compromise of policy positions.

In most political systems, political parties are limited in their policy-making roles by the exigencies of the executive branch of government. Frequently there is a gap between a party's policy positions and its government programs and actions. As a general rule, party activists are more seriously committed to party philosophy and the ideology behind policies than are elected officeholders. Elected members who hold Cabinet positions have a broader constituency and must gain rapport not just with party ideologues but with a plurality of voters, who generally relate more to political action than to abstract ideology. In most parties, candidates view success at the polls as the primary party objective because without electoral victory the party cannot implement its programs. The overriding desire to win seats in a legislature or to form the political executive reduces ideological consistency. Nevertheless, political parties do influence policy by shaping legislators' voting behaviour and the attitudes of political leaders toward specific issues.

In democratic party systems membership in a political party usually produces a high degree of cohesion* when legislators vote for bills. Generally, left-wing* parties demonstrate a stronger party cohesion in legislative voting than do right-wing* parties, partly because they take their ideology more seriously.[15] This division has also been true in Canada, where the New Democratic Party demonstrates stronger legislative and caucus loyalty than do the Conservative and Liberal parties. But in Britain the reverse is true: Labour MPs tend to split into more divisive policy-based factions* than do the Tories. In the1980s, this factionalism led to a partial disintegration of the Labour party when thirteen Labour MPs formed the Social Democratic party. In the United States, Republicans and Democrats reveal weaker legislative cohesion than do Canadian or West European parties, mainly because the parliamentary system necessitates greater party discipline to sustain the government in office.

In the Soviet Union, until *demokratizatsiya*, the enactment and implementation of government policy was dominated by the ideological perspective of the CPSU, particularly the Politburo. Ministries and their bureaucracies were the implementing agencies of party policies. The *soviets* (councils) – which are the formal equivalents to legislative bodies in democratic systems – functioned as legitimators after the decisions on policies had already been reached. *Demokratizatsiya* decentralizes decision-making authority away from the traditional command and order style of the Communist party to the soviets at the municipal, regional, republic, and national levels, as well as to other competing parties and groups.

In Canada, the policy-making and implementing process is highly complex. It is true that parties do generate and compete in the making of public policy, but the conversion process from party platform to government policy is restricted by bureaucratic and parliamentary procedures. Opposition parties advance policies of job creation but quickly temper the implementation of these policies when they become governing parties. Actually, the Liberal and Progressive Conservative parties are the only two parties that have governed Canada at the national level.[16] In both cases, upper-echelon civil servants (deputy ministers and assistant deputy ministers) greatly influence the adaptation of party policy to public policy. Departmental officials reformulate the bulk of party policy within the administrative realities of budgets and implementation. Civil servants sensitize their political masters to the limited number of policy alternatives available to a government in the face of fiscal and monetary restrictions.[17] In addition, before any policy decision is implemented, there are many consultations that must take place among Cabinet ministers, advisory committees in Parliament, and provincial premiers.

Political-Party Systems

There are many ways to classify political parties. Numerous typologies have already been designed: all the existing ones are largely impressionistic, e.g., personalistic parties, revolutionary parties. Another type of classification involves the number of parties in the party system. In this typology, it is assumed that legislative representation is a meaningful reflection of real party influence in the national system, the only exceptions being those parties that are outlawed or denied representation, and those exceptional circumstances when parties decide not to participate for strategic reasons. It is important to note that legislative representation is not always a reflection of party popularity. Parties may be popular but cannot win representation. In fact, representation is more than anything a reflection of the impact of an electoral system (i.e., single-member district or proportional representation) upon the success of parties. And in the case of most authoritarian states, no assumption should be made that legislative representation is an indication of power, for legislatures in non-democratic states are not usually powerful. Nevertheless, parties do compete for legislative representation, which is an important factor in determining a party's relationship with other parties, if not with the institutions of government.[18] The classification of party systems adopted in this study distinguishes single-party systems from pluralistic-party systems.

One-Party States

The concept "party system" implies competition between two or more political parties. States without political parties or with only one political party are therefore not systemic in terms of party competition. Prior to World War II, one-party systems appeared for the first time under communist and fascist regimes. They were unique because they outlawed all political competition and served as instruments of social control. They adhered to one all-encompassing orthodox ideology that outlined the conditions of political recruitment and determined the economic, military, and social strategies of the state.

Today, this type of party continues to flourish in non-democratic socialist states. In states such as China and Vietnam, the party has ceased to be a mere reflection of contemporary political values in the Western sense and functions instead as a permanent institution for which the government serves as an administrative agency. In these states, the party has established itself as a sort of supragovernment, a supreme decision-making and policy-making authority. This peculiar and historically novel scheme has merited the label "party state."[19] This accords with the Marxist dictum that the state is a mere instrument of the ruling class. In some of these states, such as Poland and Hungary, the traditional legitimacy of the communist party has been challenged in democratic elections that have shifted popular representation to competing groups, i.e., to the Polish union, Solidarity.

Party-centred decision making maintains the monolithic and monopolistic position of the party, claiming singular legitimacy and legality. In states where this framework exists, if decision making were in the government, the party would have less social status, while the government, with its specialized functions, would be more subject to interest-group pressures and party influence. In these political systems it is imperative to keep authority within the party framework in order to maintain a coherent, organized elite group, bound by ideological purpose, to control and supervise the state and ensure the necessary unity of the political system. Sometimes very strong rulers such as Castro, Stalin, and Tito have taken decision making entirely onto themselves, concentrating decision making almost entirely into the personalistic style of their leadership.

Since World War II, single-party systems have appeared and spread throughout the Third World, creating a number of versions of one-party systems. Less ideologically orthodox and disciplined than in one-party socialist states, these parties do not penetrate or extensively control all levels of the social infrastructure. However, in the political realm they monopolize the recruitment of political elites and permit no other party competition. As in states where the official party aspires to communism, only one party is legal, yet in a few instances, one or more additional government parties may be authorized, provided they are regime-sponsored and operate within the strict guidelines established by the government.

Single-party systems also differ in their internal organization, leadership, and their degree of authoritarianism. They are usually more elitist than mass parties, more personalistic than bureaucratic and collectivist in their decision making, and, once in power, surrender the policy-making and implementation functions to the government and state apparatus. Ideologically, these types of parties combine nationalism with an eclectic philosophy of modernization, mixing elements of traditional agrarian societies*. These parties advance the need for dictatorship in order to overcome problems of corruption, disunity, or separatism, and counter such difficulties with enforced political integration, socialization, and repression.

Many one-party states are civilian regimes, most of which appear in Africa, the Caribbean, and the Middle East, such as Guinea-Bissau, Guyana, and South Yemen. African military regimes with one-party systems include Angola and Ethiopia; in Central and South America they include Guatemala, Paraguay, and Peru; and in the Middle East and Asia they appear in Algeria, Iraq, Libya, Syria, Afghanistan, Bangladesh, Burma, Indonesia, Taiwan, and South Korea.

Two-Party Competitive Systems

A two-party political system is one in which political power and governmental offices tend to fluctuate between two major political parties. This structure does not preclude the presence of minor parties in electoral competition. In all political systems where it has evolved, the two-party system has never remained pure. Numerous third parties have formed to challenge one or both of the dominant parties. And although these third parties may tend to disappear with time, their presence is seldom without influence. The chief function of minor parties in a two-party competitive system has been to bring new issues, or new ways of looking at old issues, to the political agenda. As they succeed in forcing new policies on the older, established parties, these third parties tend to disappear. This process is one of the ways in which the party system stays alive and remains responsive to changing conditions and issues.

Some analysts have attempted to quantify the system, not so much for precision as to locate the parameters in which two dominant political parties compete: for Ronald McDonald, a two-party competitive system reveals two dominant parties each receiving approximately 40 percent of the seats but not more than 60 percent of the total number of seats in the legislature.[20] The two-party competitive system exists only in some English-speaking democracies, and appears in some twenty countries. The British party system is frequently cited as the classic example.[21] Even so, over a dozen minor parties also compete with the British Conservative and Labour parties. The bipolar character of the British party system appears in other states that have at one time or another come under direct British influence, including the United States and the Commonwealth countries, such as Barbados, Jamaica, and Malta. In Ireland, the United Ireland party (Fine Gael: party of the Irish) and the Republican party (Fianna Fáil) have been the two dominant parties.

As for the United States, it is not difficult to imagine a multiparty system in a country so diverse. There could feasibly be a party of labour, of southern whites, of blacks, chicanos, of western agriculture, and so on. In fact, the contrast between the galaxy of American interest groups and the presence throughout their political history of only two parties is striking, notwithstanding the fact that at different times the United States has had more than two parties competing in its federal election. The two-party competitive system has an extraordinary heritage: the Democrats descend from the party of Thomas Jefferson founded for the election of 1800, and the Republican party has its roots in the time of Abraham Lincoln. Three factors set the United States on the road to biparty politics. First, since the War of Independence, two main political groupings (initially known as the Federalists and the Jeffersonian Democrats) organized around conflicting economic interests and built coalitions of support within the country. Second, the adoption of the single-member legislative district (plurality) has worked to discourage lasting third-party movements,

Party standings in the Canadian House of Commons 1900-1988

Date of Election	Liberal	Unionist* Conserv.	Pro-gressive	CCF NDP	Social Credit	Ralliement Creditists	Indepen-dents	Total Seats
Nov. 7,1900	133	80						213
Nov. 3,1904	138	75					1	214
Oct. 26,1908	135	85					1	221
Sept. 21,1911	87	134					1	221
Dec. 17,1917	82	153*						235
Dec. 6,1921	116	50	64				5	235
Oct. 29,1925	99	116	24				6	245
Sept.14,1926	128	91	20				6	245
July 28,1930	91	137	12				5	245
Oct. 14,1935	173	40		7	17		8	245
Mar. 26,1940	181	40		8	10		6	245
June 11,1945	125	67		28	13		12	245
June 27,1949	193	41		13	10		5	262
Aug. 10,1953	171	51		23	15		5	265
June 10,1957	105	112		25	19		4	265
Mar. 31,1958	49	208		8				265
June 18,1962	100	116		19	30			265
Apr. 8,1963	129	95		17	24			265
Nov. 8,1965	131	97		21	5	9	2	265
June 25,1968	155	72		22		14	1	264
Oct. 30,1972	109	107		31	15		2	264
July 8,1974	141	95		16	11		1	264
May 22,1979	114	136		26	6			282
Feb. 18, 1980	147	103		32				282
Sept. 4,1984	40	211		30			1	282
Nov. 21,1988	83	169		43				295

*Unionist: The conscriptionist Conservative government of Robert Borden, formed from a coalition of English Liberals and Conservatives.

Source: Adapted from Paul Fox and Graham White, *Politics Canada*, 6th ed. (Toronto: McGraw-Hill Ryerson Ltd. 1987), 416.

Table 11.1

because only those parties that have a chance of attracting the most votes have the political momentum to continue functioning as independent groups.[22] Finally, a major institutional incentive for preserving the two-party system has been the presidency. Because only one party can win the presidency in any given election, there is little point in voting for the presidential candidate of a party that has no chance of winning.

Canada's party system retains its biparty character despite the consistent representation of minor parties in the House of Commons over the past three decades.[23] In fact, the Liberals and the Conservatives are the only two parties that have ever governed at the federal level. However, if we look at Canada's party system from the perspective of party competition, a multiparty system is discernible. For example, in the 1988 federal election, twelve registered parties competed for seats in the House of Commons but only three were successful at electing candidates. The single-member-district (plurality) electoral system almost eliminates the representation of smaller parties in Canada's parliamentary institutions. In addition, only three parties, the Liberals, Progressive Conservatives, and New Democrats (NDP) ran candidates in 295 ridings. Minor parties, also called "small" or "fringe" parties run substantially fewer candidates and consequently reduce their chances of winning

Registered minor parties in Canada
Federal elections 1984 and 1988

Party	Number of candidates 1984	Number of candidates 1988
Rhinoceros	89	74
Parti Nationaliste du Québec	75	0
Libertarian party	72	88
Party for the Commonwealth of Canada	65	59
The Green Party of Canada	60	68
Confederation of Regions Western party	55	51
Communist party	52	52
Social Credit	51	9
The Reform party	0	72
Christian Heritage Party (first election campaign, 1988)	0	63

Table 11.2

seats.[24] With these parties the political message ranges from the extreme right to the extreme left to the just plain silly.

Many of the small parties are driven by a cause: for the Libertarians the goal is to cut dramatically the size of government, and to reduce taxes and social services. The Party for the Commonwealth of Canada follows the writings of the convicted American extremist, Lyndon LaRouche, who forecasts global financial collapse. The Green Party of Canada is committed to cleaning up the environment and to making a mainstream issue in the Canadian political system. The Christian Heritage party, which ran candidates for the first time in 1988, wants a return to Christian values, is opposed to abortion, is for capital punishment, wants to toughen immigration laws, and would like to balance the budget. The Reform party is after a stronger voice for the West and believes that western Canada will never achieve equal treatment within Confederation without Senate reform. For the Confederation of Regions Western party one of the issues was language, to unite English speaking people of Canada against government-mandated bilingualism. The Communist party called for curbing the power of big business as the real guarantee of independence for Canada. For all these parties the goal is to be taken seriously by targeting discontented voters. But with the Rhinoceros party, mania is the message, and their campaign was strictly for laughs. They satirize big-party policies and mock the political process in Canada. In 1980 the Rhinoceros party came close to getting elected in two Quebec ridings, stood as Canada's fourth most popular party in 1984, and called itself the fringe party to beat in the 1988 election.

On the provincial level one encounters a variety of party systems, not all of which are examples of the classic two-party type. British Columbia, Nova Scotia, and Manitoba reveal interparty competition between, and the representation of, two parties. In British Columbia the action is between the Social Credit and the NDP; in Nova Scotia and Newfoundland the electoral struggle is between the Liberals and the Conservatives; and in Manitoba, the Conservatives, Liberals, and the NDP fight for the reins of government. In Quebec, three parties have governed the province in the post-war period, the Liberals, Parti Québécois, and the now-defunct Union Nationale. The case of the Parti Québécois served to illustrate how a provincial minor third party could stun itself, as well as the country, by springing to power, weathering political storms, and staging impressive recoveries until the Liberals were returned to power under the leadership of Robert Bourassa. And in Ontario, the Liberals last won a provincial election in 1937; the Conservatives ("Big Blue Machine") had governed continuously since 1943. Until June 1985, when the Liberals, with assistance from the NDP, gained power on a vote of no confidence, Ontario was a singular provincial example of a one-party-dominant system. In its 1987 election Ontario gave the Liberals a strong majority with 95 of the 130 seats and realigned the province in the direction of two-party competition. But in the same year in New Brunswick a rejuvenated Liberal party under the stewardship of Frank McKenna won all the 58 seats in the provincial legislature, a first-time political occurrence in that province.

On examination, Canadian politics deviates from a pure two-party model not only because of the presence of third parties, but also because one party – the Liberal party – has dominated federal government in Canada throughout most of this century (see table 11.1). Of the twenty-six federal governments since 1900, the Liberals formed nineteen of them. If we think that the two most successful parties should be roughly equal in the two-party system, that they should alternate frequently in power, and that almost every federal election is "up for grabs," the Canadian experience will likely disappoint us. Instead of being a relationship of two roughly equal competitors, the relationship between Canada's two government parties has been that of dominant to dominated. That is, one party has repeatedly formed a government, controlled the Senate, selected most of the Supreme Court justices, and elaborated public policy during its dominance, with relatively few interceptions of power by the other party.

Nevertheless, the two-party system, as it persists in Canada, has been extolled as a model of political stability. As in its British and American versions, the Canadian system is considered to be a source of continuity and compromise. The ideological distance between the two parties is very slight, driving the party system toward moderation at the centre. Narrow ideological distance among the successful competing parties means that there is a general agreement on fundamentals, to which all represented parties subscribe. Historically, Canada's electoral system has favoured the larger parties, so that the Liberals and Progressive Conservatives together usually capture over 80 percent of the seats in the House of Commons. In 1988, both parties together gained almost 75 percent of the seats in the House of Commons. This result confirms that parliamentary politics at the federal level is two-party, even if that of the whole country is not.

A stable biparty system has emerged in other states. Even though proportional representation is the applied formula in its electoral system, West Germany has produced a stable two-party system within a multiparty structure. Since 1961, two major parties – the Christian Democratic Union, with its Bavarian affiliate the Christian Social Union (CDU/CSU), and the Social Democratic Party (SPD) – have accounted for over 75 percent of the popular vote. However, the smallest of the established parties, the Free Democratic Party (FDP) has captured between 5 and 10 percent of the vote, and has often controlled enough votes to have a pivotal role in forming government coalitions. The business-oriented FDP generally acts as a moderating influence, limiting the leftist tendencies of the SPD or the conservative leanings of the CDU/CSU. In 1983 and 1987, the FDP formed such a coalition with the CDU/CSU led by Chancellor Helmut Kohl. In Costa Rica, proportional representation tends to create a disproportionate influence of minor parties on the two major parties, the governing National Liberation party and the Social Christian Unity Party. And, in Colombia, a biparty system between its Conservative and Liberal parties has existed for over 100 years.

Pluralistic-Party Systems

A multiparty system exists where three or more parties contest elections, gain representation, and/or form coalitions with the governing party. Such a system may host a variety of major parties as well as minor parties that vie for political power and government offices. It is often necessary for a coalition of interests to work together in order to carry out a program of government. The number of organized political parties varies in each multiparty system. In the 1988, Israeli elections, over twenty parties competed. Spain has fifty-five organized parties running candidates when elections are held.

Many factors converge to generate a multiparty system. The adoption of proportional representation and the expansion of the suffrage usually encourage its development. A lack of political consensus also contributes to the formation of a multiparty system. The widespread presence of conflicting political values and philosophies usually fosters the emergence of opposing groups who seek to change the structure of institutions or the formal policy-making process itself. Socio-economic factors, such as ethnicity, language, or religion, contribute to the development of a pluralistic-party system. In Belgium, for example, different parties represent the French-, Flemish-, and German-speaking people. And with regard to religious orientations, Christian democratic parties appear in most Western European states, as well as in a large number in the Caribbean and Latin America. Some parties are also formed to represent the interests of special groups, such as labour and women. But multiparty systems are more reflective of the ideological differences that evolve in a given society, as witnessed by the presence of anarchist groups, communist parties, nationalist parties, revolutionary parties, and socialist parties. These parties perceive concrete events in light of abstract ideas. Ideology is at a premium, while bargaining and compromise are superfluous. This general situation is both the cause and effect of a pluralistic party system and thus runs counter to the basic dualist tendency in two-party systems.

Multiparty systems can be *one-party dominant* and *multiparty competitive*. In a one-party-dominant system, a single party wins approximately 60 percent or more of the seats in a legislature and two or more other parties usually win less than approximately 40 percent of the seats.[25] Mexico has been a good example of a country with a one-party-dominant multiparty system. The Partido Revolucionario Institutional (PRI) has never had one of its nominees for president or governor defeated in elections since the party was founded in 1929. Only since the 1970s have other parties been able to win appreciable numbers of seats at municipal levels and in the lower house of Congress. But in the 1988 national elections the PRI turned in its worst performance in 59 years, plunging from its traditional 70 percent to 50.36 percent of the presidential vote, and even losing seats in the Senate for the first time. In the Chamber of Deputies the PRI won 260 of the 500 seats, thus at least temporarily generating a more multiparty character to Mexico's party system. Other examples of single–party dominance are India, with its Indian National Congress Party, and the Bahamas, with its Progressive Liberal party.

In some multiparty systems, one party is sufficiently strong to dominate the others but the dominance of the system is much weaker than in the one-party-dominant multiparty system. There is a greater amount of challenge from opposition parties and a higher frequency of fluctuation of power among competing parties. When one party appears to dominate the system, incentives arise for opposition parties to form coalitions, either to minimize the strength of the government party or to form a government in order to prevent the dominant party from coming to power. For example, in the national elections held in El Salvador in 1982, José Napoleon Duarte's Christian Democrats won 35.3 percent of the votes or 24 of the 60 seats in the Constituent Assembly. The ultraconservative National Republican Alliance (ARENA) won 25.7 percent or 19 seats, but managed to form a working coalition with other right-wing groups to take control of the assembly. In the elections held in 1988, Duarte's ruling Christian Democratic Party was ousted from power, and ARENA formed a government under the leadership of Alfredo Cristiani, capturing 55 percent of the popular vote and 31 seats. Duarte could not successfully form a winning coalition with any of the other parties competing in the election. Thus, even though one party may dominate in terms of the attraction of popular votes, coalition governments are formed with great difficulty, and may vary in their composition from government to government.

Multiparty-competitive systems can also demonstrate high fragmention when no single party dominates the system. In this looser expression of party competition no single party wins more than 40 percent of the legislative seats.[26] As a general rule, parties enter and exit the electoral system with relative ease. Party formation and cohesion is often based on personalities, transient issues, or economic and political events that encourage ephemeral party organizations. Within these multiparty systems, coalitions are formed with ease. Opportunism, pragmatism, and mutual self-interest are the primary forces that encourage coalitions, which usually break down and result in frequent general elections or the interference and dominance of a strong overriding executive. Denmark, for example, with its more than two-dozen parties, has averaged one general election every two years since the 1960s. Other states, such as Bolivia, the Dominican Republic, Ecuador, Finland, the Netherlands, Spain, Thailand, and Turkey, have experienced varying degrees of political instability in their multiparty systems.

The most extreme cases of fragmentation have been France and Italy. Because of the large number of weak parties in both countries, most parties represent only a small segment of the electorate. Many parties simply cannot hope to claim to represent the interests of the entire electorate. In the 1986 French parliamentary elections, the Socialist party, which has never been strong enough to assume control of the government itself, held more seats (216) than either of the two parties (Rally for the Republic 148 and the Union for French Democracy 128) that formed a coalition government in the Chamber of Deputies. The multiplicity of Italian parties has been the major factor contributing to political instability in that country, resulting in nearly fifty governments since World War II. The Christian Democratic party has led all government coalitions for over 40 years but usually is unable to organize a parliamentary majority without the co-operation of the left-of-centre parties, as exemplified in the centre-left coalition of 1988.

In most multiparty systems, the maintenance of coalitions between elections is exceedingly difficult. "Gentlemen's agreements" based on ideology, personalism, friendship, money, and patronage are frequently offered to induce post-election allegiance. There is little doubt that parliamentary instability is often the by-product of intense ideological competition in multiparty systems. However, if political stability is defined as orderly constitutional change of government, without violence or extra-parliamentary intervention, then multiparty systems are neither the most stable nor the most unstable. But if political stability is defined in terms of the constitutional tenure of governments and their ability predictably to carry out their policies, then countries in this category tend to demonstrate more frequent instability than one-party, biparty, and dominant-multiparty systems.

Party Organization and Structure

Political parties represent three distinct entities: candidates and officeholders, citizens who are party members or identify with the party, and the formal party organization. This last can range from a few legislators who co-ordinate strategies and policies under a shared party label to a decentralized party structure open to anyone interested in becoming a candidate to a highly centralized and almost closed party organization characteristic of single-party state systems.

Political parties reflect essentially two organizational arrangements: *hierarchy* or *stratarchy*. Hierarchically organized parties are structured so that the distribution of power, privilege, and authority is systemic and unequal, with control of the party organization by a few people at the top. Robert Michels was the first student of organizational behaviour to note the iron law of oligarchy* in party structures.[27] Under this arrangement a full-time professional staff dominates the party organization and the perspectives of the leader may not necessarily be those of the members. Stratarchy is characteristic of democratic political parties where power is shared by the leader with several layers of the party organization.[28] The downward deference of the party leadership is a result of the need for mass support, the voluntary nature of the party organization, the few who are dedicated to working for the party between elections, and the absence of punitive measures party leaders have over party workers who are indifferent or recalcitrant. The leader depends on the policy input and support of the membership below, while party leaders at the lower levels need the stewardship skills of the national leader.

The organization of political parties usually reflects the organization of the state, i.e., unitary or federal. In most federal states, national parties are really confederations of subnational party organizations, held together by national committees. The degree to which the national party regards itself as "integrated" or "federated" with the subnational party organizations will vary from one electoral system to another. Factors that can determine the affiliation of national and subnational party organizations are (a) the popularity and co-operation of the national and subnational party leaders, (b) the criteria of party membership, (c) the degree of personnel interaction between the national and subnational organizations, (d) integrated or separate fund-raising strategy, (e) the congruence of party policy and ideology, and (f) the allegiance of voters within the federal system.

In the United States there is generally little contact between state and national party organizations. In a majority of states, party chairpersons are not frequently involved in national committee affairs. Of the two political parties, the Republicans at the state level tend to receive more staff assistance, financial help, research and polling data, and campaign instructions from the national party organization than do state Democrats from their national organization. But in both parties, the national organization tends not to intervene in state activities, unless asked.[29] In Canada, the co-ordination of political strategies between the federal and provincial wings of the same party tends to vary from province to province, but in general can be characterized as independent. Parties of the same name may, from time to time, share workers and facilities but generally tend to keep their distance at the highest levels of party organization.[30] Interprovincial party ties also tend to be weak, with the exception of the New Democratic Party, which maintains more organizational and financial linkages between provincial parties as well as with the national party.

The organization of Canada's three parliamentary parties is quite similar. Each has a *parliamentary wing*, which consists of the leader and the party caucus who are the front-line in the legislative battles in the House of Commons and the Senate. There is also an *extra-parliamentary wing*, consisting of the national party headquarters and a national executive and its committees, which are dominated by the party leader whose image and performance affects the party organization at three levels. The first is the grass-roots organization at the *constituency level*. From here, federal candidates are nominated, delegates to conventions are elected, volunteer personnel and members are recruited, and fund-raising campaigns are initiated. The *provincial level* is next on the pyramid of the national party organization. At this level, party faithfuls plan and co-ordinate the strategies that are employed at the constituency level. Members of the executive at this level are responsible for all the federal constituencies in the province. The apex of the extra-parliamentary party organization is the *national level*. The national association normally organizes a biannual convention to stimulate debate, consider new policy directions, and elect party officials.[31] Conventions are also the platforms for electing party leaders. Because the main impact of contemporary parties comes through elections, the party organization is an apparatus oriented toward the convention and the selection or retention of a national leader. The predictable occurrence of party conventions provides an opportunity for competitive party members to bring about change, as well as for those who want to protect the status quo. In the final analysis, conventions are vehicles for important communications among competing political parties, their membership, and the independent voter.

Party Membership

From an organizational point of view, a political party in Canada is a small inner circle composed of officeholders, candidates, a professional staff, and a few party faithfuls. But we often hear that someone is a "member" of the Liberal Party of Canada, or the New Democratic Party. Yet generations of political scientists, lawyers, judges, and politicians have been unable to agree on exactly what it means to be a member of a party. Some see membership as party identification – a voter's sense of psychological attachment to a party that goes beyond merely voting for the party. Although this concept is useful to social scientists, party identification has no legal significance. A second definition of membership has to do with the process of "joining" a political party by meeting a set of criteria such as registration, dues, committee work, etc. In some European states people "apply" for membership in the Christian Democratic party, and the Socialist party, are accepted, pay dues, and carry a membership card. In the United States legal membership in some states involves registration as a Democrat or a Republican. The main purpose of registration in these states is to prevent adherents of one party from voting in another party's primary. Some parties, such as the Communist party, have strict criteria so that they can exclude people who do not meet their ideological standards.

In general, membership in a party is engaging in its activities, with or without the process of formal admission procedures. A party consists of all those people who participate in any of the following activities: running for office under the party label, seeking nomination for candidacy, contributing money, working for a candidate, attending meetings, voting as a delegate.

Party Finance

Party organizations, activities, and campaigns take huge amounts of money. Money is needed to pay for office space or the purchase of land and building, staff salaries (administration and research), telephone bills, computers, postage, travel expenses, campaign literature, polling, and advertising in the mass media. In the 1990s most political parties in democratic political systems must make strenuous and systematic efforts to broaden the base of their contributors. In most democratic states there are four primary classes of contributors: individuals, corporations, interest groups (defined broadly to include trade unions and private organizations), and the public treasury. For political parties the ability to attract money is related to (a) the quality of candidates offered, especially the leader, (b) the party organization between elections and the campaign organization during elections, (c) performance in past elections and standing in the polls, (d) the capacity to present issues, and (e) promises put forward by the leader and the candidates.

Financial contributions to political parties are the most common form of political activity. But it is difficult to generalize about money and political parties because so many governments have different rules and laws to regulate party financing and spending. However, the reasons for drafting legislation to regulate party financing tend to be similar among governments. The first is public disclosure: the amount of money parties raise and spend is brought out in the open; second, regulations place limitations on the amounts of money parties can spend on elections and other activities, thus reducing the influence of money on politicians; third, to reduce the dependence of political parties on wealthy donors by partially subsidizing election costs with public funds; fourth, to require parties to record their financial activities and to audit their books; and fifth to discourage corruptions of party fund-raising by internal and external auditing requirements.

In Canada, the *Elections Expenses Act* 1974 (with its 1983 amendments) is the legal instrument that governs how political parties raise and spend their funds.[32] Prior to this act, corporate donations were the source of most (75–90 percent) of the money raised by the two major political parties in Canada. The New Democratic Party was the exception because it drew most of its support from members, trade unions, and grass-roots fund-raising strategies. Since the passage of the Elections Expenses Act, all parties have gained greater access to individual contributions because tax credits for political donations are embodied in the legislation,(allowing 75 percent on contributions up to $100, 50 percent between $100 and $550, and 33.3 percent on amounts over $550). Also important in the law are the provisions for disclosure, requiring parties to file financial reports and to name contributors donating $100 or more. The legislation has reduced the financial burden of political parties by providing reimbursements of half the permissible spending for candidates who win 15 percent of the total votes cast in their ridings.

The major effect of regulatory legislation on political-party finance in Canada has been to facilitate a more equitable access to donors in categories such as corporations, individuals, and interest groups. Both the Liberal and Progressive Conservative parties have lessened their dependence on contributions from corporations since the mid 1970s from as much as 90 percent to 50 percent or less. Not surprisingly, the NDP raises very little money from corporations but relies heavily on individual and union donors. Contributions from individuals have grown substantially but the higher costs of administering this kind of fund-raising campaign can override the benefits it would appear to provide to a political party.

In order to avoid some of the spending restrictions in the legislation, all three parliamentary parties have increased expenditures outside the designated campaign periods when expenditures are limited only by a party's ability to raise money. The growth of non-election spending indicates a higher level of interparty competition and reflects the importance that party leaders assign to maintaining strong party organizations between elections.

Money is a frequently misunderstood aspect of politics. Without adequate financing a political party's chances of success are seriously hampered. Money buys attention, not necessarily votes. Parties must be able to reach the electorate not only by door-to-door campaigning, but also by the expensive process of slick media advertising, targeted mailings, and the use of trained public-relations specialists. If a party spends a large sum of money, the important variables are how well it is spent and how expenditures compare with those of competing parties.

Communist Parties

Among all ideological parties that have ever won power or that compete with other political parties in competitive-party systems, communist parties are ideologically the most rigid, and organizationally the most structured.[33] The principles of communism are drawn from the philosophies and practices of Karl Marx (1818–1883), his collaborator Frederick Engels (1820–1895), V.I. Lenin (1870–1924), Joseph Stalin (1879–1953), and Mao Tse Tung (1893–1976). No communist party is ideologically identical to any other, but all party members are expected to master the principles of Marxism-Leninism, as interpreted by national party elites. Thus, notwithstanding the post-World War II emergence of different national roads to communism, most communist ideologies accept Marx and Lenin as their philosophical forefathers. Regardless of which communist system one studies – the

Chinese, Cuban, Soviet, or Vietnamese – all political leaders use Marxism-Leninism to justify their public policies. The Communist Party of Canada, formed in 1921, is also a Marxist-Leninist organization. Under the leadership of Tim Buck, the party adapted its strategies and tactics to the prevailing Soviet line. Like its counterpart in the United States, the Communist Party of Canada has played a minor role in the Canadian electoral system. In both the 1984 and 1988 federal elections, the party unsuccessfully ran fifty-two candidates, attracting less than 1 percent of the electoral vote. Perhaps more important than its electoral presence is the party's involvement in the trade-union movement. Yet the party has only a marginal impact on Canada's political system.

Today, communist parties in Italy, France, Finland, Ireland, Spain, and Portugal receive electoral support from manual workers and intellectuals because they advocate a command economy*. Where they hold power, communist parties run the economy. There may be variations in the application of socialist economic planning, particularly in China where peasants are the backbone of the Communist party. In Latin America, all political systems host communist parties that operate either openly when legal or clandestinely when outlawed. Although communist parties are small in size, constituting only about 1 percent of the total population, they draw most of their support from urban wage earners, labourers, the lower middle class, and students – and not from the peasantry.

All governing communist parties have come to power by the violent overthrow of the previous regime or as a consequence of major international conflict. No communist government has ever been "democratically" elected. In Albania, China, Cuba, the USSR, Vietnam, and Yugoslavia an indigenous Communist party ascended to power. But in Afghanistan, Bulgaria, Czechoslovakia, the German Democratic Republic, Hungary, Mongolia, North Korea, Poland, and Romania the Communist party came to power with the external assistance of the Soviet army. Puppet regimes* were established in Cambodia, Laos, and Vietnam.

In most communist states there is only one governing party that usually excludes any other political groups from legitimately challenging its position. Some communist political systems such as North Korea's have permitted "allied parties" that are subordinate and may join with the governing communist party in a "national front". A growing number now permits the competition of other parties. No communist party-controlled political system admits to having achieved communism to date: the implementation of a communist society is a goal of the future.

The rigidity of communist ideology is fostered and protected by a hierarchical and pyramidal party structure. At the top of the organization is a small group of party officials called the *politburo* (as in Cuba and the Soviet Union) or the *presidium* (as in Yugoslavia). This inner circle of powerful decision makers determines the direction of party doctrine and transmits its directives down through lower party levels and across to the state and governmental apparatus. The party *secretariat* maintains the purity of the ideological and policy decisions of the politburo by supervising lower party organizations and monitoring internal party loyalty and discipline. Below the central level of the party organization are the local-party and primary-party organizations that scrutinize the application of ideological goals. Communist parties also encourage the development of *cadres* – community leaders that agitate and mobilize public support for the party at the local levels. The Chinese have been particularly successful in organizing cadres for ideological purposes, to apply thought-reform to "correct" the ideas of recalcitrant party members and intellectuals who deviate from the official party line.

Socialist Parties

In "communist" states, socialism is a historical phase that must be completed before communism emerges as the final political synthesis in human social development. China is officially "a socialist state of the dictatorship of the proletariat led by the working class and based on the alliance of workers and peasants." But the socialist parties that have formed in Western democratic states view socialism as the highest stage of political and economic development. They attract the greatest support in the democratic states of Europe: Austria, Belgium, France, Great Britain, Holland, Scandinavia, and West Germany. They are also units of political strength in Australia, Canada, New Zealand, and many of the states of Africa, Asia, and Latin America.

In contrast to the communist parties, the democratic-socialist parties seek to secure greater economic equality without the violent overthrow of the capitalist system. Political democracy is the primary goal of all democratic-socialist parties. When forming a government or in coalition with other political parties, socialist parties enact comprehensive social-service programs: old-age pensions, family allowance, health care, income supplements, and unemployment compensation. They also believe that economic growth should be stimulated largely through government investment in a modified market economy made up of public and private enterprises. In this way, democratic-socialist parties work toward peacefully transforming capitalist-based economies in the Western economic tradition into a more equalitarian* socialist mode of production.

All socialist parties adopt any one of three approaches to the economic order: *corporate socialism*, *welfare-state socialism*, and *market socialism*. Parties that promote corporate socialism, such as the Partido Socialista de Ecuador (PSE), assume that experts and professionals – economists, engineers, managers, and scientists – can best plan the economy to serve the public good. They see the role of a socialist government as a co-ordinator of public and private corporations to achieve full employment, low inflation, and the provision of social programs to the disadvantaged. Welfare-state socialists, as in Canada, Sweden, and West Germany, reject the state-planning corporate brand of socialism. Government should act as a referee in the economy, balancing the goals of public and private enterprises in a mixed economy.[34] Socialist parties that advocate market socialism, such as the Socialist Party of Peru and the Argentine Socialist party, want an economy in which the government owns the means of production but yields control of production decisions to decentralized workers' councils. Workers decide on investment and production goals in the marketplace. The role of the government is to rectify market inequalities in a decentralized market system controlled by workers.

Socialism in Canada

In Canada, democratic socialism maintains a low ideological profile.[35] When it first appeared on Canada's political horizon, socialism was a movement that became a party. The Co-operative Commonwealth Federation (CCF) was formed in 1932 and drafted its Regina Manifesto, which declared the party's ideological positions founded on the principles of democratic socialism.[36] Led by J.S. Woodsworth, the party attracted the support of farmers and workers and contested federal and provincial elections in the 1930s and 1940s. Its first major success was in Saskatchewan where it took power in 1944. The following year the party captured an astounding twenty-eight seats in the federal election. Following World War II, economic prosperity and the tensions of the Cold War gradually eroded the prewar electoral support for the party. The Winnipeg Declaration of 1956 indicated the party's abandonment of the dream of a North American socialist commonwealth by its support for a mixed economy made up of private and public corporate units.

The CCF attempted to broaden its popular support by adopting a new label and image. In 1961 the New Democratic Party (NDP) was founded.[37] In order to expand its popularity, the NDP united with major labour unions in the Canadian Labour Congress, thus taking on a more industrial image and departing somewhat from its rural and agrarian base of support. In effect, the NDP took action to become a mass party in Canadian politics, presenting itself as a competitive alternative to the Liberals and Progressive Conservatives.

Ideologically, the NDP never fully embraced socialism. During the late 1960s and the early 1970s, a number of academics and intellectuals (the Waffle Movement) challenged the pragmatic and centrist tendencies of the party leadership to return to fundamental socialist principles with an emphasis on Canadian nationalism.[38] The Waffle called for an independent socialist Canada based on a policy of nationalization of key industries and an expanded program of Canadian content in the media and educational institutions. The Waffle movement was defeated in 1973 and other factions, such as the B.C. Socialist Fellowship, the Ontario Ginger Group, and the Left-Caucus, unsuccessfully attempted to move the party toward a firm commitment to socialism. Today, ideological moderation seems to prevail in the party. What might be described as a pragmatic left-of-centre platform characterizes the ideological dimension of the NDP.

The party has only been marginally successful at the federal level. In the 1979, 1980, 1984, and 1988 federal elections, the NDP captured 26, 32, 30, and 43 seats respectively. The party's caucus still constitutes only about 15 percent of the membership of the House of Commons and has barely exceeded 20 percent of the popular vote in federal elections. Provincially, the NDP does not form a government but has formed governments in Manitoba (1981–88), in British Columbia (1972–75) and Saskatchewan (1944–64, 1971–81). By 1989 in the territories, Yukon hosted the only NDP government in the country. In Ontario, the NDP has been a strong political contender and was instrumental in bringing down the Conservative government by joining with the Liberals in 1985. But no major inroads have been made by the party in the Atlantic provinces or Quebec. The 1988 federal elections distinguished the NDP as the most regionalized of the three parliamentary parties with all but four of its forty-three seats concentrated in British

Columbia, Saskatchewan, and scattered pockets in Ontario. The NDP continues to have difficulty establishing itself as a national party.

Throughout its history the CCF/NDP has had seven party leaders: J.S. Woodsworth, M.G. Caldwell, Hazen Argue, T.C. Douglas, David Lewis, Ed Broadbent, and Audrey McLaughlin. The average tenure of the party's leadership is 8.5 years, compared with 12.8 years for Liberal leaders and 5.7 years for Conservative leaders.[39] Ed Broadbent, who served as leader for over 14 years, led his party to its best showing in terms of seats and popular vote since 1961, but his campaign stumbled and staled as the issue of free trade commanded the 1988 election. Broadbent and his party's organization entered a period of soul searching to re-examine the direction the party should take, ultimately prompting Broadbent to step down as leader in 1989. The NDP's main thrust – to work toward a decentralization of political and economic power – is a far cry from the Co-operative Commonwealth assertions of the 1933 Regina Manifesto. Recognizing the growing fears of Canadians regarding the national consequences of "big government" and "big labour," the NDP has stressed the need for stronger provincial and local governments to check these tendencies. This stance gives Canadian socialism, as articulated through the ideology and policies of the NDP, a unique character when contrasted to socialist parties in other parts of the world.

Liberal Parties

The Industrial Revolution, which began in the mid-eighteenth century, stimulated a demand to free the taxpayer from arbitrary government action. This demand for liberty and individual freedom of action came primarily from the rising industrial and trading class and was directed against restrictions imposed by government (in legislation, common law, and judicial action) upon the freedoms of economic enterprise.

The origin of liberal political parties in the modern sense – those groups organized for the purpose of electioneering and controlling government through a representative assembly – lies in the chaotic years of European history between 1700 and 1800. In Great Britain, whigs* and tories* were the remote political heirs of the parliamentarians and royalists of the seventeenth century. In turn, they became the ancestors of the Liberals and Conservatives, the Democrats and Republicans of two centuries later.

Liberal parties were formed in many European countries and most of the countries of the Western hemisphere by the end of the nineteenth century. They reflected positive assumptions about human nature, asserting faith in the basic goodness and reasonableness of people, and in their perfectibility. Liberal parties promoted liberty itself, maximizing individual freedom and advocating laissez-faire attitudes to achieve the greatest social good.

The first liberal parties opposed any state intervention in the economy and emphasized free enterprise, individual initiative, and free trade. In the twentieth century, as governments were more democratized, liberal parties shifted this position to a more optimistic role for the state in regulating, administering, and promoting society's affairs for the public good. Modern liberal parties advance economic and social reform through government regulation and stimulation of the economy and from positive social-welfare programs. They stand firm on their support for political and legal equality. Under this assumption, the laws and political freedoms of a society should apply equally to all people. However, before the twentieth century, English liberals restricted suffrage to the propertied, taxpaying, and well-educated citizens. Today, Liberal parties uphold the right of all adults to vote and run for public office.[40] Such twentieth-century liberals as John Dewey and Frederick van Hayck bridged the old liberal values of trust in human nature and reason, a belief in the idea of progress, and compassion for the downtrodden to the modern liberal tenets of economic development through government intervention in the economy.[41]

In the contemporary world of liberal political parties, it is possible to identify three ideological positions: *libertarianism, corporate liberalism,* and *reformist liberalism*. Libertarians, as found in the Libertarian Party of Canada, for example, adopt the classic laissez-faire position that accords people maximum individual liberty. They call for the resurrection of the "minimal state" in which government plays a passive role, operating only to protect individuals from force, fraud, and theft, to secure law and order, and to enforce binding contracts. Corporate liberals, such as the Democratic party in the United States, recognize the importance of individual freedom but protect the role of large-scale institutions, such as government, business corporations, and trade unions, as important centres of decision making. The social good results from the interplay of all of these individual and corporate forces.[42] Reformist liberals, such as the Liberal Party of Canada and the Liberal Party of Australia, place the greatest stress on government intervention to encourage and protect the values of freedom and equality. From their perspective, the government should represent the interests of the disadvantaged: the unemployed, the disabled, low-income senior citizens, consumers, and minorities. The role of the government is to redistribute wealth, develop programs directed at economically deprived groups and regions, and stabilize cycles of economic boom and bust through fiscal, monetary, and tax policies. Through such policies as medicare, public education, income maintenance, family allowance, and old-age pensions, the government can foster the freedom and equality of individuals in a social context.

The Liberal Party of Canada

In the election of 1874, Alexander Mackenzie led his Grits* to electoral victory over the Macdonald Tories with the support of rural and small-town Canadians, especially moderate reform groups in Ontario and antibusiness, anticlerical reform elements in Quebec. The Liberals were defeated in 1878 and two other successive national elections primarily because a new flock of voters, brought into the electorate by the accession of Manitoba and British Columbia to the BNA Act, had different economic and social demands from the rest of the country.

The Liberals worked vigorously to broaden their base of support, building on urban and rural grass-roots* strengths in most of the provinces. By the time it came to power under the leadership of Wilfrid Laurier in 1896, the Liberal party governed every province except Quebec. And, the new western provinces of Alberta and Saskatchewan contributed to the tenure of Liberal success to 1911. However, the party suffered deep divisions over the issue of conscription for overseas service during World War I, splitting the support of English-speaking and French-speaking party members in Quebec and Ontario. Laurier retired and at its leadership convention in 1919, the party chose William Lyon Mackenzie King as leader. By 1921, he had led the party to form a minority Liberal government and was to serve as prime minister for over twenty-one years. King set the Liberal party on its pragmatic reformist path, constructing an industrial-relations and welfare-state platform that influenced Canadian practices and laws governing health care, pensions, trade unions, the franchise, and taxation.[43] He viewed the party primarily as a machine for winning elections and only secondarily as an instrument to advance the principles of liberalism.

His successor, Louis St. Laurent, strengthened the support of the party in Quebec and Ontario and greatly expanded the industrial and economic base of the Canadian economy. Liberals had come to accept the role of government as a major actor in the Canadian economy and, under St. Laurent's stewardship, projected the idea that their party was the governing party of Canada.[44] St. Laurent retired in 1958 and was succeeded by Lester B. Pearson, who during his tenure as prime minister never commanded a Liberal majority in the House of Commons. As a result he was not in a strong position as a party leader to influence the direction of Liberal policies. In a minority government situation, Pearson and his ministers did not venture to develop a system of policy priorities.[45] Instead, flexibility and pragmatism abounded, so that when reformist political philosophy was resisted by members of the Cabinet, it was either withdrawn to avoid conflict, or was resubmitted with modifications that substantially altered the intent of the original policy proposal. The avoidance of political controversy and the reluctance to create and debate during the Pearson period produced an almost apolitical Liberal party. Unable to win a majority of seats, Pearson gave way to new leadership.

His successor, Pierre Elliott Trudeau, was the first Liberal leader to assume that position with a previously articulated philosophy of policy making.[46] Trudeau introduced what he called "rational" liberalism, which was to increase institutionalization* as the primary instrument of government in the policy-making process. This meant creating and expanding the role of bureaucracy to develop rational policies and decisions in all areas of the economic and social environment. It also meant enlarging and strengthening the chief advisory bodies around the prime minister, namely the Privy Council Office and the Prime Minister's Office.[47] In the years during his tenure as leader of the Liberal party, the size of Canada's public service grew enormously. Under successive Trudeau governments, Canada took on many of the characteristics of an administrative state* by (1) expanding the sphere of government into areas traditionally under private control; (2) increasing government involvement and regulation of the economy; (3) increasing bureaucratic specialization and professionalization.[48]

Under Trudeau's stewardship, the Liberals remained faithful to the party's traditional tenets such as the universality of social programs (keeping family allowances and old-age security payments free of means tests); they advanced Canadian economic and cultural nationalism, protected French language rights, and mapped out the constitutional destiny of the country.

Liberal fortunes fluctuated under Trudeau's leadership.[49] An astounding victory in 1968 was followed by near defeat in 1972 and the struggle to maintain a minority government in the House of Commons. The Liberals enjoyed another substantial victory in 1974 but suffered electoral defeat in 1979. Trudeau announced his resignation, but in December 1979 the controversial austerity budget introduced by John Crosbie was defeated. Trudeau was persuaded to stay on as party leader and subsequently led the Liberals to a majority victory in the 1980 election. In his final three years as prime minister, the Liberal party slipped to its lowest levels of popularity, stigmatized by budgets that failed to reduce unemployment and an uncontrollable deficit, and ostracized by a public increasingly cynical of its leader. Before his resignation, Trudeau had not prepared the party for his succession. Federal Liberal governments had reigned for sixty-two years in the twentieth century. Party members had grown accustomed to winning elections in the face of dwindling popularity. Many believed that Trudeau's successor, whoever he or she might be, could – by tinkering with party reorganization, some policy renewal, and procedural reform – return the party to power.

Such was the bravura of the party elite at the Liberal leadership convention in June 1984 when John Turner was chosen as the Liberals' glittering political star. Turner, who had served in the Commons for fourteen years, ten of them in the Cabinet, broke with Trudeau in 1975 and had brilliantly divorced himself from the legacy of the tarnished Liberal record. From a distance the star glistened with looks, personality, and intelligence. But on the hustings, he sparkled nervously, appearing awkward and dull to the merciless eyes of the TV camera. Turner served as prime minister for eighty days, from June to September 1984. In that brief period the public could not discern where he stood on the ideological spectrum. In both campaigns he swung from the right (on the need to tackle the federal deficit) to the left (with proposals to tax the wealthy). This uncertain ideological direction coupled with lack of leadership moxy led to the stunning electoral defeat that traumatized the Liberal party in every part of the country. After the 1984 election, the party was in debt, its membership reduced by low morale.

Turner, and the remnants of his parliamentary caucus, embarked on a comprehensive reconstruction of Liberal policies and finances from the grass roots to the party elite. On policy, the national party executive decided to hold regional conferences followed by national policy-reform conventions. The organization of national and regional conferences engaged the talents of academics, lawyers, journalists, and communications experts to research the roots of liberalism and past party policy so as to reset the path of future party doctrine. But, at these conferences many Liberals expressed the fear that a reconstituted liberalism would be difficult to distinguish and sell to the Canadian electorate now that the Conservatives and the NDP had crowded the traditional liberal ground in the centre of the political spectrum. Turner's inability to unite the party around him resulted from his controversial positions on issues such as the Meech Lake Accord and the free-trade agreement. Turner's quick support of the Meech Lake Accord distanced him from many of the old guard Liberals who agreed with Trudeau that the accord was seriously flawed.

And his promise to tear up the free-trade agreement divided the party and angered traditional financial supporters. Lingering doubts about Turner's leadership skills persisted well into the 1988 election campaign, only temporarily recessed by Turner's outstanding performance during the debates but resurfacing again after the election. In 1989 Turner resigned.

The Liberals were also concerned about the financial condition of the party. In 1984, the party decided to build a new $1.2 million headquarters on land it owns in Ottawa. The new facilities house a state-of-the art communications centre on the model of the U.S. Democratic party headquarters in Washington, D.C, capable of instantaneously sending party literature to party offices around the country by electronic mail on computer screens. The Liberal defeat in September 1984 left the party with a $3.5 million debt that had swollen to over $5 million by the time of the 1988 election. A direct-mail appeal to raise money barely broke even. Despite reconstruction efforts in the years between the 1984 and 1988 elections the Liberals experienced corrosive internal rivalries that affected their ability to raise money.

Meanwhile, beneath the struggle for a unified national Liberal party, provincial party machines began to show impressive successes. At the end of 1984 there were no Liberal governments in Canada. But in 1985, Liberal fortunes took a turn for the better in two important provinces. In Ontario, where the last Liberal government was a pre-World War II memory, the Liberal party came close to defeating the Conservatives in the 1985 provincial election, when they gained 20 seats and reduced the Tories to minority-government status. Not long after, the Liberals and the NDP signed an agreement to topple the Conservative government and form a minority Liberal government for at least two years. Then, in 1987, David Peterson's Liberals won a resounding victory at the polls, capturing 95 of 130 seats to form the first Liberal majority government in Ontario since 1937. The success of the Ontario Liberals was a shot in the arm for Liberals everywhere in the country, who were still reeling from the defeat of the federal party a year earlier. Another good turn for the Liberals had come in Quebec, with the return of Robert Bourassa and a strong Liberal government, reversing the barren trend of Liberal electoral success on Canada's political landscape. Bourassa Liberals were returned to power again in 1989, but with a reduced majority (99) and a drop in the popular vote from 55 percent to 50 percent, The Parti Québécois took 23 seats and raised its popular support to 40 percent from 38 percent. The English-language rights Equality Party won 4 seats and 4 percent of the popular vote.

In Prince Edward Island, Joe Ghiz led the Liberals to power after years of Conservative rule. Ghiz kept his Liberals entrenched in office by winning 30 of 32 seats in the May election of 1989, more than in the 1986 election. In New Brunswick, Frank McKenna gave the entire provincial legislature to his Liberal colleagues in a rare sweep of electoral victories. In Manitoba, Sharon Carstairs, the sole Liberal in the provincial legislature since 1986, led twenty of her party's candidates into the assembly as Her Majesty's Loyal Opposition. In Nova Scotia in September 1988, Vince MacLean increased the strength of the Nova Scotia Liberal party from 6 seats to 21 seats in the 52-seat legislature. In British Columbia the

Liberals have manoeuvred toward the political centre, given the polarized nature of B.C. politics between the Social Credit and the NDP. And, in Newfoundland, voters swept the Liberal party back into power, ending seventeen years of political isolation. In Alberta and Saskatchewan, membership increases and better financial health have made Liberal party prospects more optimistic. The Liberals doubled their representation in Alberta's 1989 provincial election and severely weakened the morale of the dominant Conservatives by winning Premier Donald Getty's seat in Edmonton. In Saskatchewan, the Liberals revitalized their provincial image by electing a new leader, Lynda Haverstock.

Small-l liberalism runs deep in the Canadian political psyche.[50] It has advocated government intervention to "help" protect individual freedom, but also to curb it. In practice, it is often difficult to accomplish the one without the other. The Liberal penchant for pragmatism over doctrinaire solutions has made philosophical liberalism an ambiguous yet popular creed. What is certain is that liberalism in the post-Trudeau era is still a powerful political force in Canada.

Conservative Parties

In the early nineteenth century, the first conservative parties were formed in many countries in Europe and Latin America. The conservatives, having much to conserve, championed the vested interests of the landed aristocracy and the church. At first, conservative parties were almost exclusively preoccupied with the defence of the monarchy and hereditary ruling classes against the demands of popularly elected assemblies.[51] But conservative parties shared other, more formal, ideological positions, possessing both political and historical depth.

Many of the theoretical political ideas of the early conservative parties were drawn from Edmund Burke (1729–97), a brilliant Irishman who served as a member of the British House of Commons for thirty years and was widely recognized as a Romantic writer and thinker.

Early conservative parties emphasized the existence of natural distinctions in wealth, opportunity, ability, intelligence, and privilege in the economic order of society.[52] Their chief concern was the defence of traditional wealth against the onslaught of the Industrial Revolution. Conservative parties were deeply committed to the concept of private property as the fundamental dynamic of the economic order. The economy was viewed as the interaction of government, institutions, landed aristocracy, and different classes of people as they related to the pursuit and ownership of private property. Conservative parties subscribed to the concept of a natural economic elite comprising those who held property and whose positions were protected by government. Property was the basis of the economic order for generations of citizens. Both time and survival were the principal tests for the endurance of conservative economic principles.

The first conservative parties tended to see social justice achieved in a society that permitted social, economic, and political inequality, if only because these were the characteristics of all societies throughout recorded history. But in Europe, conservatives did not equate inequality with social and political exploitation. For these conservatives, the justification of elite groups was the concern of the dominant classes for the welfare of the whole society. Conservatism had not been so presumptuous as to identify the well-being of all citizens with the conservative's own self-interest. Upper classes carried an obligation to others of inferior status, an obligation of noblesse oblige from previous times.

Politically relevant conservative parties operating in Europe and North America have a classical liberal, not a Burkean root. Many modern conservative parties advocate small government, and the laissez-faire values of classical liberalism. Some conservative parties continue to be pessimistic about human nature and dubious about the effectiveness of government expenditures for domestic welfare programs. They believe that people are better off being left alone and that government power tends to restrict liberty without solving social problems. They point to the decades of liberalism in the twentieth century during which time poverty has not been erased, social unrest has not been calmed, and wealth has not been effectively redistributed. They rate the private sector of society much more highly and assert that social improvements are more likely to arise from the work of voluntary associations and private business. At a more abstract level, conservatives tend to resist fundamental changes in social or governmental arrangements, believing that meaningful improvement in the human condition will come only slowly and naturally, like evolution. They believe that the future must be built on the past and, therefore, they believe in maintaining traditions.

In Canada, conservatives see the role of political parties as "conciliators," aggregating coalitions of interests to achieve a national consensus, harmonizing regional conflicts, and strengthening the fabric of society within the traditional framework of government institutions.[53] They stress social and legal order based on fundamental principles of conservation and preservation to protect the national interest. The conservative penchant for order requires the presence of a strong and effective government but with a limited or restricted role so as not to undermine self-reliance and individual freedom. As a balance to highly centralized government authority, conservative party policies encourage the vitality of countervailing forces of power, such as the provinces, trade unions, farm organizations, trade associations, and the media, to check the arbitrary tendencies of federal institutions.

As we can see, both the Liberal party and the Progressive Conservative party believe in protecting individual rights. This view emerges because Canadians are fundamentally pragmatic, regardless of their political persuasion. Both parties want to protect the liberties of the individual citizen. But each sees the threats to individual liberties as coming from a different direction, and therefore each adopts a different strategy aimed at what is essentially the same end. Those we call Liberals typically wish the government to aid the needy, control the powerful, and give freedom to critics and non-conformists. Those we call Progressive Conservatives typically want the government to support free enterprise, to control those who threaten the good order of society, and to give freedom to business and professional leaders, whom they see as contributing most to the prosperity in the economy.

Canadian conservatives do not ask ultimate questions and hence do not expect final answers. But they remind people of the institutional prerequisites of social order. At the Conservative Party Leadership Convention held in Ottawa in June 1983, David Crombie summed up his feelings on what it means to be a conservative: "I am a Tory. I glory in the individual. I cherish community. I seek liberty. I neither trim nor track to every social whim. I honour tradition and experience. I exalt faith, hope, and fairness. I want a peaceful, ordered, well-governed Canada. I am a Tory."[54]

It is important to point out that statements like this one reflect the weak ideological character of Canadian politics. It is a vague statement: if "tradition and experience" were removed, it could have been uttered by a Canadian Liberal. Most Canadians have a very low level of ideological consciousness.[55] What is more, people who call themselves Conservatives often do not take the conservative position on specific issues, just as many self-declared Liberals stray from the liberal side of many issues. *Conservative* and *Liberal* are handy labels that many people apply when talking about politics. These terms are used far beyond our ability to define them. Even at the doctrinal level within a political party, Canadians do not have internally consistent, fully coherent political ideologies. Both for citizens in general and for the most involved and informed observers of Canadian politics, the terms conservative and liberal have always been a source of confusion. Upon close examination, we can see that conservative and liberal belief patterns overlap one another greatly in their basic values, and that each contains internal contradictions of its own. For most Canadians, political ideology is a series of felt assumptions and vaguely held beliefs.

The Progressive Conservative Party of Canada

In 1854, a coalition comprising business, professional, and church leaders in Ontario and French Catholic and business elites in Quebec was constructed by John A. Macdonald to unite the British North American colonies into a single political unit. Under his leadership, this amorphous partnership of business and church elites was the genesis of the Conservative party (first called the Liberal-Conservative party). Macdonald, who became the first prime minister of the Dominion of Canada, won six out of eight federal elections held in the latter part of the nineteenth century. Canadian conservatism took shape as a powerful pragmatic political force, the result of a series of modernization measures that Macdonald called the "National Policy."[56] The chief component of the policy was the construction of the transcontinental railroad, completed in 1885. Other components included an industrialization plan nurtured by protective tariffs, primary resource development in the Maritimes and the West, and the encouragement of interprovincial trade.

At first, Macdonald succeeded in maintaining the tenuous coalition of political loyalties in Quebec and Ontario. But in 1885, Macdonald's decision to execute Louis Riel, a francophone Catholic Métis who had led an armed rebellion in Saskatchewan, placed bitter strains on the Quebec segment of the Conservative coalition. The support of the Conservatives in Quebec was further eroded by the party's hedging on its commitment to provide financial support to Catholic schools. These issues, the death of Macdonald, and the desperate succession of new leaders between 1891 and 1896 (John Abbott, John Thompson, Mackenzie Bowell, and Charles Tupper) led to the rout of the Conservatives.

The party remained out of power until 1911 when its leader Sir Robert Borden defeated the Liberal government of Wilfrid Laurier. Support for the Conservatives was drawn from an alliance of anti-American and protectionist forces in Ontario, combined with isolationist Quebec Conservatives who had come to an understanding with Borden that some from their ranks would be selected as Cabinet ministers in the new government.[57] This alliance disintegrated over the conscription crisis of 1917 that embittered many French Canadians because of Borden's insistence on conscripting men for overseas service in World War I. It soon became apparent to Quebeckers that none of the French Canadians in Borden's Cabinet had much influence over his decisions. The party subsequently lost its support base in Quebec.

Arthur Meighen, Borden's successor as prime minister, carried on the legacy of Quebec's abandonment. Like Borden, Meighen failed to understand the sentiments of French Canadians.[58] The Conservatives were quickly stigmatized as an English-speaking Protestant party by the Quebec electorate and Conservatives would not see a revival of French-Canadian support until John Diefenbaker's landslide victory in 1958. Lacking substantial support in Quebec, the Conservatives were defeated in 1921, and except for a brief period between 1925 and 1926, were to remain out of office until 1930. The party's new leader and prime minister, R.B. Bennett, like Arthur Meighen, did little to expand the support base of the Conservative party. He continued to antagonize Quebec by failing to keep the lines of political communication open to that province, and divided his own party when he brought forward his New Deal program, based on Roosevelt's American package, without consulting his Cabinet colleagues.[59] Under Bennett these two weaknesses – the inability to nurture support in Quebec and a proclivity to generate internal divisions and factionalism – became symptomatic of what was later called "the Tory syndrome."

Bennett was soundly defeated in 1935 and three years later he turned over the leadership of the party to R.J. Manion. Successors Ed Arthur Meighen, John Bracken, and George Drew were unsuccessful in broadening the support base of the party, especially in Quebec, and could not defeat the Liberals in the period between 1940 and 1957. That accomplishment was left to Drew's successor, John Diefenbaker.

In the election of 1957, Diefenbaker led the Progressive Conservatives to a minority-government victory. The following year Diefenbaker led them to the greatest electoral victory in Canadian history. Perhaps the most ideological of any Canadian prime minister, Diefenbaker resuscitated conservatism in Canada and gave it a most discernible North American character. His "vision" of Canada, his devotion to the monarchy and the Commonwealth, his penchant for strong national government, the National Development Policy, the Bill of Rights, and his pro-Canadianism, were all hallmarks of Diefenbaker's toryism.[60] But by 1962, Diefenbaker's personal charisma and strong electoral support had suffered a sharp reversal. He antagonized his party colleagues in Quebec by his reluctance to appoint them to important Cabinet positions and by his indecisiveness in handling the Munsinger scandal*. And internal divisions in both the Cabinet and the caucus grew out of Diefenbaker's demand for unwavering loyalty and adulation in the face of growing public discontent. The remarkable national coalition that he led in 1957 was no longer cohesive by 1963 and his government was defeated in the election of that year. It was not long before serious intraparty divisions surfaced over the quality of Diefenbaker's leadership, leading to his replacement by Robert Stanfield in 1967.

Stanfield took the reins of a deeply divided party that was unable to rally its unity to oust the Liberals in 1968, 1972, and 1974. His style of party leadership was much less exciting and more subdued than his predecessor's. But Stanfield held a deep regard for conservative ideology, espousing the honest ideals of national purpose, order, and a reverence for Canada's institutions and symbols.[61] Stanfield lacked the popular appeal necessary to convert his political philosophy into electoral support, and he retired under pressure in 1976.

Of the eleven candidates at the hotly contested leadership convention called in 1976, Joe Clark emerged the winner at age 36, with only four years of parliamentary experience under his belt. But nearly three years later, Clark led the party to a narrow victory in the May 1979 election. Clark resisted ideological pigeonholing, preferring to be judged as a pragmatic tory rather than a party leader acting in accordance with preconceived conservative philosophy. Although his tenure as prime minister and party leader was short-lived, it is possible to discern both conservative and liberal tenets in Clark's political thinking. He held that big government was much more of a detriment to Canada than were big business and big labour. Clark expressed confidence in the private sector to create jobs and to stimulate the recovery of the Canadian economy. But Clark's expressed desire to privatize Petro-Canada, sell other crown corporations, relocate the Canadian embassy in Israel, and support a tax policy governed by the principle of "short-term pain for long-term gain" generated serious doubts about the new tory minority government.[62] In December 1979, the Clark government's austerity budget and his government were defeated.

For the next three years Clark struggled to maintain his leadership of the party. In the eyes of many, his failed political record and weak public image continued to hurt the Conservative party.[63] At two successive biennial meetings of the party in 1981 and 1983, 33 percent of the delegates voted to call a leadership convention. Notwithstanding the fact that 66 percent of the party's delegates seemed satisfied with Clark's leadership, he knew that the minority against him was large enough to perpetuate doubts in the eyes of the party and in the mind of the general public that he was not solidly supported. Clark, therefore, announced his resignation and at the same time declared his candidacy in the upcoming leadership race.

It was billed as the largest political convention in Canadian history. As many as one-third of the voting delegates were undecided when they arrived at the convention, which fielded eight candidates. Clark led the other candidates on the first three ballots, but was defeated by Brian Mulroney on the fourth ballot.[64]

From the outset of his successful leadership campaign, Mulroney's personality and style changed the image of the Progressive Conservative party. The party had selected its first leader from Quebec since Sir John Abbott. But unlike other Conservative leaders Mulroney promised to bring Quebec in, not merely as a foothold, but as an ongoing constituency of support for the Progressive Conservative party.

During the 1984 election campaign, Mulroney demonstrated to Quebeckers that he was as committed to furthering the lot of his native province as had been Pierre Trudeau. Mulroney's reputation as a competent conciliator (based on his career as a labour lawyer) boosted the stolid image of the party and had an enormous political pay-off in his bid for Quebec support. Because of his adept conciliatory skills, not only did legions of Levesque supporters work for Mulroney but the former premier complimented him for choosing so many "authentic Quebecois candidates." In the process of political conciliation within Quebec, the Tories were able to crush the once impregnable Liberal stronghold, claiming 58 of the province's 75 seats in 1984 and 63 of its seats in 1988. Under Mulroney, the Conservatives penetrated every region of the province. This strong francophone presence in the party caucus did a great deal to mend the traditional English/French cleavage within the party. Across the country, the same powerful tide of support permitted Mulroney to give his party a national constituency and a unified image.

Ideologically, Mulroney is a pragmatic centrist. He won the federal elections in 1984 and 1988 not only because he succeeded in uniting a fractious party, but also because ideologically he surfed the crest of a conservative wave sweeping the country. When Mulroney first ran for the leadership of the party in 1976, some members of the party prematurely identified him as a red tory*. But by 1983, when 57 percent of the delegates placed themselves on the right of the political spectrum, Mulroney moved pragmatically for their support, opting for compromise over ideological combat. For the 30 percent of the delegates who placed themselves on the left, Mulroney vowed to keep Canada's extensive net of welfare programs intact. But for the majority of party delegates, he promised to revive Canada's sluggish economy by relying on the private sector, not on the government, to provide the economic stimulus for recovery.

Once in power, Mulroney entered the twilight zone of Canadian pragmatism, adopting a political strategy to solve the country's problems that defies ideological identification. Canada's massive deficit after the 1988 election approached the $29 billion mark, leaving little room for the application of doctrinaire solutions. Mulroney saw the only way out as economic growth: by creating new wealth, by unfettering the private sector in an atmosphere of deregulation, by federal/provincial cooperation and by generating jobs out of the newly implemented Free Trade Agreement.

The Progressive Conservatives have suffered from scandals, fumbles, and indecisiveness: conflict of interest charges, seedy land deals, and questionable behaviour led to numerous ministerial resignations and plunged the government's standing in the public opinion polls to a historic low (17 percent in March 1987). Initially, Mulroney was able to placate provincial interests, having been elected partly on the promise to end disputes between Ottawa and the regions. But the scandals and controversial policy decisions weakened Ottawa's influence and eroded much of its conciliatory posture.

In his book *Where I Stand*, Mulroney revealed his preference for political skill over philosophical prescription as a guide to governing the country.[65] As a "centrist, open to all discussions," he has dismissed the use of confrontation in his dealings with the provinces as witnessed by the Meech Lake negotiations. And as leader of a party that historically has been seen as pro-big business, anti-labour, anti-women, anti-youth, and anti-ethnic, Mulroney has tried to reset the public image of the Progressive Conservatives on social issues as it approaches the twenty-first century.

The Future of Political Parties

In the history of governmental experience, political parties are very young institutions. Those that appeared in the United States in the late 1790s are the oldest in the world. These parties were the offspring of equalitarianism – the institutional response to the idea of popular sovereignty and the belief that the rank and file citizen should have final authority in the business of governing. Less than 200 years later, political parties are found throughout the world. But parties did not evolve without ambivalent regard for their role, function, and future in the processes of democratic and non-democratic government. In the eighteenth century, philosphers and politicians had doubts about a permanent role for political parties. Political theorist Henry St. John, Viscount Bolingbroke, saw parties as "a political evil."[66] They were regarded as divisive and elitist, representing special interests against national interests, and blocking the pursuit of the common good.

Prior to the nineteenth century only one prominent theorist, Edmund Burke, defended the idea of political parties as essential instruments of representative government. As a philosopher and politician, Burke advanced the case for a mature party system long before one came into existence. Once established and organized, political parties would become the links between citizens and governmental institutions. Even in the United States where they first matured, political parties were not well received. American federalist James Madison did not envision a place for them in the constitutional order and criticized their factious effects on national unity. Thomas Jefferson held similar views even though he constructed one of the first permanently organized political parties: the Republicans, later called the Democratic-Republicans, and eventually called the Democratic party.

Ambivalence about the complementarity of political parties and democratic goals continued in the early years of the twentieth century when studies by professors Michels and Ostrogorski portrayed parties as manipulative and elitist.[67] A swell of optimism in the mid twentieth century glorified the functions of parties and regarded them as the custodians of liberal democracy. But this optimism quickly waned in the latter years of the century. Some political scientists in Canada and the United States became increasingly sceptical about the assumed functions of political parties and noted the opportunistic tendencies of these institutions to be publicity-oriented rather than issue-oriented, to be poll-driven rather than representative, and to be fixated on leadership style, imagery, and winability.[68]

A growing body of professional opinion is concluding that the party system is less than adequate because of a number of contributing social, economic, and political factors. One is that the media has displaced the party as the means of communication between people and their government and as the institution capable of reaching a large number of people quickly. Another factor has been the rise of a professional public (civil) service with its objective hiring standards and its criticisms of the old-style patronage system that contributed so much to the success of political parties in the past. As well, since the 1950s in democratic states, researchers have noted the steady weakening of party identification and the accompanying decline in the ranks of the party faithful. An additional factor frequently cited is that most democratic governments have legislated strict limitations on party fund-raising methods and spending practices. Finally, the effectiveness of interest groups in influencing the direction of public policy on behalf of a cohesive body of opinionated citizens has challenged the existing party system by luring precious campaign resources and public support.

All these factors may or may not contribute to the demise of political parties as modern agents of democracy. But if parties are not in decline they are certainly in transition. The challenge to the traditional party system is not that the things parties do will not get done, but that they will be done differently and perhaps by different agents. The gloomiest predictions are that political parties are outmoded institutions, to be observed in a sort of death vigil by analysts. Others believe it is conceivable that parties will limp along for many more years. They see a continuing role for political parties as psychological reference points for many individuals, and as conventional instruments for selecting candidates in elections. Parties may well persist as the most significant, though not the only, institutions on which political power is organized. Parties are not as strong as they once were, but in view of many of the useful functions they continue to perform it may be premature, if not unwarranted, to suggest that they are doomed.

Pressure Groups

Political parties are not the only decisive forces in shaping policy outcomes. If politics is to be comprehensive to us, we need to see the roles played by pressure groups as vehicles of public participation. In perhaps less obvious ways than political parties, pressure groups articulate the interests* of people who want to influence decisions about public policy.[69] This kind of popular participation in the political process is less familiar and apparent – and certainly less official – than voting, but it is nonetheless just as real and important. When a group of neighbours becomes exercised about the need for a stop sign on the corner of its street and circulates a petition to present at City Hall, it is a pressure group taking political action. Moreover, its efforts to influence the municipal government are considerably more direct, and likely to be more effective in achieving its goal, than reliance on the electoral machinery would be. In fact, all that the public can usually do to influence any government through its participation in political parties is to alter the tone and emphasis of general policies and programs.

All political systems have within them groups that make demands. During the past century, as societies have industrialized and modernized, the scope of group activity has widened and the quantity and variety of pressure groups have grown proportionately. In the 1990s, individuals the world over are more conscious of themselves as belonging to groups that have the potential of exercising political influence. To some degree, everyone is a member of a culture, race, religion, age and sex group, and a professional, occupational, or labour group. Even if one professes no religion, one is part of a group of atheists or agnostics. If one disavows membership in a political party, one is a member of a group that thinks the same way. Group consciousness and the political patterns of group interaction, then, become important – perhaps even more important than the sets of common characteristics that bring people together in the first place.

Many social scientists analyse why people do what they do as members of groups. Political scientists are interested in those groups that are organized to make their opinions known and to have an influence on the process of government. By definition, a pressure group or interest group is any collection of people organized to promote some objective it shares in common that somehow relates to the political process. A women's club is not, therefore, a pressure group unless its membership decides to demand equal rights with men in such things as property law, education, employment, and promotion. The Canadian Medical Association (CMA) is a pressure group by our definition even though its members are ostensibly organized for professional reasons. However, the association frequently concerns itself with public matters. The CMA was certainly involved in the political process of decision making during the establishment of medicare and it continues to press for influence in administering such programs. In the United States, the National Rifle Association (NRA), a group of over 1 million members, seeks to advance the safe use of firearms. Since 1968, it has been registered as a lobby, and it has operated as one of the most powerful and influential groups operating on the Washington scene, with an elaborate network of offices throughout the United States.

Most organizations that are national in scope have as a major objective the protection of a narrow cluster of interests or the advancement of a public interest they deem to be important. Accordingly, they relate to the political process as they attempt to influence the passage or defeat of legislation before Parliament and provincial legislatures. Numerous pressure groups of this kind – business, labour, professions, trade, religious, and other types – exist in order to promote their own objectives in the political process. Pressure groups constitute an extra-institutional aspect of politics. They are intimately related to the daily functioning of legislatures, executives, and courts and political parties. One cannot understand the dynamics of any democratic political system without understanding the deep involvement of pressure groups at all levels of society.

As a democratic state, Canada is an excellent society for the study of pressure-group activity.[70] Canada is a multigroup society: its numerous associations, groups, institutions, and organizations put pressure on governments for legislative and administrative concessions. Canadian society is so group oriented that anyone who wants to have an impact on policy decisions must either become a part of the government apparatus itself or lend support to one or more groups trying to influence government in particular ways. Canadians are joiners: we belong to a variety of groups reflecting countless interests and political demands. In an environment of flourishing pluralism, patterns of pressure-group interaction have become important. Because of their multiplicity, pressure groups are played off against each other by federal and provincial executives. The essential problem in Canada's highly competitive democratic system is to balance all these various group demands within an ordered, yet free, society.

Pressure-group activities do not flourish in non-democratic states. In authoritarian states, the status of pressure groups varies widely, depending upon the prevailing political system and the level of economic and political development that has been achieved. For example, in South Africa, despite extreme racial discrimination and political repression, there is a black trade-union movement. In Latin America generally, peasants (who constitute the largest numbers of any group) are commonly the least organized and the least politically articulate, although in a number of Central American countries – El Salvador, Honduras, and Guatemala – peasants have organized in the face of heightened political and military repression.[71] In authoritarian states, most pressure groups exist defensively; that is, they do not try to influence government positively but try to prevent the government from affecting their groups adversely.

In some totalitarian states, the party does not allow the development of autonomous pressure groups. Formal organizations exist – such as labour unions, industrial and commercial associations, guilds, and specialized societies – but they must affiliate with the party apparatus. In the Soviet Union the degree of influence enjoyed by pressure groups is increasing under *glasnost'*.[72]

Types of Pressure Groups

Identifying the types of pressure groups in a society requires a knowledge of the society's ideology and political structures. Most democratic states are pluralistic societies of great diversification, widespread heterogeneity, and a multiplicity of interests. Their political institutions are receptive to a variety of group demands. In non-democratic states, where interest articulation is closely monitored and controlled by a governing elite or a party apparatus, pressure-group formation may be difficult if not officially considered subversive. Among the pressure groups that operate in the Soviet Union are artists, scientists, educators, peasants, non-Russian nationalities, religious groups, and workers. Such groups as consumers, wage earners, and collective farmers form coalitions with institutional interest groups in the government, bureaucracy, and the party.

In democracies, political parties and pressure groups are relatively separate. In some countries, such as Britain and Canada, trade unions may support a particular political party but the party may act quite independently of trade-union pressure. Hundreds, sometimes thousands, of pressure groups with some stake in the political and economic system stand up and are heard. The great advances in industry, communications, science, and technology have brought more organized groups into the process of decision making.

Gabriel Almond developed a classification of pressure groups that applies to both democratic and non-democratic societies. These are anomic, non-associational, associational, and institutional pressure groups.[73]

Anomic Groups

Anomic groups are spontaneous gatherings of people whose behaviours demonstrates public concern and a demand for political action. Such anomic groups (*anomie* means being separated from social norms) do not feel bound to any need of organizing beyond the immediate expression of frustration, disappointment, or anger about a government policy or lack of government response to a question of public policy. Without previous organization or planning, anomic pressure groups vent their emotions as the news of government action or inaction sweeps a community and triggers a public reaction. These groups rise as flashes of support or non-support and, as suddenly, subside. In Canada, anti-abortion crusaders and right-to-lifers reacted strongly to Dr. Henry Morgentaler's arrests and acquittals. Well-organized and representative advocates on both sides of the issue gained a great deal of public visibility, and as a result attracted anomic support in those provinces where abortion clinics had been opened or were about to open. For these people, the opportunity to demonstrate their political positions on abortion to the provincial and federal governments came only once and they did not attempt to extend their involvement any further. Their actions did not lead to violence, but there were frequent incidences of civil disobedience.

In other political systems, anomic pressure-group behaviour occurs because political parties, governments, and organized pressure groups have failed to provide adequate representation of their interests. In Mexico, Chile, and Brazil, food riots swept the countries in the 1980s as people protested an increase in government-regulated food prices. In 1989, the Venezuelan government had to declare a state of emergency to quell the spontaneous riots of citizens protesting price increases on oil and other basic commodities. In the same year a state of siege was declared in Argentina to control anomic behaviour. And, in Beijing, China, the largest public protest in over forty years had revolutionary consequences for the Communist government. Some countries including Iran, India, Italy, and the United States have been marked by high frequencies of such spontaneous pressure-group behaviour. The pressure effect of anomic political activity flows from its spontaneity and the ultimate threat that it could result in widespread anti-government behaviour.

Non-Associational Pressure Groups

Non-associational groups, like anomic groups, are not formally organized. But these groups are more aware of themselves as distinctive from other groups because they possess a common activity, characteristic, or interest. Members of non-associational groups share a feeling of identification without the cohesive interplay of leadership and organization. Examples are the unorganized unemployed; prisoners and former inmates; people who inherit their ethnicity, such as Polish Canadians; consumer groups, such as vegetarians; and normative groups, such as non-smokers and non-drinkers.

These groups can be important in politics. For example, an increasing number of governments at all levels in Canada have moved to protect the rights of non-smokers by means of legislation, municipal by-laws, and agency regulations. The political influence of this group is derived from its mere presence and from the widespread support for its interests in government and in the general population. But also, non-associational groups that are poised in society as reference groups can be rapidly transformed into well-organized associational ones. Groups may organize around ethnic interests, such as the National Congress of Italian Canadians Foundation and the Italian-American Foundation in the United States, or around a common interest, such as the Non-Smoker's Rights Association in Toronto. Any group may be represented by a wide variety of associations, bureaus, unions, or other organizations. The potential supporters of an organized interest group are frequently dispersed throughout society, living in different areas and occupying different roles. The likelihood that they will unite in a collective effort to place demands on government is always there. Modern channels of communication can instantaneously unite a group that otherwise would remain non-associational. Non-smoker's rights groups recently have been organized in almost every city in Canada; yet, just a few years ago, such groups were essentially people who were aware only that other non-smokers existed. They are making their demands effectively because the channels of communication exist to project the health rights of the public as a political issue.

Associational Pressure Groups

Associational pressure groups include business, industrial, and trade associations, labour groups, agricultural groups, professional associations, and public-interest groups. These pressure groups represent the expressed interests of a particular group, maintain a full-time professional staff, and use effective procedures for formulating and processing interests and demands.

Despite their very real political interests, it is important to remember that most pressure groups do not exist exclusively, and often not much at all, for political purposes. A labour union is not organized primarily to bring political pressure; neither is the Canadian Food Processors' Association, the Canadian Federation of Independent Business, or the Canadian Manufacturers' Association. The importance of political pressure to these groups does vary a great deal, for all of them it is essentially a by-product of their central concerns, not their basic reason for being. Moreover, the first requirement for interest-group leaders is to keep their membership happy. A union leader who fails to produce a good contract may be defeated at the next election. An official of the Canadian Food Processors' Association who takes a public position that the members dislike may be silenced or dismissed. Similarly, the head of the Canadian Manufacturers' Association must be cautious when making public remarks because members will begin to drop out of the association if the public is offended by its leadership. It is only after the basic requirements of members' satisfaction have been met that group leaders can begin effectively to exercise political pressure.

In Canada and the United States, professional groups of teachers, lawyers, physicians, and others are as numerous as business, consumers', women's, and senior-citizens groups; they actively pressure governments in promoting their interests. In fact, the list of associational pressure groups grows longer and more varied each year, reflecting the pluralistic and open character of these societies. These numerous pressure groups are active participants in the political process and are instrumental in implementing changes of policy or initiating new ones. For example, the Canadian federal government sets numerous regulation standards on the food industry through three important pieces of legislation: the Canadian Agricultural Products Act, the Food and Drug Act and the Consumer Packaging and Labelling Act. Frequently these standards must adapt to new products, equipment, and technology introduced by the food-processing industry. The Technical Committee of the Canadian Food Processors' Association educates as well as pressures the government to harmonize its regulations so that the industry functions in the public interest.

In other countries, such as France, Italy, and the Latin American republics, associational pressure groups tend to be less likely to protect their narrower interests, such as the rights of renters, taxpayers, bankers, and peasants. In many countries, associational pressure groups are not nationally organized and play only a limited role in national politics. They lack autonomy and independence because they are controlled by other groups, such as political parties or the Church. In France and Italy, many associational pressure groups, such as trade unions and peasant organizations, are controlled by the Communist party or the Roman Catholic Church. Usually these groups, because of their lack of independence, can mobilize only the extent of the support enjoyed by the political or religious institutions that control them. The subordination of pressure groups to other organizations restrains their capacity to operate in the wider national interest.

Institutional Pressure Groups

Institutional pressure groups are well-established social structures such as the bureaucracies, business firms, churches, and universities. These highly self-conscious groups can and do make a stream of specific demands on government.

Most people do not perceive the institutional character of businesses. But businesses make up the largest number of institutions in our society. Business firms, acting independently or in concert, are probably the most important and active of all pressure groups operating for their own economic interests in the body politic. Businesses tend to pressure all facets of the political system, sometimes concentrating on the regulatory agencies of government administration and at other times acting directly on the politicians who draft the laws that affect commercial practices. Businesses as institutional entities have a number of advantages in dealing with government in Canada. First they have a pre-existing organization. This structure is a ready-made instrument for providing and receiving information about public policy, and for creating wider networks of associations in pursuit of business goals. Second, business organizations, whether they are individual firms or large corporations, generally have an ample supply of money. This advantage enables businesses to purchase advertising and the services of professional lobbyists to press their interests on government. The business community generates the largest amount of money for lobbying tactics, as well as the largest number of active pressure groups operating on the federal, provincial, and municipal governments in Canada.

Pressure-Group Methods

All pressure groups try to influence key decision makers. Groups may use both formal (lobbying) and informal methods (demonstration) to articulate their interests to policy makers. Within each political system, pressure groups vary in the tactics they employ and in the ways they organize and direct their influence. The available avenues for expressing group demands in a society have a great deal of importance in determining the range, effectiveness, and methods used by pressure groups. Thus, the strategies and techniques used by pressure groups are determined by the character of the government they seek to influence, as well as by the nature of the groups' goals and means.

Quite often in democratic states, pressure-group activity is conducted by *lobbying*. The term lobbyist developed in the United States from the practice of speaking to legislators about pending matters in the lobby just outside the congressional chamber. A regular occupant of the lobby, whose function was to influence legislators, came to be known as a lobbyist. Standard lobbying tactics, including appearances and testimony before legislative committees, are common practices in many countries.[74] Pressure groups lobby to induce legislators to introduce, modify, pass, or kill legislation. Professional lobbyists are sometimes hired on a part-time or full-time basis by interest groups that are preoccupied with the professional representation of their membership.

In Canada, the Lobbyists Registration Act, proclaimed in 1989, requires lobbyists to register with the federal government so that there is public knowledge about who is trying to influence policy makers. Under the act, individuals who, for payment, communicate with federal public officeholders for the purpose of influencing the development, introduction, passage, defeat, or amendment of legislation are considered to be lobbyists. Two types of lobbists are recognized: professionals, who are in the business of lobbying for a client; and "others," who lobby on behalf of an employer. There is another group of lobbyists who do not have to register because they work on a voluntary basis, usually for a cause. The act only requires lobbyists to register but does not attempt to regulate their activities. The Registrar of Lobbyists is appointed by the Registrar General of Canada.

Most lobbyists who work to influence policy in Ottawa gained their professional credentials in private industry, inside government, or by espousing special interest causes. Many lobbyists have worked closely with their governments and some are former politicians. For example, the chairman of Government Consultants International Inc. is a former premier of Newfoundland, and the chairman of Public Affairs International was Joe Clark's chief of staff and a former vice-president of the Canadian Imperial Bank of Commerce. They are on a first-name basis with hundreds of politicians and reporters and are major spokespersons for the interests they represent. Hiring a lobbyist (sometimes a prestigious law firm, public relations firm, or a legislative consultant) helps ensure that the group's interests are professionally made known to the decision makers in government, and – through a kind of watchdog function – that pending government action is brought to the attention of the group.[75]

If the pressure group is large enough, its lobbying component may be quite sizable. Numerous organizations maintain offices in the national capital and many of them employ more than a dozen people to co-ordinate the political relations of the group. The lobbying staff may include, in addition to a director and assistants, a number of liaison officers, researchers, copywriters, an editorial staff, and specialists with contacts in the different branches of government. The larger the interest represented, the more sophisticated its lobbying operation can be.

Influencing public officials in the lobbies of their workplace is still very much a part of pressure-group activity in Canada. But pressure groups employ many other means besides lobbying to aggregate citizen influence for the purpose of affecting public policy. In recent years, there have been accelerating changes taking place in Canadian practices regarding pressure-group tactics, some of which involve direct action. They include demonstrations, organized boycotts and strikes, advertising, writing books, and staging various events to attract the attention of the media and to inform the general public. As well, pressure groups will sometimes penetrate political parties to get closer to decision makers. Associations of campers, conservationists, environmentalists, bird watchers, and naturalists have used all these methods, which have proved very successful in their communications with agencies such as Parks Canada.[76]

Mass demonstrations, providing information, and propaganda are becoming standard tactics for some pressure groups like peace organizations. Embracing more than 1000 organizations and claiming a membership of over 300 000, the Canadian peace movement has staged mass demonstrations across the country. In the 1980s, many peace demonstrators were arrested but millions of Canadians were drawn into the immediacy of their message. Another dramatic but direct pressure on government was staged by Greenpeace protestors, when they lofted balloons carrying nets toward the flight path of cruise missiles in an attempt to abort the military operation. Changing circumstances, needs, and technology have encouraged an ever-increasing array of pressure groups to use demonstrations to articulate their demands and grievances and to pressure authorities into taking remedial action. With respect to the feminist movement in Canada, it is increasingly evident that the public is taking notice.

Any survey of pressure-group tactics and techniques must also include illegitimate and coercive ones, like violence and terrorism. No society has escaped the use of violence and vandalism by pressure groups. In Canada, violence has marked group struggles between labour and management since it became an independent country. The consequences of continued physical violence are alarming to contemplate, but violence is, nevertheless, always a possibility with pressure-group activity. Terrorism has taken the form of deliberate assassination of diplomatic representatives, armed attacks on other groups or government officials, the provocation of bloodshed, and the threat of bombing. The attack on the Turkish embassy in Ottawa by Armenian terrorists in the mid 1980s was an example of the extremes some groups are prepared to go to in order to bring national and international attention to their cause. Shortly after, it was widely believed that self-styled Armenian terrorists – the Armenian Secret Army for the Liberation of Our Homeland – had threatened to blow up Toronto's busy subway system if the three Armenians arrested after the Ottawa hostage siege were not freed. The terrorists were successful in drawing world attention to their cause, but at the same time lost the support of most Canadians and created a great deal of anguish within the Armenian community in Canada.

Here, of course, lies the great dilemma of direct action; it is the point around which debate on the propriety of some pressure-group activities revolves. Some would argue that violent protests are never appropriate in a democracy such as Canada, where other more peaceful channels exist. They point out that protest and violence are not always the same thing and should not be tolerated as an inalienable political right when one leads to the other. Both are political acts engaged in by individual citizens or groups, who want to pressure the government to respond. In this sense, we must judge them not only by the righteousness of the goals, but also by the morality and legality of the tactics used. It is difficult to judge the extent to which violent protest is more effective than the slower processes of citizen participation. Many – particularly government leaders who would like to discourage extreme practices – claim that they pay no attention to such acts. Others – particularly leaders of protest groups – claim that violence and quasi-violence are the only effective means of political activity.

Usually the squeakiest wheel gets oiled. But violent protests sometimes flash quickly and then fade, leaving behind only bad memories and a more defensive political system. Often the most effective pressure activity is a well-organized assertive protest. An urban demonstration bordering on mayhem, a massive descent on Ottawa of the outraged unemployed, attempts by citizens to block the infiltration of pornographic materials – all such activities may cause government leaders to change their course sharply.

Pressure-group protests are likely to be particularly effective as signalling devices. The urgency demonstrated by the protest and the vast coverage received through the media make pressure groups powerful vehicles for signalling discontent to political leaders. And they are also signalling devices to potential participants as well. Such overt and powerful manifestations of discontent may help to mobilize others to become more active.

As might be expected, the network of relationships that links pressure groups with government and the policy-making process generally is a highly complex one. The ballot box is by no means the only channel of access that people have to their government; the mass of activity that falls under the heading of pressure-group politics supplements election politics in most democratic societies. Even a sampling of the avenues of access available to pressure groups confirms that, in sheer bulk, not to mention flexibility, these groups rival political parties as guarantors of popular sovereignty. Pressure groups, however, provide people with an alternative route to the decision-making process. Sometimes the Cabinet or the responsible minister can be more favourably persuaded by a pressure group than by the combined tactics of the parliamentary opposition.

The factors that most interest political scientists about political systems – equality, freedom, participation, revolution, security, and stability – are very much a consequence of the performance of political parties and pressure groups. When they fail to aggregate and articulate for people, political systems end in failure. For unaccommodated interests rarely dissipate, and the means used by people to seek retribution are likely to grow more disruptive throughout the body politic.

REFERENCES

1. Lily Ross Taylor, *Party Politics in the Age of Caesar* (Berkley, CA: University of California Press 1961), 6–23.
2. See R.H. Blank, *Political Parties: An Introduction* (Englewood Cliffs, NJ: Prentice-Hall 1980).
3. Sir Randol Fawkes, *The Faith that Moved the Mountain* (Nassau: Nassau Gaurdian 1979), 211.
4. Leon Epstein, *Political Parties in Western Democracies* (New York: Frederick A. Praeger Inc. 1967), 9.
5. Maurice Duverger, *Political Parties and Pressure Groups* (New York: Thomas Nelson & Sons Ltd. 1972), 5.
6. See Janine Brodie and Jan Jenson, "Piercing the Smokescreen: Brokerage Parties and Class Politics," in Alain Gagnon and Brian Tanguay, eds., *Canadian Parties in Transition* (Scarborough, ON: Nelson Canada 1989), 24–44; H. Clarke et al., *Absent Mandate: The Politics of Discontent in Canada* (Toronto: Gage Educational Publishing 1984), 10–16.
7. Roy Macridis, *Modern Political Regimes Patterns and Institutions* (Boston: Little, Brown & Co. 1986), 64–70.
8. Gabriel Almond and G. Bingham Powell Jr., eds., *Comparative Politics Today: A World View* (Glenview, IL: Scott, Foresman & Co. 1988), 82–88.
9. Mervyn Matthews, *Education in the Soviet Union: Policies and Institutions since Stalin* (London: Allen & Unwin 1982).
10. Jon Pammett and Michael Whittington, eds., *Foundations of Political Culture: Political Socialization in Canada* (Toronto: Macmillan 1976), 288–315.
11. See David Roth and Paul Warwick, *Comparative Politics* (New York: Harper & Row Publishers 1989), 209–55.
12. Richard Van Loon and Michael Whittington, *The Canadian Political System* (Toronto: McGraw-Hill Ryerson 1987), 305–70.
13. David Lane, *The End of Social Inequality? Class, Status and Power under State Socialism* (London: Allen & Unwin 1982), 93.
14. Richard Rose, *Do Parties Make a Difference*? (Chatham, NJ: Chatham House 1980).
15. G. Bingham Powell Jr., *Contemporary Democracies: Participation, Stability, and Violence* (Cambridge, MA: Harvard University Press 1982), 186–200.
16. Robert Alexander, ed., *Political Parties of the Americas: Canada, Latin America, and the West Indies I* (Westport, CT: Greenwood Press 1982), 192–7.
17. See Kenneth Kernaghan and T.H. McLeod, "Mandarins and Ministers in the Canadian Administrative State," in O.P. Dwivedi, *The Administrative State in Canada* (Toronto: University of Toronto Press 1982), 17–29.
18. G. Bingham Powell Jr., "Political Systems and System Performance in Contemporary Democracies," *American Political Science Review 75* (December 1981): 861–79.
19. Giovanni Sartori, *Parties and Party Systems: A Framework for Analysis* (London: Cambridge University Press 1976), 42–7.
20. Ronald McDonald and J. Mark Ruhl, *Party Politics and Elections in Latin America* (Boulder, CO: Westview Press 1989), 20–35.
21. S.E. Finer, *The Changing British Party System, 1945–1979* (Washington, D.C,: American Enterprise Institute for Public Policy Research 1980).
22. Steven Rosenstone et. al. *Third Parties in America* (Princeton: Princeton University Press 1984).
23. Janine Brodie and Jane Jenson, *Crisis, Challenge & Change: Party & Class in Canada* (Toronto: Methuen 1980), passim; and Joseph Wearing, *Strained Relations: Canada's Parties and Voters* (Toronto: McClelland & Stewart 1988).
24. See Alain Gagnon and Brian Tanguay, "Minor Parties of Protest in Canada: Origins, Impact, and Prospects," in

Gagnon and Tanguay, eds., *Canadian Parties in Transition,* 220–48.

25. Ronald McDonald, *Party Systems and Elections in Latin America* (Chicago: Markham Publishing Company 1971), 17.
26. Ibid., 17.
27. See Robert Michels, *Political Parties* (New York: Free Press 1962).
28. See Harold Lasswell and Abraham Kaplan, *Power and Society* (New Haven, CT: Yale University Press 1950), 219–20.
29. See Cornelius Cotter et al., *Party Organizations in American Politics* (New York: Praeger 1984), 63.
30. See Rand Dyck, "Relations between Federal and Provincial Parties," in Gagnon and Tanguay, eds., *Canadian Parties in Transition,* 186–219.
31. See George Perlin and Hugh Thorburn, "The National Party Convention," in H.G. Thorburn, ed., *Party Politics in Canada,* 5th ed.,(Scarborough, ON: Prentice-Hall Canada 1985).
32. See W.T. Stanbury, "Financing Federal Political Parties in Canada, 1974–1986," in Gagnon and Tanguay, *Canadian Parties in Transition,* 354–83; *Report of the Chief Electoral Officer Respecting Election Expenses,* 1980, 1981, 1982, 1983, 1984, 1985, 1986.
33. See Almond and Powell, eds., *Comparative Politics Today: A World View,* 392–5, 406–7.
34. David Miller, "Socialism and the Market," *Political Theory 5* (November 1977): 473–9.
35. See Thorburn, ed., *Party Politics in Canada,* 41–59.
36. Leo Zakuta, *A Protest Movement Becalmed: A Study of Change in the CCF* (Toronto: University of Toronto Press 1964),163–73; and Nelson Wiseman, *Social Democracy in Manitoba: A History of the CCF- NDP* (Winnipeg: University of Manitoba Press 1984).
37. W.D. Young, *The Anatomy of a Party: The National CCF 1932–61* (Toronto: University of Toronto Press 1969); for a history beyond 1961, see Desmond Morton, *The New Democrats 1961–1986: The Politics of Change* (Toronto: Copp Clark Pitman 1986).
38. See John Bullen, "The Ontario Waffle and the Struggle for an Independent Socialist Canada: Conflict within the NDP,"*Canadian Historical Review* LXIV (June 1983): 188–215.
39. See Alan Whitehorn, "The CCF-NDP: Fifty Years After," in Thorburn, ed., *Party Politics in Canada,* 199.
40. See David Miller, "Democracy and Social Justice," *British Journal of Political Science* 8 (January 1978): 1–19.
41. Kay Lawson, *The Human Polity: An Introduction to Political Science* (Boston: Houghton Mifflin Company 1985), 99.
42. For a critique of corporate liberalism, see Christian Bay, *Strategies of Political Emancipation* (South Bend, IN: University of Notre Dame Press 1981).
43. Leo Panitch, "Elites, Classes and Power in Canada," in Michael Whittington and Glen Williams, eds., *Canadian Politics in the 1980s* (Toronto: Metheun 1981), 184.
44. Reginald Whitaker, *The Government Party: Organizing and Financing the Liberal Party of Canada 1930–58* (Toronto: University of Toronto Press 1977); Reginald Whitaker, "The Liberal Party and the Canadian State," *Acadiensis* 12, 1 (1982) 145–63.
45. W.A. Matheson, *The Prime Minister and the Cabinet* (Toronto: Methuen 1976), 164–9.
46. See P.-E. Trudeau, *Federalism and the French Canadians* (Toronto: Macmillan of Canada 1968).
47. See Christina McCall-Newman, *Grits: An Intimate Portrait of the Liberal Party* (Toronto: Macmillan of Canada 1982).
48. See R.W. Phidd, "The Administrative State and the Limits of Rationality," in Dwivedi, *The Administrative State,* 233–50.
49. See Joseph Wearing, *The L-Shaped Party: The Liberal Party of Canada* (Toronto: McGraw-Hill Ryerson Ltd. 1981).

50. See William Christian and Colin Campbell, *Political Parties and Ideologies in Canada* (Toronto: McGraw-Hill Ryerson Ltd. 1983), 40–81.
51. See N.K. O'Sullivan, *Conservatism* (New York: St. Martin's Press 1976).
52. See Robert Lindsay Schuettinger, ed., *The Conservative Tradition in European Thought* (New York: Putnam's Press 1970).
53. See Robert Stanfield, "Conservative Principles and Philosophy," in Paul Fox, ed., *Politics Canada,* 6th ed. (Toronto: McGraw-Hill Ryerson Ltd. 1987), 376–81.
54. Quoted from the CBC program, "The House," aired June 11, 1983.
55. William Christian and Colin Campbell, "Political Parties and Ideologies in Canada" in Gagnon and Tanguay, eds., *Canadian Parties In Transition,* 45–63.
56. See Rod Preece, "The Political Wisdom of Sir John A. Macdonald," *Canadian Journal of Political Science* VII, (September 1984): 459–86.
57. See John English, *The Decline of Politics: The Conservatives and the Party System,* 1901–1920 (Toronto: University of Toronto Press 1977).
58. Roger Graham, *Arthur Meighen: A Biography* (Toronto: Oxford University Press 1968), passim.
59. See J.H.R. Wilbur, ed., *The Bennett New Deal: Fraud or Portent* (Toronto: Copp Clark 1968).
60. George Grant, *Lament for a Nation* (Toronto: McClelland & Stewart 1965); George Perlin, *The Tory Syndrome: Leadership Politics in the Progressive Conservative Party* (Montreal: McGill-Queen's University Press 1980).
61. See E.D. Haliburton, *My Years with Stanfield* (Windsor, NS: Lancelot Press 1972).
62. Jeffrey Simpson, *The Conservative Interlude and the Liberal Restoration* (Toronto: Personal Library Publishers 1980), 118.
63. See Aileen McCabe, "Workshops Reveal Deep Party Divisions," *Ottawa Citizen,* March 2, 1981, 7.
64. See Patrick Martin, Allan Gregg, and George Perlin, *Contenders: The Tory Thrust for Power* (Toronto: Prentice-Hall Canada Inc. 1983).
65. See Brian Mulroney, *Where I Stand* (Toronto: McClelland & Stewart 1983).
66. Henry Saint-John Bolingbroke, *A Dissertation upon Parties,* in *The Works of Lord Bolingbroke,* vol.2 (Philadelphia: Carey and Hart 1841).
67. R. Michels, *Political Parties,* trans. by E. Paul and C. Paul (New York: Free Press 1915); and M. Ostrogorski, *La democratie et les partis politiques,* textes choisis par P. Rosanvallon (Paris: Seuil 1902).
68. See David Broder, *The Party's Over* (New York: Harper & Row 1971); W. Crotty, *American Parties in Decline,* 2nd ed. (Boston: Little, Brown 1984); G. Amyot "The New Politics," *Queen's Quarterly* 93 (Winter 1986): 952–5; Paul Pross, *Group Politics and Public Policy* (Toronto: Oxford University Press 1986); and John Meisel, "The Decline of the Party in Canada," in Thorburn, ed., *Party Politics in Canada,* 98–114.
69. See Allan Cigler and Burdett Loomis, eds. *Interest Group Politics* (Washington, D.C.: CQ Press 1983); J. H. Faulkner, "Pressuring the Executive," *Canadian Public Administration* 25, no 2 (1982): 240–53.
70. See Paul Pross, ed., *Pressure Group Behaviour in Canadian Politics* (Toronto: McGraw-Hill 1975); Hugh Thorburn, *Interest Groups in the Canadian Federal System.* vol 69 (Toronto: University of Toronto Press 1986).
71. Gary Wynia, *The Politics of Latin American Development* (London: Cambridge University Press 1984), 63–70.
72. See Gordon Smith, *Soviet Politics: Continuity and Contradition* (New York: St.

Martin's Press 1988).

73. See Almond and Powell, eds., *Comparative Politics*, 62–8.

74. See Suzanne Berger, ed., *Organizing Interests in Western Europe* (New York: Cambridge University Press 1981), ch. 12; Paul Best et al., *Politics in Three Worlds* (New York: Macmillan Publishing Co. 1986) 212–250.

75. See F. Thompson and W.T. Stanbury, "The Political Economy of Interest Groups in the Legislative Process in Canada," *Occasional Paper* no. 9 (Montreal: Institute for Research on Public Policy 1979).

76. See Paul Pross, "Pressure Groups: Talking Chameleons," in Whittington and Williams, eds., *Canadian Politics in the 1980s*, 221–42; "The Persuaders," *Maclean's*, February 24, 1986.

SUGGESTED READINGS

Jeffrey Berry, *Interest Group Society* (Glenview, IL: Scott, Foresman & Co. 1988).

Hans Daalder, *Party Systems in Denmark, Austria, Switzerland, The Netherlands and Belgium* (New York: St. Martin's Press 1987).

Kevin Featherstone, *Socialist Parties and European Integration* (New York: St. Martin's Press 1988).

Stephen Frantzich, *Political Parties in the Technological Age* (Mississauga, ON: Copp Clark Pitman 1989).

Alain Gagnon and Brian Tanguay, *Canadian Parties in Transition: Discourse, Organization and Representation* (Scarborough, ON: Nelson Canada 1988).

Ronald McDonald and Mark Ruhl, *Party Politics and Elections in Latin America* (Boulder, CO: Westview Press 1989).

Desmond Morton, *The New Democrats 1961–1986: The Politics of Change* (Mississauga, ON: Copp Clark Pitman Ltd. 1988).

Frank Sorauf and Paul Allen Beck, *Party Politics in America*, 6th ed. (Glenview, IL: Scott, Foresman & Co.1988).

Michael Waller, *Communist Parties in Western Europe: The End of Bolshevism?* (Oxford: Basil Blackwell 1988).

Alan Ware, *Political Parties: Electoral Change and Structural Response* (Oxford: Basil Blackwell 1988).

GLOSSARY

franchise: In the field of politics, this means the right to vote.

class: A category of persons sharing a similar level of privilege and social status by virtue of their occupational roles.

pluralism: A political doctrine that contends that political power is distributed among a variety of groups and institutions such that no group in society has a monopoly over resources.

aggregating: The group process of bringing together a range of demands across many levels of society on some issue, e.g., tax reform, social-welfare programs.

party coalitions: A combination or temporary alliance of political parties united for some specific purpose.

nationalization: State ownership of certain means of production.

platform: A publicly announced program of action or statement of principles adopted by a political party or a political candidate.

conventions: An assembly of official delegates representing a political party in the discharge of some official duty, such as the choice of party candidates, the adoption of platform statements, or the selection of delegates to represent the party at a higher-level meeting.

party cohesion: A term used to refer to the extent to which members of a political group co-operate.

left wing: The political designation of persons, parties, or groups supporting extremely liberal or radical economic and political programs within a social system.

right wing: The political term used to indicate persons, parties, or groups supporting extremely conservative or reactionary economic and political programs.

faction: A small, relatively homogeneous group of individuals within a larger organization, such as a political party.

traditional agrarian societies: Such societies are primarily rural and agricultural, characterized by little division of labour beyond sex and age, and widely shared ideas, customs, and habits. The great majority of people are illiterate and the standard of living is low and often precarious.

iron law of oligarchy: The principle that any organization will tend to be dominated by a few individuals at the top because of the structural characteristics of the organization.

command economy: A mode of economic organization in which three fundamental economic functions – what goods will be produced, how they will be produced, and who will receive them after production – are determined by a central planning agency or government directive.

puppet regimes: A regime controlled by officials acting in the interests of and under instructions from the government of another state, usually accompanied by threats of violence or other forms of coercion.

egalitarian: The concept of equality that refers to the degree of similarity between two or more individuals, populations, or larger groups with respect to some specified characteristic, such as a condition, a right, a duty, or a treatment.

whigs: A term used in reference to Scottish rebels in the 1670s and from 1680 onwards referring to the English Liberal political faction that sought to transfer power from the monarch to Parliament. Eventually the term applied to the British Liberal party.

tories: A word derived from the Irish *toraighe* who terrorized English settlers in Ireland. Gradually the term was used in reference to the English Conservative party, committed to free trade, a market economy, democracy, and human rights.

grits: An American slang term referring to the stuff a person is made of. It was used to label members of the Reform party in Canada in the 1840s and because of the merger of that party with the Liberal party is frequently used to describe contemporary Liberals.

grass roots: A term referring to the base of a political pyramid, usually the general electorate or riding associations.

institutionalization: The process whereby cultural values, norms, and relationships become highly structured and routinized within an established framework governed by rules and a predictable pattern of operation.

administrative state: The terms used to describe a system of governance through which public policies and programs ostensibly created by elected politicians are, in fact, influenced by the decisions of bureaucrats who are the principal agents in the formulation and implementation of the public agenda.

Munsinger scandal: A political controversy during the Diefenbaker period raising questions of national security resulting from an alleged affair between Associate Minister of Defence Pierre Sevigny and East German prostitute Gerda Munsinger.

red tory: A left-wing faction of the Progressive Conservative party of Canada that advocates economically egalitarian policies that one might expect to be more exclusively championed by Liberals or socialists.

interests: The desires, values, or objectives held in common by any number of individuals and groups.

12

Elections and Electoral Systems

Iranian women vote

Voting

ELECTIONS ARE ONE OF HUMANKIND'S oldest social institutions. Anthropologists have traced the practice to ancient Sumeria nearly 6000 years ago, when people living along the Tigris and Euphrates rivers elected leaders to bring them through emergencies and natural disasters.[1] Elections first took a formal central role in politics much later, during the fifth and sixth centuries B.C., in the Greek city-states of the eastern Mediterranean. The Greeks elected people in popular assemblies to fill offices of political authority. They voted sometimes by a show of hands, sometimes with written ballots* in the form of pebbles (psephite). Hence, the modern term psephology* – the study of voting and elections.

Today, elections mean different things in different political systems, but even the most authoritarian and totalitarian states are hard pressed to stage them. Although the frequency of elections may vary within political systems, states that hold no elections are the exception to the rule. In the modern world of governments, elections are omnipresent political practices, even among the most repressive regimes.[2] Many authoritarian as well as democratic states make voting obligatory: Belgium pioneered compulsory voting* in 1893, followed by the Netherlands in 1917 and Australia in 1924. Other states that have adopted compulsory voting are Argentina, Brazil, Italy, Liechtenstein, Nauru, Paraguay, Peru, Spain, and the USSR. In Italy it is not legally compulsory but is regarded as a civic duty, and failure to vote is recorded for five years on an elector's identity card. Italy also provides its citizens with free rail transportation to vote. Some states, such as Uruguay, have compulsory voting laws but do not enforce them. Even though voting is one of the simplest political activities, the percentage of electoral turnout varies from country to country (table 12.1).

Voter turnout in national elections
Selected nation-states

State	Compulsory Voting	Average turnout since 1945
Australia	yes	94.3
Belgium	yes	92.6
Canada	no	76
Denmark	no	85.5
France	no	78.7
Israel	no	81.1
Italy	yes	92.4
Japan	no	72.8
Luxembourg	yes	90.7
Nigeria	no	41
United Kingdom	no	77
United States	no	47.1
USSR	yes	99

Source: Keesing Archives, 1979–89, and United Nations, *Demographic Yearbook* (New York: UN 1988). For comparative data since 1945, see Thomas Mackie and Richard Rose, *The International Almanac of Electoral History* (London: Macmillan1982), 406–12; Dick Leonard and Richard Natkiel, *World Atlas of Elections* (London: Economist Publications 1986).

Table 12.1

In most states today, the electorate is 21 years of age and over, an age qualification that usually permits the majority of citizens to vote. Table 12.1 illustrates a wide range in the percentage of voter turnout among the states selected: between 41 and 99 percent. In many states, the high proportion of eligible non-voters is a persistent concern to government leaders because, despite the simplicity of the voting process, the implications of the vote are profound. When people withdraw from an election or feel no political anchorage in the system, the resulting apathy* can lead to political discontent. Studies cannot really pinpoint all the causes of non-voting, but indifference is certainly among the most influential.[3] The groups usually cited as apathetic and alienated are women, the young, the uneducated, the poor, and those generally disfranchised from the political system. In Canada, where voter turnout is relatively high in comparison to other democratic states, political alienation expressed as non-voting is often related to a region's economic weakness. In such an area, many non-voters feel that one government is as helpless as another to make any difference in reversing economic insecurities.[4] Many non-voting Canadians feel alienated even while possessing an advanced education, working in a high-status occupation, and enjoying a comfortable income.

In the advanced industrialized nation-states, non-voting is often the result of other factors related to the complications of living in a highly mobile society.[5] Common reasons given by eligible non-voters for failing to go to the polls include a recent change of job or residence, not knowing where the polling places are, conflicting hours of work and family obligations, or sickness and disability.

In totalitarian states, such as the Soviet Union and China, where voter turnout at national elections has traditionally been expected and "directed," the problem of non-voting is penalized by fines, the publication of names at places of employment or recreation, and even the exclusion of public-service benefits. In states such as these, elections are considered to be a mechanism for demonstrating citizen support of the political system, as well as support for the slate of leaders running for government and party positions. However, in the late 1980s throughout the Soviet Union and many East European countries, people have called for more political competition by permitting parties other than the Communist party to rally the support of the masses. At Beijing's Square of Heavenly Peace in May 1989, students and workers demanded democratization to enable (among other demands) the forces of pluralism to organize into political groups competitive with the Chinese Communist party.

Suffrage

Most states of the world whether democratic or non-democratic, apply the principle of universal suffrage*, whereby every *qualified* person in the community, rather than everybody who happens to be in the community on election day, has the right to vote. The history of suffrage has been similar in all states: gradually, restrictions to voting have been removed with respect to age, sex, property requirements, and race.[6] As a result, ever-larger proportions of the population have been included in the electorate*. In the first Canadian election in 1867, only about one in every thirty adults was eligible to vote. Women were the largest single ineligible group. Through succeeding decades, restrictions on suffrage were removed one by one. Women gained the right to vote in 1918; in 1960 legislation amended the Canada Elections Act and the Indian Act to grant federal voting rights to Indians.

All political systems have established certain suffrage qualifications for people who want to vote in elections. One is *citizenship*. Most states permit only native-born and naturalized citizens to vote. People with dual citizenship* or multiple citizenship* are usually allowed to vote in the country where they have taken up permanent residence and have demonstrated some loyalty toward the political system in which they wish to participate. Several Latin American states permit foreigners to vote in municipal elections after a five-year period of residence. Venezuela has permitted foreigners to vote in a number of its presidential elections. A certain minimum *age* is another requirement in all states extending the right or privilege of voting in governmental elections. The most common age limit is 21 years. But many states have lower limits. In 1989, Brazil lowered its voting age to 16. The Cuban Constitution of 1976 permits persons aged 16 or older to vote for municipal councils, which are the only popularly elected bodies. Eighteen years of age is the limit in Canada, Great Britain, Israel, the United States, and Uruguay. Some Latin American states that use 21 as the voting age for most people will allow married persons to vote at age 18. Denmark has the highest limit at age 25. And Italy permits persons who are 21 and over to elect deputies to the Chamber of Deputies, but permits only citizens over 25 to vote for senators. Another important qualification for voting in elections is *registration*. Most states compile voters' lists against which the names of people asking for ballots can be verified. There are basically two registration systems practised by states: one places the responsibility of registration on the voter; the other uses state-appointed officials to enrol eligible voters. In the United States, each voter must take the initiative by going to a registration office and applying. In Canada, the preparation of voters' lists is the responsibility of the Chief Electoral Officer, an independent civil servant chosen by the House of Commons to administer the Canada Elections Act, who issues writs of election to the returning officer* in each riding*.[7] These officials direct the preparation of voters' lists by supervising enumerators who canvass door to door, beginning forty-nine days before the election. Finally, *literacy* continues to be a requirement in some countries. Literacy requirements can disfranchise many persons from voting. Brazil and Ecuador disfranchise large numbers of illiterate Indians and peasants by literacy testing.

Besides these four qualifications, many states exclude certain people for various reasons. By law in South Africa, blacks are restricted from voting. The official reason used by the South African government is that blacks are citizens of the homelands and not of South Africa, and non-citizens are not permitted to vote.[8] In many states, electoral laws exclude people in prisons, jails, mental institutions, judges, and the Chief Electoral Officer. In Canada a judgement of the Federal Court in 1988 reversed the disqualification of federal judges from voting. In the same year the Federal Court struck down as unconstitutional the section of the Canada Elections Act that denied the vote to the mentally ill. But returning officers are permitted to vote only in the case of a tie vote in a riding. One Canadian inmate challenged the Canada Elections Act on the grounds that the Charter of Rights and Freedoms gives every citizen – including prisoners – the right to vote. However, the Supreme Court of Canada turned down the prisoner's appeal on a ruling of the federal appeal court, which had denied the inmate the right to vote in the 1984 federal elections because he was a prisoner.

Functions of Elections

Elections perform a variety of political and social functions in all states.[9] In democratic electoral systems, elections are the primary mechanisms for *recruiting* political leaders and representatives. As the special democratic events that link the institutions of government with people who aspire to a political career, elections are the vehicle of *political succession*, a peaceful process that transfers power from one set of political leaders to another. Therefore, elections have a *homeostatic** function in a political system: they provide a process for orderly political change while preserving the basic continuity of political and governmental institutions.

Another function of elections is to aggregate* individual choices into a *collective decision*. In all societies there is a continuous, often intense, political struggle to influence what collective goods will be provided, who will mostly pay for them, and who will benefit from them. In democracies, elections determine which majority will command the reins of power to authoritatively allocate these collective goods. And, because no society stands still, new social challenges constantly provoke the need for the widest possible *consensus** on social problems: on the public agenda today are the issues of abortion, crime, drug abuse, defence, environmental protection, unemployment, and many others. Elections not only provide the channel for expressing new social concerns about these issues, but are also an outlet for shifting public sentiment. Elections enable societies to capture changing *public attitudes* and to respond collectively to social exigencies.

Still another function of elections is *political socialization*.[10] Elections provide one of the few opportunities in most societies for all citizens to learn about the issues and personalities in the political system. The 1988 federal election provided an opportunity for Canadians to learn about the free-trade agreement and its potential impact on the economy. Thousands of copies of the agreement were sent to individuals, MP constituency offices, radio and TV stations, libraries, and universities for distribution and discussion. The televised debates between the three parliamentary leadership candidates stimulated an unprecedented and lively exchange of views across the country. Although it is true that elections offer citizens only the minimum amount of voting participation with some impact on policy making, they are an important means of political education for both the people and their representatives. Election campaigns (usually of two or more months' duration) offer politicians an opportunity – and an obligation – to educate the public and to justify their positions. It is increasingly important to the citizenry (with access to both domestic and international sources of information) to learn about and judge the quality of a regime's activities at home and abroad. Elections are one of the few genuine learning experiences that people, as a community, go through together.

In Canada, almost everyone develops partisan attachments based on party identification, ethnicity, religion, socio-economic status, ideology, and general social issues. The public is continuously exposed to political information conveyed by newspapers, television, and radio during the election campaign, usually followed by a substantial amount of media analysis after the election is over. In most states this process constitutes a total-immersion political learning experience for the citizenry. The learning process provided by elections may also include the reinforcement of positive attitudes towards authority and political obligation. In most authoritarian and totalitarian political systems, voting plays an important role in political socialization, serving as the symbolic input of citizen support for the undisputed authority and legitimacy of the party and the government.

In many authoritarian states, elections are confused, hectic, and often negative learning experiences for citizens. In these kinds of political systems, the coup d'état is still a widespread method of governmental change. Elections are held as uninvited, displaced events that further accelerate the propensity toward political violence and corruption. This factor was particularly dramatized during the elections held in Panama in 1989. At a rally of opposition parties protesting the widespread exercise of electoral larceny in Panama, the Defence Forces of president General Manuel Antonio Noriega appeared on the scene with clubs and metal pipes slashing and striking anyone in their way. The ordered brutality was political revenge on people who had supported opposition candidates before the election was annulled by the government. People are exposed to electoral manipulation and fraud, obscurantist campaigning, military intervention, proliferating candidacies, and last-minute political fiascos. They learn that *personalism* is rampant and that candidates magnify their own popularity and appeal by viciously attacking their political rivals, by slanderous name calling, or by identifying them as puppets of Marxists and communists.

In many Latin American states, people are exposed to flagrant corruptions of the electoral process.[11] The media are particularly vulnerable to official interference because they are subsidized by the government. In Mexico, it is not uncommon for the government to forgive loans to newspapers if the editorials appearing around election time are favourable. Since the military came to power in 1964 in Brazil, until 1985 when it withdrew from politics, censorship was institutionalized and was particularly restrictive against the press and popular candidates when elections were held. And in Paraguay, the 1988 landslide victory of General Alfredo Stroessner was achieved through widespread fraud as witnessed by the absence of opposition ballots at polling stations, a lack of closed booths to provide secret balloting, voting by underaged voters, and ballot-box stuffing. The following year Stroessner was forced into exile for reasons of massive government corruption.

In many authoritarian states, registration procedures are used to manipulate the electoral process and to discourage all but the most dedicated voters. Poor people, who are less interested in politics to begin with (because they have so many other immediate problems to worry about), must face the costs of needed documents and photographs. In countries with peasants*, the long journey from the countryside to urban polling stations is a strong deterrent to voting. In addition, there are also the well-known practices of buying votes, threatening voters, and fraudulently tallying the votes cast.

Nevertheless, millions of people in authoritarian states turn out at the polls whenever elections are held. This occurs, at least in part, because they need to keep a job, to maintain the support of a superior, or to avoid fines imposed in states with compulsory voting regulations. In these political systems, people are voting in ever-increasing numbers despite what they have learned about fraudulent electoral practices. The almost universal enfranchisement of women and increasing urbanization have contributed to greater electoral participation all over the world. Urban dwellers are more easily reached by competitive political parties; voting is physically easier in cities than in the countryside and the election experience itself socializes and politicizes more people now than ever before. Whenever elections are called in the authoritarian regimes of Africa, Asia, and Latin America, people have increasingly shown considerable sagacity in choosing their leaders.

Finally, elections can foster a sense of *personal efficacy*, a feeling of psychological satisfaction derived from the belief that the political system is affected and must respond to the aggregate results of voting behaviour. For those who vote in elections, personal efficacy means a perception that no matter how insignificant a single vote is, it may actually be part of a groundswell of identical messages to political leaders or aspiring political recruits. Such was the case in the 1989 Polish elections in which the Solidarity trade-union movement won 99 seats in the new 100-member Senate and all 161 opposition Seats in the 460-seat Sejm (lower house), where 299 seats were set aside prior to the election for members of the Communist party. Much national research has shown that political participation is closely related to feelings of personal efficacy.[12]

Major Electoral Systems

An electoral system consists of all the customs, laws, methods, and institutions used to elect representatives in a political system. A comprehensive description of an electoral system would include the customs and practices of campaigning and voting, the rules regulating the behaviour and funding of candidates, the methods of calculating and representing the popular vote, and the institutions (political parties, conventions, electoral colleges, and government agencies) that administer, recruit, and compete when elections are held.

Most states have evolved an electoral system of their own to choose a government and its representatives. The size of the electoral district, the number of political parties that compete, and the timing of elections are all variables affecting the performance of any electoral system. For purposes of analysis and classification, political scientists divide electoral systems into two main types: majority systems* and proportional-representation* systems. Majority systems are designed to produce either a simple plurality* or an absolute majority* for one candidate representing a single constituency. Where more than one candidate is elected to multi-member constituencies, the candidates with the largest pluralities are declared elected. Majority systems appear as single-member constituencies, multi-member constituencies, and constituencies using the preferential* and run-off* ballots. Proportional representation (PR) systems are designed to give the minority political viewpoints a share of the seats in the legislature based on their proportion of the popular vote. PR systems appear in constituencies using party–list systems and the single-transferable vote.

Majority Systems

THE SINGLE-MEMBER CONSTITUENCY

The single-member district/simple-plurality electoral system is the easiest to understand and the most widely utilized among the democratic nation-states of the world. It is used extensively in many countries, including Canada, France, Great Britain, India, and the United States. The single-member district is based on a geopolitical principle that divides a country or its subnational units into relatively equal constituencies, with one representative elected from each district. The candidate who gains a plurality of popular votes wins the election. This winner-take-all system usually means that the candidate who wins a plurality of support does not necessarily command the majority of votes cast in the constituency. In fact, a minority win often occurs in a single-member district when a successful candidate merely wins more votes than his or her opponents and does not get more than 50 percent of the total. For example, in the Toronto riding of St. Paul's in the 1988 Canadian federal election, the Progressive Conservative candidate won with 25 206 votes; the Liberal candidate received 21 655 votes, and the New Democratic Party (NDP) candidate got 5303 votes. Thus, the winner (Barbara McDougall) with her 25 206 votes had a grand total of 26 958 votes against her. When this kind of situation is repeated in riding after riding, the net effect is to over-represent the majority and under-represent the minority. When the Conservatives under Brian Mulroney won the federal election in 1988, they polled 43 percent of the popular vote but won 57.2 percent of the seats in the House of Commons. The Liberals under Turner polled 31.9 percent of the popular vote but won only 28.1 percent of the places in the Commons. The New Democratic Party under Ed Broadbent polled 20.4 percent of the popular vote and won only 14.5 percent of the seats in the House.

In Canada, the single-member constituency rarely produces a government that has the support of the majority of Canadians.[13] Even with what has been billed as the return of a powerful majority in the House of Commons after the 1988 election, the Progressive Conservatives represent less than half the voters, and when the percentage of votes to opposition and other parties is taken together, over 50 percent of the electorate voted against the government. Because plurality is the contingent of success in single-member constituencies, only on rare occasions will a majority of popular support be produced.

MULTI-MEMBER CONSTITUENCIES

Another type of constituency used in majority electoral systems is the multi-member district. In these circumstances, two or more representatives are elected from the same riding. The multi-member constituency is used to elect members to Turkey's National Assembly, as well as to a number of subnational and local legislatures in Canada, Great

Britain, and the United States. Most people are unaware of the fact that U.S. senators represent multi-member districts; two are elected from each state. Because one-third of the Senate is elected every two years, U.S. citizens rarely have the opportunity to vote for two senators simultaneously, which produces the popular misconception that senators are elected from single-member constituencies.

In Canada, many of the provinces that hosted multi-member constituencies abolished them. For example, Newfoundland in 1972, Nova Scotia in 1981, Saskatchewan in 1965, and Manitoba in 1958 all abolished multi-member districts. But in Prince Edward Island, all the sixteen constituencies are multi-member, each electing two members to the Legislative Assembly. In British Columbia, seven constituencies in the Vancouver area are multi-member ridings; all the rest in that province are single-member constituencies. In multi-member constituencies, the electorate is permitted to vote for as many candidates as there are posts to be filled. As in the single-member district, the candidates with the highest pluralities are declared elected.

PREFERENTIAL AND RUN-OFF BALLOTS

Some states – concerned that the plurality principle rarely achieves an absolute majority of support for successful election candidates – use a number of ballot techniques to guarantee that every elected representative wins with the approval of more than half the electorate. One of these techniques is the preferential ballot, which is currently used to elect representatives to the Australian House of Representatives and to four of its eight states and territories. On the preferential ballot, the voter ranks the candidates contesting a constituency in order of preference, by placing numbers rather than Xs beside their names. In order to be declared elected, a candidate must obtain a majority of first-choice votes on the ballot. If no candidate gains a majority on the first count, the candidate with the fewest first-choice preferences is dropped and his or her ballots are redistributed based on the second-choice preferences on each. This time-consuming process is continued until an absolute majority of support is obtained by a candidate. He or she is then declared elected.

Another technique is to use a run-off or second ballot in order to facilitate an absolute majority victory for successful candidates. In France, for example, candidates for legislative and executive posts compete in run-off elections that continue until a candidate polls a majority, unless they receive a majority on the first ballot. In the 1988 French presidential election, for example, none of the six candidates won a majority on the first election. This circumstance necessitated a second election between the two leading candidates, incumbent socialist President François Mitterand, and the neo-Gaullist premier Jacques Chirac. In the second election, Mitterand received 53.9 percent of the votes; Chirac received 46.1 percent.

Run-off elections are held in ten southern U.S. states in which a second primary election is held between the two top candidates when no candidate in the first primary gains a majority vote. In these states, where the Democratic party is dominant, winning the primary is tantamount to winning the election. The run-off election guarantees that the candidate who wins the primary will have the majority support of the voters, rather than determining a victory by a mere plurality when three or more candidates are contesting an election.

Proportional Systems

In the 1988 federal election, 57 percent of the votes cast by Canadians were against the Progressive Conservative party. Not all these votes went unrepresented. After all, the Liberals gained 31.9 percent of the popular vote and won 83 seats in the House of Commons; the New Democratic Party polled just over 20 percent of the popular vote and won 43 seats; and others polled 4.7 percent of the popular vote, gaining no seats. But on closer examination, we must conclude that the electoral system Canadians use to choose their political leaders under-represents their votes when they vote against the winning party.[14]

With a system of proportional representation, the votes that would remain under-represented or wasted in other electoral systems are given legislative representation in proportion to the total popular vote. Hypothetically, had the principle of proportional representation been employed in Canada's federal election of 1988, the Progressive Conservatives would have won only 127 seats based on 43 percent of the popular vote; the Liberals would have gained 94 seats; the NDP could have claimed 60 seats; and others were entitled to 14 seats.

Proportional representation is an attempt to give legislative expression to the dispersion of minority votes as they accrue in a democratic electoral system. The proponents of PR believe that a truly democratic assembly should reflect every representative point of view in a policy. PR is designed to preserve the diversion of political philosophies according to their relative strengths in the electorate.[15]

Many states employ a system of proportional representation: Denmark, Eire, the Federal Republic of Germany, Israel, and Sweden. Basically, these states allot seats in their legislatures in direct proportion to the distribution of votes. In fact, it can be argued that all PR systems now operative in modern democracies are variations of two basic types, the *list system* and *single-transferable-vote system*.

PARTY-LIST SYSTEMS

Party-list systems operate on the principle that all qualified political parties are awarded seats in the legislature in proportion to the percentage of popular votes they attract in an election.[16] Party lists are prepared by the leaders or executive committees of various parties and submitted to the electorate in multi-member constituencies. The size of the constituencies and the methods of counting and distributing seats vary from one state to another. But three distinct variations of the party–list system are detectable.

One variation gives the voter no choice among the candidates once the list is prepared. Israel is the best example of this take-it-or-leave-it party-list system. There is only one multi-member constituency in Israel – the entire country, which elects 120 members to the unicameral Knesset (parliament). All contending political parties must get 750 signatures from eligible voters before they can prepare their lists, numbering up to

120 candidates. Once the list has been made, no independent candidates are able to get on the ballot as they can in some other states such as Denmark and Finland. Even the order in which the candidates appear on the list cannot be changed. At the polling station the voter selects the ballot paper of his or her party as is, and deposits it in the ballot box. Each party is entitled to a number of seats in the Knesset according to its percentage of the total popular vote. In Israel's system it is the party, rather than individual candidates, that is the primary attraction of voter support. The voter knows what the ideological position of his or her party is and that only the most experienced and influential candidates of those on the party list will occupy the seats the party is awarded on the basis of proportional representation.

Another variation of the party-list system is to give the voter some choice among the party's candidates. The voter may decide not to alter the party list and to vote for it in its entirety, or may move preferred candidates to the top of the party list. When a majority of voters indicate preference for certain candidates other than those originally listed by the party, the seats are allocated in accordance with popular preference if the party wins enough votes at the polls. Belgium, Denmark, and the Netherlands permit voters to indicate their preferences for only one candidate; Norway and Sweden permit voters to choose up to four candidates.

The final variation in the party-list system gives voters complete freedom to choose among candidates running in a multi-member constituency. The voter has as many votes as there are seats to be filled in the constituency. He or she may choose to expend those votes on one particular candidate or may place one vote for several different candidates. The voter may also vote for different candidates or different party lists. When the votes are totalled, each party is allocated seats in proportion to the total votes for all lists. This system is used in Switzerland and Finland.

THE SINGLE-TRANSFERABLE VOTE

The single-transferable vote is a system of balloting that combines the principle that voters should have maximum choice of the candidates with a formula that guarantees all votes will be used to select representatives.[17] Voters in multi-member constituencies indicate their preferences by writing numbers in the boxes beside the names of the candidates. A quota is established for each constituency to determine the minimum number of votes a candidate must have to be declared elected. The *Droop quota* is often employed. This quota (Q) is derived by dividing the total number of votes cast (V) by the number of seats to be filled (S) plus one, and adding one to the result:

$$Q = \frac{V}{S+1} + 1$$

Thus, in a three-member constituency with 100 000 votes cast, the quota would be 25 001. Initially the ballots are sorted according to the first choices among voters. If no candidate obtains enough first-place votes to meet the quota, the candidate with the fewest first-place votes is eliminated. His or her ballots are then *transferred* to the candidates who received the largest number of first-, second-, and third-choice votes, but who may not have had enough votes to satisfy the quota. Eventually the quota is satisfied by the single transfer of votes from eliminated candidates. This system is used in Australia (Senate) Eire, Northern Ireland (Senate of Ulster), Malta, and other states.

The Hare quota, named after Thomas Hare, a Victorian lawyer and associate of John Stuart Mill, is also commonly used. This quota (Q) is derived by simply dividing the total number of votes cast (V) by the number of seats to be filled (S):

$$Q = \frac{V}{S}$$

Seats are allocated on the basis of a system that uses the largest remainder from the votes cast for a party. For example, in a four-member constituency where 20 000 votes have been cast the quota would be 5000 (table 12.2). Only two of the four parties (A & B) succeeded in surpassing the quota of 5000, thus each is directly entitled to receive one seat. But under the largest-remainder system the third seat also goes to party A and the fourth seat to party C.

Four-member constituency: 20 000 votes cast
Hare Quota: 5000

Party	Votes	Quota	Seats	Remainder	Seats	Total Seats
A	8200	5000	1	3200	1	2
B	6100	5000	1	1100	0	1
C	3000	—	0	3000	1	1
D	2700	—	0	2700	0	0
total	20 000		2		2	4

Table 12.2

A nineteenth-century Belgian lawyer, Victor D'Hondt, devised a system that divides each party's votes by successive divisors, and then allocates the seats in decending order of quotients (table 12.3). The first seat will go to party A, the second to party B, the third to party A, and the fourth to party B.

Four-member constituency: 20 000 votes cast
Division by D'Hondt divisors

Party	Votes	Divisor:1	Divisor:2	Divisor:3	Total seats
A	8200	8200(1)	4100(3)	2733	2
B	6100	6100(2)	3050(4)	2033	2
C	3000	3000	1500	1000	0
D	2700	2700	1350	900	0
total	20 000				4

Table 12.3

Canada's Electoral Process

Once the governor general dissolves a parliament on the request of the prime minister, the machinery for administering a federal election in Canada is put in motion. The Cabinet (governor in council) instructs the Chief Electoral Officer* to issue writs of election to the returning officer in every federal riding in Canada. Returning officers are responsible for preparing voters' lists, appointing deputy returning officers to the subdivisions in every riding, receiving the nomination of the candidates, and authorizing the printing of ballots.

The preparation of voters' lists is conducted by enumerators under the supervision of the returning officers. In urban centres, two enumerators (one from each of the two parties that in the last election obtained the highest pluralities in the constituency) go from door to door to register voters. Only one enumerator is required to compile lists in each rural riding. The final revision of voters' lists should be completed twelve days before the election.

The returning officer also designates the location of polling stations in each riding. At these stations, a deputy returning officer and a poll clerk watch over the polling process under the scrutiny of two agents representing each candidate. The voter is given a ballot on which are listed the names of the candidates running for office, two detachable serial numbers on the back, and the initials of the deputy returning officer (see sample ballot). For purposes of verification, the deputy returning officer tears off the first identical serial number. Once the voter has marked an "X" beside the name of the preferred candidate (in the voting booth), he or she folds the ballot paper so that the initials and the remaining serial number on the back can be read without unfolding it. The ballot is then handed back to the deputy returning officer, who confirms, by verifying the initials and the remaining serial number, that it is the same ballot paper given to the voter. If it is the same, the deputy returning officer then detaches the other identical serial number and deposits the ballot in the box. When the polls are closed, the ballots are counted by each returning officer in front of a poll clerk and party scrutineers. The ballots are locked in the ballot box and given to the returning officer who issues a declaration of election in favour of the winner. If there is a tie, the returning officer may cast the deciding vote in favour of one of the candidates.

All candidates for election to the House of Commons must be Canadian citizens, 18 years of age or over. In order to file nomination papers, a candidate must be endorsed by twenty-five other electors and provide a $200 deposit to the returning officer for the constituency. The deposit is refunded if the candidate obtains at least half the number of votes polled by the winning candidate. Otherwise the deposit is forfeited to the Crown. For example, in the 1988 election, 835 candidates lost their deposits, returning $167 000 to the Crown. Political parties register with the Chief Electoral Officer provided they had members in the previous House of Commons or have at least fifty candidates in the current election.

General elections appear to be expensive political theatre in Canada. The Chief Electoral Officer's requirements for staff and supplies amounted to an estimated $91 000 715 for the 1988 election. In addition, an estimated $20 million was set aside to reimburse some candidates' and political-party expenses, bringing the total estimated cost

to $112 002 074.[18] Over one-third of these expenses go to the preparation, enumeration, revision, and printing of lists and notices. About 20 percent of the cost of the election is spent on the operation of polling stations and the printing of ballots. Then there are the fees and allowances of returning officers and election clerks. Added to these are headquarters expenses, cost of postage, wages and extra staff, and special voting for the Armed Forces and the public-service electors (such as embassy staffs) overseas.

Do Canadian elections really cost so much? We can compare the cost of Canada's federal elections to the cost of national elections held in other nation-states (table 12.4). Actually, compared with United States, Ireland, Israel, and West Germany the cost to each elector of a Canadian federal election is quite high.

Canada's electoral system is one of the best in the world, notwithstanding the relatively high per voter cost in a country as large as it is. But there is always the possibility of improving a system that works well most of the time. Some shortcomings such as human error are unavoidable but others are correctable. In the 1988 election thousands of Canadians were denied the right to vote because of flawed procedures to register electors. Enumerators did everything from soliciting political donations to showing voter lists to candidates before returning officers had accepted them. Approximately 85 percent of the 295 returning officers named by Cabinet in the 1988 election had no prior experience as election administrators. Should the government appoint returning officers or should the Chief Electoral Officer?

Comparative cost of national elections per eligible voter
Selected states

state	$ cost per elector
Canada	6.29
Ireland	3.93
Israel	4.34
West Germany	3.20
United Kingdom	0.50
United States	
Congressional	1.51
Presidential	1.74

Source: American Institute for Public Policy Policy Research; Canada, *Elections Canada* (Ottawa: Elections Canada 1988), data for the 1988 federal election

Table 12.4

Canada's Election '88

Unlike the 1984 election, when no single issue dominated the electoral campaign more than leadership, Election '88 focussed clearly on one issue, free trade, and only subsequently on the environment, Meech Lake, the image and winability of party leaders, and the economy. But as in other recent federal elections, "leadership image" was one of the most important short-term factors contributing to voter preference and defection.[19] On the hustings*, the three party leaders put forward newer, more refined images of their leadership styles.

The Progressive Conservatives

Campaign '88 saw a newly-modelled Brian Mulroney, who departed from his old penchant for what the critics called "blarney" and for taking fierce shots at the opposition. The game plan for the 1988 campaign was for Mulroney to look more positive, restrained, and prime ministerial – to avoid the kind of dangerous "ad libs" and verbal dog-fights that had hurt his image in the past. On the most salient issue – free trade – Mulroney tried to deflect exclusive public attention from the trade agreement by pointing to the government record and making Canadians feel good about the economy and insecure about what would happen if an opposition party got elected. A private poll commissioned by the Conservatives just before the campaign showed that most Canadians (75 percent) felt they were better off in 1988 than they had been in 1984.

Mulroney had begun his campaign long before he called the election: between May and late September 1988 he and his Cabinet colleagues announced over seventy federal projects, totalling about $8 billion in pre-campaign promises. This so-called game plan proved to be very successful for the first three weeks of the campaign until the televised debates moved the free-trade issue out of the control of party strategists. From the perspective of the prime minister and his top advisers, the debates unleashed a confidence vacuum around the free-trade issue.

The sands had shifted and the Mulroney campaign needed to abandon the quiet propriety of its initial re-election strategy for a more aggressive counterattack against the Liberal thrust. Mulroney quickly linked free trade with nation building, job creation, and economic prosperity. Then he attacked Turner for what he called Turner's negative political rhetoric and his lack of a clear alternative for the economic future of the country. In the final three weeks of the campaign Mulroney was able to focus the electorate on leadership and to allay the fears of undecided voters, at least about the immediate impact of a comprehensive trade partnership with a superpower. By engineering the campaign as a one-dimensional event around the free trade issue, Mulroney succeeded in becoming the first Progressive Conservative to win a back-to-back Commons majority since John A. Macdonald in 1891.

The Liberals

At the outset of the 1988 campaign there was a new image plan for John Turner as well. Liberal organizers wanted voters to forget Turner's rusty, stumbling performance in the 1984 campaign. The Liberals expected Turner to surpass low public expectations and surprise Canadians by a smooth and forceful performance. Normally, in the TV age, a leader's image counts for more than specific stands on policies. But in 1988 Turner wanted to change that by making free trade the biggest single election issue. The Liberals tried to stir up as much passion and controversy over the trade agreement as possible to help bury doubts over Turner's leadership. The lingering issue of Turner's ability to win an election plagued the Liberal campaign from the beginning. Turner unvailed a 40-point policy platform that contained some poorly prepared budget estimates. For example, the day care program proposed by the Liberal party ranged in cost from $4 billion to $10.1 billion and drew strong criticism both inside and outside the Liberal party. Inside the party, some Liberal strategists and members of the caucus began to turn on their leader as the campaign proceeded. At one point during the campaign the party appeared to be stabbing its leader in the front as well as the back.

But Turner held ground tenaciously, carefully preparing for the televised confrontations that would change the course of the election campaign: the debates. Polls were showing that more Canadians were opposed to free trade than for it: Turner was able to attract their support temporarily by his strong showing during the debates, appearing as a credible alternative to free traders and, thus, recovering the respect of his party for the remaining part of the campaign. The Turner challenge threatened to carry the country when a Canadian Gallup poll showed the Liberals with 43 percent of the popular vote and the Conservatives trailing with 31 percent. For a brief time after the debates, Liberal rallies across the country attracted unexpected legitimacy as greater numbers of supporters and more money poured into the coffers of the party. But in the end, the free-trade issue would only rescue the honour of John Turner. The Liberals, having gained much stronger representation from their showing in the previous election, were unable to ride to power on the crest of the wave of popular doubt they had created on the free-trade issue.

The New Democrats

The NDP used glossy posters of Ed Broadbent to portray him front and centre in the NDP campaign. NDP strategists knew that Ed Broadbent was a lot more popular than their party and more popular than the other leaders just before the election. On free trade, Broadbent, like the Liberals, tried to blunt Mulroney's thrust by claiming that the Tories had widened the gap between rich and poor while squeezing the middle class. The main theme of the NDP in the election was a personalized one – that only Broadbent could be trusted to deliver integrity and fairness.

By concentrating on promoting the image of their leader the New Democrats made a strategic campaign error: they minimized the importance of the free-trade issue. The media perceived the omission and noted the offstep of the New Democratic campaign. Broadbent talked about the environment, supermailboxes, family allowances, old-age pensions, and the demise of the Liberal party – almost everything except free trade. Even after the campaign was exhausting its energies on the free-trade issue, Broadbent persistently stuck to his own agenda. Not until party strategists warned Broadbent that a serious drift in the direction of their campaign would give support away to the Liberals did free trade take on a more prominent position in the NDP platform. But it was too late: the undecided Canadian electorate was concluding that the NDP had missed its chance to take a stand on free trade.

The leaders' debates were unkind to Ed Broadbent. He stammered embarrassingly throughout the French-language debates and failed to make his presence felt in the English-language debates, appearing cranky during statements and distant from the issues being discussed. Broadbent was unable to recover the ground lost on his image as a national leader or on the party as a credible alternative to the other two parties. In the last week of the campaign the NDP had dropped to its traditional third place.

During the months that followed the election Broadbent reviewed the options for both the party's future and his own. By March 1989 his decision was to resign. In his fourteen years as leader of the party the NDP more than doubled its support from voters who identify themselves as strong party members (9 percent in 1975 to 18 percent in 1989). In the 1988 election the NDP won a record 43 seats in the House of Commons and increased its party membership in Quebec from a scant 300 in 1984 to over 20 000 in 1989.

The Results

The early returns did not confirm the pre-election projections of both private and independent pollsters that another national Progressive Conservative government would prevail. In the four Atlantic provinces with 32 seats in the House of Commons, 24 Conservatives went down to defeat, while the Liberals won 20 seats, an increase of 13 from the 1984 election. Much of the switch was due to regional apprehensions about the impact of the free-trade agreement on jobs and the social network. (See table 12.5.)

Quebec revealed the good fortune of the Mulroney strategy by returning 63 Progressive Conservatives to Ottawa and by giving the Liberals their worst showing since Confederation. The government's strong performance in Quebec was largely an expression of gratitude for the "distinct society" clause in the Meech Lake Accord, strong popular support for the free-trade agreement, and the powerful electoral endorsement of Robert Bourassa and his party machinery. The Liberals were humiliated, losing 5 additional seats since the devastating 1984 election, thereby reducing their representation in that province to its lowest since Confederation.

Ontario, the largest electoral prize, now with 99 seats, proved to be the most competitive battleground among all the political parties. The Conservatives lost considerable ground from the sweep of 67 in 1984. The anti-abortion Christian Heritage party and the anti-bilingualism Confederation of Regions party stole votes away from the Conservatives to allow Liberal or NDP candidates to finish first in five ridings. The Liberals gained support not only from disgruntled Tory supporters but also by splitting the vote in many ridings with the New Democratic Party over the issue of free trade. Of all the parties, the Liberals gained the most seats in Ontario but failed to reach their target of 55, despite the appeal and support of Premier David Peterson.

In traditionally Conservative Western Canada, the battle shifted from the Liberals and the Conservatives to the NDP and the Conservatives. One exception was Manitoba, where the Liberals increased their representation from one seat in 1984 to five in 1988 – at the expense of both the Conservatives and the NDP. But, two noteworthy surprises were the surge of the NDP in Saskatchewan and British Columbia. In Saskatchewan, the NDP doubled its representation at the expense of the Conservatives. In British Columbia the NDP more than doubled its representation, its best performance in any province in the country. The NDP also won in Yukon, while the Liberals took the two seats in the Northwest Territories. Other parties seriously challenged the perceived dominance of the Progressive Conservatives in the West.

The western-based Reform party of Canada and to some extent the Christian Heritage party also made inroads in the popular vote. In fact, the Progressive Conservative Party faced a challenge from across the political spectrum, even though it won 48 of the 86 seats in the "region." Appealing to expressions of western alienation, the Reform Party attracted about 15 percent of the Alberta vote, almost always at the expense of the Progressive Conservatives. Just four months after the federal election the Reform Party's candidate, Deborah Grey, stunned the Conservatives by winning Alberta's sprawling Beaver River riding in a by-election called after the death of Conservative MP John Dahmer.

The 1988 election gave the Progressive Conservatives another mandate to implement their strategies for the country. The free-trade agreement became a reality for Canadians. The Progressive Conservative's focus on the deficit, the national debt, and role of government in the Canadian economy, the Meech Lake Accord, and the thrust of Canada's external relations were reaffirmed in the results.

One of the most notable outcomes of the elections in 1984 and 1988 was the breakthrough of women into the area of federal politics. In 1984, twenty-nine women won

Election results by provinces 1984 and 1988

	1984			1988		
province	**PC**	**L**	**NDP**	**PC**	**L**	**NDP**
Newfoundland	4	3	0	2	5	0
Prince Edward Island	3	1	0	0	4	0
Nova Scotia	9	2	0	5	6	0
New Brunswick	9	1	0	5	5	0
Quebec	58	17	0	63	12	0
Ontario	67	14	13	46	43	10
Manitoba	9	1	4	7	5	2
Saskatchewan	9	0	5	4	0	10
Alberta	21	0	0	25	0	1
British Columbia	19	1	8	12	1	19
Yukon	1	0	0	0	0	1
Northwest Territories	2	0	0	0	2	0
		(281)			(295)	

Source: Canada, *Elections Canada*, results by provinces, 1984, 1988 (Ottawa: Elections Canada 1988).

Table 12.5

seats in the House of Commons – about double the number of the previous Parliament – and an unprecedented six women were appointed to Mulroney's first Cabinet. In some ways the myths of political prejudice may have been shattered once and for all, although compared with other states, Canada is relatively low in terms of the percentage of the representation of women in its lower House (see table 12.6) In 1988, thirty-nine women were elected but the number of women called to the Cabinet still remained at six. The social and psychological barriers that have prevented women from participating in Canada's male-dominated federal institutions may have begun to crumble. But the fact remains that women, who represent 50 percent of the gender population, only hold about 13 percent of the seats in the House of Commons. Since 1921, when they were declared "persons" under the British North America Act, only seventy-eight women have ever been elected to the House of Commons. Of these, only fifteen have made it into the Cabinet.

In the 1980s, women's issues attained public visibility to a much greater degree than at any previous time in Canada's electoral history.[20] Since the early 1970s, the executive of the National Action Committee on the Status of Women had challenged the three federal party leaders to debate women's issues, and the three leaders have felt compelled to say yes. This, too, was a turning point: the recognition of women's equality in Canada's political system.

In 1984 the main indicator of the ascendancy of women into the hitherto male preserve of national politics was the Cabinet appointments, making up an unprecedented 15 percent

Percentage of women in the single or lower chamber of parliament, selected states

state	% of women
Albania	28.8
Austria	10.9
Bangladesh	9.1
Canada	13.0
Denmark	29.0
German Federal Republic	15.4
German Democratic Republic	32.2
Lebanon	0
USSR	34.5
U.S.	5.3

Source: Inter-Parliamentary Union, Geneva, Switzerland, 1988.

Table 12.6

of the political executive. But no further increases took place after the 1988 election. For the first time in the history of the Canadian political executive, there is at least one woman on every Cabinet committee, putting women firmly in the inner circles of government power, notwithstanding the under-representation of women at every level of Canadian politics.

Women, formerly considered a passive political force in Canada, are now regarded as constituent contributors to the political culture of the country. The 1984 election demonstrated that the contemporary Canadian electorate is beginning to love its daughters as much as its sons. But as Canadian women look ahead only a few years to the next century, they may wonder whether the promises of equal pay for equal work and the amendment of all discriminatory legislation against women at the federal level will happen in the twentieth century. Where this agenda will lead, no one can say precisely – except that it will entail much more than a simple redefinition of political equality. Indeed, political equality is still a long-term goal.

Elections in the United States

As in Canada, elections to public office are dramatic events in American political life. With the possible exceptions of assassination and public scandal, they command more attention from more people than any other political phenomena. Thousands of candidates take part in the numerous elections that characterize the American political scene.

The excitement of elections and electioneering is not limited to campaigns for the presidency. All members of the U.S. House of Representatives and one-third of the senators are up for re-election every two years. Many state and local officials are elected in the years between federal elections. In addition, there are many referendum elections held on school taxes, bond issues, state constitutional amendments, and other municipal questions.

Elections in the United States are complicated events. Candidates and their supporters expend a lot of energy and money on a wide range of campaign activities. Presidential campaigns, for example, usually consume a full year of electioneering, and sometimes as many as four years.[21] Many aspiring candidates manoeuvre and posture to test the political waters before they declare their intentions for party nominations. These nominations are won only after arduous and expensive presidential primary campaigns during which candidates amass convention delegate support. In the 1988 Democratic primary campaign, there were the seven original Democratic candidates who competed for 3900 delegates, of whom 1967 were needed to win the presidential nomination. Finally, after a formidable and bitter nomination battle that continued even as the Democratic convention was in progress, Michael Dukakis emerged as his party's candidate in the nationwide presidential election. This kind of extended campaign is expensive. Candidate organizations spend several hundred million dollars to elect a president. In the 1988 presidential election the candidates and their parties spent $140 million, occasionally skirting official rules. Campaign supporters offer their time as well as their money for their candidates.

Throughout the campaign period, speeches are made, issues are debated, images are projected, personalities are revealed, and voters finally choose their government decision makers. The electoral process is, therefore, critical for the recruitment of candidates and to the operation of the political system. Even though elections by no means determine what the U.S. government does, they can have enormous impact on public policy. The first election of Ronald Reagan in 1980 reversed the direction of American public policy over the preceding half-century by large tax cuts, reductions in domestic program spending, and deregulation.

One very important aspect of U.S. elections is that they occur regularly: federal elections take place at the exact times specified in the Constitution, regardless of convenience or partisan advantage. They have never been postponed. State and local elections, though governed by different constitutional calendars, also are held regularly, as are primary elections held by states to nominate candidates. The regularity of elections guarantees that public officeholders are accountable to their constituents.

These elections in the U.S. are structured in another important way. Most election activities – filing for candidacy, selection of nominees, raising and spending money, and a host of campaign activities – are shaped and regulated by law. Many of these laws are state regulations; they vary somewhat from one state to another. The patterns that emerge provide a basis for the study of U.S. electioneering practices.

Primaries

In the early years of the American republic, party nominees were chosen by the caucus, an informal meeting of leaders who selected a candidate to carry the party banner in the election. Presidential candidates were selected by caucuses of party senators and congresspersons. As the electorate expanded, so did the complexity of party organizations at the grass-roots level. The method of caucus selection gradually became inadequate and party *convention* in the 1830s, made up of delegates elected by local party organizations, were established to choose party nominees for president, vice-president, and other elective offices. The conventions greatly democratized the nominating process, but by 1900, party bosses* gradually took control of the conventions. Conventions of this period often were rigged and dominated by certain party factions. The reformers of the progressive era at the turn of the century demanded that nominations be made directly by the people, not by politicians or party organizers. The mechanism for so doing was the *direct primary*. The primary, taken from the Latin word for "first," is the first election taking place within the party. Primary elections are the means of involving party followers in the nominating process. They are followed by a general election where competition transpires between parties.

Some primaries held in about forty states are *closed*, requiring voters to declare in advance that they are registered members of the party. Other primaries are *open*, and do not force partisan declarations: people can decide when they enter the voting booth on election day in which party's primary they will participate. Voters are given each party's primary ballot; they vote on one. Idaho, Michigan, Minnesota, Montana, North Dakota, Utah, Vermont, and Wisconsin have open primaries. Some states have a run-off primary; when no candidate gets a majority of the primary votes, there is a run-off between the two candidates with the most votes. Two states, Alaska and Washington, provide a variant of the open primary called a *blanket primary*, which permits a voter to mark a ballot that lists the candidates for nomination of all the parties. Thus, the voter can help select the Democratic candidate for one office and the Republican candidate for another.

The South was the first region of the United States to institute the direct primary; however, its purpose was to prevent a coalition of poor blacks and poor whites from presenting their candidates for public office. By appealing to racism, dominant economic groups aligned with rural whites to sustain one-party domination in the region. In contrast, the political structure of the urban northeast was characterized by sharp competition between parties.

The primary system has greatly influenced the structure of party competition and the outcome of presidential elections in the United States.[22] When they were first used in many states, it was widely believed the primaries would be a more democratic way to nominate candidates, because they involve many more people than the handful who participate in conventions or *caucuses**. Later, primary elections were formed to involve party followers in the nomination process. Reformers felt that a larger dose of democracy would bring about mass political participation of truly representative character. But today the voters in primary elections are far from a simple cross-section of the population. Usually older, wealthier, and better educated, they tend to be more politically aware and ideologically conscious than people who vote only in general elections.[23] Therefore, primaries retain an elitist character.

The primary system today is confusing because each state has its own rules for presidential primaries. The variations are considerable and can have extraordinary consequences for the fortunes of presidential candidates. In Texas, a voter must vote once on Saturday morning and once more in the evening to have the vote count for local delegates. Because of the many issues in each state, candidates find it difficult to enunciate national policies. In New England, candidates must talk about the price of heating oil. In New York, candidates must cultivate Jews, blacks, and Italians, to the exclusion of other groups. In Texas and California, they court Hispanic voters. In the farm and industrial states, they must woo farmers whose needs conflict with those of steelworkers in Ohio and Pennsylvania.

Many candidates say, off the record, that the direct-primary nominating system is too important to be left to disparate state practices and that Congress should step in to standardize the system across the country by law. Unquestionably, the primary permits voter participation in the selection of candidates. It permits unknowns to compete for office, and it gives candidates opposed to the party leadership a chance to win. The primary also gives great emphasis to image and personality and enhances the power of money and the media. In these ways, it has contributed both to democracy and to demagogy* in American party politics.

National Conventions

Conventions are the next step in the process of selecting a presidential candidate.[24] But unlike in Canada, where conventions actually choose the party's candidate, most conventions in the U.S. tend to ratify the choice of the candidate who has succeeded in committing the most delegates* during the primaries. Even before the convention meets, the leading candidate usually has enough delegate votes to remove any doubt about the outcome. But in the hotly contested seven-man Democratic leadership race in 1988, Michael Dukakis was never able to remove all doubts within his party that he was a shoo-in at the convention. Even on the eve of the convention Jesse Jackson braced some Democrats with the thought that a black man could win the nomination. In this case, the choice for president was not predetermined.

Delegates to the presidential nominating convention are selected in a variety of ways. In some states, delegates are bound to the candidate winning the primary election, while in other states delegates can exercise their discretion about voting for the winner of the state primary at the national convention. In yet other states, delegates are selected by state party committees. Because not all the fifty states hold primaries, these states send delegates to the convention who have been selected by party committees and caucuses. The results of committee and caucus action are not always telling. Consider the caucuses held in Iowa in early February of a presidential election year. Anyone who does badly in Iowa is at a disadvantage because of the predictive analyses provided by the media. In 1988, the first real test of the Republican candidiates in Iowa showed Senator Robert Dole coming first, the evangelist Pat Robertson second, and Vice-President George Bush finishing third. Few would argue that making sense of the bewildering array of primaries and caucuses to determine candidates for presidential conventions in the United States is easy.

Conventions perform other important functions in addition to the glamorous selection of a presidential candidate. They are the supreme governing body of their respective parties.

They formulate rules for the party and write the platform. All this is done in less than a week by several thousand people, most of whom do not know each other, and in all likelihood may never meet again.[25]

For the first day or two, the convention is concerned primarily with the work of the Committee on Credentials and the Platform Committee. The Committee on Credentials works out conflicts that arise between rival groups of delegates from the same state or when rival groups are pledged to different candidates. The Platform Committee works hard to placate all factions in the party and attempts to put together a statement of national party policies.

Conventions are also forums for keynote speakers. These orations are stylized political spectacles in which the speaker points to his or her party's achievements, views with alarm the sinister plans of the rival party, and attempts to excite the delegates to a state of high emotion.

When all the candidates are before the convention, balloting begins. The roll of the states is called and the world watches to see where the delegates' support will go. Party politicians prefer to decide the contest on the first ballot, thereby minimizing the danger of exposing party divisions and reducing the risk of the convention choosing a dark horse* nominee. The candidate who begins slipping is usually deserted like a sinking ship. At a crucial time, a switch in an important state can start a bandwagon effect. California is always an important state to watch because it combines the advantages of having many votes and is called to the roll near the top of the alphabet. As soon as the nominee has received enough votes to win, it is customary for rivals to move that the nomination be unanimous.

The nomination for the vice-presidency is usually an anticlimax because it is left to the determination of the party leaders. The considerations marking the choice are the personal preferences of the presidential candidates, the number of political IOUs resulting from the campaign, and the observance of the political maxim to "balance the ticket." In 1984, Walter Mondale's choice of Geraldine Ferraro had broken the mould of U.S. politics, by balancing women as equals with men. In 1988 George Bush had no idea that his choice of Dan Quayle for vice-president would generate so much controversy. Many people had doubts about Quayle's ability to assume the presidency, should the death, illness, or resignation of Bush necessitate the political succession of the vice-president. Eight times in American history a vice-president has become president because of the death of his predecessor and once because of a presidential resignation.

After the excitement of the nominating process, candidates have about six weeks to get their second wind before beginning the dash to the election finish line. By the end of September, the campaign is in full swing, and the candidates spend fifteen to twenty hours a day making speeches, shaking hands, travelling, and meeting with the media.

Elections are won and lost by a combination of long-term forces such as party identification and short-term forces such as the issues and the personal appeal of the candidates.[26] The mass media have become a crucial factor in influencing major shifts in electoral support toward candidates. Party identification seems to have lost much of its power. Even though the characteristics of people identifying themselves as strong

Democrats and strong Republicans have remained stable since the early 1950s, Americans are voting in more widely diverse ways. It is not uncommon, for example, for a party's candidate for president to receive 30 or 40 percent more or less votes than the same party's candidate for governor or senator. The 1988 presidential election showed this practice of ticket splitting in state after state. At the gubernatorial* level, Republicans are still in the minority: Democratic governors presently control most of the statehouses.

Many politicians and journalists think that the public issues in a political campaign are not important. Instead they stress candidate image, party loyalty, and get-out-the-vote drives. Other scholars and politicians concede the potency of all of these factors but nevertheless argue that in recent years, more and more people have come to base their choices on the closeness of fit between their own issue positions and the candidate's stand on policy. Increasingly, the American electorate is judging candidates in terms of the policies their candidates stand for.[27] But the issues themselves have become exceedingly complex, all sprayed over with contradicting statistics: disputed factoids of missile and nuclear capability, of budget entitlements, and of thunderhead effects that could prove anything any candidate wanted to prove.

The other side of the coin is exhibited by repeated findings that many voters do not have opinions – or have only weak and unstable opinions – about most issues. Voters are often ignorant of the candidates' positions or of issues, and vote solely on candidate image. There is also a detectable tendency for American voters to rationalize their choice of candidates by misperceiving where they stand. Many will support a favorite candidate by thinking mistakingly that he or she agrees with their policy preferences. At the same time, these voters dismiss other presidential candidates by imagining that the candidates disagree with them even when they do not. Some voters even change their minds on issues so as to be consistent with the candidate they prefer. In other words, the candidate is perceived as more important than the issues.

One way of attracting broad support in recent presidential elections is to engage in personality politics. Projecting a strong personal image appeals to diverse interests, and television is ideally suited to reinforce this purpose. A candidate's appeal may be based on a non-political record and experience, for example, Reagan's acting career.[28] To the extent that Americans do base their votes on personality, the crucial question is whether burning national and international issues are sacrificed for personal appeal. American elections affect public policy in complex and indirect ways that are hard to chart and nearly impossible to measure. Elections clearly are not policy and issue referenda. Rather, they determine which personalities will govern – but not how or to what ends. Amidst the drama and heros of a presidential campaign, elections are often seen as a struggle of personalities – of good guys against bad guys. Because of this, public comprehension of the more difficult underlying realities is lessened.

Election '88

Canada had a national election in 1988 and so did the United States. Americans made George Bush their 41st president: he piled up a 40-state victory, tallying 426 votes in the

Electoral College. This was an impressive national showing for a presidential candidate in the shadow of Ronald Reagan, who had won a landslide of 49 states. There have only been three occasions in American history when a vice-president has been able to win the presidency without his president having died in office: Martin Van Buren (1836), Richard Nixon (1968), and George Bush (1988). It was also the first time since 1928 that the Republican Party won a third consecutive term in the White House. Dukakis won 112 electoral votes with 46 percent of the popular vote. His support was drawn in large numbers from urban blacks, Hispanics, union households, women, and people who earn less than $10 000 a year. Bush took everyone else, attracting every category of voter in the suburbs and in the rural areas: the young, middle-aged, and elderly; the low-, middle-, and upper-income groups; Protestants, Jews, and Roman Catholics; and professionals, business, white-collar workers, and union members. In fact, Bush won over 85 percent of the voters who had supported Ronald Reagan.

From the start the Democrats had a major uphill battle into the White House. They had lost four of the preceeding five presidential elections and, in the wake of Ronald Reagan, the economy was perceived to be healthy by Americans who felt more prosperous in 1988 than they did in 1984 and much better off than they had felt in 1980. As well, the electoral calculus was mounting against the Democrats: successful Democratic presidential candidates had carried all or most of the southern states. But since 1968, the Republicans had become very strong in the South. Another disadvantage for the Democrats at the national level was that they were widely viewed as being too liberal. Dukakis tried to displace this perception in the primaries when he ran as a moderate against Jesse Jackson, who was seen as very liberal. And, by choosing a conservative Texan, Senator Lloyd Bentsen (the first time since 1960 a southern Democrat was the chosen nominee for vice-president), as his vice-presidential running mate, Dukakis beckoned to the South. From the beginning, Dukakis campaigned on his record as governor of Massachusetts, focussing on competence, character, and a departure from the Reagan administration's approach to government and the economy. He tried to sell the idea that he was a good manager, someone who could replicate the magic he professed to perform for Massachusetts, for all of America.

George Bush campaigned with two important advantages: a growing economy and a country at peace. His challenges were to establish himself as a distinctive leader after serving eight years as Reagan's vice-president and to endear himself to the same people who had become addicted to Reagan's ideology. As well, Bush had to distance himself diplomatically from the unsightly side of Reagan's legacy while still vice-president: the corruptions of the Iran-contra affair, the inhumane character of Reaganomics among the less fortunate in America, and the public perception that Reagan did not grasp the issues. Bush appealed to America's altruism, for "a kinder and gentler" nation, a new compassion for the world, while going for the jugular against the Democrats.

The tone of the 1988 campaign was negative: Bush portrayed Dukakis as a knee-jerk liberal, whose propensities were evident in the Massachusetts prison-furlough program, and whose positions on abortion, the death penality, pollution, and taxation would return Americans to the chaos of the 1960s. Bush's tough posturing was designed to reverse the limp public image he acquired while vice-president. He appealed to *retrospective voters* – constituents who evaluate the recent past and then vote for the party that controls the White House if what has happened is perceived as favourable. Retrospective voting does not require the electorate to have a lot of information – only, when looking back, to feel that they are better or worse off. In 1980 retrospective voters wanted change; in 1984 and 1988 they wanted continuity. Bush was close enough to Reagan as vice-president to be the next best thing to an incumbent*. He portrayed himself as the candidate who would continue the conservative policies that generated prosperity and he characterized Dukakis as a the "closet liberal" who would upset the lasting effects of those policies.

Dukakis, in contrast, was appealing to *prospective voters* – those who look forward, want change, and rationally compare the rhetoric and policies of the presidential candidates before making their decision. In the United States they are the minority of all voters. Even so, Dukakis was unclear about the future directions of his policies and, thus, was unable to attract many of his targeted constituents. And, his campaign suffered more from its omissions than its actions. Dukakis shrugged off Republican charges that he was flaky, too liberal, elitist, tax-prone, and unpresidential. For one who had repeatedly called the campaign a "marathon" Dukakis proved to be a man too late with his sprint. His delays would turn impressions into imagery and convince an observant electorate that the devil they knew was better than the devil they did not know.

The two presidential debates did little to alter the electoral mind-set. Dukakis was awarded the spoils of the first debate, but the impact of the debate was fleeting. Bush was generally considered to have come out ahead in the second debate, which helped foster a marked swing to him in the days following that media event. Since the famous Lincoln-Douglas debates in the 1850s, face-to-face confrontations between political candidates have held a special place in the lore of American politics. But only in unusual circumstances could a debate be decisive in a contemporary presidential election. Debates provide opportunities and dangers, but are only one component of a long and elaborate election campaign.

On the second Tuesday of November George Bush scored a decisive victory, winning 54 percent of the popular vote. The results seemed to confirm the belief that in presidential elections, the incumbent party has significant advantages during good economic times. But even with such a strong showing for the White House, the Republicans did not improve their position in Congress, which seemed to confirm that in prosperous times voters rarely make major changes.

One important question to ask is how much of a realigning* effect Ronald Reagan's eight-year tenure will have on long-term Republican victories in the White House? There is growing evidence to support the hypothesis that a realignment may have taken place. The percentage of voters identifying themselves as Republicans rose by five points from 1980 but still only constitutes about 35 percent of the electorate. To a great extent, realignment was a possibility that depended on how successful President Reagan was in his second term. The 1984 election challenged the long-held assumption that an increase in voter participation favours the Democrats. The policies of the Reagan administration – lower taxes, a stronger military, antipathy toward abortion and affirmative action, continued the realignment that had apparently started in 1980. By 1988 southern white voters had solidified their movement out of the Democratic party and into the Republican party. There were 5 million more voters in 1988 than in 1980 and most of this new voter support went to Bush. In addition, the president won approximately two-thirds of the votes cast by people between the ages of 18 and 24.

The American electoral process has fulfilled its basic function of giving citizens a periodic opportunity to review the performance of political leaders. However, there is little indication that even presidential elections are important enough to many Americans to increase voter participation much above 50 percent. Recent presidential elections have not involved flaming issues that inspire voter turnout or divide the nation into rival political camps. As in Canada, leadership seems to dominate the decision of the American voter. The Democratic and Republican parties still play an important role, even though voters are increasingly likely to make independent judgements about the leadership qualities of presidential candidates. The parties are also still a major force in local, state, and congressional races. Thus, from the standpoint of encouraging executive responsiveness to the people, the American political party system appears to be effective.

REFERENCES

1. T.H. Jacobson, "Primitive Democracy in Ancient Mesopotamia," *Journal of New Eastern Studies* 11 (1943): 159–72.
2. Jon H. Pammett, "Elections," in Michael Whittington and Glen Williams, eds., *Canadian Politics in the 1980's* (Toronto Methuen 1981), 206.
3. Sidney Verba et al., *Participation and Political Equality: A Seven-Nation Comparison* (New York: Cambridge University Press 1978); and Richard Leonard and Richard Natkiel, *World Atlas of Elections: Voting Patterns in 39 Democracies* (Ann Arbor, MI: The University of Michigan Press 1986); and G. Bingham Powell Jr., "American Voter Turnout in Comparative Perspective," *American Political Science Review* 80 (March 1986): 17–44.
4. David Elkins and Richard Simeon, *Small Worlds: Provinces and Parties in Canadian Political Life* (Toronto: Methuen 1980), 60–70; and George Perlin, *Ambivalent Canadians* (Toronto: Butterworths 1982); see also "Determinants of Provincial Voting Behaviour," in Allan Kornberg et al. *Representative Democracy in Canadian Provinces* (Toronto: Prentice-Hall 1982).
5. Gabriel Almond and G. Bingham Powell Jr., eds., *Comparative Politics Today: A World View* (Glenview, IL: Scott, Foresman & Co. 1988), 49–56.
6. Richard Rose, ed., *Electoral Participation: A Comparative Analysis* (Beverly Hills, CA: Sage Publications Inc. 1980), 5–34; and Charles Vaughan, *Franchising: Its Nature, Scope, Advantages, and Development* (Lexington: MA: Lexington Books 1979).
7. "Electing a Canadian Government" in Paul Fox, ed., *Politics: Canada,* 5th ed. (Toronto: McGraw-Hill Ryerson Ltd. 1982), 368.
8. Brian Tennyson, *Canadian Relations with South Africa: A Diplomatic History* (Washington, D.C.: University Press of America 1982), 179–200.
9. Dell Gillette Hitchner and Carol Levine, *Comparative Government and Politics* (New York: Harper & Row Publishers 1981), 127–62; and Alan Ball, *Modern Politics and Government,* 4th ed (London: Macmillan Education 1988), 119–28.
10. Harold Clarke et al., *Political Choice in Canada* (Toronto: McGraw-Hill Ryerson Ltd. 1980), 242–51.

11. Ronald McDonald and Mark Ruhl, *Party Politics and Elections in Latin America* (Boulder, CO.: Westview Press 1989); and Howard Wiarda and Harvey Kline, *Latin American Politics and Development* (Boulder, CO: Westview Press 1989).
12. Sidney Verba et al., *Participation and Political Equality: A Seven-Nation Comparison* (New York: Cambridge University Press 1978); and Samuael Barnes et al., *Political Action: Mass Participation in Five Western Democracies* (Beverly Hills, CA: Sage Publications 1979).
13. W.P. Irving, *Does Canada Need a New Electoral System?* (Kingston: Institute of Inter-governmental Relations, Queen's University 1979).
14. A. Westell, "Election System Undemocratic," *Star-Phoenix* (Saskatchewan), June 9, 1979.
15. Paul Fox, "P.R. for Canada," in Fox, ed., *Politics: Canada*, 6th ed. (Toronto: McGraw-Hill Ryerson 1987), 417–24.
16. Alan R. Ball, *Modern Politics and Government*, 90–93.
17. Thomas Mackie and Richard Rose, *The International Almanac of Electoral History*, 2nd ed. (London: Macmillan 1982), 406–12.
18. Canada, *Estimated Cost of the 1988 General Election* (Ottawa: Chief Electoral Officer 1988).
19. Jon H. Pammett, "Elections," in Whittington and Williams, eds., *Canadian Politics in the 1980's*, 208–13.
20. See Janine Brodie, *Women and Politics in Canada* (Toronto: McGraw-Hill Ryerson Limited 1985); Nancy Adamson et al., *Feminist Organizing For Change* (Toronto: Oxford University Press 1988) 3–26.
21. William Flanigan and Nancy Zingale, *Political Behavior of the American Electorate* (Boston: Allyn and Bacon, Inc. 1983), 115–40; Seymour Martin Lipset, "A Reaffirming Election: 1988," *International Journal of Public Opinion Research 97* (January 1989).
22. Harold Barger, *The Impossible Presidency* (Glenview, IL: Scott, Foresman & Co. 1984), 65–72; Wayne Parent, C. Jillson, and R. Weber, "Voting Outcomes in the 1984 Democratic Party Primaries and Caucuses," *American Political Science Review* 81 (March 1987): 67–84.
23. Austin Ranny, "Turnout and Representation in Presidential Primary Elections," *American Political Science Review* 66 (March 1972): 21-37; see also E. Ladd, and K. Keene, "Attitudes Toward Government: What the Public Says," *Government Executive* 22 (January 1988) 11–16.
24. Robert Lineberry, *Government in America*, 4th ed. (Glenview, IL: Scott, Foresman & Co. 1989), 267–91.
25. Lock Johnson and Harian Hahn, "Delegate Turnover at National Party Conventions," in Donald Matthews, ed., *Perspectives on Presidential Selection* (Washington: Brookings Institution 1973); Paul-Henri Gurian, "Resource Allocation Strategies in Presidential Nomination Campaigns," *American Journal of Political Science* 30 (November 1986): 802–21.
26. Flanigan and Zingale, *Political Behaviour of the American Electorate*, 24–30.
27. David Hill and Norman Luttbeg, *Trends in American Electoral Behaviour* (Itasca, IL: F.E. Peacock Publishers Inc. 1983), 30–58; 1980, 1984, and 1988 data from the *New York Times*/CBS News exit polls.
28. Ronnie Dugger, *On Reagan, The Man and His Presidency* (New York: MacGraw-Hill 1983), 1–25, 254–68.

SUGGESTED READINGS

Arturo Alvarado, *Electoral Patterns and Perspectives in Mexico* (San Diego, CA: University of California Press 1987).

John Booth and Mitchell Seligson, *Elections and Democracy in Central America* (Chapel Hill, NC: University of North Carolina Press 1988).

Michael Lewis-Beck, *Economics and Elections: The Major Western Democracies* (Ann Arbor, MI:

University of Michigan Press 1988).

Thomas Mackie and Richard Rose, *The International Almanac of Electoral History* (New York: Facts on File, Inc. 1988).

Howard Penniman, ed., *Canada at the Polls, 1984* (Washington: American Enterprise Institute 1988).

Gerald Pomper, Ross Baker et al., *The Election of 1988: Reports and Interpretations* (Chatham, NJ: Chatham House Publishers 1989).

James Reichley, *Elections American Style* (Washington: Brookings Institute 1988).

Larry Sabato, *Campaigns and Elections: A Reader in Modern American Politics* (Glenview, IL: Scott, Foresman & Co. 1989).

Frank Sorauf, *Money in American Elections* (Glenview, IL: Scott, Foresman & Co. 1988).

Joel Swerdlow, *Media Technology and the Vote* (Boulder, CO: Westview Press 1989).

GLOSSARY

ballot: Derived from the term ballotta, a round bullet; eventually, came to mean a voice or a lot used in the act of voting, usually in secret by balls or by written or printed tickets or slips of paper.

psephology: One of the most highly developed areas of behavioural political science that uses quantifiable methods to study elections and voting.

compulsory voting: Electoral participation by qualified voters that is required by law and is used in Australia, Belgium, the Netherlands, Austria, Brazil, Italy, and other countries.

political apathy: A sense of diffused responsibility regarding political matters: the individual does not feel personally involved or has become convinced that he or she is not able to influence political outcomes.

universal suffrage: The right of qualified voters to participate in the electoral process of a political system through the use of the vote.

electorate: All persons taken as a group who have qualifications to vote in an election.

dual citizenship: Citizenship that is officially recognized by two states.

multiple citizenship: A person has multiple citizenship when three or more states officially recognize his or her citizenship.

returning officer: A person from each riding appointed by order in council to supervise the conduct of the election after writs of election are issued by the Chief Electoral Officer.

riding: A legislative constituency from which an individual is elected with the charge to act in a public fashion on behalf of the people residing within the constituency.

homeostasis: The tendency in a social or political system to stabilize by means of self-adjustments (such as elections) that counter or compensate for disruptive and destabilizing influences.

aggregate: The process by which two or more individuals or groups combine their demands to seek a common political objective.

consensus: A decision-making procedure in a group that seeks agreement or acquiesence by all members of the group.

peasant: An agricultural worker in an agrarian society.

majority system: An electoral system requiring either a plurality or an absolute majority to elect representatives to an organization or political institution.

proportional representation: A multi-member electoral system in which each qualified party wins seats in a legislature in proportion to its total popular vote.

plurality: The number of votes secured by a candidate that is more than the number obtained by any rival candidates for office and is less than a majority of total votes cast.

absolute majority: A number of votes equal to more than 50 percent of the eligible votes cast.

preferential ballot: An electoral form that

permits the voter to mark the candidates in the order of his or her preference by placing numbers rather than Xs beside their names.

run-off ballot: A final election to break a tie or to force a majority of support for one candidate.

Chief Electoral Officer: In Canada, an independent official who is responsible to the House of Commons and sets the election machinery in motion.

hustings: Any place where political campaign speeches are made.

party boss: A person who heads a political machine and who manipulates political power in a particular area (state, county, city), especially through the use and control of patronage.

caucus: A closed meeting of the members of a political party, either to select a candidate for office or to agree on a legislative position.

demagogue: A person who takes political advantage of social and political unrest through the use of highly emotional and prejudiced appeals to the general population or a particular segment of the general population.

delegate: A person authorized or sent to act for others in a constituent assembly or party convention.

dark horse: An unexpected compromise candidate, who is nominated for office by a political party after a series of deadlocks over more conspicuous contenders.

gubernatorial: Of or relating to the office of governor whose functions include the management of state government in the United States and other countries.

incumbent: The person currently in office.

realigning election: Amidst widespread social change caused by past economic dislocations and a lack of response by the majority party, the minority party seizes upon the new issues, as millions of voters switch to its support and demand fundamental policy changes in government.

13

The International System

Amnesty International supports human rights world-wide

What is the International System?

THINK OF THE WORLD AS AN ECONOMIC and political community made up of state and non-state actors.[1] Today, this global community is complexly interdependent. The actions of one actor on any number of participants can touch and affect the lives of people anywhere. By the 1990s Canada was supporting more than 4600 development projects in over 100 countries. In Bhopal, India, the leaking of toxic gas from a multinational pesticide plant killed more than 3320 people by 1989. The Supreme Court of India ruled that the multinational corporation had to pay $470 million (on claims totaling $3 billion) in damages to surviving victims and their families. In Lockerbie, Scotland, Pan American Flight 103 is blown out of the sky by a concealed bomb planted by terrorists. In Canada, an organization called MATCH International Centre supports projects that help women in the developing world obtain better health care, child-care options, occupational training, and employment. In 1989 a United Nations-sponsored treaty to control the proliferating trade in hazardous waste is unanimously approved by 116 states including Canada. Peter Lown and Yevgeny Chazov, cofounders of International Physicians for the Prevention of Nuclear War are two individuals who have affected the international system by their will and energies to work for peace.

The above examples serve to identify the six types of actors in the contemporary global system: states, international organizations, multinational corporations, non-governmental organizations, trans-national groups, and individuals.

Until the twentieth century, most students of global and comparative politics assumed that the state was the core unit of the international system and that knowledge of interstate relations was all that was necessary to understand and explain events in the global political system. Most present-day students of global politics still recognize the importance of a state-centric perspective in world affairs, but they are also aware that the global political system consists of many other autonomous actors interacting in patterned ways to influence the character of the system.[2] We still accept the principal role played by states, but it is no longer possible to ignore the presence of non-state actors and the challenges they make to the dominance of states in the global system. There is a growing recognition that the vast majority of states are no longer able to cope with the new global problems emerging from development, energy, food, space, and technology. Some states, such as Canada, the Soviet Union, and the United States, may be in a superior position to deal with these issues, but as time goes on, even their resources will succumb to the need for an inter-global effort to resolve world problems of such great magnitude.

States

The predominant actors in the international system are sovereign and independent states. For the most part, the international system is an aggregation of their behaviour and decisions. States create the rules of the system: they trade, aid, and invest with each other; they form international organizations; they host multinational corporations; they exchange diplomats; their citizens interact with foreign nationals; they sign treaties and go to war. They also set the tone and establish the character of relations within the international system. They can engage in relations of consensus*, relations of overt manipulation, or relations of coercion.[3]

In the latter part of the twentieth century, the viability of the state has been challenged by many factors. The destructive power of contemporary weapons, the interdependence of the global economy, the international character of environmental pollution and energy conservation, the internationalization of the mass media – all these challenge the capacity of individual sovereign states to survive as independent autonomous members in the international system.

These global challenges now affect the laws and customs of the international community and may lead to the creation of new international instruments for the resolution of conflict*. The state, as it first evolved, was a response to challenges that were beyond the problem-solving capacity of small principalities and kingdoms. The present character of human problems on the global scale is likely to produce an increase in the building of new regional* and global international institutions.[4] The state is not likely to wither away in the face of these challenges, but it may have to surrender more of its autonomous decision-making capacities to supranational institutions.

The twelve member European Communities (EC) is a regional approach to trade, political, and economic integration. With a 410-member European Parliament, a system of courts, a Common Agricultural Policy (CAP), and a European Monetary System (EMS), the EC is pledged to complete its integration of currencies and services by 1992, creating, in effect, a United States of Europe. Other supranational efforts have begun in Central and South America, as well as in the Caribbean. Likewise, the proliferation of multinational corporations like the Exxon Corporation, International Telephone and Telegraph (ITT), and International Business Machines (IBM) has created new international approaches to trade, the flow of capital and labour across national boundaries, and the planning of production for the global marketplace. Many of these massive corporations, with their enormous assets, escape national regulation simply because their decision-making centres are beyond the reach of individual states.

The predominance of the state is also threatened internally by decentralizing tendencies. As large centralized bureaucracies, modern states are domestically pressured to respond to the special needs of certain regions and groups. The internal adjustments required to accommodate these kinds of pressures have strengthened the functions of subnational and regional governments. The efficient management of national resources and the response to language, religious, and minority rights have all weakened the traditional sovereign preserves of national governments. In order for people to accomplish their purposes, they have had to form even larger political and economic associations. The modern state as we know it, with its strong tendency toward autonomy and independence, is required to accommodate these new forces of international co-operation.

International Organizations

International organizations are unique constructs within the world community. They are formed solely on the consent of states, groups of non-governmental organizations (NGOs), and the private associations of individuals with transnational* goals. Once formed, international organizations take on a life of their own, establishing a global presence greater than the sum of their parts. They perform a multiplicity of functions that give the international system rules, structures, and interdependence.[5] These functions involve collective security*, conferences, cosmopolitanism, cultural ties, diplomacy, international administration, international economic co-operation, international law, international social co-operation, international trade, peaceful settlement of disputes, scientific exchanges, world business, world communications, and world travel. All international organizations establish permanent organizations staffed by international civil servants whose ideas and attitudes transcend national interests. The frequent interactions of these people gradually build attitudes and customs that foster an ideology of internationalism.

International Governmental Organizations (IGOs)

International governmental organizations are voluntary associations of two or more sovereign states that meet regularly and have full-time staffs. IGOs may be described according to their size of membership or scope of their goals. Only one organization, the United Nations, approaches global membership, with over 160 member-states (see also fig. 13.1). Regional organizations, such as the Organization of American States (OAS), the Organization of African Unity (OAU), and the Association of Southeast Asian Nations (ASEAN), are multi-purpose IGOs that have limited memberships based on the geographical proximity of states sharing common interests (table 13.1). Many IGOs are formed as voluntary associations of independent states from various regions of the world that have some common purpose for co-operating with one another. For example, the fifty-nine members of the Commonwealth of Nations are drawn from Africa, Asia, Europe, Oceania, and the Western hemisphere. These countries were once part of the British Empire and freely co-operate and assist each other without formal agreements. Another example is the Organization of Petroleum Exporting Countries (OPEC), which is a functional* IGO

Principal multi-purpose IGOs

NAME	FORMED	MEMBERSHIP
Organization of American States (OAS)	1948	31[a]
Organization of African Unity (OAU)	1963	49
Commonwealth	1926	59
Council of Europe	1949	21
Organization of Central American States (ODECA)	1952	5
Andean Group	1969	5
Association of Southeast Asian Nations (ASEAN)	1967	5
Nordic Council (NC)	1952	5
Council of Europe	1949	21
League of Arab States	1945	21
Common Afro-Mauritian Organization (OCAM)	1966	11

[a] Canada joined in 1989.

Source: Yearbook of International Organizations: Global Action Networks (Brussels: Union of International Associations 1988/89)

Table 13.1

Principal functional-regional IGOs

NAME	FORMED	MEMBERSHIP
Benelux Economic Union (Benelux)	1948	3
European Coal and Steel Community (ECSC)	1952	10
European Communities (EC)	1967	12
European Free Trade Association (EFTA)	1960	6
European Atomic Energy Community (Euratum)	1958	10
Organization for Economic Co-operation and Development (OECD)	1961	24
Latin American Free Trade Association (LAFTA)	1961	11
Central American Common Market (CACM)	1961	5
Council for Technical Co-operation in South and Southeast Asia (Colombo Plan)	1950	26
Caribbean Community (CARICOM)	1973	13
Economic Community of West African States (ECOWAS)	1975	12
Council for Mutual Economic Assistance (COMECON or CEMA)	1949	10
Inter-American Development Bank (IDB)	1959	43
African Development Bank (AFDB)	1964	47
Asian Development Bank (ASDB)	1966	42
Central American Bank of Economic Integration (CBEI)	1961	5
European Investment Bank (EIB)	1958	9
Organization of Petroleum Exporting Countries (OPEC)	1960	13
Arab Monetary Fund (AMF)	1973	14
Nordic Investment Bank (NEB)	1976	5

Table 13.2

consisting of a group of thirteen oil-exporting countries that formed an intergovernmental cartel to regulate the production, distribution, and pricing of oil (table 13.2). A number of IGOs have a security orientation and collectively form a military alliance system for defence (table 13.3).

At the turn of the century, fewer than 10 IGOs existed. By World War I there were 50 IGOs. The rapid expansion of IGOs has taken place in the post-World War II era: from 1945 to the present, the number of IGOs grew from 90 to over 350.[6] There has been an enormous development of international organizations in a very brief period of human history. The international system has become highly interactive and bureaucratized. What Marshall McLuhan described as the "global village" is under construction at the international level.

There are several reasons for the impressive proliferation of international bodies at this time in human history. One is the realization in the minds of most national policy makers that no state acting alone can prevent war and that a world composed of autonomous and

Principal collective-security IGOs

NAME	FORMED	MEMBERSHIP
North Atlantic Treaty Organization (NATO)	1949	16
Warsaw Treaty Organization (WTO)	1955	8
Australia, New Zealand, United States Security Treaty Organization (ANZUS)	1952	3
Western European Union (WEU)	1954	7

Source: Yearbook of International Organizations (Brussels: Union of International Associations 1988/89)

Table 13.3

nationalistic actors greatly enhances the possibility of violent conflict. The mass destructive powers of modern conventional and nuclear weapons have made war between any two states a global concern. No longer is it possible to isolate the destructive effects of contemporary warfare from all humankind or from all living things on this planet. Many of the IGOs created since World War II address themselves to the issues of war and peace – applying their skills to negotiation and communication rather than to the technologies of war.

Another reason for the rapid growth of IGOs has been the great advances made in the technology of human communication. Instantaneous global telecommunication informs and alerts people about events in every corner of the world. Governments have immediate access to one another. As well, the ability of diplomats and policy makers to travel long distances in short periods of time has been an impetus for governments to participate in international organizations and to co-operate on solutions to international problems.

Other reasons for the increasing number of IGOs as actors in the international arena have been global problems of poverty, starvation, underdevelopment, and disease. Governments have involved themselves in controlling these problems on a co-operative global level through the vehicles of international organizations. While humanitarianism may appear to be the main thrust behind the inclinations of governments to use international instruments to attack these problems, many governments are also motivated by practical expediency, as when developed states apply their aid programs to developing economies so as to create new markets for their manufacturing and service sectors.[7]

Yet another factor contributing to the widespread recognition that multinational organizations are needed to address complex human problems of great magnitude is the expansion of the international civil service.[8] By the 1990s, over 60 000 people on a worldwide scale were employed on a full-time basis by IGOs. They administer the resolutions and international policies of global and regional institutions. International civil servants tackle the world's pressing problems with solutions that rise above national perspectives. They are much less inclined to accept the narrow nationalistic approaches to international difficulties than are bureaucrats of autonomous governments.

The United Nations

The United Nations (UN) is the world's first IGO ever to gain the membership of over 90 percent of the states in the international community.[9] It is the most representative intergovernmental forum ever organized by humankind. No other public institution in history has been mandated to accumulate and correlate information about every kind of global concern. The United Nations and its related agencies gather data on the frequency of international co-operation and conflict; on human rights; on variations in the key indicators of the international economic system – trade, investment, and development assistance; on world population trends; on the global demography of disease; on the global ecology; and on food, energy, and development. In short, the world is a United Nations' study.

The United Nations owns twenty acres of land donated by John Rockefeller for use as international territory. As an organization, the United Nations makes its own rules, has its own flag, and operates its own police force. It also owns a multilingual radio station, a post office, and a stamp mint. It uses six official languages: Arabic, Chinese, English, French, Russian, and Spanish. The United Nations is not a supranational organization*, nor is it a world government. There are no citizens, taxes, or a regular army. It is the voluntary association of sovereign independent states for the purpose of dialogue to keep peace in the world. It serves as the only IGO capable of global decision making. Through its organizations, it attempts to foster peaceful relations among states and to promote economic equality and human rights for all people.[10]

Prime Minister Mackenzie King signed the United Nations Charter on June 26, 1945. Even before the charter was drafted, Canada played an important role in the formulation of the United Nations system. Canada participated in the Dumbarton Oaks Conferences in 1944 and at the United Nations Conference on International Organizations in 1945 at San Francisco. Canada also participated in the establishment of the principal organs of the United Nations. Presently, Canada contributes nearly $125 million to the general operation fund of the United Nations (not including its financial committments to UN peace-keeping or specialized agencies).

Of these, the *Security Council* has the primary responsibility, under the charter, for the maintenance of international peace and security. In general, the council is charged with

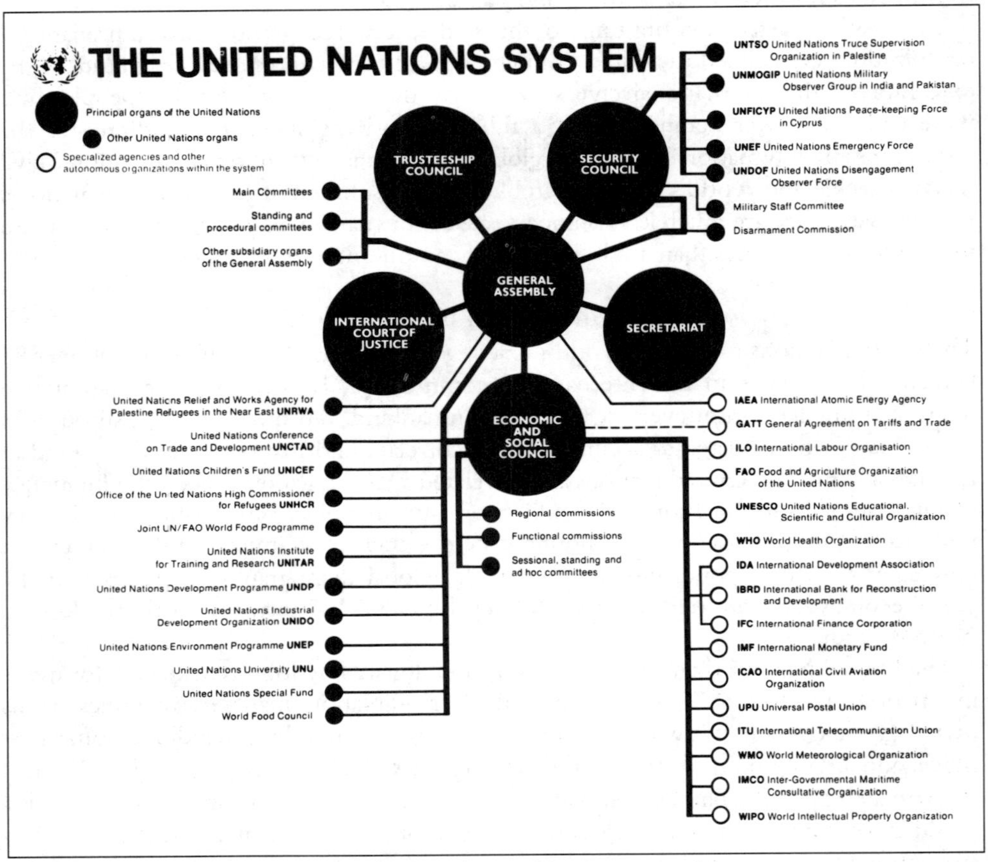

Figure 13.1

implementing the peaceful settlement of disputes* and may consider any action viewed by its members as a threat to peace, a breach of peace, or an act of aggression subject to investigation. After investigating a dispute, the council is empowered to make recommendations for the peaceful resolution of conflict. In 1987 a Security Council resolution (598) was adopted unanimously, calling for a cease-fire and an end to all military actions between Iran and Iraq in the Gulf region by a withdrawal of forces to internationally recognized boundaries.

The Security Council consists of five permanent members (China,[11] France, Great Britain, the Soviet Union, and the United States) and ten non-permanent members elected by the General Assembly for two-year terms. Each of the five permanent members can veto an action deliberated by the council. In order for the council to take an action against a violator of the charter, the five permanent members must be in agreement on that action. In addition, a minimum of four non-permanent members must concur with the same action. Since 1945, Canada has been on the Security Council four times for two-year periods in 1948–49, 1958–59, 1967–68, and 1977–78. In 1988 Canada was once again elected to the council for a fifth time, after having vigorously campaigned on its general role in the United Nations and on its four decades of peace-keeping.

The second principal organ of the United Nations is the *General Assembly*. This is the only body of the United Nations in which all member-states are represented. Each of the member-states has one vote (except South Africa, whose credentials have been rejected because of its continuing apartheid policies). The General Assembly may discuss any question that falls within the scope of the United Nations Charter or that relates to the powers and functions of any other organ of the world forum. It may recommend to member states, as well as to the Security Council. In 1989 for the first time, the assembly moved to Geneva for a few days during its regular session. It did so to hear the chairman of the Palestine Liberation Organization (PLO), Yasir Arafat, after the United States refused to grant him an entry visa.

Decisions of the assembly have no binding legal force on governments, but they do have a quasi-legal character because these decisions carry the weight of international opinion as expressed by members. Three instruments are used by the General Assembly to formulate a consensus of world opinion. The first is a General Assembly *declaration*: a broad statement of general principle on an important global concern. The Universal Declaration of Human Rights passed in 1948, the Declaration of the Establishment of a New International Economic Order (NIEO) in 1974, and the Declaration of the Right to Development in 1986 are examples of such an instrument generating world expectations. A General Assembly *resolution* is another quasi-legal instrument of world opinion. Resolutions recommend that member-states follow a particular policy action. For example, in the 1980s the General Assembly has passed resolutions to implement the UN plan for the independence of Namibia (1989), to acknowledge the proclamation of the Palestinian state (1989), and to implement the Afghanistan peace settlement (1989). In the first forty years of assembly business, it has adopted countless resolutions and declarations establishing the norms of international conduct. For example during that time the assembly has passed nearly seventy resolutions on the subject of disarmament and proclaimed the 1990s as the Third Disarmament Decade. Finally, a General Assembly *convention* is a legally binding instrument because it is a treaty requiring the ratification of signatory states that are then bound by its terms. There are two types of conventions: multilateral treaties passed by the General Assembly and ratified by member-states, and a United Nations treaty with a state, as when Egypt in 1956 signed a treaty with the world body to allow multinational peace-keeping forces to enter Egyptian territory.

The assembly also has assumed the power to conciliate international disputes and to make recommendations for collective measures against an aggressor. The Uniting for Peace

Resolutions* of 1950 gives the assembly a back-up role to the Security Council when that body is prevented from taking action by a veto of a permanent member. A series of stalemates in the Security Council led to special emergency sessions of the General Assembly to deal with Afghanistan (1980), Palestine (1980 and 1982), Namibia (1981), the Occupied Arab Territories (1982), and apartheid in South Africa (1989).

The 1950 Resolution gives the General Assembly a critical role in peace-keeping when the Security Council is unable to fulfil its responsibility to maintain peace and security. Peace-keeping is not mentioned in the charter, but the organization has developed this method of dealing with conflict. Canada is the only state in the world that has participated in some way in every peace-keeping operation of the United Nations system. Canada has participated in such operations in the Middle East, India/Pakistan, West New Guinea (West Iran), Yemen, the Congo, and Cyprus. Canada also participated in non-UN peace-keeping activities in Indochina and Nigeria. Canada's major participation in peace-keeping began with the establishment of the United Nations Emergency Force (UNEF), which was established after the Suez crisis in 1956. By 1988 Canada had contributed personnel to fifteen peace-keeping missions since 1945, with its most recent commitments to Afghanistan and Iran/Iraq.

The third major organ of the United Nations is the *Secretariat*. This is a body of international civil servants, numbering over 20 000 people, one-third of whom work at United Nations headquarters in New York. The rest are dispersed in the Geneva office, as well as in the regional commissions operating in over 130 countries. The Secretariat organizes conferences such as the United Nations Convention against Illicit Traffic in Narcotic Drugs and Psychotropic Substances (1988); collects and publishes data on world cultural, economic, and social trends; administers United Nations peace-keeping actions; and performs administrative, budgetary, and housekeeping functions. The Secretariat is headed by a secretary general, who is appointed by the General Assembly following a nomination by the Security Council. Javier Perez de Cuéllar of Peru, appointed in 1982 and reappointed for another five-year term in 1987, was the first person from a Latin American country to direct the secretariat. The job of the secretary general is a complicated one that verges on the impossible. He presides over a budget of $1 700 000 000 for 1988–89 with $1 760 000 000 approved for 1990–91; is the chief administrator for the United Nations and for all its specialized agencies; and is also accredited as a diplomat plenipotentiary to the world in that the secretary general is expected to bring parties in dispute to a peaceful settlement by means of the mediating and conciliating instruments at the disposal of the United Nations. The secretary general is held responsible for the professional actions of thousands of international civil servants and must work to keep their loyalties in the face of mounting criticism that the United Nations is an ineffective IGO. The secretary general's personality and his or her political diplomatic skills are crucial to the success of the United Nations as a credible world forum.

The fourth principal organ of the UN is the *Economic and Social Council* (ECOSOC). It was established at the insistence of the developing states that participated in the drafting of the United Nations Charter in San Francisco. They justifiably saw the Security Council as dominated by the great post-war powers and considered the General Assembly too unwieldy to promote the welfare of the smaller powers. The present-day importance of ECOSOC is seen by the dramatic enlargement of that body from eighteen members originally, to twenty-seven after 1965, to fifty-four members after the charter amendment of 1971. All members are elected by a two-thirds vote of the General Assembly for three-year terms, eighteen elected each year. Canada was elected to ECOSOC in 1987 until December 31, 1989.

ECOSOC conducts research on economic, educational, social and cultural problems: it drafts conventions that, when adopted by the General Assembly and ratified by member-states, become international law. It co-ordinates the activities of thirteen United Nations agencies. To assist in its operations, the council established eight functional commissions (Human Rights, International Commodity Trade, Narcotic Drugs, Population, Prevention of Discrimination and Protection of Minorities, Statistics, Status of Women, and Transport and Communications). The council also administers four regional economic commissions: Economic Commission for Africa (ECA), Economic Commission for Europe (ECE), Economic Commission for Latin America (ECLA), and the Economic Commission for Western Asia (ECWA).

Of the principal organs of the United Nations, ECOSOC is linked most with all levels of the international community. It is authorized to advise and co-ordinate international programs with private organizations, generally referred to as non–governmental organizations (NGOs). By the 1990s, 700 or 20 percent of the NGOs operating in the United Nations member-countries were listed on the ECOSOC roster, sending observers to its meetings, submitting written and oral statements to the council's commissions, and influencing the direction of its programs around the world.

Finally an appreciation of the importance and complexity of ECOSOC's global influence is seen in its consultative role to a number of other United Nations bodies offering programs in the economic and social fields. These bodies include (1) the United Nations Development Program (UNDP); (2) the United Nations Children's Fund (UNICEF); (3) the United Nations High Commissioner for Refugees (UNHCR); (4) the United Nations Conference on Trade and Development (UNCTAD); (5) the World Food Program; and (6) the United Nations University (UNU), which began operations in 1975 at its headquarters in Tokyo.

Another of the six principal organs is the United Nations *Trusteeship Council*. This body is also charged with the international supervision of trust territories*. The membership of the council is composed of all trust-administering states, non-administering permanent members of the Security Council, and elective members drawn from the General Assembly. After World War II, the non-self-governing territories of the former League of Nations became trust territories. The Trusteeship Council has worked to prepare these territories for eventual independence, to hear petitions from trust-territory representatives, and to send visiting missions from time to time for on-the-spot supervision. For example, the trust territory of British Togoland merged with Ghana in 1957, Tanganyika became Tanzania in 1961, and New Guinea became Papua New Guinea in 1975. By 1982, ten of the eleven United Nations trust territories administered since 1946 had gained independence or had united with a neighbouring nation-state. The only remaining territory is the Trust Territory of the Pacific Islands, generally known as Micronesia or "land of the small islands." In 1946, the United States agreed to administer these former Japanese-mandated islands of the Caroline, Marshall, and Mariana groups as a United Nations trusteeship. The Pacific Islands are currently negotiating the status of free association with the United States. Free association is a step towards independence: it would permit the United States to defend the islands in return for U.S. financial support to assist the territory in its efforts to become independent.

The sixth organ of the United Nations is the *International Court of Justice* (ICJ). The functions of this court are discussed in chapter 14 (International Law). The ICJ was founded in 1945 as the judicial arm of the United Nations to rule on disputes arising between states and to advise the UN on matters of international law. In practice, however, the ICJ has been the least productive organ of the United Nations: in four decades of existence, it has reviewed only seventy cases (excluding advisory opinions), most of them concerning minor disputes such as establishing boundaries or determining fishing rights. Less than one-third of the members of the United Nations have accepted the compulsory jurisdiction of the court, demonstrating a lack of confidence on the part of most states in conflict to seek a legal remedy from such a highly visible and respected body.

During the 1980s, the United Nations experienced a decline in prestige and influence in world affairs. Perhaps unfairly, the world had expected too much from the resources it was providing to the UN. It blamed the United Nations for the failure to force South Africa to disgorge Namibia, to get the Cubans out of Angola, to get the Vietnamese out of Kampuchea, and for its own financial crisis as a global institution. But these assessments were unrealistic. The United Nations could never force peace on disputing parties without a collective change of attitude among its members, especially among the five permanent members of the Security Council.

An extraordinary outburst of common sense among the so-called gang of five led to a great improvement in the international climate by the late 1980s. Gorbachev's embrace of the United Nations to support his new initiatives of multilateralism and his announcement that the Soviet Union would pay off its peace-keeping debts, which it had previously refused to do, gave a tremendous push to the new spirit of co-operation in the world body. Soon after, former U.S. president Reagan disclosed that the United States would release the funds it was withholding from the operating budget of the United Nations. These actions reflected the new maturity among members of the Security Council and led to international detente among members of the General Assembly. Increasingly, states in conflict have come to recognize that when they want the violence to stop, they go to the United Nations.

Under the auspices of the UN, the INF agreement between the United States and the Soviet Union, banning short- and medium-range nuclear missiles, was finally concluded in 1987. In Central America co-operation between the OAS and the UN strengthened the stability of the region and demonstrated that the world community wants peace to come to this embattled area. The blue helmets of United Nations peace-keeping forces were visible in the Persian Gulf in the late summer of 1988. Iran and Iraq decided to accept UN Resolution

598 to work out a peace plan. In that year South Africa, Angola, and Cuba agreed to a cease-fire. Morocco and Algeria came to terms over their dispute and the Frente Popular para la Liberación de Saguía el-Hamra y de Rio de Oro (POLISARIO) guerrillas in the Western Sahara agreed to stop fighting. At the close of the 42nd session of the General Assembly, diplomats from around the world toasted their successes and celebrated the awarding of the Nobel Peace Prize to their peace-keeping forces.

As an international organization, the United Nations is more than the sum of its parts. Since its conception during World War II, it has come to be regarded as an autonomous international actor. Its members speak and react to a common theme as if the UN was an independent entity, expressing itself authoritatively through its various organizations. No one of its members has the capacity nor even the will to eradicate world problems. But as a global forum, each state is made aware of the need to do so. The UN is an effort on the part of the community of states to concur on norms of international conduct to outlaw war and to reduce conflictive behaviour. It provides for the peaceful settlement of international disputes, the regulation of armaments, the supervision of trust territories, and the co-operation of members in dealing with global economic and social problems.[12] It is a human institution, reflecting the successes and failures of people in their daily lives. Because it is a unique experiment in human political ingenuity, with no other models for comparison, its shortcomings have gained more visibility than most of its achievements.

Other International Organizations

The United Nations is the singular example of a broad-purpose world organization. All other IGOs neither approach global membership, nor take the world perspective of the United Nations. Public international organizations with varying degrees of integration exist for the purposes of collective security, economic advancement, and multi-purpose regional alliances. The United Nations Charter supports the formation of regional IGOs as complementary institutions to the goals of the UN world organization, provided their actions are consistent with the Charter (Articles 52–54). Examples of IGOs are the North Atlantic Treaty Organization (NATO), the Council on Mutual Economic Assistance (COMECON or CEMA), and the Organization of American States (OAS).

NATO

Since 1949, the North Atlantic Treaty Organization has functioned as a collective-security alliance of Western states against the perceived threat of communist aggression in the North Atlantic area.[13] Its sixteen members –Belgium, Britain, Canada, Denmark, France, Greece, Iceland, Italy, Luxembourg, the Netherlands, Norway, Portugal, Spain (since 1982), Turkey, the United States, and West Germany – form the largest and most highly organized international defence system in the world. All these signatories of the North Atlantic Treaty agree that "an armed attack against one or more of the parties to the treaty in Europe or North America shall be considered an attack against them all." This collective-security provision legally requires member-states to honour their commitments to take military action if aggression occurs against the alliance.

Collective security is supported by an extensive network of political and military structures designed to co-ordinate communications and decisions among members. The supreme governing organ of NATO is the North Atlantic Council, chaired by the secretary general of NATO in Brussels. The council consists of ministers of foreign affairs or defence and an ambassador from each of the NATO members. It meets at the ministerial level at least twice a year and at the ambassadorial level on a weekly basis. Its discussions and decisions flow from political/military matters, as well as from the financial and scientific aspects of defence planning.

In 1966, France decided to pull its armed forces out of the integrated military organization of NATO, but retained its political seat on the North Atlantic Council. Because of France's withdrawal, the other NATO states created a new committee, the *Defense Planning Committee*, to determine military policy.

The military-command structure has three major organs: Allied Command Europe (ACE), headquartered at Costeau, Belgium, takes responsibility for the defence of Europe, except of France and Portugal; *Allied Command Atlantic* (ACLANT) provides security for the North Atlantic Ocean from the Tropic of Cancer to the North Pole; and the *Allied Command Channel* (ACCHAN) controls the English Channel and the south sector of the North Sea.

Another separate organ of NATO is the *Nuclear Planning Group* (NPC), which meets twice a year to develop NATO's nuclear policy. France, Iceland, Luxembourg, and Spain have not joined this group for various domestic reasons.

In over forty years of existence, NATO has undergone stresses and strains in addition to a continuing consensus of support from its members.[14] From time to time, European members have pushed to gain more control of the command structures of NATO because of the primacy of the United States and the often difficult defence relationships that member-states have with this nuclear superpower.

In the past, a number of members have asserted their independence: the French withdrawal in 1966, for example. Canada reduced its NATO forces in Europe from 10 000 to 5000 in the early 1970s but by 1990 had increased these numbers to 7500; and Greece withdrew its forces from NATO after Turkey's invasion of Cyprus in 1974, resuming full participation in 1980.

The European policy of NATO on nuclear deterrence* is under review for three reasons. First, on examining the consequences of nuclear war, many Europeans do not like the idea that Europe will be the theatre* for such a war; second, there is widespread doubt about the credibility of that deterrent in preventing a Soviet first strike at the United States and in preventing an attack on Europe because nuclear weapons are also installed there; third, reforms in the Soviet Union have transformed the East Bloc by the unilateral reduction of huge armies and weapons in Central Europe and through the changing character of the state systems of Eastern Europe. Any consideration of disintegrating military alliances leads to the question of German re-unification. The vision of a new Europe that extends to the Soviet border and beyond will determine the future of NATO and the Warsaw Pact.

One alternative to nuclear deterrence being considered is to increase NATO's conventional capability, which would involve using conventionally armed ballistic and cruise missiles to deter the occupation of European territory from enemy forces. Increasing numbers of Europeans hold that defence ultimately depends on the capacity to protect territory – not on the capacity to inflict damage on the territory of an adversary or to punish an aggressor with weapons of mass destruction. Thus, the strategy presently advocated is that the most stable military role for NATO in Europe should be one that does not pose a serious nuclear threat to an adversary and, at the same time, is essentially invulnerable to attack by the possession of conventional-weapons' technologies.

Despite a disparity of opinion on its role, NATO still enjoys widespread support in Europe, as well as in North America, as an IGO essential for the collective security of its membership and as a deterrent to possible Soviet aggression. Most Europeans, Americans, and Canadians agree on the need to participate in such an organization to protect the security of the North Atlantic community and to balance competitive military forces in Europe.[15]

COMECON (CMEA)

The Council of Mutual Economic Assistance was founded in 1949 as a Soviet response to the U.S.-sponsored Marshall Plan, which sent billions of dollars of economic aid to Western Europe to restore Europe's war-shattered economy and to prevent the expansion of communism.[16] As an IGO composed solely of communist-bloc states, it is unique among international organizations established for economic co-operation. Originally it was organized to plan the development of the national economies of the East European states. Its founding members were Albania, Bulgaria, Czechoslovakia, East Germany, Hungary, Poland, Romania, and the Soviet Union. But in 1959, the Charter of COMECON was amended to permit the admission of non-European members: Mongolia joined in 1962, Cuba became a member in 1972 and Vietnam was admitted in 1978. Other states such as Afghanistan, Angola, Ethiopia, Laos, Mexico, Mozambique, Nicaragua, and Yemen carry an observer status*. Albania is listed as a member, but has not participated since it withdrew in 1961. Since 1964, Yugoslavia has only taken part in a limited number of economic programs.

The highest organ of COMECON is the council, which meets at least once annually to discuss comprehensive economic and scientific co-operation among member-states. It co-ordinates "the international socialist division of labour" so as not to duplicate the process of industrialization already under way in each country, and to plan complementary projects from an international perspective. All member-states send delegates to the sessions of council, and decide on economic planning strategies. For example, in 1979 council members signed an agreement in Moscow to convert power generation from oil to nuclear power as the main source of energy over the period 1981 to 1990.

The next body of importance is the executive committee, which meets four times each year to supervise the implementation of council decisions and to receive economic proposals from member-states. The secretariat administers the directives of the executive committee, develops statistics and economic forecasts, and carries on the day-to-day operations of COMECON.

COMECON has operated as an economic association of socialist states within the Soviet sphere of influence.[17] The flow of trade, the planning of production, and industrialization created a high degree of interdependence so that any break with the group by a member would require extensive and costly readjustments. By the 1990s, a large proportion of the trade among satellite states was with the Soviet Union, from about one-half to four-fifths in the cases of East Germany and Bulgaria. This arrangement was advantageous to most of the East European states. They received Soviet raw materials more cheaply than available on world markets and had an assured market for their industrial goods. COMECON is under transformation because many of its members are adopting market economies independent of Soviet control. The fate of COMECON will depend on the ability of these transforming economies to trade and invest with each other more freely and competitively.

ORGANIZATION OF AMERICAN STATES (OAS)

In many respects the OAS is the classic example of the type of multi-purpose regional organization endorsed by the Charter of the United Nations.[18] The OAS is the most important IGO within the inter-American system*. This hemispheric system now incorporates over 100 permanent and ad hoc bodies, which include committees, institutes, academies, congresses, conventions, courts, economic associations, and treaties. In effect, a system of international relationships has developed since the early nineteenth century based on the regular interaction and interdependence of the states of the Western hemisphere. It is noteworthy that all these organizations set the Western hemisphere apart from the rest of the world as a regional international system.

The leading formal decision-making institution in this inter-American system is the OAS, established by the Ninth International Conference of American states at Bogota, Colombia, in 1948. Today the headquarters of the OAS are in Washington, D.C., where thirty-one American republics meet to discuss regional economic, political, and military matters. After many invitations, Canada has joined the OAS and participates as a full member in eight inter-American organizations. In 1972, Canada became a permanent observer at the OAS; it acceded to the Charter of the OAS on January 1, 1990.

The largest decision-making body of the OAS is the General Assembly. It sits annually as a general conference of all members and has jurisdiction to consider any regional problem that a majority of its members wish to debate. The Permanent Council carries out directives of the assembly and performs pacific-settlement functions when disputes among members are considered by the OAS. Two other bodies, the Inter-American Economic and Social Council and the Inter-American Council for Education, Science and Culture sponsor conferences, draft treaties, and co-ordinate inter-American programs. When regional international disputes arise, the Meeting of Consultation of Ministers of Foreign Affairs is summoned at the request of a majority of members. The Inter-American Juridical Committee is a judicial advisory body of the OAS and promotes the codification and development of international law in the Western hemisphere. In addition, special agencies, such as the Inter-American Development Bank (IDB), the Pan American Institute of Geography and History (PAIGH), and the Inter-American Institute of Agricultural Science (IAIAS) (Canada participates as a full member in all three) function autonomously in support of general OAS objectives. The General Secretariat of the OAS, headed by a secretary general, employs nearly 1400 staff workers and is the administrative arm of the OAS.

While the OAS functions as a general regional multi-purpose IGO, it also operates as a collective-security defence organization. All signatories to the Charter of the OAS are automatically parties to the Inter-American Treaty of Reciprocal Assistance of 1947 (Rio Pact)*. This pact was originally drafted to deal with the threat of communism in the Western hemisphere. The collective-security provisions of the treaty have been invoked on a number of occasions since it was adopted at Bogotá in 1948: concerning Cuba (1961–62), and the intervention of an OAS peace force in the Dominican Republic in 1965. The United States has played a dominant role in the application of this treaty because most Latin American governments depend on its superior military capacity to meet the perceived threats of aggression.

In the area of the peaceful settlement of disputes, the OAS has played an important role, with the Permanent Council, the Meeting of Consultation of Ministers of Foreign Affairs, and the Inter-American Peace Commission serving as instruments through which mediation* and conciliation* were attempted. Among the disputes considered by the OAS were Costa Rica and Nicaragua (1948–49, 1955–56, 1959); Honduras and Nicaragua (1957); Venezuela and the Dominican Republic (1960–61); Venezuela and Cuba (1963–64, 1967); the Dominican Republic and Haiti (1950, 1963–65); and Panama and the United States (1964 and 1989). The OAS was instrumental in resolving the "soccer war" between El Salvador and Honduras in 1969–70, and in 1980 a peace treaty between these states was deposited with the OAS. Argentina and Chile requested the Holy See* (a permanent observer of the OAS) to mediate their disputes over the future of various island territories and maritime areas. And in 1981, the good offices* of the OAS were used to restore peaceful relations between Ecuador and Peru. In 1982, the OAS adopted resolutions in support of Argentina during the Argentine-British war over the Falkland Islands. Latin American states upheld the provision of the Rio Pact "that an armed attack by any state against an American state shall be considered as an attack against all the American States." But the United States supported Great Britain during the dispute and persuaded the Latin American members of the OAS to express mild denunciations of British military action in the General Assembly.[19]

The OAS has served as a hemispheric instrument of economic and cultural co-operation.[20] Through its various inter-American agencies, it has played a role in conducting research on economic and social problems, making recommendations directly to member governments, such as for the contadora peace initiative*. It has supported the work of the United Nations Economic Commission for Latin America (ECLA) and encouraged the founding of the Latin American Free Trade Association (LAFTA), the Central American Common Market (CACM), the Andean Group, and the Inter-American Development Bank (IDB).

There is no question that the overpowering presence of the United States, so enduring and so obvious in its effects on Latin American states, has generated a great deal of disillusionment among the other members of the OAS. The United States has used the OAS to provide a multilateral* legitimacy to the implementation of its foreign policy goals in the Western hemisphere. Free from the veto power of the Security Council of the United Nations, the United States converts its unilateral* actions to the status of regional international "peace-keeping," immune from the veto of the Soviet Union and well within its own politically and economically controlled sphere of influence.

Multinational Corporations (MNC)

Since World War II, multinational corporations (MNCs) have become major international actors. More than any other actors in the international community, MNCs have transformed the global economy through their increased influence of four resources in the world economic system: the technology of production and distribution, capital, finance, and marketing. As corporations with a world focus, MNCs are the first institutions in human history, with the exception of the Vatican, dedicated to central planning on a global basis. According to Barnett and Müller: "The rise of the planetary enterprise is producing an organizational revolution as profound in its implications for modern man as the Industrial Revolution and the rise of the nation-state itself."[21]

Multinational corporations are international actors because they conduct business activities and own assets beyond the jurisdiction of one state. They have political as well as economic impact on the international system because they move and control goods, services, money, personnel, and technology across national boundaries. As actors in the international economy, MNCs have tremendous bargaining powers with governments and international organizations.[22] For example, International Telephone and Telegraph (ITT) used its influence at the World Bank, the inter-American Development Bank, and the International Monetary Fund to make it difficult for the Allende government to fund certain development projects, thereby creating stresses on the Chilean economy.[23] Evidence surfaced to show how one multinational corporation undermined the economy of Chile by encouraging credit and loan terminations, causing fuel and weapons shipment delays, organizing copper boycotts, intervening in the internal political affairs of a sovereign government, and sponsoring a global anti-Allende propaganda effort. Actions such as these demonstrate the power of global corporations to challenge successfully the invariable geographical character of nation-states. The power of international companies is measured by their world-wide financial flexibility and influence, whereas the power of governments is essentially territorial and measured by what happens within the territories they administer.

If we think of these two types of international actors as economic units competing for dominance in a global economic system, we can make some interesting observations (table 13.4). The annual sales of MNCs are comparable to the gross national product (GNP) of national economies. General Motors, for example, is bigger than the combined GNPs of Israel,

The 100 principal economic actors in the world, comparing MNC sales with the GNP of nation-states, 1988 (in billions of U.S. dollars)

1.	United States	4194
2.	Soviet Union	2062
3.	Japan	1962
4.	West Germany	895
5.	France	724
6.	Italy	599
7.	Great Britain	495
8.	Canada	393
9.	Brazil	270
10.	China	262
11.	Poland	240
12.	India	196
13.	Mexico	177
14.	German Dem. Rep.	175
15.	Iran	168
16.	Austrialia	166
17.	Spain	161
18.	Czechoslovakia	136
19.	Switzerland	135
20.	Sweden	131
21.	Yugoslavia	129
22.	Romania	125
23.	Netherlands	124
24.	*General Motors*	102
25.	South Korea	98
26.	Austria	94
27.	Indonesia	86
28.	Belgium	81
29.	Hungary	80
30.	*Royal Dutch Shell*	78
31.	Saudi Arabia	77
32.	*Exxon*	76
33.	Turkey	75
34.	Nigeria	74
35.	*Ford Motor Co.*	72
36.	Finland	71
37.	Norway	70
38.	Argentina	64
39.	South Africa	62
40.	Taiwan	59
41.	Bulgaria	58
42.	Denmark	57
43.	*IBM*	54
44.	*Mobil*	51
45.	Venezuela	50
46.	Algeria	48
47.	*British Petroleum*	45
48.	Thailand	42
49.	*Toyota*	41
50.	*IRI*	41
51.	Greece	40
52.	*General Electric*	39
53.	*Daimler-Benz*	38
54.	Iraq	35
55.	*American Tel & Tel*	34
56.	*Texaco*	34
57.	Hong Kong	34
58.	Colombia	33
59.	Pakistan	33
60.	Philippines	31
61.	*Du Pont*	30
62.	*Fiat*	30
63.	*Hitachi*	30
64.	*Volkswagen*	30
65.	Cuba	29
66.	Israel	28
67.	Malaysia	28
68.	Libya	27
69.	*Siemens*	27
70.	*Matsushita*	27
71.	*Unilever*	27
72.	United Arab Emirates	26
73.	*Chevron*	26
74.	*Chrysler*	26
75.	*Nissan*	26
76.	*Philips*	26
77.	Egypt	25
78.	*Renault*	25
79.	North Korea	24
80.	*ENI*	24
81.	*Nestlé*	24
82.	New Zealand	22
83.	*BASF*	22
84.	*Philip Morris*	22
85.	Portugal	21
86.	*Bayer*	21
87.	*CGE*	21
88.	*Elf Aquitaine*	21
89.	*Hoechst*	21
90.	*Samsung*	21
91.	Kuwait	20
92.	*Amoco*	20
93.	*Peugeot*	20
94.	*Toshiba*	20
95.	Ireland	18
96.	*Imperial Chemical*	18
97.	Chile	17
98.	*Honda Motor*	17
99.	*Occidental Petroleum*	17
100.	*Procter & Gamble*	17

Source: For nation-states, *World Statistics in Brief* (New York: UN Publications 1988; and Victor Showers, *World Facts and Figures* (New York: John Wiley & Sons 1989); for MNCs, *Fortune Magazine*, August 1, 1988, D2–3

Table 13.4

New Zealand, and Venezuela; and Ford is bigger than South Africa.

By the 1990s over $200 billion of the world's gross economic product was produced by the largest 450 MNCs: 40 of the world's 100 principle economic actors were MNCs, and out of 175 nation-states, over 100 states had less economic strength than did these 40 global enterprises.[24] Today over 7500 MNCs control and operate more than 27 000 subsidiaries that employ 3 percent of the world's labour force. Even socialist states host MNCs, or one of their subsidiaries.

Because of their enormous sales figures and profits, MNCs collectively aggregate large amounts of international currencies and are in the position to influence exchange rates. By the mid 1970s, MNCs controlled more than twice the total of all international reserves held by all central banks and international monetary institutions. By 1988, MNCs accounted for about one-quarter of the activity in the world's market economies and a staggering 80–90 percent of the exports in advanced countries such as Britain, Canada, and the United States.[25] One scholar has estimated that by the year 2000, MNCs will produce over half the world's gross economic product.[26] Another analyst forecasts that before the turn of this century, 200–300 global corporations will control 80 percent of all productive assets of the non-communist world.[27]

The economic power of MNCs often translates into political and social power. Politically, MNCs promise investment, jobs, the raising of living standards, and the introduction of technology to assist developing countries to modernize and industrialize. In return they demand political stability and concessions on taxation and government regulations. When national interest and corporate interest conflict, MNCs challenge the political decisions of governments from every possible vantage point.

In the social sphere, the global marketing strategies of MNCs serve to homogenize consumer tastes the world over. Because MNCs have created the "global shopping centre," there is a resulting tendency for people all over the world to adopt the same tastes and the same consumption habits. The proliferation of communications satellites has made global advertising a reality, with the result that world enterprises can now suggest new needs to new consumers anywhere and reinforce old needs for old consumers in established markets.

The rise of the global corporation has launched an important integrating force within the international community. As agents of political, social, and economic change, MNCs are creating a world society that transcends geography, race, and nationalism. Once considered economic outcasts, MNCs are now viewed increasingly as harbingers of development and growth around the world. The debate between the critics and supporters of MNCs rages on, but both groups agree that global corporations have entered the world arena as permanent and powerful actors in a competitive international system.

Non-Governmental Organizations (NGOs)

We have identified the three dominant classes of actors in the contempory international system: states, international organizations, and multinational corporations. But there are other actors, not always recognized by states and IGOs, that stimulate international co-operation on all levels of human interaction. NGOs are specialized organizations that work to develop national interest and involvement in world affairs. These types of international organizations are created from every conceivable field of human endeavour, from agriculture to science and technology. By organizing workshops, seminars, and conferences, and by publishing information on various aspects of their activities, these organizations have created a social basis for international relations.

Non-governmental organizations perform an educative function in the countries where they operate: they contribute to the gathering and dissemination of information about international problems. At the same time, they generate an internal domestic interest in world affairs. In the process of mobilizing public and private support for global concerns, NGOs create a flow of ideas, materials, and people across national boundaries. Many organizations make contributions in the forms of money, food, clothing, books, equipment, and expertise to promote co-operation and development in the international system.

By the 1990s there were nearly 5000 NGOs of diverse size, composition, and purpose functioning in the world. This number is expected to double by the year 2000.[28] Many of these organizations have high visibility and are widely known in all countries: for example, the International Olympic Commission, the International Red Cross, and the International Chamber of Commerce. But others are not so prominent, such as the International Council for Philosophy and Humanistic Studies or the Council for International Organizations of Medical Sciences.

In Canada, nearly 200 NGOs encourage and provide domestic links with all world areas.[29] Organizations such as World Vision of Canada, Foster Parents Plan of Canada, and the Salvation Army are among them.

Some NGOs are organized as professional associations that seek to protect the interests of their members but exercise an important role in the international community. For example, the Association of Canadian Medical Colleges (ACMC), with headquarters in Ottawa, has international affiliations with the Pan American Federation of Associations of Medical Schools and with the Pan American Health Organization. The International Federation of Airline Pilots' Association, with headquarters in Montreal, represents the interests of pilots in over fifty countries and functions to gain international agreements on the intricate patterns of interactions in the area of world air transport.

Still other NGOs undertake humanitarian efforts. In the field of human rights, Amnesty International is the best known. Its Canadian office (in Ottawa) has been operating since 1973. Founded in England in 1961, it has devoted its major efforts in over 160 countries toward the protection of prisoners of conscience, and collects information on the incidence of torture, arbitrary arrest, and capital punishment around the world. For example, in 1983 an Amnesty International mission visited Canada to investigate allegations that prisoners at Archambault Prison in Quebec had been subjected to torture and ill treatment following a prison riot in July 1982.[30] The allegations, supported by the sworn statements of seventeen prisoners, referred to beatings, spraying tear-gas into prisoners' mouths, keeping inmates naked for weeks, depriving them of sleep, and adulterating food. Amnesty International found reasonable grounds to believe that cruel and inhuman treatment occurred and asserted Canada had an international obligation under the United Nations Declaration on Torture to undertake a full, impartial inquiry. Another humanitarian group is the International Committee of the Red Cross, founded in Geneva in 1963. It has gained global recognition for upholding the Geneva conventions on the rules of warfare and has provided humanitarian services on behalf of civilians in most of the countries of the world.

Trans-National Groups and Movements

Religious movements, trans-national political organizations, and terrorist groups must also be included in a composite of the contemporary international system. In this century, trans-national actors have added a new dimension of complexity to that system because they participate in a web of global interactions that affect the behaviour of governments, international organizations, individuals, and corporations. They can play a major role in international relations.[31]

Perhaps the most apparent example of an organized religion that has taken a leading role in world affairs is the Catholic Church. The Vatican is the government of the Catholic Church and represents the pope's authority. Pope John Paul II is the religious leader of one-sixth of the world's population and the world's most visible moral leader. He is also often very political: when the Solidarity union threatened to resort to violence in Poland, he tried to calm the situation. He is the only world leader ever to draw 5 million people to see him at one place (Mexico City 1984).

The pope and the Church he leads play a unique role in the contemporary international arena. Peace has been a recurrent papal theme: in 1982 the pope visited both Argentina and Great Britain in an attempt to help end the Falkland Islands War. He also visited strife-torn Central America and Ireland, bringing with him the moral and political pressures of a neutral Vatican to settle disputes peacefully. Another enduring papal theme is human rights. Throughout the 1980s, the pope was concerned with human-rights questions arising out of the struggle between the Polish trade union Solidarity and the Polish government. In the next two years, his message of human rights as an international concern was taken to South Africa, Indonesia, Nicaragua, and Canada.

In Canada, this most-travelled pope in Catholic Church history (40 trips to 73 different countries in 10 years), and the first pope ever to kiss Canadian soil, added many politically charged statements to his "essentially pastoral" visit. At Flat Rock, Newfoundland, the pope raised a storm of controversy when he spoke against the pursuit of profits by the few at the expense of the workers and supported the co-operative ownership of the fishery. In Edmonton, John Paul II assailed the neglect of the poor economies by the rich economies. He challenged political leaders the world over on the issues of the arms race, human-rights infringement, ethnic and minority rights, economic deprivation, and exploitation. He condemned the "imperialists" who monopolize economic and political powers at the expense of the poor economies of the Third World and called on Canada to take the lead in sharing its affluence in the North-South* context. He issued a firm appeal for publicly funded religious education – an issue that is much more inflammatory in the United States and Latin America than in Canada. The pope's visit was no less controversial in Canada than in the numerous other countries he had visited. Women's groups expressed their disappointment at his lack of flexibility regarding the role of women in a patriarchal Catholic Church. The issues of abortion and birth control continue to press the Vatican to modernize Catholic Church doctrine.

As his Canadian visit demonstrated, the pope takes his role as a world diplomat and political leader very seriously. John Paul II placed himself and his Church in the position of being a primary mediator in what he sees as a "troubled planet"; he uses his role as a world leader to influence international affairs in the wealthy northern states, the Third World, and the totalitarian socialist countries.

Many political groups and movements transcend national boundaries, appeal to an international clientele, and thus influence the global political system. Anarchism, communism, and socialism are international movements that have influenced most national political systems. In the latter part of the nineteenth and early twentieth centuries, communist internationals (Cominterns) were established to bring world communists together in the goal of uniting workers and destroying capitalism. In 1947, the Communist Information Bureau (Cominform) was organized, a revival of the old Cominterns, dedicated to the spread of revolutionary communism throughout the world. Today, the Euro-communists of France, Italy, and Spain disagree on many fundamental issues but share an international camaraderie.

In Latin America, *aprista*-type parties share the international goals of *aprismo**, which include land reform; nationalization of key industries; the solidarity of oppressed classes; the political representation of Indians, peasants, students, and intellectuals; and opposition to communism. Leaders of aprista parties are known to each other and agree on general principles of political, economic, and social change in Latin America. This international dimension of *aprismo* makes it a significant regional trans-national political movement.

All ideologically kindred parties and movements of this kind seek to build systematic links in the international community. The founding session of a world-wide organization of conservative parties took place in London in 1983: the International Democratic Union has 20 members, including the Progressive Conservative Party of Canada. The Socialist International is a similar organization of 49 full members, including Canada's NDP. For liberal parties there is the Liberal International with 31 members, which met in Ottawa in September 1987 to consider a range of global issues where consensus could be achieved.

Finally, terrorists are also actors in the international system.[32] In a world where many different groups and organizations are prepared to use violence to achieve political ends, terrorism almost eludes definition. Diverse groups – armies, insurgents, mercenaries, freedom fighters, religious and national-liberation parties, and even individuals – are frequently identified with terrorism as users of violence and psychological weapons in international affairs. The terrorists label seems to be a matter of perception of the objectives of political violence. For the Nicaraguans, the U.S.-backed *contras* engaged in acts of terrorism against Nicaraguan peasants and their government, while to the Reagan administration, the contras were freedom fighters attempting to overthrow an undesirable government by conducting their military operations from bases on the Honduran border.

The Palestinian Liberation Organization (PLO) is differentially perceived as a national liberation movement, a state, and a terrorist group. The United States condemns the Democratic Revolutionary Front and the Farabundo Marti National Liberation Front of El Salvador as guerrillas using terrorist tactics against the government, but hailed the anti-communist guerrillas in Afghanistan as "freedom fighters."

State terrorism consists of the use of violence or the threat of violence by governments against their own populations as an instrument of political and social control. Almost always, state terrorism has international consequences resulting in the mass exodus of refugees or the intervention of other governments, as with Nazi Germany in the 1940s and in Cambodia in the 1970s. Amnesty International reports that in the 1980s no fewer than ninety-eight countries practise torture on suspected dissidents. In some of these nation-states, such as Syria and Uganda, tens of thousands of civilians have died in massacres by their government's use of military forces.[33] *Revolutionary terrorism* is seen as radical social and political movements that resort to violence across national boundaries to achieve their goals. Revolutionary terrorism tends to attract much more international attention because it targets prominent citizens, airlines, airports, embassies, and is usually reported globally in the media.

Terrorist organizations exist all over the world and today number about 3000. Among the most prominent and recently active terrorist groups are Italy's Red Brigade, which kidnapped and killed former Italian prime minister Aldo Moro in 1980; the Red Army Faction, which bombed the Munich Oktoberfest in 1980; the Islamic Jihad Organization, which destroyed the American Embassy in Beirut in 1983; Uruguay's Tupamaros; various Cuban exile groups; the Fatah in the Middle East; the Bader-Meinhof group in West Germany, the Basque separatists in Spain, and the Provisional Wing of the Irish Republican Army (IRA).

The activities of organizations such as these have international consequences and challenge the stability of the global community. Intimidation and random violence are unique features of these non-state actors: assassination, abduction, hijackings, hostage taking, and murder seriously defy the structures and routine interactions of international relations. Some Western governments have responded to the threat of terrorism by training anti-terrorist combat units. The Canadian Security Intelligence Service* and the emergency response teams of the Royal Canadian Mounted Police (RCMP) and Canada's newly formed National Security Investigations Directorate, Great Britain's Special Air Services, Israel's 269 Headquarters Reconnaissance Regiment, the U.S. Delta Team, and West Germany's Group Nine are examples of counter-terrorist and intelligence-gathering groups.

The use of terrorism typically reflects the desire of some groups to change the rules and structures of international politics.[34] Violent tactics are used by groups who feel that they have least to lose from chaotic upheaval and whose expectations of the international system cannot be achieved by legitimate means.

With reality outdoing fiction, the media have come to play an important role for terrorist groups the world over. In international political society, the media provide terrorists with instant public access and an escape from anonymity. The impact of terrorism on world affairs is measured by column inches and screen time. In March 1985, Armenian terrorists successfully used the media to draw world-wide attention to their cause when they stormed the Turkish embassy in Ottawa, taking hostages and wounding the Turkish ambassador; a security guard was killed in the incident. The Armenian Revolutionary Army, a spin-off group of the Armenian Justice Commandos, at first only wanted to deal with the media, not the police, in order to expose the massacre of 1.5 million Armenians by the Turks in 1915 and to demand the return of Armenian homelands in eastern Turkey. This was the third Armenian terrorist act in Ottawa over a three-year period: the first occurred in April 1982 when a commercial attaché to the Turkish embassy was gunned down in an Ottawa parking lot, and another followed in August 1982 when a military attaché to the same embassy was ambushed and killed by three Armenian gunmen. But the seizure of the Turkish embassy in 1985 was the most dramatic and successful in terms of media exposure. In the weeks following the attack, the media documented the history of the Armenian people and their "holocausts" from the decline of the Ottoman Empire to World War I.

Pope John Paul II, the first pope since John XXIII to add the media to his divine ministry, also stumbled onto the other side of world exposure when, in front of the cameras, he became the object of an assassination attempt by a young Turkish far-rightist, Mehmet Ali Agca. The whole incident was steeped in the world of the media, not only for the victim, but equally for the aggressor and his international conspirators. What better opportunity to propel a terrorist and his act to spectacular notoriety! Indeed, in 1980 an ailing Marshall McLuhan was summoned by Italian authorities to unravel the troubled dialectic between the media and terrorism. He summed it up in one succinct comment: "Without the media there would be no terrorism."

Individuals as International Actors

The role that private individuals play in the international system often goes unnoticed because the actions and achievements of people are identified with the states and organizations to which they are attached.[35] But individuals do have an impact on international affairs and examples abound. American industrialist Andrew Carnegie willed US$10 million for the abolition of war between civilized states. Swedish soldier Count Gustaf von Rosan created the Biafran Air Force during the Nigerian civil war. Argentine revolutionary Ché Guevara attempted to start a series of revolutions in Latin America. Bishop Desmond Tutu, who won the Nobel Peace Prize in 1984 for his unifying role in the campaign to resolve peacefully the problem of apartheid in South Africa, travelled extensively, calling for support to work against the South African government. American actor Ed Asner, star of television's "Lou Grant," raised over US$1 million for medical aid, food, and clothing to be sent to the people of El Salvador in opposition to U.S. military assistance for the Salvadorian government. In 1985, Live Aid, the near-global musical extravaganza that raised over US$60 million for African famine relief was the brainchild and organizational achievement of one man, Bob Geldof. In Canada, Terry Fox received over $25 million from all over the world in his unique fight against cancer. Another Canadian, Steve Fonyo, took up the same challenge and successfully completed Terry Fox's dream of running across Canada, attracting financial support from people and governments in Canada and around the world. And, Vancouver wheelchair athlete Rick Hansen completed a 40 000 kilometre world tour to raise money for spinal research in the international community.

Each day millions of tourists travel to foreign places bringing with them money that translates into local jobs and industries. On a global basis the impact of tourism is considerable, not only in dollar terms but also in terms of the trans-national perceptions and interactions that take place. The cumulative effect of individuals who decide to emigrate to other countries is also a significant influence on the international system. Large migrations of people the world over to the great industrial countries are still occurring in the latter part of the twentieth century: Pakistanis and West Indians to Great Britain and Canada, North Africans to France, Turks and Yugoslavs to West Germany, Mexicans and Central Americans to the United States, Greeks to Australia, and Polynesians to other parts of the Pacific. At the individual as well as the social level, these population shifts may pose insoluble political problems for the host state, confounding classical "democratic" institutions like universal suffrage, equal education, and social-welfare programs. But these relocations also make the world a more integrated community.

Individuals in their private capacity – as artists, business persons, journalists, professionals, and writers, are independent actors able to behave autonomously in the global arena. In recent years, individuals – in addition to states and international organizations[36] – have been given some recognition internationally as subjects of world law under certain circumstances. The International Covenant on Civil and Political Rights contains fifty-three articles conferring rights directed at individuals and groups. Under the protocol, individuals and groups may register human rights complaints before the United Nations Commission on Human Rights.

Such a right was exercised by Sandra Lovelace, Maliseet Indian from New Brunswick's Tobique reserve. In Geneva she charged Canada with legislative discrimination under the Indian Act, which strips only native women of their status if they marry non-natives and denies them the benefits of federal money, housing, education, land and burial rights. The United Nations Human Rights Committee agreed with Sandra Lovelace and cited Canada with a human-rights violation. As a result of her efficacious action in the international community, the Canadian government changed its legislation to comply with the international instrument and in accordance with its own Charter of Rights and Freedoms.

In short, individuals are an integral part of the contemporary international community. They are not, therefore, merely cogs in the large bureaucratic machinery of states and international organizations: they have a capacity, through their actions, of influencing the character of world affairs. So proved American Michelle Alexander, who at age 12, invented a board game she called "Give Peace a Chance" and went on to play former Soviet President Andrei Gromyko and India's Prime Minister Rajiv Gandhi. Her efforts brought her the World Children's Day Foundation Award and led to her being invited to address the United Nations General Assembly in 1988.

The Future of the International System

In the twentieth century, the international system has undergone enormous transformation.[37] Many new actors have entered the arena, each with different capabilities, values, and goals. Most of these new actors, unlimited by the present territorial divisions of the world, are raising demands that challenge the very principle of centralized state power.[38] Modern states are increasingly drained of their power and sovereignty. All are subject to the laws of the world market: the tyranny of market prices and interest rates; the difficulties of providing work, food, housing, and security to more and more people; the problems of the global physical environment.

These weaknesses of states are also sharpened by geographical disparities and internal divisions. Few of the newer states – Egypt, Madagascar, Vietnam – are located in a clearly defined natural geographic space. Most are quite artificial political creations, like the states around the Sahara or the scattered islands of the Caribbean, the South Pacific, and the Indian Ocean, where a multitude of "statelets" find it nearly impossible to manage their own social and economic space or to function as autonomous members of international society. Many peoples who are denied an identity by existing states (Inuits, Lapps, Samoyeds, and the North, Central, and South American Indians) are laying claim to historical rights of place that antedate present territorial divisions. They are demanding the return of their land and self-government, and they are resisting forcible assimilation. This new awakening has coincided with the rise of radical movements in the West since the 1960s (feminism, ecology, counter-cultures, anti-militarism). These trans-state socio-cultural currents are increasing resistance to the dominance of territorial structures and the state-centric principle. From the broad perspective, these contemporary forces seriously challenge the idea of a single model of modern state development and suggest that many different future paths are possible.

Several other categories of actors have recognized the vulnerability of states in their present form of organization. Global corporations market an ideology that justifies their world management role and their executives make the same basic claim: nationalism and territoriality are passé. To these corporations the world is an integrated marketplace that is hindered by the economic nationalism and protectionism of the state. The secretariats of intergovernmental organizations argue that autonomous governments must transfer more sovereignty to supranational organizations if regional and global problems are to be successfully resolved. Similarly, non-governmental organizations advance the principles of international co-operation and development as an alternative to national self-sufficiency.

In the contemporary international system, only a few states are in a position to control their own destinies. The eight most industrialized economies – Britain, Canada, France, Italy, Japan, West Germany, the Soviet Union, and the United States – are able to convert their national wealth and economic growth into independent international behaviour in matters of aid, investment, and trade. But for the majority of the other states of the world, independence is both a political and legal fiction. They see their destinies as tied to the advanced capitalist and socialist economies, which for reasons of protectionism are increasingly centralizing the global economic system to their own advantage.[39]

In the wider context of international relations*, which involves the fullest expression of trans-national human interaction (such as business, cultural and scientific exchanges, tourism, and technological advancement), there is a growing tendency among people and their governments to seek a regional approach to problem solving.[40] Latin America and the Caribbean provide rich examples of the movement toward a regional system of international co-operation and integration. In 1960, the Latin American Integration Association was established in response to the European Common Market to reduce tariffs among member states until a regional free-trade zone* was reached. That same year, the Central American Common Market (CACM) was founded to promote regional economic development in Central America through a customs union* and industrial integration. In 1969, a six-member-nation economic group created a subregional market, known as the Grupo Andíno (Andean Group), to eliminate all trade barriers, establish a common external tariff on imports, and develop a mechanism to co-ordinate investment as a common market*. This Andean common market supports the ideas of regional co-operation, central planning, and directed economies for achieving economic integration in the Andean region. The Caribbean Free Trade Association (CARIFTA) spawned the creation of the Caribbean Community and Common Market (CARICOM), which in 1973 established a regional organization designed to achieve a higher level of economic and political integration among Caribbean countries, based on the European community model. The Latin American Economic System (SELA), established in 1975, is a regional organization similar in its purposes, tactics, and goals to the Organization of Petroleum Exporting Countries (OPEC). It is an effort on the part of many Latin American countries to develop an advantageous regional strategy for producing, selling, and pricing primary products, such as bauxite, chrome, coffee, nickel, and sugar on the world market. When all these organizations are seen in the context of the entire inter-American system, a pattern of regional international integration is observable as a gradualist approach to the building of political and economic communities in the Americas beyond that of the state.

This pattern occurs elsewhere, too. The prolific growth of limited-member organizations since World War II has been a global phenomenon and stems from new emphasis being placed on regional integration as a means of achieving national objectives.[41] For the foreseeable future, the world appears to be moving in this direction.

On the level of intergovernmental relations, contemporary observers of international politics* detect other changes in the character of the global community. Since World War II, the proliferation of state and non-state actors has altered the structure of the international system and the distribution of power within it. The analysis of the balance of power* within the global state system in defined by the number of major actors or poles in that system. A pole is the term used to refer to a "great power," usually measured in terms of military strength.

Analysts have described the variations of the balance of power in the global state system as *unipolar*, *bipolar*, *tripolar*, *multipolar*, and *multibloc* or *oligopolar*.[42] At one hypothetical extreme, this power could be a world government and this system would be unipolar. But there is only a very slight probability of a global governmental system being realized.[43] Just as improbable is another unipolar variation in which one superpower acquires world hegemony*. A bipolar balance-of-power system is one where two superpowers dominate rival military, political, economic, and ideological camps – e.g., the United Sates and the Soviet Union. In a bipolar system, international tensions and conflicts are intensified because each of the protagonists perceives any gain of power for the other as a loss of power for itself and takes action to prevent this imbalance. The rising significance of China in contemporary international politics could lead to a tripolar political structure, where three poles – not necessarily equal in power – manoeuvre and shift their alliances in order to avoid isolation. In a tripolar structure the international system is much less rigid and much more flexible and political: each pole tries to prevent the emergence of a dominant coalition of the other two poles. Détente* and rapprochement are sought by the three competing powers, thus contributing to a more stable international political system based on superpower alliances and diplomatic compromise. A multipolar system exists when more than three powers function as major competing actors in the international system. The more numerous the actors, the more complex and flexible is the balance-of-power system. According to some theorists, in addition to the United States, the Soviet Union, and the People's Republic of China, the present balance-of-power system must also include Brazil, India, and Japan as significant players in the contemporary game of international politics. The multipolar bloc model goes one step further and portrays the international system divided into many spheres of influence, with many actors. It views the world as a composite of large, autonomous, integrating regions, such as North America, Central America, South America, Western Europe, Eastern Europe, the Middle East, and the various regions of Asia.[44] These emerging regional units may be the forces that will replace states as the primary actors in global affairs. Increasingly, political scientists have challenged the credibility of a model that does not include all the actors in the system. In short, the conditions that might have facilitated the view that states are the only poles of power in the contemporary world of international relations have changed dramatically. The state as a pole of power will probably remain a central characteristic of the international community in the future, but its pre-eminence has eroded and will, in all probability, continue to lessen as other actors gain power and influence. From the perspective of the 1990s, MNCs, IGOs, trans-national groups and organizations, and supranational organizations are all ascendant international powers.

Two of the most tangible elements of power – economic and military capacity – are now exercised by other actors in competition with states. MNCs, trans-national groups, individuals, and some IGOs and NGOs have access to great wealth that challenges both the viability and solvency of states. The world is no longer made up simply of rich states and poor states; rather it is composed of strong actors and weak actors. A similar situation exists with respect to military capacity. Conventional and nuclear technologies are no longer the sole possession of states. The recent proliferation and subsequent diffusion of nuclear arms have irreversibly altered the post-1945 nuclear bipolar balance. As we approach the twenty-first century, more and more states will come to possess nuclear weapons – and we can expect that other actors will, as well.[45]

All these factors lead us to conclude that the future international system should not be described in terms of poles of power. Instead, we may be more accurate to analyse the system as a multi-level network of contending actors, each with a certain degree of power and influence, each with a capability to contribute to the system's stability or instability. At present, the international system seems to be made up of numerous national actors. Closer examination reveals that every one of its working parts, including us as individuals, is interdependently connected to all the other working parts. It is, to put it one way, the only truly closed political system any of us know about. And to put it another way, it is the ultimate human organization. As evolutionary time is measured, the system appeared only moments ago and has a lot of growing up to do. At present, despite its "youth," the international system is the brightest spot on the horizon.

Canada in the International System

A decade ago John Holmes remarked that "Canada is an inescapably international country."[46] From the geographical perspective, Canada appears to be locked into the Western hemisphere as a North American country. But while it is true that Canada is geopolitically consigned to interact with the United States, the network of Canada's international relations were never historically contained in a geographically delimited hemisphere. Andrew Burghardt says that "because of the continued predominance of the North Atlantic in world commerce, because of the early development of the Maritimes and Quebec, because of ethnic ties, because of the broad St. Lawrence gateway and the extension of landmass eastward towards Europe, Canada has been heavily oriented toward the North Atlantic."[47] All these factors encouraged Canada's political and economic ties with Great Britain, the states of continental Europe, and the Commonwealth. Historically, the Commonwealth tie expanded Canada's international relations with Asia, Africa, the Caribbean, and Europe. These linkages introduced Canada to a network of global bilateral and multilateral interactions that earned Canada the widespread reputation of a good world citizen. As Barbara Ward observed, Canada was the "first international nation."[48]

Today, Canada continues to advance foreign policies with a global focus. In addition to purely historical and geographical explanations of Canada's *internationalist tradition*, some analysts have pointed to sociological characteristics lodged in Canada's political culture.[49] Early in its statehood Canada developed a diplomatic culture based on a respect for negotiation and the resolution of international conflict by legal means. The Canadian preference for pragmatic compromise in international matters flowed from the experience of constructing a nation-state containing the widest differences of political and economic interests. Canada's skills in solving political disputes legally and peaceably has gradually gained world-wide recognition as an international asset.

Perhaps the most revealing component of Canada's reputation as an important international actor is its support and *involvement in international organizations*. In this regard, Canada's active participation in the creation of the United Nations, the Commonwealth, NATO, NORAD, L'Agence culturelle et technique de la langue français (L'Agence)*, the General Agreement on Tariffs and Trade (GATT)*, the International Monetary Fund (IMF)*, the Organization for Economic Co-operation and Development (OECD)* and most recently the Organization of American States (OAS), is an insight into the enormous scope of Canada's global presence. Internationalist engagement marked by a commitment to international institutions has continued under successive Canadian governments since 1945. By 1990, the number of international institutions that Canada joined grew to over 250. The number of national economies with which Canada traded continued to expand, as did the number of Canadian representative missions abroad. In 1945, Canada had diplomatic missions in 22 states; by the 1990s, this number had grown to over 160, of which 82 were embassies.

Canada's openness to the world community is driven by its need to trade. Judged as a percentage of gross national product (GNP), Canada is the world's largest international trader. In the 1990s, 33 percent of its GNP is aggregated in trade, compared with 25 percent for the German Federal Republic and the United Kingdom, 20 percent for France and the United States, and (surprisingly) only 15 percent for Japan. Approximately four-fifths of Canada's world trade is with the United States.[50] The economic exchange between these two states is the largest bilateral trade relationship in the world, and was so even before the implementation of the Free Trade Agreement in 1989.

In the 1980s, the global recession shook the stability of Canada's international trade performance. In an economically depressed world, many governments introduced measures to protect their nascent or ailing industries against foreign imports. At the same time they have aggressively marketed their exports, competing for the same trade partners as Canada. This disheartening climate in the international economy is further clouded by other interrelated economic problems threatening the viability of trade: high levels of inflation, high unemployment, high interest rates, sagging investments, and almost universal balance-of-payments* deficits.[51] The combined impact of these complex economic forces has stimulated Canada's international instinct. At the annual GATT meetings, Canada has actively supported resolutions to liberalize international trade and encourages the reduction of protectionist measures. But, in Montreal in 1988, members of GATT could not agree on an acceptable strategy of further multilateral trade liberalization against the forces of protectionism in the international economy. At the regular meetings of the International Monetary Fund (IMF) and the International Bank for Reconstruction and Development (World Bank)*, Canada has supported the provisions of credits, loans, and subsidies to international importers in the developing countries. At all the economic summits throughout the 1980s, Canada lobbied the United States to lower interest rates and, thus, reduce pressures on its own economy, as well as on the domestic economies of the Third World debtor states. At the June 1988 economic summit in Toronto, Canada played a major role in the agreement to reduce the debt burden of the world's poorest economies, particularly in Sub-Saharan Africa. Within the framework of the United Nations Conference on Trade and Development (UNCTAD), Canada has been a protagonist for adopting guidelines to control restrictive business practices (RBPs) that result in adverse effects on international trade.

It remains Canada's view that *co-operative multilateral efforts* can be of major importance in addressing national problems and in resolving many international problems of global significance – for example, the creation of a New International Economic Order (NIEO), international environmental issues, the food crisis, and human rights. Since the 1970s, Canada has urged other developed states to accept basic changes recommended by the less developed countries (LDCs) in the international economic system. As a proponent of NIEO, Canada has advocated the stabilization of international commodity markets, the expansion of development loans and assistance through the international banking system, and the preferential treatment of Third World products in international trade. One major component of NIEO to which Canada maintains a strong commitment is North-South dialogue. At the Tokyo round of Multilateral Trade Negotiations (MTN) in 1980, Canada agreed to the gradual implementation of non-tariff-barrier codes that would open markets of the rich northern countries to the exports of the developing southern countries. In 1981, Canada was a principal contributor to a Common Fund for Commodities to assist developing countries adversely affected by volatile price fluctuations in the international marketplace.[52] The dependence of the developing economies of the South on volatile commodity markets is an ever-increasing complaint.

At Cancun in 1981, twenty-two states – including the world's richest and poorest – met in Mexico to search for a solution to the North-South economic-disparities gap. Canada and most of the other attending delegates were united in the need to move towards NIEO to address global problems in aid, trade, food, energy, and international debt resulting from the growing inequalities between the North and the South. The Canadian government promised to increase its aid program to 0.5 percent of GNP. But this falls well below Lester Pearson's suggestion in the 1960s that Canada and other developed economies should donate 1 percent of their GNP as foreign aid. This target was later lowered to 0.7 percent and among the OECD member states only four (Denmark, Norway, Sweden, and the Netherlands) have given more than 0.7 percent of their respective GNP to assist developing economies. In 1989, Canada's strong austerity budget slashed its development-assistance programs, causing its aid contribution to actually plummet to 0.43 percent of GNP in 1989–90, a lower ratio than when the Mulroney government took office in 1984. It is very unlikely that the long overdue goal of 0.5 percent of GNP will be reached by Canada in the first half of the 1990s.

The most compelling arguments for narrowing the gap between the North and the South at the Cancun Conference were directed at financing *the international debt*. Developing states feed their people, fuel their economies, and compete in the world-trade markets by means of loans and long-term repayment schedules negotiated with international lending institutions, such as the World Bank and the IMF. The IMF is usually the last resort for financially strapped Third World countries. In 1982, the World Bank and the IMF met in Toronto. Canada played a major role in the establishment of a special soft-loan fund for the International Development Association, an affiliate of the World Bank. At the 1988 economic summit Canada proposed that debtor states should repay their debts based on different combinations of terms, partial write-offs and soft-loan provisions. In the spirit of NIEO, soft loans feature a low cost (no interest, except for a small annual service charge), a long repayment schedule (usually fifty years), and a slow amortization rate (usually a ten-year period of grace, followed by 1 percent of the loan repayable annually for the next ten years and 3 percent repayable annually for the next thirty years).

On *international environmental questions*, Canada was a major player in the negotiations that led to signing of the United Nations Convention on the Law of the Sea in 1982. Canada, as the largest coastal state in the world, was successful in obtaining recognition of the need to manage offshore living and non-living resources, as well as for the provision of international legal measures to prevent marine pollution, particularly in arctic waters. The creation of an International Seabed Authority to protect the resources of the deep seabed from indiscriminate exploitation and pollution was spearheaded by Canada.[53] In pursuit of its environmental objectives, Canada took part in many international meetings in the 1980s, particularly those sponsored by the United Nations Environment Program (UNEP). Canada was instrumental in the establishment of EarthWatch, UNEP's key program which keeps an eye on all corners of the planet day and night. UNEP's observations are passed on to governments, scientists, and industrialists in all regions. The Canadian delegation initiated work on a convention for the protection of the stratospheric ozone layer that was signed by forty-five states in March 1985. Canada also ratified a United Nations Convention on Long-Range Transboundary Air Pollution (LRTAP), which recognizes acid rain as a major international environmental problem. And, in 1989, Canada was one of twenty-five states to sign the Convention on Air Pollution to limit the emissions of carbon dioxide gases. Canada also contributed to the establishment of the World Atmospheric Trust Fund.

In 1984, the *food crisis* in Africa jolted international attention to the spectre of a global food shortage. By 1990 the situation had actually worsened, even though the cameras of journalists were not focussed on Africa's starving populations to the extent they had been in the mid 1980s. The food situation in Africa is a regional manifestation of a world-wide problem of massive food shortages and the need for thousands of tonnes of food aid and millions of dollars in development assistance. Emergency relief from Canada has been crucial in averting mass starvation not only in Africa, but in Asia, Latin America, and the Caribbean. Many people in disaster-stricken areas of the world would not have survived if Canadian grain had not been delivered on time or had not been given at all. Through food aid and funding for longer-term development projects that lead to the production of food, the Canadian International Development Agency (CIDA) administers food aid and other forms of development assistance using three main channels: government-to-government aid; multilateral aid, in which Canada supports the efforts of international organizations; and aid to Canadian non-governmental organizations that work through their affiliates in the receiving state. Canada endorsed the 1987 Beijing Declaration which reaffirmed the international commitment to eradicate hunger and malnutrition by a world food strategy. Canada called for the replenishment of the International Fund for

Agricultural Development and supported the General Assembly resolution that targeted $1.4 billion in voluntary contributions to the World Food Programme for 1990.

In the field of *human rights*, Canada has not hesitated to ratify all relevant international conventions: the International Covenant on Economic, Social and Cultural Rights (1976), the International Covenant on Civil and Political Rights and its Optional Protocol (1976), and the Helsinki Agreement of 1975. In January 1982, the International Convention on the Elimination of All Forms of Discrimination against Women came into force. Canada was instrumental in drafting and supporting this convention and is a member of the committee that monitors the implementation of it provisions. Because of strong domestic pressures to speak out on human-rights violations in Poland, El Salvador, Guatemala, South Africa, and Afghanistan, Canada was a member of a working group that drafted the Convention against Torture and Other Cruel, Inhuman or Degrading Treatment or Punishment, which entered into force on June 26, 1987. One of the provisions of the convention is that a torturer may be prosecuted in any state, regardless of his or her nationality, the nationality of the victim, or the place where the torture occurred. Canada also initiated the United Nations Working Group on Enforced or Involuntary Disappeared Persons, which in urgent cases authorizes the chairman of the group to make immediate contact with the government concerned.

Given Canada's vested interest in *an orderly international system*, its government has no option but to continue on the path of vigorous international engagement. Few states are as sensitive as is Canada to the trends in the international system, the linkages among NGOs, the business manoeuvres of MNCs, the growth of IGOs, and the general condition of the international economy. Most of the domestic sources of Canadian foreign policy are clearly oriented toward the international system.[54]

Canada and the United States in the International Context under Free Trade

The complexity and constancy of Canada's relations with the United States are unique in international relations.[55] No other two states in the world share the intimacy of an undefended border 30 000 kilometres long where over 85 million people cross each year and over which nearly $200 billion in international trade is exchanged annually. This two-way trade exceeds two-way trade between the United States and Japan and between the United States and any four of its European trading partners combined. Just one province – Ontario – buys more from the United States than either Japan, the United Kingdom, France, or West Germany. Given the increasing intimacy of both economies, neither of the national governments on either side of the 49th parallel takes this sort of trading relationship for granted.[56] *Trade* between Canada and the United States translates into about 1.3 million jobs in each country. Prior to the implementation of the Canada-United States Free Trade Agreement (FTA) in 1989, both economies had already enjoyed a very large measure of free trade. Successive rounds of multilateral trade negotiations under GATT had eliminated tariffs on about 75 percent of goods and services flowing both ways across the border. A great deal of this success had resulted from sectoral trade agreements. The historic

Canada-U.S. Automotive Agreement of 1965 brought tremendous economic benefits in increased production and employment in both countries. Since the implementation of the auto pact, two-way trade in automotive products skyrocketed from less than a billion dollars annually to over $25 billion. At the Quebec Summit in March 1985, Prime Minister Mulroney and U.S. President Reagan committed themselves to reduce and eliminate the existing barriers on roughly 25 percent of trade that remained subject to tariffs. The gruelling negotiations that followed led to the signing of a historic 1407-page accord, the Canada-United States Free Trade Agreement, implemented January 1, 1989. This bilateral treaty eliminates all trade barriers (i.e., tariffs, duties, fees, quotas, or trade restrictions) between both economies by 1999, thereby initiating the largest free-trade zone in the world.[57]

Trade restrictions by each state would be permissible under certain conditions according to the terms of the agreement: when there are critical domestic shortages of food or other essential products; when domestic cuts are required to prevent diminishing natural resources; to stabilize lower domestic prices on a commodity; and to secure other products in short supply.

Government negotiators on both sides of the border saw that unhindered access to each market, including the purchases of the U.S. and Canadian governments, would permit each economy to expand by attaining increases in productivity, generate more domestic employment, enhance efficiency by sharper competition, and stimulate greater research and development at the corporate level.[58] Consumers would gain from lower prices resulting from the removal of trade barriers and governments would reap the harvest of taxes from augmented growth.

The FTA will eventually touch almost all means of production and services in the markets of Canada and the United States. New international rules and regulations will apply to many sectors in addition to business and manufacturing: agriculture, energy, financial services, government procurement, investment, and services. In some sectors exports will grow disproportionately higher in one country over the other, generating the need or the incentive to specialize in the production of certain goods and services. But a balance is anticipated, as an adjustment of industries will take place on both sides of the border: The US will gain in chemicals but Canada will gain in paper.

Canada and the United States are two of the world's largest net exporters of food. Yet, because of the complementary character of agriculture in each country, trade in farm products remained at less than 5 percent of total bilateral trade. Under the FTA some barriers to agricultural trade will disappear, stimulating a larger percentage of exchange over a ten-year period. This process will inevitably trigger the need to reform North American farm policies so that both Canada and the United States will remain competitive in the global market for agricultural products.[59]

The FTA ensures that Canada will be the largest supplier of energy to the United States. By 1987 Canada had already achieved that status for oil exports. In addition to petroleum products, Canada exports electricity, natural gas, and uranium. Prior to the FTA, quotas, taxes, and price restrictions were used to control the flow of energy trade and to protect the domestic market and producers. The FTA gives North American consumers access to energy supplies regulated essentially by market forces rather than government-imposed restrictions. Major obstacles to New England's demands for hydroelectric power from Quebec will diminish under the FTA.[60] All barriers to the export of Canadian uranium will be lifted, eliminating a source of bilateral friction in the nuclear-power industry.

Economic nationalism usually shows its possessive character around financial institutions by massive federal regulations and public-policy restrictions. The FTA attempts to give greater freedom to banks, security and trust companies, and other lending institutions to penetrate the financial markets in Canada and the United States. Canadian dealers operating in the United States would be permitted to sell government securities. In return, the FTA does away with Canada's 25 percent limit on foreign ownership of financial institutions for U.S. investers. However, no individual, corporation, or group of connected persons or companies – foreign or domestic – may own more than 10 percent of a single Canadian bank. But individual American investors, who are not affiliated, could own a series of 10 percent share positions in a Canadian bank such that American investors could hypothetically come to own or control a Canadian bank. Finally, the 16 percent ceiling on the total assets that foreign banks operating in Canada may own will be lifted to exempt American banks under the FTA.

Trade liberalization will also affect American and Canadian government contracts. Cross-border bidding on government business will expand trade opportunities for suppliers on goods and services subject to competitive tender. Potential suppliers on both sides of the border are entitled to equal information about government business, as well as fair and non-discriminatory consideration under the provisions of the FTA. Certain restrictions will remain: the provisions of FTA do not apply to state, local, or provincial governments or to departments of government that fall into the category of national security, such as some businesses under the jurisdiction of the Department of Defence in Canada and the Pentagon in the United States.

Trade is not the only part of the continuing international dialogue under free trade; *foreign investment* is another major component of this complicated agreement.[61] Americans have invested nearly $100 billion in Canada, representing about 70 percent of all foreign investment in the economy at present. By 1987, Canadians, in turn, had invested about $45 billion in the United States, or about half Canada's total investment abroad. No two economies in the world are so closely integrated in their business relations. In 1984, the Mulroney government instituted Investment Canada to replace the Foreign Investment Review Agency (FIRA), which had functioned under the Trudeau governments. Investment Canada was given a much more positive face than its predecessor and is primarily targeted to attract the confidence of the American investor. The main features of Investment Canada's mandate are that (1) foreign investments in new Canadian businesses are no longer automatically reviewed as had been the case under FIRA; (2) a review of foreign direct acquisitions of Canadian firms is conducted only if the target Canadian company has assets of over $5 million (this stricture would apply to American acquisitions in the natural gas, oil, and uranium industries); 3) foreign indirect purchases of a Canadian firm by taking over its foreign parent is reviewed if the Canadian assets involved exceed $50 million. But under the Free Trade Agreement, by January 1992, Investment Canada would no longer review indirect takeovers where an American parent of a Canadian subsidiary is taken over by another American company.

The establishment of such a comprehensive trading regime will inevitably result in fundamental differences of opinion regarding the interpretation of the FTA or the behaviour of Canadians and Americans in acting out its provisions. Persistent charges of unfair trading without the availability of a dispute-settlement mechanism would seriously threaten any long term international agreement that attempts to regulate cross-national economic behaviour. The FTA contains a binational dispute-settlement mechanism that can hear conflicts of interests flowing from bilateral trade and investments.[62] The FTA instituted two separate dispute settlement mechanisms: (1) a Canada-U.S. Trade Commission, composed of trade ministers and representatives from each government who supervise the operation of the agreement and try to resolve overriding disputes between both economies; (2) binational panels to review disputes about subsidies and to review antidumping or countervailing duty decisions that go through the courts. Both these groups can uphold the decision of a tribunal or overturn a decision with binding power on disputants.

The FTA made certain deferences on matters of cultural significance to Canada that constitute the non-economic implications of bilateral free trade.[63] Article 2005 of the FTA firmly states: "Cultural industries are exempt from the provisions of this Agreement." Cultural industries are broadly defined as publishing, radio and television, film, and audio/visual recordings. A number of exceptions to the FTA are significant: (1) Canada will remove tariffs on tapes and records; (2) a foreign-owned cultural enterprise may be sold to non-Canadians in the absence of a Canadian buyer; (3) after 1990 Canadian cable TV companies will have to pay for U.S. programs they capture and retransmit; (4) U.S. advertisers will qualify for Canadian tax deductions on publications printed in the U.S. for distribution in Canada if the magazines or periodicals meet Canadian content rules.

Beyond the FTA, *environmental protection* has appeared over recent years as a major question of international concern between Canada and the United States.[64] Acid rain is at the forefront of the issues of bilateral concern between both states. Scientists have provided much evidence to show that acid rain is formed from emissions of sulphur dioxide and oxides of nitrogen that mix in the atmosphere to produce acids that eventually fall to earth in rain, dew, snow, and dust. Acid rain causes annual damages in excess of $350 million to Canadians; environmental groups such as the Canadian Coalition against Acid Rain say it threatens fishing, tourism, and farming in many parts of Canada and the United States. Two major sources of the problem are auto emissions and pollution from smelters. With time, legislated emission controls, and $2 billion in public monies on both sides of the border, acid rain may become a treatable problem.

Previous U.S. administrations have consistently opposed undertaking a costly clean-up program until more is known about the causes and effects of acid rain. But the Bush administration promised to take immediate action on the problem. In 1989 President Bush announced his intention to cut U.S. sulphur dioxide and nitrogen oxide emmissions by one-half for the mid 1990s. The Mulroney government accepted the U.S. contention that Canada trailed the United States in cutting emissions and made a commitment to cut Canadian emissions of sulfur dioxide and nitrogen oxides by 2.3 million tonnes by 1994. But the Canadian government believes that perfect knowledge about the extent and consequences of acid rain is not a prerequisite to immediate public-policy action on the problem. Canada's federal plan aims at adopting and enforcing auto-emissions standards and providing government assistance to attack the smelter problem. Canadians and many northeastern Americans believe that enough is now known to move bilaterally against acid rain even as further research is being conducted. The United States has indicated its willingness to reverse its position of cautious action as Canada demonstrates substantial progress in cutting emissions that cause acid rain.

Resource management and development are two other areas high on the agenda of both states. Free water, taken for granted by North Americans as an inexhaustible and free natural endowment, is now considered a long-range resource issue on the continent. Given the growing awareness of the effects of acid rain, the quality of both surface water and ground water is already a great concern in some places. But quantity of supply is also a resource-management concern because of rising demand anticipated over the next decades. For that reason, it requires a different kind of bilateral response than acid rain now seems to be receiving. Although water seems to be plentiful in North America, drinkable water is in much shorter supply. The long-range supply of water is not only threatened by increased consumption but also by pollution and spoilage. Other resources such as nickel and zinc, as well as such energy resources as oil and natural gas, are all in finite supply and eventually will be exhausted. Long-term planning is recognized by both governments as essential to their national interest.

Defence is another cornerstone of Canada-U.S. relations. Since the 1930s, Canadians have been aware that Canada is strategically one with the United States.[65] After World War II, it became increasingly evident that Canada had a major military role to play in the defence of the North American continent. Thus, it was natural for Canada to enter into the NORAD (North American Air Defense) agreement with the United States in 1958. Cross-border collaboration between Canadian and American military forces intensified with the installations of the Distant Early Warning (DEW) system. For nearly three decades, the DEW line served as Canada's main contribution to hemispheric defence and entwined Canadian military commitment with American strategic theory and practice. Recognition of Canada's strategic bond to the military security of the United States was demonstrated in the agreement, giving the United States permission to conduct cruise missile tests on Canadian territory. But this was just the beginning of a much more concrete contribution to continental defence.

By the 1980s, Soviet intercontinental bombers armed with nuclear cruise missiles could fly over the polar cap in the Canadian high arctic, slip through radar gaps over Labrador, and skirt detection by the DEW-line installations. That possibility is the main reason why Canada and the United States agreed in 1985 to a massive overhaul of the NORAD system, involving a $1.5 billion modernization program for air defence that includes a new North Warning System to replace the obsolete DEW line. The new system, which will be fully in place by the 1990s, will see an end to most of the radar stations at the southern arc of the arctic circle and will erect a series of detection and warning stations around the North American continent capable of tracking aircraft and cruise missiles penetrating the Northern hemisphere. Unlike the DEW-line system, which was controlled by the U.S. Air Force, the North Warning System is Canadian controlled, giving Canada sovereign decision-making authority over its use and development.

Finally, the high degree of interdependence between both countries has raised concerns over questions of *national identity and cultural diversity*. Canadians may not be the most nationalistic people but they are the most identity-conscious people in the world. The preoccupation with national identity is intimately tied to Canada's relations with the United States. But as Arthur Siegel says: "If Canadians had any choice in the matter, they would probably pick the United States as a neighbor."[66] Unlike most other bilateral relationships in the world, Canadian interaction with the United States goes well beyond government-to-government dealings between Ottawa and Washington or between the provinces and the states. Indeed, Canada's intimacy with the United States goes beyond history and geography. The contacts at every level, among businesses, individuals, and families, and between academic and other institutions constitute a symbiotic socio-cultural relationship that defies definition.[67] There have been mutual benefits to these ties.Bothcountries share two of the highest standards of living in the world, a rapid rate of industrial and technological development, and a dynamic daily exchange of communications, ideas, and people.

This close interaction, however, has also created some serious anxieties and problems in many sectors, especially national identity and cultural diversity. For English-speaking Canadians, this concern is derived from the overwhelming influence of American culture on Canada; for French-speaking Canadians, it results from living among 260 million American and Canadian anglophones. In both cases there is a genuine fear of cultural and political assimilation, which has led to the development of public policies explicitly designed to protect and nurture indigenous cultural activities.[68] The American influence is still especially noticeable in television; the most popular U.S. programs enjoy top TV ratings in Canada. American products are equally pervasive in books and films. *Cultural protectionism* has been resisted in the United States by private industry and Congress. Americans have interpreted Canadian government support for indigenous cultural activities as an impingement on U.S. economic interests. Both states have carefully negotiated to minimize irritations in the sensitive areas of national identity and economic nationalism.

REFERENCES

1. For comprehensive analyses of the "actors" in the international systems, see Theodore Couloumbis and James Wolfe, *Introduction to International Relations: Power and Justice* (Englewood Cliffs, NJ: Prentice-Hall Inc. 1982); Walter Jones and Steven Rosen, *The Logic of International Relations* (Boston: Little, Brown & Co. 1982); Charles Kegley Jr. and Eugene Wittkopt, *World Politics: Trend and Transformation* (New York: St. Martin's Press Inc. 1981); Bruce Russett and Harvey Starr, *World Politics: The Menu for Choice* (San Francisco: W.H. Freeman & Co. Publishers 1981).
2. Daniel S. Papp, *Contemporary International*

Relations: Frameworks for Understanding (New York: Macmillan Publishing Co. 1984), 13–38; and Richard Mansbach, Yale Ferguson, et al., *The Web of World Politics: Non-State Actors in the Global System* (Englewood Cliffs, NJ: Prentice-Hall Inc. 1976), 20–31.

3. K.J. Holsti, *International Politics A Framework for Analysis* (Englewood Cliffs, NJ: Prentice-Hall Inc. 1988), 79–81; and Seyom Brown, "The World Polity and the Nation-State System: An Updated Analysis," *International Journal XXXIX* (Summer 1984): 509–28, pub. by Canadian Institute of International Affairs, Toronto.
4. John T. Rourke, *International Politics on the World Stage* (Guilford, CT: Dushkin Publishing Group 1989), 105–09.
5. Harold Jacobson, *Networks of Interdependence: International Organizations and the Global Political System* (New York: Alfred A. Knopf Inc. 1981); H. Jacobson, W. Reisinger, and T. Mathers, "National Entanglements in International Governmental Organizations," *American Political Science Review* 80 (March 1986): 142–58.
6. *Yearbook of International Organizations: Global Action Networks*, 4th ed. (Brussels: Union of International Associations 1986/87).
7. Press Release, "The Mulroney Program and the Third World Institutional Highlights, Employment, and Other Links," January 4, 1985, North-South Institution/L'Institute Nord-Sud, Ottawa.
8. A. Leroy Bennett, *International Organizations Principles and Issues* (Englewood Cliffs NJ: Prentice-Hall Inc. 1988), 384–410.
9. *Basic Facts About the United Nations* (New York: United Nations 1988).
10. Robert Riggs and Jack Plano, *International Organization and World Politics* (Chicago: Dorsey Press 1988); see also Paul Diehl, *The Politics of International Organizations: Patterns and Insights* (Chicago: Dorsey Press 1989).
11. Until October 25, 1971, the Chinese seat on the Security Council was occupied by the Republic of China (Taiwan). After that date, the Chinese seat was occupied by the People's Republic of China.
12. Peter Fromuth, ed., *A Successor Vision: The United Nations of Tomorrow* (Lanham, MD: University Press of America 1988).
13. NATO, *Facts and Figures* (Brussels: NATO Information Service 1989).
14. Desmond Ball, *Targeting for Strategic Deterence,* Adelphi Papers no. 185 (London: The International Institute for Strategic Studies 1985).
15. Steve Chan, *International Relations in Perspective: The Pursuit of Security, Welfare, and Justice* (New York: Macmillan Publishing Co. 1984), 59.
16. John Spanier, *Games Nations Play* (New York: Holt, Rinehart and Winston 1984), 229–31.
17. See "Socialist Integration: What Has Been Done and What Remains to be Done," *World Marxist Review* 25 (January 1982): 71–5.
18. Bennett, *International Organizations,* 357–60.
19. S.J. Rubin, "Falklands (Malvenas), International Law and the OAS," *American Journal of International Law* 76 (July 1982): 594–5.
20. Alejandro Orfila, "Can the Crisis Gripping the OAS Be Overcome?" *Vital Speeches of the Day* 48 (March 15, 1982): 329–31.
21. Richard Barnett and Ronald Muller, *Global Reach – The Power of the Multinational Corporations* (New York: Simon & Schuster 1974), 15.
22. Michael Bliss, "Our Vanishing Borders," *Financial Times of Canada,* January 2, 1989; see also John Kenneth Galbraith, "The New Improved Industrial State," *Business Month,* January 1989.
23. George Modelski, ed., *Transnational Corporations and the World Order: Readings in International Political Economy* (San Francisco: W.H. Freeman 1979), 241; and

Jane Spero, *The Politics of International Economic Relations* (New York: St. Martin's Press Inc. 1985), 230–3.

24. John Stopford and John Dunning et al., *The World Directory of Multinational Enterprise* (New York: Facts on File 1980), XXV; U.S. Central Intelligence Agency, *The World Factbook 1982* (Washington: U.S. Government Printing Office 1982).
25. United Nations Centre on Transnational Corporations, *Transnational Corporations in World Development: Trends and Prospects* (New York: UN Publications 1988).
26. Modelski, ed., *Transnational Corporations*, 240; and David Blake and Robert Walters, *The Politics of Global Economic Relations* (Englewood Cliffs N.J.: Prentice-Hall 1987).
27. Howard Perlmutter, "Super-Giant Firms in the Future," *Wharton Quarterly* 24 (Winter 1968); see also Spero, *The Politics of International Economic Relations*.
28. Frederic Pearson and Martin Rochester, *International Relations: The Global Condition in the Late Twentieth Century* (Reading, MA: Addison-Wesley Publishing Co. 1984), 318; Harold Jacobson et. al., "National Entanglements in International Governmental Organizations," *American Political Science Review* 80, no. 1 (1986): 142–59.
29. *A Directory of Canadian Peace Organizations with International Concerns* (Winnipeg: Mennonite Central Committee 1982).
30. *Amnesty International Report 1984* (London: Amnesty International Publications 1984).
31. Papp, *Contemporary International Relations*, 77–90.
32. See Neil Livingstone, *The War against Terrorism* (Lexington, MA: Lexington Books 1982); and Yonah Alexander and Kenneth Meyers, eds., *Terrorism in Europe* (New York: St. Martin's Press Inc. 1982).
33. See P. Grantham, *Torture in the Eighties* (London: Amnesty International Publications 1984); and n.a. *Terrorism*, Report Series 7, no. 4 (College Park, MD: Center for Philosophy and Public Policy, University of Maryland 1987).
34. Martin Slann and Bernard Schechterman, *Multidimensional Terrorism* (Boulder, CO: Lynne Rienner Publishers 1987).
35. Robert Isaak, *Individuals and World Politics* (North Scituate, MA: Dixbury Press 1975); and J. Rourke, *International Politics and the World Stage* (Guilford, CT.: Dushkin Publishing Group 1989), 16–19, 101–3.
36. Hugh Kindred et al., *International Law: Chiefly as Interpreted and Applied in Canada* (Toronto: Emond Montgomery Publications 1987), 122–30.
37. W. Ladd Hollist and James N. Rosenau, eds., *World System Structure: Continuity and Change* (Beverly Hills, CA: Sage 1981); see also Steven Haggard and Beth Simmons, "Theories of International Regimes," *International Organization* 41, no. 3 (1987): 497–517.
38. See Yale Ferguson and Richard Mansbach, *The State, Conceptual Chaos, and the Future of International Theory* (Boulder, CO. Lynne Rienner Publishers 1989).
39. Leonard Silk, "A Growing Interdependence," *New York Times*, February 8, 1981, section 12; see also David Blake and Robert Walters, *The Politics of Global Economic Relations* (Englewood Cliffs, NJ: Prentice-Hall 1987).
40. See Robert Keohane, "The Demand for International Regimes," *International Organization* 36, no. 2 (1982) 325–56; and Robert Riggs and Jack Plano, *The United Nations: International Organization and World Politics* (Chicago: Dorsey Press 1988).
41. Bennett, *International Organizations*, 347–83.
42. William Thompson, "Polarity, the Long Cycle and Global Power Warfare," no. 4: *Journal of Conflict Resolution* 30, no. 4: (1986): 587–615; I. Kim, ed., *The Strategic Triangle: China, United States, and the*

Soviet Union (New York: Paragon House Publishers 1987); and M. Perry et. al., *Civilization, Ideas, Politics, and Society* (Boston: Houghton Mifflin Co. 1989).

43. Peter Bernholz, *The International Game of Power* (Berlin, GFR: Mouton Publishers 1985), 210.

44. Couloumbis & Wolfe, *Introduction to International Relations*, 291–310.

45. For a comprehensive analysis of the proliferation of nuclear weapons, see Stockholm International Peace Research Institute, *World Armaments and Disarmament, SIPRI Yearbook 1987* (London: Taylor & Francis 1987);and Jozef Goldblat and David Cox, *Nuclear Weapon Tests: Prohibition or Limitation?* (Oxford, England: Oxford University Press 1989).

46. John Holmes, *Canada: A Middle-Aged Power* (Toronto: McClelland & Stewart Ltd. 1976), 66; and Kim Richard Nossal, *The Politics of Canadian Foreign Policy,* 2nd ed. (Scarborough, ON: Prentice-Hall Canada 1989).

47. Andrew Burghardt, "Canada and the World," in John Warkentin, ed., *Canada: A Geographical Interpretation* (Toronto: Methuen Publications 1968), 571.

48. Barbara Ward, "The First International Nation," in William Kilbourn, ed., *Canada; A Guide to the Peaceable Kingdom* (Toronto: Macmillan 1975), 45–8.

49. Michael Tucker, *Canadian Foreign Policy: Contemporary Issues and Themes* (Toronto: McGraw-Hill Ryerson Ltd. 1980), 2–3; and Denis Stairs, "Political Culture in Canadian Foreign Policy," *Canadian Journal of Political Science* 15 (December 1982): 667–90.

50. Allan Gotlieb, Roy Cottier, et al., "Canadian Business Representation in the United States," *Behind the Headlines* XII, no. 1 (1984): 1; Canadian Institute of International Affairs Toronto; and Gotlieb, "Notes for an Address: Ambassador of Canada to the United States," Oxford and Cambridge dinner, New York, May 6, 1987.

51. Robert Rothstein, "Dealing with Disequilibrium: Rising Pressures and Diminishing Resources in Third World Nation-States," *International Journal* XXXIX, no. 3 (1984): 1; Canadian Institute of International Affairs, Toronto.

52. Spero, *The Politics of International Economic Relations*, 200–15.

53. Barry Buzan and Dan Middlemiss, "Canadian Foreign Policy and the Exploitation of the Seabed," in Barbara Johnson and Mark Zacher, eds., *Canadian Foreign Policy and the Law of the Sea* (Vancouver: University of British Columbia Press 1977).

54. Kim Richard Nossal, "Analyzing the Domestic Sources of Canadian Foreign Policy," *International Journal* XXXIX, no. 1 (1983–84): 1–22.

55. See Charles Doran, "The United States and Canada: Invulnerability and Interdependence," *International Journal* XXXVIII, no. 1 (1982–83): 128–46; see also Norman Hillmer, ed., *Partners Nevertheless* (Toronto: Copp Clark Pitman Ltd. 1989).

56. See Denis Stairs and Gilbert Winham, eds., *The Politics of Canada's Economic Relationship with the United States* (Toronto: University of Toronto Press 1985).

57. See Bruce Wilkinson, "Canada-United States Free Trade: Setting the Dimensions," in Allan Maslove and Stanley Winer, *Knocking on the Back Door:Canadian Perspectives on the Political Economy of Freer Trade with the United States* (Halifax: Institute for Research on Public Policy 1988), 7–26.

58. See Jeffrey Schott and Murray Smith, eds., *The Canada-United States Free Trade Agreement: The Global Impact* (Washington, DC: Institute for International Economics 1988), 3–64.

59. Canada, Department of Finance, *The Canada-US Free Trade Agreement: An Economic Assessment* (Ottawa: 1988); and Dale Hathaway, "Agriculture and the GATT: Rewriting the Rules," *Policy Analyses in International Economics* 20

(September 1987), Institute for International Economics, Washington.

60. See Alex Netherton, "Hydro in the Free Trade Agreement," *International Perspectives* XVI, no.1 (1988): 11–14.

61. Alan Rugman, *Outward Bound: Canadian Direct Investment in the United States* (Toronto and Washington: Canadian-American Committee, 1987).

62. See Gary Horlick et al., "Dispute Resolution Mechanisms," in Schott and Smith, *The Canada-United States Free Trade Agreement: The Global Impact*, 65–86.

63. See Denis Stairs, "Free Trade – another View," *International Perspectives* (May/June 1987): 3–8.

64. See Don Munton, "Dependence and Interdependence in Transboundary Environmental Relations," *International Journal* XXXVI, no. 1 (1980–81): 161–79; and K. Curtis and J. Carroll, "Transboundary Environmental and Resources Issues," in Norman Hillmer, ed., *Partners Nevertheless*, 194–205.

65. See R.J. Sutherland, "Canada's Long-Term Strategic Situation," *International Journal* XVII, no. 1 (1962): 199–223.

66. Arthur Siegel, *Politics and the Media in Canada* (Toronto: McGraw-Hill Ryerson Ltd. 1983), 3.

67. Andrew Malcolm, *The Canadians* (Toronto: Fitzhenry & Whiteside 1985).

68. See John Meisel, "Escaping Extinction: Cultural Defence of an Independent Border," in D.H. Flaherty and W.R. McKercher, *Southern Exposure: Canadian Perspectives on the United States* (Toronto: McGraw-Hill Ryerson 1986), 152–67.

SUGGESTED READINGS

Tim Brodhead, et al., *Bridges of Hope? Canadian Voluntary Agencies and the Third World* (Ottawa: North-South Institute 1988).

Innis Claude, *States and the Global System* (New York: St. Martin's Press 1988).

Karl W. Deutsch, *The Analysis of International Relations,* 3rd ed. (Englewood Cliffs, NJ: Prentice-Hall 1988).

Kail Ellis, *The Vatican, Islam and the Middle East* (Syracuse, NY: Syracuse University Press 1987)

John Holmes and John Kirton, eds.,*Canada and the New Internationalism* (Toronto: Canadian Institute of International Affairs 1988).

Steven Lamy, *Contemporary International Issues: Contending Perspectives* (Boulder, CO: Lynne Rienner Publishers 1988).

Walter Laqueur, *The Age of Terrorism* (Boston: Little, Brown & Co. 1987).

Steven Luper-Foy, *Problems of International Justice* (Boulder, CO: Westview Press 1988).

Olav Stokke, *Western Middle Powers and Global Poverty* (Uppsala, Sweden: Scandinavian Institute of African Studies/Norwegian Institute of International Affairs [Oslo] 1989).

Sylvia Woodby and Martha Cottam, *The Changing Agenda: World Politics since 1945* (Boulder, CO: Westview Press 1988)

GLOSSARY

consensus: The converging of opinion upon a common judgement as sometimes displayed by members of international organizations.

conflict: In the international system it is a type of interstate interaction, characterized by antagonistic encounters or collisions of interests, ideas, policies, programs, and persons, or other entities, sometimes involving the use of armed force.

regionalism: The international-relations concept that nation–states situated in a definable geographic area can co-operate with each other on matters of economic, social, political, and military concern.

transnational: Extending beyond the borders of a single country, sometimes applied to a political movement, issue, organization, or some event.

collective security: A concept that provides

for a global or regional defence system based on the agreement of members to take collective action against an aggressive and belligerent state or group of states.

functional intergovernmental organizations: IGOs that promote economic, social, and political collaboration with little or no regard to collective security.

supranational organization: An international organization to which members surrender some sovereignty or jurisdiction to a higher authority in order to achieve a degree of political and economic integration.

peaceful settlement of disputes: The resolution of international disputes, using legal and political procedural techniques such as arbitration, adjudication, diplomatic negotiation, good offices, inquiry, meditation, and conciliation.

Uniting for Peace Resolution: A resolution that authorizes the General Assembly to take collective action against aggression when the Security Council is paralysed from ordering action by a permanent member's veto.

trust territories: Non-self-governing territories placed under the United Nations trusteeship system.

deterrence: A political and military strategy based on the theory that the best way to prevent war and aggression is to build up such a massive and threatening arsenal of weapons that no other nation-state would risk an attack.

theatre: In the language of nuclear warfare, theatre refers to an extended area or region of attack as distinct from tactical theatre, which refers to the battlefield.

observer status: A formal arrangement between an international organization and a non-member-state, allowing the latter to observe without voting privileges the former's decision-making councils.

inter-American system: The network of international relations among the nation-states of the Western hemisphere based on American international law, international institutions, commitments, and agreements through which regional co-operation and integration are achieved.

Inter-American Treaty of Reciprocal Assistance: A permanent collective-security agreement, establishing a defence zone from the North to the South Pole, that provides for military assistance among signatories in case of an armed attack within the zone or any form of aggression against a signatory from outside the zone.

mediation: A procedure to peacefully settle disputes, whereby an impartial third party assists the disputants to resolve a conflict by offering its good offices, recommendations, and diplomatic skills to reconcile opposing claims.

conciliation: a procedure to peacefully settle disputes in which representatives of a group of impartial nation-states establish the facts and base recommendations on them to the disputants.

Holy See: This refers to the office or jurisdiction of the pope.

good offices: As viewed from the perspective of international law, this is an instrument used for the peaceful settlement of disputes by which a state not party to a dispute offers the perceived neutrality of its territory and official resources to parties in conflict so as to facilitate a negotiated settlement.

contadora peace initiative: A proposal produced by the so-called contadora countries – Colombia, Panama, Mexico, and Venezuela – calling for a regional non-aggressive treaty to end hostilities among Central American countries and requiring the support of the United States.

multilateral: A course of action taken by three or more states to foster co-operation in trade, collective security, or any economic, political, or military endeavour established by treaty, convention, or other international instruments.

unilateral: An independent action or policy taken by a state from its own resources to advance its national interest.

North/South axis: The growing tension between the few economically developed economies of the North and the many deprived economies of the South.

aprismo: The democratic revolutionary movement spawned by the American Popular Revolutionary Alliance (APRA), founded by Victor Haya de la Torre of Peru, which came to be the prototype for other revolutionary parties of the democratic left in the Latin American region.

Canadian Security Intelligence Service: A special intelligence agency of the Canadian government that came into being in July 1984, with a legal mandate to place under surveillance anyone suspected of terrorism, espionage, sabotage, and foreign-influenced threats to national security or domestic subversion.

international relations: The term used to refer to all forms of interaction between and among members of separate societies whether government sponsored or not.

free-trade area: The eliminatation of tariffs among member-states but each member is permitted to set its own external tariff for imports from the outside world.

customs union: Eliminates tariffs among members but goes beyond the free trade area by erecting a common external tariff against imports from the outside world.

common market: A step closer to economic integration: in addition to free trade among members and a common external tariff: common markets either eliminate or substantially reduce restrictions on the movements of labour and capital among member states. They may even co-ordinate fiscal, monetary, and exchange-rate policies.

international politics: The term used to refer to all forms of official governmental relationships exclusive of other human trans-national relations.

balance of power: A concept used to denote several types of interstate relations in the context of shifting alliances and alignments.

hegemony: The domination of one state over another state, region, or the world.

détente: A diplomatic term indicating a situation of lessened tension in relations between two or more nation-states.

L'Agence culturelle et technique de la langue française (Agency for Cultural and Technical Co-operation): An international association of French-language nation-states concerned with cultural and technical co-operation.

General Agreement on Tariffs and Trade (GATT): An international organization formed at Geneva in 1947 that promotes trade among members and provides a forum for negotiating the reduction of tariffs, quotas, and other trade barriers.

International Monetary Fund (IMF): A specialized agency of the United Nations, established in 1944, to promote exchange-rate stability and provide monetary services to help its more than 130 members overcome short-term disequilibria in the balance of payments.

Organization for Economic Co-operation and Development OECD: A regional international economic organization established in 1961 to study and promote economic growth and free trade among its twenty-four members.

balance of payments: A statistical record of all economic transactions that have taken place during a given time period between a state's residents and the rest of the world.

International Bank of Reconstruction and Development IBRD: A specialized agency of the United Nations, established in 1944 as the World Bank to assist states to achieve their development goals by providing loans and technical assistance to foster economic development.

14

International Law

A terrorist car bomb scatters debris in a New York street

Law and Order in the International Community

IN THE 444 DAYS PRECEDING January 20, 1981, the world witnessed one of the most blatant violations of international law that could be committed by a state. Under the new regime headed by the militant religious leader Ayatollah Khomeini, Iran held fifty-two Americans hostage in Tehran in order to extract concessions from the U.S. government and to expose the corruption of the ousted Shah. The protracted incident sent shock waves through the diplomatic corps of the entire international community as the principle of diplomatic immunity, which protects diplomatic personnel from seizure and punishment, was reduced to a form of terrorist ransom by the Khomeini regime. For Canadians, events in Iran held a special significance because Ambassador Ken Taylor arranged the chilling escape of six American diplomats during the hostage crisis, making him the international hero of the diplomatic world.

In its unprecedented violation of a sacred rule of international law, Iran has not legally answered for its conduct. And, in all probability, it may never have to. This incident is a vivid illustration of the dilemma of international law in an increasingly violent and potentially explosive international society. In 1989, the same leader, Ayatollah Khomeini, ordered the death sentence for author Salman Rushdie, a British citizen, thereby committing yet another fundamental breach of international law. Other than political, economic, and military sanctions, there are no compulsory enforcement instruments for bringing a recalcitrant government to justice in the international system. There is no international legislature for making laws; there is no regular international police force to stop illegal behaviour; and there is no compulsory adjudication* to force a legal violator to appear in court and respect the law.

It would appear that international law is a powerless deterrent against deviant behaviour* in the international community. But this is a misconception. In reality most states do not violate international law. Compliance* with the laws of the international community is often greater than the degree of compliance and enforcement found in centralized national legal systems, where institutions to legislate and enforce laws are present and developed. In the United States, for example, only three murders out of ten are followed by conviction[1]; and of all serious crimes reported (except murder), only 19 percent of the cases result in arrests, less than 10 percent of those arrested are convicted, and only 2.5 percent of those convicted spend time in a correctional institution.[2] In Great Britain, some 59 percent of all serious crimes known to the police never result in convictions. In Canada, police do not gain convictions on 63 percent of most known offences and record as few as one out of every twenty-three crimes committed.[3] Yet these three legal systems are among the most highly developed in the world.

Compliance with international law tends to be greater than with municipal law* because states comply out of national interest. States are themselves the architects of systems of law and order in international affairs and so are willing to tolerate constraints on their own behaviour in the absence of strong legislative and enforcement mechanisms. In addition, in the international community (which is composed of only 175 members) there are enormous pressures on governments to comply with the expected rules of behaviour. By means of legal challenges, diplomatic manouevres, and political jabs, violators are made to face the judgements of their peers. When a state violates international law, it is almost always detected by other states, which may take extra-legal as well as legal measures against the perpetrator. For example, the international community expressed strong disapproval on learning that the United States was responsible for illegally mining Nicaragua's harbours in February and March 1984. The mining stopped in April of that year after the Sandinista government introduced a resolution before the United Nations Security Council in New York City calling for an immediate halt to such practices. Even though the United States vetoed the resolution, it had suffered a severe blow to its legal credibility in Central America: a long-time champion of the rule of law, the United States was seen to be breaking it. While the deterrent effect of law is less formal and less institutionalized in the international system, most states have learned that their compliance to it avoids chaos in the complex world of international commerce, travel, and politics.

What Is International Law?

International law has been defined as "a *system* of law containing *principles, customs, standards* and *rules* by which relations among states and other international persons are governed."[4] As with most definitions, key terms demand elaboration. International law is "systematic" because it endeavors to establish persisting patterns of legal relationships among all members of the international community, which are interdependent and need a peaceful and orderly environment to survive. The systematic nature of international law results from its universal design, intended to invite compliance from all members of the international community. The legitimacy* of international law is based on the consent of states to regard its authority as binding on their behaviour. Because of this need for consent, the probability of compliance increases significantly when a great number of states accept a rule of conduct. Thus, a multilateral treaty ratified* by 150 states has greater legitimacy than one that only 25 states have ratified.

International law is made up of generally accepted principles* governing the conduct of states. Principles are fundamental rules of conduct that guide the legal behaviour of states. One such principle is the *jus cogens** (law of pre-emptory norms), as stated in articles 53 and 64 of the Vienna Convention of the Law of Treaties, whereby a treaty becomes void if it is contrary to norms recognized by the international community as a whole.[5] For example, a treaty signed and ratified by some states to exterminate a racial or ethnic group runs contrary to general principles of international law and thus is void. Another accepted principle is the legal equality of independent states. This principle is generally recognized and upheld as international law. For example, Bolivia's vote in the General Assembly of the United Nations carries the same legal weight as Canada's, despite the differences in the size and wealth of both states.

Customs form a substantial body of international law. In a landmark case of international law – *The Paquette Habana v. The Lola* (1900) – U.S. Supreme Court Justice Horace Gray defined custom as "ancient usage ripening into law." The incorporation of customs into codified law* has occurred frequently in the twentieth century. Customs that are widely practised as binding on states still continue to surface, as with international behaviour on diplomacy and in outer space. For example, a growing number of states are placing restrictions on some of the codified rules regarding diplomatic immunities (see chapter 15). And outer space is being researched and tested for the use of defensive and offensive military technology, despite the presence of treaties and conventions that have previously designated outer space a non-military area of scientific research.

Standards of conduct refer to the generally accepted procedures by which states reach agreements and apply solutions to resolve conflicts. Rather than resort to the use of force to settle disputes, states are expected to negotiate, adjudicate, and arbitrate when conflicts arise. States are obliged to employ peaceful instruments and skills in their relations with the other members of the international community.

Until the twentieth century, only states were considered as "persons," i.e., entities with rights and obligations under international law. Today, legal personality is extended to international organizations and individuals. For example, diplomatic immunities are enjoyed by international organizations such as the United Nations and the Organization of American States, and are protected by international convention. In addition, the general conduct of international organizations is accountable under international law. These organizations have rights and duties similar to those of states. Under international law, individuals have legal personality only in a limited set of circumstances. Since most individuals possess a nationality*, their own states either act as agents to protect them or to prosecute them for behaviour that has international consequences. When individuals become refugees or stateless*, international law directs a limited measure of legal personality to them. The bases for the legal protection of refugees were developed during the Convention Relating to the Status of Refugees in 1951. This convention determined the rights of refugees to work, education, social welfare, religious freedom, and legal processes. Article 15 of the Universal Declaration of Human Rights (1948) established standards for dealing with stateless persons. International law encourages states to adopt a flexible approach to the conferment of nationality on stateless persons and to provide them with proper identity documents to enable their legal admission to other states.

Finally, international law is a very special kind of law because of its consensual nature. It is intimately tied to the presence of the decentralized international system that emerged in Europe in the sixteenth and seventeenth centuries. Since the Treaty of Westphalia in 1648, most states that comprise this decentralized international community have shown a willingness to abide by the law of the majority and have developed habits of compliance with international norms. This international system has been successful in developing an identifiable process for creating legally binding rules of conduct, even in the absence of a complete set of formal institutional lawmaking machinery. The sources of this process of law are officially recognized by the states of the world and have been documented as Article 38 of the Statute of the International Court of Justice, which is attached to the United Nations Charter.

Sources of International Law

The international legal system consists of a substantial body of law derived from five sources: (1) widely recognized and practised customs of states; (2) international treaties and conventions signed and ratified by states; (3) general principles of law recognized by states; (4) judicial decisions of national and international courts and tribunals; and (5) writings and teachings of qualified legal experts.

Some scholars have noted that the progressive development of international law is at present established by a sixth highly visible and identifiable source, namely, the acts of international organizations, particularly the United Nations and its specialized agencies.[6]

Each of these sources has contributed to international legal development by either giving recognition to historical compliance with the rules of international conduct or by establishing new laws (figure 14.1). Ultimately, however, states themselves are the principle source of international law. They hold the power of consent to the norms and customs that have evolved over a long period of time and they ultimately become parties to the treaties that bind them to the codified laws of international behaviour.

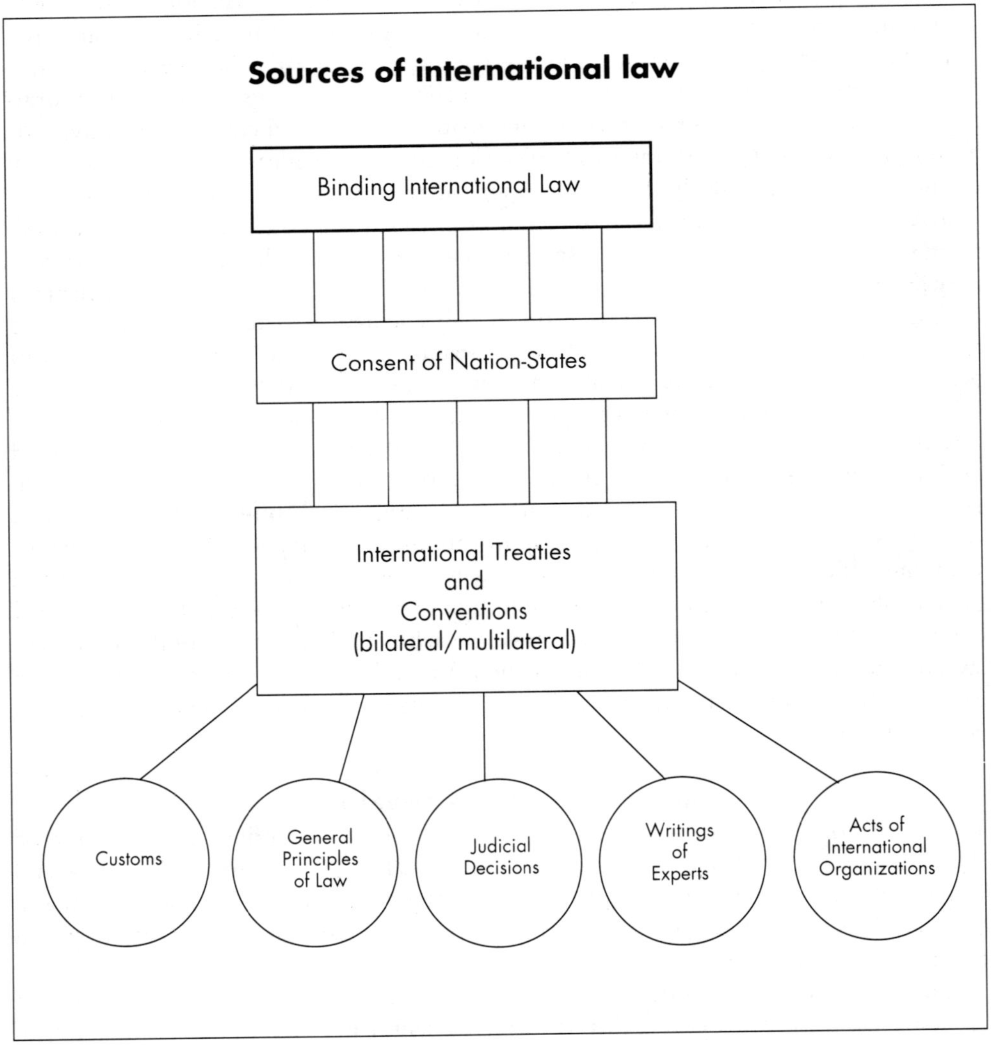

Figure 14.1

CUSTOM

With the emergence of modern European states in the mid–seventeenth century, the vast majority of transactions among independent political units were governed by customs. This body of observable usages and practices in international conduct became widely accepted by states as obligatory and binding* as law. Habitual, constant, and uniform conduct evolved in many areas of international behaviour. Rules of conduct in times of war, standard practices of navigation and maritime safety, diplomatic immunity, the observance of treaties, and the jurisdictions of states are examples of law built on the actual practices of states. Customs were transformed into legal rules because states recognized the expediency of order in a largely decentralized and lawless international community. The technical name for this psychological motivation to respect custom as law is *opinio iuris sive necessitatis** (*opinio iuris* for short) – legal forms of conduct are necessary if chaos is to be avoided.

Until the twentieth century, custom formed the bulk of international law among states. Major and minor inconsistencies in state practices created difficulties in the interpretation and compliance with customary international law.[7] For example, in the sixteenth and seventeenth centuries, states began to make conflicting claims about their jurisdictions within the territorial sea. Many states adopted the custom of regarding the border of the sea to be three miles – the range of a cannonball fired from the low-water mark on shore. Many states accepted this "cannon-shot" rule, but Scandinavian states claimed four miles of territorial sea and Spain and Portugal claimed six. In the twentieth century, the codification of international law has done much to clarify these types of inconsistencies in the practices of states.

The Third United Nations Conference on the Law of the Sea (adopted on April 30, 1982) went a long way toward clarifying these kinds of ambiguous practices.[8] Article 3 of the convention reads that "every state has the right to establish the breadth of its territorial sea up to a limit not exceeding twelve nautical miles." When the convention is finally ratified by the required number of states (in this case 60, out of which 37 had ratified by 1990), it will have transformed hundreds of years of conflicting customs on maritime jurisdiction into an intelligible body of codified legal prescriptions.

Today, customary law continues to form an important part of international law, but treaties have displaced custom as its major source.[9] In a rapidly changing and more highly integrated international community, custom has come to be regarded as a scattered and imprecise source for determining rules of conduct. The younger states in the global community in Asia, Africa, Latin America, and the Caribbean demand more exacting instruments to consolidate and create law. The confusion in locating the existence of, and determining the consent toward, customary law has increasingly motivated states to negotiate lawmaking treaties.

INTERNATIONAL CONVENTIONS

Conventions are sometimes called treaties, covenants, accords, pacts, charters, declarations, statutes, or protocols. Regardless of the name, all conventions are international law and have a binding effect on the parties that consent to them, based on the legal principle *pacta sunt servanda** (pacts are binding).

By definition, conventions are formal international agreements between two or more states. When they are entered into by only two states, the treaty is bilateral; when many states sign and ratify a treaty, it is said to be multilateral. As sources of international law, multilateral treaties perform two important functions: (1) the codification of existing rules of customary international law (e.g., the Vienna Convention on Succession of States in Respect of Treaties, 1978), and (2) the creation of new international law (Outer Space Treaty, 1967).

Such treaties have global significance and are widely viewed to make world law because of their general and universal effect. Some international law experts have even identified multilateral conventions with the legislation of laws in municipal legal systems.[10] One noteworthy exception in this analogy is that conventions legally apply only to those states that consent to their provisions. Yet even under circumstances where a state does not ratify a treaty because it objects to some of its provisions, there are extra-legal pressures on non-consenting states to comply at least with the spirit of a lawmaking treaty, if not with the letter of the law in the treaty. The U.S. decision not to sign the 1982 Law of the Sea (LOS) convention does not exempt that state from respecting most of the internationally agreed-upon provisions involving the laws of navigation, fishing rights, conservation, the continental shelf, and the self-proclaimed establishment off U.S. shores of a 200-mile Exclusive Economic Zone (EEZ) that is compatible with many of the provisions of the convention. Because 130 states adopted the LOS convention, the United States is sensitive to the near-global consensus on this regime of maritime law and recognizes the rights of other states in the waters off its coasts, as outlined in the convention. To behave otherwise would run contrary to the general will of the international community and ultimately would have negative consequences for U.S. national interests.

Article 102 of the United Nations Charter requires that all treaties be registered with the Secretariat of the United Nations so that they are known to the world. This requirement adds another important dimension of legitimacy to all treaties, bilateral as well as multilateral. Open publication of treaties is not only intended to discourage the practice of secret conventions, but to demonstrate the levels of consensus achieved concerning international norms and expectations. Lawmaking treaties are barometers of world opinion. To resist compliance with the expected behaviour of states is to run against the common will of the international community.

The continuing development of international law has been greatly enhanced since 1947, when the General Assembly of the United Nations created the International Law Commission (ILC). The ILC is charged with the tasks of studying, recommending, and codifying international law. Its thirty-four international law experts – who represent most of the world's legal systems – research and codify customary law in the area of recognition, state succession, diplomatic immunities, state jurisdictional immunities, law of the sea, nationality, statelessness, and arbitral procedures. They consolidate their legal research and prepare drafts that are reported to the General Assembly, which has often convened international conferences to adopt lawmaking treaties. The ILC did the preparatory work for a convention on diplomatic relations at Vienna in 1961; a convention on consular relations at Vienna in 1963; a convention on the law of treaties at Vienna in 1969; the convention on state succession at Vienna in 1978; and on the law of the sea at Geneva in 1958 and at the United Nations in 1982. The writing of draft articles of agreement by the ILC has been instrumental in summarizing international laws that have evolved over a period of 2500 years. By gradually displacing the uncertainties of disparate customs practised by states, lawmaking treaties have injected a high degree of precision in the application of international law. Indeed, the twentieth century will be remembered by students of international behaviour as a period when detailed written codes of conduct agreed to by a majority of states added much to the binding authority and competence of international law.

GENERAL PRINCIPLES OF LAW

In cases where treaty law and customary law do not provide guidance in international disputes, the Statute of the International Court of Justice (ICJ) points to "the general principles of law recognized by civilized nations." To avoid the possibility of a case remaining undecided and to insure that justice is done when other sources of law provide no assistance, states in conflict will sometimes invoke generally recognized principles of national and international law to settle disputes.

Some of these general principles of international law revolve around the concepts of sovereignty, legal equality of states, territorial integrity, and non-interference in the internal affairs of other states. They have also been drawn from principles of justice derived from *natural law*.[11] The essence of law itself is discovered from the meticulous organization of the universe, which demonstrates that order (in this case, legal order) is required if the human race is to survive. Thus, as a general principle, prescriptions for human behaviour are necessary if order is to be maintained among interacting states. The concept that each side in a dispute is entitled to a fair hearing and that judicial decisions should be made *ex aequo et bono** (out of justice and fairness) when no exacting codes of law are applicable are examples of general principles of law applied in international tribunals.

The practice of incorporating international law into domestic municipal legal systems is another general principle linking national and international law. Canada, the United States, Belgium, France, and Switzerland, to name but a few, have practised the adoption, incorporation, and harmonization of international law with domestic lawmaking processes. This has important legal consequences for nationals of one state contesting an international dispute in another domestic legal system. In the case *The Paquette Habana v. The Lola,* Supreme Court of the United States (1900), the court reasoned that "international law is part of our law and must be ascertained and administered by courts of justice of appropriate jurisdictions." In *West Rand Central Gold Mining Co., Ltd., v. The King*, King's Bench Division, Great Britain (1905), the court ruled that "it is true that whatever has received the common consent of civilized nations must have received the consent of Great Britain, and that to which the latter has assented . . . could properly be called international law."

In Canada, over 20 percent of the Revised Statutes of Canada incorporate the rules of international customary and treaty law.[12] But Canadian courts have not ruled consistently on the relationship of international law to domestic law. In some early cases, such as *The Ship "North" v. The King* (1906) it appeared that Canada was following court practices in the United Kingdom to take "judicial notice" of the rules of international law and to interpret the rules of domestic law in a manner compatible with them. In 1943, however, in two cases (*Reference re Power of Municipalities to Levy Rates on Foreign Legations and High Comm'rs Residences and Reference re Exemption of U.S. Forces from Canadian Criminal Law*), a number of justices of the Supreme Court argued that even customary international law is part of Canadian law only if those customs are formally "incorporated" by Parliament or given judicial notice. In a more recent case, *Republique Democratique du Congo v. Venne* (1971), the Supreme Court clearly supported the principle that customary international law is part of Canadian law. Similarly, in 1969, the Quebec Court of Appeal, in *Penthouse Studios Inc. v. Government of Venezuela*, recognized that even the changing character of custom is enforced in Canada.

There is no question that different systems of national law try to conform to general principles of law as derived directly from the international community or from within themselves. The problems of seeking and interpreting general principles of law result from the isolated traditions of law throughout the world. The Anglo-American system, the Napoleonic Code, the Islamic system, and the system of law most communist states follow are based on different philosophical and cultural premises. But the disparity of fundamental legal systems does not take away the political need to foster legal uniformity. There exists a tacit understanding in the world community that international order is safeguarded by specific rules of common acceptance. The Statute of the International Court of Justice has recognized the imperative character of these rules as a primary source of international law. And among states we can detect a conscious subordination of state activity to the general welfare of the international community.

JUDICIAL DECISIONS

Judicial decisions are cited in Article 38(1) (d) of the statute "as subsidiary means for the determination of rules of law." The problem international law presents is twofold: in the absence of formal lawmaking institutions, it is always necessary first, to establish agreement as to the very idea of international law, and second, constantly to reassess the effectiveness of international law itself. This problem is significant for judicial decisions because they are viewed primarily as an indirect and subsidiary source of international law.

But, upon close examination, the value of domestic and international court decisions as sources of international law can be discovered. If a court in a domestic legal system or an international tribunal interprets a contentious question of international law, its judicial opinion includes the rationale for the decision, the *ratio decidendi**. It indicates what the rule is held to mean at the time the decision is drafted. This provides the international community with a ruling on international law, a kind of precedent, to which analogous cases may conform. Even though, in international law, there is no doctrine of *stare decisis** *et non quieta movere* (to stand by decisions and not to move what has been settled) to affirm the obligatory character of previous decisions as precedents, most court systems take judicial notice* of them and usually take them into account. In time, as precedents are rendered by a series of similar judicial decisions, a body of legal opinions is formed. As early as 1815, Chief Justice John Marshall of the Supreme Court of the United States ruled in the case of *Thirty Hogsheads of Sugar v. Boyle* that "the decisions of the Courts of every country show how the law of nations, in the given case, is understood in that country, and will be considered in adopting the rule which is to prevail in this." In the *Barcelona Traction* case, the ICJ made reference to the rulings on nationality in an earlier case (the *Nottebohm* case) in order to distinguish the nationality of a Canadian company that was controlled by Belgian shareholders and that incurred injuries inflicted by Spain.[13]

The ICJ has not only taken judicial notice of previous cases in affirming the existence of customary and codified law but has, in some cases, created new law. In the *Reparation for Injuries Suffered in the Service of the United Nations* case (1949), the court certified the legal personality of the United Nations and affirmed the capacity of that international organization to assert claims against other entities in the international system for injuries suffered by its agents. Similarly, in the *Anglo-Norwegian Fisheries* case (1951), the ICJ stated new criteria for the delimitation of base lines from which to determine the width of the territorial sea. These criteria were adopted by the Geneva Convention on the Territorial Sea and Contiguous Zone (1958) and included in the Law of the Sea Convention in 1982.

There is no question that international law is both summarized and created by judicial decisions rendered by domestic and international tribunals. The dramatic legal battle in 1984/85 between Ariel Sharon, a prominent Israeli politician, and *Time* magazine, a multinational corporation, in a Manhattan federal court had international legal consequences. At issue in the $50 million lawsuit was the international reputation of an Israeli citizen who was directly linked to the vengeful massacre by Lebanese Christians of as many as 800 Palestinians in two Beirut refugee camps in a seven-page cover story of *Time*, headlined, "The verdict is guilty." As a result of the news story, Sharon was forced to resign as Israel's defence minister and claimed that his world-wide reputation was destroyed. The three rulings of the U.S. federal court – two in favour of Sharon – decided that the *Time* article was false; one vindicated *Time* of malice to libel Sharon and affirmed a growing tendency in the present century to recognize that individuals and companies have some degree of international legal personality.[14] Individuals and corporations have not only acquired rights and duties under special treaties, but have also had specific rights and duties identified by domestic courts, as in the case of Ariel Sharon and *Time*.

Each decision carries its own prestige, which – when combined with the traditional and legal authority of the courts in question – creates a subsidiary but nonetheless important source of international law. The framework of national judicial power often extends far beyond the limited binding application of judicial decisions to the contesting parties in a legal dispute. In effect, all judicial decisions of international consequence contribute to the substance of international law, providing trans-national and cross-cultural norms in the international community.

WRITINGS OF LEARNED EXPERTS

In addition to being a legal system, international law is also a formal academic field of study, drawing expertise from the disciplines of history, law, philosophy, and political science. The academic study of international law developed concurrently with the modern nation-state system in the sixteenth and seventeenth centuries. Learned writers, or "publicists," as they were once called, began to analyse and interpret the evolution of international law.

Hugo Grotius (1583–1645), widely acclaimed as the founder of international law, published his *De jure belli ac pacis Libri Tris (Three Books on the Law of War and Peace)* in 1625. It was the first modern study of the law of states. Other noteworthy publicists to follow Grotius were Richard Zouche (1590–1660), Samuel Pufendorf (1632–1694), Emmerich de Vattel (1714–1769), and John Austin (1790–1859). In 1790, Jeremy Bentham invented the term "international law" to designate what had previously been called "the law of nations" (*jus gentium, droit des gens*) in his book, *An Introduction to the Principles of Morals and Legislation*, which was published in 1789. In more recent times, names such as Hans Kelsen, Josef Kunz, James Brierly, Richard Falk, and Michael Akehurst come to mind as modern legal publicists. Contemporary writers conduct comparative research into the behavioural aspects of international law. They plot trends in the legal expectations of states and monitor the international system for new sources of law in codified form, for any legal or academic reference is a major unofficial contribution to the body of scholarly materials on international law. Today, almost every state has a pool of international legal experts who publish work on a regular basis. These publications have created a vast and instructive body of opinion and analyses for use by justices who deliberate upon international cases.

Acts of International Institutions

The Statute of the International Court of Justice does not list the acts of international organizations as a source of international law. However, a growing number of scholars now detect a substantial body of international law directly emerging from the work of numerous international institutions.[15] Most international organizations are institutional forums in which legal norms are debated and generated by member-states. Many of these organizations pass resolutions and declarations that carry quasi-legal* authority and promote world law (see table 14.1). It is true that these resolutions and declarations are not as binding as are ratified treaties. But they do represent a consensus of membership expectations on important matters of international behaviour. In the inter-American system*, resolutions and declarations adopted at conferences are regarded as binding by Latin American states and thus create legal obligations among them. For example, the Charter of Bogotá, proclaimed at the Ninth Inter-American Conference in 1948, established the Organization of American States (OAS), which creates an obligation for all signatory states to use peaceful settlement procedures – including diplomacy, good offices, mediation, investigation, conciliation, arbitration, and adjudication – to resolve disputes.

In the General Assembly of the United Nations, resolutions are not necessarily binding on member-states, but often call for the creation of an international conference to draft a multilateral treaty that would bind signatories. The consensus expressed through resolutions and declarations in the United Nations can lead to the creation of a new rule in conventional law or may reflect the presence of a new principle of international custom. For example, in 1963, the General Assembly passed its Declaration of Legal Principles Governing Activities in Outer Space based on a unanimous proclamation that "international law, including the Charter of The United Nations, applies to outer space" ... and that "Outer Space" and celestial bodies are free for exploration and use by all States in conformity with international law, and are not subject to national exploitation." Later, in 1966, these principles were embodied in the Outer Space Treaty, which came into force

Major international organizations and agencies promoting world law

Amnesty International (London)
European Commission of Human Rights (Strasbourg, France)
European Court of Human Rights (Strasbourg)
Inter-American Council of Jurists (Juridical Committee) (Rio de Janeiro)
Inter-American Commission on Human Rights (Washington)
International Chamber of Commerce (Paris)
International Commission of Jurists (Geneva)
International Court of Justice (ICJ) (The Hague)
International Labor Organization (ILO) (Geneva)
Organization of American States (Washington)
Organization of African Unity (Addis Ababa, Ethiopia)
The Institute for World Order, Inc. (New York)
The World Peace Through Law Center (Geneva)
United Nations Commission on Human Rights (Geneva)
United Nations Commission on International Trade Law (Vienna)
United Nations Economic and Social Council (ECOSOC) (New York)
United Nations Educational, Scientific and Cultural Organization (UNESCO) (Paris)
Untied Nations General Assembly (New York)
World Federalists Association (Washington)
World Health Organization (WHO) (Geneva)

Table 14.1

for ratifying states in 1967. And, in 1988, The Draft Convention on the Rights of the Child was completed by the United Nations Working Group and was adopted by the UN General Assembly.

Another international organization that has played a pioneering role in creating new international law has been the International Labor Organization (ILO). Since its establishment in 1919, it has built a body of law known as the International Labor Code. In the 1990s, the code consists of the work of nearly 160 conventions that have dealt with a wide range of ratified recommendations in the area of workers' rights, wages, insurance benefits, and the protection of women, young people, miners, and indigenous peoples. For example, the ILO drafted the revised Indigenous and Tribal Populations Convention, 1989. In a similar way, the World Health Organization (WHO) created the Code of International Health Regulations, adopted in 1969, to establish legal controls on hundreds of drugs used throughout the states of the world.

Another specialized agency of the United Nations, the International Civil Aviation Organization (ICAO), headquartered in Montreal, has been an active body in the development of international law in the area of air transportation. The ICAO has established regulations governing information standards, facilities, and services in world air transportation. For example, as a result of deep concerns expressed by the International Federation of Airline Pilots Associations (IFALPA) over the downing by a Soviet military jet of a Korean passenger plane that had "strayed" into Soviet territory on September 1, 1983, the ICAO passed a resolution deploring the incident and calling for a clearer set of standards to regulate the identification of all aircraft in the future.

The International Court of Justice

The International Court of Justice, sometimes called the World Court, is one of the six principal organs of the United Nations, with headquarters at The Hague, Netherlands. The court is attended by fifteen judges who are paid US$82 000 a year, serving nine-year terms, and elected by a concurrent vote of the General Assembly and the Security Council. In order to provide fair representation, no two judges of the same nationality may sit on the bench at the same time. And if parties to the dispute do not have national judges elected at the time the case is heard, they may appoint their own judge with full voting rights. Cases are decided by majority vote, and in the event of a tie the president of the court casts the deciding vote.

According to ICJ statute, only states are entitled to appear as litigants before the court. When contesting states permit the court to make a judgement in a case, that judgement binds the parties. For this reason many states have been reluctant to register their legal complaints with the court. And sometimes states that submit to the court simply ignore the decision. Several states, including such outstanding international citizens as Iceland, India, and France, have refused to submit to the panel's rulings. In 1980, Iran ignored a judgement from the court to pay reparations to the United States for seizing its embassy in Tehran.

Since the ICJ lacks compulsory adjudication, whereby states would be compelled to appear before the world tribunal to defend their actions, the court can only hear those cases that states choose to bring before it. To strengthen the position of the court in this regard, Article 36 of the statute provides the *Optional Clause*. Under this clause, states agree in advance to accept the compulsory adjudication of the court involving questions of treaty interpretation, international law, breaches of international obligations, and reparations. Recently Canada and the United States accepted the compulsory adjudication of the court to settle a question of jurisdiction on the North American east coast. In 1984, the World Court ruled on a boundary dispute that had been raging for seven years between Canada and the United States over the rich resources and fishing grounds on the Georges' Bank off the coasts of Maine, Massachusetts, and Nova Scotia. The disputed jurisdictions resulted when both countries extended their territorial limits 200 nautical miles to sea. In its decision, the ICJ dismissed the arguments of both countries, and developed its own criteria for drawing a new boundary line between Massachusetts and Nova Scotia, asserting that Canada and the United States had based some of their claims on false premises. The decision was binding in accordance with a 1981 Canada-U.S. agreement that registered the dispute with the ICJ and accepted its jurisdiction to rule on the Georges' Bank with no appeal.

The court's ruling was unexpected by both parties and, in effect, created new law that will likely affect five other maritime disputes in which Canada is involved – three with the United States, one with France over St.-Pierre et Miquelon, and one with Greenland. Canada has proposed a line based on the principle of equidistance* and disregarded the existence of Cape Cod and Nantucket Islands, arguing that they constituted unusual geographic protrusions of the U.S. coastline. Washington claimed all the Georges' Bank with a proposed line that came as close as 25 nautical miles to Yarmouth, Nova Scotia. The World Court awarded Canada one-sixth of the bank – only half the territory it claimed – but unexpectedly Ottawa got the northeast edge where there are concentrations of scallop beds, vital to Nova Scotia's $60-million-a-year scallop industry. The area awarded to the United States amounts to five-sixths of the Georges' Bank, over which Washington claimed total jurisdiction. Despite the dislocation and economic hardship generated by the decision on people in the fishing industries of both countries, the court's ruling was accepted as international law. Of the 160 states that are parties to the Statute of the International Court of Justice, only 47 adhere to the Optional Clause, most with reservations* that have the effect of rendering its acceptance meaningless. Since its creation in 1946, the court has rendered judgements in only seventy cases. Twenty-seven cases have been removed without judgement because the defendant states refused to submit to the court's jurisdiction or because the plaintiffs removed the case to settle out of court. Besides hearing and deciding on this small number of cases since 1946, the ICJ has been utilized for only eighteen advisory opinions, most of which were requested by the United Nations General Assembly.

As witnessed by the declining docket of cases since the 1950s, states are reluctant to submit to the jurisdiction of the World Court. There are several reasons why states appear to distrust the court as a legal instrument for resolving conflict:

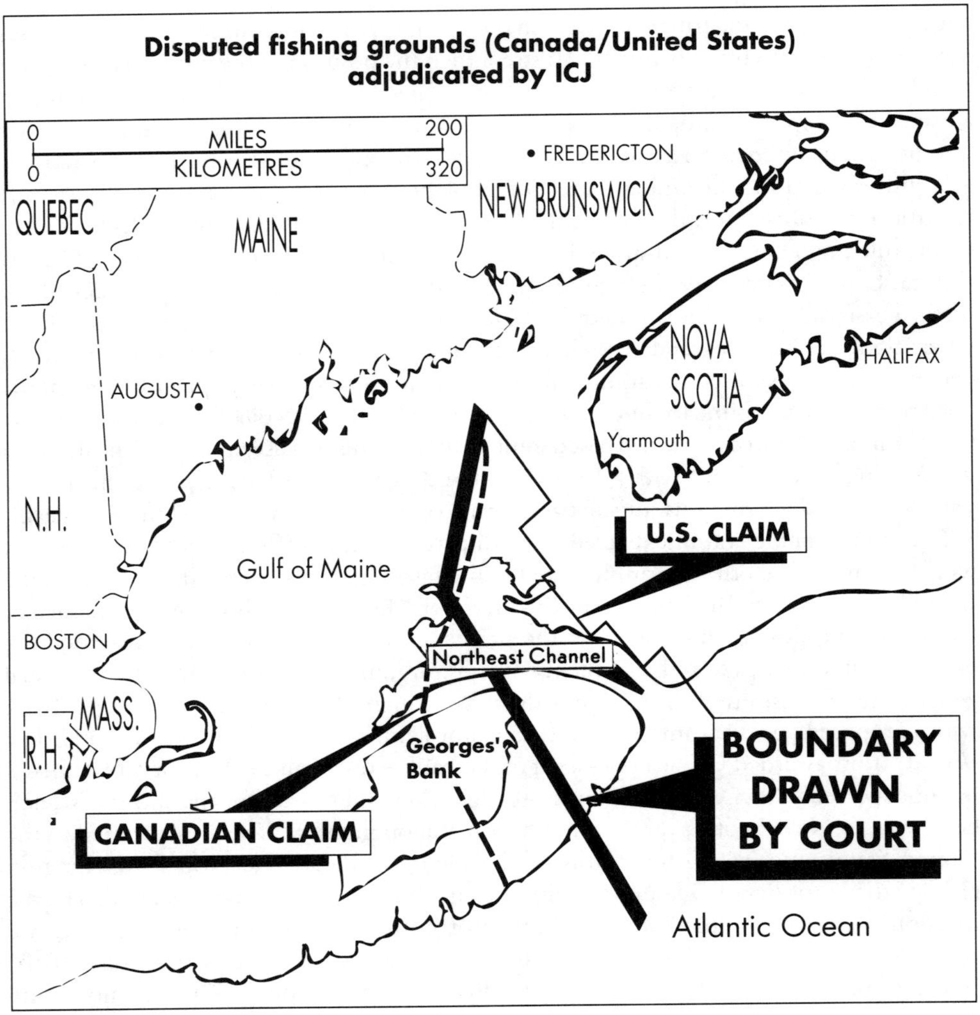

Figure 14.2

- Powerful states tend to avoid the embarrassment of a legal judgement on their behaviour. They are unwilling to entrust matters of national importance to a non-national legal body with high international visibility.
- States are more inclined to resort to political instruments such as negotiation, conciliation, and mediation to arrive at the peaceful settlement of disputes.
- Many states, of different rank in power, sense that the application of international norms to their disputes are alien to the legal principles in their domestic systems; consequently they distrust the judicial process of the World Court.

For reasons such as these, the court has not remedied* major international disputes. In their long-running boundary dispute over the waters surrounding the islands of St-Pierre et Miquelon, both Canada and France avoided the use of the ICJ in 1988 and opted instead to have a mediator help settle their differences over fishing quotas, while negotiators continued to seek agreement on geographical boundaries (France claimed 320-kilometre territorial waters and Canada recognized only a 19-kilometre boundary). Mediation, rather than adjudication, was more acceptable to authorities in both states, even after the arrest by Canada of seventeen French island fishermen and four politicians for illegally fishing in Canadian waters and the French retaliation shortly thereafter that seized a Newfoundland trawler for fishing in the disputed waters off the islands of St-Pierre et Miquelon. However, in 1989 Canada and France agreed to resolve their twelve-year territorial dispute by sending it to binding international arbitration. The international tribunal is composed of five judges – one each from Canada, France, Uruguay, Italy and the United States.

Since 1945, international bodies other than the ICJ have been used to address serious international questions – parties to crises in Korea, the Congo, the Middle East, Suez, Cyprus, Zimbabwe, and Afghanistan did not request ICJ judgements. Political and military power have been the primary methods employed by states in major conflicts such as Vietnam, Biafra, the Cuban missile crisis, Northern Ireland, and the Middle East. Generally, international confidence in the court is weak and this diminishes the legitimacy of the highest tribunal in the world. Until states are willing to place justice above politics and national interest, the court will remain basically an advisory legal institution of the United Nations.

Acts of the International Law Commission

The work of the International Law Commission (ILC) is a principal instrument for codifying and developing international law. The procedures the ILC employs clarify and standardize existing international law, as well as help to draft the results of research for consideration as new law. The commission uses the following steps to execute its mandate in all areas of codifying modern international law:

- Researches and selects a relevant topic
- Submits this topic to the General Assembly for approval
- Appoints a commission rapporteur as liaison with the General Assembly
- Reports preliminary drafts to the General Assembly
- Meets to discuss and revise the submission
- Receives feedback from governments
- Incorporates suggestions into the draft
- Submits the revised draft to the General Assembly

The General Assembly then decides whether to convene an international conference to consider the commission's draft. If a conference is held, the participating delegates may make further revisions before the document is prepared for consenting governments to sign. Then follows the slow process of state ratifications before the new convention comes to force. By way of example, such were the procedures used by the commission for the Convention on the Reduction of Statelessness (1961) and the Convention on Liability for Damage Caused by Objects Launched into Outer Space (1971).

Despite what appear to be enormous obstacles, the track record of the ILC is impressive. Most of the multilateral treaties signed and ratified since 1950 have been drafted by the ILC. Its main achievements are in the codification of international customary law; but because of its direct link to world legal opinion it has great potential to make major breakthroughs in the creation of new laws. The codification and accompanying globalization of international law – a phenomena witnessed only in the twentieth century – has provided more opportunities and incentives for states to resolve international conflict peacefully rather than violently.

International law continues to evolve as we enter the challenges of a new century. Notwithstanding its many imperfections the international legal system has come a long way in the twentieth century. No legal system, regardless of its enforcement capabilities, can completely deter violations of the law. International law proscribes genocide, yet Idi Amin of Uganda and Pol Pot of Kampuchea both ignored that proscription, killing thousands of their own citizens. Despite the unanimous condemnation of Iran by the General Assembly and the International Court of Justice in 1980, Iran's behaviour toward the United States' diplomats was not remedied. International norms were again disregarded in 1979 when the Soviet Union invaded Afghanistan and China invaded Vietnam; in 1982 when Israel invaded Lebanon, in 1983 when the United States invaded Grenada; and in 1984 when Vietnam again invaded Cambodia (now Kampuchea). Yet in all these recent cases of invasion, it is important to note that the protagonist states attempted to justify their actions in terms of international legal standards. For example, both the Soviet and the American invasions were defended as military actions in response to legitimate invitations to rescue deteriorating political systems. In another example, Argentina sought to legitimize its capture of the Falkland Islands in 1982 in accordance with the United Nations Charter.

States believe it is of paramount importance that they not appear to be in violation of international law so that they can appeal to international morality and world public opinion in support of their actions. Every world leader is aware that the international system is a fish bowl into which all states can look to observe and judge the behaviour of their legal peers.

In past centuries, international law merely served as a normative constraint on the exercise of certain types of power practised by states. But in the twentieth century, there exists the largest number of legally binding bilateral and multilateral treaties governing the behaviour of states in human history. We also see more international organizations dedicated to the promotion and codification of world law than in any previous period. Today, a comprehensive set of binding rules, rights, obligations, and principles has immediate global impact on the national interest of states. Most states of the world deliberately weigh every action they take in an attempt to comply with the general principles of international law and with the provisions of the treaties to which they are parties. In the sphere of international relations, it is no longer possible for states to view themselves as the highest authorities, absolutely free from restraint. As in all major legal systems, states as subjects are free to determine their own interests but they must do so in conformity with international and community law. Throughout this century, the organization of states into large and small groups, pursuing common goals, has generated the creation of a formidable legal regime, clearly recognizable by the international community as a coherent and effective legal order.

REFERENCES

1. United States Department of Commerce, *Bureau of the Census Statistical Abstract of the United States*, 1976 (Washington, D.C.: U.S. Government Printing Office 1977), 159.
2. David V. Edwards, *The American Political Experience*, 1st ed. (Englewood Cliffs, NJ: Prentice-Hall Inc. 1979), 289.
3. See P.J. Griffen, "Official Rates of Crime and Delinquency," in W.T. McGrath, ed., *Crime and Its Treatment in Canada*, 2nd ed. (Toronto: Collier Macmillan 1976), 73; see also Gwynn Nettler, *Explaining Crime* (New York: McGraw-Hill 1974), 66.
4. See Hugh Kindred et al., *International Law Chiefly as Interpreted and Applied in Canada*, 4th ed., (Toronto: Emond Montgomery Publications 1987), 1–10.
5. Chrostos Rozakis, *The Concept of Ius Cogens in the Law of Treaties* (Amsterdam: North-Holland Publishing Co.1976), 1–10; see also Theodor Meron, "On a Hierarchy of International Human Rights, "*American Journal of International Law* 8.0, no. 1 (1986): 13–23.
6. Ibid., 22; A. Leroy Bennett, *International Organizations* (Englewood Cliffs, NJ: Prentice-Hall Inc. 1988), 175.
7. See Michael Akehurst, "Custom as a Source of International Law," *British Yearbook of International Law* 47 (1974–5): 12–21.
8. R.P. Barston and P. Birnie, *The Maritime Dimension* (Boston: Allen & Unwin 1980), 45–6.
9. Gerhard von Glahn, *Law among Nations* 3rd ed. (London: Collier Macmillan 1976), 17; see also Theodor Meron, "The Geneva Conventions as Customary Law," *American Journal of International Law* 81, no 2 (1987): 348–70.
10. Theodore Couloumbis and James Wolfe, *Introduction to International Relations* (Englewood Cliffs, NJ: Prentice-Hall Inc. 1982), 242.
11. Wolfgang Friedmann, "The Uses of 'General Principles' in the Development of International Law," *American Journal of International Law* 57, no. 2 (1963): 279–99; and Josef L. Kunz, "Natural Law Thinking in the Modern Science of International Law," *American Journal of International Law* 55, no. 4 (1961): 951– 8.
12. S.A. Williams and A.L. de Mestral, *Introduction to International Law* (Toronto: Butterworths 1979), 27.
13. See *Barcelona Traction case*, International Court of Justice Reports (1970), 3, 42.
14. Akehurst, "Custom as a Source of International Law," 71–4.
15. See M.S. McDougal, and M. Reisman, eds., *International Law in Contempory Perspective* (Mineola, NY: Foundation Press 1981); and Robert Turner, "International Law, the Use of Force, and Reciprocity: A Comment on Professor Higgins' Overview," *Atlantic Community Quarterly* 25, no. 2 (1987): 160–74.

SUGGESTED READINGS

Lief Carter, *Reason in Law*, 3rd ed. (Glenview, IL: Scott, Foresman & Co. 1988).

Anthony Carty, *The Decay of International Law?* (New York: St. Martin's Press 1988).

Innis Claude, *States and the Global System* (New York: St. Martin's Press 1988).

Sheldon Cohen, *Arms and Judgment: Law, Morality, and the Conduct of War in the Twentieth Century* (Boulder, CO: Westview Press 1989).

Margaret Doxey, *International Sanctions in Contemporary Perspective* (New York: St. Martin's Press 1987).

Anthony Ellis, *Ethics and International Relations* (Manchester, Eng.: Manchester University Press 1989).

Walter Jones, *The Logic of International Relations* (Glenview, IL: Scott, Foresman & Co. 1988).

W.L. LaCroix, *War and International Ethics: Tradition and Today* (Washington, D.C.: University Press of America 1988).

J.G. Merrills, *The Development of International Law by the European Court of Human Rights* (Manchester, Eng.: Manchester University Press 1989).

Steven Luper-Foy, *Problems of International Justice* (Boulder, CO: Westview Press 1988).

GLOSSARY

compulsory adjudication: The judicial process to compel the attendence in court of a legal person (state), wanted there as a witness or otherwise.

deviant behaviour: In the international community, deviance can be defined as behaviour that is contrary to the standards of customary and legal conduct (which are widely accepted as contributing to the stability of the system in interstate relations).

compliance: Conduct that demonstrates an acceptance of legal authority, and a willingness to conform to the rules, regulations, and laws of international relations.

municipal law: The technical term used by international lawyers to refer to the national or domestic law of a state.

legitimacy: The perception held by a majority of people that the exercise of power and the system of law are based on "rightful" authority and should be respected and obeyed.

ratify: The procedures used by states to approve and sanction treaties, conventions, and other instruments of international law requiring formal legal adoption by sovereign governments or international organizations.

principle: A comprehensive rule or doctrine that furnishes a clear basis or origin for others unless contradicted by a proposition that is still clearer.

ius cogens: The law of unnatural norms, which holds that a treaty is void if, at the time of its conclusion, it conflicts with a pre-emptory norm of general international law.

codified law: The process of collecting and arranging the laws of a state into a code, i.e., into a complete system of positive law, scientifically ordered, and promulgated by legislative or executive authority.

nationality: That quality or character which arises from the fact of a person's belonging to a particular nation or state, by birth or naturalization.

statelessness: The condition of an individual who has lost the legal claim to nationality and who no longer has the protection of any state.

binding: To bring or place under definite duties or legal obligation, particularly by treaty, convention, or custom, which can affect states in a constraining or compulsory manner.

opinio iuris sive necessitates: Literally means "legal attitudes are necessary" and asserts that legal forms of conduct are required by international law.

pacta sunt servanda: Literally means "pacts are binding" and is the basic postulate on which the whole structure of positive international law is founded.

ex aequo et bono: Literally means "in justice and fairness" and is used when a court is permitted to apply the doctrine of equity in the determination of a case.

ratio decidendi: Literally, "the reason for the decision"; in cases of international consequences, court rulings contribute to the general principles of international law.

stare decisis: "Let the decision stand." The principle of precedent in the Anglo-American tradition of law. In international law, there is no doctrine of *stare decisis* but the International Court of Justice and many domestic court systems do take judicial notice of previous judicial opinions.

judicial notice: The act by which a court in conducting a trial, or framing its decision, will of its own motion, and without the production of evidence, recognize the existence and truth of certain facts that have a bearing on the matter before it.

quasi-legal: This term is used in legal phraseology to indicate that one subject or action resembles what is law by comparison, but because of its non-binding affect, there is an intrinsic and material difference between the two.

inter-American system: All the regional institutional structures created by the Pan American movement in the Western hemisphere. The Organization of American States (OAS) is the largest of these.

equidistance: Boundaries for lakes, oceans, rivers, and straits based on the principle that the line is drawn down the geographical centre, giving each side equal and equally usable portions.

reservation: A clause in a treaty or other instrument of international relations whereby a signatory retains a right or exception to one or a number of provisions comprising the agreement.

remedy: The means by which a legal right is enforced or a violation of a right is prevented under international and municipal law.

15

Diplomacy

Canadian Ambassador Yves Fortier presents his credentials to UN Secretary-General Javier Perez de Cuellar

A Privileged Profession

ONE BRITISH EXPERT ON DIPLOMACY, Sir Harold Nicholson, guessed that the first diplomat was probably a hairy primitive, who, after licking the wounds he suffered from battling his neighbours, decided to negotiate a truce with his enemies. Since the Stone Age, the world's diplomats have been motivated by the same instinct - negotiate* or perish. In ancient China, Egypt, and India, heralds, envoys, and orators engaged in forms of diplomatic behaviour. They conveyed messages and warnings, defended causes, and delivered gifts to distant places. From the first, these negotiators demanded *immunity* from harm, having taken the risk that their presence before the enemy could result in their own demise. Because they were foreigners, they were considered impure: they submitted to the rituals of purification to assure their doubtful hosts that they could be trusted and worthy of credibility. Once the message was delivered and accepted, the earliest envoys left to report the sentiments of their hosts to their superiors. But there were no embassies or standard diplomatic practices accepted by the governments of ancient peoples. There was simply the recognized need to contact and communicate with both friends and enemies in order to survive. In the words of Abba Eban, Israel's distinguished statesman: "It can certainly be said of diplomacy, as of few other human occupations, that mankind has never been able to live without it."[1]

Although all civilizations have conducted diplomatic activities, it is generally regarded that modern diplomacy has been influenced primarily by ancient Greece. The Greeks made passports, called *diplomas*, from double metal plates folded and sewn together. Diplomas granted the bearer travel privileges and special treatment when presented to officials in foreign places. The Greeks called their messengers *angelos*, or angels, and accorded them the patronage of Zeus, the father of the gods, and Hermes, the messenger and herald of the gods, who was, as well, the god of cunning ruses and pretences.

The Greeks chose exceptional people to represent them in foreign places. Their envoys were the finest orators, well versed in the knowledge of theatre, the arts, literature, philosophy, and the general principles of law. They were drawn from the highest levels of polite society, usually from an aristocratic background. Since the polis* was a republic, controlled by an assembly, they were appointed with popular approval to negotiate the affairs of state with other city-states, as well as the foreign places such as Sparta and Rome.

The Greeks believed that envoys had the power to negotiate on equal terms with one another and that they should possess immunity from local customs and hostilities.[2] They believed that envoys enjoyed the immunities of the gods to protect them from the harmful impact of human disputes. But they also developed the secular political practice of respecting the dignity and integrity of visiting envoys and expecting reciprocal treatment for their diplomatic representatives when travelling abroad. For example, the Greeks advanced the idea that an ambassador represented the person of the sovereign, being entitled to the same respect that the sovereign would receive if he or she were personally present. Because sovereigns were so sensitive to embarrassment when visiting foreign places, the practice grew to accord diplomatic representatives the highest courtesy – that of personal inviolability*. If a diplomatic delegation was in the unfortunate circumstance of being in a place where war was declared, they would be accorded *safe conduct** from hostilities, as when Sparta voted for war against Athens while the Athenian delegation was present negotiating a trade treaty. Gradually, the Greeks elaborated a system of constant diplomatic relations based upon accepted practices of diplomatic privilege and immunities*. They established an institutional style of diplomacy that spread far beyond the Aegean corner of the Mediterranean Sea. Greek diplomatic practices influenced and shaped the diplomacy of the high Middle Ages, when the newly formed state system adopted them as customary international law.

Unlike the Greeks, the Romans had very little respect for the principle of equality in negotiation. The goals of the Roman Empire were not open to compromise. Roman ambassadors, called *nuntii*, travelled abroad as quasi-governors who treated their foreign colleagues more like colonists than equal negotiators.

Because of the dominance of the empire, the Romans were highly selective of the foreign envoys they received. When a representative from a foreign land came to Rome he was kept outside the city gates until his credentials were carefully scrutinized and his diplomatic status verified. Nowadays, this humiliating system of receiving and accepting emissaries has been replaced and refined by the practice of requesting agrément* (agreement): that is, the sending state does not announce the appointment of its ambassador until the receiving state signifies its acceptance of the individual chosen. When followed by the two states this procedure is called *agréation*.

In the early Middle Ages, Byzantium rose as a world power. Chicanery, sharp dealing, and suspicion characterized Byzantine diplomacy. The Byzantines used diplomacy to weaken their adversaries by fomenting rivalry among them. Envoys acted as a fifth column* in the lands where they were sent, engaging in sabotage* and buying support by bribery and flattery. The Byzantines used their envoys to spy wherever they were sent, a practice not uncommon today in many capitals of the world. History confirms that Byzantine practices had a corrupting influence on the evolution of diplomacy.

What we would recognize as modern diplomacy – that is, an independent profession with qualified practitioners and resident missions – originated in Italy in the fourteenth and fifteenth centuries. At that time, diplomats no longer worked solely as messengers of their prince. Mediaeval ambassadors functioned as permanent representatives of the state, gathering information, advising, and negotiating on behalf of the home government. Of course, treachery, deceit, and intrigue continued to characterize mediaeval diplomacy. In France, Louis XI advised his ambassadors: "If they lie to you, see to it you lie much more than them." In England, foreign diplomats were so distrusted that members of Parliament would be deprived of their seats in the House of Commons if found talking with them.[3]

One crude expediency of diplomacy during the medieval period was best summed up by Niccolò Machiavelli in *The Discourses*: "For where the very safety of the country depends on the resolution to be taken, no consideration of justice or injustice, humanity or cruelty, nor of glory or of shame should be allowed to prevail, but putting all other considerations aside, the only question should be what will save the power and the liberty of the country."[4] But the practice of extreme self-interest in a world of competing sovereignties was itself a restraining force. Diplomats quickly learned that corruption and deceit were condoned but impractical because negotiations could not be conducted in good faith. Pragmatism and reason dictated honesty in diplomatic affairs. Intelligent diplomats recoiled from deception in the same way that politicians eschewed unpopularity.

Despite the amoral character of diplomacy during this period, diplomats made valuable contributions to their profession, some of which have survived to the present time. The first resident embassy was opened at Genoa in 1455. Permanent embassies soon became acknowledged as inviolable sanctuaries for the records and files of diplomats and they became the depositories for treaties and for diplomatic reports. Custom dictated that the host state respect the sovereign integrity of the embassy. As permanent embassies began to replace travelling diplomatic missions, the practice of stealing or confiscating diplomatic records from envoys grew less and less acceptable. Italian diplomats were the first to write periodic summaries of events taking place in the countries to which they were accredited.

They expected these reports to remain confidential within the security of their embassy.

The methods and procedures of Italian diplomacy spread throughout Europe, first to France, then through the Hapsburgs to the rest of the continent. The growing diplomatic community viewed its members as trustees of interstate relations. Privileges and immunities belonged to them as a special class of negotiators, not as individuals.

By the seventeenth century, the professional status of diplomacy was well established. In 1626 under Louis XIII, Cardinal Richelieu opened the first ministry of external affairs to exercise French diplomatic leadership in European affairs through one government agency. The French recognized diplomacy as an ongoing part of state policy. French became the leading language in diplomatic communication, with most of its nomenclature still in use today.

The Peace of Westphalia (1648) generated twelve of the first independent states in Europe. Gradually a complex code of diplomatic procedures grew out of the international relations among these states. Nevertheless, conflicts arose regarding different interpretations of diplomatic rules and customs. As the number of sovereign states increased, it became necessary to standardize the practices of international diplomacy. At the Congress of Vienna (1815) and Aix-la-Chapelle (1818), attending states ratified a règlement* governing diplomatic titles and order of rank: (1) ambassador extraordinary and plenipotentiary, and from the Vatican, papal legate and nuncio; (2) envoy extraordinary, minister plenipotentiary, and from the Vatican, papal internuncio, (3) minister resident; and (4) chargé d'affaires, and chargé d'affaires ad interim. The Congress of Vienna determined that the rank of ambassador is the highest that a diplomat can hold. From this time on, ambassadors or ministers were recognized internationally as chiefs of diplomatic missions. Official diplomatic quarters were designated an *embassy* when headed by an ambassador, and a *legation* when headed by a minister. The congress was the first multinational statement on the rules of diplomacy. It gave diplomacy an international stamp of approval as a profession distinct from that of a statesman and legitimized the widely accepted immunities enjoyed by diplomats in the European world of politics.

The century 1825–1914 was marked by relative peace and stability in international affairs. The six great empires of Europe – Austria-Hungary, Czarist Russia, Ottoman Turkey, Germany, Britain, and France – entered a period of diplomatic grace. This concept of Europe gave diplomats a sense of achievement and elevated their profession to a distinguished and specialized vocation. A dozen European states together with the United States formed an intimate and cohesive diplomatic community, the *corps diplomatique*. Diplomats associated as a small privileged group, insisting on immunities, practising discretion, and avoiding the political brush-fires of domestic politics.

Twentieth-Century Diplomacy

Four important factors have influenced the character of diplomacy in this century. The first is the explosion of new states, each sending and receiving diplomats and struggling for a place in the international arena. At the turn of the century, there were less than

1000 embassies and legations in the world; now there are well over 4000. This increase has greatly expanded the size of the diplomatic corps and complicated the process of negotiation. Diplomats of old were not encumbered by the entourage of specialized personnel that today constitute a formidable bureaucracy within an embassy. Experts from every field of government are now attached to embassy staffs in each country, and modern negotiation has become a complex process of internal consultation whereby diplomats rely on technical expertise before a decision can be made or a report submitted. For example, in addition to an ambassador, the Canadian embassy in Washington has seventy-five full-time diplomatic officers and representatives, apart from the other embassy staff members. These include ministers resident, minister/counsellors, commercial counsellors, general counsellors, first secretaries, second and third secretaries, and attachés. One of the jobs of the ambassador is to co-ordinate the work of all these people so that they can represent the policies of the Canadian government.

A second factor that has had a far-reaching effect on the world's diplomatic system is the ever-present and intrusive *communications media*. In every Western country, the media have claimed the right to inform the public about all levels of government decision making, and large press contingents, armed with batteries of microphones and television cameras, and intent on discovering and revealing what is going on, descend on diplomatic meetings. This makes political compromise very difficult, and diplomats regard the media as an intrusion into the delicate balance of the negotiating process. Those with a professional commitment to diplomacy say that press surveillance inhibits the strategy of the negotiator.[5] Secrecy provides negotiators with opportunities for making concessions without the fear of creating unnecessary anxiety in the public domain. In 1979, Moshe Dayan, after travelling in disguise, met with Egyptian authorities in Morocco to lay the groundwork for negotiations at Camp David. President Carter ensured the seclusion of the negotiating parties by withholding invitations to the media. If he had not, public indignation in Egypt and Israel at what was being compromised may have scuttled the agreement. And, for obvious reasons, at the London Summit Conference in June 1984, the seven leaders refused to publicly discuss the agreement they had reached for dealing with the problem of international terrorism. But diplomats also use the media for their own purposes, e.g., planting stories and carrying on negotiations through the media. In modern diplomacy, the presence of the media is not entirely unwelcome.

The third major influence on the modern world of negotiation has been *multilateral conference diplomacy*, in which negotiations take place among many states simultaneously.[6] Until the latter part of the nineteenth century, most diplomatic communications were bilateral. Whenever multilateral conferences were held, they tended to conclude peace treaties to terminate major European wars. But by the turn of the century, governments had started to send diplomats to multilateral conferences dealing with such subjects as agriculture, codification of international law, liquor traffic, navigation, tariffs, and weights and measures. Diplomats were expected not only to represent the interests of their own states, but also to contribute to the formation of international law. Under the League of Nations, ongoing conference machinery was established that gave international diplomacy a new institutionalized framework. After World War II, the United Nations and its specialized agencies provided a permanent forum for multilateral diplomacy. Since that time, thousands of conferences have been hosted by the United Nations and other international organizations such as the Organization of American States (OAS) and the Organization of African Unity (OAU).

Today, an ever-increasing portion of diplomatic communications is conducted through multilateral organizations. This in no way reduces the importance of bilateral relations between states, but it does tend to complicate the control of diplomatic news and activities for the embassy ambassador and staff. Keeping abreast of diplomatic relations within the framework of international organizations is a complex and monumental task. Each year, the UN spends over US$35 million to print millions of pages of reporting on its diplomatic activities. Press releases to delegations run up to 10 000 pages a year. In addition to the rushed routine of embassy business, today's diplomat is expected to be aware of the complicated trends in multilateral diplomacy.

Inside the United Nations and other international organizations around the world, diplomats are given the opportunity to communicate with representatives of countries with whom they may not share bilateral diplomatic exchanges. A lot of bilateral negotiations occur within the walls of these organizations, providing an atmosphere as private and secret as that afforded by traditional diplomacy. But the multilateral diplomat is a new breed, a product of twentieth-century internationalism. He or she is not only representing the narrow interests of a state, but also participating as an architect of a much wider community, concerned with the global issues of population, malnutrition, nuclear proliferation, and world peace.

Much of Canada's multilateral diplomacy is conducted through its ambassador to the United Nations. In July 1988, Yves Fortier, a notable Canadian lawyer, inherited the prolix title Ambassador Extraordinary and Plenipotentiary and Permanent Representative of Canada to the United Nations, replacing Stephen Lewis who had served in that capacity for 46 months. Fortier was educated at the Université de Montréal, McGill Law School, and Oxford University, where he received a Bachelor of Letters as a Rhodes Scholar. Yves Fortier brought with him a long list of legal accomplishments, having acted as counsel to several royal commissions, served as Canada's representative at the International Court of Justice at The Hague, been chief negotiator in Canada's fishing dispute with France, and the chief lawyer in the Canada-U.S. marine boundary dispute. In 1987 Fortier turned down an offer to sit on the Supreme Court of Canada after former Justice Julien Chouinard died.

Yves Fortier assumed his new position at a time of unparalleled opportunities for Canadian diplomacy at the United Nations. He can apply his inexhaustive energies to the task of propelling Canadian foreign policy to new heights at the UN, where Canada enjoys a superb reputation. At the same time the United Nations itself has regained credence among world leaders and global popular opinion. Increasingly, international issues are being successfully addressed by the UN system, and sovereign states have reached a mature realization of the crucial role for this global multilateral organization. Notwithstanding all this, Fortier joins an international organization facing severe financial and personnel problems. The reforms agreed to by the General Assembly placed a freeze on hiring and cuts in overall staff positions by 15 percent, largely by attrition. The remaining staff are carrying the extra load, making more difficult the job of any new diplomat trying to grasp quickly the labyrinthine complexities of the United Nations. On taking his appointment Fortier was in the midst of leading Canada's campaign to gain the two-year non-permanent membership on the Security Council, the inner circle of global power.

From his office on the United Nations Plaza, Yves Fortier has almost instant access to diplomats representing 160 nation-states. Because there are so many diplomats in one place, constantly passing each other in the corridors and lounges, eating and drinking together, and meeting in the debating chambers of the UN, important contacts can be made between an ambassador and other individuals and groups. The UN provides Canada's ambassador with a mixture of open conference diplomacy and secret talks and negotiations. It gives Yves Fortier near-global coverage from a single office.

A UN ambassador follows a crowded schedule. The range of Ambassador Fortier's work is no less comprehensive than that of a diplomat accredited to a traditional embassy. Yves Fortier must conduct representation involving a heavy social itinerary; communicating his government's views to the councils of the United Nations, as well as to individual governments; reporting; public relations; and gathering information.

The following is an example of one day's work for Ambassador Fortier, taken from his program for the day of February 24, 1989.

8:45 a.m.	Various telephone calls
9:00 a.m.	Interview with Wendy Mesley of CBC-TV
9:35 a.m.	Depart mission for Intercontinental Hotel
9:50 a.m.	Depart Intercontinental with secretary of state for External Affairs (SSEA) back to mission
10:00 a.m.	Coffee in the Conference Room with SSEA and mission personnel
10:20 a.m.	Meeting with SSEA and officers of the mission
11:30 a.m.	Depart mission for United Nation Headquarters
11:45 a.m.	Accompany SSEA to meeting with the president of the Security Council.
12:00 a.m.	Meeting with under-secretary general for Special Political Affairs, Mr. Goulding, Room S-3853 followed by:
12:30 p.m.	Coupe de champagne in Mr. Goulding's office
13:30 p.m.	Meeting France-Canada: Marriot Hotel (La Guardia Airport)
16:30 p.m.	Drinks with SSEA and Ms. Capeling (UNICEF), ambassador's office.
18:30 p.m.	Reception: Ambassador of Mexico, Dr. Gorge Montano, Ambassador Fortier, and Mrs. Carol Fortier

The fourth development of major significance in modern international politics is *summit diplomacy**, a phrase coined by Winston Churchill. Occasionally summit meetings of great historic value took place before the twentieth century, such as the Congress of Vienna (1815) and the Congress of Berlin (1878). But diplomatic mythology has always held as undesirable the direct communication between heads of state. Today, in the Age of

Summitry, many observers are critical of diplomacy at the highest levels because political executives are not often trained in the skills of negotiation. Diplomats advise that compromise is difficult when the prestige of the negotiating parties is at stake. The main argument against summiteering is that face-to-face meetings among leaders are much too dramatic and politically charged to provide a rational environment for delicate negotiations. Dean Rusk warned that "summit diplomacy is to be approached with the wariness with which a prudent physician prescribes a habit-forming drug...the experienced diplomat will usually counsel against the direct confrontation of those with final authority."[7]

It has been conceded by students of international relations that summit diplomacy has no greater possibility of success than the traditional avenues of diplomatic communication.[8] For example, in Vienna in 1961, a summit meeting took place between Nikita Krushchev and John Kennedy that ended in failure and increased world tensions until 1963. Both leaders met face to face to discuss the arms race, each returning home determined to accelerate military buildups. Nearly 25 years later a similar dramatic diplomatic encounter took place at the Reagan-Gorbachev Summit in Geneva in November 1985, Reykjavik in 1987, and with Western world leaders at Toronto in 1988 and at the 15th economic summit in Paris in 1989. Gorbachev's meeting with president Reagan and president-elect Bush in New York in 1988 was widely reported as a confidence-building measure to facilitate long-term détente on matters related to disarmament.

But the idea that only heads of state can settle intractable disputes or negotiate complicated international instruments has not been supported by much evidence, although there have been some notable successes for summitry. One of the most successful in terms of positive international relations was the so-called Shamrock Summit between Reagan and Mulroney at Quebec city in March 1985. Both leaders inaugurated the institution of annual summit meetings. The idea was to bring regular top-level management to Canada-U.S. affairs. The first working session between George Bush and Brian Mulroney in 1989 departed from the ceremonial trappings of the Reagan era and gave way to informality and a pragmatic approach to the issues without a highly scripted agenda.

The visits to China of U.S. presidents Nixon in 1972 and Reagan in 1984 established a U.S.-Chinese rapprochement* that was possible only because of contacts at the highest levels of power. The Camp David Accords of 1979 showed how the intimacy of secluded summitry could successfully accomplish in just a few days what lower levels of negotiation had failed to do after years of effort. And in Malta in 1989, the first Bush-Gorbachev summit successfully rekindled the expanding U.S.-Soviet relationship, laying the groundwork for the completion of the Strategic Arms Reduction Talks begun in Geneva in 1982, and for the reduction of conventional forces in Europe and the integration of the Soviet Union into the world economic system. Another victory for summitry took place in November of 1989, when Gorbachev conferred with the Pope, ending seventy years of antagonism between the Kremlin and the Holy See. The Soviet leader promised to guarantee religious freedom in the Soviet Union and to reopen diplomatic relations with the Vatican.

The spectacular increase in the frequency of summit meetings indicates the new importance political leaders attach to them. In these times of instant communications and rapid travel, many leaders have discovered the political advantages of world exposure by bypassing traditional diplomatic machinery and maintaining direct contact among themselves. Despite the widespread denunciation of summitry by the global corps diplomatique, the increase in personal diplomacy by heads of state is a fact of life in the modern world of negotiation. Any analytical definition of diplomacy today must include the whole process of policy making by heads of government, as well as through normal diplomatic channels. Summitry has permanently invaded the domain of diplomacy.

The Protocol of Modern Diplomacy

Today, diplomatic relations between states are conducted according to a vast code of behaviour embodied in the Vienna Convention on Diplomatic Relations.[9] The Vienna conference (1961) was a major international effort to codify international law in the area of diplomatic privileges and immunities. It was attended by eighty-one states that drafted a comprehensive agreement covering diplomatic activities; the convention came into force by 1964. The conference was called because of the length of time over which customs and rules had been accumulating and because of the changing circumstances in which these rules were applied. It was time to reach an agreement on the differing interests and interpretations of the rules by various countries. At Vienna, the attending states set forth the rules of diplomatic practice to conform to contemporary conditions and standards of diplomacy. The heads of diplomatic missions were divided into three general categories. The first two categories are ambassadors and ministers respectively. These diplomats are accredited* to the head of the host state. The third category is comprised of chargés d'affaires. These lower-ranking diplomats are accredited to the foreign minister of the host state.

The Appointment of an Ambassador

Before an ambassador is appointed to a post, the sending state seeks the approval or agrément of the receiving state. Approval is usually granted when the discretionary authority of the receiving state determines a diplomat is *persona grata** (a person in good grace). A receiving state may also declare a diplomat of another state to be *persona non grata* when that diplomat is found to be unacceptable after initial investigation, or when a diplomat engages in criminal and antisocial behaviour or interferes in the internal affairs of the host state. But such a practice is exceptional and contrary to the spirit of international relations. This reciprocal procedure of confidential application and acceptance is an important instrument of protocol* that builds trust and confidence in interstate relations. There is, however, one notable exception. Former Liberal Cabinet Minister Bryce Mackasey was appointed ambassador from Canada to Portugal as one of three patronage rewards made by John Turner before he went to the polls in the late summer of 1984. Portugal did not accept Mackasey as Canada's diplomatic representative, making it clear it would not do so until after a new government was elected. The eleven-week delay by Portugal was highly unusual and widely interpreted as a signal that Mackasey's appointment would have to be reviewed by the new Canadian government. After the Conservative landslide in 1984, External Affairs Minister Joe Clark appointed Lloyd Francis, a former speaker of the House of Commons, to the post without incurring any objections from Portugal.

Once agréation is reached, an ambassador is given credentials to present to the head of state. In Commonwealth countries where the sovereign is the head of more than one state (e.g., the Queen for Canada, New Zealand, and Australia), ambassadors are provided with a letter of introduction from prime minister to prime minister. In accordance with diplomatic protocol, *letters of credence* (see Fig. 15-1) are provided for the exchange of ambassadors outside the Commonwealth.

On arrival, an ambassador will inform the minister of foreign affairs or secretary of state that he or she is ready to assume the duties of the embassy. In a letter referred to as the *copie d'usage*, the ambassador indicates a willingness to present the letters of credence to the head of state and includes the predecessor's *letter of recall** that terminated the mission. Once a

In the Name and on Behalf of	Aux Nom, Lieu et Place de
Elizabeth II	**Elizabeth II**
by the Grace of God of the United Kingdom, Canada and Her other Realms and Territories Queen, Head of the Commonwealth, Defender of the Faith	par la grâce de Dieu, Reine du Royaume-Uni, du Canada et de ses autres royaumes et territoires, Chef du Commonwealth, Défenseur de la Foi
Ramon Hnatyshyn	**Ramon Hnatyshyn**
Governor General and Commander in Chief of Canada	Gouverneur général et Commandant en chef du Canada
Your Excellency,	Excellence,
Wishing to promote the relations of friendship and good understanding which happily exist between our two countries, I have decided to accredit to You	Désireux de poursuivre les relations d'amitié et de bonne entente qui existent entre nos deux pays, J'ai décidé d'accréditer auprès de Vous
in the character of Ambassador Extraordinary and Plenipotentiary of Canada.	en qualité d'Ambassadeur Extraordinaire et Plénipotentiaire du Canada.
The experience which I have had of his talents and zeal assures Me that the selection I have made will be perfectly agreeable to You, and that he will discharge his important duties in such a manner as to merit Your approbation and esteem.	La connaissance que J'ai de ses talents et de son dévouement Me sont autant de garanties que Mon choix Vous sera agréable et qu'il s'acquittera de ses hautes fonctions de façon à mériter Votre estime et Votre bienveillance.
I, therefore, request that You will give entire credence to all that he shall say to You in My name, more especially when he shall convey to You the assurances of the lively interest which I take in everything that affects the welfare and prosperity of Your country.	Je Vous prie donc de bien vouloir lui accorder entière créance en tout ce qu'il Vous transmettra de Ma part, surtout lorsqu'il Vous renouvellera l'assurance du vif intérêt que Je porte à tout ce qui concerne le bonheur et la prospérité de Votre pays.
Given at My Government House,	En Mon Hôtel du Gouvernement,
Your Good Friend,	Votre Grand Ami,

Figure 15.1

diplomat presents credentials to the head of state, he or she is considered officially to represent the sending state, unless the ambassador is recalled for a specific reason. For example, Canada withdrew its Ambassador from Beijing to protest the Government of China's repressive military operations in Tiananmen Square in 1989.

Sometimes the ambassador and members of the diplomatic staff are assigned to more than one state. For example, Canada's ambassador to Costa Rica and his or her staff are also accredited to El Salvador, Nicaragua, and Panama. No state maintains a diplomatic mission in every capital of the world.[10] For economic reasons, most states are selective, balancing national interests against the costs involved in maintaining a permanent presence in a country. Canada has embassies in 82 capitals but conducts diplomatic relations with over 160 states. In effect, Canada has virtually doubled its diplomatic presence in the world by accrediting many of its heads of missions as non-resident or visiting diplomats to other states.

Multi-accreditation or plural representation, as it is sometimes called, can cause difficulties between states. Those states where the ambassador does not reside may feel that the sending state considers them inferior to states where embassies are permanently established. Problems arise when two or more states covered by the same ambassador engage in hostilities or break diplomatic relations. Parties in dispute will usually doubt the objectivity of the multi-accredited ambassador. These situations are potentially embarrassing both for the ambassador and for the states involved.

Privileges, Exemptions, and Immunities

It is a well-established and widely accepted rule of international law that all categories of diplomatic personnel are immune from civil jurisdiction of the courts of the host country. This rule has never meant that immunity should give diplomats a licence to violate laws of the receiving state. Although every state's diplomatic corps can report cases of envoys who conspire to break local laws, the majority of the world's diplomats readily comply with these laws. Most governments are aware that lawbreaking foreign diplomats who try to escape local jurisdictions can be dealt with through political channels. And, generally speaking, governments rarely, if ever, institute criminal suits against diplomats. In cases of flagrant criminal activity by a foreign diplomat, the host state will declare the individual persona non grata. Since the end of World War II, Canada has declared fifty-nine people, nearly all of them Soviet-bloc diplomats and consuls, personae non gratae. In the summer of 1988 Canada expelled eight Soviet diplomatic officials in Canada and banned nine former officials from re-entry because they were found to have engaged in activities threatening to the security of the state. In retaliation, the Soviets expelled two Canadian diplomats from Moscow and banned the return of three others who had already left the Soviet Union.

Sometimes diplomats are expelled from their posts because of sudden strains between governments. Such was the case between Great Britain and the Soviet Union in 1985 when a KGB officer, Oleg Gordievski, defected in London after spying for the West for at least fifteen years. The British Foreign Office expelled over thirty-five Soviet citizens and diplomats who were believed to have taken part in spying operations. The Soviets retaliated by expelling an almost equal number of British citizens and representatives, causing diplomatic relations between both states to suffer for some time. Another diplomatic practice used when tension develops between states is recall. In 1989, Canada recalled its chargé d'affaires from Tehran to express outrage at Ayatollah Khomeini's death threats against Salman Rushdie, author of *The Satanic Verses*. Similarly, Britain recalled its entire embassy staff and simultaneously expelled the Iranian chargé d'affaires because of the death threat to at least one of its citizens.

Not all states recognize immunities and privileges as an absolute right. In April 1984, for example, the British embassy in Tripoli was surrounded by Libyan militia units, which prevented the diplomatic staff from leaving. Libyan officials indicated that the units would remain at the embassy until Libyan detainees, held by British police for killing a police officer and wounding demonstrators, had been freed. The restrictions imposed on the British embassy staff limiting their freedom of movement were finally lifted after negotiations between the British foreign office and the Libyan government. The United States also holds exceptions to the inviolability of a diplomat when an envoy's conduct threatens the safety and security of the republic.[11] In such cases, a diplomat will be restrained, although in time he or she will normally be sent home. In 1982, U.S. law permitted the State Department to establish the Office of Foreign Missions to give the government more control over foreign diplomats. The law permits the United States to retaliate against diplomats from governments that mistreat U.S. envoys or whose diplomats habitually violate U.S. laws. In taking off its diplomatic gloves, the U.S. is now empowered to disconnect telephones in Washington embassies, hold up shipments of goods, and refuse to allow foreign diplomats to buy property. In 1984, a Chinese request for permission to buy an apartment building in Washington was denied because the United States is barred from owning property in China. The Soviets were denied permission to buy eight condominium apartments in New York for the same reason. And the Czechoslovaks were refused permission to build an apartment on land they own in Washington because of their failure to respond to property acquisition and maintenance needs of the United States in Prague. The Office of Foreign Missions levies income taxes on the diplomats of states that tax the incomes of U.S. emissaries overseas. Diplomats are now required to get red, white, and blue licence plates for their automobiles, as well as titles (proof of ownership) and liability insurance.

All these actions reflect changes in the official attitudes of some states toward traditional diplomatic privileges and immunities. Even though most states adhere to diplomatic protocol as codified by the Vienna Convention, many governments are legislating limitations on diplomatic privileges and immunities. With regard to criminal behaviour, it remains to be seen whether any state would honour the diplomatic immunity of an envoy who sought the audience of the head of state, and then, as a premeditated act, performed an assassination.

One of the most impressive statements on the question of national security* and diplomatic immunity was made by Justice Bissonette of Canada in the widely publicized case of *Rose v. The King*.[12] Justice Bissonette reasoned that diplomatic immunity is relative, not absolute, and that if a diplomat commits a crime against the security of a state, he or she renounces the privilege of inviolability. Even though the *Rose* case occurred long before the Vienna Convention, it is certainly possible that Justice Bissonette's legal arguments could be again cited in today's courts.

In 1977, Canada proclaimed the *Diplomatic and Consular Privileges and Immunities Act*. This act enabled Canada to ratify the 1961 Vienna Convention while imposing several limitations on its application within Canada. By Section 2(4) the secretary of state for External Affairs can withdraw privileges and immunities from foreign diplomats if those privileges are not properly accorded to Canadian diplomats in their state. And, under Section (5), when a question arises as to whether a person is entitled to diplomatic immunities, the matter is decided by the secretary of state for External Affairs.

Diplomats enjoy personal inviolability as well as inviolability of premises and property. Full diplomatic privileges and immunities apply to diplomats and members of their families and staff in all official as well as most private activities, provided they are not nationals or classed as permanent residents of the state to which the diplomat is accredited.

The Vienna Convention asserts that diplomats and those properly associated with the mission are immune from civil and administrative jurisdictions of the host state. In most circumstances a diplomat can sue but cannot be sued. However, if legal proceedings* are initiated by a diplomat, he or she is subject to counterclaims*. Under the convention, a diplomat is subject to legal action on private immovable property and on any commercial transactions undertaken outside official diplomatic functions.

All property held on behalf of the sending state for the purpose of the mission is inviolable. The host state is obligated to protect the persons and property of a diplomatic mission and is not permitted to seize, search, or confiscate documents wherever they may be. Because the premises of the mission and the private residences of the head of the mission and staff are inviolable, they may not be entered by agents of the host state without special permission from the sending state. The diplomatic bag* may not be opened or detained whether it is carried by an envoy, a diplomatic courier, or a designated national official who is making a special journey to the sending state. Diplomats and their families are also exempt from the inspection of personal luggage.

In addition to inviolability, diplomats enjoy a wide range of exemptions from national, regional, and municipal taxes. Except for services such as electricity, gas, refuse collection, water, and sewerage, the premises of diplomatic missions are tax exempt. Any articles that are imported for the official use of the mission are also exempt from customs and excise duties, provided they are not sold or otherwise disposed of for profit in the host state.

Consular Immunity

Like diplomats, consuls* are specialized agents of one state in another state. Unlike diplomats, however, consuls do not conduct political relations or negotiations between states. They are not accredited by one head of state to another to represent the person of the sovereign in a foreign state. The consul represents the sending state in a different way from diplomats. Consuls are concerned with assisting nationals of their state and furthering

Canada

Elizabeth the Second, by the Grace of God of the United Kingdom, Canada and Her other Realms and Territories QUEEN, Head of the Commonwealth, Defender of the Faith.

TO ALL TO WHOM these Presents shall come,

GREETING:

WHEREAS We have thought it necessary for encouraging Canadian citizens trading to the Republic of the Ivory Coast to appoint a Consul of Canada at Abidjan with jurisdiction in the Republic of the Ivory Coast to take care of Canadian citizens and to aid and assist them in all their lawful and mercantile concerns.

NOW KNOW YE that reposing special trust and confidence in the discretion and faithfulness of Our Trusty and Well-beloved

We did, on the day of in the year of Our Lord one thousand nine hundred and eighty-five and in the thirty-fourth year of Our Reign, constitute and appoint,

CONSUL OF CANADA AT ABIDJAN

with jurisdiction as aforesaid, thereby giving and granting unto him full power and authority by all lawful means to aid and protect those Canadian citizens who may trade or visit or reside within his Consular District, and to hold the said office during Our Pleasure with all rights, privileges and immunities thereunto appertaining.

AND We do hereby strictly enjoin and require all Canadian citizens to take due notice of this Our Commission and yield obedience thereto.

IN TESTIMONY WHEREOF there is affixed hereunto the Seal of the Registrar General of Canada.

WITNESS:

Elizabeth Deux, par la Grâce de Dieu, REINE du Royaume-Uni, du Canada et de ses autres royaumes et territoires, Chef du Commonwealth, Défenseur de la Foi.

À TOUS CEUX qui les présentes verront,

SALUT:

ATTENDU QUE Nous avons jugé nécessaire, en vue d'encourager les citoyens canadiens qui se livrent au commerce avec la République de Côte d'Ivoire de nommer un consul du Canada à Abidjan ayant juridiction en République de Côte d'Ivoire pour s'occuper des citoyens canadiens et pour les aider et les assister dans toutes leurs entreprises légitimes et commerciales.

SACHEZ MAINTENANT QUE, en raison de la confiance particulière que Nous mettons dans la discrétion et la loyauté de Notre Féal et Bien-aimé

Nous avons, le jour de en l'an de grâce mil neuf cent quatre-vingt-cinq, le trente-quatrième de Notre règne, constitué et nommé,

CONSUL DU CANADA À ABIDJAN

ayant juridiction comme il est dit plus haut et lui donnant et lui conférant par ces présentes pleins pouvoirs et autorité pour aider et protéger par tous moyens légitimes les citoyens canadiens autorisés à se livrer au commerce dans les limites de sa circonscription consulaire ou à la visiter ou y résider, et pour remplir ladite charge pendant Notre bon plaisir avec tous les droits, privilèges et immunités qui s'y rattachent.

ET par ces présentes Nous enjoignons et prescrivons strictement à tous les citoyens canadiens de tenir dûment compte de Notre présente Commission et de s'y conformer.

EN FOI DE QUOI les présentes ont été revêtues du sceau du Registraire général du Canada.

TÉMOIN:

BY COMMAND, PAR ORDRE,

DEPUTY REGISTRAR GENERAL OF CANADA
SOUS-REGISTRAIRE GÉNÉRAL DU CANADA

DEPUTY ATTORNEY GENERAL OF CANADA
SOUS-PROCUREUR GÉNÉRAL DU CANADA

Figure 15.2

the commercial, economic, cultural, and scientific relations between the sending state and the receiving state. They issue passports, visas, and appropriate travel and judicial documents to nationals. Consuls safeguard the interests of their nationals as individuals and corporations in a foreign state, particularly by acting as notary, civil registrar, and administrative agent for the sending state. They also exercise certain rights of supervision and inspection over crews of vessels having the nationality of the sending state.

Unlike embassies, consulates are not necessarily located in the capital city of the host state. They are usually opened in cities and towns that have special commercial significance to the sending state. In the United States, Canada has consular posts in fourteen cities,[13] and each consulate provides consular services to a designated territory that includes a number of U.S. states. For example, the Canadian consulate in Boston services a territory that includes the states of Maine, Massachusetts, New Hampshire, Rhode Island, and Vermont. Canada's consular posts in the United States are operated by about 750 people – about 300 are from Canada and the rest are hired locally. Not including the salaries of Canadian diplomats, the thirteen offices (including the Canadian embassy) have an annual operating budget of close to $40 million.

Consular officers are appointed by their governments through diplomatic channels in the host state. They are given a commission (see figure 15.2), which is a written document showing the consul's name, rank (e.g., consul general, consul, or vice–consul), the consular district, and the post. The host government issues an exequatur* that approves and authorizes the appointment. The exequatur entitles the consul to certain privileges and immunities in respect to acts performed in the exercise of consular duties.

The Vienna Convention on Consular Relations (1963) codified most of the pre-existing rules of customary international law regarding consular immunities. Under the convention, the privileges and immunities enjoyed by a consular officer are similar to those enjoyed by members of a diplomatic staff. They apply, however, to a lesser degree. The host state is obliged to protect consular officers, but personal inviolability and immunity from jurisdiction apply only to acts performed in the exercise of consular functions. A consul must respond to civil actions by third parties for damages arising from acts of personal negligence. Consuls must appear before proper authorities if criminal charges are brought against them. If found guilty of criminal acts, consuls are liable to imprisonment in the host state. In the event that a consular agent is charged with a "grave crime," the Vienna Convention states that a consul may even be detained pending trial. In Canada, the Diplomatic and Consular Privileges and Immunities Act of 1977 provides that a "grave crime" is any offence determined by an act of Parliament for which an offender may be sentenced to imprisonment for five or more years.

In the Canadian case of *Maluquer v. The King*, it was ruled that a foreign consul is not entitled to the same degree of immunity enjoyed by a person who occupies a diplomatic position.[14] When acting as a private person, a consul has the same legal rights as any other resident alien. This restrictive theory applied by Canadian courts in cases involving consular immunity has been widely shared throughout the international system. The Canadian position has been clarified further in the act of 1977, which firmly distinguishes the application of civil and criminal jurisdictions to diplomats and consular officers.

Despite conventional and judicial restrictions of consular immunities, all governments want to ensure the effective fulfilment of consular functions.[15] Thus, consulates, their archives, and their documents are inviolable and may not be entered by local authorities without the permission of the head of the consular post. The consular premises, including the residence of the head of the post, are tax exempt. All career income is tax exempt to consuls and so are fees for consular services that generate income to the consulate. All consular personnel are exempt from local regulations concerning residence permits and the registration and employment of aliens.

The host state is obligated to give consuls access to nationals who are arrested or detained. Consuls also have the right of access to information in cases of death, guardianship, shipwrecks, and aircraft accidents. Finally, consuls have the right to communicate with appropriate authorities in the receiving state in order to perform official duties.

Profile of an Ambassador

In the complicated world of international relations, today's ambassador needs to possess the specialized talents of many professionals: the survival instinct of a business person, the organization of an administrator, the charm of an actor, and the intellectual curiosity and objectivity of a social scientist.

Foreign services in all states, therefore, seek to recruit people of unique character and high training. There is no question that the corps diplomatique has traditionally been elite. But today it is an elite not of breeding, but of talent. The academic qualifications of most diplomats are very high. Almost invariably they are university educated, holding professional degrees to the level of Ph.D. By the 1990s, for example, 80 percent of Canadian diplomats had two degrees or more. They have had extensive experience in government, usually in the public service, and have made a career of climbing to the rank of ambassador. Many diplomats are multilingual: Europeans excel in this qualification because of the geographical proximity of people speaking many different languages. Canada is officially bilingual and many of its foreign representatives are as well. Education and language skills are to a great extent personal achievements. But most of the formal training a diplomat receives is usually provided by the diplomatic corps of the sending state.

The formal procedure and protocols of diplomatic practice are a product of training, both at the home office and on the job. Yet all the formal training a diplomat receives cannot extrude the innate qualities of character – moral integrity, flexibility, loyalty, courage, and political sense – required for the job. Most diplomatic observers seem to agree that the personal attributes of the envoy, rather than his or her formal qualifications, have a decisive influence on the outcome of diplomacy. The intellectual context in which an envoy is trained is often not relevant to many of the issues conducted among governments. J.W. Burton has observed that "languages and history are no longer sufficient as equipment [for diplomats]."[16] Today's practitioners require, in addition to these traditional skills, knowledge of the latest technologies of peace and war. They must be aware that their negotiations transcend the interests of the governments they represent and that nuclear-age decision making has global consequences. Above all, ambassadors need to have what Sir Harold Nicholson called "the main formative influence in diplomatic theory ... common sense."[17]

In diplomacy, common sense is as much a skill as it is a gift. Although such a quality may only on rare occasions change history, it is a vital ingredient in the daily operation of any embassy, whether in London, England, or Kuala Lumpur, Malaysia.

The art of negotiation requires a person who is an empathetic communicator – one who listens and understands. After all, the purpose of diplomacy is communication; everything connected with diplomacy – representation, protocol, procedures – is designed to facilitate communication with people. Diplomats have to be observant, pragmatic, and intuitive with the people they meet. Diplomats will make accommodations not because they are impressed with political rhetoric and argumentation, but because they believe that making a concession will be more useful or less harmful than refusing it.[18] Thus, the strategy of diplomats is not so much to be eloquent in defence of their government's interests as it is to provide convincing incentives that rivals will perceive as concessions in their self-interest. In effect, the force of logic is more desirable than the logic of force in the negotiating process.

In addition to negotiating with the host country and handling sensitive or secret material, an ambassador takes responsibility for a large operating staff that depends on his or her leadership. This amounts to maintaining a complicated network of people above and beyond the important political relations with the officials of the host country. Every embassy maintains a mission staff made up of accountants, translators, chauffeurs, secretaries, cipher clerks, radio operators, gardeners, and hospitality personnel. Today's ambassadors are no longer considered too high up the ladder to get involved in the organization of a smoothly running embassy. Indeed, those with large staffs of diplomats, experts, and locally employed workers now have to fulfil a managerial role in addition to their negotiating functions.

Despite the glamour the public is anxious to attach to diplomacy, it is a profession much like other professions. It is filled with routine and protocol, and meeting people is the essence of the diplomat's craft. Activities include attending luncheons and receptions, giving speeches, hosting guests, giving interviews, and being present at celebrations of the host state's national holidays.

Derek Burney is Canada's ambassador to the United States. A native of Thunder Bay, Ontario, he holds an MA degree in political science from Queen's University. Burney joined the Department of External Affairs in 1963. His assignments in Canada and abroad include: ambassador to the Republic of Korea; administrator to the 1980 economic summit held in Ottawa and Montebello; assistant under-secretary for commercial policy and general economic relations; assistant deputy minister for United States affairs; and associate under-secretary of State. In 1987, he was appointed chief of staff to the prime minister. His appointment as ambassador to the United States of America was effective January 1, 1989. From that time on he became the manager of the 320 employees who operate the Canadian embassy in Washington. Like most diplomats he follows a very tight schedule that usually begins at 8:00 a.m. and ends late in the evening. The following is the schedule of a typical day in Ambassador Burney's life.

Thursday March 2, 1989

	Ambassador Burney:
8:00 a.m.	Arrives at Embassy: Meets with staff to discuss schedule, makes a number of telephone calls.
9:00 a.m.	Conference Information Program for the Northern Virginia Business Community. Opening Statement "Doing Business with Canada under the FTA" Marriott Crystal Gateway Hotel Crystal City B. Craig/L. Legault Drafters: B. Oak/B. Dymond
11:30 a.m.	Meeting with Senator David Durenburger (R-Minn.) Room 154, Russell Senate Office Bldg. J. Fried (to accompany)
12:30 p.m. – 2:00 p.m.	Ambassador and Mrs. Joan (Peden) Burney: Hosts at the residence in honour of Mr. and Mrs. Belzberg in conjunction with the opening of Master Drawings from the National Gallery of Canada at the National Gallery of Washington. R. Picard
3:00 p.m.	Ambassador Burney: Courtesy call on Ambassador Rawdon Dalrymple, Embassy of Australia 1601 Massachusettes Ave. N.W. Marilee Doust P. Barton
4:30 p.m.	Meeting with Senator Bennett Johnston (D-VA) Room 136, Hart Senate Office Bldg. J. Fried(to accompany)
5:30 p.m.	Meeting with the Honourable David Russell Deputy Premier of Alberta Ambassador's Office G. Tyerman J. Osler
6:00 p.m.– 8:30 p.m.	Ambassador and Mrs. Joan (Peden) Burney: Reception in recognition of Master Drawings from the National Gallery of Canada; hosted by the Board of Trustees, National Gallery East Building R. Picard

8:00 p.m. Ambassador and Mrs. Joan (Peden) Burney
Dinner hosted by Ambasssador and Mrs Duemling
in honour of Ambassador and Mrs. Burney
Black Tie

Almost everything an ambassador does is related to representation, but going to a party or a dinner is really going to work. Entertaining (or representation) by diplomats is important because (1) social functions convey a positive image for the country concerned; (2) entertainment provides an opportunity for obtaining information; and (3) while entertaining, important contacts are made. Of a total annual operating budget of $7.5 million, the Canadian embassy in Washington spends $2 million on representation. The ambassador and his wife attend approximately 200 social functions annually and host over 150 events, both at the embassy and their residence. These functions include breakfast briefings, meetings, lunches, receptions, dinners, and meeting groups that are invited to the residence for tea or drinks. This is an important part of the information-gathering function of the diplomatic mission. Social gatherings provide an atmosphere that projects friendship and good public relations. They are opportunities for nation-states to give their best representation in a relaxed setting. But we should not assume that vital information concerning the affairs of state is a direct result of hosts pouring alcoholic beverages into their guests. Most information upon which an embassy will act comes from open sources and conventional channels. Formal meetings, conversations, newspapers, and public statements by governing officials all form the main sources of information needed to make or adjust foreign policy.

Usually the functional division of the mission provides the organizational framework for the acquisition of information.[19] At Canada's new embassy in Washington, the political section (headed by a minister who answers to the ambassador) attempts to acquire information on subjects relating to the political trends and foreign-policy positions of the United States. The economic and commercial sections, each headed by a minister (also answerable to the ambassador), seek to gain information that might be of interest to Canadian government officials concerned with trade and economic policy. The Canadian embassy also has attachés concerned with military, scientific, cultural, and agricultural matters that affect both states.

The role of the ambassador is crucial in the process of receiving and transmitting information. It is the ambassador who usually reports to Ottawa any changes that may affect Canada's relations with the United States. Because information comes in endless flows, what the ambassador chooses to send the Department of External Affairs, as well as the other departments of government, is important. His ability to give priority to certain trends and events and to press his views to Ottawa determines whether the Cabinet can adjust its policies to meet new conditions in the United States.

At the same time the ambassador must be aware of the long-term changes taking place in the state to which he or she is accredited. Burney has to identify those significant political and constitutional changes in the United States that have taken place over the past ten years and have far-reaching implications for Canadian interests.[20] For example, the system of checks and balances in the United States among the three branches of government has become increasingly complicated. There is a strong spirit of congressional independence from the presidency, demonstrated by the much greater involvement of the legislative branch of government in foreign affairs. The U.S. Congress is much more ready to assert its prerogatives and less willing to follow the lead of the White House. At the same time, Congress has become less cohesive and unified through the proliferation of committees and subcommittees, which are particularly receptive to professional lobbyists.

The Canadian ambassador to the United States no longer deals primarily with officials of the State Department. In the 1990s, an ambassador and his or her staff must deal with a myriad of politically active individuals and groups that now have a dramatic effect on the political landscape in the United States. Washington is populated by an army of lawyers, public-relations experts, political-action committees, pressure groups, political strategists, tacticians, and fund raisers. Then there is the Congress, with over 20 000 staff members working on politics and substance. In addition to the traditional departments of government, the Canadian embassy staff must negotiate with many of the independent federal regulatory agencies and commissions established by Congress, such as the Federal Aviation Agency and the Federal Maritime Commission. Added to this is the complication of monitoring the tactics of over 15 000 lobbyists who, at any time, may pressure executive and congressional staff members and officials on matters related to Canadian interests. These can range from acid rain to special problems arising out of the Free Trade Agreement. The impact of special-interest groups can have a damaging effect on trade and employment for both economies.

The separation of powers in the United States makes negotiating an especially complicated process. The executive branch of government may enthusiastically agree to a set of concessions in a negotiation, but the Senate, responding to an effective lobby, may not ratify the agreement or may add unanticipated provisions to it. For example, some senators, in response to interest groups, were able to block Senate approval of the painstakingly negotiated West Coast Salmon Treaty. In this case, the administration in Washington took the lead in negotiating with the Canadian government. But the treaty stalled in the Senate because of congressional opposition by the representatives of one region – Alaska. It was only when Reagan and Mulroney ratified the Pacific Salmon Treaty at the March 1985 Quebec Summit that years of painstaking negotiations over fishing and dwindling stocks on the West Coast ended in a binding agreement.

On the trade side, the ambassador actively lobbies for Canadian interests. Trade between Canada and the United States creates enormous benefits to both countries. On an annual basis Canadians and Americans exchange about US$200 billion worth of goods. Under the Free Trade Agreement this bilateral trade relationship translates into jobs for over 1 million Canadians and nearly 2 million Americans.

One important role for the ambassador is to promote the most positive environment possible for free trade. This brings him into frequent contact with U.S. trade representatives and the secretary of Commerce. The ambassador also co-ordinates regular and continuing contact between Canadian Cabinet ministers and their counterparts in Washington. On January 1, 1989 the first tariff reductions took effect from the FTA. The new rights and obligations respecting trade in services, the treatment of investors, the facilitation of business travel, the reduction and elimination of non-tariff barriers, and the expansion of opportunities to compete for government procurement contracts have now been initiated.

Much of the success behind Canada-U.S. agreements can be attributed to the behind-the-scenes efforts of the ambassador and his staff. In this connection, an important aspect of the ambassador's job in Washington is that of sensitizing Congress to the effects of trade actions on Canada. Canadian negotiators learned long ago that in Congress, when the interests of a foreign state are up against the constituency imperatives of a domestic group, the foreign state, even if it is the closest ally of the United States, is at a disadvantage. Even if the targets of U.S. restrictions are Japan and Europe, and Canadian trade is not even at issue, Canada's economy is easily sideswiped by actions aimed at others. When this happens, the ambassador will attempt to inform members of Congress and their committees that trade restrictions hurt both economies.

In addition to representing Canadian interests in the American political system, the embassy staff also administers routine claims from Canadians who are visiting or who are involved in business in the United States. These run annually into the thousands. In the ambassador's office alone, the embassy processes approximately 225 pieces of mail a week, of which about 75 percent require some form of follow up. The Canadian embassy acts as a broker for its citizens, administering travel and business matters requiring official representation. The mission is required to protect those nationals who may have legal difficulties and to assist in ensuring fair treatment by the laws of the host state. An arrest or an affront to a Canadian in the United States may put strains on embassy officials who desire to settle these matters in good faith; the embassy staff never knows what political factors might be involved in a given incident. Many times the staff is faced with decisions that can have enormous consequences and must walk a difficult line between maintaining good relations with the host state and protecting the interests of Canadians.

An important factor in routine interactions is the degree of friendship or hostility that exists between states. Canada and the United States enjoy a historic friendship and maintain a large number of regular interactions, especially in the areas of tourism and business.[21] Geographic location is another extremely important factor. A common border and common bodies of water between the United States and Canada create many situations that must be handled routinely. Heavy mutual trading also creates frequent and varied interactions, which result in numerous administrative problems for the embassy because so many Canadians have a huge stake in the economic policies of the United States.

No matter how varied the duties of an embassy might be, the prime concern of an ambassador is to keep international relations as routine and as friendly as possible. Whether executed by lower-level administrative officials or conducted by ranking diplomats at the foreign-policy level, the many areas of collaboration between states must be kept viable by diplomatic means. The Canadian embassy in Washington must see that the large volume of transactions across the Canada-U.S. border is facilitated by the least amount of conflict between the two governments.

Canada has never been complacent in its lopsided relationship with its powerful and affluent neighbour to the south. It has always feared that the United States could single-handedly crush its interests without taking notice. For that reason, the Canadian government has assigned the largest single concentration of diplomatic talent it has to Washington to make sure the United States does take notice. In addition, its $90-million investment in new embassy facilities demonstrates the importance Ottawa attaches to its diplomatic operation there. In the Ottawa headquarters of the Department of External Affairs, the United States rates a branch of its own, headed by an assistant deputy minister. The U.S. branch of External Affairs includes six divisions: general relations (political and legal matters); trade and economic relations; trans-boundary matters (environment, transport, and energy); marketing; trade and investment; and programs. The U.S. branch is run by a staff of seventy-six bureaucrats with an operating budget of $5 million. All these institutional representations reflect the large volume of international transactions that take place between Canada and the United States.

Diplomacy is the centerpiece of relations between and among states. It is by means of diplomacy that human problems arising in the international system are resolved. The work of a diplomat is frequently overlooked because much of it is routine and lacks the glamour of executive and legislative decision making. But diplomacy and its human offspring – diplomats – will always be needed if states want to carry on a continuous dialogue on the inter-personal level. In a world where people still engage in personalized politics despite encroaching technologies, diplomacy by human contact is still very relevant.

REFERENCES

1. Abba Eban, *The New Diplomacy: International Affairs in the Modern Age* (New York: Random House 1983), 332; see also Karl Deutsch, *The Analysis of International Relations* (Englewood Cliffs, NJ: Prentice Hall 1988), 172–81.
2. Frank Adcock, *Diplomacy in Ancient Greece* (New York: St. Martin's Press 1975), 139–40.
3. Charles Mayer, *Diplomat* (New York: Harper & Brothers Publishers 1959), 43.
4. Quoted from Max Lerner, ed., *The Prince and the Discourses* (New York: Modern Library 1940), 60.
5. See Henry Kissinger, *Years of Upheaval* (Boston: Little, Brown & Co. 1982).
6. K.J. Holsti, *International Politics, A Framework for Analysis* (Englewood Cliffs, NJ: Prentice-Hall Inc. 1988), 163; and Eric Clark, *Diplomat* (New York: Taplinger Publishing Co. Inc. 1974), 249–63.
7. Dean Rusk, "American Foreign Policy in the Eighties," (Washington, D.C.: LTV Washington Seminar 1980); and Charles Stefan,"The Ups and Downs of Summitry," *Foreign Service Journal* 64(10) (1987): 29–31.
8. See Hedley Bull, "The Decline of Professional Diplomacy," in Bull, *The Anarchical Society* (New York: Macmillan 1980); and William Zartman, "Negotiation as a Joint Decision-Making Process," in Zartman, ed., *The Negotiating Process: Theories and Applications* (Beverly Hills, CA: Sage Publications 1978), 67–86.
9. Gilbert Winham, "International Negotiation in an Age of Transition," *International Journal* 25 (Winter 1979–80): 1–20; and Diane Bendahmane and John McDonald,

International Negotiating: Art and Science, Report of the Conference on International Negotiation, June 9–10 (Washington, D.C.: Center for the Study of Foreign Affairs 1983).

10. Canada, *Canadian Representatives Abroad* (Ottawa: Department of External Affairs 1983), 5–84; see also Chadwick Alger and Steven Brams, "Patterns of Representation in National Capitals and Intergovernmental Organizations," *World Politics* 19 (July 1967): 662.
11. Clifton E. Wilson, *Diplomatic Privileges and Immunities* (Tucson, AZ: University of Arizona Press 1967), 78–97.
12. *Rose v. The King* (1946), 88 C.C.C. 114 (Que. C.A.).
13. Atlanta, Boston, Buffalo, Chicago, Cleveland, Dallas. Detroit, Los Angeles, Minneapolis, New Orleans, New York, Philadelphia, San Francisco, Seattle, Washington, D.C.
14. *Maluquer v. The King* (1925), 38 Que. K.B.1 (C.A.).
15. See R.G. Feltham, *Diplomatic Handbook* (London: Longman Group Ltd.1980), 43–52; and Glen Buick, "The Consul's Helping Hand," *International Perspectives* (July/August 1977): 23–7.
16. J.W. Burton, *System, States, Diplomacy and Rules* (New York: Cambridge University Press 1963), 208.
17. Sir Harold Nicholson, *Diplomacy*, 4th ed. (New York: Oxford University Press 1988), 23.
18. See Dean Pruitt, "An Analysis of Responsiveness between Nations," *Journal of Conflict Resolution* 6, no. 1 (1962): 5–18.
19. Canada, *Canadian Representatives Abroad*, 74.
20. See Derek Burney, "Canada-U.S. Trade Relations under the Bush Administration: Canada Counts," delivered to the Canadian Lumbermen's Association, Montreal, February 16, 1989.
21. See Holsti, *International Politics*, 443–47.

SUGGESTED READINGS

R.B. Bartson, *Modern Diplomacy* (Essex, Eng.: Longman 1988).

Hans Binnendijk, ed., *National Negotiating Styles* (Washington, D.C.: Foreign Service Institute 1987).

Seyom Brown, *New Forces, Old Forces and the Future of World Politics* (Glenview, IL: Scott, Foresman & Co. 1988).

Grant McClanahan, *Diplomatic Immunity* (London: C. Hurst & Co. 1988).

Marin Herz, ed., *The Consular Dimension of Diplomacy: A Symposium* (Washington, D,C.: Institute for the Study of Diplomacy, University Press of America, 1983).

George McGhee, *Diplomacy for the Future* (Washington, D.C.: University Press of America 1987).

David Newsom, *The Diplomacy of Human Rights* (Washington, D.C.: University Press of America 1986).

Kim Richard Nossal, *The Politics of Canadian Foreign Policy* (Scarborough, ON: Prentice-Hall 1989).

Smith Simpson, *Perspectives on the Study of Diplomacy* (Washington, D.C.: Institute for the Study of Diplomacy 1986).

Smith Simpson and Margery Boichel, eds., *Education in Diplomacy: An Instructional Guide* (Washington, D.C.: Institute for the Study of Diplomacy, University Press of America 1988).

GLOSSARY

negotiate: A technique for settling disputes whereby each party attempts to obtain what it desires from the other party by making concessions and by demonstrating a willingness to end the dispute.

polis: Greek city-state that practised independent decision making, permitted the direct political participation of its population, and competed vigorously with its neighbours for territorial and economic status.

inviolability: The universally recognized principle that diplomatic agents and their property should be protected from harm by the host nation.

safe conduct: A guarantee or security granted by a sovereign to an envoy or a stranger for his or her safety coming into or passing out of the jurisdiction of the state.

diplomatic immunities: Exemptions applied to diplomatic representatives of one state from certain internal civil and criminal jurisdictions of the state to which the representatives are accredited.

agrément: An official gesture of response by a government of the acceptability of a foreign diplomat who will be sent to it.

fifth column: A subversive strategy to weaken a government by infiltrating its organization in order to cause division, dissent, and disorder.

sabotage: Originally referred to the practice (during the early stages of the industrial revolution) of workers placing their shoes (sabots) into machinery so as to grind production to a halt; in diplomacy the term refers to the wilful obstruction and interference with the normal diplomatic processes with the aim to inconvenience or discourage normal relations.

règlement: An agreement to establish rules, regulations, controls, and conditions to govern the conduct of officials under special circumstances.

summit diplomacy: The conduct of diplomacy by heads of state or governments instead of at the ambassadorial or ministerial level.

rapprochement: The establishment of normal diplomatic and commercial relations between rival states after a period of estrangement.

accredited: An officially acknowledged envoy or diplomat who possesses the formal credentials of a representative having the general authority to act on behalf of a foreign sovereign.

persona grata: An expression used to indicate that a particular diplomatic agent is acceptable as an official representative of a foreign state.

protocol: A document or practice serving as the preliminary to, or opening of, any diplomatic transaction.

recall: To summon a diplomat back to the sending state.

national security: A premise that each state is required to protect and promote certain basic interests if it is to survive physically and if its political, economic, and social values are to be maintained.

legal proceeding: This term includes all legal actions authorized or sanctioned by law and brought or instituted in a court of justice or legal tribunal for the acquiring of a right or the enforcement of a remedy.

counterclaim: A claim presented by a defendant in opposition or deduction from the claim of the plaintiff.

diplomatic bag: A sealed pouch or valise, clearly marked and identified as diplomatic property, that contains official records and documents for communication between an embassy and the sending state.

consul: A foreign-service official appointed to represent various commercial, minor diplomatic, and service functions on behalf of a state.

exequatur: Many states, although not required by international law to receive foreign consuls, issue a document called an exequatur, which authorizes the consul to exercise a professional jurisdiction within the territory of the receiving state, with all the privileges and immunities customarily granted to such officers.

16

Challenge and Change in the Nuclear Age

Red Army engineers prepare to destroy Soviet missiles

International Turbulence

As we enter the final years of the twentieth century most of the leaders of the great and small powers of the world talk about peace with more confidence and conviction now than they did just a few years ago. This decade began with as much international turbulence as previous decades, except that in the 1990s the margin of safety for human survival is much narrower than ever before. The destructive capacity of modern military technologies has never been so great. Up to now, despite the awesome power of contemporary weapons, the world has been lucky enough to continue its history. But the transition from limited conventional weapons to the global destruction of nuclear weapons is only a matter of pressing a different set of buttons. The British movie *Threads* was a startling vision of how a limited war in the Middle East can escalate into the dreaded nuclear holocaust.[1] As this movie vividly showed, the international community as a whole is vulnerable to the escalation of any political and military brush-fires.

By the end of the 1980s the world seemed to be moving in a direction of moderation and conciliation. In 1988 the Nobel Peace Prize was presented to an army of 10 000 from thirty-five states – including 1300 Canadian soldiers – who wore the blue berets of peace-keeping to guard the truce lines for the United Nations. In the same year Iran and Iraq accepted a peace plan to end their eight-year war of attrition that had killed millions on both sides. In 1989, the Soviet Union completed its military withdrawal from Afghanistan, ending nine years of invasion. In the same year presidents of the Central American republics reached an agreement on a regional strategy for peace. American-Soviet entente promised to move the process of disarmament beyond the reductions of the Intermediate Range Nuclear Forces (INF) treaty. And, at the United Nations, Gorbachev delivered his message of peace on earth and good will between rival power blocs. Inter-bloc tensions were further reduced in November 1989, when authorities of the German Democratic Republic permitted their citizens to pass freely through "Checkpoint Charlie" into West Berlin. Once the Berlin Wall had been breached, the entire Iron Curtain began to crumble, and the two Berlins became effectively one after twenty-eight years of enforced separations.

As we enter the 1990s, the old Eastern European question, "Can totalitarian socialism be reformed?" has become "Can it survive at all?" The domino effect of democratization shows that "people power" can penetrate the political and psychological repression of totalitarian rule. In none of the East European states caught up in the process of democratic change can totalitarian socialists find much cause for hope. Even inside the Soviet Union, democratization has transformed the Baltic states, legalizing multi-party systems in defiance of Moscow's wishes.

The Challenge of Peace

George Santayana warned us of the dangers of not remembering the past. It is perhaps even more dangerous to remember the past incorrectly. Throughout all history, every major military technology invented – including nuclear weapons – has been used in wars among groups and states. The danger of nuclear war is part of a much older problem, which is that humans will use violence to settle disputes among themselves. Long before the existence of nuclear arsenals, societies could and did destroy one another. Earlier eras are distinguished from the present not by the amount of destruction one combatant could potentially inflict on another, but rather by the options available to those that survive the destructiveness of modern military technology.

In the present era, the set of alternatives available is quite limited – if, indeed, any are left. In today's world, what invalidates the previous asymmetry of military verdicts is the fact that there is no longer any strategic superiority*.[2] Throughout any confrontation, both sides will retain the capability to destroy one another. Nuclear-armed missiles and bombers can withstand an enemy's attack and retaliate with devastating force – for all practical purposes destroying the attacker's economy, industrial base, and population, not to mention those of neighbouring states. The long-range effects on the ecology of the planet are inestimable. In the nuclear age, ultimate strategic capabilities have cancelled one another out, making the risks of global devastation unacceptable. It is ironic that the historic race to build the most destructive weapons should now lead competitors to consider an option that was available to them from the dawn of human history: peace. "Peace, which costs nothing, is attended with infinitely more advantage than any victory with all its expense" (Thomas Paine).[3] At no other time in human history has world peace been more of a challenge.

The term peace is often given a multiplicity of meanings. Some define peace narrowly as the absence of war. But to the majority of people in the West, peace is more than the mere absence of war.[4] The word has positive connotations, implying rights to pursue human happiness through economic, social, and political opportunity. Religious and political thinking reinforce this positive view. Peace and good will are definitely linked to our conception of what is morally right and politically desirable. Peace is associated with trust, mutual respect, and with living free from the reality of war. On the international level, peace means the free collaboration and interaction of nation-states. At a personal level, peace is a state of mind.

The relative character of this highly prized human goal is subject to differing and, at times, contradictory interpretations between the East and the West. Peace, like wealth or well-being, is a highly charged ideological concept. For some socialist states, peace is possible only after the conflict between capitalism and communism has been resolved. Historically, Soviet ideology accepted the role of war in promoting revolutionary change and in advancing the cause of socialism. It reserved the right to engage in war to pursue its vision of peace. In July 1963, the Central Committee of the Soviet Communist Party expressed its view of peace in an open letter to all communists: "The struggle for peace and for peaceful coexistence is organically bound up with the revolutionary struggle against capitalist imperialism."[5]

It is not difficult to infer that differing ideological perspectives of peace have generated barriers of distrust among states. The world of interstate relations is viewed by many leaders, especially those of the superpowers, as essentially predatory and anarchic. Working on this ideological presumption, states spend resources on arms in order to engage or deter aggression, and thus to achieve greater security. In these circumstances, peace is equated with military preparedness, deterrence, and arms competition.

As we approach the year 2000, the challenge to peace focusses upon the buildup and possession of weapons. After the atomic bomb was invented, the choices available to humankind became narrower and more ominous. The subsequent development of thermonuclear weapons and sophisticated delivery systems of great range and accuracy severely limited our choices. Of course, the dismantling of these weapons is an option, by far the most attractive.[6] Nuclear weapons can be dismantled, but they cannot be disinvented. In a world of such divergent ideological focus, the level of trust necessary for complete nuclear disarmament is now beginning to rise. The immediate problem is to use all available political and legal instruments to ensure that nuclear weapons are not used, and to survive international conflict engaging conventional weapons as best we can. But although nuclear weapons are widely viewed to present the gravest threat to world peace, in fact its greatest threat arises from conventional weapons. Today's conventional weapons are approaching the destructive scale of nuclear weapons without the residual radioactive effects. Recent wars in the Middle East and in the South Atlantic bear out this view. Even at the level of small-group terrorism, modern conventional technology has severe destructive potential. In any international conflict involving armed aggression, the spiral of violence blurs the distinctions between conventional and nuclear war, both because of the misery it inflicts and because it could possibly erupt into a nuclear confrontation.

The notion that adding more nuclear weapons to existing arsenals will deter aggression is under fire in nuclear- and non-nuclear-weapon states.[7] World wide, the nuclear-deterrence theory adopted by military strategists since the 1950s is being challenged by the peace movement. Peace activists are found in every country of the world and they advocate plans for nuclear-arms control ranging from unilateral disarmament* to freezes, bans, and moratoriums. The notion of *nuclear freeze* calls for an immediate halt to the development, production, transfer, and deployment of nuclear weapons. But although the idea is popular just about everywhere, there is disagreement as to whether the freeze should be "unilateral," or "mutual and verifiable."

Britain's Campaign for Nuclear Disarmament (CND) calls on all nuclear-weapon states to dismantle their nuclear arsenals. The CND is anti-military, anti-American, and anti-NATO. In Canada, groups such as the Canadian Peace Congress and Project Ploughshares want Canada to be a nuclear-weapon-free zone* (NWFZ).[8] This position includes opting out of the North Warning System for continental defence and refusing to permit U.S. Trident submarines from entering Canadian waters. The agenda of some peace activists also calls on Canada to leave NATO and proclaim its neutrality outside of the Western alliance. The Toronto Disarmament Network (TDN), formed in 1981, represents over sixty peace groups that maintain a network of organization and communication with other disarmament groups around the world. Besides this group, nearly 1000 peace groups are operating in the country.

In much the same spirit, peace activists in Europe have rallied against the presence of nuclear weapons on their continent, targeted at the Soviet Union. The European Nuclear Disarmament (END) is organized to persuade nuclear-weapon states in both the East and West to renounce the possession and use of their arsenals. They call for a zone free of nuclear weapons from Portugal to Poland. In the Soviet Union, peace advocates have called for a NWFZ in Central and Eastern Europe.[9]

Another proposal is the "zone of peace" (ZOP)*. The concept goes much further than the NWFZ. The ZOP is a regional approach to general disarmament and is not merely a ban on one particular type of dangerous weapon. States that would compose the zone agree to resolve their disputes peacefully, without resorting to conventional or nuclear arms. It is also envisioned as a zone for regional economic and social co-operation. The concept was endorsed by the UN General Assembly in 1978, but rejected by the superpowers because it would deprive them of their military bases, present in virtually every region of the world. However, in 1988 Mikhail Gorbachev suggested that the Arctic be declared a zone of peace and in 1989 the Soviet ambassador to Canada reiterated that idea to the Mulroney government. No response was forthcoming from Canada. In relation to great-power interests, the concept of the ZOP is acceptable only if the region selected neutralizes the military bases of their adversaries. The ZOP is a concept with increasing appeal.

Although millions of people from all continents have been involved in the peace movement, peace activism has not been successful, in part because its promotion of destabilizing proposals, if adopted, would weaken the strategic advantage of an alliance system. For example, if Canada became an NWFZ, it could destabilize the strategic balance in favour of the Soviet Union and would still not provide any guarantee that Canadians would escape attack. Disarmament must be linked with mutual security. The final document of the first United Nations Special Session on Disarmament in 1978 stressed that "genuine and lasting peace can only be created through the effective implementation of the security system provided for in the Charter of the United Nations": Other suitable institutions – such as the International Court of Justice and regional intergovernmental bodies – exist, but they are under-used. States in conflict all too often resort to power politics.[10]

Perhaps humankind's best chance at peace – or at least of preservation – is never to become complacent. Some people believe that humankind will muddle through, that the world's small wars will never get out of hand, and that anyone who argues otherwise is engaging in millennial ravings. But the contagious nature of conflict should rule out complacency. So long as political disputes continue to be resolved by military means, there is grave danger that some small spark – some little war far from our homes – could detonate the nuclear arsenals.

Peace is not simply something that follows war, although historically peace has been successfully imposed by stronger powers. It is a human relationship at which people choose to work. It first requires the political will to eliminate the root causes of conflict. This effort involves trust, the opening of all possible lines of international communication, and the strengthening and reform of international institutions. It requires an increase in economic and social interaction: people doing business with each other and meeting each other through a vast network of social exchanges involving the arts, the sciences, sports, and tourism. At the level of international organization, each bloc will have to recognize and respect the security of others. In the process, a gradual and balanced reduction of conventional and nuclear weapons can be obtained. After decades of distrust, the "open skies" proposal (1990) between NATO and Warsaw Pact states promises to build confidence in this new decade of arms control negotiations by making it possible for the air forces of East and West to fly over each other's territories and share surveillance aircraft and technology. However, just as arms control is essential, so is it necessary to address the global problems of population and hunger before a lasting peace is achieved. These are the immediate challenges.

The Challenge of Arms Control

Since the turn of the century numerous international efforts have been made to control the deadly game of the arms race*. Weapons of every conceivable genre were developed or acquired by most states in the international community. Even before the first atomic bomb was tested, other weapons of mass destruction (chemical* and biological*) were being stockpiled for military use.[11] As early as 1915, chemical weapons had made their appearance on the battlefields of Europe – and Canadians were among the first casualties. By the end of World War I, 1 300 000 people were victims of chemical warfare.

The Hague International Peace conferences of 1899 and 1907 were the first proposals for international arms control standards[12] (table 16.1). The Geneva Protocol of 1925 (signed and ratified by over 110 states) prohibits the use of asphyxiating, poisonous, or other gases and analogous liquids in warfare between states party to the agreement. But the protocol did not prohibit the development, production, and stockpiling of such weapons. By 1990 nearly twenty states possessed chemical weapons. In March 1988, one of those states – Iraq – unleashed mustard and cyanide gas on its own Kurdish civilians in Halabja.

During the 1950s and 1960s, progress in the negotiating rounds at the United Nations was very slow because there was no agreement on whether weapons of mass destruction should be considered separately.[13] A number of milestone treaties were initiated by the superpowers to restrain the use and proliferation of nuclear weapons[14] (table 16.1). The Antarctic Treaty of 1959 made the Antarctic the first non-nuclear continent and prohibits all military activities there. In 1963, the Partial Test Ban Treaty entered into force banning the testing of nuclear devices in the atmosphere, outer space, and under water. The 1974 Threshold Nuclear Test Ban Treaty prohibits nuclear testing underground with explosive yields over 150 kilotons. The 1976 Peaceful Nuclear Explosions Treaty controls nuclear testing for non-military purposes. At the same time, the world witnessed the development of new generations of more sophisticated and deadly weapons at an unprecedented pace. However, in 1971, Canada, Czechoslovakia, Poland, Romania, the USSR, the United Kingdom, and the United States revised a proposal made at the Conference of the Committee on Disarmament (CCD). It became the Convention on the Prohibition of the Development, Production, and Stockpiling of Bacteriological (Biological) and Toxin Weapons and on their Destruction, which was adopted by the General Assembly in 1972 and entered into force in 1975. Under the provisions of this convention, the parties renounce the development, use, and transfer of these weapons and undertake to destroy them within nine months of ratification. A review conference was held in Geneva in 1980, where most states expressed satisfaction that the convention was comprehensive enough to encompass recent technological developments for these kinds of weapons.

In 1985, the General Assembly, on recommendations by the Ad Hoc Committee on Chemical Weapons, called for the speediest conclusion of a convention banning chemical weapons and providing for their destruction. Since that time, many superpower summits placed the issue of chemical weapons on their agenda. In Paris, 1989, representatives from 149 states reaffirmed the spirit of the Geneva Protocol and pledged to move the

Conventions on arms control

Convention	Description	Date signed	Number of Signatories
Geneva Protocol	Bans the use of gas or bacteriological weapons	1925	111
Antarctic Treaty	Internationalizes and demilitarizes the continent	1959	33
Partial Test Ban	Bans nuclear tests in the atmosphere, in outer space, or under water	1963	116
Outer Space Treaty	Internationalizes and demilitarizes outer space, the moon, and other celestial bodies	1967	89
Latin American Nuclear Free Zone	Bans nuclear weapons in Latin America	1967	23
Non-Proliferation Treaty	Bans selling, giving or receiving nuclear weapons, nuclear materials, or nuclear technology for other than peaceful purposes	1968	136
Seabed Arms Control	Bans nuclear weapons in or under the seabed	1971	78
Biological Weapons Convention	Bans the production and possession of bacteriological and other toxic weapons	1972	107
SALT I	Limited the number and types of U.S. and USSR strategic weapons (expired 1977)	1972	2
ABM Treaty	U.S. and USSR agreed to limit antiballistic missile sites and to no further ABM development	1972	2
Threshold Test Ban	Limits underground tests to 150 kt for US and USSR (not ratified but its provisions are observed)	1974	2
Environmental Modification Treaty	Bans environmental modification as a form of warfare	1977	51
Salt II	Limits the number and types of U.S. and USSR strategic weapons (not ratified but its provisions are observed)	1979	2
The Moon Treaty	Bans placing nuclear weapons on or in orbit of the moon	1979	54
Physical Protection of Nuclear Material	Provides protection standards on materials during shipment and for recovering lost/stolen materials	1980	34
South Pacific Nuclear-Free Zone	Bans making and acquiring nuclear weapons in the region	1985	9
Intermediate-Range Nuclear Forces	Eliminates all U.S. and USSR missiles of inter-mediate range (500 km – 5000 km)	1987	2

Source: SIPRI Yearbook 1987 (Oxford: Oxford University Press 1987)

Table 16.1

international community towards a treaty to ban the "use" of all chemical weapons.

The acronym SALT represents the first round of Strategic Arms Limitations Talks between the United States and the Soviet Union over a two-and-a-half-year period from 1970 to 1972.[15] The SALT I Anti-Ballistics Missiles (ABM) Treaty prohibited the United States and the Soviet Union from constructing ABM defence systems at more than two sites. Both parties further agreed to freeze the number of offensive ballistic missile launches at their existing levels until 1977. The SALT II ABM Protocol, signed in Moscow in 1974, further limited the superpowers to one defensive site and committed both parties to limit the number of warheads they carry. SALT II was never ratified by the U.S. Senate even though both Jimmy Carter and Ronald Reagan were committed to arms limitations.[16] But both the Soviet Union and the United States adhere to the spirit of its provisions.

The acronym START was coined by the Reagan administration in 1980 to begin a new round of nuclear-arms negotiations as distinguished from SALT I and SALT II. The Strategic Arms Reduction Talks brought the Americans and Soviets to the bargaining table in Geneva in 1982. The talks involved not only weapons deployed by the superpowers, but also the intermediate nuclear forces (INF) in Europe. After six years of intensive negotiations, the United States and the Soviet Union signed the intermediate-nuclear-forces treaty in 1987, eliminating an entire class of nuclear weapons from Europe and from the rest of the world. These weapons comprise the intermediate-range weapons that could be deployed closer to their intended targets. The agreement called for the destruction of 1752 Soviet and 859 U.S. missiles and established rigorous on-site verification procedures, preparing the way for more comprehensive reductions under START.

A daunting challenge faces the negotiators for the United States and the Soviet Union as they sit down in the future to practise the summitry of arms control. The major offensive weapons subject to negotiations are the intercontinental ballistic missiles*, bombers, and submarine-launched missiles, all of which are deadly accurate and capable of rendering nuclear devastation on an unimaginable scale. If they fail, the incomprehensible and unacceptable spectre of nuclear war looms over all humankind. Every word exchanged behind the closed doors of disarmament negotiations has a direct impact on every citizen of this planet.[17]

Both the United States and the Soviet Union have stockpiled a variety of these weapons, and nearly all of them were deployed on the European continent. Throughout the 1960s and 1970s, Europe became a nuclear fortress with British, French, and U.S. weapons assigned to NATO states aimed at the technologically inferior Soviet SS-4 and SS-5 missiles. This state of nuclear affairs did not sit well with Soviet military strategists. In 1977, the Soviet Union set out to change the nuclear balance of power in Europe. The instrument of this change was the SS-20 missile (reduced by the INF treaty), a mobile and accurate multiple warhead missile that can be moved thousands of miles and launched from a trailer. A new Soviet ICBM – the SS-25, unveiled in the late 1980s – is as mobile as the SS-20, can cover the same targets (hitting the United States sooner), and dodges the provisions of the INF treaty.

The discussions that began in Geneva in 1982 may take years to reach a conclusion because of the enormous number of strategic weapons that have been accumulated since the 1970s. But the economic burden of an uncontrolled arms race may motivate the superpowers to come to terms on matters of trust and arms reduction sooner than expected in the 1990s.

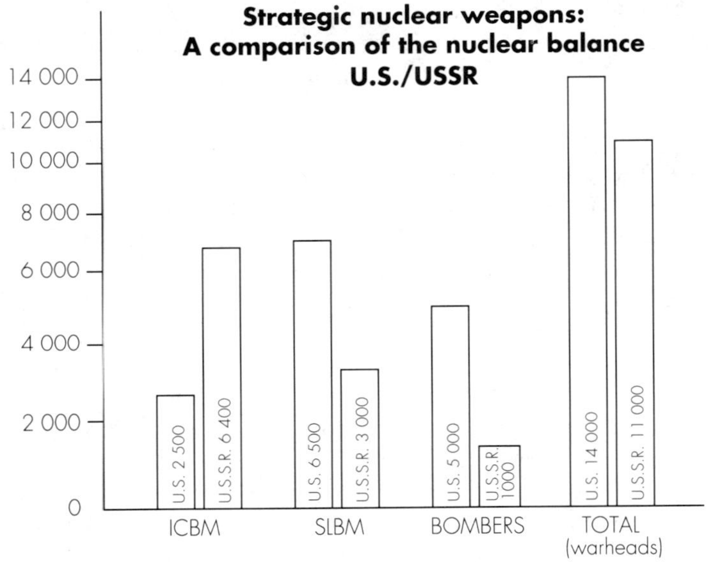

Source: International Institute for Strategic Studies, *The Military Balance,* 1987 - 1988 (London: IISS, 1988)

Figure 16.1

Strategic Weapons

The field of nuclear-arms control has accumulated more than its share of acronyms, but the most notorious one is MAD (mutually assured destruction)*. Simply put, the doctrine of mutually assured destruction holds that neither side will launch a nuclear attack so long as it knows that the other side will be able to retaliate with an equally devastating nuclear blow. MAD is the fundamental dynamic behind the concept of modern deterrence. But not all nuclear weapons provide the same deterrent value. For example, large land-based missiles and strategic bombers are not by themselves the best deterrent because the missiles are in fixed silos that could be destroyed in a first strike and the bombers take hours to reach their targets. In contrast, nuclear submarines are a very credible deterrent because they are harder to detect and to destroy at sea. Thus, they are not vulnerable to a first strike.

In the 1970s, the Americans and the Soviets developed MIRV technology (multiple independently targetable re-entry vehicles). This means that each missile is armed with more than one warhead, each independently targetable. For example, all U.S. submarine-based missiles and the MX (experimental missile) carry 8–10 nuclear warheads; the giant Soviet SS-18 missile is normally equipped to carry 10 warheads, but is capable of carrying up to 30. This multiple-warhead technology makes arms control very complicated. Now warheads have to be counted, too. By 1990, the United States could explode nearly 14 000 strategic nuclear weapons on the Soviet Union; the Soviets could explode about 11 000 nuclear weapons on the United States and Canada[18] (figure 16.1). When tactical nuclear weapons* are added to strategic* ones, the total combined arsenal of the two superpowers still equals about 50 000 nuclear weapons. Because of this unimaginable arsenal of destructive power, the fact remains that neither superpower can claim superiority in nuclear weapons.[19] Even if only 10 percent of the arsenal was used, each side would destroy the other side many times over. The irony is that nuclear weapons really provide no defence. It matters not which side strikes first and which side retaliates. Both the superpowers and many of their neighbouring countries will be destroyed utterly and completely. In effect, the superpowers are mutually inferior because there can be no superiority in mutual destruction.

Star Wars

Arms talks between the superpowers had never focussed specifically on space weapons until the Geneva negotiations began in June 1982. When former president Reagan announced his Strategic Defense Initiative (SDI) in 1983, he moved the world into a new era of nuclear competition.[20] SDI or Star Wars replaces the principle of Mutual Assured Destruction (MAD) with a theory of assured defence – a kind of high-tech shield wherein "fifth generation" computers would scan the skies to search and destroy enemy ICBMs. But SDI is only a strategic dream: it is still at least a decade and a trillion dollars away from reality. As they are conceived, space-based and ground-based systems would detect, track, and intercept Soviet ICBMs on their way to targets in the United States and Canada. Several weapons are being considered: particle beams, chemical lasers, lasers propelled by nuclear explosions, and lasers bounced off mirrors poised in space.[21] But even if all defensive systems were in place, some warheads would still reach their targets.

Supporters of the SDI systems say that this is a U.S. trump card, both in terms of deterrence and in future arms-reduction talks because the Soviets have neither the money nor the technology to match Star Wars. Opponents of SDI systems say that the Soviets will be encouraged to build a more massive arsenal of ICBMs capable of penetrating any American space-based defence system.

But there is a second category of weapons that has been the object of intense competitive research in both the United States and the Soviet Union – anti-satellite weapons (ASATs). Since the first satellite, *Sputnik*, was launched by the Soviet Union in 1957, the Americans and the Soviets have orbited more than 200 military satellites in space.[22] They constitute the strategic eyes and ears of the superpowers. It has been reported that some satellites are powerful enough to zoom in on the ground and photograph newspaper headlines. To attack these satellites would amount to blinding the enemy; such an attack would be the first step in a nuclear conflict. Both sides have been developing these anti-satellite weapons since *Sputnik* orbited the earth three decades ago.

The deployment of space weapons would contravene as many as ten international agreements. Among the most important is the Anti-Ballistic Missile Treaty of 1972. But the treaty does not specifically ban research into space weapons. SDI has altered the character of international arms negotiations well into the twenty-first century. The possibility of superpower arsenals in space could provide an obstacle, a trigger, a latch, or the key to success in achieving world peace.

Peace in Space

Since the launching of the first human-made satellites, the exploration of space moved from a dream to a challenge. With it came the beneficial opportunity to infinitely expand human knowledge. But the conquest of this new frontier was accompanied by the danger that it would one day become an extension of territorial conflict. The Soviet Union and the United States, especially, have enhanced their military strength on earth by developing numerous communications, navigation, and reconnaissance satellites. Canada has been involved in outer space for about thirty years, since the launching of the *Alouette* I satellite in 1962. A Canadian Policy for Space was adopted in 1974. It states that Canadian space technology will be used for peaceful purposes. The development of CANADARM, which was used on the U.S. Space Shuttle and the Canadian Astronaut Programme, has captured much public attention.

The peaceful benefits of space exploration involve communications, remote sensing, industry science, and interplanetary travel.[23] The International Telecommunications Satellite Organization (INTELSAT) was created in 1964 to rapidly transfer information related to news, sports, and cultural events. In 1975, only Canada, the Soviet Union, and the United States had communications satellite systems. By 1990, INTELSAT with its fifteen systems had over 100 member-states, including Canada, and formed the nucleus of the global-space based telecommunications system. Canada owns and operates four INTELSAT earth stations and has played a vital role in the international use of space for communications purposes.[24] In 1969, TELSAT CANADA was created to operate Canada's domestic satellite communications system, the backbone of which is the ANIK series.

Another non-military opportunity in space is remote sensing. In 1972, the United Nations Committee on the Peaceful Uses of Outer Space (COPUOS) gave global approval to the remote observation of the earth's surface, its weather patterns, environmental depletions, and other phenomena by means of air–borne and space-borne platforms. Remote-sensing satellites scan the topography of the planet to gather precise data to be shared by all states and international organizations. Two of the more commonly known uses of remote sensing are weather forecasting (to gather data on hurricanes, tornadoes, and other severe storms) and crop assessment (to gather data on crops, forests, grasslands, deserts, and fisheries). Canada uses information provided by the U.S. LANDSAT satellites for resource management to measure forest and crop inventories and to study ice-flow patterns.[25] The

SARSAT search and rescue program created by Canada, France, and the United States locates airplanes and ocean vessels that are in trouble.

Commercial satellites provide enormous opportunities for industrial development and experimentation. Weightlessness and airlessness in space make possible the production of certain goods that are not efficiently manufactured on earth. For example, the manufacture of homogeneous crystals, so important to the electronics industry, are much more efficiently produced in conditions present in space. New or better drugs can also be manufactured in the weightless environment of space. Almost every field of human enterprise will benefit from space exploration.

Space provides living organisms, from the microbe to the human being, with unique environmental conditions in which life forms can be studied and scientific knowledge expanded. Many biomedical, behavioural, and life-support studies have already been conducted to increase the scientific body of human knowledge.

But space has also been assigned a strategic importance by a growing number of states. In reviewing the use of commercial satellites, it is necessary to realize that they also serve both a defensive and military purpose. Over the past four decades, the Soviet Union and the United States have launched a far greater number of military satellites than commercial or civilian satellites. By the 1990s, the number of military satellites deployed stabilized at around 100 satellites a year. Early-warning satellites and other electronic intelligence satellites make it virtually impossible for any state to conceal its military preparations.

The growth in the deployment of space-based technologies spawned the development of international law[26] regarding the sovereign and military uses of outer space. There is still no internationally agreed-upon definition of where the boundary is that divides national air space and outer space. Scientists of the Committee on Space Research (COPSAR) have recommended the lower boundary of outer space be established at an altitude of 100 km. This is the altitude at which satellites can orbit freely beyond the earth's gravitational pull. Many states, including Canada, believe it is important to reach agreement on a space boundary because of the legal and practical risks in the application of a growing regime of space law.

In 1963, the Partial Test Ban Treaty (PTBT) prohibited the explosion of nuclear weapons above the atmosphere. In 1967, COPUOS drafted The Outer Space Treaty prohibiting the extension of sovereignty beyond national air space. Signatories to this treaty agree not to orbit weapons of mass destruction, install such weapons on celestial bodies, or establish military bases in space. The ABM Treaty (1972) between the United States and the Soviet Union also related to space by prohibiting each party from developing, testing, and deploying ABM systems that are air-based and space-based. Another agreement that governs the activities of states on the moon and other celestial bodies is The Moon Treaty (1979), which prohibits placing nuclear weapons on or around the moon.

The challenges of space are many and they are perceived in various ways by different governments. To a few, space is the logical arena for the projection of political and military power. To others, space is yet another opportunity for international co-operation and exploration where scientific benefits can be derived from exchanges of information, from joint efforts on the problems of space research, and from the pooling of financial, human, and material resources.

The Challenge of Nuclear Proliferation

As far back as the mid 1940s, when the first development of nuclear weapons was in process under the Manhattan Project,* U.S. scientists were arguing for the non-proliferation of nuclear-weapons' technology. By the early 1950s, the United States, United Kingdom, France, USSR, and China had begun to build and expand their nuclear programs almost solely to amass weapons, and they designed and operated nuclear facilities for that purpose.

Nuclear candidates with demonstrated capabilities

Argentina:
Has the capacity to enrich uranium and is working toward the construction of its first nuclear weapon, sometime in the 1990s.

Iran:
An ambitious nuclear strategy was initiated under the Shah. In 1981, the Khomeini regime renewed Iran's interests in developing its nuclear facilities. It is difficult to get reliable sources within Iran to confirm the progress of its nuclear-weapon capacity. But Iran will need more time to build its own bomb.

Iraq:
Israel bombed Iraq's nuclear facilities in the early 1980s and thereby delayed the progress of Iraq's nuclear capacity. But Iraq has substantial quantities of uranium and it is just a matter of time before it assembles its first nuclear weapon, quite possibly in the early 1990s.

South Korea:
This state has had a vibrant nuclear-energy program since the 1970s and promises to develop its own nuclear weapons if the United States should withdraw its military presence and guarantees.

Taiwan:
Taiwan developed an ambitious nuclear-energy program in the early 1970s and will soon possess a complete domestic nuclear-fuel cycle.

Source: Firdaus James Kharas and Helene Samson, "Nuclear Proliferation," *Briefing Paper* (Ottawa: United Nations Association, October 1984), 6; John T. Rourke, *International Politics on the World Stage* (Guilford, CT: Dushkin Publishing Company 1989), 484–9; and Leonard Spector, *Going Nuclear* (Cambridge, MA: Ballinger 1987), passim

Table. 16.2

In the 1980s, Brazil, India, Israel, North Korea, Pakistan, and South Africa all developed the capacity to assemble and stockpile nuclear weapons. These eleven states are the principal nuclear-weapons powers into the 1990s. However, estimates range from as low as eleven to over sixteen states that will have nuclear weapons by the turn of the century (table 16.2).

States desire to acquire nuclear weapons for many complex military and political reasons.[27] Among the most obvious reasons are international prestige and enhanced military power. But the possession of nuclear weapons is also viewed as the ultimate deterrence against external aggression. However, the danger of nuclear proliferation* is that the option of nuclear weapons available to a wide dispersion of political decision makers increases both the possibility and probability of their deployment. As nuclear weapons spread, there is intense pressure on many governments to develop these weapons because others have or may do so.

The miniaturization of nuclear weapons makes their acquisition more likely for transnational groups as well as for states that do not have the capacity to manufacture them.[28] Present trends point to the acquisition of nuclear weapons by international actors that may be more inclined to resort to nuclear weapons to meet their goals. Conflicts that are currently limited to the use of conventional weapons could more easily involve the use of nuclear weapons should they be in the possession of non-state actors.

The first efforts to contain nuclear proliferation concentrated on regulating the peaceful uses of nuclear power. By 1945 Canada, the United States and the United Kingdom had signed the Agreed Declaration on Atomic Energy, which resolved that nuclear proliferation was a threat to world peace. The following year at the United Nations Atomic Energy Commission, the United States proposed that an international atomic-energy agency be established to regulate and control all aspects of the uses of nuclear energy. One of the first resolutions of the United Nations created the Atomic Energy Commission (AEC) with Canada, China, France, Great Britain, the United States and the USSR as members. The AEC was finally dismantled in 1955 because of disagreements among members as to how to control the spread of nuclear weapons.

In 1957, a separate organization under the aegis of the United Nations, the International Atomic Energy Agency (IAEA), was founded with headquarters in Vienna.[29] The major aim of IAEA is to prevent the diversion of atomic materials to military uses and to disseminate information on the peaceful applications of nuclear technology. Canada was the first state in the world to renounce the possession and spread of nuclear weapons and has been represented on the board of IAEA since it was founded. *Safeguards* are applied by requiring member states to design their nuclear facilities according to international standards, to keep detailed records of nuclear operations, and to submit reports to IAEA. *Inspections* are conducted on site to verify that states are not diverting peaceful nuclear-energy facilities or materials to build nuclear weapons. Still, highly enriched weapons-grade uranium manages to slip by the eyes and ears of the IAEA. These undetected diversions of nuclear materials are a major contributing factor to proliferation. By the 1990s, 525 facilities were producing nuclear materials around the world. This growing number of nuclear-production facilities has made the monitoring of nuclear proliferation a difficult and complicated task.

At the level of international law, the United Nations drafted the Non-Proliferation Treaty (NPT), which entered into force in 1970 and is due for renewal in 1995.[30] About 140 states adhere to the provisions of the NPT, 16 of which have become signatories since 1980. They agree not to transfer nuclear weapons or assist non-nuclear-weapon states to manufacture them. And non-nuclear-weapon states agree to abide by IAEA safeguards on the peaceful application of nuclear technology. But many states have not signed the NPT, primarily because they see its provisions as discriminatory between states that have already

Non-signatories to the NPT: Selected states

Albania	China	Israel	Tanzania
Algeria	Cuba	Kampuchea	Uganda
Angola	France	Mozambique	Vietnam
Argentina	Guinea	Pakistan	Zambia
Brazil	Guatemala	Saudi Arabia	
Burma	Guyana	South Africa	
Chile	India		

Source: Firdaus James Kharas and Helene Sampson, "Nuclear Proliferation," *Briefing Paper* (Ottawa: United Nations Association, October 1984), 5; and Canada, Department of External Affairs, *NPT Signatories* (Ottawa 1989)

Table 16.3

manufactured nuclear devices and those that have not (table 16.3). They point out that nuclear-weapon states can keep, and even increase, their arsenals. Non-nuclear countries are under no obligation to submit to IAEA safeguards and inspections, but must do so on signing NPT. Despite the fact that a majority of states are parties to the treaty, the number of nuclear weapons continues to grow and concentrate among the nuclear-weapon states. Many non-nuclear-weapon states assert that those states that have already stockpiled nuclear weapons have not lived up to their obligations to stop spreading nuclear-weapons' technology and to negotiate toward general and complete disarmament.

Because of the shortcomings of the IAEA and the NPT, some states adopted their own controls to nuclear proliferation. After India exploded its nuclear device in 1974, approximately fifteen states, including Canada, formed a nuclear-suppliers cartel, named the "London Club." In 1977, the London Club drafted voluntary export guidelines, designed to ensure that the export of nuclear material be safeguarded. A so-called "trigger list" was made of all sensitive nuclear materials, the export of which require special safeguards. Canada's policy terminates the sale of nuclear materials and equipment to any state that does not apply these safeguards in all its facilities.[31] The United States has developed a similar policy under its Nuclear Non-Proliferation Act. And in Latin America, the Treaty of Tlateloco, signed in 1967, prohibits the acquisition or production of nuclear weapons anywhere in Central and South America. But perhaps the most controversial unilateral action to control nuclear proliferation was initiated in 1981 when Israel bombed a nuclear reactor under construction in Iraq.[32] Israel argued that its attack was a pre-emptive strike against Iraq to prevent developing nuclear weapons. Iraq countered by charging that such an act was extreme, given that the reactor was being constructed according to IAEA standards and Iraq was a signatory of the NPT.

There appears to be a need to improve verification of nuclear facilities wherever they are constructed, if only to avoid suspicions of violations of standards. Such suspicions not only undermine the NPT and the IAEA but also make efforts at arms-control negotiations in all areas more difficult. The threat of nuclear proliferation poses a grave danger not only to international security, but to the survival of all human beings.

Conventional and Other Weapons

While it is true that the world is ultimately threatened by nuclear military technology, it is no less threatened by the advances that have been made in conventional weapons' technology since World War II.[33] Our concern about nuclear weapons has diverted our attention from the proliferation of conventional weapons, particularly in the less developed countries. However, with the exception of the few atomic weapons used against Japan in the mid 1940s, all wars in this century have been fought with conventional weapons supplied by the major industrial powers.

Despite the current world economic recession, the trade in arms has remained buoyant. This trade is dominated by the United States and the Soviet Union, which together supply 70 percent of all arms exports in Asia, Africa, and Latin America.[34] France is the third-largest arms-exporting country in the world, accounting for 11 percent of the market. France's conventional arms sales are targeted at countries that want to avoid dealing with the superpowers. Mirage fighter bombers, Etendard naval fighters, and Exocet air-to-ship missiles are good examples of French conventional weapons being sold abroad. Approximately 60 percent of France's military sales go to the Middle East. Behind France are the United Kingdom, the Federal Republic of Germany, and Italy, which each have a share of the global arms market. Other states have established indigenous arms facilities for the production of conventional weapons and equipment; these include Brazil, India, Iran, Jordan, Libya, Singapore, South Africa, South Korea, and Taiwan.[35]

In 1990, world military expenditures exceeded $1 trillion. About 80 percent of world military expenditures are made for conventional weapons and equipment.[36] In the past decade, developing countries have contributed significantly to the rapid expansion of these purchases. Poor economies, such as Ethiopia and Somalia, spent a greater proportion of their gross domestic product (GDP) than did much wealthier ones such as Norway, Finland,

and the Netherlands. This trend of increased military spending by less developed countries led the United Nations to focus on global military expenditures. Since the United Nations was formed, the General Assembly has on many occasions considered the reduction of military expenditures as an approach to disarmament. In 1978, the United Nations held a Special Session on Disarmament (UNSSOD I). The final document became the basis of the first international arms-control agreement negotiated through special United Nations conference. The Convention on Prohibitions or Restrictions on the Use of Certain Conventional Weapons Which May Be Deemed to Be Excessively Injurious or to Have Indiscriminate Effects and three protocols were opened for signature in 1981. Nearly sixty states have signed the convention; it promises to be a major contribution to the international law of peace. A second Special Session on Disarmament (UNSSOD II) was held in 1982 to continue the development of international law in this area, but a consensus was not achieved on most agenda items and a multilateral convention was not forthcoming.

Canada contributed to the agendas of both UNSSOD I and UNSSOD II, promoting the theme of limiting and reducing conventional weapons under the aegis of the United Nations. Canada controls the export of conventional weapons by the Export and Import Permit Act, which regulates the sale of military materials abroad. The departments of National Defence and External Affairs approve all military sales outside Canada. Nearly 80 percent of Canada's military exports go to the United States and the NATO alliance. Notwithstanding its international efforts to control the conventional arms race, Canada has more than tripled its defence budget in the past decade: And now Canada has been formally invited to participate in Star Wars research, a course that received priority consideration by the Mulroney government and moves Canada into the arena of nuclear deterrence.

The available quantitative evidence on the predictors of war in history challenges the widespread assumption among many world leaders that military strength prevents war and military weakness invites aggression.[37] Some studies now conclude that when disputes are accompanied by arms races they are more likely to escalate into war than disputes that transpire in the absence of arms competition.[38] We know that arms races fail to resolve interstate differences, that they escalate into wars, and that they are – in most cases – the precursors to war. The present arms race is as unprecedented in magnitude as would be the war resulting from it.

The emerging strategic environment of the 1990s and beyond promises not only to be dangerous but also to be very expensive. All states caught up in the spiral of arms competition get less in job creation and general economic advantage from dollars spent on defence than if the same dollars were spent on civilian production. Increased defence spending creates inflation because huge payrolls and expensive weapons inject more money into the economy without increasing the supply of consumer goods.[39] Arms control or reduction does carry an economically beneficial payload. Will this realization act as a deterrent or will it be an irrelevant consideration to national leaders caught in the web of the arms race?

The Challenge of Population

In the eighteenth century, the world's first great demographic transformation began in Europe, raising the earth's total human population from about 800 million in 1750 to 3 billion in 1960 (figure 16.2)[40] Today, with nearly 5.5 billion people populating the earth, human beings number more than any other type of vertebrate, having recently pulled ahead of rats. At the present rate of annual growth of 1.7 percent, there will be one square foot of earth surface for every human being in 700 years. And in 1200 years, the human

Growth of world population (billions of people)

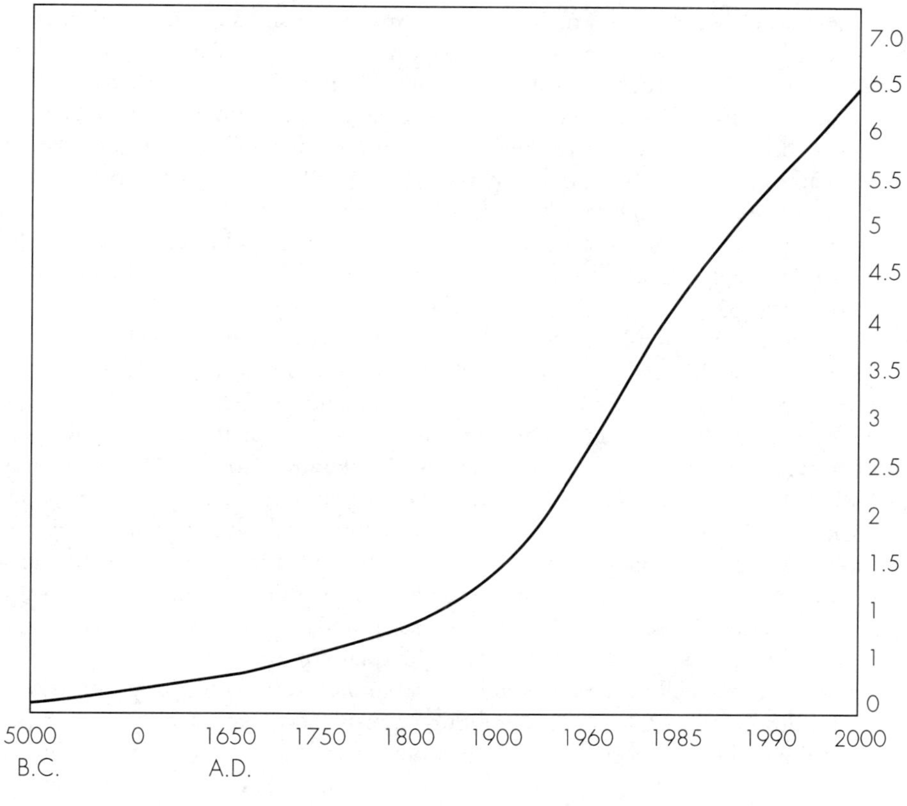

Source: Frederick Pearson and J. Martin Rochester, *International Relations, The Global Condition in the Late Twentieth Century* (Reading, MA: Addison and Wesley Publishing Company 1984), 49

Figure 16.2

population will outweigh the earth. Now that this great transformation is nearly complete, its impact can be analysed. On the surface, the results have been generally positive: the fall in the death rate* has increased life expectancy* to an unprecedented level; most infectious diseases are now medically controllable; and the level of education has risen substantially.

However, a second great demographic transformation has been under way since World War II in the developing countries, and it threatens to undermine the apparent progress of the past 200 years. Population growth in the developing world is far greater than in the developed countries, often more than 3 percent a year (doubling in about twenty years), as against just over 1 percent (doubling in about seventy years). Between 1990 and 2000, about 90 percent of the global population increase will occur in the developing countries. Of the 6.5 billion people expected to be in the world in the year 2000, 5 billion will live in developing countries. The best current estimates also suggest that the population of developing countries will likely double in the next century and thereafter remain stable.[41]

In the industrialized countries of Europe and Australia, Canada, Japan, and the United States, low mortality* has been accompanied by low fertility*. This circumstance is also well under way in countries such as Argentina, Cuba, Hong Kong, and Singapore, where economic development has reached a fairly high level. However, in most of the developing countries of Africa, Asia, and Latin America, this demographic transition has not proceeded far. The death rate has been falling rapidly over the past 40 years, but the fertility rate only began to decrease in the 1980s. It is because of this disparity in the rates that the population of developing countries is still growing rapidly.[42] It remains to be seen how closely the course of demographic transition in the developing world will resemble that of the First World countries.

We know that demographic processes have a built-in momentum that takes years to stabilize. At present, the total population of developing countries, taken as a group, is about 3.5 billion. By 2025 it will have risen to over 7 billion and to 9 billion by 2050. A century from now, the world's population will be over 11 billion.[43] If at that time a World Population Conference is held, representatives of attending states will be discussing the "population explosion" with deep concern. Over the coming decades, the consequences of population growth will challenge the pace of national economic development and the political stability of the developing countries.[44] In these countries, rapid population growth will worsen employment opportunities, exacerbate urban growth, put pressure on food supplies, widen the gap between the rich and poor, and foster non-democratic regimes.

In the years between 1980 and 2000 alone, the total number of working-age people in developing countries will have increased by 1150 million.[45] Only under the most optimal growth conditions in modern-sector labour-intensive economies could these people secure employment. In most developing countries in the 1990s, there are intensive pressures to create jobs in the public sector. In these countries government itself is the major employer. In Kenya, for example, the public sector accounts for two-thirds of the growth in new jobs. The most tangible effects of this trend will be inflation and economic stagnation unless jobs can also be created at the same pace in the agricultural, manufacturing, and service sectors of developing economies. Complicating the challenge of unemployment in developing countries is the problem that future population increases will take place in cities.

The United Nations forecasts that in the decade 1990–2000, the global urban population will grow by 662 million while rural population will grow by 219 million people.[46] The number of Third World cities with populations above 10 million will grow from three to twenty-one by the turn of the century. By the year 2000, Mexico City (31 million) will have more people than Canada; São Paulo (26 million), Shanghai (23 million), and Bombay and Jakarta (each with 17 million) will experience unacceptable levels of congestion and municipal dysfunction. Housing, sewage, garbage collection, and the maintenance of the physical urban infrastructure will all suffer the consequences of overpopulation.

High population growth rates threaten the basic social and economic organization of developing states.[47] Excessive demands are placed on credit, financial, and marketing systems; food production is not sufficient to maintain per capita consumption; illiteracy, malnutrition, and disease diminish the performance of the education and health systems. In the face of such enormous pressures created by demographic expansion, developing states move to strengthen their administrative control over the population. All problems related to rapid population growth tend to be viewed by governments as threats to social stability and political order. In such cases, an authoritarian response to people by government is almost inevitable. Since 1970 in China, for example, the government has instituted a comprehensive birth-control policy involving forced sterilization, abortion, penalties, and fines to reach the goal of one-child families and zero population growth (ZPG)*.

A growing number of states – Bangladesh, India, Kenya, Nigeria, Pakistan, and Zaire – have moved toward a more pervasive regulation of social life, particularly with respect to birth control. Some states, such as China and Cuba, restrict movement from rural to urban areas so as to control rapid population growth in certain areas of the country. And restraints on reproductive freedom may become more common where governments through incapacity or lack of awareness allow demographic pressures to build to extremes. Sheer numbers here can overwhelm national borders and administrative capacities. Some governments have adopted measures aimed at greater social responsibility in the reproductive decisions made by families without coercively intruding into the decisions themselves. Such measures largely come down to reducing fertility. They are reflected in policies to expand basic family education, to promote a social consensus favouring small families, to ensure a more equitable distribution of income, and above all else, to raise the status of women socially, economically, and politically. Brazil, Sri Lanka, South Korea, and Taiwan currently follow policy prescriptions along such lines.

While it is true that uncontrolled population can and does perpetuate poverty in a country, it is also true that a small population can keep a country poor.[48] A small population can compound and exacerbate national economic and social difficulties. Today, there are about 100 countries with populations under 12 million, about one-half of these with populations under 6 million. Most countries with less than 6 million are found in Africa (27) and in the Americas (15). States with small populations face higher costs to administer social-development programs because their tax revenues are small.[49] Their markets are not big enough to attract labour-intensive or capital-intensive industries, resulting in a low level of domestic competition, a tendency to form monopolies, and generally sluggish economic growth. As a result, the economies of countries with small populations can nurture poor standards of performance, low productivity, and technological obsolescence. These countries also reflect low levels of education and employment skills.

For the majority of independent states, including Canada, the increasing number of people in the world is a distant problem. Unless a country with a small population has high density* (such as El Salvador), its rate of population growth tends not to concern its government. Low-population countries point to the small number of major offenders that are responsible for the alarming post-World War II global population explosion. They cite China, India, Indonesia, and Pakistan as accounting for over 50 percent of the total world population increases. The obvious conclusion from their perspective is for the world to pressure the few countries with large populations to stabilize global population growth.

Few governments are willing or prepared to give serious consideration to an institutional approach to population control. Canada, for example, offers its population a family-allowance program and tax policies that encourage families to grow. While the U.S. government promotes family planning, the Canadian government has not taken a position on this issue and financially supports fertility. Japan was the first state to pass fertility laws: abortion was legalized and the country's fertility rate fell dramatically. Taiwan began one of the world's most successful contraceptive programs in 1964 and dropped its fertility rate from 5.4 in 1963 to 3.5 in 1990. But these are among the few exceptions. Throughout the international system, most states have laws drafted to increase fertility, not to reduce it.

National and global institutions are at odds on the perception of the world's population problem. Nationalists argue that population growth is a sovereign preserve in the national interest. Global institutions point to the insidious nature of national population growth and call for international co-operation to control it. The challenge for all states lies in the recognition that the space and resources of this planet are limited. Sovereign governments must reject the idea that the quantity of human beings is of value apart from the quality of their lives. Part of the remedy is to stop thinking of population as only a national jurisdiction. The world is much greater than the sum of its national parts. For the time being, a major international effort will be required to build a controllable balance between population, food production, and resource consumption. In order to prevent the disastrous consequences of global overpopulation, governments and the international organizations representing them will have to co-ordinate massive educational and informational programs designed to balance population growth with the ecological resources of the earth. Otherwise the widening gap between resource sufficiency and resource scarcity will become unmanageable.

The Challenge of Hunger

Nearly 200 years ago, Thomas Malthus alarmed the world by pointing out that the global population increase would press more and more insistently on food supply.[50] If unchecked, a geometric progression* of world population growth would result in widespread misery and starvation.[51] Until recent times the Malthusian prediction was widely discredited. But Malthus's theory may have been more premature than erroneous. During the nineteenth and the early part of the twentieth centuries, with the opening up of new land and the introduction of better agricultural methods, food production increased more than the arithmetic progression* predicted by Malthus. We now realize, however, that this growth will not continue indefinitely and world population will soon outstrip global food production. At present, if all the food produced were divided equally among the world's people, no one would die of starvation. But by the year 2000, if the amount of food currently produced were to be divided equally among 6.5 billion people, we would all gradually die of starvation. In the 1990s, the prevailing distribution system is partly responsible for hunger and starvation. Even if the states of the world perfect their distribution systems, the growth of global population at current rates will severely strain the means of subsistence for all of humankind by the early twenty-first century.

There are some who say that the situation will take care of itself, through industrialization and through the opening of new lands to cultivation, or that science will find a way out by improving food-production techniques, exploiting new sources of food resources (such as the oceans), and reducing food losses resulting from spoilage.[52] But too little is happening too late. Quite simply, there is not enough capital, skill, or time available to change the traditional habits and attitudes among the bulk of the world's people. Population is already catching up with and outstripping increases in food production. The fact is that an annual increase of over 75 million mouths to feed requires more food than can possibly be added to production year after year.[53] The growth of population has reached such dimensions and speed that it cannot help winning in a straight race against production. The situation is worsened by the fact that food production is in the race at a serious disadvantage. According to the latest estimates of the World Health Organization (WHO), at least two-thirds of the world's people are undernourished. Before food production can overtake the increase in human numbers, it must make good this large deficiency. There are also intervening variables: land-tenure systems that leave large tracts of unproductive land in the hands of a few; a high proportion of non-productive persons in the agricultural sector; the high cost of fertilizer and agricultural technology; and adverse weather conditions resulting in drought and famine.[54] Global food problems will continue to stem primarily from the production and distribution of food. Both these elements will also continue to be affected by climatic conditions, technology, farm-management practices, and government policies. Improving the global diet will be a complex and demanding challenge.

Since the early 1980s, the worst drought of the century has devastated Sub-Saharan Africa. According to the United Nations' Food and Agriculture Organization (FAO), twenty-four African countries with a population totalling 150 million are in the grip of food shortages and mass starvation.[55] In Mozambique, for example, famine is believed to have killed over 100 000 people in 1984 alone, while another 4 million of its 13 million suffer from malnutrition. In Ethiopia, the famine went unnoticed until fall 1984 when news of drought awakened the world to the long-standing food crisis on the African continent. Not until there were pictures on television of the ghastly images of pain and suffering of Ethiopian families did the world take notice. Ethiopia got most of the attention because of the sheer scale of its famine, which directly threatens 7 million people and which has turned the country's north into a dust-blown wasteland. Although successive years of drought were blamed for an ecological disaster unique in this century, other factors are involved. In Ethiopia, as in much of Africa, deforestation and overuse of land destroyed vast tracts even before the rain stopped. Undernourished, the land simply could not withstand the crisis or begin to feed an ever-growing population. The drought is simply the latest event in a tragedy many years in the making.

In Ethiopia and the Sudan, observers began using the term mega-famine, predicting deaths by the hundreds of thousands. Western states had ignored the warning. So did Ethiopia's ally, the Soviet Union. At first, only a few states, such as Canada and the United States, provided extra aid when famine struck in full force in late fall 1984.[56] Tens of thousands were to die in extreme misery before television cameras moved the world's conscience and an international relief effort was mobilized – so hastily organized and starting so late that relief barely manages to keep pace with starvation. In many areas, the attempt to move food to the stricken has been hampered in turn by the structural weaknesses of so many African countries: lack of roads, limited transport, and the chronic shortage of trained personnel. But the most outstanding weakness lies in the African governments themselves, which have in large part failed to develop agriculture properly, neglecting the countryside in favour of big projects and pampered cities.

In one sense, at least, the famine of the 1980s may have been a turning point. So enormous was the disaster that its bitter lessons alerted the aid-granting states of the world. Black African governments have finally started giving emergency priority to expanding food production, and to saving the land. Aid agencies began to drive home the message that horrors like Ethiopia will be repeated time after time unless long-term development becomes a world priority. For Western governments, there is the grim realization that Africa's crisis will not fade. There is no way to avoid an expensive prolonged commitment. Ultimately Africa could feed itself, but the time left to correct its wasted ecology is running short. At its current growth rate of 3.2 percent a year, Sub-Saharan Africa's population will double in the next 18 years. If present trends continue, Africa, which already receives 60 percent of the world's food aid, will only be able to feed less than half its population by the turn of the century. In 1990, Ethiopia and the Sudan are a startling vision of what lies ahead in Africa unless the spread of desert southward (currently at a pace of 10 km each year) is halted. Each famine is worse than the last. Vast populations are being displaced. Their search for food becomes steadily more desperate.

Apart from human extinction by war, the number of people on this planet will somehow have to adjust to the resources available for supporting them. The question is: By what means? Starvation is one means well under way. The application of new technologies is another. Production techniques, of course, can be improved; the yield per acre can be increased; unused lands in Asia, Africa, Latin America, and tropical islands can be developed; arid and semi-arid regions can be made productive when processes are economically feasible to convert sea water to fresh; and the seas can be farmed. But even if high-efficiency production were presently under way, at current rates of reproduction, human societies will still outgrow food supply early in the twenty-first century. Humans do not produce food in relation to population growth. Food production is essentially a response to a monied-market mechanism that returns profit. If you took a starving Ethiopian out of the desert and placed this person in a well-stocked Canadian supermarket, he or she would still die from starvation. Why? Because the Ethiopian would not get past the cash register. All national economies, whether of capitalist or socialist organization, produce food in response to domestic and international market demands that are usually accompanied by some kind of economic reward. Otherwise food supply is redirected to more profitable markets or the industries die and production ceases.

The vital need, therefore, is for an integrated approach to economic, social, and technological policies with a long-term perspective and global outlook.[57] We must learn how to apply humanitarian considerations to economic criteria in order to create long-term social benefits in place of short-term economic ones. Many believe that world hunger can be averted by combining competitive business practices with scientific and technological innovation. Although present total food production is not lower than that required for today's world population, national distribution systems and market mechanisms do not ensure that the poor of the world receive the minimum necessary nourishment.[58] Improved agriculture, through science and technology, cannot provide for a doubled world population unless there are fundamental changes in all economic and social systems and in international political thinking.

The problem of food production and distribution has not been addressed on a global scale. Upwards of ten years can elapse before the results of any international reforms might become fully evident. But extensive planning based on a future world outlook is essential if hunger is to be controlled. It is not difficult to predict with certainty what single desirable future we want. It is one that provides every human being with the basic dignity of enough to eat. Without a global food policy, we will reaffirm our sad destiny that derives its real limits for success from lack of political, economic, and managerial insight. Our future, if we choose to follow the same amorphous path of the past, will see much of the population of the world increasingly debilitated, diseased, aberrant, and violent. People will not curtail their birth rate sufficiently to bring population into balance with supportive resources, and per capita food production will begin to drop. As agriculture falters, states like Canada and the United States will have to apply triage* in their food diplomacy; and there will be the delicate question of how much international dole Americans and Canadians will be willing to pay for. Beyond that, farming will be carried out only to the extent of supplying those who can afford to buy food. The world's labour force, increasingly malnourished and ailing, will become less productive, the green revolution* will falter, and the effective commercial demand for food will drop. Under these circumstances the great food exporters will be unable to meet the massive dole necessary to avert widespread famine.

The Global Environment

In the latter part of the twentieth century, humanity is learning that the pollution* and destruction of the global environment have consequences second only perhaps to nuclear war. Since the eighteenth century the idea of progress led us to the dangerous conclusion that industrialization* and technological* change resulted in manageable environmental consequences.[59] Indeed, industrialization has been licensed to pollute the air and water with impunity. Most national economies are in the business of doing just that everyday, under the guise of legitimate governmental policies encouraging import-substitution industrialization* in order to increase national employment and strengthen local currencies. We know that technology can liberate us from disease, hunger, ignorance, and premature death. We may recognize that modernization has advanced us but often at incalculable environmental costs.

Global issues of the environment have only recently become politicized as governments begin to measure the deathly onslaught of despoliation within their legal jurisdictions.[60] Almost every state, regardless of wealth or ideology, now faces severe environmental problems. Underdeveloped states almost always trade off ecological* sensitivity for economic growth, allowing foreign governments and multinationals to pour chemicals into their coasts, lakes, rivers, and soil. In the United States and Canada high levels of toxic waste are steadily discharged into the oceans, creating hazardously high concentrations of arsenic, cadmium, copper, lead, mercury, nichol, polychlorinated biphenyls (PCBs), and zinc in the delicate salt-water ecology.[61] Plant and animal life absorb the toxins and die, or share these insidious contaminants with their human predators. Chronic land-based pollution that comes from chemical spillage, sewage, and garbage mixes with the agricultural run-off of fertilizers and pesticides to generate an anti-ecology, an independent toxic system that robs the environment of its benign life-sustaining forces.

The Soviet Union also ranks among the worst offenders. One tragedy of international dimensions (first reported by Swedish authorities in April 1986), was the explosion of the Soviet nuclear reactor at Chernobyl that contaminated a vast area on the European continent. Years later, livestock in northern Europe could not be slaughtered for food because of high radiation levels.

Nothing has come to symbolize the vulnerability of the environment to the selfish national goals of an industrialized civilization more than massive ocean-going oil tankers crossing the high seas. Many supertankers are over 300 000 tons and bigger ones are planned. When a supertanker cracks up and spills its oil into the ocean, fisheries and beaches are despoiled. Thousands of species are threatened and the world's delicate ecological balance is imperilled. The *Exxon Valdez* spill in 1989 was the largest in U.S. history (over 10 million gallons), covering 1000 sq. miles, and damaging the fragile ecology of Alaska probably well into the twenty-first century.

During the summer of 1988 hundreds of climatologists, lawyers, biologists, engineers and atmospheric chemists from six continents convened in Toronto to address an emergency:

radical changes in the global atmosphere. This World Conference on the Changing Atmosphere focussed on two phenomena: the destruction of the ozone layer and global warming. In both cases conference participants called for immediate individual, national, and international action if we are to face another century of industrial productivity.

Serious ozone depletion has occurred in the Antarctic: an equal-sized ozone hole around the North Pole would cover all of Canada. In reality, the ozone layer is very thin – about as thick as a pane of glass encircling the earth. Since the dawn of civilization this rarified protective layer of gas has prevented animal life from frying in the direct rays of the sun. Scientists point to chlorine, which originates from the breakdown of chlorofluorocarbons* (CFCs), as a cause of the problem. These human-made chemicals – which are very useful in aerosol cans, heat pumps, refrigerators, freezers, and air conditioners, and are rather benign at sea level – break down in the atmosphere as chlorine combines with and destroys ozone. If all states legislated a stop to the production of CFCs today it would take about 100 years for them to be cleansed out of the atmospheric system. In 1988 the Montreal Protocol established a schedule for the gradual banning of CFCs. Assuming all signatories ratify the treaty the hole over the Antarctic will only dissappear by the early part of the twenty-second century.

Dramatic environmental change called "global warming*" is also occurring at a rapid pace because of large atmospheric accumulations of carbon dioxide from fossil fuel burning and emissions of methane from agricultural and industrial practices. Scientists predict the earth is rushing toward an historically unprecedented average global warming of up to 4.5 degrees Celsius within the next fifty years. Over the past 150 years, 1987 was the warmest year globally and the four hottest years in the last 130 years have occurred since 1980.

This "greenhouse effect,"* which now appears to be well under way, has the potential for enormous environmental destruction caused by the rise of ocean levels and unpredictable changes in regional climates.[62] Many states have become concerned about acid rain*, which results from conditions that contribute to the greenhouse effect. On the pH scale, the measure of acidity in which 7 is neutral, some Canadian lakes consistently measure 5 (vinegar measures 3). One of the solutions to this crisis is for states to plant trees. Trees absorb environmental impurities and convert them to oxygen. However, the twentieth century has witnessed a tremendously extensive deforestation* on most continents. In the tropics, especially in Brazil and Indonesia, enormous areas of forest are being cleared for commercial farming, hydro-electric dams, and industrial development. These trees are usually burned, generating more carbon and killing the very trees that help keep the carbon dioxide in balance. In 1989, Brazil lost a forest with an area larger than Denmark, Belgium, Switzerland, and Austria combined.

The changing atmospheric phenomena of warming and ozone depletion from human-made chlorofluorocarbons* and other gases has dangerous consequences for agriculture. The major world food crops – wheat, rice, corn, and soybeans in particular – are really quite sensitive to ultraviolet radiation. They will respond by a drop in yield worldwide. In southern parts of Canada scientists measure a 3–4 percent decrease in ozone levels. At 10 or 15 percent ozone depletion, food production in Canada would be seriously decreased.

In 1988 the World Congress on Climate and Development met in Hamburg, Germany, and called upon all states, led by the industrial states, to take unilateral action, with the aim of reducing carbon dioxide emissions by 30 per cent by the year 2000 and 50 per cent by 2015. Environmentalists and scientists urged state participants to reduce their use of fossil fuels, to reduce their rates of deforestation, and to commence reforestation as soon as possible.

Solutions to global warming and ozone depletion are fundamentally political and international. The idea that a remarkable technological fix is waiting in the wings is unrealistic.[63] In an era of tight global connection, problems of peace, arms control, hunger, population growth,and environmental deterioration do not merely require domestic response: the international face of these problems takes solutions beyond national jurisdiction to the level of a global will. In the final analysis we are individually and socially equipped to solve the problems we have brought upon ourselves. Hunger, overpopulation, and war are not extra-human forces acting upon us. They are engineered by our attitudes, ignorance, and actions. Our greatest threat is the way we think. As cartoonist Walt Kelly's Pogo observed, "We have met the ENEMY ... an' HE IS US."

REFERENCES

1. *Threads* (London: British Broadcasting Corporation 1984).
2. See Henry Kissinger, *Years of Upheaval* (Boston: Little, Brown & Co. 1982), 1175; Seymour Melman, "Limits to Military power," no. 1 *International Security*, 11 (1986): 72–88.
3. Thomas Paine, *Rights of Man*, ed. by Henry Collins (Harmondsworth, Eng.: Penguin Books 1969), 238.
4. See H. Newcombe and A. Newcombe, eds., "Alternative Approaches to Peace Research," *Peace Research Review* 4 (February 1972): 1–23.
5. *Pravda*, July 14, 1963, 1–4.
6. See Frank Alluan, *Questions and Answers about Nuclear Weapons* (London: Campaign for Nuclear Disarmament 1981).
7. See E.P. Thompson and Dan Smith, eds., *Protest and Survive* (Harmondsworth, Eng.: Penguin Books 1980).
8. See Project Ploughshares, *Help End the Arms Race: Make Canada a Nuclear Weapons Free Zone* (Waterloo, ON: 1982).
9. See *Tass*, January 20, 1983.
10. UN Document A/S-10/4, 1978; see paragraph 13; see also Leo Gross, "Underutilization of the International Court of Justice," *Harvard International Law Journal* 27, no. 3 (1986): 572–98.
11. See Steven Rose, ed., *CBW: Chemical and Biological Warfare* (Boston: Beacon Press 1968); and Firdaus James Kharas and Helene Samson, eds., "Chemical Weapons" *Briefing Paper* (Ottawa: United Nations Association, October 1984).
12. See David Ziegler, *War, Peace, and International Politics* (Boston: Little, Brown & Co. 1984): 239–70.
13. See George Kemp et al., *The Other Arms Race: New Technologies and Non-Nuclear Conflict* (Lexington, MA: Lexington Books 1975), passim.
14. See Francis Beer, *Peace against War* (San Francisco: W.H. Freeman & Co. 1981), 247–9.
15. H. Scoville, "The SALT Negotiations," *Scientific American* 237, August 1977, 24–31.
16. G.B. Kistiakowsky, "False Alarm: The Story behind SALT II," *New York Review of Books* 26, March 22, 1979, 33–8.
17. See Burns Weston, ed., *Toward Nuclear*

Disarmament and Global Security: A Search for Alternatives (Boulder, CO: Westview Press 1984), esp. parts II and III.

18. International Institute for Strategic Studies, *The Military Balance 1987–1988* (London: IISS 1988), 25.
19. See Barry Blechman and Robert Powell, "What in the Name of God is Strategic Superiority?" *Political Science Quarterly* 97, no. 4 (1982–83): 589–602.
20. See Jonathan Stein, *From H-Bomb to Star Wars* (Lexington, MA: D.C. Heath & Co. 1984), 51–91; Steven Weisman, "Reagan Proposes U.S. Seek New Ways to Block Missiles," *New York Times*, March 24, 1983, A21.
21. See Kurt Gottfried, "The Physicists Size Up SDI," *Arms Control Today*, July/August 1987, 28–32.
22. Helene Samson, "Outer Space in the 1980s," *Briefing Paper* (Ottawa: United Nations Association 1984), 1.
23. See Frederick Ordway III et al., *Dividends from Space* (New York: Thomas Y. Crowell Company 1971), 1–62.
24. Canada, *Canadian Space Industry: Marketing Opportunities in the 80's* (Ottawa: Industry, Trade and Commerce 1980), 4–7.
25. Canada, *The Canadian Space Program: Five-Year Plan*, 80/81– 84/85 (Ottawa: Communications Canada 1980), 15–34.
26. See Hugh Kindred et al., *International Law Chiefly as Interpreted and Applied in Canada* (Toronto: Emond Montgomery Publications 1987), 405–10.
27. Steve Chan, "Incentives for Nuclear Proliferation: The Case of International Pariahs," *Journal of Strategic Studies* 3 (May 1980): 26–43.
28. Bruce Blair and Gary Brewer, "The Terrorist Threat to World Nuclear Programs," *Journal of Conflict Resolution* 21 (September 1977): 379–403; see also Lewis Dunn, *Controlling the Bomb* (New Haven, CT: Yale University Press 1982).
29. See A. Leroy Bennett, *International Organizations* (Englewood Cliffs, NJ: Prentice-Hall 1988), 213–19.
30. Stockholm International Peace Research Institute (SIPRI), *The NPT: The Main Political Barrier to Nuclear Weapons Proliferation* (London: Taylor & Francis Ltd. 1980), 9–10.
31. Canada, *Canada's Nuclear Non-proliferation Policy* (Ottawa: Department of External Affairs 1985), 1–27.
32. Bennett Ramberg, "Attacks on Nuclear Reactors: The Implications of Israel's Strike on Osiraq," *Political Science Quarterly* 97, no. 4 (1982–83): 653–69.
33. See Richard Wiggers, "Conventional Weapons," *Briefing Paper* 21 (Ottawa: United Nations Association, October 1986), 1–6; United States, Arms Control and Disarmament Agency (ACDA), *World Military Expenditures and Arms Transfers, 1986,* Publication no. 127 (Washington, DC: ACDA 1987).
34. See Uri Ra'anan et al., *Arms Transfers to the Third World* (Boulder, CO: Westview 1978); see also United States, Arms Control and Disarmament Agency (ACDA), *Arms Control Update*, no. 3 (Washington, DC: January 3, 1988).
35. See Leslie Gelb, "Arms Sales," *Foreign Policy* 25 (Winter 1976–77): 3–23; see also Stephanie Newman and Robert Harkavy eds., *Arms Transfers in the Modern World* (New York: Praeger 1979).
36. See Michael Bizoska, "Arms Transfer Data Sources," Journal of Conflict Resolution 26 (March 1982): 39–75.
37. See J. David Singer and Melvin Small, "Foreign Policy Indicators: Predictors of War in History and in the State of the World Message," *Policy Sciences* 5 (September 1974): 284–5; see also Michael Wallace, "Armaments and Escalation: Two Competing Hypotheses," *International Studies Quarterly* 26 (March 1982): 32–56.
38. Michael Wallace, "Arms Races and Escalation: Some New Evidence," *Journal of Conflict Resolution* 1 (March 1979): 3–16; and William Thompson et al., "Wars, Alliances and Military Expenditures: Two Pendulum Hypotheses,"

Journal of Conflict Resolution 23 (December 1979): 629–54; Ofer Zur, "The Psychohistory of Warfare: The Co-evolution of Culture, Psyche, and Enemy," *Journal of Peace Research* 24, no. 2 (1987) 125–34.

39. See Miroslav Nincic and Thomas Cusack, "The Political Economy of U.S. Military Spending," *Journal of Peace Research* 16, no. 2 (1979): 111; Laurence Korp, "The FY 1981-1985 Defense Program: Capital, Labor, and the Spoils of War," *Journal of Peace Research* 17, no. 2 (1980): 103–5.
40. Ansley Coale, "The History of the Human Population," *Scientific American* 231, September 1974, 41–51.
41. Davidson Gwatkin and Sarah Brandel, "Life Expectancy and Population Growth in the Third World," *Scientific American* 246, May 1982, 3–11.
42. Davidson Gwatkin, "Implications of Change in Developing Country Morality Trends: The End of an Era," *Population and Development Review* 6 (December 1980): 615–44.
43. *World Development Report* (Washington, DC: World Bank 1988).
44. See Marcel Leroy, *Population and World Politics* (Leiden, Netherlands: Martinus Nijhoff Social Sciences Division 1978), 97–123.
45. See Robert McNamara, "Time Bomb or Myth: The Population Problem," *Foreign Affairs* 62 (Summer 1984): 1107–31; Lester Brown, "Analysing the Demographic Trap," in Lester Brown et al., *State of the World 1987* (New York: W.W. Norton & Co. 1987), 21–37.
46. United Nations, *Patterns of Urban and Rural Population Growth* (New York: United Nations 1980).
47. See Robert Weller and Leon Bouvier, *Population Demography and Policy* (New York: St. Martin's Press 1981), 22–48; see also Brown "Analyzing the Demographic Trap," 21–37.
48. See Allen Crosbie Walsh, "Special Problems in the Population Geography of Small Populations," in John Clarke, ed., *Geography and Population: Approaches and Applications* (Oxford: Pergamon Press 1984), 69-76.
49. Peter Perie, "The Demographic Effects of Local Socio-economic Change on Small Populations: A Samoan Example," in L.A. Kosinski and John Webb, eds., *Population at Microscale* (New Zealand: New Zealand Geographical Society 1976), 79–92.
50. Thomas Malthus was a British professor of political economy whose major work, *An Essay on the Principle of Population* (1778) had a major impact on the social sciences and contributed to the development of the discipline of demography.
51. See Leroy, *Population and World Politics*, 55–57.
52. See Paul Ehrlich and Ann Ehrlich, *Population, Resources, Environment* (San Francisco: W.H. Freeman 1970), 101–3.
53. See United Nations, *Demographic Yearbook 1988* (New York: UN 1988).
54. See National Defense University, *Crop Yields and Climate Change to the Year 2000* (Washington, DC: U.S. Government Printing Office 1980).
55. Canada, *The Food Crisis in Africa: An Overview* Canadian International Development Agency, (Ottawa: October 1984).
56. Canadian International Agency, *The Food Crisis in Africa: An Overview* (Ottawa: October 1984).
57. Douglas Williams and Roger Young, *Taking Stock: World Food Security in the Eighties* (Ottawa: North–South Institute 1981).
58. Toivo Miljan, ed., *Food and Agriculture in Global Perspective: Discussions in the Committee of the Whole of the United Nations* (New York: Pergamon Press 1980), 7–26.
59. Irwin Altman and Martin Chemers, *Culture and Environment* (Monterey, CA: Brooks/Cole Publishing Co. 1980), 15–71; see also Jeremy Rifkin, *Entropy* (New York: Viking Press 1980), 15–30.
60. Nicholas Onuf, "Reports to the Club of Rome," World Politics 36, no. 1 (1983):

121–46; see also World Resources Institute and International Institute for Environmental Development, *World Resources 1986* (New York: Basic Books 1986).

61. John Rourke, *International Politics on the World Stage* (Guilford, CT: Dushkin Publishing Group 1989), 525–33.
62. Canada, *State of the Environment: Report for Canada* (Ottawa: Environment Canada, May 1986), 153–208; and Yves Fortier, "Sustainable Development," statement to the Canadian Club, Winnipeg, Manitoba, March 17, 1989.
63. Campbell Creighton, *Philosophy and the Ecological Problems of Civilizations* (Moscow: Progress Publishers 1983), 5–19; and David Suzuki, "Playing Russian Roulette with World Environment," in H.B. McCullough, ed., *Political Ideologies and Political Philosophies* (Toronto: Wall & Thompson 1989), 288–90.

SUGGESTED READINGS

Geoffrey Blainey, *The Causes of War* (New York: Free Press 1988).

Philip Bobbitt, *Democracy and Deterrence: The History and Future of Nuclear Strategy* (New York: St. Martin's Press 1988).

Naomi Chazan and Timothy Shaw, *Coping with Africa's Food Crisis* (Boulder, CO: Lynne Rienner Publishers 1988).

Martin van Creveld, *Technology and War: From 2000 B.C. to the Present* (New York: Free Press, 1988).

Vic George, *Wealth, Poverty and Starvation* (New York: St. Martin's Press 1988).

Charles Kegley Jr., and E. Wittkopf, *The Nuclear Reader: Strategy, Weapons and War* (New York: St. Martin's Press 1989).

Frances Lappe and Joseph Collins, *World Hunger: Twelve Myths* (San Francisco, CA: Grove Press/Food First Books 1989).

Aaron Schneider, ed., *Deforestation and "Development" in Canada and the Tropics* (Sydney, NS: Centre for International Studies, University College of Cape Breton 1989).

Paul Stares, *Space and National Security* (Washington, DC: Brookings Institute 1987).

R.B.J. Walker, *One World, Many Worlds: Struggles for a Just World Peace* (Boulder, CO: Lynne Rienner Publishers 1988).

John Warnock, *The Politics of World Hunger* (Scarborough, ON: Nelson Canada 1987).

GLOSSARY

strategic superiority: A temporary military advantage of one or a group of states arising out of the credible enhancement of their offensive and defensive capabilities.

disarmament: The decision by one or more states to destroy weapons in their possession and not to build and acquire others.

nuclear-weapon-free zone: Any country, region or zone designated as an area free of nuclear weapons as is Antarctica, the seabed, Latin America, and outer space.

zone of peace: Any country, region, or zone designated as an area free of any arms, conventional or nuclear.

arms race: Competitive armament by two or more states seeking security and protection against each other.

chemical weapons: Gases, herbicides, and other substances that can kill or paralyse enemy troops or populations.

biological weapons: Toxic substances that create diseases and epidemics when released against enemy troops or populations.

intercontinental ballistic missiles: Electronically guided land–based weapons that can deliver their nuclear payloads at distances of over 3000 miles.

mutually assured destruction: A strategic doctrine of deterrence under which each adversary preserves the capability to absorb a first nuclear strike by the other and still retaliate with devastating force - inflicting unacceptable damage on the attacker.

tactical nuclear weapons: Small-scale, short-range nuclear devices designed for use in the battlefield.

strategic nuclear weapons: large-scale, long-range nuclear weapons delivered by ICBMs and bombers.

Manhattan Project: The U.S. government-sponsored research project that produced the first atomic weapon.

nuclear proliferation: The acquisition of nuclear weapons by nation-states that formerly did not have them.

death rate: The number of deaths in any given year divided by the mid-year population and multiplied by 1000.

life expectancy: The average number of additional years a person is expected to live from birth.

mortality: The deaths occurring to a population.

fertility: Concerns the power of an individual to be productive, to produce offspring, and to have reproductive capacity.

zero population growth: A population with a growth rate of zero because births plus immigration equal deaths plus emigration.

density: The number of persons per unit of land, usually a square mile or a square kilometre.

geometric progression: A geometric progression is one in which each term is derived by multiplying the preceding term by a given number R called a common ratio. Thus if R is 2 the progression would appear as 2, 4, 8, 16, 32, 64 ...

arithmetic progression: An arithmetic progression is a sequence in which each term is derived from the preceding one by adding a given number D, called the common difference. Thus if D is 2 the progression would appear as 2, 4, 6, 8, 10, 12 ...

triage: The sorting out and classification of casualties of war or other disaster, to determine priority of need and proper place of treatment.

green revolution: A term coined in 1968 by William Guad, administrator in the U.S. Agency for International Development (AID), to describe the introduction and rapid adoption, world wide, of high-yielding wheats and rices.

pollution: To physically spoil the air, water, earth, and life environment by means of toxic matter, noise, or heat.

industrialization: The social and economic process whereby productive efforts are systematically organized to optimize output by means of power-driven machinery and a specialized labour force.

technology: A body of knowledge pertaining to the utilization of tools and processes that a group or civilization has learned to use.

import-substitution industrialization: An industrial strategy to establish domestic industries, protected by tariff and quota barriers, that produce goods and services otherwise imported by the national economy.

ecology: A term coined in the nineteenth century referring to the relationship of living things to each other and to their natural environment.

global warming: A general warming of the planet caused by a multiplicity of human-made and natural factors.

chlorofluorocarbons (CFCs)*:* Chemical emissions that have negative impacts on the levels of ozone (O_3) in the atmosphere.

greenhouse effect: A global warming effect caused by an accumulated presence of carbon dioxide levels in the atmosphere, which blocks the radiation of heat reflecting from the earth into space.

acid rain: Rainfall contaminated by high levels of sulfur dioxide (SO_2), usually emitted from the burning of fossil fuels and industrial processes.

deforestation: Loss of forests due to harvesting, expanding farm, and urban acreage, soil erosion, acid rain, and other deleterious impacts.

Appendix

Canadian Charter of Rights and Freedoms

Whereas Canada is founded upon principles that recognize the supremacy of God and the rule of law:

Guarantee of Rights and Freedoms

1. The *Canadian Charter of Rights and Freedoms* guarantees the rights and freedoms set out in it subject only to such reasonable limits prescribed by law as can be demonstrably justified in a free and democratic society.

Fundamental Freedoms

2. Everyone has the following fundamental freedoms:
(a) freedom of conscience and religion;
(b) freedom of thought, belief, opinion and expression, including freedom of the press and other media of communication;
(c) freedom of peaceful assembly; and
(d) freedom of association

Democratic Rights

3. Every citizen of Canada has the right to vote in an election of members of the House of Commons or of a legislative assembly and to be qualified for membership therein.
4. (1) No House of Commons and no legislative assembly shall continue for longer than five years from the date fixed for the return of the writs at a general election of its members.
(2) In time of real or apprehended war, invasion or insurrection, a House of Commons may be continued by Parliament and a legislative assembly may be continued by the legislature beyond five years if such continuation is not opposed by the votes of more than one-third of the members of the House of Commons or the legislative assembly, as the case may be.
5. There shall be a sitting of Parliament and of each legislature at least once every twelve months.

Mobility Rights

6. (1) Every citizen of Canada has the right to enter, remain in and leave Canada.
(2) Every citizen of Canada and every person who has the status of a permanent resident of Canada has the right
(a) to move to and take up residence in any province; and
(b) to pursue the gaining of a livelihood in any province.
(3) The rights specified in subsection (2) are subject to
(a) any laws or practices of general application in force in a province other than those that discriminate among persons primarily on the basis of province of present or previous residence; and
(b) any laws providing for reasonable residency requirements as a qualification for the receipt of publicly provided social services.
(4) Subsections (2) and (3) do not preclude any law, program or activity that has as its object the amelioration in a province of conditions of individuals in that province who are socially or economically disadvantaged if the rate of employment in that province is below the rate of employment in Canada.

Legal Rights

7. Everyone has the right to life, liberty and security of the person and the right not to be deprived thereof except in accordance with the principles of fundamental justice.
8. Everyone has the right to be secure against unreasonable search or seizure.
9. Everyone has the right not to be arbitrarily detained or imprisoned.

10. Everyone has the right on arrest or detention
(a) to be informed promptly of the reasons therefor;
(b) to retain and instruct counsel without delay and to be informed of that right; and
(c) to have the validity of the detention determined by way of *habeas corpus* and to be released if the detention is not lawful.

11. Any person charged with an offence has the right
(a) to be informed without unreasonable delay of the specific offence;
(b) to be tried within a reasonable time;
(c) not to be compelled to be a witness in proceedings against that person in respect of the offence;
(d) to be presumed innocent until proven guilty according to law in a fair and public hearing by an independent and impartial tribunal;
(e) not to be denied reasonable bail without just cause;
(f) except in the case of an offence under military law tried before a military tribunal, to the benefit of trial by jury where the maximum punishment for the offence is imprisonment for five years or a more severe punishment;
(g) not to be found guilty on account of any act or omission unless, at the time of the act or omission, it constituted an offence under Canadian or international law or was criminal according to the general principles of law recognized by the community of nations;
(h) if finally acquitted of the offence, not to be tried for it again and, if finally found guilty and punished for the offence, not to be tried or punished for it again; and
(i) if found guilty of the offence and if the punishment for the offence has been varied between the time of commission and the time of sentencing, to the benefit of the lesser punishment.

12. Everyone has the right not to be subjected to any cruel and unusual treatment or punishment.

13. A witness who testifies in any proceedings has the right not to have any incriminating evidence so given used to incriminate that witness in any other proceedings, except in a prosecution for perjury or for the giving of contradictory evidence.

14. A party or witness in any proceedings who does not understand or speak the language in which the proceedings are conducted or who is deaf has the right to the assistance of an interpreter.

Equality Rights

15. (1) Every individual is equal before and under the law and has the right to the equal protection and equal benefit of the law without discrimination and, in particular, without discrimination based on race, national or ethnic origin, colour, religion, sex, age or mental or physical disability.
(2) Subsection (1) does not preclude any law, program or activity that has as its object the amelioration of conditions of disadvantaged individuals or groups including those that are disadvantaged because of race, national or ethnic origin, colour, religion, sex, age or mental or physical disability.

Official Languages of Canada

16. (1) English and French are the official languages of Canada and have equality of status and equal rights and privileges as to their use in all institutions of the Parliament and government of Canada.
(2) English and French are the official languages of New Brunswick and have equality of status and equal rights and privileges as to their use in all institutions of the legislature and government of New Brunswick.
(3) Nothing in this Charter limits the authority of Parliament or a legislature to advance the equality of status or use of English and French.

17. (1) Everyone has the right to use English or French in any debates and other proceedings of Parliament.
(2) Everyone has the right to use English or French in any debates and other proceedings

of the legislature of New Brunswick.

18. (1) The statutes, records and journals of Parliament shall be printed and published in English and French and both language versions are equally authoritative.

(2) The statutes, records and journals of the legislature of New Brunswick shall be printed and published in English and French and both language versions are equally authoritative.

19. (1) Either English or French may be used by any person in, or in any pleading in or process issuing from, any court established by Parliament.

(2) Either English or French may be used by any person in, or in any pleading in or process issuing from, any court of New Brunswick.

20. (1) Any member of the public in Canada has the right to communicate with, and to receive available services from, any head or central office of an institution of the Parliament or government of Canada in English or French, and has the same right with respect to any other office of any such institution where

(a) there is a significant demand for communications with and services from that office in such language; or

(b) due to the nature of the office, it is reasonable that communications with and services from that office be available in both English and French.

(2) Any member of the public in New Brunswick has the right to communicate with, and to receive available services from, any office of an institution of the legislature or government of New Brunswick in English or French.

21. Nothing in sections 16 to 20 abrogates or derogates from any right, privilege or obligation with respect to the English and French languages, or either of them, that exists or is continued by virtue of any other provision of the Constitution of Canada.

22. Nothing in sections 16 to 20 abrogates or derogates from any legal or customary right or privilege acquired or enjoyed either before or after the coming into force of this Charter with respect to any language that is not English or French.

Minority Language Educational Rights

23. (1) Citizens of Canada

(a) whose first language learned and still understood is that of the English or French linguistic minority population of the province in which they reside, or

(b) who have received their primary school instruction in Canada in English or French and reside in a province where the language in which they received that instruction is the language of the English or French linguistic minority population of the province, have the right to have their children receive primary and secondary school instruction in that language in that province.

(2) Citizens of Canada of whom any child has received or is receiving primary or secondary school instruction in English or French in Canada, have the right to have all their children receive primary and secondary school instruction in the same language.

(3) The right of citizens of Canada under subsections (1) and (2) to have their children receive primary and secondary school instruction in the language of the English or French linguistic minority population of a province

(a) applies wherever in the province the number of children of citizens who have such a right is sufficient to warrant the provision to them out of public funds of minority language instruction; and

(b) includes, where the number of those children so warrants, the right to have them receive that instruction in minority language educational facilities provided out of public funds.

Enforcement

24. (1) Anyone whose rights or freedoms, as guaranteed by this Charter, have been infringed or denied may apply to a court of competent jurisdiction to obtain such remedy as the court considers appropriate and just in the circumstances.

(2) Where, in proceedings under subsection (1), a court concludes that evidence was obtained in a manner that infringed or denied

any rights or freedoms guaranteed by this Charter, the evidence shall be excluded if it is established that, having regard to all the circumstances, the admission of it in the proceedings would bring the administration of justice into disrepute.

General

25. The guarantee in this Charter of certain rights and freedoms shall not be construed so as to abrogate or derogate from any aboriginal, treaty or other rights or freedoms that pertain to the aboriginal peoples of Canada including (a) any rights or freedoms that have been recognized by the Royal Proclamation of October 7, 1763; and (b) any rights or freedoms that may be acquired by the aboriginal peoples of Canada by way of land claims settlement.

26. The guarantee in this Charter of certain rights and freedoms shall not be construed as denying the existence of any other rights or freedoms that exist in Canada.

27. This Charter shall be interpreted in a manner consistent with the preservation and enhancement of the multicultural heritage of Canadians.

28. Notwithstanding anything in this Charter, the rights and freedoms referred to in it are guaranteed equally to male and female persons.

29. Nothing in this Charter abrogates or derogates from any rights or privileges guaranteed by or under the Constitution of Canada in respect of denominational, separate or dissentient schools.

30. A reference in this Charter to a province or to the legislative assembly or legislature of a province shall be deemed to include a reference to the Yukon Territory and the Northwest Territories, or to the appropriate legislative authority thereof, as the case may be.

31. Nothing in this Charter extends the legislative powers of any body or authority.

Application of Charter

32. (1) This Charter applies

(a) to the Parliament and government of Canada in respect of all matters within the authority of Parliament including all matters relating to the Yukon Territory and Northwest Territories; and

(b) to the legislature and government of each province in respect of all matters within the authority of the legislature of each province.

(2) Notwithstanding subsection (1), section 15 shall not have effect until three years after this section comes into force.

33. (1) Parliament or the legislature of a province may expressly declare in an Act of Parliament or of the legislature, as the case may be, that the Act or a provision thereof shall operate notwithstanding a provision included in section 2 or sections 7 to 15 of this Charter.

(2) An Act or a provision of an Act in respect of which a declaration made under this section is in effect shall have such operation as it would have but for the provision of this Charter referred to in the declaration.

(3) A declaration made under subsection (1) shall cease to have effect five years after it comes into force or on such earlier date as may be specified in the declaration.

(4) Parliament or the legislature of a province may re-enact a declaration made under subsection (1).

(5) Subsection (3) applies in respect of a re-enactment made under subsection (4).

34. This Part may be cited as the *Canadian Charter of Rights and Freedoms*.

Index